Risk Management Strategies in Public-Private Partnerships

Peter Adoko Obicci
POA-Kittim Consultants, Uganda

A volume in the Advances in Business Strategy and Competitive Advantage (ABSCA) Book Series

IGI Global
DISSEMINATOR OF KNOWLEDGE
www.igi-global.com

Published in the United States of America by
IGI Global
Business Science Reference (an imprint of IGI Global)
701 E. Chocolate Avenue
Hershey PA, USA 17033
Tel: 717-533-8845
Fax: 717-533-8661
E-mail: cust@igi-global.com
Web site: http://www.igi-global.com

Library of Congress Cataloging-in-Publication Data

Names: Obicci, Peter Adoko, 1971- author.
Title: Risk management strategies in public-private partnerships / by Peter Adoko Obicci.
Description: Hershey : Business Science Reference, [2017]
Identifiers: LCCN 2017003791| ISBN 9781522525035 (hardcover) | ISBN 9781522525042 (ebook)
Subjects: LCSH: Public-private sector cooperation. | Risk management. | Strategic planning.
Classification: LCC HD3871 .O25 2017 | DDC 658.15/5--dc23 LC record available at https://lccn.loc.gov/2017003791

This book is published in the IGI Global book series Advances in Business Strategy and Competitive Advantage (ABSCA) (ISSN: 2327-3429; eISSN: 2327-3437)

British Cataloguing in Publication Data
A Cataloguing in Publication record for this book is available from the British Library.

For electronic access to this publication, please contact: eresources@igi-global.com.

Advances in Business Strategy and Competitive Advantage (ABSCA) Book Series

Patricia Ordóñez de Pablos
Universidad de Oviedo, Spain

ISSN:2327-3429
EISSN:2327-3437

Mission

Business entities are constantly seeking new ways through which to gain advantage over their competitors and strengthen their position within the business environment. With competition at an all-time high due to technological advancements allowing for competition on a global scale, firms continue to seek new ways through which to improve and strengthen their business processes, procedures, and profitability.

The **Advances in Business Strategy and Competitive Advantage (ABSCA) Book Series** is a timely series responding to the high demand for state-of-the-art research on how business strategies are created, implemented and re-designed to meet the demands of globalized competitive markets. With a focus on local and global challenges, business opportunities and the needs of society, the **ABSCA** encourages scientific discourse on doing business and managing information technologies for the creation of sustainable competitive advantage.

Coverage

- Tacit Knowledge
- Customer-Orientation Strategy
- Innovation Strategy
- Strategic management
- Strategic alliances
- Outsourcing
- Core Competencies
- Differentiation Strategy
- Strategy Performance Management
- Foreign Investment Decision Process

IGI Global is currently accepting manuscripts for publication within this series. To submit a proposal for a volume in this series, please contact our Acquisition Editors at Acquisitions@igi-global.com or visit: http://www.igi-global.com/publish/.

The Advances in Business Strategy and Competitive Advantage (ABSCA) Book Series (ISSN 2327-3429) is published by IGI Global, 701 E. Chocolate Avenue, Hershey, PA 17033-1240, USA, www.igi-global.com. This series is composed of titles available for purchase individually; each title is edited to be contextually exclusive from any other title within the series. For pricing and ordering information please visit http://www.igi-global.com/book-series/advances-business-strategy-competitive-advantage/73672. Postmaster: Send all address changes to above address.

Titles in this Series

For a list of additional titles in this series, please visit: www.igi-global.com/book-series

Handbook of Research on Small and Medium Enterprises in Developing Countries
Noor Hazlina Ahmad (Universiti Sains Malaysia, Malaysia) T. Ramayah (Universiti Sains Malaysia, Malaysia) Hasliza Abdul Halim (Universiti Sains Malaysia, Malaysia) and Syed Abidur Rahman (Universiti Utara Malaysia, Malaysia)
Business Science Reference • ©2017 • 479pp • H/C (ISBN: 9781522521655) • US $255.00

Technology-Driven Productivity Improvements and the Future of Work Emerging Research and Opportunities
Göran Roos (University of Adelaide, Australia)
Business Science Reference • ©2017 • 255pp • H/C (ISBN: 9781522521792) • US $175.00

Entrepreneurship and Business Innovation in the Middle East
Philippe W. Zgheib (Lebanese American University, Lebanon)
Business Science Reference • ©2017 • 357pp • H/C (ISBN: 9781522520665) • US $190.00

Comprehensive Problem-Solving and Skill Development for Next-Generation Leaders
Ronald A. Styron, Jr. (University of South Alabama, USA) and Jennifer L. Styron (University of South Alabama, USA)
Business Science Reference • ©2017 • 389pp • H/C (ISBN: 9781522519683) • US $205.00

Diasporas and Transnational Entrepreneurship in Global Contexts
Sanya Ojo (University of East London, UK)
Business Science Reference • ©2017 • 334pp • H/C (ISBN: 9781522519911) • US $200.00

Integrating Art and Creativity into Business Practice
Giovanni Schiuma (University of Basilicata, Italy & University of the Arts London, UK) and Antonio Lerro (University of Basilicata, Italy)
Business Science Reference • ©2017 • 260pp • H/C (ISBN: 9781522520504) • US $170.00

Sustainable Entrepreneurship and Investments in the Green Economy
Andrei Jean Vasile (Petroleum-Gas University of Ploiesti, Romania) and Domenico Nicolò (University Mediterranea of Reggio Calabria, Italy)
Business Science Reference • ©2017 • 339pp • H/C (ISBN: 9781522520757) • US $185.00

CSR 2.0 and the New Era of Corporate Citizenship
Mark Anthony Camilleri (University of Malta, Malta)
Business Science Reference • ©2017 • 398pp • H/C (ISBN: 9781522518426) • US $190.00

IGI GLOBAL
DISSEMINATOR OF KNOWLEDGE

www.igi-global.com

701 East Chocolate Avenue, Hershey, PA 17033, USA
Tel: 717-533-8845 x100 • Fax: 717-533-8661
E-Mail: cust@igi-global.com • www.igi-global.com

For my lovely children: Otunnu Norman Obicci, Ajok Esther Fiona, Kittim Peter Obicci, Obama Emmanuel, and Opira Francis Obicci with their mother Atto Mary Joyce Obicci and in loving memory of late dad, Ongom Matthew Obicci, the incorruptible genius.

Table of Contents

Preface

Good risk management is integral to delivering a successful partnership. - Sir David Omand

Risk management in a public private partnership arrangement is continuing to advance both theoretically and practically. That advance accelerated during the last quarter of the last century as governments at all levels came under increasing pressure to do more in the 'muddy-waters of financial shortage'. Indeed, all governments, irrespective of neither developed countries nor developing ones are struggling in the face of unrelenting budget constraints yet citizens demands greater quality services in an efficient, fair and equitable manner. In this book, a framework that depicts the current development in risks management in a public private partnership will be presented. Then, implication of this framework will be briefly explored. Actually, this framework became a basis for the chapter selection of this book. As public private partnership is a new unexplored area in terms of study, and as much attention has been focused on 'contracting' out searching, reflect the scope of risk management is a challenge. In the remaining part of the book, more attention will be given to new service delivery context, growing interest in public private partnership.

Governments all over the world today face a new service delivery context (Ringold, Holla, Koziol & Srinivasan, 2012). Progressive globalization 'pregnant' with excessive demand for quality services, widely exhibited to be the defining features of the late twentieth century world governments, seems set to continue into the twenty-first century and beyond (Fatemi & Behmanesh, 2012). The process of world production with overriding consumption has involved a broadening and deepening of the interrelationships between public organizations and private firms/companies (Brown, Potoski & Van Slyke, 2006). World consumption outpaced public production during the last two to three decades and governments' financial deficits falls far below the expected (Keast & Brown, 2006). Accordingly, production and quality of goods and service delivery respectively reached historically unprecedented low in the last quarter of the twentieth century (Kort & Klijn, 2011).

The onset of public private partnership (PPP) is likely to bring a permanent quick-up in the flows of rapid production that meets corresponding demands for high quality goods and services, albeit at an accelerated pace during the forthcoming periods (Forrer, Kee, Newcomer & Boyer, 2010). The outcome is the creation of "all-sector's" engagement in PPP. However, there seems to be an inherent challenge in this arrangement. A combination of factors- failing service delivery quality (through poor performance and resource wastage), increasing financial constraints, declining resources availability and increased production costs and highly sophisticated technological advancement seeking out new service delivery provision-have driven governments to team up with the private sector (Neshkova & Kostadinova, 2012). This complex process is irreversible and has revolutionary implications for service delivery.

Teaming up and collaborating with the private sector has become more important to the realization of service delivery within an integrated world economy (Cicmil & Marshall, 2005). These forces are exerting a profound influence on the behavior of public organizations as well as the environment around them by altering production processes, new product introduction, supply-chain relationship between organizations, demand conditions and regulations. This new service delivery context, based on financial capability and technical expertise of the private sector, provides an unparalleled new opportunities and poses new risks for service delivery in both developed and developing countries (Maylor, Vidgen & Carver, 2008). It has the potential to offer government organizations with access to new source of finances, new technology, skills, capital, markets and hence better service delivery and greater quality services than ever before. A lack of resources (including skills, financial and technological) and small markets at national level will pose less of a constraint to service delivery and production transformation as public organizations link up with private organizations and draw on private sector resources and markets (Antoniou, Aretoulis, Konstantinidis & Kalfakakou, 2013). At the same time, the integration between public organizations and the private organization brings about a sudden, marked increase in competition from production and use of new technological advancement with the service delivery sector to meet the demands of the citizens.

Many public organizations had previously under estimated the power of this integration and its effects on service delivery (Rees, Mullins and Bovaird, 2012). Accordingly, adjusting to increased high consumption patterns has placed an unprecedented demand on the capacities of public organizations in especially developing countries. In general, old production formula, poor institutional and structural disparities seem ill-prepared to deal with the increasing challenge of the globalized world of scarce resources (Trafford & Proctor, 2006). Not surprising, perhaps, the evidence suggests that public organizations continues to witness mixed production responses during the last two to three decades or so. A handful of newly crafted means of production (and to a greater extend involvement of the private sector in the production process) have taken advantage of the new opportunities offered by PPP and expanded their production as well as distribution capacities through ready finances, skills and expertise from the private sector (Brown & Keast, 2005). The first generation of governments, for example, Britain, Australia, USA, that had embraced PPP by the mid twentieth century have had sustained rapid service delivery improvement as a result of involving the private sector in their quest for holistic development. They have in the course witnessed rapid quality growth in their service delivery provision but with varying achievements in high technology exports (Ibrahim, Price& Dainty, 2006). Per capita service enjoyment in these countries has typically risen dramatically since the last few decades and several have become high quality service delivery countries.

However, other developing countries in Sub-Saharan Africa, South Asia, the Caribbean and the Pacific have been slow to reap benefits from PPP. With a few exceptions, this second group has had sluggish service delivery and limited production upgrading of their service standards and levels in the public sector (which are dominated by poor performance, use of substandard resources) (Gazley, 2010). A concentration on relatively poor quality services has made these developing countries vulnerable to the threat of poor unending service provision, with cheap costs and other resources, in attempt to satisfy the needs and wants of the citizens (Bovaird, 2006). Some, particularly, in Sub-Saharan Africa, have even experienced a contraction in existing production capacity and there is little sign of new capacity emerging. Public organizations which often accounts for bulk of the number of service delivery outlets/ establishments and consumption-sources in African economies-have performed poorly relative to their counterparts in the developed world (Bovaird & Davies, 2011). Equally serious is the few functioning public organizations have not flowed in the desired volumes into the provision of quality services and the bulk of them have remained at producing/providing poor services (Adisu, 2014). The developing world is thus becoming increasingly polarized into those that have succeeded into becoming countries 'specialized' in producing/delivering poor quality goods/substandard services respectively and this has continued and nothing done to outdo them to date. The prospect of service delivery marginalization is a persistent worry in policy circles in the developing world. There is an urgent need for change in government and public sector organizations' attitudes and strategies (Entwistle & Martin, 2005). Change is no longer an option but a survival algorithm.

In the move, PPP has been identified as an innovative tool for causing a desired changed. Ke, Wang and Chan (2011), contend, that PPP can be used as tool for financing major infrastructure projects and has huge potential for the near future, for example. In fact, PPP has become a vibrant key area for the socio-economic development of countries in both developed as well as developing world and remains in constant fruition (Keçi, 2015). Because of intense needs to satisfy citizens' wants and needs for socio-economic advancement, countries are forced to diversity their service delivery functions and to propose an increasing number of avenues for service delivery (Akintoye, 2006). However, countries often enter into PPP arrangement paying no close eyes to important procedural aspects of risks and may not be aware of the consequences. On the other hand, in most instances the PPP agreements often ignore risks factors (Abednego & Ogunlana, 2006). Thus, the design and deployment of resources to implement PPP projects that incorporate risk factoring are subject to uncertainties such as stalling or completed breakdown of the project (Xiao & Zhang, 2011). Questions surrounding proper risk management- together with the massive adoption of PPP in providing service delivery and increasing wants and needs of the citizenry- bring to the forefront hard questions about the future of PPP and the need to address those questions in a systematic and comprehensive manner (Brinkerhoff & Brinkerhoff, 2011). This book on "Risk management strategies in public private partnerships" fills that gap, presenting the systematic and comprehensive contrivance available to see any PPP project succeeds.

Concerns about the process of service delivery restructuring in an ever-changing and technologically advancing world economy have sparked widespread interest in the concept of PPP as applied to the relationship between public organizations and private firms/company within them (Landow & Ebdon, 2012). This interest originated in England but has recently spilled over into developing countries. Political leaders, investors and business people constantly refer to it during their discussions on business rivalries between the public and private sector (Aaronson, 2011). The media both print and electronic often makes frequent mention of it in articles and bulletins on the engagement of countries (governments) in providing those and that services (Abbott & Grady, 2011).

Policy makers produce indicators (which range from inception to execution and implementation of a PPP project) showing risk sharing matrix and rewards accruing out of a PPP arrangement (Alexander, 2012). Governments have established bodies/units to overseas, initiate and formulate policies to improve national and regional embrace of PPP principles (Emirullah & Azam, 2014). Experts and consultants of different kinds conduct studies of PPP strategy in what has become a highly profitable industry. The theoretical foundation of some of this work is questionable and its empirical basis is often weak. Thus, sheer volume of studies that have been generated to date on PPP is impressive but this may have been achieved at the expense of service quality and rigor. It is not surprising; therefore, that a lively debate is taking place among policy makers and implements on the subject of failure of PPP projects. McQuaid and Scherrer are dismissive of the idea: 'PPPs … offer genuine and sustainable increases in efficiency and effectiveness compared to the alternatives (McQuaid & Scherrer (2010, p. 33)'. McQuaid and Scherrer's critique was particularly directed at the lesser brighter side of PPP. They argue that if PPPs achieve what they are claimed to be good for, then they should have a positive impact on future public resource availability, but if they do not then they may provide short term financial and political benefits but at the cost of constraining future decision-makers and placing greater pressures on public finances in the longer term. In the premise, therefore, PPP may end up becoming a misleading approach to deliver services, hence, eroding citizens' trusts, stagnating their own development and rising the standards of the their expectation for quality services at their detriments (Appuhami, Perera & Perera, 2011). Alsudiri, Al-Karaghouli and Eldabi (2013) argue: 'once the severe limitation of PPP has been addressed and its application to the real world situations are recognized, the analytical and empirical critiques from the likes of McQuaid and Scherrer cannot stand. He concludes, 'contrary to McQuaid and Scherrer, the notion of PPP is practically meaningful and useful to the development of an area' (Baker, 2012).

Berg (2011a) admits that the concept PPP is 'often misunderstood and mostly ill-defined' but goes on to argue that 'in spite of its fairly recent appearance on the scene, the concept PPP, has long been in existence and addresses issues which have been central in public service delivery (PSD) at least during the last 1000 years, albeit under different names/headings' (Bloomfield & Ahern, 2011). Commenting on available PPP studies, Chinyere and Xu (2012) concurs that 'the purpose is of variable quality: under its aegis come serious service production as well as a quality tracts, high level service-competitiveness tracts, charming service satisfaction, consumption of impressive and high goods and services; and straightforward fulfillment of the needs and wants of the beneficiaries' and adds 'whatever its goal, the inclusion of the private party in public service delivery clearly responds to a growing ever changing citizens' demands and wants for quality goods and services'.

A central issue in the policy and implementation debate on PPP is the creation of efficient public and private partners' capacity to cope with more intense challenge in risk in the arrangement (Codescasa & Ponzini, 2011). This has drawn attention to mechanisms of risk handling in both developed and developing world, which lie well behind best practices frontiers (Brinkerhoff, 2011). The knowledge and progressive understanding of risks are not new to them, if not the world, has been as central aspect of concern (particularly to financiers/donors of PPP projects) that have often witnessed dramatic PPPs failure during rapid 'adaptation and implementation'. In order to put knowledge about risks in PPP into productive use, policy makers and implementers ought to undergo a lengthy learning process and are to be supported by coherent and systematic analogy of the subject matter (Gbadegesin & Aluko, 2014). Such interventions have not been forthcoming such that would-be-beneficiaries so far had been left in the cold. There has been but less directed attempt to close these gaps within the available literatures and other forms of documentations (Glennie & Lodhia, 2013). Unfortunately, finance market imperfection, risk aversion, externalities and collaboration as well as implementation failures are widely cited examples of PPP failures which influence the pace of PPP initiation and implementation and weak linkages to achievement of desired goals are increasingly recognized as examples of PPPs failures (Grossman, 2012). The experience of collapsed PPPs projects has turned the attention of policy makers, implementers and financiers to the appropriate risk free-environment for a successful PPP engagement.

In this vein, six key questions for a risk-free PPP are:

- What is the meaning of public service in the context of PPP in relation to concepts and practices?
- What are the respective risk management issues and practices for a PPP project to succeed and well?
- What are the specific risk management fundamentals for a PPP arrangement to work better than any other alternatives?
- What is the optimal way to design and implement a concrete risk management framework so as to make a PPP arrangement successful?
- What are the necessary conditions for success in terms of tools for successful management of risk?
- What are the roles, functions and duties of the different stakeholders in ensuring sustainable risk management in a PPP arrangement?

This book seeks to address these questions in the context of both developed and developing countries experiencing rapid 'excessive-ever-changing demands and wants of the citizens' and ever dwindling financial resources in the public sector. The individual chapters are carefully written with deeper consideration of both countries and, taken together are intended as a reader on risk management and PPP in developed and developing countries. The book attempts to apply recent developments in risk and PPP studies (especially in the areas of theoretical and conceptual considerations and most especially empirical examinations) to the study of risks and PPP in both developed and developing countries. The focus is on the design and application of specific types of PPP to fostering service delivery provision in both developed and developing countries rather than on the theories underlying them.

The book divides risk management in a PPP arrangement into two broad perspectives: public and private partners'-side perspectives. The former consist of measures (such as risk awakening, risk transfer and favorable risk allocation), which change the nature and intensity of government participation in PPP affecting its success and stimulates the urges for finding solutions unto them. The latter provides inputs and support for PPP implementation-level execution (including taking a lesser risk, providing adequate finances, and performance of obligations of the bargain). Earlier studies and writings have never attempted to emphasize the interaction of these two critical components of PPP arrangement in the midst of risk occurrences right from their inception stage and even during the rapid implementation. In contrast, this book emphasizes the role of a detailed understanding of risks in its entirety during all the stages of PPP processes but many times neglected by the policy makers and implementers alike. Where possible, the book tries to assess empirical evidence on the impact of given perspectives and incorporate examples of executed PPP projects from the developing countries and other developed countries to highlight good practices.

In line with the six questions raised above, this book was prepared based on practical objectives. These objectives were defined and addressed in the course of conducting research and preparing this book. Four critical practical objectives stood out clearly in this work. These were:-

1. To support practitioners' efforts gained by new sustainable risk management models in a fully scrutinized and broadened risk management framework.
2. To study and identify risk management opportunities through the cycle of PPP, especially for PPP projects, content and specialized tools for effective risk management.
3. To contribute to a strategy relative to socio-economic wants and needs by increasing the motivation for the deployment of cost effective and flexible solutions using risk management tools and content.

4. To provide guidelines and recommendations for utilizing different ways and tools of managing risks in PPP, as well as to mode and quantify necessary actions.

To achieve these objectives, personal knowledge and experiences of the author were intertwined with scrutiny of works from earlier researchers/writers on the various areas of risks and risks in PPP arrangement. This led to a fuller grasps on different aspects of the subject matter of this work. The major focus was on an integrated and exegetical manner on the six major themes identified and hinted in the questions posed above.

Two methodological approaches were developed and adopted for collection of materials for this work (Denzin & Lincoln, 2011). First, a comprehensive general literature review and specific literature review capitalizing on some specific case studies to identify initial lists of risks associated with PPP projects in differential infrastructural and service sectors and generally available mitigating measures for those risks (Cohen, Manion & Morrison, 2011). Secondly, evaluation of the criticality of the identified risks as well as the effectiveness of corresponding mitigation measures (Zikmund, Babin, Carr & Griffin, 2010). In all, collected data and personal experience and knowledge were then integrated into three different parts with each of the parts have three chapters. Two other chapters introduce and conclude the work respectively, making in all a work of three parts and nine chapters. Suffice to note however; the chapters are captured with a deeper exploration of their 'dedicated areas' much to the fulfillment of discursive requirements for a successful risk-free PPP projects execution and implementation. Even more, the chapters suggest promising avenues for the development of operational tool for handling PPP projects' functional reviews and proactive management strategies for various different risky domains.

With inputs from two methodological approaches used (Zohrabi, 2013), this book addresses a range of matters associated with risks and PPP, from policy considerations to implementation issues. The book is divided in to three sections and 9 chapters. Each of the sections and chapters of the book focuses on specific area of knowledge about risk and PPP. As indicated, the book has three sections. Section 1 is about introduction, service delivery and parts with two chapters of paradox of service delivery and the quest for PPP. Section 2 is on risk management issues and practice for success. It has five chapters of risks and project phases, risk sharing in a partnership, risk in a partnership, establishing boundaries for risk taking and risk management framework. Section 3 is on enticement actions for effective risk management in public private partnership. It has two chapters of risk management planning, sustainability risks management and risks shareholders, and key to partnership: building effective risk management. There is an abstract on each chapter to explain briefly what the chapter contains.

Section 1 presents the detailed introduction to the book by looking at service delivery in the context of the concept and practice of PPP, the framework for using PPP and an empirical analysis of public services in respect to themes of the book in three chapters of introduction, the paradox of service delivery and quests for public private partnerships.

Chapter 1 examines the paradox of public service delivery and the relevance of PPP in curtailing the paradox. Having introduced the subject matter, the chapter suggests that it's the public and private perspectives that play a critical role in dissuading the paradox of service delivery. These perspectives provide useful practical insights they offer fully in guiding formulation and implementation of PPPs. Furthermore, the chapter suggests that the newer PPP perspective (derived from public and private financial and risk-ownership capabilities) offers a more comprehensive policy framework in countries in both the developed and developing world because it incorporates public service delivery distortions, financial imperfection and PPP project failures. Using this framework, the chapter proposes core elements of partnership plus concrete strategy approach (which combines finances, competitiveness and skills of the private sector with risk sharing) for a successful risk-free PPP. Finally, the chapter concludes aspects considered in the chapter generally.

In Chapter 2 there is examination of the quests for PPP that has taken the world by a storm in promoting service delivery provision. The chapter argues that there is a triangular motif for adopting PPP. It these motifs that governments rely on in overcoming the disadvantages of traditional method of service delivery provision and investing in private sector inclusiveness in development agenda. Basic dynamics of PPP arrangement and public-private interactions are illustrated through rational, critical success factors (CSFs) and dangers and/or challenges in adopting PPP as a procurement and service delivery tool. The chapter thereafter suggests that upgrading PPP to solving the menace of poor service delivery of even low quality, PPP capabilities must be fostered through a process that entails clearer knowledge of the environment, legal framework and the cycle of PPP projects themselves. A conclusion ends the chapter.

Section 2 discusses risk management issues and practices for success. This is done in four chapters of risks and project phases; risk sharing in a partnership; risk in a partnership; establishing boundaries for risk taking; and risk management framework.

In Chapter 3, there is consideration of the interplay between the three cores of PPP project cycle. Following a practical analysis of the PPP project cycle, the chapter analyses the three perspectives of the basics of PPP project implementation and determining their importance for an effective, efficient and efficacious management of risks. The chapter emphasizes that selecting, planning and designing projects phase is the most critical phases in a PPP arrangement since it determines the success or failure of such a project. The chapter goes on to analyses this issues in the realm of three broader stages of selection of projects, planning projects and designing projects. The chapter takes on to look at the second most important stage of this phase which is procurement and contractual design choice phase. Under this stage, three sub-stages of traditional procurement versus partnering procurement, procurement process under PPP projects and PPP tendering are treated. Meanwhile the last stage in this phase of construction/ service delivery phases discussions were made of the sub-stages of project mobilization phase, project operation phase and project close-out and termination phase. The chapter ends with a conclusion.

Chapter 4 presents the benchmark for risk sharing in a PPP arrangement. the chapter examines widely the concept of risks, highlight several road maps for an effective risk management in a PPP arrangement. It also set out the conditions necessary for a successful PPP projects. The chapter considers risk in view of appreciating basics concepts applicable in this book. In the main, the three concepts discussed in the chapter are the elusive concept of risk, risk management and strategy. The chapter goes on to scrutinize a simple roadmap for an effective risk management based on three subcomponents (assessment, designing the sharing framework and implementation) and presents the results as effective. The detailed coverage of this roadmap provides a more comprehensive handling of risks than ever thought of before. Finally, the chapter examines potential determinations of risk management success in a PPP arrangement and concludes that sound necessary conditions for success must have a strong capabilities' of the public partner, private partner as well as the sustained private partner's commitment. The chapter ends with a summary as well as a conclusion.

In Chapter 5, a detailed discussion both general and specific is made of risk in a partnership. The chapter is expounded in three areas: risk classification, risk perspectives of parties and risk criteria. The section on risk classification navigates risks and its effects on PPP projects. It illustrates the effects of risk in a PPP project through classification. It goes on to suggest that a proper understanding of risk classification must be considered in terms of the typology of risk, risk factors and risk categories in stages of the PPP projects. This ought to be facilitated by amiable take of the prime actors in PPP projects that is the risk perspectives of the parties involved, especially the public partner, the private partner and the creditors. The chapter also examines a range of elements which constitute better risk criteria. It discussed normative approach, descriptive approach, and normative and descriptive approaches vis-à-vis other approaches. The chapter concludes with practical hints on grasping in totality numerous risks embedded in PPP projects.

In Chapter 6, establishing boundaries for risk taking is examined in greater detail. It can be argued that to overcome the challenge of managing risk, it is crystal clear there ought to be clear boundaries for risk sharing to take a noble route. These boundaries were established within the context of risk attitude, risk and returns as well as risk response. Risk attitude is examined within the realm of risk loving, risk aversion/reduction and risk neutral. This was followed by the examination on risk and return within the specific areas of risk target, risk capacity and risk appetite. Before a conclusion was derived for the chapter a deeper examination of risk utility/risk tolerance, risk avoidance and risk retention as important aspects of risk response was ably done.

Chapter 7 analyses risk management framework. It explores empirical evidences to cement the arguments put forward in the chapter. The analyses are condensed into three parts. The first part discussed risk management fundamentals in detail with deeper considerations in terms of risk estimation, risk mitigation and risk transfer/allocation. This deeper analysis is followed with detailed discussions on risk management processes. Considerations were also made on risk identification, risk assessment and risk analysis. The chapter also examined risk control and monitoring. In it, the chapter looked at risk control, risk monitoring and risk auditing and reporting.

Section 3 analyses enticement actions for effective risk management in PPP in two chapters.

Chapter 8 analyses risk management planning, sustainability risk management and risk shareholders. It explores alternative approaches to a successful implementation of PPP project. It emphasizes that an organization needs proper risk planning, be endowed with the ingredients for a sustainable risk and above all the stakeholders must be deeply involved. Risk management planning was considered within the context of process of risk management planning, risk management plan and risk budgeting. Sustainability risk management was looked at in terms of characteristics of sustainability, strategies for PPP and sustainability risks management and model of sustainability risks management. Lastly, risk stakeholders were considered in terms of their vitality; relationships and project politics and trust and their circles. A conclusion is provided to end the chapter.

In Chapter 9, an examination of the key to partnership as to building an effective risk management is carried out. The chapter stresses theoretical and empirical evidences on risk management strategy in PPP and suggests a sequence of actions that can be undertaken to have an efficient, effective and efficacious PPP project. The chapter is presented in three broad areas. The ingredients for a successful risk management is examined within the realm of operating environment of risk partnership, building blocks for successful risk partnerships and key principles for a successful risk partnerships. The contractual partnerships: the tools are considered in terms of risk mapping, risk register and risk matrix. The role of ICT for transforming risk management is discussed in terms of information needs and networks for mitigating risk, ICT best practices, and risk communication. The chapter has a conclusion at the end.

Each of the nine chapters has a list of reference which acts as a guide to further sources of information for those interested to gain a little deeper knowledge on a particular chapter. At the end, appendices and bibliography are also be provided.

The book will be useful to those interested in issues of managing risks in a PPP arrangement in developed and developing economies. It will be of particular use to the following: policy makers concerned about risk management challenges and successful PPP projects which are risk-free drawing on international best practices; public sector organization seeking strategies for effective service delivery through PPP; private sector organizations seeking means of profitable investments and strategies for enhancing their ability to grow; public-private sector partnerships to foster competitiveness; students interested in risk management and PPPs in both developed and developing economies on advanced undergraduate and post-graduate courses in risk management and PPP studies; and the public who may be curious to know more and more.

During the last few months, I have not only learned about the concepts of public private partnerships in greater depth but I had had the opportunity to work as a curious researcher with keen interest to assemble facts that can easily be comprehended during this small adventure to write a treatise on the subject of risk in public private partnership. My gratitude goes to all who have in a way or another made my life a little livable in the course of my existence so far. From the long list, I want to first acknowledge my gratitude to the persons with whom I had a particular contact during the execution of this project. I warmly thank Professor Peter Okidi Lating PhD for provided assistance. To Contemporary Philosopher, Fr. Augustine Mugarura, PhD for his useful encouragement, comments and advice for improving this project during our interactions.

Furthermore, I am particularly thankful to those persons that filled all other aspects of my life. To my wife Atto Mary Joyce Obicci for het intensive support in the most difficult moments, for their examples of self-improvement, for the encouragement in difficult times and good ones and specially for being the mother of my children. To my children Otunnu Norman Obicci, Ajok Esther Fiona Obicci, Kittim Peter Obicci, Obama Emmanuel Obicci and Opira Francis Obicci for their love and support at all times. Moreover, my eternal gratitude goes to God for giving the support in every aspect of my life and His infinite force in everyday.

Finally, I thank my parents the late Ongom Matthew Obicci (RIP) and Akidi Alice Obicci, for being the most role models, the best parents, the best mentors, for their unconditional and everlasting love, for encouraging me never to surrender, for the indefatigable support for being my light in the dark times. My everlasting gratitude go to them.

Agoro ero kumeno!

Peter Adoko Obicci
POA-Kittim Consultants, Uganda
December 2016

REFERENCES

Aaronson, S. A. (2011). Limited partnership: Business, government, civil society and the public in the extractive industry transparency initiative. *Public Administration and Development*, *31*(1), 50–63. doi:10.1002/pad.588

Abbott, L., & Grady, C. (2011). A systematic review of the empirical literature evaluating IRBs: What we know and what we still need to learn. *Journal of Empirical Research on Human Research Ethics; JERHRE*, *6*(1), 3–19. doi:10.1525/jer.2011.6.1.3 PMID:21460582

Abednego, M. P., & Ogunlana, S. O. (2006). Good project governance for proper risk allocation in public-private partnership in Indonesia. *International Journal of Project Management*, *24*(7), 622–634. doi:10.1016/j.ijproman.2006.07.010

Akintoye, A. (2006). Public private partnerships for sustainable development of infrastructure in developing countries.*Proceedings of International conference on Built Environment.*

Alexander, R. (2012). Network structures and the performance of brownfield redevelopment PPPs. *Public Performance & Management Review*, *35*(4), 753–768. doi:10.2753/PMR1530-9576350409

Alsudiri, T., Al-Karaghouli, W., & Eldabi, T. (2013). Alignment of large project management process to business strategy: A review and conceptual framework. *Journal of Enterprise Information Management*, *26*(5), 596–615. doi:10.1108/JEIM-07-2013-0050

Antoniou, F., Aretoulis, G. N., Konstantinidis, D., & Kalfakakou, G. P. (2013). Complexity in the evaluation of contract types employed for the construction of highway projects. *Procedia: Social and Behavioral Sciences*, *74*(29), 448–458. doi:10.1016/j.sbspro.2013.03.048

Baker, K. (2012). Understanding strategic service partnerships. *Public Performance & Management Review*, *35*(4), 660–678. doi:10.2753/PMR1530-9576350405

Berg, A. (2011a). Not roadmaps but toolboxes: Analyzing pioneering national programmes for sustainable consumption and production. *Journal of Consumer Policy*, *34*(1), 9–23. doi:10.1007/s10603-010-9129-2

Bloomfield, P., & Ahern, F. D. (2011). Long-term infrastructure partnerships: Contracting risks and risk-reduction strategies. *State & Local Government Review*, *43*(1), 49–59. doi:10.1177/0160323X11400435

Bovaird, T. (2006). Developing new relationships with the market in the procurement of public services. *Public Administration*, *84*(1), 81–102. doi:10.1111/j.0033-3298.2006.00494.x

Bovaird, T., & Davies, R. (2011). Outcome-based service commissioning and delivery – does it make a difference? In S. Groeneveld & S. van de Walle (Eds.), *New Steering Concepts in Public Management, IPMN Research in Public Policy Analysis and Management 21*. Rotterdam: Emerald Press. doi:10.1108/S0732-1317(2011)0000021011

Brinkerhoff, D. W., & Brinkerhoff, J. M. (2011). Public–private partnerships: Perspectives on purposes, publicness, and good governance. *Public Administration and Development*, *13*(1), 2–14. doi:10.1002/pad.584

Brinkerhoff, J. M. (2011). David and Goliath: Diaspora organizations as partners in the development industry. *Public Administration and Development*, *31*(1), 37–49. doi:10.1002/pad.587

Brown, K., & Keast, R. (2005). Social services policy and delivery in Australia: Centre- periphery mixes. *Policy and Politics*, *33*(3), 505–518. doi:10.1332/0305573054325774

Brown, T., Potoski, M., & Van Slyke, D. (2006). Managing public service contracts: Aligning values, institutions, and markets. *Public Administration Review*, *66*(3), 323–331. doi:10.1111/j.1540-6210.2006.00590.x

Chinyere, I. I., & Xu, X. (2012). Public – private partnership: The underlining principles of infrastructure investment, finance, and development projects. *International Journal of Business and Management*, *7*, 109–125.

Cicmil, S., & Marshall, D. (2005). Insights into collaboration at the project level: Complexity, social interaction and procurement mechanisms. *Building Research and Information*, *33*(6), 523–535. doi:10.1080/09613210500288886

Codescasa, G., & Ponzini, D. (2011). Public-private partnership: A delusion for urban regeneration? Evidence from Italy. *European Planning Studies*, *19*(4), 647–667. doi:10.1080/09654313.2011.548471

Cohen, L., Manion, L., & Morrison, K. (2011). *Research methods in education* (7th ed.). New York, NY: Routledge.

Denzin, N. K., & Lincoln, Y. S. (2011). *The Sage handbook of qualitative research* (4th ed.). Thousand Oaks, CA: Sage.

Emirullah, C., & Azam, M. (2014). Examining public private partnerships in ASEAN countries: The role of investment climate. *Theoretical and Applied Economics*, *2*(591), 67–76.

Entwistle, T., & Martin, S. (2005). From competition to collaboration in public service delivery: A new agenda for research. *Public Administration*, *83*(1), 233–254. doi:10.1111/j.0033-3298.2005.00446.x

Fatemi, M., & Behmanesh, M. R. (2012). New public management approach and accountability. *International Journal of Management Economics and Social Sciences*, *1*, 42–49.

Forrer, J., Kee, J. E., Newcomer, K. E., & Boyer, E. (2010). Public private partnerships and the public accountability question. *Public Administration Review*, *70*(3), 475–484. doi:10.1111/j.1540-6210.2010.02161.x

Gazley, B. (2010). Linking collaborative capacity to performance measurement in Government- Nonprofit Partnerships. *Nonprofit and Voluntary Sector Quarterly*, *39*(4), 653–673. doi:10.1177/0899764009360823

Gbadegesin, J. T., & Aluko, B. T. (2014). Public private partnerships/private finance initiatives for financing infrastructure in public tertiary institutions in Nigeria. *Built Environment Project and Asset Management*, *4*(2), 199–215. doi:10.1108/BEPAM-04-2013-0010

Glennie, M., & Lodhia, S. (2013). The influence of internal organizational factors on corporate- community partnership agendas: An Australian case study. *Meditari Accountancy Research*, *21*(1), 52–67. doi:10.1108/MEDAR-07-2012-0022

Grossman, S. A. (2012). Introduction: The emerging role of partnership governance. *Public Performance & Management Review*, *35*, 575–577. doi:10.2753/PMR1530-9576350400

Ibrahim, A. D., Price, A. D. F., & Dainty, A. R. J. (2006). The analysis and allocation of risks in public private partnerships in infrastructure projects in Nigeria. *Journal of Financial Management of Property and Construction*, *11*(3), 149–163. doi:10.1108/13664380680001086

Ke, Y., Wang, S. Q., & Chan, A. P. C. (2011). Equitable risks allocation of projects inside China: Analyses from Delphi survey studies. *Chinese Management Studies*, *5*(3), 298–310. doi:10.1108/17506141111163372

Keast, R., & Brown, K. (2006). The government service delivery project: A case study of the push and pull of central government coordination. *Public Management Review*, *4*(4), 1–21.

Keçi, J. (2015). Public Private Partnership for Infrastructure Projects: Mapping the Key Risks, *International Journal of Social, Behavioral, Educational, Economic. Business and Industrial Engineering*, *9*(9), 3085–3095.

Kort, M., & Klijn, E.-H. (2011). Public–private partnerships in urban regeneration projects: Organizational form or managerial capacity? *Public Administration Review*, *71*(4), 618–626. doi:10.1111/j.1540-6210.2011.02393.x

Maylor, H., Vidgen, R., & Carver, S. (2008). Managerial complexity in project-based operations: A grounded model and its implications for practice. *Project Management Journal*, *39*(1), 15–26. doi:10.1002/pmj.20057

McQuaid, R. W., & Scherrer, W. (2010). *Changing reasons for public–private partnerships (PPPs). Public Money and Management Journal*. doi:10.1080/09540960903492331

Neshkova, M. I., & Kostadinova, T. (2012). The effectiveness of administrative reform in new democracies. *Public Administration Review*, *72*(3), 324–333. doi:10.1111/j.1540-6210.2011.02483.x

Rees, J., Mullins, D., & Bovaird, T. (2012). *Third sector partnerships for public service delivery: An evidence review*. Third Sector Research Centre Working Paper 60.

Ringold, D., Holla, A., Koziol, M., & Srinivasan, S. (2012). *Citizens and service delivery Assessing the Use of Social Accountability Approaches in the Human Development Sectors*. Washington, DC: The World Bank.

Trafford, S., & Proctor, T. (2006). Successful joint venture partnerships: Public-private partnerships. *International Journal of Public Sector Management*, *19*(2), 117–129. doi:10.1108/09513550610650392

Xiao, H. J., & Zhang, G. (2011). Modeling optimal risk allocation in PPP projects using artificial neural networks. *International Journal of Project Management*, *29*(5), 591–603. doi:10.1016/j.ijproman.2010.07.011

Zikmund, G. W., Babin, B. J., Carr, C. J., & Griffin, M. (2010). *Business Research Methods* (8th ed.). London: South-Western, Cengage Learning.

Zohrabi, M. (2013). Mixed method research: Instruments, validity, reliability and reporting findings. *Theory and Practice in Language Studies*, *3*(2), 254–262. doi:10.4304/tpls.3.2.254-262

Section 1
Introduction, Service Delivery, and Partnerships

Chapter 1
Paradox of Service Delivery

ABSTRACT

This chapter reviews the literature on the paradox of services as a cause for the necessity of PPP. First, the chapter discusses why governments pursue PPPs form the perspectives of both the private and public and how this has brought about the urge for PPPs throughout the world. Second, the chapter reviews the principles of PPP from a current development and management perspectives. Three core elements are crucial for PPP to thrive, and these are finance, skills of the private sector and risk sharing are reviewed. This chapter analyses papers, case-studies and reports concerning the challenge of service delivery provision in the current and concludes that, from a practical perspectives, it is proper that governments ought to rethink their mode of service delivery provision, and that PPP seems to be the right answer in the scenario.

Reality is that which, when you stop believing in it, doesn't go away. - Philip K. Dick

INTRODUCTION

After more than dozen decades of wanting public service provisions and dismay, the inclusion of the private parties has finally taken off. Now, we are witnessing the first signs of evidence of what might become the explosion of private parties' involvement and interplays that will be shaping service delivery provision of the future. Similar to the public collaborations in service delivery provision, the new 'marriage' will become more relevant in the face of dwindling public finances. Within the cistern of development discourse, the urge and desire for public private partnership (PPP) in the paradox of service delivery is very real, alive and kicking. The clearest reality is that the prospects of actionable course either 'conventional' or 'non-conventional' ought to be undertaken as a noble approach to tackle the twin evils of scarce resources and insatiable human quests for more and more quality services. Thus Governments and PPP practitioners as active initiators and implementers of PPP projects respectively may leverage the unending quests for more and more quality services are examples of a 'conventional case', while the citizens/populace with high 'value-added' demands for quality services would be one

DOI: 10.4018/978-1-5225-2503-5.ch001

of a 'non-conventional' case. This chapter will discuss the different perspectives corrugated in the paradox of service delivery. It specifically tackles individually the perspectives of the private, public, and a combination of public and private under the umbrella of a partnership. It will also deal with the core elements necessary to exist for the partnership strategy in handling the paradox of service delivery become of relevance. A summarized version of the chapter shall together with a conclusion end the chapter.

PUBLIC AND PRIVATE PERSPECTIVES

No one, Diana (2014) contemplates can dispute the immensity with which the demand of quality services has tripled and duly engulfed the whole world. By the turn of the 21st century, the demand for quality services has reached a disproportionate level in terms of resources which could be used to provide those services (Garcia, 2014). Its continual enragements will even the more see dwindling scarce resources yet there would continue to be an explosion of fuller exploitation of available resources (Eggers & Macmillan, 2013). Numerous examples could be mentioned: new products, content produced and individualized spent-thrift consumptions, productivity application in line with continual technological advancement, or health and physical solution to increase quality of life (Robinson, 2015). Every human being now yearns for personal enjoyment to harness inner quests for good life as sole point of inspiration.

In the main, Government that traditionally has a role and primary function of providing services to the citizens/populace finds itself in an awkward position (Marty & Voisin, 2005). As the demands of the citizens weighs it down, similarly inadequacy of resources are also taking their toll at the same time. Many of the new challenges will require access to finances in an orderly and meaningful manner. This means governments must concerns themselves with purely their financial health indicators. Garcia (2014) suggests that the indicators are majorly three: sustainability, flexibility and vulnerability. By sustainability indicator, its meant "… the degree to which a government can maintain its existing financial obligations both in respect of its service commitments to the public and financial commitments to creditors, employees and others without increasing the relative debt or tax burden on the economy within which it operates" (p.364). By flexibility, its meant "… the degree to which a government can change its debt or tax burden on the economy within which it operates to meet its existing financial obligations both in respect of its service commitments to the public and financial commitments to creditors, employees and others" (p. 364). And by vulnerability, its meant "…the degree to which a government is dependent on sources of funding outside its control or influence or is exposed to risks that could impair its ability to meet its existing financial obligations both in respect of its service commitments to the public and financial commitments to creditors, employees and others" (p.364). In the conclave of financial crunch, the government finds itself in a compromising position such that these indicators bedeviled the government into a paradox of service delivery (Ringold, Holla, Koziol & Srinivasan, 2012).

Currently, the vulnerability financial health indicator of government functioning has become a bedrock of all activities in both developed and developing countries (Abels, 2007). This is because there are lots of risks involved in whatever undertaking the government might want to, so as to meet the demands of the citizenry. Overcoming these risks, which are already gateways to failure in meeting assigned obligations- public value and good-, has seen governments taking steps that has previously been ignored generally (Akintoye, 2008). It has created a paradox which will therefore become (is already becoming) the mean to reach appropriate content and applications of development strategies, and to provide additional value to service delivery provision in a number of sectors (Fatemi & Behmanesh, 2012). It exploits the fact that the finances can be obtained from elsewhere rather than the public purse and these finances can be used to fund public infrastructure and provide services (Pârvu & Voicu-Olteanu, 2009). These facts are very pertinent for development initiatives to realize their goals. The realization of the noble roles the private sector can play in development of the public domain enables context-aware search service in current and future ambient financial environments (for example, making use of available finances in the hands of the private sector organizations as well as their unique management techniques for profit maximization) (Tetřevová, 2006). In short, the paradox of public service delivery as of now could easily be turned into pieces of historical museum or even more critical in the garbage domain than in the lucrative future public service provision (McCann, 2014).

As a result, the use of financial resources from the private sector as well as their skills and knowledge on management for profit maximization is becoming an attractive expansion markets for all governments and investors (Cankar & Petkovšek, 2013). It is a clash in many respects: different business cultures (public good versus profit maximization); governance influences (bureaucratic versus non-bureaucratic); procurement model (collectively-based versus privately-based) and the relationship between the user and service provider (value-based versus innovation-based) (Cumming, 2007). However, in this clash, two main protagonists do exist: the public and the private whose interest and longings must be catered for. An understanding of the perspectives of the public as well as the private, thenceforth, can provide a deeper appreciation of these protagonists.

Public Perspective

The viewpoint of the public perspective in the paradox of service delivery is rooted in the origin of the term "public". From the Latin verb publicus (also poplicus), public is from populous which generally, denotes loosely some mass population ("the people") in association with some matter of common interest. One of the primary concerns of the public is to ensure simultaneous balances in the achievement of the common interest for all. In this vein, Alastair (2005) contends public is a group of individual people who associate to achieve a common goal. A public then can well be described as the highest possible level of cooperation and collaboration consistent with a tolerable level of individual interested charted onto the common good at a given level of convenience, equated with collective equilibrium (Bloomfield, 2006).

In the paradoxical service delivery situation, the public can be thought of as real collaborative and cooperative spirit, which in combination with the requisite measures, achieve individual and collective balance (Hope, 2005). This implies organization on the part of a group of people who in facing a similar problem; recognizes it and make all efforts to address it by themselves. It means they organize about the situation just as in the case of the world of production and consumption that has gone into some deficit for enormous reasons (Hefetz & Warner, 2012). The public would then be linked into four main categories: nonpublics, latent publics, aware publics, and active publics. According to the situational theory of publics (Matei, 2006), nonpublics are those who have no problems- these are never 'affected' by the paradox of public service delivery; the latent publics are those who have a problem, for example, failure to enjoy quality services due to challenges in service delivery provision; aware publics are the ones who recognize that they have a problem, for example, they feel the pinch of say poor service delivery but are impotent to redress it; and active publics are those who so something about their problem, for example, these are people who recognizes the reality of a situation and actively take a step to remedy the darker side. Here, the public is taken to mean the active ones (Adeyemi, Oladapo & Akindele, 2005). It's therefore considered as a collection of individuals that develop a group consciousness around a problematic situation and act to solve the problematic situation. It can also be comprehended as a group of people who relate to an organization, who demonstrate varying degree of activity-passivity, and who might (or might not) interact with others concerning their relationship with the organization (Skietrys, Raipa, & Bartkus, 2008).

As the demands of the public for quality services increases and that of their production decreases, service delivery provision shift from weirdly wanted to loss of trust in the public sector organizations that provide them (Singaravelloo, 2010). This case implies a public turns out to be a subset of the set of stakeholders that comprise those people concerned with specific issues. As

Koppenjan (2005) sees it, a public does not necessarily have an exchange relationship but it's both self-creating and self-organizing. This is why when the demand of the public is not met as ought to be, loss of trust in the provider becomes inevitable. In this case, the public become either target or intervening but at most influential. Target publics are those publics whose involvement is necessary for achieving organization's goals while intervening publics are opinion formers and mediators who pass information to the target publics (Maseko, 2014). The influential publics on the other hand, are those that are the target turns to for consultation, whose value judgments are influential upon how target publics will judge anti public relations material.

In service delivery, the public are either gainers or losers, and no general presumption that the occurrence of any of these conditions can fail to be registered. But one can legitimately say that the world of service delivery has become less responsive to the public as gainers (Bing, Akintoye, Edwards & Hardcastle, 2005a). There has been a general loss in the production processes with daring consequences on the consumption levels. In due course, the current deficit cannot be adjusted since there has been too much confusion as to the understanding of the concept-public. There has been a retrogressive understanding of the term-public, such that it had been used interchangeably with client, customer and citizen (Grimsey & Lewis, 2005). This interchangeability has only helped to heap more confusion as it came to service delivery provision. Thus, from a service delivery perspective, public has largely been ill-understood and at most ill-defined (Haran, Alastair, Berry, McGreal, Smyth, Kashayap & Hutchison., 2013). The association of the public with the real service delivery raises the issue of its understanding. As mentioned above, it can be suggested that attempts needed to be made to discuss and agree to a shared understanding of the relationship between public as client or as customer or as citizen. The understanding must be placed within a broad conceptual framework which can be used later for systematic analysis of the content of this book. An escalation in this understanding indicates an appreciation of the position of the public in service delivery and a plummet denotes downgrading the importance of publics which is very unhealthy for a fuller grasps of the content of this book. One of the difficulties with this term of the Public is that it was impracticable to attempt definitive expositions of the term public, which would rather attract universal acceptance and be invariably applicable across different communities (McCann, Aranda-Mena & Edwards, 2014). Given that this may not possible, the discussions in these sub section of chapter two, is to seek to provide a logically consistent and comprehensively simple basis for assessing the development of PSD systems (Brzozowska, 2006).

In practice, therefore, it's important to resort to the real life situation which is derived from the concept of the public as client or as consumer or as a customer or as a citizen. The real effective position in service delivery has for long been taken as a client (Trafford & Proctor, 2006). This conception has its origin in the traditional professional model; where there was a tendency of dominating the server-served relationship (Egnell & Halden, 2013).). Differential attitudes abound at this stage, because officials and politicians often referred to public services as clients or collectively as client groups (Gupta & Biswas,

2010). This raised some costs in terms of the best attitude to the public then tended to predominates as officials and politicians often referred to their shared perception of the public interest but without any meaningful engagement with that very public (Brinkerhoff & Brinkerhoff, 2011). Owing to the conceptual and attitudinal limitations, the public could not have a real bearing on the kinds of services provided to them. Interests of the officials and politicians were the most easily available commodity as nearly all public interests were catered for as secondary. According to Aziz (2007), the key characteristics of the client relationship are that the client is, on the whole, dependent on the professionals since all power lies with the professionals. However, this included a large number of crude feelings of impotence on the part of the public in relation to a particular service demanded or wanted. The main demerit with such a conception was that there could be sudden changes in key service delivery areas without any consideration of the interests and demand of the public (Delmon, 2009). The difficulties in the conception are noticeable in two-fold: connotation with closed making decision making in regard to service delivery a nuisance and the often established paternalistic decision making including in social services with all its ills (Estache & Wren-Lewis, 2009).

The perspective of a public as a customer has been used extensively to examine the competitiveness of the public demands and interest and those of the private sector (Kamarkar, 2014). This conception highlights the link between the unsatisfactory character of client's encounter in real service delivery provisions, and a shift in encounters with professional service providers. It underlines the fact that the preference of the public as customers is rooted in the shortcomings of public as client in particular the comparative impotency of the public under the client system (Banerjee, Oetzel & Ranganathan, 2006). Large current discontent with service delivery relies on the taking the public as customer something that originated from the management thinkers in the private sector with the ideas enthusiastically extended to the delivery and management of service delivery (Akintoye, 2006). Hence, this conception of the public suggests that it is desirable to avoid some members of the public who might demonstrate some bias towards a service provided to them. In effect, the conception of the public as customer brought about the idea of customer-driven government based on an approach which strives to meet the needs of the customer rather than the bureaucracy (Iossa & Martimort, 2015). It's hankered on the belief that the customer is always right because the customer can chose, criticize or reject. This is completely divorce of the public as client, because in it the client gives up all the privileges of a customer and instead accepts the superior judgment of the professional. It thus derives the claims of professionals for monopoly of wisdom and proficiency (Kuppusamy, 2010). Given the unsatisfactory situation, customer service model has been adapted to public service context by reorienting it to set service for the public as the key organizational values that must be upheld (Jomo & Chowdhury, 2009). However, creating a 'customer-first' culture requires not just major investment in improved delivery systems and staff training to develop good interpersonal skills but also fundamental organizational change (Chowdhury, Chen & Tiong, 2011).

The conception of the public as a consumer is but despite being a mixed blessing has been criticized on various grounds (Trebilcocka & Rosenstocka, 2015). A major pitfall is equating it with the presumption that the remaining clients as customers would enjoy the power exercised by purchasers in the market place but this is ridiculous because the buyer-seller relationship rarely exists in the public sector (Vining & Boardman, 2008a). In spite of this, experiences have suggested that this conception calls for an inventive approach to customer relation so as to win loyalty and strong support for services. Another closely related pitfall is that narrow scope for active role of the public within the diverse environment to service delivery provision (Osborne, 2010). This is because the customer care approach does not tip the balance of power strongly in favor of the user (Barber, 2008). It is because the customer may turn out to be a form of organization sleight of hand in which bureaucratic paternalism disappears only to be replaced by a new, more subtle form of managerial paternalism (Roehrich, Lewis & George, 2014). It relies heavily of course, on the basis of citizenry which reliance has more to offer because in different ways, they focus more sharply on empowering the public users and funders of services (Jomo, Chowdhury, Sharma & Platz, 2016). Perry, Hondeghem and Wise (2010) articulate that the concept of consumers refers essentially to the relationship of a person to a product or service. They also note that as concept, consumerism has advanced steadily and focused its arguments around the five key principles of access, choice, information, redress and representation. Ramalingam (2013) retorts consumers in the private sector may be able to exercise considerable influence on the quality and development of the services they use, the situation is often far less clear cut with public services.

Real service delivery provision characterized with satisfaction to the expectation of the citizens is a necessary and a sufficient condition to register gradual improvement in the socio-economic status of the public as citizens (Nafukho, 2008). A satisfied, trustful citizenry signals to existence of service delivery which is competitive, rewarding, enjoyable and likeable. By itself, a vital ingredient in a coherent service delivery with marked impact on a host of other impediments to quality service delivery such as inefficient workforce, inadequacy of funds, poor quality infrastructure and lack of service delivery skills (Osborne, Radnor & Nasi, 2013). According to Bovaird (2005), taking the public as citizens is because of the involuntary and monopolistic character of many public services that can be a key factor inhibiting consumer preferences and limiting the validity of a consumerist model. This invites a deeper consideration for the empowerment strategies by keeping focus on the citizens (Martin & Parston, 2006). It requires balancing measures that foster attitudes that go beyond self-interest if the government is have meaningful concentration on consumerists contention with emphasis on individual and material needs. It has to be comprehended that even though a public service is provided on a mandatory basis, it does not absolve the provider from the requirement to treat its fellow citizens with dignity and respect (Osborne, 2006).

In essence, the myriad services and taxes administered by the civil service affect hundreds of thousands of individual on an annual basis (Awodele, Ogunlana & Motawa, 2010). Every individual who forms part of the public must therefore be happy with the service, her/she receives. It would be amazing if the poor image of the services were not in part the result of the justified anger and frustration of these individuals justified not because their claims were rejected but rather by how their claims were handled (Singaravelloo, 2010). The public have the right and ought to enjoy public services provided with courtesy, consideration, information and speed (Munya, 2010). By the mere fact that the public can expect as of right certain tangible standards of services from public bodies, they must also own the responsibility for ensuring that the system that administers them is guided by objectives policies aimed at meeting social rather than personal needs (Takim, Ismail, Nawawi & Jaafar, 2009). Every public organization ought to have a goal of transforming its administration into a 'service' responsive model to the requirements of the market mechanism and to the public interest (Matei, 2006). Such a model should make the public act as private 'consumers' to size in a genuine way the public need, to decrease the public expenditures and increase the quality of public service (Jun, 2009).

Private Perspective

The private perspective on the paradox of service delivery comes from the realm of the private sector rather than the public one and is concerned with the issue of profit maximization and the approaches that private firms/companies employ in coming out with clean profit (Chan, Lam, Chan, Cheung, Ke,

2010b). This sector is destined to be the central point upon which all service delivery provisions whose mandates were previously 'assigned' to the public sector get to no more. Worldwide, the private firms/companies/organizations are slowly but surely becoming responsible for public and private businesses (Kwak, Chih & Ibbs, 2009). Competition from new entrant-private firms/companies/organizations, in the domain of the public provides a rationale for service delivery strategy at firm-level as well as individual-levels. The private firms/companies/organizations have responded the 'calls' for addressing the hiccups embedded in failed service delivery (Armitage, 2006). They have as well responded to the dynamic need by proposing a variety of generic strategies for enterprises to maintain (or increase) market share in an industry and maximize profits.

Following Christensen and Laegreid (2007b), private can broadly be classified into: profit-oriented (involving major preoccupation of soliciting, investing and engaging for money) for example, registered business companies (RBCs), small medium enterprises (SMEs); nonprofit-oriented (emphasizing service delivery without iota of profit making). Subsequent private sector strategists have refined these two levels tactics and combined them under various slogans though with a tendency to PPPs. Some of these slogans include, for instance, talks about 'total global strategy' for example, multinational corporations, 'strategy for a borderless world' for example, international non- governmental organizations (NGOs); 'core social justice delivery' for example civil society organizations (CSOs); and 'local touch ownership', for example, local or regional NGOs or community based organizations (CBOs) (Christensen & Laegreid, 2011). Most of these manifestations of private organizations are thus concerned with manipulating the nuts and bolts of profit and service delivery (for example, business ventures, investment, service delivery) to handle the quest of the public and has since moved to the domain of functions (for example, infrastructure and services) which had previously been reservoirs of the public sector organizations.

Generally, according to Dewulf, Blanken and Bult-Spiering (2012), private denotes a belonging to or for the use of one particular person or group of people only. It is synonymous with a meeting or discussion involving only a small number of people and dealing with matters that are not to be disclosed to others. In terms of service or industry, private implies provision or ownership by an individual or an independent, commercial company rather than by the government. It generally refers to or relating to a system of service delivery conducted outside the system of government and charging fees to the individuals who make use of it (Gorodnova, 2012). It also relates to or denotes a transaction between individuals and not involving commercial organizations. A private company, for example, operates in the private (non-public) sector of an economy, controlled and operated by individuals (and not by civil servants or government-employees) (Christensen & Laegreid, 2007a). Many, however, of these private organizations have applied micro-level implementation strategy to cater for their needs. This has not been forthcoming as noted by Liu and Wilkinson (2014). In this vein, the public services have been particularly influential. Alonso-Conde, Brown and Rojo-Suarez (2007) argue that 'the only meaningful contribution the private can make and as well as gain from is to enter into partnership with the public sector. A rising awareness of collaboration with the public sector has seen the emergence of concepts like PPPs (Broadbent & Laughlin, 2005). This is aimed to achieve high levels of productivity and to increase the profitability of the private organizations in the most.

The primary task here is to understand the realm of the private and its relation to provision of service delivery given the paradoxical nature of services currently in play (English, 2007). Private can be explained as that which exists and operates in the segment of the economy known as the private sector. It is a sector of the part of a country's economic system that is run by individuals and companies rather than government (Kaul & Conceicao, 2006). This suggests that private sector organizations are run with the intention of making profit. Therefore, the competitive advantages of privates arise from private-level efforts to innovate in a broad sense (that is develop new products, improve production processes and introduce new brands). This stems from an idea deeply embedded in business-inclined formation of these organizations. Those successful private organizations in achieving dominant shares in world markets do so not only because they possess some unique resources but also because of their ability in leveraging on these resources (Warner & Hefetz., 2008). In essence, though, their operations and intentions seem to suggest that innovations they often make, in a technical sense can take any form geared towards making/maximizing profits (Sagalyn, 2007). To this end, in a free enterprise economy, like the USA, Australia, the private sector is large. This is because in such an economy, the government imposes very few restrictions on businesses. On the other hand, in an economy with more government control, for example China, the public sector makes up the larger part of the economy (Adam, Young & Zhihong, 2006).

According to Dal Bó, Finan and Rossi (2013) whether free enterprise or closed government control, but private organization exists, the functionality of any such private organization is a result of availability of four elements constituting a quadruple-framework, which are as follows:

1. Factor conditions (the private organization's endowments of production factors like human resources, physical infrastructure, administrative infrastructure, physical resources, e.g., finances);
2. Demand conditions (the nature of local demand for the private organization's product or services);
3. Related and supporting organizations (the availability of suppliers, distributors and ancillary organizations that are locally and international competitive);
4. Organization strategy, structure and rivalry (the circumstances in the country determining how private organizations are created, organized and managed and the intensity of domestic competition).

Having set out a wide-ranging framework for the determinants of its functionality, the private organization has to take a distinctive stand on the production and/or service dedicated to do (Robinson, 2007). The ability to produce/offer services in a highly competitive world of business can only be possible in an environment via each of the four attributes of the quadruple-framework (Bennett & Iossa, 2006). Private organizations would therefore, be in a better position to influence further service delivery by investing in new skills and infrastructure; demand conditions by limiting public procurement of goods and services; relating and supporting industries by supplying specialized skills and infrastructure particularly to reinforce existing industry clusters; and firm strategy, structure and rivalry through free trade and domestic competition policies (Abonyi & van Slyke, 2010). Compared with the public perspective in the paradox of service delivery, there is a broader role for private organizations though the emphasis is on indirect actions rather than a more comprehensive and integral role related to private-level and collective engagement processes (Perry, 2007).

It has to be noted, however, that in many countries, there is considerable overlaps between public and private sector players/industries (Andrews, 2013). Examples of enterprises that are often run cooperatively include waste management, water management, security services, and health care e.t.c. According to Anvuur and Kumaraswamy (2007), an industry or business may start out in one sector and move to the other. The act of turning a publicly-run enterprise over to private citizens is known as privatization (Dunleavy, Margetts, Bastow & Tinkler, 2006). The opposite movement, from private to public, is known by various names, including nationalization or muncipalization, depending on the level of government involved (Grimsey & Lewis, 2007).

Digest

Perspectives of the two central characters in the paradox of service delivery provide insights on service delivery complexity in both developed and developing countries (Agranoff, 2006). Each is useful depending on the angle of analysis. At one extreme, the public perspective deals with aggregate, collective, whole-level issues and links the availability of resources, for example finance, to production of quality goods and/or services and to consumption of high value goods and services by the end users (Bangura & Larbi, 2006). It also emphasizes prudent real change in the service delivery provision to foster user's competitive satisfaction in the world of globalization and ever-changing technological advancement (Nutt, 2006). Few would disagree, for example, with the view that the traditional service delivery provision, for instance, of making available goods and services at the pleasure of the bureaucrats can no longer enrich the current ever changing demands and needs of the public (Bourgon, 2011). The surest thing is that evidences abound to show that change from the traditional closet in service delivery provision matter for competitiveness and could be even a fundamental ingredient of success (Poole, Mansfield & Gould-Williams, 2006). More so, empirical evidence suggests that real trends of service delivery ought to match with the semantic approaches, cognitive approaches and aesthetics derivations (Besley & Ghatak, 2007). And those micro-level specific modalities are invited for developing that can render services fitting of the changing demands and needs. This has the potential of making the paradox of service delivery to change for the better which is very important for the contemporary demands and wants of the public (Batley & Mcloughlin, 2009). It follows that a comprehensive competitive strategy for service delivery provision should include high standardization of desired and expected services (van der Wal, de Graaf & Lasthuizen, 2008). This must be exhibited in the progressing and matching of demand-need-awakening which ought to augment the reality to invest maximally including the use of high techs to enrich the quality of services demanded and wanted by the public.

At the other extreme, the private perspective focuses on micro-level behavior of private firms/companies/organizations in the arena of service delivery paradox (Bayart, 2009). It is concerned with the involvement of the private party in areas traditionally taken as reservoirs of the public sector but now by virtue of inevitable factors open to the world outside the public sector (Besley & Ghatak, 2005). It is perhaps, the contributions of the quadruple-framework for the functioning of a private party that adds additional dimensions by applying business strategy concepts to the service delivery functions of public sector organizations (van der Wal, & Huberts, 2008). This perspective offers a bottom-up view of service delivery provision and gives some scope for improvements. Its emergence relies on the criticism of the traditional service delivery formula. Taking the private perspective into the puzzle of the paradox of service delivery vis-à-vis traditional formula, criticisms on the traditional formula can be level on three grounds (Besley & Ghatak, 2006). First, that it is misleading to think and believe that the government can continue to all the goods and services and even to the required standards in the midst of ever-changing technological advancement in face of limited resources, for example and especially finances in the hand of government. Second, that the definition of service delivery is currently unclear and that service delivery itself is defined for an empirical purpose and that it has drastically changed from that which used to be (availability and 'quantity') to in-time and superior quality (McCourt, 2005). Lastly, that the limited and inadequate capacity of government to provide all the services/infrastructure needed by the public lacks financial and skills rationale in the given scenarios of inadequate finances in the hands of government and lack of contemporary skills requisite for production of goods and services

(McCourt, 2013). It is not by mistake that the private party has to come in to solve the puzzle of the paradox of service delivery (Bingham, Nabatchi & O'Leary, 2005).

The traditional way of executing government function has to take a complete overhaul (Goldstein & Naor, 2005). To dismantle the paradox of service delivery, therewith, there is an urgent need for the identification of worthy models of executing government functions, use of sophisticated tools and machines, change in the location and market of goods and services, security in the production and consumption chains (Meier & O'Toole, 2007). Most of these require advanced technological building blocks entailing very adequate finances. Thus, governments world over continue to wake in the new changing reality of complex demands and needs requiring complicated assurance of their fulfillment (Eaton, Kaiser & Smoke, 2011). However, many governments have not yet come to term with the reality to the extent of failing to make use of commercial services and applications as detailed in the private sector functioning (Booth, 2011). Thus it can be argued that, in the short to medium term, there is no missing "critical financial component". Instead, the main financial challenge is to better integrate (existing) public finances with those of the private sectors if at all the ends of services delivery provision is to reckon with the ever changing demands and needs of the public. In other words, financial integration and technological interoperability is the key to success, rather than to the development of a new "hard-core-insatiable demands and needs of the public" (Denhardt & Denhardt, 2011). With regard to the long-term prospects, financial integration is particularly challenging, i.e., getting the necessary components cooperation from the private sector is difficult and hard to come by (Bourgon, 2007). In addition, current and future networks will also be interoperable whenever a non-clearer arrangement is put in place. Such is the tale of this work to coming nearer to an appreciation and understanding of the changing trend of service delivery, PPPs with a capitalization on infrastructures.

The next section examines the public private partnerships that take on the board the major criticisms of traditional approaches to service delivery provision, dismantling it in preference of a new arrangement-presumed to be a marked answer to the challenge of financial inadequate in the public sector and risk sharing.

Public Private Partnership Perspective

Other perspectives which seem to echo the essence of collaborative workings between the public and private perspectives is that of PPP perspective. In the context of service delivery per se, Eaton and Akbiyikli (2009) views the role of PPP as a procurement tool that is complex to provide needed infrastructure and services. Leiringer (2006) opines PPP as a mean of overcoming challenges embedded in the traditional mode of service delivery. According to Ismail and Harris (2014), PPP presents a framework that- while engaging the private sector-acknowledges and structures the role for government in ensuring that social obligations are met and successful sector reforms and public investments achieved. To the limitless extent that PPP brings about reforms in the public sector, Adam, Young and Zhihong (2006) see PPP as a liberator to the inability of the public sector to provided needed infrastructure/services. Sanda and Anigbog's (2016) article on conceptual framework for managing risks in PPP projects and related works on PPP as a strategy for development have attracted some attention in the literature on the perspective of PPP in the paradox of service delivery. In their line of argument, PPP as a policy initiative is an attempt to attract and encourage private sector participation upon realization that neither the government nor the private sector can provide the adequate infrastructures/services required. To them, as form of procurement, PPP is fitting recognition as an effective way of delivering value-for-money public infrastructure or services.

Akintoye and Chinyio (2005) takes exception to the proposition put forward by protagonists of PPP that it combines the advantage of competitive tendering and flexible negotiations between the parties. They add that PPP aid in allocation of risk on an agreed basis between the public sector and the private sector. And according to them, the most important thing about PPP is that in the world of intense competiveness, broad-based opportunities and technological advancement, the traditional role of government in infrastructural development and service delivery provision is left archaic. Not gain to any public can be ascertained any more from such a role. Another line of argument is concerned with Wibowo and Mohammed's (2008) definition of PPP in terms of risk transfer. They contend that PPP is a long-term arrangement where risks are transferred to the private sector, for which they (risks) are financially compensated. Burger and Hawkesworth (2011) assert that the private sector has been known to be better at managing risk compared to the public sector. Liu and Wilkinson (2011) argue that it's hardly disputable in that in PPP, there is something unique about closing the gaps between poor service delivery performance and the needs of the public through a private intervention. Hayford and Partner (2006) suggest that in theory, allowing the private sector to manage the risks should result in lower project costs mainly because the private sector is profit driven which makes them better at managing the risks at a lower end. At the same time, however, Cheung, Chan and Kajewski (2010) argue that it is by every means obvious that being the most effective of procuring goods and services makes PPP the right choice to raise the standard of production and consumption in an economy.

A related point is that Zhang (2005a, 2005b), PPP is not just any tool to be used anyhow. It requires appropriate allocation and management of risks from both parties to avoid depletion and wastage of resources (Murphy, 2008). In this vein, it should be taken that PPP is a process that combines the principles of managing public services together with those provide by the private entities (Brown, Potoski & Van Slyke, 2006). Making services delivery to be guided by these principles therefore, means for example, equitable treatment and allocation of resources according to needs. It stresses the principles of fairness and equity when considering the concept of quality (Raisbeck, Duffield & Xu, 2010). It further takes equality of treatment as very important whose sight should not be lost when efficiency measures, including, for example, contracting out of public services are being implemented.

Others suggest that the link between the public and private partners in a PPP arrangement is centered on a party willfully shoulders a risk (Ball, Heafey & King, 2007). Quiggin (2005) contends that this assertion lacks quality service delivery rationale. He instead argues that the private sector is always unwilling to bear risks when the risks are of high magnitudes and beyond their influence. This would therefore require allocation of some risks to the government. In essence, an appreciation of the position of the public and private is normally indicative of a fuller comprehension of the essence of PPP in the paradox of service delivery (McLaughlin, Osborne & Ferlie, 2005). Within the realm of public service delivery, private sector firms would not normally be obliged, because of their primary obligations to provide financial returns to the shareholders, to maintain nonviable services to geographically or financially disadvantaged groups (Boyne & Law, 2005). Next two subsections provide such an understanding.

Origin and Link to Service Delivery

PPP has long been practiced as an important means of providing services since as far back as the Roman Empire two thousand years ago in Europe (Brinkerhoff & Brinkerhoff, 2011). Even after the fall of the

Roman Empire, era of industrialization brought rapid urbanization and expansion of public networks in transport, for example, railways, tramways, water supply, whose costs of construction and maintenance could not be borne by the government then alone. This is the main driver of PPP in all perspectives as well as the theoretical conception of development in the face of shortages of resources in the hands of government. Following in this tradition, the more recent perspective in the modern development of PPP can be traced back to the period after the First World War. At that time new public infrastructure was mainly designed, constructed and financed from public funds. However, prior to 1982, there was very limited private financing of transport infrastructure in developing or transition countries (Bloomfield, 2006). Significant advances in the idea of PPP saw the emergence of United Kingdom's Private Finance Initiative (PFI) which began in 1982.

Associated then with then PPP public services' established activities were that did not make a clear distinction what the arrangement meant-whether it was a total surrender of government functions to the private sector or not. In this vein, it should be noted that the government had been collaborating with the private entities to develop and catchy relationship in the field of improving service delivery provision (Weber & Khademian, 2008). For example, public services' established activities would be contracted out operationally in some cases to private firms though the delivery of such services might continue to be funded from taxation and remained governed by public service criteria. Examples of this kind of arrangement can be contracting out of local government services such as refuse collection and local transport to private companies, as well as privatization of some government services like prison service.

This was a composite indicator that the government was, however, incapable of providing all the services the public needed. It was inevitable to 'give out' some of these functions to those who could manage them better (Roll, 2014). Gradually, this led to a growing competition between the ranks and files of those who had the potentials of providing the needed services. But this wasn't easier to come by. Essentially, the provision of public services was often complex and indirect in terms of the relationship between the provider and customer (public) as shown in Figure 1.

From Figure 1, payment is not normally made directly for the service received and so customer (public) is weakened. Public choice is very limited when provision is monopolistic (Bozeman, 2007). From the providers' viewpoint, ability to pay is often not a key determinant of demand and accordingly market disciplines of price control frequently do not apply. Indeed, the providers' ability to supply is likely to be determined by budgetary funding outside its direct control.

Meanwhile, in the private sector, the common perception was that the successful enjoying of services could be encouraged by the smooth flow of profits (revenue) from the customer to the private producer,

Figure 1. Customer (public) relationship: Public service
Source: Google search

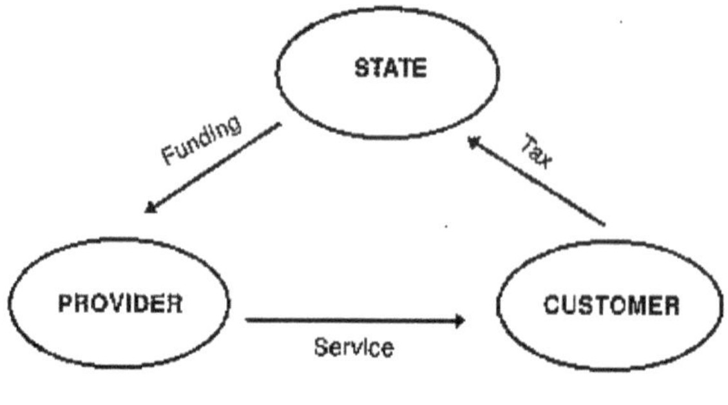

for example, through payment for goods and services on an individual basis (Sarker, 2006). In the traditional form of service delivery, the private does not have a role to play, but on their own, are incapable to ensure continuous process of quality service delivery required by the public. On strand of phenomenon concerned with lesser motivation to participate in the public services provision was that concern of 'excess demand' (Moulton, 2009). This phenomenon which often led to queues and rationing would decrease the motivation to improve quality in other ways too, for example, if one customer dislikes the service and goes elsewhere (if they can) there is usually another one waiting in the queue. Large scale desertion ('exit') may be unlikely because the public provider occupies monopolistic or oligopolistic position (there are few if any alternative to exit to). This restriction on behavior is, of course, likely to be felt most acutely by low-income consumers. Another strand (bureaucratic form) mostly practiced in the public sector, was primarily concerned with creating situations which could easily compromise service delivery. This had the potentials of spill over to the works of the private sector. For example, negativism outpouring from a defined department or division; an administrative hierarchy of control; a set of procedures designed to ensure uniformity of treatment and groups of professionals or specialists to perform tasks (Buxbaum & Ortiz, 2007). In this kind of situation, service delivery systems might seek to ensure fairness and impartiality but may end up characterized by inflexibility, and the type of top down professional client relations unhealthy for service delivery provision (Saxena, 2011). In spite of these strands, though, the relationship between the customer and the private sector is usually that of a comparative freedom of the consumers (public) to choose between competing service providers. Figure 2 presents the scenario.

As shown in Figure 2, to select on the basis of price or quality, as well as to express satisfaction (or otherwise) with the service provided, means that customer (public) needs are paramount in services by the private sector.

Figures 1 and 2 give a bird-eye view of the differences between services provided by the public and those of the private. These differences can be seen in a number of ways, for example, public services do not normally operate for financial profit or require immediate payment for goods or services prior to delivery. Also, if public services are charged for, then they are not usually sold to customers at commercial prices set to produce profits (Fiszbein, Ringold & Rogers, 2011). Meanwhile, where private sector firms are contracted to public bodies for the provision of services, for example, for the provision of transport to the general public, charges may be subsidized for social policy reasons.

Time and again, evidences have abounded to show that public sector organizations do 'generate' weak performance, that the public services are nor innovative and not flexible enough. Coupled with these challenges, is the endemic problem of inadequate finances to fund most activities and programmes of public sector organizations. This scenario has not been helped as Lamech (2012) asserts, organizational structures characteristics to the public sector, reflected in hierarchical way, are rigid. Implicitly,

Figure 2. Customer relationship: Private sector
Source: Google search

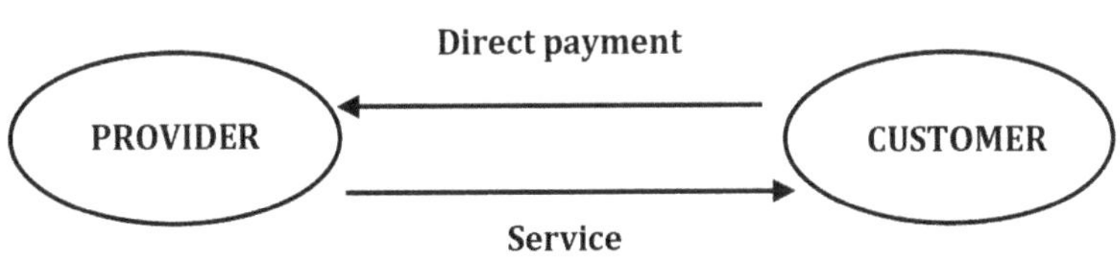

the traditional service delivery is unstable and unyielding, in sharp dissimilarity to the private sector which is innovative, and it easily adapt and change over time in conformance with prevailing situations. Cankur and Petkovšek (2013) suggest that theories and practices in the private sector ought to be used in the public sector domain in order to increase the quality and provision of public services. It therefore appears critical for this option to be explored as it might reduce the budgetary allowances for the public services to become public-friendly and increase the efficiency and effectiveness of the public sector.

The main reason for the great interest in this kind of cooperative framework is that many governments can obtain necessary funds for financing fundamental, for example, infrastructure projects, by resorting to partnership with the private sector (Rakić & Rađenović, 2014). This has been precipitated by the unresponsive public services bureaucracies that had been common especially in the 1970s. Consequently, a number of development initiatives using the form of cooperation with the private sector have been growing rapidly since the beginning of the 21st century (Van der Wal, 2013). To this end, the current public debt crisis has put additional emphasis on partnership with the private sector as it provides public budget relief and meets public needs. Therefore, developing and emerging countries see in PPP the potential for developing infrastructure and augmenting economic growth (Ho, 2012). Such a framework can and only will be achieved through following a threefold typology of public service reform strategies by focusing on people as consumers, customers and citizens.

Singaravelloo (2010) affirms that governments are inevitably faced with the problem of a rise in the demand for better services and to produce these with the limited revenue resources available. With the current levels of ever changing demands for quality public services, it is useful to describe the relationship of considerable prime actors: the public and private. It has to be noted that in any given environment and in which none of the actors controls the situation completely; thus, both collaboration and competition occur at the same time. Today's public services arena is characterized- in general terms- by an increasingly intense competition at the delivery platform level. With respect to previous periods, the focus of the public service industry has shifted from just any services towards quality control and value-for-money issues (Lee & Shamsul Haque, 2006). The changing trend seems to suggest that there ought to be a new model for any public service delivery or application, which can be adapted also to the public service in general.

The role of the government in the new public service delivery can be broadly divided into three main stages: information processing (Heeks & Bailur, 2007), delivery and capture/use/integration. This three-layer action structure is typical of contemporary public service delivery. For each of the action area requires a well calculated approach to ensure that services are provided as required in the right quality and quantity (Quah, 2013). However, any attempt in such a direction has majorly often been frustrated by lack of finance at the disposal of the public sector organization for service delivery provision. Gupta and Biswas (2010) though classified the constraints faced by governments as financial, technical, and human resources. These constraints hamper the governments' ability to efficiently deliver services to their communities.

According to Chan, Yeung, Yu, Wang and Ke, (2011), following the 2007-2008 global financial crises, there has been an increasing interest in the adoption of PPP by governments in both developed and developing countries. Cheung, Chan and Kajewski (2012) argue that many governments across the globe are now seeking to tap the private sector's expertise and capital to minimize their infrastructure deficit. Such an inter-sector collaboration consolidates itself as an extended practice in order to compensate and soften the lack of resources needed for optimal quality service delivery competence and effective performance. Public service delivery becomes a key are for collaboration practices (Kelsall, 2011). Under the new arrangement, an inevitable worldwide change in public service delivery is taking place advocating different service delivery strategies that allow the provision of public services and infrastructure in the less risky manner, while assuring citizen's satisfaction (Koppel, 2010).

Collaboration and cooperation between the public and private sector organizations has led to the establishment of the favored organizations models resulting to be, in this way, the catalyst for establishing PPP (Weihe, 2006). Since its inception, PPP gained popularity even though this has remained imprecise with obscured defining features. According to Weihe (2006), the level of ambiguity is also negatively reflected at the operational level since policy guidelines remains unclear. In the face of the changing role of government in service delivery provision, there is completely no unique solution and no single model can be followed. Matei (2008) conversely, proposes that a probable model than can be pursued is by the government coming to form an association of decisions and public and private means within the framework of the game system of action, aiming to comply simultaneously the consumers' and citizen's expectation. He opinioned that such an arrangement can best be possible to execute under public-private partnership, to which we turn next.

Distinctive Features of the PPP Perspective

The PPP perspective to the paradox of service delivery is that the public sector can have access to private finances and as well share risks. The distinctive feature of this perspective is its focus on the private organizations as the main actors in the process of provision of service delivery. It emphasizes the notion that governments have to undertake conscious steps to involve the private sector in its functions to deliver services. This new form of service delivery has a large tacit element embodied in solving the puzzle of inadequacy of resources and the devastating effects of risks. It may seem difficult to rewrite all potential challenges in the arrangement, but currently this seems to be the way to go.

According to Rakic and Radjenovic (2011), the most important distinctive feature of PPP can be gleaned from its nature. The nature of PPP is that of cooperation between public and private participants of a permanent sort. It requires the development of a mutual products and/or services with shared risk, expenses and profit. Leavitt and Morris (2007) elaborates to indicates PPP includes a private partner investing in public infrastructure, and providing related non-core services to the government or to the community on the government behalf. Siemiatycki (2007) intimates another key feature of PPP is that the government retains responsibility for the delivery of core services such as teaching and clinical services, and the government and private party working together under long-term arrangements. According to Aaronson (2011), the payments to the private sector party depend upon its continuing to deliver the specified services to the agreed performance standards. Appuhami, Perera and Perera (2011) warn that failure to meet these standards results in the private partner not being paid.

Elsewhere, Baker (2012) describes the feature of PPP as a considerable use of capital expenditure by the contractor (the private party). This implies that the contractor is usually expected to invest heavily in productive assets such as buildings, roads, tunnels, or other physical infrastructure including Information Technology (IT) systems. The investments are often financed by private sources involving the issuing of equity and debt securities. Yang, Hou and Wang (2013), asserts PPP is featured by the bundling of different operational tasks within a partnership. This means rather than outsourcing each activity separately, for example, cooking, cleaning, heating, they can be combined into several or most operations together. This normally constitute a package of services within one long-term contract. In this way, it enables the contractor to seek innovative solutions for costs reductions within a longer planning horizon and enjoyment of economy of scale. Chinyere and Xu (2012) talk of PPP major feature as being that of performance-based payment schemes. This is perhaps what appeals to the private party the more because payments are always assured at the specified time period. This is especially helping in that PPP normally rely on competitive tendering. More still, its contracts make payments during the contract period dependent on a set of performance measures evaluated at regular time intervals. Kociemska (2010) reminds that PPP contracts typically set requirements regarding the quality of outcomes (rather than quantity of input or output) and leave the contractor freedom as to who to meet them.

In the process of building up a workable PPP arrangement, earlier writers have indicated different features, however, five of them which stand out are worthy of mention in our context here. According to Mauldin (2012), the process of acquiring quality services is unpredictable. This is because investments say in infrastructures which should produce those quality services, for example, roads carry considerable risk and the outcome is uncertain. Public and private organizations face technical difficulties and financial uncertainties, especially in construction activities in this case. Moreover, rarely can these organizations ensure against failure to tackle such risks. The implications of fundamental uncertainty, as indicated by Parashar (2014) are clear; the reality cannot be fully modeled and the direction of change never achieves equilibrium minus the public and private parties working together.

PPP is an incremental and cumulative process meaning the arrangement instantaneously develops the capabilities needed to handle complex infrastructures, nor can it jumps into completely new area of competence (Seitanidi, 2010). Instead, it proceeds in an incremental manner building on private sector experience and moving from simple to complex activities. According to Sharma (2012), PPP involves close cooperation between the public and private partners. Partnerships rarely succeed in isolation. When engage in fulfilling their obligations under the agreement (for example, securing land by the public partner or providing finances by the private partner) in attainment of the objectives of the project. Hence, interaction and interdependence between parties (i.e., collaborative action) in the implementation of a project is a fundamental characteristic of PPP.

Turhani (2013) discovered that successes in executing a PPP project to its logical conclusion can spillover into quality service delivery. The major theories of comparative advantage-notably the factor proportion theory, theories of economies of scale and neo-technology theories- offer powerful explanations on the causes and evolution of PPP (Siddiquee, 2011). The technology and innovative perspective adds an additional insight to previous theories of comparative advantage. By contrast, the technology and innovative perspective holds that comparative advantage may arise from 'minor learning' in weak countries and that this process is costly, unpredictable and cumulative (Solana, 2014). Hence, differences in the efficiency with which public-private-level capabilities are created are themselves a major source of differences in outcomes of the PPP project. Strong countries with relatively efficient PPP-level learning processes will witness rapid project implementation and up-grading while weak implementation processes in others will be associated with poor quality services.

PPP is affected by a host of national policy and institutional factors (Trangkanont & Charoenngam, 2014). The implementation of a PPP project can be stimulated by adequate finances, secured land, and application of requisite skills. In general, political stability, outward-oriented economic conditions and investment policies, ample supplies of general and technical manpower, ready access to required finances and comprehensive support from credit institutions are conclusive to PPP project implementation (Tserng, Russell, Hsu, & Lin, 2012). The details of these measures along with practical examples must be properly understood and executed by the partners. And these form the core elements of PPP arrangement as discussed below.

Determinants and Policy Implications

The last point highlights the determinants of PPP at project level and has a direct bearing on the formulation of policies to enhance PPP project implementations (Wang, 2015). Perhaps, the best way to analyze the influence on PPP project implementation is to view them as being part of a system of a collaborative and inter-connected elements that are all geared to collective workmanship and, hence, attaining PPP success. This scheme is called Special Purpose Vehicle (SPV) or systems of executing a PPP project as shown in Figure 3.

The SPV approach emphasizes that initiation and execution of a PPP project are processes that involve more than firms/companies, credit institutions, governments and other actors because of the synergies and systems effects. It also suggests that initiation and execution of a PPP project's processes hinge on the internal interactions between the actors in the system and the external links of the system.

There are three levels of the initiation and execution of any PPP project. The first level is made up of infrastructural and/or service clusters within a public sector. This contains all the organizations (central and local governments, regional governments, government corporations) engaged in provision of service delivery. In turn, these clusters can be linked to various players (for example, private firms/companies, credit institutions, experts) in global service delivery clusters (represented by all the parties in lower part of Figure 3). As they provide access to finances, technical and managerial skills and availability of other resources, these external links are crucial to PPP initiation and execution.

The second level is the set of institutions and factor markets which support PPP project implementation in the infrastructural and/or services clusters. There is a strong emphasis on processes of interactive engagement, that is, the sharing of risk and the exchange of knowledge and information between the parties involved in the implementation of a PPP project. These institutions and factor markets include: finance, banks, lending institutions, consultancy firms, technical support and physical infrastructure.

Figure 3. Agreements between PPP Participants
Source: (Gupta, Trivedi & Kansal, 2013)

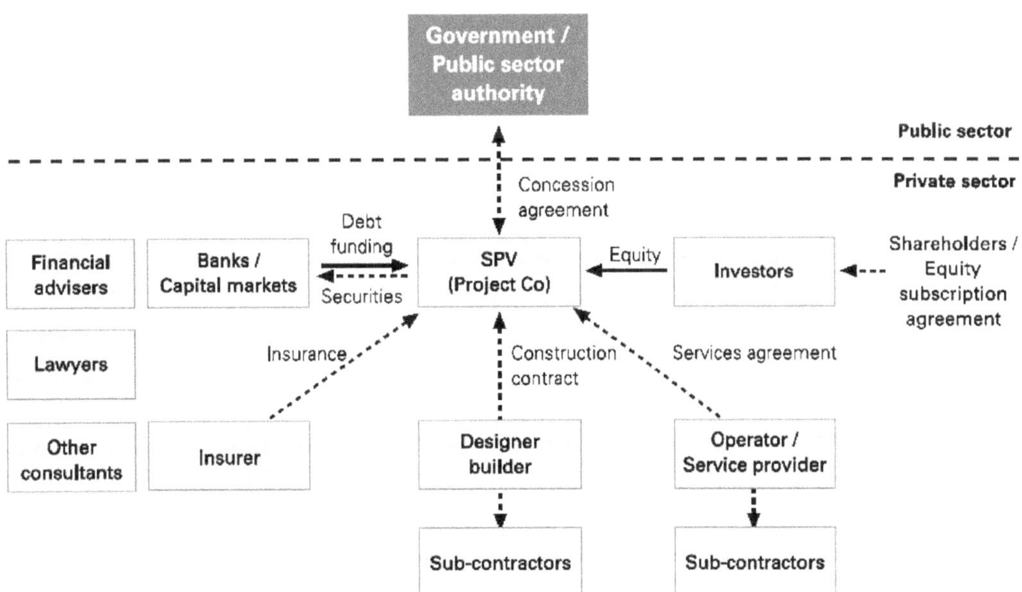

The third level is the set of policies that stimulate the PPP project implementation processes between the infrastructural and/or services clusters and the institutions and factor markets. A range of policies which influences technological and managerial activities fall under this heading including: political and macroeconomic environment, trade and competition regime, business and project transaction costs, tax regime and the legal regime.

SPV differ markedly in implementing a PPP project in the financial, technological and managerial strengths embedded with it (ability to obtain finances, availability of technical and skilled personnel and integrated skilled management), the efficiency of its operation, system effects and the intensity of its external links (Wang & Zhao, 2014). It take a few moment to have in place a SPV that has a good base of technologically and managerially competent firms and personnel and have developed extensive external links with third parties' sources of finances and skills. Requisite incentive and regulatory frameworks (characterized by exposure to competitive pressures and low implementation costs) have also stimulated concrete PPP project implementation processes in an efficient SPV system. As a result, this innovation system has witnessed smoother implementation of PPP projects to a higher level of providing good infrastructure and quality services (Yang, Hou & Wang, 2013). This means moving from a stage of conception of a PPP project to acquisition of capable firms to execute the project to marked improvement in production processes and eventually consumption of quality goods and services (Appuhami, Perera & Perera, 2011). Higher levels of SPV capability development are in turn associated with better PPP project implementation, technologically and managerially advanced production and satisfactory consumption of high quality goods and services.

CORE ELEMENTS OF PARTNERSHIP STRATEGY

The PPP perspective of service delivery provision provides strong theoretical and practical grounds for a different service delivery agenda than the public and private strategies perspectives (Alsudiri, Al-Karaghouli & Eldabi, 2013). In common with the previous approaches, the PPP perspective emphasizes sound macroeconomic management and predictable policy framework, a favorable operational regime, a strong and efficient legal framework conducive for a SPV to operate and a pivotal role for efficient risk mechanism in risk sharing. However, in order to remedy pervasive weaknesses in SPV, it also makes the case for a more holistic approach with additional policies to support PPP project implementation. According to Abdel Aziz (2007), an assuredly successful service delivery strategy from the PPP perspective can be expressed in terms of three core elements: a) a national partnership involving complementary actions by government and the private sector for service delivery provision; b) a 'liberalization plus strategy' involving a mix of policy instruments; and c) where appropriate an economic grounds, micro-level policies to promote active role and/or engagement of the clusters indicated in Figure 3 above.

Flinders (2005) states the importance of the first element is self-explanatory. The successful implementation of any set of PPP projects (including their operations) requires a national consensus goals and broad policy direction amongst the principal social partners (that is the government, the private sector, and the creditors). Whilst noting the importance of private sector organizations, it is important to focus on the interaction between the government and the private sector as well. The private organization, however, needs to contribute actively, alongside government, to the implementation of the PPP project.

Obermann (2007) warns that the second element is somewhat more complicated and can be classified into two sets of policy measures. The first, incentive policies are instruments to remove economic distortions created by past traditional systems of service delivery discouraging their perpetuation and use. Restriction on private participation and removal of redundant bureaucratic procedures on private sector activity all fall under this heading. The second, supply-side policies are geared to overcome arrangement failures which impede implementation processes and the creation of innovative channels to improve on the achievement of the outcomes of the PPP projects (Sadka, 2007). These include technological support, financial leverages, and involvement of qualified and skilled personnel. The point to stress is that it is the interaction of incentive and supply-side policies that develop success in PPP projects.

Whereas the second element involves largely non-specific measures, the third element emphasizes detailed actions to improve the implementation of the PPP project. Intervention at the micro-level is often directed towards acquiring technological and financial capabilities, promoting use and improving links between the different parts of the PPP project implementation process. Successful implementation strategy might range from project-specific measures to the provision of specialized institutional support facilities for a particular project (Pessoa, 2008). Joint actions (for example, sharing operational costs) between the government and the private partners are also commonplace. The remainder of this section explores these three core elements in terms of finances, skills of the private partner and risk sharing in more details.

Finances

Xie and He (2006) identifies finances as core driver of a PPP arrangement due to constraints by government to provided needed services and improving the quality and elements to enhance service delivery provision to the public. Gehrt, Klatt and Beckers (2010) claim this is the rationale upon which protagonists of PPP based themselves as the need for quality services has recently adopted a higher quality-oriented, value-satisfying stance. According to Bing, Akintoye, Edwards, Hardcastle (2005b), that at stake at the moment, is no government is able to finance all projects wanted and needed by their citizens. There is therefore an urgent need to find adequate finances elsewhere which is why the involvement of the private sector becomes inevitable and very necessary. However, to be able to gain access to such finances some important conditions must prevail in order for PPP projects to succeed.

A stable, predictable macroeconomic environment and political stability are *sine qua non* for access to finance. Ye (2009) contends that would lead to improved implementation of a PPP project but the situation is asymmetric: macroeconomic and political stability cannot ensure PPP project implementation but macroeconomic and political instability inevitably hurts PPP projects implementation. Experience suggests that implementers of PPP projects embark on a series of corrective measures (or even for that matter a measure to seal gaps created by the instability) in the hope of succeeding in implementing a PPP project. In such circumstances, an overhaul real turn of the prevailing environment might also arise from devastating effects of the occurrences. Macroeconomic and political instability is likely to send confusing signals about the profitability of investing in a PPP project, then the processing of implementing a new PPP project may itself become difficult to sustain. Much has been written about what constitutes good macroeconomic and political policy which enables acquisition of finances for development purpose (Angelides & Xenidis, 2009). Regardless of the author, in essence, the medicine would be the same in developed and developing countries as well- there ought to be a stable macroeconomic and political environment in the country. Much emphasis is also placed on consistency, flexibility, coherence, and continuity of macroeconomic and political policies, so claims Xenidis and Angelides (2005)

A stable and conducive macroeconomic and political condition in the country itself may be insufficient to the acquisition of necessary finances for implementing a PPP project. An efficient financial infrastructure is necessary for a successful PPP project implementation (Moulton, 2009). Persistent financial infrastructural problems in a given economy can significantly raise its lending costs for its enterprises relative to those in a non-problem-prone financial infrastructure. For example, bottlenecks in the loan processing criteria and imposition of high loan interest, short or rather reduced loan repayment period feed into complication of loan acquisition. Further, examples could be missed customer appeals, poor institution's reputation and cancellation of loan processing activities. Similarly, long delays in accessing loan processing facilities, like banks and other lending financial institution during PPP project initiation phase or later costing of the project for risk allocation raise projects implementation cost and wastage of management time. In most cases financial institutions may not be willing to cover such expenditures. Shaoul (2005b) believes that its recommendable for ease of access to finance from the private sector, there must be in place institutions typically formed to invest a given percentage of their capital in initiating and maintaining a culture of timely and calculative lending. Other recommendation might include:- liberalization of the financial lending institutions to allow many players to participate that way would narrow the current complications in loan acquisitions as suggested by Maskin and Tirole (2008). All these require putting in place as an effective regulatory framework, so advised Kriześ-Dobieszewska (2014)

Boardman and Vining (2012) avows development experience suggests that a financial institution's lending policy has a great deal of influence on its viabilities. Financial analysts typically classify financial institutions by their lending policies inward and outward-oriented institutions. The difference between them is in terms of the effective protection granted to the development loan borrowers compared to non-development loan borrowers. An inward-oriented lending policy grants significant protection for non-development borrowers and is biased against development loan borrowers where outward-oriented policy has unlimited protection and favors development borrowers. Financial analysts agree that an outward-oriented lending regime is better associated with improved financing of PPP projects than an inward-oriented one. An outward-oriented-lending regime induces better financial accessibility according to need; the realization of economic of scales; access to new technologies; improved productions inputs and subsequent outputs due to protection; and less load defaulting behavior.

According to Harris and Tadimalla (2008), access to finance at competitive interest rates (for example, for working capital and capital investment as in the case of PPP projects) is an obvious requirement for creating and sustaining a PPP project. Yet organizations, especially SPV, in most countries would complain about high interest rates (in part due to oligopolistic banking practices) and a lack of access to bank credit. It would therefore, be prudent that each country ought to have an effective, efficient and efficacious monetary policy management, competition into the banking sector and training schemes for banking staff on assessing PPP project credit. Burger and Hawkesworth (2011) suggest that there could also be in place specialist 'soft terms' funding windows for PPP projects schemes. It appears once the financial system has been deepened, there could be scope for introducing different financing mechanisms including venture capital requirements, something Demirag and Khadaroo (2008) deeply advocates for, for a successful risk-free PPP project implementation.

Skills of the Private Sector

Skills of the private sector to promote private sector development have been widely applauded in many developed and developing countries. For example, the idea of new public management (NPM) arose as a result of management theories venturing into the intricacies of efficient and effective private sector management by borrowing those principles to the public sector domain. As defined by Camilleri (2011), skills refer to the set of expertise' acts that aim to stimulate and support the performance of assigned tasks, strengthening achievement of the goals of the tasks and increase value-addition of the performance. These acts have been applied to the private sector with lots of successful outcomes. As a result, the private sector has often been equated with efficiency and effectiveness providing a menu to be envied by the public sector which is often inefficient and ineffective (Akintoye & Chinyio, 2005). However, this is rarely the case in practice, as the public sector tends to shun anything coming from the private sector, as it claims those would be geared for profits rather than public value. Most skills applied in the private sector are implemented in a more disoriented framework in the public sector such that they are often ignored and not made to form the bulk of policy derivations. Thus, pressures from the public for quality services form the backdrop for the application of skills much engrained in the private sector to public sector.

Thus, within a PPP-oriented country, the aim of applying skills of the private sector is to improve the performance of PPP projects. As earlier on indicated, the intervention at the levels of skills of the private sector is an embodiment of a strategic move that the cause of taking PPP as a new development tool has taken (Quiggin, 2005). Skills of the private sector are clamored for in the PPP arrangement to acquire necessarily managerial capabilities, promotion and improving the links between the public and private sector in the PPP engagement (Pârvu & Voicu-Olteanu, 2009). These links can be cemented through; providing strategic skills to the PPP projects implementation via SPV; removing bureaucratic regulations that hamper the emergence of innovation brought by experience from the private sector, helping to bring together the public and private partners to act as a block; facilitating joint actions (for example, setting up a specialized unit within the SPV) entrusted with effective framework development and implementation of the project; and attracting the private partner to hold nothing back but bring all to the fore for a successful implementation of the PPP project.

Whilst application of skills in the private sector offers a means to enhance the success of implementing a PPP project, it should not be applied in an *ad hoc* manner as there is high risk of failure of the PPP project. However, Loosemore (2007) sounds a consoling tone laying bear the suggestion that there are principles which can be borne in mind while applying these skills. These principles include: - the choice of the skills should be guided by far future comparative advantage rather than short term comparative advantage; interventions should be at a broad framework-level rather than at a micro-level and justified by arrangement perfections; clearly defined performance measures should be used to evaluate the success of the interventions; and the interventions should be bounded by best practices and local content. According to Diana (2014), all these requires application of a more robust boosts to theses skills as what is dearly needed to what works and does not and the conditions for successful PPP project implementations.

Risk Sharing

According to Sanda and Anigbogu (2016), the elusive effects of risk are the prime cause of entering into a PPP arrangement. This idea has widely been accepted and defended as the prime mover for setting up PPP projects. Its build on the premise that the traditional role of government in providing services to its citizens has been scaled down due to risk. To overcome the challenge, many policy makers suggested transferring this risk to another party (Bing, Akintoye, Edwards & Hardcastle, 2005a). Others proposed sharing of these risk instead because in some circumstances if might be impracticable to transfer the risk. As a result, there has been contention to take a move of adopting PPP as mean of overcoming the challenges of risk in service delivery provision. Proponents of this idea have packaged their arguments into a cluster of two major viewpoints. First, PPPs are set up to produce and distribute quality goods and services at the lowest possible cost to achieve two purposes (Loosemore, 2007). On the one hand; achievement of the dire need of public value for the side of the public partner and profits on the side of the private partner. However, in this move, the main challenge is that of the existence of risk that can corrode every effort made towards the achievements of these noble goals (Hoppe & Schmitz, 2013). Entering into a PPP arrangement is a struggle to create an environment where though risk might occur in the provision of services, it might not have serious devastating effects. Those PPP arrangements that successfully share risk equally will survive while the less conscious to share risk will go under (Ng & Loosemore, 2007). Over time, sharing risk is the only formula to overcome the challenges in the delivery of services.

Secondly, PPPs are set up as an amiable arrangement by the public and private partners to further the interest of and respond to daring call for quality service delivery (Cicmil & Marshall, 2005). These consist of maintaining the superiority of the public values and at the same time the profit motives of the private partner. On behalf of their longings, the public and private partners in a PPP present their risk sharing viewpoints and interest on the sharing ratio which they deliberate on and in the end find a neutral position that does not compromise the achievement of the interest of any party (Tang, Shen & Cheng, 2010). It is on this basis that the parties come together and enter into a PPP arrangement which would help them to forge a joint venture to pursue their courses.

Wibowo and Mohamed (2008) applaud PPP as a venture that makes the public and private sector complement each other in service delivery provision. It is a mean through which the parties come together to pull risks together and finally cornered them to harmless arena. Where this synergy works well, there can be significant gains for the parties as a whole (Trafford & Proctor, 2006). A similar analogy can be applied to the relationship between the private sector as a whole and the government in any economy. If PPP is to work well, there must be less of the threat of risks; and they must not be allowed to flourish. If the PPP fails and no party in the arrangement intervene, then there can be no further gains. When the public and private partner shares risk together, the whole is likely to be greater than the sum of the individual as evidenced by the success of PPP projects in economies like those of Britain, Australia, France, USA (Zaharioaie, 2012). In an event of a withering of risk sharing formula (as evidence by stalling, un-completion of PPP projects as in the case of most developing countries like Uganda, Nigeria, Ghana, Malaysia) and a rising disparity in risk sharing, both parties increasingly need to contribute actively to the initiation of long-term PPP projects.

Successful risk sharing experience indicates that the public and private partners make at least four important contributions to the final implementation of the PPP projects. First, Hosman (2011) articulates that sharing risk help weaker partners to help themselves. In developing countries, for example, both the public and private sectors are characterized by a dualistic production structure with a small base of efficient organizations and staffed with a long tail of under-performers. The challenge is how to raise the efficiency of these weaker organizations to the best practice levels of risk sharing. Although many, government organizations and to some extent private organizations do engage in this venture, their dealings in terms of appropriate risk sharing while entering into a PPP arrangement is far below the recommended standard. To show the way for a successful PPP, would entail actively assisting in upgrading the risk sharing capabilities of each partner; carrying out a productive benchmarking exercises and consequence awareness; and providing taking cautious risk sharing matrix. Sharma (2012) advices that actively attempting to develop an acceptable risk sharing matrix is another important way of transferring risk to a party who is able to contain and handle them. Likewise, all the parties can play a pivotal role in fostering 'ownership' of the accepted risk sharing matrix; and directly providing the saps necessary for the PPP project to succeed.

Secondly, risk sharing help the parties to plug the implementation gaps. Risk is virtually the only threat that can derail implementation of a PPP project. That this gap is reduced by proper sharing of the risk, is itself an indicator of the success of the PPP project. Access to timely and detailed information on the implementations gaps is a key determinant of party-level action but such information tends to be unevenly given to the other party in a PPP arrangement (Sadka, 2007). Owing to its profits interest, the private sector has better access than the public sector to information about a host of risks that could cause an implementation gap in a PPP project. Active public sector participation in identifying these risks in the implementation gaps and charting solutions forthwith are possible ways of making this knowledge effective. Hence, both parties' specific knowledge on risk in the implementation gaps would be valuable inputs to formulating a plan of action for the risk sharing matrix. Both parties can further contribute to effective PPP implementation by carrying out regular review of the risk sharing matrix and its performance over the couple of the pre-review period.

Thirdly, proper risk sharing public partner's capabilities which would be helping for a PPP project to succeed. That the private sector has developed a solid base of modern management, financial, technical and marketing skills, is indisputable, so claims Siddiquee (2011). Not a surprise though, the public partner continuous to be weak in these areas; probably due to the attitude of indifference which is very common in public sector organizations. In part this may be due to relatively higher compensation packages in the private sector (which attracts the best qualified and skilled personnel) and investments in employee's personal development in private sector organizations. It would seem the private party is better endowed to work out a risk sharing matrix strategy due to that fact that its personnel are well experienced and better managers as well as technicians who might well be in the know of all it takes to have a PPP project free of risk (Keçi, 2015). Nevertheless, another route may be to undertake joint public-private sector risk sharing matrix based on the inputs of the private partner but duly accepted and taken as well as complimented by the public partner.

Fourthly, risk sharing requires active participation of the public and private parties in the infrastructural or service projects (Kamarkar, 2014). A wide range of infrastructural and service gaps characterizes many public and private organizations. These gaps range from, for example, the infrastructures, power fluctuations to uncompetitive utility costs and are faced with the challenge of investing in new infrastructure and maintaining the quality of the existing infrastructure. The challenge here is failure to come up with a good risk sharing formula. This is because infrastructure investments often involve very high project costs which debt-ridden governments are unable to meet. Quiggin (2005) suggests that one solution might be joint-ventures between government and the private sector to develop new infrastructure projects. But is itself subject to risk. The simple reason is that it may involve arrangements, which call for some private sector funding and private sector management with government funding and financial guarantees. All these are incubators of risks. Siemiatycki (2010) articulates that it would be better to take a variants position for a number of these arrangements called the PPPs. Chapter four gives a pointer to such a scheme.

It is worth emphasizing that an active public private partnership is a necessary condition for an efficient and practical strategy of overcoming challenges embedded in partnership agreements. In turn, a successful strategy will fuel future PPP implementations success, high value production and quality consumption of goods and services. Thus, a more satisfying service delivery provision will generate a 'win win' situation for both the government and the private sector.

CONCLUSION

The notion of the paradox of service delivery is likely to be shrouded in academic and policy controversy for the foreseeable future. At the same time, it is being tackled in different forms to examine the best way of answering the insatiable quests for more and more quality services by the public and to guide policy making in developed and developing countries. Whilst the output of these exercises are of variable quality, a carefully defined concept of who to provide the services remains useful for analyzing comparative performance of the public and private partners and formulation policies for improving their engagements to deliver services.

Different approaches to service delivery do exist (for example, public and private perspective) offer insights into these issues but the relatively recent PPP perspective seems to provide the optimal framework for evaluating performance and designing policy remedy for poor service delivery experienced at the moment. This perspective emphasizes that the public and private perspectives have to come together and undertake conscious investments decisions to convert poor service delivery into good ones and they are to cooperate and collaborate in this venture. In turn, sustained collaboration and cooperation are associated with enhance high quality production and quality consumption. The process of collaborative and cooperative is themselves affected by systematic weaknesses in PPP (for example, relational imperfections, breached contracts, poor incentives, high interest rates, poor regulatory policy).

Remedying the paradox of service delivery is the principal aim of a PPP strategy. The central elements in a PPP strategy are: a) a national partnership involving complementary actions by the government and the private sector; b) a liberalization plus approach involving a mixture of incentive and supply-side policy measures; and c) where appropriate on service delivery grounds, policies to promote PPP projects initiations and implementations. A well-designed and management PPP is necessary but not sufficient for handling the paradox of service delivery. Clearly, even the best managed and coherent PPP project require a deeper stride in curtailing the devastating effects of risk. The next chapter gives a direction for handling risks in PPP projects.

REFERENCES

Aaronson, S. A. (2011). Limited partnership: Business, government, civil society and the public in the extractive industry transparency initiative. *Public Administration and Development*, *31*(1), 50–63. doi:10.1002/pad.588

Abdel Aziz, A. (2007). Successful delivery of public-private partnerships for infrastructure development. *Journal of Construction Engineering and Management*, *133*(12), 918–931. doi:10.1061/(ASCE)0733-9364(2007)133:12(918)

Abels, G. (2007). Citizen involvement in public policy-making: Does it improve democratic legitimacy and accountability? The case of PTA. *Interdisciplinary Information Sciences*, *13*(1), 103–116. doi:10.4036/iis.2007.103

Abonyi, G., & van Slyke, D.M. (2010). Governing on the edges: Globalization of production and the challenge to public administration in the Twenty-first century. *Public Administrative Review*, *70*(S1), S33-S45.

Adam, J., Young, A., & Zhihong, W. (2006). Public Private Partnerships in China: System, constraints and future prospects. *International Journal of Public Sector Management*, *19*(4), 384–396. doi:10.1108/09513550610669202

Adeyemi, A. Y., Oladapo, A. A., & Akindele, O. (2005). Balancing globalization and the sustainable development equation in the Nigerian construction industry.*Proceedings of the 3rd Postgraduate Conference*, 289-302.

Agranoff, R. (2006). Inside collaborative networks: Ten lessons for public managers. *Public Administration Review*, *66*(1), 56–65. doi:10.1111/j.1540-6210.2006.00666.x

Akintoye, A. (2006). Public private partnerships for sustainable development of Infrastructure in developing countries. *Proceedings of International Conference on the Built Environment.*

Akintoye, A. (2008). Project risk management practice: The case of a South African utility company. *International Journal of Project Management*, *26*(2), 149–163. doi:10.1016/j.ijproman.2007.03.011

Akintoye, A., & Chinyio, E. (2005). Private finance initiative in the healthcare sector: Trends and risk assessment. *Engineering, Construction, and Architectural Management*, *12*(6), 601–616. doi:10.1108/09699980510634155

Alonso-Conde, A. B., Brown, C., & Rojo-Suarez, J. (2007). Public private partnerships: Incentives, risk transfer and real options. *Review of Financial Economics*, *16*(4), 335–349. doi:10.1016/j.rfe.2007.03.002

Alsudiri, T., Al-Karaghouli, W., & Eldabi, T. (2013). Alignment of large project management process to business strategy: A review and conceptual framework. *Journal of Enterprise Information Management*, *26*(5), 596–615. doi:10.1108/JEIM-07-2013-0050

Andrews, M. (2013). *The limits of institutional reform in development: Changing rules for realistic solutions*. Cambridge, UK: Cambridge University Press. doi:10.1017/CBO9781139060974

Angelides, D., & Xenidis, Y. (2009). PPP Infrastructure Investments: Critical Aspects and Prospects. In A. Akintola & M. Beck (Eds.), *Policy, Finance and Management for Public-Private Partnerships*. London: Wiley-Blackwell. doi:10.1002/9781444301427.ch9

Anvuur, A., & Kumaraswamy, M. (2007). Conceptual Model of Partnering and Alliancing. *Journal of Construction Engineering and Management*, *133*(3), 225–234. doi:10.1061/(ASCE)0733-9364(2007)133:3(225)

Appuhami, R., Perera, S., & Perera, H. (2011). Coercive policy diffusion in a developing country: The case of public-private partnerships in Sri Lanka. *Journal of Contemporary Asia*, *41*(3), 431–451. doi:10.1080/00472336.2011.582713

Appuhami, R., Perera, S., & Perera, H. (2011). Management Controls in Public–Private Partnerships- An Analytical Framework. *Australian Accounting Review, 21*(1), 64–79. doi:10.1111/j.1835-2561.2010.00122.x

Awodele, O. A., Ogunlana, S. O., & Motawa, I. (2010) Understanding and managing risks necessary condition for success and sustainability of privately financed market projects in Nigeria.*Proceedings of ARCOM Doctoral Researcher Workshop on Sustainability Strategies in the UK Construction Industry at University of Wolverhampton on 25th June.*

Aziz, A. M. A. (2007). Successful delivery of public-private partnerships for infrastructure development. *Journal of Construction Engineering and Management, 133*(12), 918–931. doi:10.1061/(ASCE)0733-9364(2007)133:12(918)

Baker, K. (2012). Understanding strategic service partnerships. *Public Performance & Management Review, 35*(4), 660–678. doi:10.2753/PMR1530-9576350405

Ball, R., Heafey, M., & King, D. (2007). The Private Finance Initiative in the UK: A value for money and economic analysis. *Public Management Review, 9*(2), 289–310. doi:10.1080/14719030701340507

Bangura, Y., & Larbi, G. A. (Eds.). (2006). *Public sector reform in developing countries: capacity challenges to improve services.* Houndmills, UK: Palgrave.

Barber, M. (2008). *Instruction to Deliver: Fighting to transform Britain's public services.* London: Methuen.

Batley, R., & Mcloughlin, C. (2009). State capacity and non-state service provision in fragile and conflict-affected states. GSDRC Issues Paper. Birmingham: Governance and Social Development Resource Centre. From. Retrieved from http://www.gsdrc.org/go/display&type=Document&id=3175

Bayart, J.-F. (2009). *The State in Africa: The politics of the belly (2nd ed.).* Cambridge, UK: Polity Press.

Bennett, J., & Iossa, E. (2006). Building and managing facilities for public services. *Journal of Public Economics, 90*(10-11), 2143–2160. doi:10.1016/j.jpubeco.2006.04.001

Besley, T., & Ghatak, M. (2005). Competition and incentives with motivated agents. *The American Economic Review, 95*(3), 616–636. doi:10.1257/0002828054201413

Besley, T., & Ghatak, M. (2006). Public goods and economic development. In Understanding poverty. Oxford, UK: Oxford University Press.

Besley, T., & Ghatak, M. (2007). Reforming public service delivery. *Journal of African Economies, 16*(Supplement 1), 127–156. doi:10.1093/jae/ejm026

Bing, L., Akintoye, A., Edwards, P., & Hardcastle, C. (2005a). Perceptions of positive and negative factors influencing the attractiveness of PPP procurement for construction projects in the UK – Findings from a questionnaire survey. *Engineering, Construction, and Architectural Management, 12*(2), 125–148. doi:10.1108/09699980510584485

Bing, L., Akintoye, A., Edwards, P. J., & Hardcastle, C. (2005b). The allocation of risk in PPP construction projects in the UK. *International Journal of Project Management*, *23*(1), 25–35. doi:10.1016/j.ijproman.2004.04.006

Bingham, L., Nabatchi, B. T., & OLeary, R. (2005). The new governance: Practices and processes for stakeholder and citizen participation in the work of government. *Public Administration Review*, *65*(5), 547–558. doi:10.1111/j.1540-6210.2005.00482.x

Bloomfield, P. (2006). The challenging business of long-term public private partnerships: Reflection on local experience. *Public Administration Review*, *66*(3), 400–411. doi:10.1111/j.1540-6210.2006.00597.x

Bloomfield, P. (2006). The challenging business of long-term public-private partnerships: Reflections on local experience. *Public Administration Review*, *66*(3), 400–411. doi:10.1111/j.1540-6210.2006.00597.x

Boardman, A. E., & Vining, A. R. (2012). The political economy of public-private partnerships and analysis of their social value. *Annals of Public and Cooperative Economics*, *83*(2), 117–141. doi:10.1111/j.1467-8292.2012.00457.x

Booth, D. (2011). Introduction: Working with the grain? The Africa power and politics programme. *IDS Bulletin*, *42*(2), 1–10. doi:10.1111/j.1759-5436.2011.00206.x

Bourgon, J. (2007). Responsive, responsible and respected government: Towards a new public administration theory. *International Review of Administrative Sciences*, *73*(1), 7–26. doi:10.1177/0020852307075686

Bourgon, J. (2011). *A new synthesis of public administration: Serving in the 21st Century*. Montreal, Canada: McGill-Queen's University Press.

Bovaird, T. (2005). *Public Sector Performance*. University of West England. doi:10.1016/B0-12-369398-5/00475-8

Boyne, G. A., & Law, J. (2005). Setting public service outcome targets: Lessons from local public service agreements. *Public Money and Management Studies*, *25*(4), 253–260. doi:10.1080/09540962.2005.10600128

Bozeman, B. (2007). *Public values and public interest: Counterbalancing economic individualism*. Washington, DC: Georgetown University Press.

Brinkerhoff, D. W., & Brinkerhoff, J. M. (2011). Public–private partnerships: Perspectives on purposes, publicness, and good governance. *Public Administration and Development*, *13*(1), 2–14. doi:10.1002/pad.584

Brinkerhoff, D. W., & Brinkerhoff, J. M. (2011). Public–private partnerships: Perspectives on purposes, publicness, and good governance. *Public Administration and Development*, *13*(1), 2–14. doi:10.1002/pad.584

Broadbent, J., & Laughlin, R. (2005). The Role of PPP in the UK Governments modernization agenda. *Financial Accountability and Management*, *21*(1), 75–97. doi:10.1111/j.0267-4424.2005.00210.x

Brown, T., Potoski, M., & Van Slyke, D. (2006). Managing public service contracts: Aligning values, institutions, and markets. *Public Administration Review*, *66*(3), 323–331. doi:10.1111/j.1540-6210.2006.00590.x

Brzozowska, K. (2006). *Advantages and threats of public – private partnerships in larger infrastructure projects*. Warszawa: CeDeWu.PL.

Burger, P., & Hawkesworth, I. (2011). How to attain value for money: Comparing PPP and traditional infrastructure public procurement. *OECD Journal on Budgeting, 2011*(1), 1- 56.

Buxbaum, J. N., & Ortiz, I. N. (2007). Protecting the public interest: The role of long-term concession agreements for providing transportation infrastructure. Los Angeles, CA: U.S.C. Keston Institute for Public Finance and Infrastructure Policy.

Camilleri, E. (2011). *Project Success: Critical Factors and Behaviors*. Surrey, UK: Gower Publishing Limited.

Cankar, S. S., & Petkovšek, V. (2013). Private and public sector innovation and the importance of cross-sector collaboration. *Journal of Applied Business Research*, *29*(6), 197–1606.

Chan, A. P. C., Lam, P. T. I., Chan, D. W. M., Cheung, E., & Ke, Y. (2010b). Privileges and attractions for private sector involvement in PPP projects. In Challenges, Opportunities and Solutions in Structural Engineering and Construction. Taylor & Francis Group.

Cheung, E., Chan, A. P. C., & Kajewski, S. (2010). Suitability of procuring large public works by PPP in Hong Kong. *Engineering, Construction, and Architectural Management*, *17*(3), 292–308. doi:10.1108/09699981011038088

Chinyere, I. I., & Xu, X. (2012). Public – private partnership: The underlining principles of infrastructure investment, finance, and development projects. *International Journal of Business and Management*, *7*, 109–125. doi:10.5539/ijbm.v7n1p109

Chowdhury, A. N., Chen, P. H., & Tiong, R. L. K. (2011). Analyzing the structure of public– private partnership projects using network theory. *Construction Management and Economics*, *29*(3), 247–260. doi:10.1080/01446193.2010.537354

Christensen, T., & Laegreid, P. (2007a). The whole-of-Government approach to public sector reform. *Public Administration Review*, *67*(6), 1059–1066. doi:10.1111/j.1540-6210.2007.00797.x

Christensen, T., & Laegreid, P. (2007a). *Transcending the new public management: The transformation of public service reforms*. Burlington, VT: Ashgate.

Christensen, T., & Laegreid, P. (2011). Complexity and hybrid public administration- theoretical and empirical challenges. *Public Organization Review*, *11*(4), 407–423. doi:10.1007/s11115-010-0141-4

Cicmil, S., & Marshall, D. (2005). Insights into collaboration at the project level: Complexity, social interaction and procurement mechanisms. *Building Research and Information*, *33*(6), 523–535. doi:10.1080/09613210500288886

Cumming, D. (2007). Government policy towards entrepreneurial finance innovation investment funds. *Journal of Business Venture*, *22*(2), 193–235. doi:10.1016/j.jbusvent.2005.12.002

Dal Bó, E., Finan, F., & Rossi, M. A. (2013). Strengthening state capabilities: The role of financial incentives in the call to public service. *The Quarterly Journal of Economics*, *128*(3), 1169–1218. doi:10.1093/qje/qjt008

Delmon, J. (2009). *Private sector investment in infrastructure project finance - PPP projects and risks* (2nd ed.). Austin, TX: Wolters Kluwer.

Demirag, I., & Khadaroo, I. (2008). Accountability and value for money in private finance initiative contracts. *Financial Accountability & Management*, *24*(4), 455–478. doi:10.1111/j.1468-0408.2008.00462.x

Denhardt, J. V., & Denhardt, R. B. (2011). *The New Public Service: Serving, not steering* (3rd ed.). Armonk, NY: M. E. Sharpe.

Dewulf, G., Blanken, A., & Bult-Spiering, M. (2012). *Strategic Issues in Public-Private*. London: Wiley-Blackwell. doi:10.1002/9781119968306

Diana, M. (2014). Sustainable performance of public organizations: Shaping a coherent system for implementing and measuring the concept. *Studies in Business and Economics*, *9*(3), 50–56.

Dunleavy, P., Margetts, H., Bastow, S., & Tinkler, J. (2006). New public management is dead— long live digital-era governance. *Journal of Public Administration: Research and Theory*, *16*(3), 467–494. doi:10.1093/jopart/mui057

Eaton, D., & Akbiyikli, R. (2009). Innovation in PPP. In A. Akintoye & M. Beck (Eds.), Policy, Finance & Management for Public Private Partnerships. West Sussex, UK: Blackwell Publishing.

Eaton, K., Kaiser, K., & Smoke, P. (2011). *The political economy of decentralization reforms: implications for aid effectiveness*. Washington, DC: The World Bank. doi:10.1596/978-0-8213-8840-2

Eggers, W. D., & Macmillan, P. (2013). *The Solution Revolution: How business, government and social enterprises are teaming up to solve society's toughest problems*. Boston: Harvard Business Review Press.

Egnell, R., & Halden, P. (Eds.). (2013). *New agendas in state building: Hybridity, contingency, and history*. Abingdon, UK: Routledge.

English, L. M. (2007). Performance Audit of Australian Public Private Partnerships: Legitimizing Government Policies or Providing Independent Oversight? *Financial Accountability and Management*, *23*(3), 313–336. doi:10.1111/j.1468-0408.2007.00431.x

Estache, A., & Wren-Lewis, B. (2009). Towards a theory of regulation for developing countries: Following Jean-Jacques La®onts Lead. *Journal of Economic Literature*, *47*(3), 730–771. doi:10.1257/jel.47.3.729

Fatemi, M., & Behmanesh, M. R. (2012). New public management approach and accountability. *International Journal of Management Economics and Social Sciences*, *1*, 42–49.

Fiszbein, A., Ringold, D., & Rogers, H. (2011). *Making services work: indicators, assessments, and benchmarking of the quality of public service delivery*. Policy Research Working Paper No. 5690, The World Bank.

Flinders, M. (2005). The Politics of Public-Private Partnerships. *British Journal of Politics and International Relations*, *7*(2), 215–239. doi:10.1111/j.1467-856X.2004.00161.x

Forrer, J., Kee, J. E., Newcomer, K. E., & Boyer, E. (2010). Public private partnerships and the public accountability question. *Public Administration Review, 70*(3), 475–484. doi:10.1111/j.1540-6210.2010.02161.x

Garcia, F. M. (2014). Developments and challenges in public sector accounting, *Journal of Public Budgeting, Accounting &. Financial Management, 26*(2), 345–366.

Gehrt, J., Klatt, J. P., & Beckers, T. (2010). *Refinancing in public-private partnerships conceptual issues and empirical results from the UK and Germany*. WIP-Working Paper No. 2010-02, Workgroup for Infrastructure Policy (WIP) at Berlin Institute of Technology (TU Berlin).

Goldstein, S. M., & Naor, M. (2005). Linking publicness to operations management practices: A study of quality management practices in hospitals. *Journal of Operations Management, 23*(2), 209–228. doi:10.1016/j.jom.2004.07.007

Gorodnova, N. (2012). The integration of state and private business: The development of a socially oriented economy. *Finance and Credit, 6*(486), 20–30.

Grimsey, D., & Lewis, M. (2007). Public private partnerships and public procurement. *Agenda (Durban, South Africa), 14*(2), 46–58.

Grimsey, D., & Lewis, M. K. (2005). Are public private partnerships value for money? Evaluating alternative approaches and comparing academic and practitioner views. *Accounting Forum, 29*(4), 345–378. doi:10.1016/j.accfor.2005.01.001

Gupta, A. K., Trivedi, M. K., & Kansal, R. (2013). Risk variation assessment of Indian road PPP projects. *International Journal of Science. Environmental Technology, 2*(5), 1017–1026.

Gupta, O., & Biswas, N. (2010). Public private partnership: Indian economy. *SCMS Journal of Indian Management, 7*, 44–53.

Haran, M., Alastair, A., Berry, J., McGreal, S., Smyth, C., Kashayap, A., & Hutchison, N. (2013). The global infrastructure challenge: The role of PPP in a new financial and economic paradigm. London: Royal Institution of Chartered Surveyors (RICS).

Harris, C., & Tadimalla, K. (2008) Financing the boom in public-private partnerships in Indian Infrastructure: Trends and policy implications. Gridlines 45, World Bank/PPIAF.

Hayford, O., & Partner, C. U. (2006). *Successfully allocating risk and negotiating a PPP contract*. Paper Presented at the 6th Annual National Public Private Partnerships Summit: Which way now for Australia's PPP market? Syndey, Australia.

Heeks, R., & Bailur, S. (2007). Analyzing E-government research: Perspectives, philosophies, theories, methods, and practice. *Government Information Quarterly, 24*(2), 243–265. doi:10.1016/j.giq.2006.06.005

Hefetz, A., & Warner, M. E. (2012). Contracting or public delivery? The importance of service, market, and management characteristics. *Journal of Public Administration: Research and Theory, 22*(2), 289–317. doi:10.1093/jopart/mur006

Ho, P. (2012). *Governing for the future: What governments can do.* RSIS Working Paper, No. 248. Retrieved from www.rsis.edu.sg/wp-content/uploads/rsis-pubs/WP248.pdf

Hope, K. R. Sr. (2005). The New Public Management: A perspective from Africa. In K. McLaughlin, S. P. Osborne, & E. Ferlie (Eds.), *New public management: Current trends and future prospects*. London: Routledge.

Hoppe, E. & Schmitz, P. (2013). Public-Private partnerships versus traditional procurement: Innovation incentives and information gathering, *The RAND Journal of Economics*, *44*, 56-74.

Hosman, L. (2011). View from practice: Making the transition from pilot to scale: examining sustainability and scalability issues in a public–private telecenter partnership in Sri Lanka. *Information Technology for Development*, *17*(3), 232–248. doi:10.1080/02681102.2011.568225

Iossa, E., & Martimort, D. (2015). The Simple Microeconomics of Public-Private Partnerships. *Journal of Public Economic Theory*, *17*(1), 4–48. doi:10.1111/jpet.12114

Ismail, S., & Harris, F. A. (2014). Challenges in implementing public private partnership (PPP) in Malaysia. *Procedia: Social and Behavioral Sciences*, *164*, 5–10. doi:10.1016/j.sbspro.2014.11.044

Jacobson, C., & Choi, S. O. (2008). Success factors: Public works and public-private partnerships City of Manhattan Beach, Manhattan Beach, California, USA. *International Journal of Public Sector Management*, *2*(6), 637–657. doi:10.1108/09513550810896514

Jin, X.-H., Zhang, G., & Yang, R. J. (2012). Factor analysis of partners commitment to risk management in public-private partnership projects. *Construction Innovation*, *12*(3), 297–316. doi:10.1108/14714171211244550

Jomo, J. K., & Chowdhury, A. (2009). Reconsidering public-private partnerships in developing countries. *International Journal of Institutions and Economies*, *1*(2), 191–205.

Jomo, K. S., Chowdhury, A., Sharma, K., & Platz, D. (2016). *Public-private partnerships and the 2030 agenda for sustainable development: Fit for purpose*? DESA Working Paper No.148,ST/ESA/2016/DWP/148.

Jun, J.L. (2009). The limits of post-new public management and beyond. *Public Administration Review*, *69*(1), 161-165.

Kamarkar, R. (2014). Public Private Partnerships (PPP's)-A future intentions to development. *International Journal of Marketing and Financial Management*, *2*(7), 144–147.

Kaul, I., & Conceicao, P. (2006). *The New Public Finance: Responding to Global Challenges*. New York: Oxford University Press. doi:10.1093/acprof:oso/9780195179972.001.0001

Keçi, J. (2015). Public Private Partnership for Infrastructure Projects: Mapping the Key Risks, *International Journal of Social, Behavioral, Educational, Economic Business and Industrial Engineering*, *9*(9), 3085–3095.

Kelsall, T. (2011). Rethinking the relationship between Neo-Patrimonialism and economic development in Africa. *IDS Bulletin*, *42*(2), 76–87. doi:10.1111/j.1759-5436.2011.00213.x

Kociemska, H. (2010). Public – private partnership project success circumstances. *Journal of Modern Accounting and Auditing*, *6*, 53–58.

Koppell, J.G S. (2010). Administration without borders. *Public Administration Review, 70*(S1), S46-S55.

Koppenjan, J. F. M. (2005). The formation of public-private partnerships: Lessons from nine transport infrastructure projects in The Netherlands. *Public Administration*, *83*(1), 135–157. doi:10.1111/j.0033-3298.2005.00441.x

Kriześ-Dobieszewska, J. (2014). Managing public-private partnership market in the times of economic crisis. *Oeconomia Copernicana*, *5*(2), 63–73. doi:10.12775/OeC.2014.014

Kuppusamy, S. (2010). PPP: The right marriage between local government and the private sector in Malaysia. *International Journal of Institutions and Economics*, *2*(2), 142–166.

Kwak, Y. H., Chih, Y., & Ibbs, C. W. (2009). Towards a comprehensive understanding of public private partnerships for infrastructure development. *California Management Review*, *51*(2), 51–78. doi:10.2307/41166480

Leavitt, W. M., & Morris, J. C. (2007). Public works service arrangements in the 21st century: The Multiple-sector partnership as an alternative to privatization. *Public Works Management & Policy*, *12*(1), 325–330. doi:10.1177/1087724X07302588

Lee, E. W., & Shamsul Haque, M. (2006). The new public management reforms and governance in Asian NICs: A comparison of Hong Kong and Singapore. *Governance: An International Journal of Policy, Administration and Institutions*, *19*(4), 605–626. doi:10.1111/j.1468-0491.2006.00330.x

Leiringer, R. (2006). Technological innovation in PPPs: Incentives, opportunities and actions. *Construction Management and Economics*, *24*(3), 301–308. doi:10.1080/01446190500435028

Liu, T., & Wilkinson, S. (2011). Adopting innovative procurement techniques: Obstacles and drivers for adopting public private partnerships in New Zealand. *Construction Innovation: Information, Process Management*, *11*(4), 452–469.

Liu, T., & Wilkinson, S. (2014). Large-scale public venue development and the application of public-private partnerships. *International Journal of Project Management*, *32*(1), 88–100. doi:10.1016/j.ijproman.2013.01.003

Loosemore, A. N. M. (2007). Risk allocation in the private provision of public infrastructure. *International Journal of Project Management*, *25*(1), 66–76. doi:10.1016/j.ijproman.2006.06.005

Martin, C., & Parston, G. (2006). *Unlocking public value. A new model for achieving high performance in public service organizations*. London: John Wiley and Son, Inc.

Marty, F., & Voisin, A. (2005). The contracts of public-private partnerships in prison: The British experience. *Policy and Public Administration Review*, *23*, 21–42.

Maseko, M. (2014). *Analysis of critical success factors for public-private partnerships in infrastructure development in South Africa*. The 6th International Platinum Conference, 'Platinum–Metal for the Future', The Southern African Institute of Mining and Metallurgy.

Maskin, E., & Tirole, J. (2008). Public-private partnerships and government spending limits. *International Journal of Industrial Organization*, *26*(2), 412–420. doi:10.1016/j.ijindorg.2007.05.004

Matei, L. (2006). Empirical approaches of the public-private partnership in the services of public utility. *Theoretical and Applicative Economics*, *10*(505), 3–14.

Mauldin, M. D. (2012). A new governance explanation for the creation of a minority economic development public – private partnership in Florida. *Public Performance & Management Review*, *35*(4), 679–695. doi:10.2753/PMR1530-9576350406

McCann, S. (2014). *A public sector governance model for public private partnership: Integrating partnership, risk and performance management in the operating phase* (Unpublished Masters' Thesis). RMIT University, Melbourne, Australia.

McCann, S., Aranda-Mena, G., & Edwards, P. J. (2014). Delivering value-for-money in the operating phase of public private partnership: Interview findings. *International Public Management Review*, *15*(2), 91–110.

McCourt, W. (2005). New public management in developing countries. In K. McLaughlin, S. P. Osborne, & E. Ferlie (Eds.), *New public management: Current trends and future prospects*. London: Routledge.

McCourt, W. (2013). *Models of public service reform: A problem-solving approach.* Policy Research Working Paper, No. 6428. Washington, DC: The World Bank.

McLaughlin, K., Osborne, S. P., & Ferlie, E. (Eds.). (2005). *New public management: Current trends and future prospects*. London: Routledge.

Meier, K., & OToole, L. J. Jr. (2007). Modeling public management: Empirical analysis of the management-performance nexus. *Public Management Review*, *9*(4), 503–527. doi:10.1080/14719030701726630

Moulton, S. (2009). Putting together the publicness puzzle: A framework for realized publicness. *Public Administration Review*, *69*(5), 889–900. doi:10.1111/j.1540-6210.2009.02038.x

Munya, A. (2010). *Advantages and Risks of Pursuing P3s for Elements of Express Lane Networks in California*. Lessons for Developing Countries, 46th ISOCARP Congress 2010, Nairobi, Kenya.

Murphy, T. (2008). The case for public-private partnerships in infrastructure. *Canadian Public Administration Journal*, *51*(1), 99–126. doi:10.1111/j.1754-7121.2008.00006.x

Nafukho, F. M. (2008). Consensus building dialogue and spirituality principles of the learning organization paradigm. Implications for Kenya Public Service reform agenda. *Journal of Third World Studies*, *25*(2).

Ng, A., & Loosemore, A. M. (2007). Risk allocation in the private provision of public infrastructure. *International Journal of Project Management*, *25*, 66–76.

Nutt, P. (2006). Comparing public and private sector decision-making practices. *Journal of Public Administration: Research and Theory*, *16*(1), 289–318.

Obermann, G. (2007). The role of the state as a guarantor of public services – Transaction cost issues and empirical evidence. *Annals of Public and Cooperative Economics*, *78*(3), 475–500. doi:10.1111/j.1467-8292.2007.00343.x

Osborne, S. P. (2006). The new public governance? *Public Management Review*, *8*(3), 377–388. doi:10.1080/14719030600853022

Osborne, S. P. (2010). *The new public governance*. London: Routledge.

Osborne, S. P., Radnor, Z., & Nasi, G. (2013). A new theory for public service management? Towards a (Public) Service-Dominant Approach. *American Review of Public Administration*, *43*(2), 135–158. doi:10.1177/0275074012466935

Parashar, D. (2014). The Governments role in private partnerships for urban poor housing in India. *International Journal of Housing Markets and Analysis*, *7*(4), 524–538. doi:10.1108/IJHMA-08-2013-0049

Pârvu, D., & Voicu-Olteanu, C. (2009). Advantages and limitations of the public private partnerships and the possibility of using them in Romania. *Transylvanian Review of Administrative Sciences*, *27*, 189–198.

Perry, J. L. (2007). Democracy and the new public service. *American Review of Public Administration*, *37*(1), 3–16. doi:10.1177/0275074006296091

Perry, J. L., Hondeghem, A., & Wise, L. R. (2010). Revisiting the motivational bases of public service: Twenty years of research and an agenda for the future. *Public Administration Review*, *70*(5), 681–690. doi:10.1111/j.1540-6210.2010.02196.x

Pessoa, A. (2008). Public-private partnerships in developing countries: Are infrastructures responding to the New ODA Strategy? *Journal of International Development*, *20*(3), 311–325. doi:10.1002/jid.1416

Poole, M., Mansfield, R., & Gould-Williams, J. (2006). Public and private sector managers over 20 Years: A test of the 'Convergence Thesis'. *Public Administration*, *84*(4), 1051-1076.

Quah, J. S. T. (2013). Ensuring good governance in Singapore: Is this experience transferable to other Asian countries? *International Journal of Public Sector Management*, *26*(5), 401–420. doi:10.1108/IJPSM-05-2013-0069

Quiggin, J. (2005). Public private partnerships: Options for improved risk allocation. *The Australian Economic Review*, *38*(4), 445–450. doi:10.1111/j.1467-8462.2005.00388.x

Raisbeck, P., Duffield, C., & Xu, M. (2010). Comparative Performance of PPPs and Traditional Procurement in Australia. *Construction Management and Economics*, *28*(4), 345–359. doi:10.1080/01446190903582731

Rakic, B., & Radjenovic, T. (2011). Public private partnerships as an instrument of new public management. *FACYA UNIVERSITATIS Series: Economics and Organizations*, *8*(2), 207–220.

Ramalingam, B. (2013). *Aid on the edge of chaos*. Oxford, UK: Oxford University Press.

Ringold, D., Holla, A., Koziol, M., & Srinivasan, S. (2012). *Citizens and service delivery assessing the use of social accountability approaches in the human development Sectors*. Washington, DC: The International Bank for Reconstruction and Development / The World Bank.

Robinson, M. (2007). The politics of successful governance reforms: Lessons of design and implementation. *Commonwealth and Comparative Politics*, *45*(4), 521–548. doi:10.1080/14662040701659944

Robinson, M. (2015). *From old public administration to the new public service implications for public sector reform in developing countries*. UNDP Global Centre for Public Service Excellence #08-01.

Roehrich, J. K., Lewis, M. A., & George, G. (2014). Are public-private partnerships a healthy option? A systematic literature review. *Social Science & Medicine*, *113*, 110–119. doi:10.1016/j.socscimed.2014.03.037 PMID:24861412

Roll, M. (Ed.). (2014). *The politics of public sector performance: Pockets of effectiveness in developing countries*. London: Routledge.

Sadka, E. (2007). Public-private partnerships - A public economics perspective. *CESifo Economic Studies*, *53*(3), 466–490. doi:10.1093/cesifo/ifm013

Sagalyn, L. B. (2007). Public/private development. *Journal of the American Planning Association*, *73*(1), 7–22. doi:10.1080/01944360708976133

Sanda, Y. N., & Anigbogu, N. A. (2016). A conceptual framework for managing risks in public private partnerships projects in Housing Estate department in Nigeria. *International Journal of Regional Development*, *3*(1), 50–63. doi:10.5296/ijrd.v3i1.8144

Sarker, A. E. (2006). New public management in developing countries: An analysis of success and failure with particular reference to Singapore and Bangladesh. *International Journal of Public Sector Management*, *19*(2), 180–203. doi:10.1108/09513550610650437

Saxena, N. C. (2011). *Virtuous Cycles: The Singapore public service and national development*. Singapore: UNDP.

Seitanidi, M. M. (2010). *The politics of partnerships: A critical examination of nonprofit business partnerships*. New York, NY: Springer Science-Business Media. doi:10.1007/978-90-481-8547-4

Shaoul, J. (2005b). A critical financial analysis of the Private Finance Initiative: Selecting a financial method or allocating wealth. *Critical Perspectives on Accounting*, *16*(4), 441–471. doi:10.1016/j.cpa.2003.06.001

Sharma, C. (2012). Determinants of PPP in infrastructure in developing economies. *Transforming Government: People. Process and Policy*, *6*, 149–166.

Siddiquee, N. A. (2011). Rhetoric and reality of public-private partnerships: Learning points from the Australian experience. *Asian Journal of Political Science*, *19*(2), 129–148. doi:10.1080/02185377.2011.600163

Siemiatycki, M. (2007). Whats the secret? Confidentiality in planning infrastructure using Public-Private partnerships. *Journal of the American Planning Association*, *73*(4), 388. doi:10.1080/01944360708978520

Siemiatycki, M. (2010). Developing transportation infrastructure through public-private partnerships. *Journal of the American Planning Association*, *76*(1), 43–58. doi:10.1080/01944360903329295

Singaravelloo, K. (2010). PPP: The right marriage between local government and the private sector in malaysia? *International Journal of Institutions and Economics*, *2*(2), 142–166.

Skietrys, E., Raipa, A., & Bartkus, E. V. (2008). Dimensions of the efficiency of public–private partnership. *Economic Engineering*, *3*, 45.

Solana, E. F. O. (2014). Public private not-for-profit partnerships: Delivering public services to developing countries. *Procedia Engineering*, *78*, 259–264. doi:10.1016/j.proeng.2014.07.065

Takim, R., Ismail, K., Nawawi, A. H., & Jaafar, A. (2009). The Malaysian private finance initiative and value for money. *Asian Social Science*, *5*(3), 103–111. doi:10.5539/ass.v5n3p103

Tang, L. Y., Shen, Q., & Cheng, E. W. L. (2010). A review of studies on Public–Private Partnership projects in the construction industry. *International Journal of Project Management*, *28*(7), 683–694. doi:10.1016/j.ijproman.2009.11.009

Tetřevová, L. (2006). Theoretical and practical aspects of PPP Projects. *Vadyba/Management, 3–4*(12–13), 105-110.

Trafford, S., & Proctor, T. (2006). Successful joint venture partnerships: Public-private partnerships. *International Journal of Public Sector Management*, *19*(2), 117–129. doi:10.1108/09513550610650392

Trangkanont, S., & Charoenngam, C. (2014). Critical failure factors of public-private partnership low-cost housing program in Thailand. *Engineering, Construction, and Architectural Management*, *21*(4), 421–443. doi:10.1108/ECAM-04-2012-0038

Trebilcocka, M., & Rosenstocka, M. (2015). Infrastructure Public–Private Partnerships in the Developing World: Lessons from Recent Experience. *The Journal of Development Studies*, *51*(4), 335–354. doi:10.1080/00220388.2014.959935

Tserng, H. P., Russell, J. S., Hsu, C. W., & Lin, C. (2012). Analyzing the role of national PPP units in promoting PPPs: Using new institutional economics and a case study. *Journal of Construction Engineering and Management*, *138*(2), 242–249. doi:10.1061/(ASCE)CO.1943-7862.0000398

Turhani, A. (2013). Governance of public-private partnerships: Lessons learned from an Albanian case. *Journal of East European Management Studies*, *18*, 371–385.

Van der Wal, Z. (2013). Mandarins versus Machiavellians? On differences between work motivations of administrative and political elites. *Public Administration Review*, *73*(5), 749–759. doi:10.1111/puar.12089

van der Wal, Z., de Graaf, G., & Lasthuizen, K. (2008). Whats Valued Most? Similarities and differences between the organizational values of the public and private sector. *Public Administration*, *86*(2), 465–482. doi:10.1111/j.1467-9299.2008.00719.x

van der Wal, Z., & Huberts, L. (2008). Value Solidity in Government and Business - Results of an empirical study on public and private sector organizational values. *American Review of Public Administration*, *38*(3), 264–285. doi:10.1177/0275074007309154

Vining, A., & Boardman, A. (2008a). Public-private partnerships. Eight rules for governments. *Public Works Management & Policy*, *13*(2), 149–161. doi:10.1177/1087724X08323843

Wang, Y. (2015). Evolution of public–private partnership models in American toll road development: Learning based on public institutions risk management. *International Journal of Project Management*, *33*(3), 684–696. doi:10.1016/j.ijproman.2014.10.006

Wang, Y., & Zhao, Z. (2014). Motivations, obstacles, and resources: Determinants of public- private partnership in state toll road financing. *Public Performance & Management Review*, *37*(4), 679–704. doi:10.2753/PMR1530-9576370407

Warner, M. E., & Hefetz, A. (2008). Managing markets for public service: The role of mixed public/private delivery of city services. *Public Administration Review*, *68*(1), 155–166. doi:10.1111/j.1540-6210.2007.00845.x

Weber, E. P., & Khademian, A. M. (2008). Wicked problems, knowledge challenges, and collaborative capacity builders in network settings. *Public Administration Review*, *68*(2), 334–349. doi:10.1111/j.1540-6210.2007.00866.x

Wibowo, A., & Mohamed, S. A. M. (2008). *Perceived risk allocation in public private partnership (PPP) water supply projects in Indonesia*. Paper Presented at 1st International Conference on Construction in Developing Countries (ICCIDC-I), Karachi, Pakistan.

Xenidis, Y., & Angelides, D. (2005). The financial risks in build-operate-transfer projects. *Construction Management and Economics*, *23*(4), 431–441. doi:10.1080/0144619050004155

Xie, W. D., & He, W. (2006). PPP pattern financing in urban mass transit realm of China. *Urban Transit Transportation*, *3*, 1–4.

Yang, Y., Hou, Y., & Wang, Y. (2013). On the development of public–private partnerships in transitional economies: An explanatory framework. *Public Administration Review*, *73*(2), 301–310. doi:10.1111/j.1540-6210.2012.02672.x

Ye, S. (2009). Patterns of Financing PPP Projects. In A. Akintola & M. Beck (Eds.), *Policy, Management and Finance of Public-Private partnerships*. London: Wiley-Blackwell. doi:10.1002/9781444301427.ch10

Zaharioaie, M. (2012). The utility of using public private partnership for local governments. *Journal of Public Administration, Finance and Law,* 17-24.

Zhang, X. (2005a). Critical success factors for public private partnerships in infrastructure development. *Journal of Construction Engineering and Management*, *131*(1), 3–14. doi:10.1061/(ASCE)0733-9364(2005)131:1(3)

Chapter 2
Quests for Public–Private Partnership

ABSTRACT

This chapter critically reviews seminal literature on PPPs, in order to identify core congruent issues, motif, basics and environment as necessity to answer the quests for quality service delivery so rampant world over. It draws out a number of key themes to better understand why the quest for PPP has turned out to be the 'driving tone' for all governments, even though successive reports/news prints, have uncovered many challenges in their implementation. Acknowledging that there is no one clear definition, strategy or template for the effective partnering, findings from extant literature highlight principles and critical success factors (CSFs) deemed integral to augmenting PPP performance and success. So, whilst governments invariably conducts their businesses with a smaller ration of strategic partnerships than commonly believed, and accepting private partners dominance has predominantly remained, it is advocated that there is an exigent need to disentangle the PPP initiative through some form of proper risk analysis in the project phases. The case for this is presented through a relationship schema that maps the fabric, reliance and drivers for PPP success.

The purpose of life is to collaborate for a common cause; the problem is nobody seems to know what it is. - Gerhard Gschwandtner

INTRODUCTION

There is a growing interest in policy circles in both developed and developing world in promoting better production to produce quality goods and services and obtaining a suitable strategy to achieve this (Bovaird, 2010). Policy makers are typically concerned with how their economy has been performing in relation to: a) quantity of production; and b) quality of goods and services produced vis-à-vis thee high and ever changing demands of the public for quality goods and services. Similarly, academicians and researchers have since the turn of the century embarked on a series of investigations with constant

DOI: 10.4018/978-1-5225-2503-5.ch002

research on the costs and benefits of production in relation to consumption of quality goods and services on a worldwide basis. The interest has fueled several attempts to devise an integral development indicator at country level, a composite measure combining the organizations in the public and private sectors of an economy according to their areas of operations. The numbers of projects implemented under such arrangements are growing by the day; experts and consultants involvement as well as interventions from financial institutions is growing and even becoming increasingly influential in policy formulation and implementation of such projects.

Against this backdrop, this chapter appraises some insights on the literature on PPP and puts forward the current quests for PPP that seems to; had taken the world as a storm. The first section on "Triangular motif for public private partnership" examines three key reasons for the urge for adopting PPP in any development discourse, those are: the need for broader public sector reforms, mobilization of private capital to meet development needs; and greater efficiency. Each of these motifs shall be analyzed within the context of PPP and their strength and weaknesses will as well be captured. The section on "Basics of public private partnerships" constructs a simple analysis of three main sub components of PPP (rationale/critical success factors, principles/benefits, and dangers/challenges) and presents the results by illustrations and examples. This is thought to provide the most core of the most basic knowledge needed on a PPP. The section on "The process of public private partnership" examines potential determinants of a successful PPP projects and concludes that the environment, legal framework, and the cycle of the PPP project are closely associated with each other for a better results-oriented success of a PPP project. Reference materials for this chapter shall be provided though after a precise conclusion had been drawn.

TRIANGULAR MOTIF FOR PUBLIC-PRIVATE PARTNERSHIP

According to Hayford (2013), the core of any partnership is the idea of shared authority and responsibility, joint investment, sharing liability/risk taking and mutual benefits. As a result of these, Shen, Platten and Dang (2006) claims that a PPP is characterized by involvement of two or more actors (at least one from the public and another from the private sector) with each party being a principal. Cheung, Chan and Kajewski (2009b) attest that PPP is an establishment of an enduring and stable relationship among actors implying that the parties enter into a long-term relationship. Delmon (2010) maintains there is transfer of resources from both parties. These resources could be material, authority or other symbolic values meaning that no matter how small, each participant brings something to the partnership. Trafford and Proctor (2006) articulate that there is usually a shared responsibility for outcomes or activities which closely relates it to the core highlighted above.

In spite of these, anyhow, the global quests for PPP are dominated by three triangular motifs, each of which is related to the other. These motifs: public sector reforms, private capital and greater efficiency have attracted attentions of policy makers and well as implementers and generated lots of debate in the development circle both in the developing and developed world. Scholars and researchers have been publishing articles and papers on PPP since 1980. At the heart of these publications is PPP that shows the relative positioning of a new avenue for authentic service provisions. Wettenhall (2010) terms it a 'tool of procurement' while Kamarkar (2014) calls it 'a new mode of service delivery'. Both terms suggest that PPP involves a thorough assessment of the existing level of service delivery in any country and provides a realistic basis for designing future development policies to promote PPPs. The focus of these exercises is not to compute a measure of service delivery performance of the public sector per se; instead they adopt a more direct approach of looking at a large assortment of factors affecting PPP projects in a broad sense of the word. Using their ultimate ends, PPP is presumed by Murphy (2008) as a mode quite diverse of the traditional methods of providing services. It is quite detached from such a much which were common in the traditional service delivery provision, though 'unfortunately in some areas or sections' the practice is still prevalent. The changing trends of demand for goods and services had dictated adoption of a strategy in which the long-term nature of PPP is very much relevant and wanted. The next sub sections look at these motifs in turn.

Broader Public Sector Reform

Silvester and Aroujo (2012) contend that governments are always on the look out to find catalysts that can provoke a greater commitment to revive the public sector reform agenda. According to Gorodnova (2012), one of such catalysts is PPP. This is because a reform program that includes PPP provides an opportunity to reconsider the assignment of sector roles to remove any potential conflicts and to consider a private entity as a possible sector participant (). This would dictate a reexamination of the roles in the public sector through restructuring and clarifications. Jin, Zhang, and Yang (2012) claim specific attentions would be required in reexamining the roles of key actors, for example, policy makers, regulators and service providers. The purpose of such reexamination is solely for the mobilization of capital so as to achieve efficiency in service delivery.

Hodge and Greve (2007) assert events of marked magnitudes forced governments to act to salvage the challenge of service delivery. For example, implementing a specific PPP transaction often forces concrete reform steps to support the new allocation of sector roles such like the passage of laws and establishment of separate regulatory bodies. Robinson (2008) seems to suggest that because of globalization the politic of state capacity has led to public discontent. Lufuunyo (2013) attributes the discontent to political, social, economic and technological challenges. These challenges have often brought with them insensitive outcomes. Osborne, Radnor and Nasi (2013) claim that together with a growing political consensus that the public services needed to develop more cost effective and responsive approaches, led to calls for reform both within and without the public service. Out of this discontent, two marked approaches arose. According to Abonyi and van Slyke (2010), the first approach emphasized the importance of exposure to market forces and competition. It stressed individual choice and the needs of consumers (Perry, 2007). McCourt (2013) asserts this led to radical reforms in the organization and delivery of public service. Elsewhere, Osborne (2010) indicates a different rhetoric and *mondus operandi* developed, which emphasized the needs of the communities. This second approach to service delivery sought to strengthen the voice of service users as citizens and increase their direct involvement with those services and their development (Osborne, 2006). Between these two comparative extremes of public service reform policy and strategy lies a more managerial approach (Christensen & Laegreid, 2011). According to Bourgon (2011), the managerial approach draws ideas and approaches from both sides of the political spectrum, but aims to replace unresponsive public service bureaucracies by more flexible and responsive systems geared to the needs of public service customers. Christensen and Laegreid (2007a) allege the emphasis is not so much on the imperative of market forces or the urge to give greater give greater voice to the communities served. Somewhere else, Christensen and Laegreid (2007b) indicate that it is on the drive for internal self-improvement. Weber and Khademian (2008) argue that the aim is to provide a more modern public service which is far more responsive to the competing pressures of the outside world. According to Andrews (2013), this will equip the public service more effectively to meet changing national socio-economic needs.

Diverse studies (Cheung, 2011) have shown many countries have drawn to varying degrees, at different points in time, upon these three strands. Even though this seems to be true, the origin of service quality initiatives in any country appears to vary, so suggested by Denahrdt and Denhart (2011). For example, in some countries a budget pressure was the determining factor; in others it was general dissatisfaction with government services (Agus, Barker & Kandampully, 2007). Some countries had a combination of origins (Bovaird, 2007). In spite of their origins, though, there were two protagonists behind their emergence. These were the politicians and the civil services. For example, in the UK the initiative was developed and promoted by political leaders (Bouckaert, 2008). Instead in Canada, it was initially developed and promoted by civil servants (Bouckaert, Van de Walle & Kampen, 2005). Eggers and Macmillan (2013) aver in a number of countries (for example, Australia, Sweden and New Zealand), management and staff of individual government organizations initiated service quality improvements as part of internal management reform and in the absence of a centrally driven initiative. For all intents and purposes, Dalton (2005) shows that service quality initiatives reflect a general acceptance of the importance of responsive and efficient government to economic and social progress. Usually, this happens even within a general context of budgetary constraints (McGovern, 2011).

The urge for a broader public service reform is something that has rocked the world of service delivery like a storm in an oceanic area. Dunleavy, Margetts, Bastow and Tinkler (2006) avow the fan of the storm is being promoted by governments of various political persuasions. Taylor-Gooby (2006a) opines that service quality initiatives are not necessarily part of 'smaller government' initiatives, although they may be when competition in service delivery is introduced. Somewhere else, Taylor-Gooby (2006a) proclaims that service quality initiatives should be consistent with an ongoing role for the public sector and with defending and instilling confidence in the public sector.

Based on the ever changing needs of the public surprise production of poor quality goods and provision of low quality services, service delivery initiatives must be tailored to that which answers the inner quests of the public. Bangura and Larbi (2006) suggest that the key components of responsive service delivery must include: transparency, accessibility, participation and satisfying user requirements. In his master piece on the transformation of British public service, Barber (2008) stresses the key components of responsive service delivery cited above must be cultivated and promoted at all levels of public service delivery if at all the public were to enjoy the outcomes of their public service delivery. Van Ryzin (2007) seems to recommend that the public participates in or are consulted about decisions on what level and type of services is to be provided. Meanwhile, Kelsall (2011) outlays information provision to the public about what level and types of services to be provided is very critical to the success of service delivery provision. The riding outcome from such intervention is likely to lead to the public being in a position of reasonable expecting to receive the desired level of service (Wang & Montgomery, 2007). Van Ryzin (2011) concurs and advocates that the public must have the right of complaints and redress if the appropriate level of service is not provided. In the intervening time, Houston (2006) proposes that service delivery agencies must set service quality targets and to report their performance against them. On his part, Vining and Boardman (2008a) articulates that the achievement of such a target is possible through PPP. He indicates that PPP targets both the public and private sectors, sectors which have potentials of engaging in amiable service delivery provision. It acts as a first point of contact for investors and permits active networking among the players in the public as well as private sectors plus other key stakeholders.

Keeping tap in entering into and promotion PPP engagements would ensure approval of active participation of partners who matters in the process, their elaborate contributions and eventual success of the PPP projects undertaken by the parties. Kahwajian, Baba, Amudi and Wano (2014) adds that partnering between the public and private sectors is a way to bridge the financial gap between developing for instance infrastructure projects and the financial ability of governments specialized in developing these projects with preserving the public rights. They continue to state that partnership between the public and private sectors is the key to achieve economic and social development. For example, investment through partnership can establish large scale projects that will enhance development, achieve economic progress and increase local products.

Mobilization of Private Capital

Xenidis and Angelides (2005) put plainly, governments often face daunting challenges due to an ever-increasing need to find sufficient financing to produce and provide quality services required to support growing populations. For example, governments are challenged by the demands of increasing urbanization, the rehabilitation requirements of aging structure (Ndandiko, 2006), the need to expand network to new populations (Akintoye, 2006), and the goal of reaching previously unserved or underserved areas (van Dijk, 2008). Owusu and Badu (2009) designate an additional drain on public resources is exhibited, for example, by the provision of infrastructure services often at an operating deficit. In combination with limited Government's financial capability, the pressures drive the government 'crazy' and tickle its desire to mobilize private sector capital for infrastructure and service investments (Steijin, Klijn & Edelenbos, 2011). It's through PPP that previously untapped resources from the international, local or regional private sector players that capital for investment can be realized (Drew 2005).

While partners may enter in an arrangement in fulfillment of providing quality services as suggested by scholars (Krześ-Dobieszewska, 2014), it would this is threatened with numerous bottlenecks. The most notable of the bottlenecks is the inadequacy of finances in the hands and for use by the public sector. This issue has presented numerous methodological problems to any sort of development initiative which could have been thought of undertaking in the public sector. Apart from being inadequate, lack of finances in the public sector poses serious challenges in as far as delivery of services are concerned (Sabolová & Tetrevová, 2010). Among other serious challenges, it does not permit public sector organizations to fulfillment its mandate in providing quality services to the public. It has continuously acted as a cog in the wheel of service delivery provision in many, but especially, the public sector. Furthermore, public sector's organizations can neither assists nor act in combination to salvage the state of poor quality service delivery and poor performance. Considerable care, however, needs to go into designing policy 'pregnant' with measures to overcome the deficits of finances. Maskin and Tirole (2008) offers some insight into this. To him, involving the private sector in the schemes of soliciting finances is something very acceptable; however, all such efforts should be more directed on those able to meet the demand.

Shrivastava (2011) suggests focusing on those private sector organizations that are capable of either providing finances on their own or have the capability of raising finances. Tetřevová (2006) avers finances from the private sector organizations can revamp the inadequacy of finances in the public sector. This is much so as the private sector organizations can be more modest in claiming to quantify their activities in the hopes of making profits in the end. Nevertheless, obtaining finances from the private sector is a phenomenon that is too multifaceted and complex to permit ease of access. Taking this suggestion on board, Liu and Wilkinson (2014) developed a simple mean of attaining money from the private sector.

This approach emphasizes the rapid pace of borrowing of resources, for example from financial institutions. For quite sometimes even more as far back as the down of civilization, financial borrowing has been a continuous process. This strong root of acquiring perspective is always available and can be extended at all level.

Aside from borrowing, finances can be obtained from the private sector through getting private sector organizations themselves involved in the execution of, for example, PPP project using their finances. At the first glance, Kamarkar (2014) points out that this seems like quite a difficult notion to translate into practicality as perhaps, a public sector organization would want it to be. Yet, some private sector organizations have the capacity to implement very huge projects as required under PPP arrangement, single handedly. Mobilizing finances from the private sector is therefore, focused on the possibility of raising finances from a bunch of millionaire who sees such lending as a source of increasing on the quantity of resources at their disposal for a pleasurable use (Ibem, 2010). Accordingly, a more competitive approach must therefore characterize the process of acquiring finances from the private sector (Grimsey & Lewis, 2005). For example, such competition can for instance, the arranged as to when and how potential private organization capable of providing the desired services can ably participates. In conjunction with borrowing approach, which can be viewed as a proxy for the extent to which a private sector organization can meet its demand for finances, this provides a multi-faceted yet relatively simple notion of acquisition of finances (Gunawansa, 2010). In using this simple approach, the public sector can hope to improve its functional capability to produced desired goods and services. Given the focused notion of mobilization of capital finances from the private sector as outlined above, and the desire for obtaining required finances, the final acquisition of finances from the private sector can be constructed as critical for implementing a project leading to the closer of the gaps in service delivery provision (Glasbergen, 2011).

Greater Efficiency

Diana (2014) shows most governments especially in developing often provide poor quality services and majorly their performances are of low standard, compared to for example, the privates sector. There has been a greater concern among policy makers, implementers and beneficiaries of government services on the wanting service quality and performance (Farquharson, de Mästle, Yescombe & Encinas, 2011). Studies have shown that efficient use of scarce resources is a critical challenge for governments- and one in which many governments fall far short of goals. The reason for this, as claimed by Eaton, Akbiyukli and Dickinson (2006) is that the public sector typically has few or no incentives for efficient structured into its organization and processes and is thus poorly positioned, for example, to efficiently build and operate infrastructure. According to Angerer and Hammerschmid (2005), however, injecting incentives into an entrenched public sector is difficult, though not impossible. As Banerjee, Oetzel and Ranganathan, 2006) demonstrated by suggesting the development of a government-wide dedication to efficiency while maintaining many critical services with the public domain.

The beauty of PPP arrangement is that it promotes private sector participation which is normally translated into greater efficiency (Siemiatycki, 2010). For example, the private sector enters into the investment or contracting opportunity with the clear goal of maximizing profits. According to Forrer, Kee, Newcomer and Boyer (2010), these profits are generated in large part by increased efficiency in investments and operations. This means if the PPP is structured to let the operator pursue this goal, the efficiency of, say, the infrastructure services will likely to be enhanced. Likewise, Weihe (2006) retorts improving the efficiency of the services and operations also increases the chances that those services are economically sustainable and provided at affordable rates-even after satisfying the profits requirements of the private operators.

In furtherance, Singaravelloo, (2010) asserts PPP allows government to pass operational roles to efficient private sector operators while retaining and improving focus on core public sector responsibilities, such as regulation and supervision. Properly implemented, Cheung, Chan & Kajewski (2012) demonstrates, this approach should result in a lower aggregate cash outlay for the government, and better and cheaper service to the consumer. Usually, this holds true even if the government continues to bear part of the investment or operational cost since government's cost obligation is likely to be targeted, limited, and structured within a rational overall financing strategy (Yang, Hou & Wang, 2013).

As a tool for reforming infrastructure or service delivery, PPP also has the potential to promote greater efficiency (Zaharioaie, 2012). Skietrys, Raipa and Bartkus (2008) testify that PPP is most effective to create efficiency if it is accompanied by other reform activities as to underpin and reinforce and to support sustainable improvement. Sharma (2012) reiterates that a successful PPP is designed with careful attention to the context or the enabling environment within which the partnership will be implemented. Steijin, Klijn and Edelenbos (2011) indicate that where the operating environment can be reformed to be more conducive to the goals of PPP-that efficiency promotion and enhancement-this should be accomplished. While Shendy, Kaplan and Mousley (2011) insinuate where elements of the operating context cannot be changed, the PPP design must be tailored to accommodate existing conditions. As a sure case to promote and enhance efficiency, Matei (2006) recommends that in designing a PPP process and selecting a form of PPP, it is important to consider the reform objectives; policy environment; the legal, regulatory and institutional frameworks. Grimsey and Lewis (2005) supplement by bringing in the elements of financing requirements and resources of the sector and the political constraints and stakeholder concerns. The only thing that Hahn (2010) persuasively tells about PPP is that it may be an effective tool to address some, but probably not all sector issues, with the exception perhaps of promoting and enhancing greater efficiency.

BASICS OF PUBLIC-PRIVATE PARTNERSHIP

Jomo and Chowdhury (2009) articulate the goal of PPP as exploitation of the synergies in the joint innovative use of resources and in the application of management knowledge, with optimal attainment of the goals of all parties involved. Ismail (2013a) cherishes that these goals cannot be attained to the same extent without the other parties.

However, as highlighted earlier on, there is not widely recognizing definition of PPPs (Keçi, 2015). This makes it increasingly difficult to understand all appreciate all its precepts. Although there is no clear agreement on what does and what does not constitute a PPP, as it is sometimes sued to describe a wider range of arrangement, Abdel Aziz (2007) notes that proper understanding of PPP is a first step to appreciate how deep the discipline has moved. Whilst the overall outlines of PPP is only slightly larger than to be contained in this book, for the purpose of this book, limitations shall be restricted to only the basics. This feature get help us get along to have further more interest on the theme of this book as well as provide an index to the main thesis of the book-risk management (Zitron, 2006).

There are only three important issues which shall be deliberated upon in this section. The rationale epitome by the critical success factors forms the basis for this choice and subsequent argument for the quest for PPP. This shall be followed by principles as well as benefits for choosing PPP as a service delivery tool. Dangers/challenges in the use of PPP shall also be highlighted in another sub section to this section. Next we determine how these are very important for taking up a PPP arrangement.

Rationale and Critical Success Factors

As intimated earlier on, even more reviews of literature on PPP does not provide any hard of fast definition of the term (Cankar & Petkovšek, 2013). This seems to suggest that there could probably hundred definition of PPP out there. However, it has to be noted that the philosophical underpinning of the choice of PPP as a tool for development and quality service delivery is premised on a number of substantial arguments. Walker (2007) argues that PPP is an arrangement between a public sector organization and the private sector organization for the provision of public sector activity. He continues to say the activity will be provided, owned by the public organization for a specified period before reverting to the public body. Zhang (2005a) suggested PPP is to be treated as a term with very 'persuasive definition'. This is because it draws on the positive connotations of the term 'partnership'. According to Jui-Sheng and Pramudawardhani (2015), the most basic thing about PPP is that the provision of publics services shall inevitably involves interaction with the private sector partners. These partners could be suppliers, contractors or just joint ventures. Ismail and Harris (2014) advice that it is very important to consider what kind of relationship is to be involved in the PPP and whether it can achieve the benefits typically associated with the partnership.

Coming into partnership, Cheung (2009) claims is an assured mean and ease of designing, planning, financing, constructing and/or operating projects for public good which would have been regarded traditionally as falling within the remit of the public sector. Good examples of such projects are roads, bridges, buildings and such like. Sometimes it might be hard for the government to take all the responsibilities to say construct and operate a road. In this case, PPP can come in handy and set a framework for treating this dilemma. For example, through PPP, the private sector can contributes design, construction, operation, maintenance, finance and risk management skills. These skills may be lacking in government. Meanwhile, government may be responsible for strategic planning and industry structure, obtaining permits, some customer interface issues, regulation, community service obligations and (sometimes) payment on behalf of the service users (Babatunde, Opawole & Akinsiku, 2012).

Bloomfield (2006) highlights the transactional nature of PPP. This provides an avenue for both the government and the private sector organization to benefits. For example, the private sector may provide design, financing and/or construction and the delivery of services in exchange for publically-owned assets or user fees (Leiringer, 2006). Whilst acknowledging the transaction base, Koppenjan (2005), broaden the scope to include a 'working together approach' that relies upon cooperation to meet objectives in return for mutual gain through the sharing of risks, costs, resources and responsibilities. In its collaborative endeavors Smyth and Edkins (2006) articulate that PPP involves public and private partners developed through the expertise of each partner in order to meet identified public needs through appropriate resource, risk and reward allocation.

Apanavičienė and Rudžianskaitė-Kvaraciejienė (2010) contend that the wisdom of PPP is founded on the conception of it being an important pillar in the implementation of national strategic goals for development. Since its emergence in the earliest civilization as claimed by Wettenhall (2010), PPP only got a buzzword status in the 1990s with the rise in the importance of involving private partners in the course of development. From then on, the renewed quests for social and economic transformation have been under surveillance of the public expenditures as cherished by Bovaird (2010). At this juncture the centre of redesign was the cutting back of public sector expenditure, delegating responsibilities to the private for-profit sector and the fostering of voluntary engagement aiming at providing local public goods.

Driven by the argument that the hierarchical bureaucracy in the public sector is inherently inefficient, Jacobson and Choi (2008) proclaim that PPP was a mean of introducing market mechanism into the workings of the public sector. This was especially necessary as the politicians and bureaucrats were wanted to act in public interest at all times instead of pursuing their own interests or those of powerful interest groups. This eventual shift resulted into an expansion to involve greater range of actors including civic organizations and the private sector organizations. In the process though, Jefferies (2006) argues the focus had to heavily rely on the institutional and managerial consequences of the mixed economy of care in service delivery provision that required a managerial mode of coordination in a multi-provider system. Basically, the rationale behind PPP is the contractual obligations entered into during the agreement between the parties (Bennett & Iossa, 2006). The nature of the agreement is such that the skills and assets of each of the partners are to be brought on board for the realization of the goals set about during the agreement time (Aziz, 2007). The parties are to share rewards and risk equally in this arrangement. In addition to sharing reward and risks, the parties are to share resources as well. For example, the private partner is required to provide the services and/or project and assumes substantial financial, technical and operational risks (Ng, Wong & Wong, 2012). Similarly, this could be the sharing ratio for the public organization also. Sabolová and Tetrevová, 2010) elucidate that the public sector gets a better quality for equal costs or equal quality for lower costs while the private sector gets a long-term (and to a large extent very stable) income security. Kim, Lee, Lee and Lee (2013) cautions though, for the private partners to obtain equitable outcomes there must be rigorous definitions of their roles and what is meant by the public and private sectors. Also, Clayton (2013) suggests that the notion of associated action and how horizontal power relations among the partners must be ensured more importantly, the mediating role of the state to enable and regulate the partnership must be very clear.

According to Jin, Zhang and Yang (2012), the rationale of embracing PPP is informed by two critical factors. First, an enablement of the public sector to harness the expertise and efficiencies that the private sector can bring to the delivery of certain facilities and services traditionally procured and delivered by the public sector. Secondly, is structured so that the public sector seeking to make a capital investment does not incur any borrowing. ModuKumshe, Badiya Yusuf Magaji and Bani (2015) declare that since borrowing is incurred by the SPV implementing the project, PPP becomes an "off-balance sheet" method of financing the delivery of new or refurbished public sector assets. To them, PPP is neither a promotion of privatization and subsidies to private entrepreneurs nor promotion of a free market economy, but corporatism. Such that the conception in the like manner has to go beyond concentrating on "complementarity" as the case in most developing countries (Atkinson, Crawford & Ward, 2006) to include "embeddedness" (Chen & Partington, 2006).

While there is considerable probable rationale for engagement in PPP as suggested in the literature (Singewar & Deshmukh, 2016), likewise several of such literature do exist for factors that can enable PPP to succeed (Singewar and Deshmukh, 2016). These factors commonly regarded as critical success factors (CSFs) are those few key areas of activity in which favorable results are absolutely necessary for a manager to reach his/her goals (Hardcastle, Edwards, Akintoye & Li, 2005). Since the early 1990s, CSFs has been used as a management measures in majorly construction industry, for example in competitive tendering, negotiation and management of public clients (Hardcastle, Edwards, Akintoye & Li, 2005). CSFs have been identified by many researchers to improve the success rate of PPP projects around the world (Ogunsanmi, 2014; Olaniyan, 2013; Dada & Oladokun, 2012; Helmy, 2011;Shrivastava, 2011; Cheung, Chan, Lam & Chan, 2010). Using factor analysis approach, Hardcastle, Edwards, Akintoye and Li (2005) studied CSFs for PPP/PFI projects in the UK construction industry. They identified seventeen factors from past studies and grouped them into five principal groups: effective procurement, project implementatibility, government guarantee, favorable economic conditions and available financial markets. These groupings though ignore the political support factors and even those of technology yet they are very critical for the success of a PPP project. Somewhere else, Ismail and Ajija (2013) used a survey to rank the CSFs for PPP implementation in Malaysia. They found the top factors to be: good governance, commitment and responsibility of public and private sectors, favorable legal framework; sound economic policy and available financial markets. They also illustrated that only four factors signified the ranking difference between the public and private sectors: multi-benefit objectives, competitive procurement process, and government involvement by providing guarantee, and finally shared authority between public and private sectors.

Categorization or groups of CSFs for PPP is beyond the scope of this book. Suffice to note the importance attached to knowing these factors so as to be able to even identify possible risks involved in them. This way, it would prove a better tool to management risks in a PPP project. A summary list of probable CSFs for PPP was developed from past studies. Table 1 shows CSFs for PPP success and their corresponding references.

In his study on the CSFs for infrastructural development Zhang (2005) identified sub success factors for PPP and grouped them under five main CSFs as indicated in Table 2.

Principles and Benefits

Drawing on the possibility of choosing the right combination of the CSFs and their sub success factors does not guarantee success to any PPP project. Successes will then entirely rely on whether the principles have been followed or not. One of the challenges facing PPP project implementation is the dearth of unclear information on the relevant variables that make adherence to principles in PPP projects tick. There are no proxies in doing this, as a partnership is a process not a product (Chowdhury, Chen & Tiong, 2011). For that reason, successful navigation through the process often results in net benefits for all the parties involved (Eggers & Startup, 2006). For example, the public partner can leverage and maximize public assets, increase its control over the development process, and create a vibrant environment for development to thrive. While the private partner on the other hand will be given greater access to public resource(s), for instance, land and infill sites and receive more support throughout the development process.

It's important to note that where private partner tally with the public partner there is a likelihood of developing an opportunity to create public goods. In their study on principles that can guide community leaders and public officials together with private investors and developers throughout the development process, Humbene, Hudnut III, Levitt, Stainback, Ward and Witenstein (2005) developed ten principles for a successful PPP. According to them, the principles endeavor to ensure the most efficient use of public and private resources in the pursuit of mutual gains through PPP. Their discovery suggests that the principles are pertinent to the success of a PPP project. Elaborate explanations of the principles follows suit.

First and most important is the proper preparation for the PPP. This entails creating and constantly updating a plan for development showing specific sites for private investment opportunities. It elicits responsibilities of both the public as well as the private partners. It requires the public partner to identify

Table 1. List of success factors in a PPP

Critical Success Factors	Source
Strong private consortium	Jefferies et al. (2002) Tiong (1996) Birnie (1999)
Appropriate risk allocation and risk sharing	Qiao et al. (2001) Grant (1996) Arthur Andersen and Enterprise LSE (2000)
Competitive procurement process	Jefferies et al. (2002) Kopp (1997) Gentry and Fernandez (1997) Arthur Andersen and Enterprise LSE (2000)
Commitment /responsibility of public/private sector	Stonehouse et al. (1996) Kanter (1999) NAO (200 lb)
Thorough and realistic cost/ benefit assessment	Qiao et al. (2001) Brodie (1995) Hambros (1999)
Project technical feasibility	Qiao et al. (2001) Tiong (1996) Zantke and Mangels (1999)
Transparency in the procurement process	Jefferies et al. (2002) Kopp (1997) Gentry and Fernandez (1997) Arthur Andersen and Enterprise LSE (2000)
Good governance	Qiao et al. (2001) Frilet (1997) Badshah (1998)
Favorable legal framework	Bennett (1998) Boyfield (1992) Stein (1995) Jones et al. (1996)
Available financial market	Qiao et al. (2001) Jefferies et al. (2002) McCarthy and Tiong (1991) Akintoye et al. (200 lb)
Political support	Qiao et al. (2001) Zhang et al. (1998)
Multi-benefit objectives	Grant (1996) Stonehouse et al. (1996)
Government involvement by providing guarantees	Kanter (1999) Qiao et al. (2001) Zhang et al. (1998)
Sound economic policy	EIB (2000)
Stable macro-economic environment	Qiao et al. (2001) Dailami and Klein (1997)
Well organized public agency	Boyfield (1992) Stein (1995) Jones et al. (1996) Finnerty (1996)
Shared authority between public and private sectors	Stonehouse et al. (1996) Kanter (1999)
Social support	Frilet (1997)
Technology transfer	Qiao et al. (2001)

Source: Past studies as indicated in the source column

Table 2. Critical Success factors and Success sub factors for PPP projects

Critical Success Factor	Success Sub Factors
Favorable investment environment	Stable political system; Favorable economic system; Adequate local financial market; Predictable currency exchange risk; Predictable and reasonable legal framework; Government support; Supportive and understanding community; The project is in the public interest; Predicable risk scenarios; The project is well suited to privatization; and Promising economy.
Economic viability	Long-term demand for the products/services offered by the project; Limited competition from other projects; Sufficient profitability of the project to attract investors; Long-term cash flow that is attractive to lender; Long-term availability of suppliers needed for normal operations.
Reliable concessionaire consortium with strong technical strength	Leading role by a key enterprise or entrepreneur; Effective project organization structure; Strong and capable project team; Good relationship with host government authorities; Partnering skills; Rich experience in international PPP project management; Multidisciplinary participants; Sound technical solution; Innovative technical solution; Cost-effective technical solution; Low environmental impact; and Public safety and health considerations.
Sound financial package	Sound financial analysis; Investment, payment, and drawdown schedules; Sources and structure of main loans and standby facilities; Stable currencies of debts and equity finance; High equity/debt ratio; Low financial charges; Fixed and low interest rate financing; Long-term debt financing that minimizes refinancing risk; Abilities to deal with fluctuations in interest/exchange rates; Appropriate toll/tariff level(s) and suitable adjustment formula.
Appropriate risk allocation via reliable contractual arrangements	Concession agreement; Shareholder agreement; Design and contract construct; Loan agreement; Insurance agreement; Supply agreement; Operation agreement; Off-take agreement; and Guarantees/support/comfort letters

Source: (Zhang, 2005a)

development goals and resources including commitments for inducements and incentives for prioritized project in the plan. This can best be done through assessment of the capabilities of the public partner, for example, by creating a redevelopment authority or a quasigovernmental agency (Hodge, 2010). Also create a public vision which should come out as a result of consensus-building process that identifies the opportunities, objectives and ultimate goals of the community (Owusu & Badu, 2009). The public partner ought to be legislatively prepared by ensuring that codes and regulations formulated support the vision established for the PPP project including the potential for streamlining codes and regulations to remove potential obstacles to effective partnerships. It is critical that the public partner should be resourceful with funding given that with the increasing scarcity of public sector funds, the complexity of financial package will necessarily increase (Dada & Oladokun, 2012). The public partner as well needs to examine its ability to assemble the necessary land, for example by consideration of the potential for land banking. It is also during this stage, that the public partner ought to establish a schedule that clarifies the expectation of the public decisions makers. Usually, it's a good idea to craft public awareness program to inform stakeholders of the goals of the development strategy and the specific projects that are identified. The public partner at this stage needs to be prepared for a transparent process as it makes its numbers, names, and itself open to public scrutiny (Flyvbjerg, 2014). This can best be achieved by establishing the feasibility, for example, through meeting with investors to explain the nature of PPP. It's as well important to know the other partners, for example, a developer should assess the public partner's ability to deliver and to commit its resources up front (Cuttaree, 2008). More critical, the private partner should get the right team- a team that will bring insight and experience with the public partner.

Second, creation of a shared vision because a successful projects start with a vision. A vision is a framework for the project goals and serves as the benchmark to ensure the realization of joint objectives. Maylor (2005) reminds that without a vision, the project will most likely fail. It's important to create a vision that can be shared, hence, elicits involvement of all the parties. Once created, a vision ought to be sustained. This involves the use of a strategy for implementation which includes funding mechanisms (public and private), potential partners (and their responsibilities), and an agenda or time frame for achieving the vision (making the project a reality).

Third, proper understanding of the partners and key players is one of the principles that can ensure success of a PPP project. Hodge and Greve (2007) remind that PPPs are a four-legged stool. They involve government, nonprofit organizations, for-profit interests, and stakeholders. Humbene, Hudnut III, Levitt, Stainback, Ward and Witenstein (2005) advice that Government should understand, for example, that the private partner needs a positive bottom line, while the private partner should understand the government does not move fast, is not necessarily profit driven, and has broader constituencies to deal with. Any such deal, must therefore, answer the fundamental questions of financial feasibility and approval.

Fourth, there must be proper clarification on risks and rewards since 'nothing ventured, nothing gained'. The essence of PPP is based on sharing risk and rewards (Zitron, 2006). This is the only way through which tangible results can be realized when each parties understand and appreciate their nature and scope of their opposite party's potential risks and rewards, as well as its own. This is good for achieving mutual success.

Fifth, establishment of a clear and rational decision making process is yet another crucial principle for the success of a PPP project (Kahwajian, Baba, Amudi & Wanos, 2014). All the parties must articulate and agree upon the process to be followed and the rules of engagement to be used to structure the deal with public and private dimensions. This must be as early as possible. Agreeing on the process helps to ensure partnerships establish effective policies and implement them efficiently and collaboratively

(Ismail & Ajija, Sh, 2013). It calls for creation of a roadmap, definition of the roles and responsibilities and creation of checks and balances.

Sixth, ensure all the parties do their homework at the outset as well as throughout the project. Parties must be ready to invest their time, energies and resources in all the phases of the project (Hardcastle, Edwards, Akintoye & Li, 2005). To achieve this, necessitates continuous diligence and sharing information. It also demands for adoption of scenario planning, that is, for example, understanding the partner's limitations and pursuance of creative public/private finance plan.

Seventh, securing consistent and coordinated leadership aids in defining clear goals; building broad constituencies; brining the right parties around the table and coordinating process. Good leadership helps a PPP project to succeed especially when such a leadership bridge private project management with political leadership (Trafford & Proctor, 2006). This provide stakeholder who are not financially involved but have an interest in, and expectations about, a project, with a forum to express their views. It will also aid to keep everyone on point and not let a project languish. It is through good leadership that a possible change can be created. Moodley, Smith and Preece (2008) recommend that a leader must possess the following qualities for a successful realization of PPP. These qualities includes:- integrity ("Behavior is the only score that's kept"), vulnerability ("Trust in the abilities of others, letting them do their best"), discernment (What kind of antennae do you have? Can you detect nuance and perceive changing realities?), awareness of the human spirit ("Person skills always precede professional skills"), courage (Face up to tough decisions, resolve conflicts, define and carry out justice, and say what needs to be said), compassionate sense of humor (It is "essential to living with ambiguity"), intellectual energy and curiosity (Accept "the responsibility for learning frantically"), respect for the future, regard for the present, understanding of the past ("The future requires our humility in the face of all we cannot control. The present requires attention to all the people to whom we are accountable. The past gives use the opportunity to build on the work of our elders"), predictability (Leaders "are not free to follow a whim", they are "especially responsible for the vision and values of an organization"), breadth ("Leaders are people large enough to contain multitudes"), comfort with ambiguity (A leader makes sense out of chaos), and present ("Leaders stop-to answer questions, to be patient, to listen to problems, to seek a nuance, to follow up a lead"). In brief, leaders stand alone, take the heat, bear the pain, and tell the truth.

Eight, communicating early and often assists in the recognition of joint interests and ensures the more efficient decision-making and implementation process (Zhang, 2005). Communication has to be both internal and external. Internal communication is essential to the internal dynamics of complex partnership structure. It allows the distribution of information and implementation of compatible efforts. It's therefore important that partners should communicate overarching project objectives, such as downtown revitalization or increased real estate values, to find common ground within the partnership (Westland, 2006). External communication with a broad array of actors external to the PPP project is integral to ensure widespread support and diverse perspectives within the process. The endearment here is that the partners need to reach out, listen and respond to stakeholders and the community, elected and appointed officials, the media as well as the investors. In a precise and concise manner, communicate the project values and objectives and its guiding principles. Communication is also a mean to create and build a transparent process in the PPP project implementation (Akintan & Morledge, 2013). This will aid in increasing potential for broad support for PPP projects, particularly from non-stakeholders.

Ninth, negotiate a fair deal since 'fairness' is a value desired by all the parties in the deal. Fair deal can be arrived at by agreeing beforehand the terms all the parties consent to (Hayford & Partner, 2006). Much important to observe the notation of fair deal is that because not all future changes can be anticipated, it only possible that fairness will often remain an elusive goal. Fairness in negotiating a deal structure means that all parties are reasonably satisfied (Cheung, Chan, & Kajewski, 2012). Its necessarily follows that parties must a party that accepts in exchange for taking significant financial risk, will have to accrue proportionate future financial returns.

Tenth, build trust as a core value because of the complex nature of PPP process and structure. It is only trust between the multiple partners and entities that can enable a shared decision making and the taking of financial risks (Jefferies, 2006). It is therefore crucial that parties must ensure that other stakeholders, such as financial investors, as well as the public are dedicated to and trust the project and the partnership. Trust needs not only be built, but must be sustained as well. Sustaining trust demands incremental builds up of trust through small efforts within the partnership. This creates a sense of small successes that support bigger strides. In other words, success breeds confidence, and confidence breads trust (Babatunde, Opawole, & Akinsiku, 2012).

Having gotten these principles right, Maseko (2014) indicates that PPP will not only provide the public partner with access to resources but also provides opportunities to share risk with the private sector. In fact, the benefits of a PPP project are themselves promising and yet this aspect has often been neglected especially in developing countries, where the number of PPP projects has never increased to half of its potential. The requisite needs for PPP projects though can be gauged from a number of benefits that can accrue from the arrangement. Moreover, it is seen as a way to create more value for money compared to conventional projects (Bing, Akintoye, Edewards & Hardcastle, 2005) especially in the short term. For example, the ability to transfer risk to whichever of the public or private partner is better able to manage the risk is a source of value for money. Kurunmäki and Miller (2011) show PPP involve the private sector providing a 'bundle' of services. Bundling can provide value for money that contracting services separately cannot. PPP can contain incentives for the private sector party to perform well. For example, under a contract to contract a road, a developer has an incentive to the minimum necessary to meet the contract terms.

Grimsey and Lewis (2005) attest that PPP can offer numerous benefits to the public partners, private partners and the community as a whole in the delivery of public services and realization of public projects compared to traditional public procurement. They indicate that when choosing to realize public projects through PPP, public partners seek to determine whether this will enhance the efficiency of the public sector and whether these projects offer better value for tax payers' money as compared to traditional state investment. Assuredly, parties to a PPP project would want to ensure that the project provides cost-efficient, reliable, and on-time services at the agreed price and in accordance with the arranged quality standards, as defined by the contract. This effectively means that the PPP project has to be cost-efficient, and this is what the public sector is mostly interested in. On the other hand, the private sector is mainly interested in the long-term financial benefits that come from the partnership. Valimarsson (2007) alleges that benefits that can be derived by the public partner from a PPP include: transfer of risk to the private partner, minimizing of government activities, possibility for multiple uses of the facilities and constant cash flows.

Zimmermann and Eber (2014) claims that by both transferring risk and imposing verifiable quality standards, a PPP contract can induce efficiency-increasing reductions in cost via two avenues: "Bundling" responsibility for multiple project phases incentivizes the private partner to capture cost savings across phases, such as by making long-view investment choices in earlier phases of the project that reduce costs in later phases. For example, using higher quality but more expensive paving material on a road might prevent potholes and reduce maintenance costs. In conventional procurement, such incentives are absent because different parties are typically responsible for the construction and maintenance phases. Bundling can also encourage accelerated project delivery; if the private partner is responsible for the construction, operation, and financing of the project, and receives a share of project revenues, then it will have increased incentives to complete construction and begin operation as early as possible in order to start providing a return to both debt and equity investors. Malone (2005) argues that contractually obligating the private partner to meet minimum asset and service quality standards can improve efficiency and produce further cost savings. Minimum standards can prevent the deferral of maintenance and resulting asset deterioration, therefore lowering the costs to users imposed by a degraded asset, for example, potholes on a road increase vehicle wear-and-tear.

Chen, Partington and Wang (2008) insinuate that much as there are a number of reasons usually advanced by proponents of PPP including delivering services through partners which can being significant benefits as well as bring about successful innovation in service delivery, there are failing occurrences around the design. This insinuation corroborates earlier study conducted by Brzozowska (2006) who warned that there are risks involved much as these benefits/advantages may look good in themselves. He drew up these advantages of PPP with corresponding risk as indicated in Table 3.

Leung and Hui (2005) contend that the advantages of public private partnership are to bring together the complementary skills of both public and private sectors to the completion of projects, with varying levels of involvement and responsibility. Public private partnership offers value propositions: access to private finance, reduced operational risk for the public sector, faster delivery of capital projects, improved service delivery to citizens, project management skills, and optimum utilization of government resources, entrepreneurship and innovation. Tang, Shen and Cheng (2010) asserts further that many projects in broad range of infrastructure sectors have been successfully developed through public private partnership: roads, bridges, ports, airports, railways; power, water supply; schools, hotels and even military facilities. According to Glasbergen (2011), public private partnership offers greater certainty of contract value before construction as a result of functional brief finalized prior to tendering; development of designs by bidders; complete integration of design, construction, operational, maintenance and refurbishment costs with potential to achieve value for money; enables greater transfer of risk at each phase, including cost,

Table 3. Advantages and risks of public private partnerships

Advantages	Risks
Possibility for smaller investments	Limited influence of public authority over the investment
Possibility for conducting other public investments	Increase of the prices charged to the users of the infrastructure
Savings to the budget	Reduction of bargaining position of public authorities
Transfer of new technologies	High transaction costs
Sharing the risk	Poorer quality of the services
More competition on market	Limited accessibility to services
More competition on market	Decrease of employment in the public sector
Guarantee of the services for a longer term	Financial risk for public partner
Decrease of the political influence in economy	Opportunity risk for public partner
More transparency in the economy	Political risk for private partner

Source: (Brzozowska, 2006, p. 24)

to the private sector; provides opportunity to fashion innovative solutions; the assumption of 'whole of life' cost risk encourages efficient design and attention to construction and material finishes; contractor bears design and 'fit for purpose' risk; during the design phase, public private partnership construction contractor can inform design team on building issues to facilitate integrated planning of construction and operations; operating and maintenance standards agreed and costs approved for period of concession; and payment for the services dependent on delivery of facilities and services to agreed standards.

For Bloomfield (2006) the most cited advantages are substantial public benefits, cost savings and the risk sharing opportunities. Majamaa, Junnila, Doloi and Niemistö (2008) avers the benefits from PPP can be achieved in four main areas: increasing efficiency in the execution of projects; enhancing implementation capacity; reducing risk for the public sector; and mobilizing financial resources by freeing scarce public funds for other uses. Generally, public private partnership reduces government's financial obligations. It instead provides a long-term source of revenue to the government through rent or user fees. It also provides construction opportunities at prevailing wages as well as provides workforce equity programs, including workforce training (apprenticeships), goals for participation by women and people of color, minority-owned, woman-owned, and emerging small businesses (Maskin & Tirole, 2008). It further promotes green requirements, including reduction in energy, water and green-house gases and the development of eco-districts. It also provides to affordable housing and additional development opportunities through development options. Meanwhile the private partner has its own goals and objectives including the following contributions and assistance from the public side: contribution of land or assistance in land assemblage (including the use of eminent domain); low-cost loans or grants, including use of tax increment funds; property tax freezes; freedom to construct both the public and private portion of the project through an exemption from the normal public building process; protection against environmental liability for publicly owned property transferred to the project; and assistance in coordinating necessary governmental approvals (Akintoye, 2007). Other evidences from various studies show that PPP is very beneficial to service delivery. For example, Aziz (2007) found out that PPP projects are not subject to political interference and deferred payments for the government. In their study on the expansion of Madrid-Baraja's subway network to the international airport, Soliño and Vassallo (2009) found that nonintegrated PPP contracts have important advantages for the urban rail PPP, particularly for conventional subway networks. According to them, these advantages are notable in terms of encouraging economies of scale and density, boosting competition, and reducing financial costs. These benefits/advantages, though, should not 'blind' to see challenges and dangers in adopting PPP as a new tool for infrastructural development as well as service delivery provision.

Dangers and Challenges

Not all is rosy with PPP. There are pervasive weaknesses in PPP, which inhibit its processes and prefigured outcomes. As marked progress is being registered in the move to take on PPP as a tool for procurement and service delivery provision, it has increasingly been recognized that, despite benefits, it can bring potential downside especially in a long-term relationship. Studies, for example, Akintoye (2006) cites challenges experienced with PPP to include: polarized perspectives on risks; difficulty in generating a sense of ownership of action to address risks; lack of clarity about what risks had been transferred, leading to unhelpful behavior when risks materialize (with a lack of willingness to accept responsibility for taking action); and an optimistic view of how much risk can be transferred to the private sector many services are delivered through Executive Agencies or other public-sector bodies such as government agencies and semi-autonomous government bodies (SAGB). These may have their own separate statutory responsibilities and, in the case of government agencies, separate lines of accountability. The terms of any agreements between the partners may be less explicit than in a typical contract, and in particular there may well have been very little explicit agreement of risk-management responsibilities (Demirag & Khadaroo, 2008). There is a specific challenge here in being clear about where partners' objectives overlap (and can be aligned to address a common goal, with common risks) – as opposed to where they are fully independent. A further challenge is to adapt, as far as possible, the good practice established for contractual relationships for use with other partners. An example here is seeking to achieve the clarity of objectives in a good commercial contract, including its necessary compromises between partners.

Chen, Partington and Wang (2008) vie that PPP can lead to a higher level of uncertainty (especially when working with new partners), and introduce different, and potentially unfamiliar, risks inherent in the partner's business service delivery chains are often complex. They augment that PPPs are becoming risky to undertake more so – defining responsibilities for handling risks is a major challenge. They continue to argue that the diversity of different cultures in partnerships brings with it a need to understand diverse perspectives on risks and arrangements. They suggest that there must be proper tools for managing risks in PPP contracting arrangements, because public finance initiative (PFI) and public private partnership, have traditionally emphasized an 'arms length' approach, to avoid confusing responsibilities between customer and contractor, to maintain a level playing field for competitors and to reduce the risk of impropriety.

Wang (2006) compliments the dangers which can be garnered from PPP as its enablement of the investor to charge a higher tariff on the services provided is a possibility which cannot be doubted. Although PPP projects often have high costs and take up a long time in contract negotiation with the hope of representing good values to the parties, it's the beneficiaries who usually pay for the services who suffer. More so, Chan, Lam, Cheung and Ke (2010) point out that the usual result would be that the deal may not materialize in the beginning or may falter in the end.

The introduction of PPP has also exerted much pressure on the legal frameworks of many countries. For example, Zhang (2009) found that in China, the PPP regulatory systems such as cost auditing, tariff regulation, responsibility scope and boundary regulation agencies have not been fully developed. These subsequently lead to a great deal of resistance from the conservative wing and are already slowing down some key reform projects. In addition to lack of established legal frame, Singewar and Deshmukh (2016) elaborate, the many challenges faced by PPP projects include: inability to raise business interest by public sector making private sector to remain aloof from participating; and the most well structured projects are scraped or delayed due to obstacles created by people.

Innocenti (2015) classifies constraints and challenges to PPP into two major areas: political and economical. Political constraints are manifested in the form of perceived misuse of taxpayer money, past failures in technology investments, private profits in exchange for service quality, lack of capacity to management and build, political election cycle and lack of political spokesperson. Financial constraints on the other hand, are exhibited through a combination of public finance, corporate finance, and project finance. Public finance is characterized by a direct lending to the project, or by a government guarantee provided to the private sector lenders, or a combination of the two as illustrated in Figure 1.

Innocenti (2015) further indicates that corporate finance can be a constraint on PPP. This is because corporate finance involves providing the lender(s) with recourse to the Borrower's, or if the Borrower is a new SPV company that has been established to become the operator then, both the Borrower's and the Borrower's Parent Company's, assets to secure loan repayment. Sometimes, repayment of the loan may

Figure 1. Liability of Government's list of financial obligations
Source: (Innocenti, 2015)

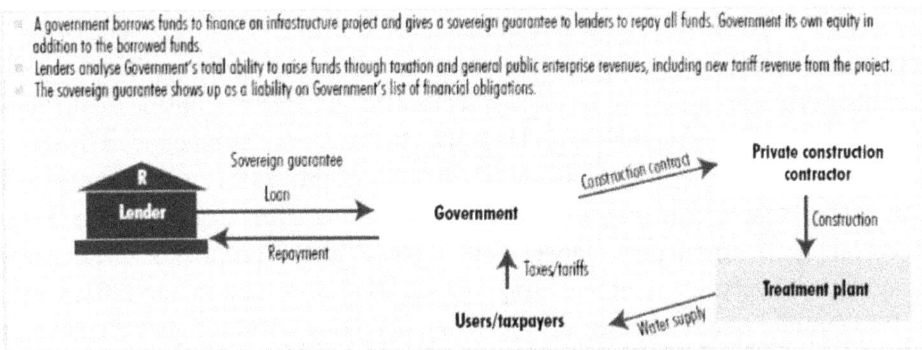

prove difficult or impossible leading to default and subsequent confiscation of thee security. Innocenti (2015) observes that project finance can be either "non-recourse" or "limited resource" financing that may act as a challenge to PPP implementation. Project finance means the lender's access to the asset and revenue streams of the borrower and/or its parent company is entirely or partially limited. Funds to repay the loan are supposed to come entirely or partially from the project but most times project fail along the way especially during implementation and even so failed to raise the expected output after commissioning as illustrated in Figure 2.

According to Innocenti (2015), other financial constraints to PPP include payment mechanisms which are various in PPP project, for example, loans that often becomes senior debt have to be repaid regardless of the financial performance of the project. Another constraint is the incentives for investors, for example, tax holidays, tax exemptions, labor training grants, import duties exemptions, subsidized land and/or building provisions, all may have negative effects on the PPP project and more especially the quality services targeted by the PPP. Lastly, Innocenti (2015) specifies PPP funding facilities can also act as a challenge to PPP. For example, facilities in form of project development facility (PDF) which

Figure 2. Projected future revenue of a PPP project
Source: (Innocenti, 2015)

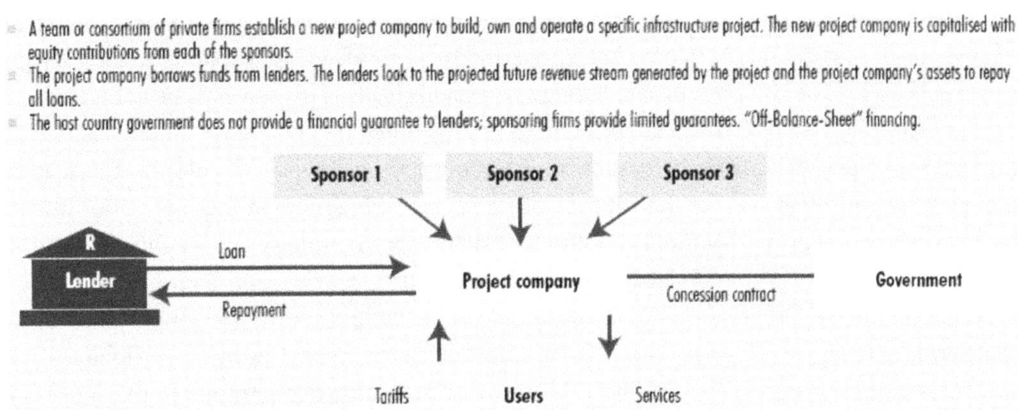

is a pool of money, usually donor grant funded with possibly some contributions from the government, always have strings attached.

Zhang (2005a, 2005b) demonstrates that the implementation of PPPs have given rise to a number of challenges, with many expectations that are not met. According to Jing-Feng, Skibniewski and Zheng (2010), the challenges are due to a combination of factors that need to be considered and managed during the project life cycle. They continue to add that the challenges are compounded by the inclusion of multiple participants in addition to the inherent challenges in projects. Some of these challenges are related to cost; quality, schedule, management ability and slow progress in the implementation of PPPs. Bender and Gibson (2010) affirm poor management of these factors lead to cost overruns, poor quality of products, and late delivery. On their part, Jing-Feng, Skibniewski and Zheng (2010) allege some of these factors lead to unforeseen increases in capital and operating cost or higher than expected service delivery and maintenance costs.

It's unsurprising that PPPs have come under sharp criticisms from some sections of the civil society organizations, public interest groups, the media, and other stakeholders. For example Gupta and Biswas (2010) discovered that trade unionists were very critical of PPPs due to the lack of trust in the role of the private sector in public service provision. In South Africa, for example, a number of PPP projects resulted in increased tariffs such as in the Dolphin Coast Water supply project, where the tariff increase in some communities was 119%. Concerns raised by critics include tariff increases, layoffs, high procurement costs that deter small players, and faulty, rushed, non-competitive, and nontransparent application of PPP principles (Zou & Fang, 2008).

Siemiatycki (2010) seems to suggest that challenges exhibited in PPP are due to the very nature of PPPs. To him, PPPs are often inflexible arrangement as they involve long-term contracts and in a large number of cases, prolonged conflicts arise between partners, which have the potential of even ending the partnership before the contract finishes. Because of this, past studies designate varied challenges to PPPs. Chen, Hubbard and Liao (2013) decries the numerous problems in the process of concluding the legal transaction, and finalizing the government's stake is inclined to take too long characteristic of the conservative bureaucratic nature of governments especially in developing countries. Batley (2006) shows that capacity and understanding of the PPPs process is still a major problem that faces most countries that have PPP projects. Bloomfield (2006) maintains that PPPs in developing countries, for example, are underutilized as vehicles for infrastructural developments. Macário (2010) illustrates that even though the primary objective of PPP is shared between both the public and private entities, synergies are polarized with regard to other objectives, such as skills and social responsibilities. In most countries with devolved systems of governance, the local level governments often lack the capacity to identify potential PPPs or to create PPPs even on pure public service responsibilities. This is very common in developing countries, for example, Nsasira, Basheka and Oluka (2013) notes this challenge in the case of Uganda.

Institutional deficiencies and ineffectiveness in most countries, especially developing ones, have posed substantial negative implications for the success of PPPs. Notable amongst them are poor negotiations driven by fraud and corruption (Meunier & Quinet, 2010), lack of strategy and vision (Costantino, Pellegrino & Sciancalepore 2011), technological transfers (Zhang, 2005a), and lack of quality or skilled personnel (Garcia, 2014). Others are: - an unconducive environment (Akintoye, 2008), lack of decisive transformation (Al-Kharashi & Skitmore, 2009), and too much biased political influences (Nsasira, Basheka & Oluka (2013) are still prevalent problems proving serious constraints to the success of PPP projects. In addition, Assaf and Al-Hejji (2006) reveal that clarity on the part of government in terms of principles governing PPP is lacking. For example, objectives and expectations are not clearly set out at the conception of a project. Even then, Fedderke, Perkins and Luiz, (2006) illumines the question of unavailability of capacity within countries to run successful PPPs. There are also the problems of monopolies of state-owned enterprises acting as stumbling blocks in particular services, as in the case of Eskom in South Africa (Shaik & Niketa, 2011). Apart from these, challenges also come from disparity in salaries between the public and private sectors (Bracey & Moldovan, 2006). In most countries, if not all, the private sector rewards their employees much better than their counterparts in the public sector. The disparities with their antecedent consequences have the likelihood of affecting PPPs. There is also the issue of reduced autonomy for the technical specialists in the public sector (Delmon, 2009) compared to the private sector. There is usually serious negative political interference in the public sector than deserved, while in the private sector, there is nearly none of such interference. Toor and Ogunlana (2008) imbue lack of transformation in the private sector as well as unwillingness to transfer skills as also having a negative impact on PPPs. Other common reasons for challenges in PPPs are (Cuttaree, 2008): poor legal framework and enforcement; weak institutional capacity and public private partnership strategy; unrealistic revenue and cost estimations; lack of thorough financial and economic analysis; inappropriate sharing of risks; lack of competitive procurement; and public resistance (willingness to pay not assessed).

Much as there are challenges in effecting a successful PPP, the earlier two sub sections of this section provided incentives to uphold PPP as a viable tool for high value production and quality service delivery. In making good use of this tool, however, certain conditions must exists in order to reap success from a PPP project initiative. This forms the basis of the section, to which we turn and the last under this chapter.

ENVIRONMENT OF PUBLIC PRIVATE PARTNERSHIP

Traditionally, PSD has been perceived as belonging to the function of government through its public sector organizations. In other words, only public sector organizations are responsible for providing public services and no others else. This is a very narrow view of the complexity of public service currently in the ever changing environment characterized by technological advancement and globalization (Kasala & Burra, 2016). In reality, for certain public sector organizations cannot do all is required for high value and quality public services. For a better provision of PSD, Governments all over the world have brought on board private sector organizations in an arrangement, commonly referred to as PPP. Three questions then emerge, if at all the arrangement is to see the light of success. First, what should the environment for its operation be like? Secondly, what sort of a legal regime is required? Thirdly and last, what socio-economic conditions are critical for the mission of the arrangement to be attained? Moreover, answers to these questions may not be forth coming easily given the complexity of the arrangement, but they are critical to take proper decisions in handling risks that may come about in the course of executing the conditions and obligations assigned by the arrangement. Finally, this section presents just exactly that, getting to fully appreciate the conditions under which PPP can thrive well.

Legal and Regulatory Framework

A growing body of international evidence points to the importance of a favorable legal and regulatory environment for the success of PPP projects (Christensen & Laegreid, 2007a). Petersen (2010) intimates that the experience of public agencies and their capacity to select, evaluate and implement PPP transactions also has a bearing on project viability, as does the investment climate and availability of financial instruments for long-term financing. These critical activities can only be satisfactorily done if there is a sound and proper legal and regulatory framework (Fiszbein, Ringold & Rogers, 2011). According to Petersen (2011), initiating and subsequent activities prior to and actual implementation of a PPP project, demands a favorable legal and regulatory environment. This ensures that the private partners can operate with a (low) level of production costs and a reduction in public sector restraints. A good legal and regulatory environment for success of a PPP must have at least four essential elements.

First and foremost is the consistency and quality of the PPP laws and regulations as the "rule of the game". At the outset suffice to note, an acclamation from Robinson and Scott (2009) that the introduction of PPPs has exerted an unprecedented pressure on the legal systems of virtually all countries. As Abednego and Ogunlana (2006) reveals, laws and regulations provide assurance to especially the private partners for safeguarding their interests and alleviating risk. Tranfied, Rowe, Smart, Levene, Deasley and Corley (2005) point outs that laws and regulations act as barricades for the public partner to enter into contracts that are only enforceable and not to incur costs unplanned for. Gupta and Biswas (2010) depict good legal systems as one that assists in ensuring the efficient operation of partnerships in accordance with broader policy objectives. In contrast, Ismail and Harris (2014) established that in absence of the rule of law, insolvable disputes are inevitable, frequent, and painful for both parties given the complexities of PPP projects.

The second element of a favorable legal and regulatory framework is an effective PPP selection and decision-making. Proper selection of a PPP project is very important for success. Likewise, effective decision making is very critical, PPP cannot work without a thorough understanding of the available potential projects and taking appropriate decision in the circumstance. Improper selection of a PPP project frequently occurs where all the concerned parties are not involved. It is therefore necessary that there ought to be a sound legal and regulatory framework to guide and direction the process of selection and decision taking. Cheung (2009) reminds that proper decision making usually imposes heavy obligations on the parties. For example, for a good selection of a PPP project to be made, there must be improvement of openness, fairness, and transparency in the selection process; the enforcement of promotion of high standard of ethics and strengthening selection process and performance. This will aid in avoidance of corruption rearing its ugly head in the process. In Easter Europe, for example, Neshkoya and Kostadinova (2012) find that administrative reform facilitates transparent governance, which contributes to curbing corruption and attracting foreign investment. This can only be made possible if there is a strong and functional legal and regulatory framework.

Another very important third element of a good legal and regulatory framework is the fairness/openness of bids and contract changes. PPP is a highly complex procurement tool and process. It demands the highest level of observance of the principles of fairness and competitiveness (Meadowcroft, 2007) lest the very purpose for which it's conceived would be amiss. Liese and Beisheim (2011) divulge a good legal and regulatory system upholds the principles of fairness and openness. This allows those with potentials to participate are able to do so and also it gives stakeholders upper hand to know about the project without being in the dark of all those happening.

Dispute often results whenever a risky situation is not handled well. For PPP to thrive well therefore there is need to have in place a proper dispute-resolution mechanism. Such a mechanism can be well catered for through inscription in the legal or regulatory framework of the country. Brown, Potoski and

Van Slyke (2006) found that absence of a workable dispute-resolution was the cause of PPP projects failure. In another study, Bryde (2005) specified having in place a good dispute-resolution mechanism is a mean to successful implementation of PPP project.

Apart from these elements, Zhang (2007) notes that the legal environment refers to the broad legal framework that governs all PPP project activities, including development and research (regulations dealing with safety and health of new products), manufacturing (safety and health regulations at workplace and pollution control), finance (regulations dealing with disclosure of information), marketing (regulations dealing with deceptive advertising and disclosure of product characteristics), personnel (regulations dealing with equal opportunity for women and minorities), and contract law. Indeed, most aspects of PPP project contract such as contract requirements, disputes, and breach of contract are governed under the same contract law. Andres and Guasch (2008) warns that where legal systems are not comprehensive, for example, in developing countries, government contracts may need detailed clauses defining basic principles. Darnall and Preston (2010) cautions as since a contract administration includes all relationship between the public partner and the private partner and the contractor, the legal rights and duties of the parties should determine the proper course of action.

A sound PPP project implementation process needs to have a good laws and regulations. In theory and practice, PPP laws and regulations have been considered as one of the most important pillars of a sound PPP project implementation process, as evidenced in past research, publications and practices. PPP laws and regulations lead to PPP project efficiency or inefficiency. There have been debates and efforts to identify and discard laws/regulations and/or their provisions that hinders or helps PPP disintegration. Ideally, PPP laws and regulations should be clear, consistent, comprehensive and flexible. According to Hayford (2013), clarity requires the primary sources be carefully drafted to ensure that basic principles are clear but do not prevent the use of more efficient procedures or new technology. Cicmil and Marshall (2005) recommend that all procedural details should be included in implementing regulations consistent with the primary sources. Klinj (2010) advices delegation of regulatory responsibilities at the national government, political subdivision, or agency levels should be clearly defined, as appropriate. Klinj and Teisman (2005) aver consistency can be achieved when PPP contract provisions contained in different sources are well coordinated (that is, there is no overlap or conflict, the hierarchy of the sources is clear, new provisions are promptly incorporated, and outdated provisions are repealed). Comprehensiveness, according to Mouraviev and Kakabadse (2012), entails that all relevant aspects of the PPP project process are addressed (there are no gaps in the regulatory framework which allow "personal" or "distorting" interpretation of aspects of the process). Flexibility requires that primary sources set forth only principles, basic features of the system, an outline of the procurement methods, and conditions for use (Mouraviev, 2012b).

Suffice to note that depending on prevailing conditions, there may be several layers of regulatory authority, including SPV issued codes or rules regulating aspects which are peculiar to the SPV. It's at that lower level in the hierarchy of the partnership that there should be practical guidance to implementers in carrying out their work and should be easily regularly updated. PPP laws and regulations clearly cover the whole scope of PPP project, all stages of the PPP project processes, methods and procurement, ethics, and transparency. In addition, PPP laws and regulations have to be easily accessed by both parties. Kurunmäki and Miller (2011) points out that access to the PPP rules and regulations contribute to transparency thereby resulting in more successful PPP projects.

Institutional Framework

According to Akintoye (2006), the massive move to PPP has brought with it the importance of a robust institutional framework for developing sustainable and efficient PPP projects. Cankar and Petkovšek (2013) reechoes that PPP has brought on board redefinition of the role of government in public service delivery. This is very critical in the ever-changing world of 'unsatisfied' demands for quality services. Gupta and Biswas (2010) ring a bell that PPPs do not necessary imply "less government" but rather pose a different role for government. For example, Quiggin (2005) discloses that the stronger position held by the private partners say in technology, information and capital, requires more skilled government participation, particularly with regard to negotiation, operation and supervision. Singaravelloo (2010) states that the government (agencies), whether it participates as a partner or regulator, must possess the appropriate aptitude in terms of expertise, knowledge, and information, as well as the means to acquire appropriate aptitudes if it does not yet possess them. Kort and Klijn (2011) indicate that in a PPP project, the managerial capability of the government is more important than organizational form in terms of performance enhancement.

One crucial feature to enhance government performance is the existence of a credible institutional framework. To facilitate a smooth PPP project implementation, a government must demonstrate its credibility through the institutions it has. For example, Neshkoya and Kostadinova (2012) opine in such institutions there could be the elements of political checks and balances through an independent judicial system and an independent regulation about all issues related to PPP project. However, as noted by Ho (2006), lack of government credibility is prominent in most cases, especially transition countries. This does not act as an incentive to attract foreign investors. And in usual cases of frequent change of government most times violently, there is a tendency by new government officials to find ways of terminating any agreements believed to be unfair or unreasonable. All these are pointers that a government needs a credible and a functioning institutional framework. After all, Weihe (2006) advices a government can actively participate as a partner in a PPP project, if it has a consolidated mechanism for a solid institutional framework.

Davies and Eustice (2005) argue that a successful PPP requires a strong government institution structure to steer and guide policy implementation. Such a structure eases finding solutions to problems that can dissuade private partners to invest in public facilities. It's therefore important that there must be proper administrative arrangement conducive to PPP projects. There must be a very clear channel of authority, for example, to negotiate and sign PPP contracts for ensuring their enforcement (Ho, 2006). Helmy and Lindergh (2011) while evaluating development strategies for PPP projects in Kuwait, discovered that a comprehensive PPP institutional framework elicits effective procurement, project implementaibility and government guarantee.

Political and Socio-Economic Conditions

Cherevykov (2013) states that the general environment in terms of political, social and economics, is that which affects all organizations in a given society. Mahalingam (2011) argues that the general environment has also within it a physical aspect. The physical environment includes weather and other natural phenomena such as landslips and earthquakes. It can have a significant negative impact on the PPP project process. Despite the fact that risks which come out of this environment; may sometimes prove very devastating, Delhi, Palukuri and Mahalingam (2010) declare that they cannot be controlled. This means damages that those risks that produce can only be mitigated. On the other hand, risks that arise due to political, social and economic conditions are partially controllable. This is because these risks come out of events within a particular country for which the government has control. While the physical risks are not in this world, no government can control but mitigate them. No environmental risk can be ignored (Jooste, Levitt & Scott, 2010). Although pressure can be brought to bear upon the government to influence or change decisions, in general, most events are uncontrollable by the private partner. In these circumstances, Hanh (2010) recommends that attention must be given to evaluating the risk exposure.

Akintoye and Beck (2009) intimate economic conditions have a great influence over the PPP project system's effort to maximize competition. Moreover, the market determines whether or not socio-economic objectives of PPP projects are accomplished, whether or not a government entity cal fulfill its needs; the timeliness of fulfillment; and the quality and costs of purchased goods, services, and capital assets. Regan, Love and Smith (2015) opine that it is very important to consider the market conditions prevailing then. This is because the market contains a large number of buyers and sellers of approximately equal importance. Thus when entering into a PPP arrangement, therefore, consideration as to be made as to the kind of market to which a proposed PPP project falls. For example, in a project whose products are homogeneous, consumers/publics would not desire just only one particular product other than any others. Heybati, Roodposhti, Nikoomaram and Ahmadi (2011) avow consumers will always act rationally and producers (private partner) are free to learn to enter into a PPP arrangement or not. Under this market conditions, the supply and demand principles dictates the deal, and producers (private partners) compete for the PPP project by the offer of the most favorable terms as to price, quality, promptness of delivery, or service.

The political environment must be stable and conducive, one that up holds democracy (Bäckstrand, 2006). In such environment, many individuals, groups and organizations in the private sector including trade associations, professional associations, and business firms/companies (commonly known as interest groups) (Gawel, 2011) are actively involved in all aspects of the PPP project activities. Having various interests, objectives, and beliefs, interest groups are involved in the PPP project, influencing implementation and influencing budget authorization and appropriation processes. Normally, a PPP project implementation activity that is eventually adopted is a compromise among different views of interest groups, policy makers, and management.

Weihe (2008) argues that a free media, vibrant civil society, engaged local communities, and an independent citizenry are crucial component of the good governance process of a PPP arrangement. This is because they had a unique place with respect to holding PPP project implementers accountable for PPP project transparency, fairness, and efficiency. Although PPP project transparency can help to facilitate participation and oversight, more proactive engagement of society is also vital. Meier and O'Toole (2007) confers that the engagement creates concrete opportunities for participation and oversight. For example, through participatory development of PPP regulations and policy, PPP budget allocations, civil society and media oversight over PPP, monitoring of income and assets declarations, and other arrangements that empower legitimate social groups. According to Provan and Kenis (2008), the engagement also enables the development of the independent and competitive media that can investigate and report on the PPP process, including corruption.

CONCLUSION

Actualization of the idea of PPP across countries has become an increasingly popular pursuit among government actors, private investors and policy makers. While earlier work focused on implementing it in all sectors, there is greater attention being paid to the urges for establishing a new PPP arrangement. Currently, many governments through their policy makers are engaged in ensuring the triangular motif of PPP is recognized and well realized. However, a close scrutiny of the motifs revealed that there are three main drivers in the urges underlying their adoption including broader public sector reforms, mobilization of private capital, and greater efficiency. In an attempt to deal with these gaps in knowledge, this chapter presented further a simpler but clearer and more intuitive basics of PPP based on three sub-components (rationale and critical success, principles and benefits, and challenges/dangers of PPP) and gave examples and illustrations. Thus focusing on the motifs and basics of PPP alone is insufficient to ensure success in any country be it developed or underdeveloped. Instead, the available evidence points to the need for a combination of legal/regulatory, institutional, and political and socio-economic factors to deliver a positive outcome. These factors must be in existence in the area where the PPP is to operate. The environment in which PPP is to operate must be that which is conducive enough to not only encourage adoption of PPP as a tool of procurement for high valve production and quality services provisions but also promotes and sustains it. An environment of such nature must have a proper legal and regulatory framework operated in and by a good institutional framework in amiable political and socio-economic conditions. The next chapter digs deeper into unearthing risks imbued in all the activities of PPP projects, right from inception to final delivery.

REFERENCES

Abdel Aziz, A. (2007). Successful delivery of public-private partnerships for infrastructure development. *Journal of Construction Engineering and Management*, *133*(12), 918–931. doi:10.1061/(ASCE)0733-9364(2007)133:12(918)

Abednego, M. P., & Ogunlana, S. O. (2006). Good project governance for proper risk allocation in public–private partnerships in Indonesia. *International Journal of Project Management*, *24*(7), 622–634. doi:10.1016/j.ijproman.2006.07.010

Abonyi, G., & van Slyke, D.M. (2010). Governing on the edges: Globalization of production and the challenge to public administration in the Twenty-first century. *Public Administrative Review*, *70*(S1), S33-S45.

Agus, A., Barker, S., & Kandampully, J. (2007). An Explanatory Study of Service Quality in the Malaysian Public Sector. *International Journal of Quality & Reliability Management*, *24*(2), 1777–190. doi:10.1108/02656710710722284

Akintan, O. A., & Morledge, R. (2013). Improving the Collaboration between Main Contractors and Subcontractors within Traditional Construction Procurement. *Journal of Construction Engineering*.

Akintoye, A. (2006). Public private partnerships for sustainable development of Infrastructure in developing countries. *Proceedings of International Conference on the Built Environment*.

Akintoye, A. (2007). Developments in the UK Public Private Partnerships: Lessons for the New PPP Ventures. *Proceedings of the 2007 International Conference on Concession Public / Infrastructural Projects (ICCPIP)*.

Akintoye, A. (2008). Project risk management practice: The case of a South African utility company. *International Journal of Project Management*, *26*(2), 149–163. doi:10.1016/j.ijproman.2007.03.011

Akintoye, A., & Beck, M. (2009). *Policy, finance & management for public-private partnerships*. London: Wiley-Blackwell.

Al-Kharashi, A., & Skitmore, M. (2009). Causes of delays in Saudi Arabian public sector construction projects. *Construction Management and Economics*, *27*(1), 3–23. doi:10.1080/01446190802541457

Andres, L., & Guasch, J. L. (2008). Negotiating and Renegotiating PPPs and Concessions. In G. Schwartz, A. Corbacho, & K. Funke (Eds.), *Public Investment and Public-Private Partnership: Addressing Infrastructure Challenges and Managing Fiscal Risks*. International Monetary Fund. doi:10.1057/9780230593992_13

Andrews, M. (2013). *The limits of institutional reform in development: Changing rules for realistic solutions*. Cambridge, UK: Cambridge University Press. doi:10.1017/CBO9781139060974

Angerer, D. J., & Hammerschmid, G. (2005). Public private partnership between euphoria and disillusionment. Recent experiences from Austria and implications for countries in transformation. *Romanian Journal of Political Science.*, *5*(1), 129–159.

Apanavičienė, R., & Rudžianskaitė-Kvaraciejienė, R. (2010). *Analysis of evaluation methodologies for public-private partnership (PPP) projects in infrastructure construction*. Paper Presented at the 10th international conference on modern building materials, structures and techniques, Vilnus, Lithuania.

Assaf, S. A., & Al-Hejji, S. (2006). Causes of delay in large construction projects. *International Journal of Project Management*, *24*(4), 349–357. doi:10.1016/j.ijproman.2005.11.010

Atkinson, R., Crawford, L., & Ward, S. (2006). Fundamental uncertainties in projects and the scope of project management. *International Journal of Project Management*, *24*(8), 687–698. doi:10.1016/j.ijproman.2006.09.011

Aziz, A. M. A. (2007). Successful delivery of public-private partnerships for infrastructure development. *Journal of Construction Engineering and Management*, *133*(12), 918–931. doi:10.1061/(ASCE)0733-9364(2007)133:12(918)

Babatunde, S. O., Opawole, A., & Akinsiku, O. E. (2012). Critical success factors in public– private partnership (PPP) on infrastructure delivery in Nigeria. *Journal of Facility Management*, *10*(3), 212–225. doi:10.1108/14725961211246018

Bäckstrand, K. (2006). Multi-stakeholder partnerships for sustainable development: Rethinking legitimacy, accountability and effectiveness. *European Environment*, *16*(5), 290–306. doi:10.1002/eet.425

Banerjee, S. G., Oetzel, J. M., & Ranganathan, R. (2006). Private provision of infrastructure in emerging markets: Do institutions matter? *Development Policy Review*, *24*(2), 175–202. doi:10.1111/j.1467-7679.2006.00321.x

Bangura, Y., & Larbi, G. A. (Eds.). (2006). *Public sector reform in developing countries: capacity challenges to improve services*. Houndmills, UK: Palgrave.

Barber, M. (2008). *Instruction to Deliver: Fighting to transform Britain's public services*. London: Methuen.

Batley, R. (2006). Engaged or divorced? Cross-service findings on government relations with non-state service-providers. *Public Administration and Development*, *26*(3), 241–251. doi:10.1002/pad.422

Bender, P., & Gibson, S. (2010). *Case Study for the 10 years of the Mbombela (Nelspruit) Water and Sanitation Concession South Africa Department: National Treasury, South Africa*. Retrieved from http://www.ppp.gov.za/Legal%20Aspects/Case%20Studies/Nelspruit%20Case%20Study %20Final%2029%20 May%202010.pdf

Bennett, J., & Iossa, E. (2006). Building and managing facilities for public services. *Journal of Public Economics*, *90*(10-11), 2143–2160. doi:10.1016/j.jpubeco.2006.04.001

Bing, L., Akintoye, A., Edwards, P. J., & Hardcastle, C. (2005). The allocation of risk in PPP/PFI construction projects in the UK. *International Journal of Project Management*, *23*(1), 25–35. doi:10.1016/j.ijproman.2004.04.006

Bloomfield, P. (2006). The challenging business of long-term public-private partnerships: Reflection on local experience. *Public Administration Review*, *66*(3), 400–411. doi:10.1111/j.1540-6210.2006.00597.x

Bouckaert, G. (2008). *Managing Performance: International Comparisons (New Edition)*. London: Routledge.

Bouckaert, G., Van de Walle, S., & Kampen, J. K. (2005). Potential of Comparative Public Opinion Research in Public Administration. *International Review of Administrative Sciences*, *71*(2), 229–240. doi:10.1177/0020852305053882

Bourgon, J. (2011). *A new synthesis of public administration: Serving in the 21st Century*. Montreal, Canada: McGill-Queen's University Press.

Bovaird, T. (2007). Beyond engagement and participation: User and community Coproduction of public services. *Public Administration Review*, *67*(5), 846–860. doi:10.1111/j.1540-6210.2007.00773.x

Bovaird, T. (2010). A brief intellectual history of the public-private partnership movement. In *International Handbook on Public Private Partnership*. London: Edward Elgar Publishing. doi:10.4337/9781849804691.00010

Bracey, N., & Moldovan, S. (2006). *Public-private partnerships: Risks to the public and private sector*. Paper presented at the 6th Global Conference on Business and Economics.

Brown, T., Potoski, M., & Van Slyke, D. (2006). Managing public service contracts: Aligning values, institutions, and markets. *Public Administration Review*, *66*(3), 323–331. doi:10.1111/j.1540-6210.2006.00590.x

Bryde, D. J. (2005). Methods for managing different perspectives of project success. *British Journal of Management*, *16*(2), 119–131. doi:10.1111/j.1467-8551.2005.00438.x

Brzozowska, K. (2006). *Advantages and threats of public – private partnerships in larger infrastructure projects*. Warszawa: CeDeWu.PL.

Cankar, S. S., & Petkovšek, V. (2013). Private and public sector innovation and the importance of cross-sector collaboration. *Journal of Applied Business Research*, *29*(6), 197–1606.

Chan, A. P. C., Lam, P. T. I., Chan, D. W. M., Cheung, E., & Ke, Y. J. (2010). Potential obstacles to successful implementation of public-private partnerships in Beijing and the Hong Kong Special Administrative Region. *Journal of Management Engineering*, *26*(1), 30–40. doi:10.1061/(ASCE)0742-597X(2010)26:1(30)

Chen, C., Hubbard, M., & Liao, C.-S. (2013). When public–private partnerships fail. *Public Management Review*, *15*(6), 839–857. doi:10.1080/14719037.2012.698856

Chen, P., & Partington, D. (2006). Three conceptual levels of construction project management work. *International Journal of Project Management*, *24*(1), 412–421. doi:10.1016/j.ijproman.2006.02.009

Chen, P., Partington, D., & Wang, J. N. (2008). Conceptual determinants of construction project management competence: A Chinese perspective. *International Journal of Project Management*, *26*(1), 655–664. doi:10.1016/j.ijproman.2007.09.002

Cherevykov, I. L. (2013). *Institutional environment for public-private partnership in Ukraine: Do institutions really matter?* MPRA Paper No. 62110. Retrieved from http://mpra.ub.uni-muenchen.de/62110/

Cheung, A. B. L. (2011). New public management in Asian countries. In P. Laegreid & T. Christensen (Eds.), *Ashgate Research Companion to new public management*. Ashgate.

Cheung, E. (2009). *Developing a best practice framework for implementing Public Private Partnerships (PPP) in Hong Kong* (Unpublished doctoral dissertation). Queensland University of Technology, Queensland, Australia.

Cheung, E., Chan, A. P. C., & Kajewski, S. (2009b). Reasons for implementing public private partnership projects: Perspectives from Hong Kong, Australian and British practitioners. *Journal of Property Investment & Finance*, *27*(1), 81–95. doi:10.1108/14635780910926685

Cheung, E., Chan, A. P. C., & Kajewski, S. (2012). Factors contributing to successful public private partnership projects, comparing Hong Kong with Australia and the United Kingdom. *Journal of Facility Management*, *10*(1), 45–58. doi:10.1108/14725961211200397

Cheung, E., Chan, A. P. C., Lam, P. T. I., & Chan, D. W. M. (2010). Critical success factors for PPPs in Infrastructure Developments: Chinese Perspective. *Journal of Construction Engineering and Management*.

Chowdhury, A. N., Chen, P. H., & Tiong, R. L. K. (2011). Analyzing the structure of public– private partnership projects using network theory. *Construction Management and Economics*, *29*(3), 247–260. doi:10.1080/01446193.2010.537354

Christensen, T., & Laegreid, P. (2007a). The whole-of-Government approach to public sector reform. *Public Administration Review*, *67*(6), 1059–1066. doi:10.1111/j.1540-6210.2007.00797.x

Christensen, T., & Laegreid, P. (2007a). *Transcending the new public management: The transformation of public service reforms*. Burlington, VT: Ashgate.

Christensen, T., & Laegreid, P. (2011). Complexity and Hybrid public administration- Theoretical and empirical challenges. *Public Organization Review*, *11*(4), 407–423. doi:10.1007/s11115-010-0141-4

Cicmil, S., & Marshall, D. (2005). Insights into collaboration at the project level: Complexity, social interaction and procurement mechanisms. *Building Research and Information*, *33*(6), 523–535. doi:10.1080/09613210500288886

Clayton, U. (2013). *Improving the outcomes of public private partnerships*. Sydney, Australia: Academic Press.

Corrigan, M. B., Humbene, J., Hudnut, W. III, Levitt, R. L., Stainback, J., Ward, R., & Witenstein, N. (2005). *Ten Principles for Successful Public/Private Partnerships*. Washington, DC: ULI–the Urban Land Institute.

Costantino, N., Pellegrino, R., & Sciancalepore, F. (2011). Evaluation of different tolling systems for a transportation PPP project. In Towards New Horizons in Public Procurement. Boca Raton, FL: Academics Press.

Cuttaree, V. (2008). *Successes and failures of PPP projects. Europe & Central Asia Region*. Warsaw: WB.

Dada, M. O., & Oladokun, M. G. (2012). Analysis of critical success sub-factors for public- private partnership in Nigeria. *Alam-Cipta*, *5*(2), 13–26.

Dalton, R. J. (2005). The social transformation of trust in government. *International Review of Sociology*, *15*(1), 133–154. doi:10.1080/03906700500038819

Darnall, R., & Preston, J. M. (2010). *Project Management from Simple to Complex*. Flat World Knowledge, Inc.

Davies, P., & Eustice, K. (2005). *Delivering the PPP Promise. A Review of PPP Issues and Activity*. London: PricewaterhouseCoopers.

Delhi, V. S. K., Palukuri, S., & Mahalingam, A. (2010). *Governance issues in Public Private Partnerships in infrastructure projects in India*. Paper presented at the Engineering Project Organizations Conference, South Lake Tahoe, CA.

Delmon, J. (2009). *Private sector investment in infrastructure project finance - PPP projects and risks* (2nd ed.). Austin, TX: Wolters Kluwer.

Delmon, J. (2010). *Understanding options for private-partnership partnerships in Infrastructure*. Policy Research Working Paper 5173, World Bank.

Demirag, I., & Khadaroo, I. (2008). Accountability and value for money in private finance initiative contracts. *Financial Accountability & Management*, *24*(4), 455–478. doi:10.1111/j.1468-0408.2008.00462.x

Denhardt, J. V., & Denhardt, R. B. (2011). *The New Public Service: Serving, not steering* (3rd ed.). Armonk, NY: M. E. Sharpe.

Diana, M. (2014). Sustainable performance of public organizations: Shaping a coherent system for implementing and measuring the concept. *Studies in Business and Economics*, *9*(3), 50–56.

Drew, J. (2005). Public Private Partnerships – Opportunities and Challenges. *Proceedings of the Conference on Public Private Partnerships – Opportunities and Challenges.*

Dunleavy, P., Margetts, H., Bastow, S., & Tinkler, J. (2006). New public management is dead— long live digital-era governance. *Journal of Public Administration: Research and Theory*, *16*(3), 467–494. doi:10.1093/jopart/mui057

Eaton, D., Akbiyukli, R., & Dickinson, M. (2006). An evaluation of the stimulants and impediments to innovation within PFI/PPP projects. *Construction Innovation*, *6*(2), 63–77. doi:10.1108/14714170610710668

Eggers, W. D., & Macmillan, P. (2013). *The Solution Revolution: How business, government and social enterprises are teaming up to solve society's toughest problems*. Boston: Harvard Business Review Press.

Eggers, W. D., & Startup, T. (2006). *Closing the Infrastructure Gap: The role of public- private partnerships*. New York: Deloitte.

Farquharson, E., de Mästle, C., Yescombe, E. R., & Encinas, J. (2011). *How to engage with the private sector in public-private partnerships in emerging markets*. Washington, DC: World Bank. doi:10.1596/978-0-8213-7863-2

Fedderke, J. W., Perkins, P., & Luiz, J. M. (2006). Infrastructural investment in long-run economic growth: South Africa, 18752001. *World Development*, *34*(6), 1037–1059. doi:10.1016/j.worlddev.2005.11.004

Fiszbein, A., Ringold, D., & Rogers, H. (2011), *Making services work: indicators, assessments, and benchmarking of the quality of public service delivery.* Policy Research Working Paper No. 5690, The World Bank.

Flyvbjerg, B. (2014). What you should know about megaprojects and why: An overview. *Project Management Journal*, *45*(2), 6–19. doi:10.1002/pmj.21409

Forrer, J., Kee, J. E., Newcomer, K. E., & Boyer, E. (2010). Public private partnerships and the public accountability question. *Public Administration Review*, *70*(3), 475–484. doi:10.1111/j.1540-6210.2010.02161.x

Garcia, F. M. (2014). Developments and challenges in public sector accounting, *Journal of Public Budgeting, Accounting &. Financial Management*, *26*(2), 345–366.

Gawel, E. (2011). *Political drivers of and barriers to Public-Private Partnerships: The role of political involvement*. University of Leipzig, Faculty of Economics and Business Management, Working Paper, No. 098.

Glasbergen P. (2011). Understanding partnerships for sustainable development analytically: the ladder of partnership activity as a methodological tool. *Environmental Policy and Governance, 21*, 1-13.

Gorodnova, N. (2012). The integration of state and private business: The development of a socially oriented economy. *Finance and Credit*, *6*(486), 20–30.

Grimsey, D., & Lewis, M. K. (2005). Are public private partnerships values for money? Evaluating alternative approaches and comparing academic and practitioner views. *Accounting Forum*, *29*(4), 345–378. doi:10.1016/j.accfor.2005.01.001

Gunawansa, A. (2010). *Is there a need for public private partnership projects in Singapore*? Paper presented at the Construction, Building and Real Estate Research Conference of the Royal Institution of Chartered Surveyors, Paris, France.

Gupta, O., & Biswas, N. (2010). Public private partnership: Indian economy. *SCMS Journal of Indian Management*, *7*, 44–53.

Hahn, D. (2010). How to create a public–private partnership: A replicable project associated with business continuity. *Journal of Business Continuity & Emergency Planning*, *4*(3), 274–285. PMID:20826390

Hardcastle, C., Edwards, P. J., Akintoye, A., & Li, B. (2005). Critical success factors for PPP/PFI Projects in the UK Construction Industry: A factor analysis approach. *Construction Management and Economics, Scotland*, *23*(5), 459–471. doi:10.1080/01446190500041537

Hayford, O. (2013). *Improving the outcomes of public private partnerships*. Sydney, Australia: Clayton UTZ.

Hayford, O., & Partner, C. U. (2006). *Successfully allocating risk and negotiating a PPP contract*. Paper Presented at the 6th Annual national public private partnerships summit: Which way now for Australia's PPP market? Sydney, Australia.

Helmy, M. A. (2011). *Investigating the critical success factors for PPP projects in Kuwait*. KTH Architecture and the Build Environment Department of Real Estate and Construction Management Thesis No: 106. Stockholm: Royal Institute of Technology.

Helmy, M. A., & Lindbergh, J. (2011). *Investigating the Critical Success Factors for PPP Projects in Kuwait*. KTH Architecture and the Build Environment Department of Real Estate and Construction Management, Thesis No: 106, 46, urn:nbn:se:kth:diva-77471.

Heybati, F., Roodposhti, F. R., Nikoomaram, H., & Ahmadi, M. (2011). Developing a model for Iran about the relationship between economic freedom indices and public private partnerships. *African Journal of Business Management*, *5*(9), 3511–3522.

Ho, P. H. K. (2006). Development of public–private partnerships (PPPs) in China. *Surveyors Times, 15*(10).

Hodge, G. A. (2010). Reviewing public-private partnerships: some thoughts on evaluation, 81– 112. In G. Hodge, C. Greve, & A. Boardman (Eds.), *International Handbook on Public-Private Partnerships*. London: Edward Elgar Cheltenham. doi:10.4337/9781849804691.00012

Hodge, G. A., & Greve, C. (2007). Public-Private Partnerships: An international performance review. *Public Administration Review*, *67*(3), 545–558. doi:10.1111/j.1540-6210.2007.00736.x

Houston, D. J. (2006). Walking the walk of public service motivation: Public employees and charitable gifts of time, blood and money. *Journal of Public Administration: Research and Theory*, *16*(1), 67–86. doi:10.1093/jopart/mui028

Ibem, E. (2010). An Assessment of the role of government agencies in public private partnerships in housing delivery in Nigeria. *Journal of Construction in Developing Countries*, *15*(2), 23–48.

Innocenti, E.B. (2015). *Public-Private Partnerships in e-Government Guide*. Paper Presented during the two day workshop "PPPs in e-Government", Kyiv, Ukraine.

Ismail, S. (2013a). Drivers of value for money public private partnership projects in Malaysia. *Asian Review of Accounting*, *21*(3), 241–256. doi:10.1108/ARA-06-2013-0042

Ismail, S., & Ajija, Sh. R. (2013). Critical Success Factors of Public Private Partnership (PPP) Implementation in Malaysia. *Asia-Pacific Journal of Business Administration*, *5*(1), 6–19. doi:10.1108/17574321311304503

Ismail, S., & Harris, F. A. (2014). *Challenges in implementing public private partnership (PPP) in Malaysia*. Paper Presented at the International Conference on Accounting Studies 2014, Kuala Lumpur, Malaysia.

Jacobson, C., & Choi, S. O. (2008). Success factors: Public works and public– private partnerships. *International Journal of Public Sector Management*, *21*(6), 637–657. doi:10.1108/09513550810896514

Jefferies, M. (2006). Critical success factors of public private sector partnerships: A case study of the Sydney SuperDome. *Engineering, Construction, and Architectural Management*, *13*(5), 451–462. doi:10.1108/09699980610690738

Jin, X.-H., Zhang, G., & Yang, R. J. (2012). Factor analysis of partners commitment to risk management in public-private partnership projects. *Construction Innovation*, *12*(3), 297–316. doi:10.1108/14714171211244550

Jing-Feng, Y. M., Skibniewski, A. J., Li, Q., & Zheng, L. (2010). The driving factors of China's public-private partnership projects in metropolitan transportation systems: Public sector's viewpoint. Vilnius Gediminas Technical University, 16, 5–18.

Jomo, J. K., & Chowdhury, A. (2009). Reconsidering public-private partnerships in developing countries. *International Journal of Institutions and Economies*, *1*(2), 191–205.

Jooste, S. F., Levitt, R. E., & Scott, W. R. (2010). *Capacity, Legitimacy, and Interest: Toward a Framework for PPP Program Success*. Paper presented at the 2010 Engineering Project Organization Conference, Fallen Leaf Lake, CA.

Jui-Sheng, C., & Pramudawardhani, D. (2015). Cross-country comparisons of key drivers, critical success factors and risk allocation for public-private partnership projects. *International Journal of Project Management*, *33*(5), 1136–1150. doi:10.1016/j.ijproman.2014.12.003

Kahwajian, A., Baba, S., Amudi, O., & Wanos, M. (2014). Identification of critical success factors (CSFs) for public private partnership (PPP) construction projects in Syria. *Jordan Journal of Civil Engineering*, *8*(4), 393–405.

Kahwajian, A., Baba, S., Amudi, O., & Wanos, M. (2014). Identification of critical success factors (CSFs) for Public Private Partnership (PPP) Construction Projects in Syria. *Jordan Journal of Civil Engineering*, *8*(4).

Kamarkar, R. (2014). Public Private Partnerships (PPP's)-A future intentions to development. *International Journal of Marketing and Financial Management, 2*(7), 144–147.

Kasala, S.E., & Burra, M.M. (2016). The role of public private partnerships in planned and serviced land delivery in Tanzania. *iBusiness, 8*, 10-17.

Keçi, J. (2015). Public private partnership for infrastructure projects: Mapping the key risks. *International Journal of Social, Behavioral, Educational, Economic Business and Industrial Engineering*, *9*(9), 3085–3095.

Kelsall, T. (2011). Rethinking the relationship between neo-patrimonialism and economic development in Africa. *IDS Bulletin*, *42*(2), 76–87. doi:10.1111/j.1759-5436.2011.00213.x

Kim, S., Lee, D.-L., Lee, Y.-J., & Lee, M. J. (2013). The study on the risk factors and the success factors of public private partnership project: Focusing on China and the Middle East. *Advanced Science and Technology Letters*, *32*, 35–37.

Klijn, E. H. (2010). Public–private partnerships: Deciphering meaning, message and Phenomenon. In G. Hodge & C. Greve (Eds.), *Handbook Public Private Partnership*. Edward Elgar. doi:10.4337/9781849804691.00011

Klijn, E. H., & Teisman, G. (2005). Public–private partnerships as the management of coproduction: Strategic and institutional barriers in a difficult marriage. In The Challenge of Public-Private Partnerships: Learning from International Experience. Edward Elgar.

Koppenjan, J. F. M. (2005). The formation of public-private partnerships: Lessons from nine transport infrastructure projects in the Netherlands. *Public Administration*, *83*(1), 135–157. doi:10.1111/j.0033-3298.2005.00441.x

Kort, M., & Klijn, E.-H. (2011). Public–Private Partnerships in Urban Regeneration Projects: Organizational Form or Managerial Capacity? *Public Administration Review*, *71*(4), 618–626. doi:10.1111/j.1540-6210.2011.02393.x

Krześ-Dobieszewska, J. (2014). Managing Public – Private Partnership Market in the Times of Economic Crisis. *Oeconomia Copernicana*, *5*(2), 63–74. doi:10.12775/OeC.2014.014

Kurunmäki, L., & Miller, P. (2011). Regulatory hybrids: Partnerships, budgeting and modernizing government. *Management Accounting Research*, *22*(4), 220–241. doi:10.1016/j.mar.2010.08.004

Leiringer, R. (2006). Technological innovation in PPPs: Incentives, opportunities and actions. *Construction Management and Economics*, *24*(3), 301–308. doi:10.1080/01446190500435028

Leung, B. Y. P., & Hui, E. C. M. (2005). Evaluation approach on Public-private partnership (PPP) Urban Redevelopments. *International Journal of Strategic Property Management*, *9*(1), 1–16.

Liese, A., & Beisheim, M. (2011). Transnational public-private partnerships and the provision of collective goods in developing countries. In Governance without a state? Policies and politics in areas of limited statehood. Columbia University Press.

Liu, T., & Wilkinson, S. (2014). Large-scale public venue development and the application of public-private partnerships. *International Journal of Project Management*, *32*(1), 88–100. doi:10.1016/j.ijproman.2013.01.003

Lufuunyo, H. (2013). Impact of public sector reforms on service delivery in Tanzania. *International Journal of Social Science Tomorrow*, *2*(2), 1–26.

Macário, R. (2010). Future challenges for transport infrastructure pricing in PPP arrangements. *Research in Transportation Economics*, *30*(1), 145–154. doi:10.1016/j.retrec.2010.10.015

Majamaa, W., Junnila, S., Doloi, H., & Niemistö, E. (2008). End-user oriented public-private partnerships in real estate industry. *International Journal of Strategic Property Management*, *12*(1), 1–17. doi:10.3846/1648-715X.2008.12.1-17

Malone, N. (2005). The evolution of private financing of government infrastructure in Australia—2005 and beyond. *The Australian Economic Review*, *38*(4), 420–430. doi:10.1111/j.1467-8462.2005.00385.x

Maseko, M. (2014). *Analysis of critical success factors for public-private partnerships in infrastructure development in South Africa*. The 6th International Platinum Conference, 'Platinum–Metal for the Future', The Southern African Institute of Mining and Metallurgy.

Maskin, E., & Tirole, J. (2008). Public-private partnerships and government spending limits. *International Journal of Industrial Organization*, *26*(2), 412–420. doi:10.1016/j.ijindorg.2007.05.004

Matei, L. (2006). Empirical approaches of the public-private partnership in the services of public utility. *Theoretical and Applicative Economics*, *10*(505), 3–14.

Maylor, H. (2005). *Project Management*. Edinburgh, UK: Pearson Education.

McCourt, W. (2013). *Models of public service reform: A problem-solving approach.* Policy Research Working Paper, No. 6428. Washington, DC: The World Bank.

McGovern, K. (2011). The promise of administrative conservatorship vs. the threat of administrative evil in the mission of public service. *Public Integrity.*, *14*(1), 51–65. doi:10.2753/PIN1099-9922140104

Meadowcroft, J. (2007). Democracy and accountability: the challenge for cross-sectoral partnerships. In Partnerships, governance and sustainable development: Reflections on theory and practice. Cheltenham, UK: Edward Elgar.

Meier, K., & OToole, L. J. Jr. (2007). Modeling public management: Empirical analysis of the management-performance nexus. *Public Management Review*, *9*(4), 503–527. doi:10.1080/14719030701726630

Meunier, D., & Quinet, E. (2010). Tips and pitfalls in PPP design. *Research in Transportation Economics*, *30*(1), 126–138. doi:10.1016/j.retrec.2010.10.013

ModuKumshe, H., Badiya Yusuf Magaji, B.Y., & Bani, L.M. (2015). Public-Private Partnership and Nigeria's infrastructural development: A Panacea for Economic Growth. *International Journal of Humanities Social Sciences and Education*, *2*(10), 87–98.

Moodley, K., Smith, N., & Preece, C. N. (2008). Stakeholder matrix for ethical relationships in the construction industry. *Construction Management and Economics*, *26*(6), 625–632. doi:10.1080/01446190801965368

Mouraviev, N. (2012b). What drives the employment of public-private partnerships in Kazakhstan and Russia: Value for money? *Organizations and Markets in Emerging Economies*, *3*(1), 32–57.

Mouraviev, N., & Kakabadse, N. (2012). Conceptualizing public–private partnerships: A critical appraisal of approaches to meanings and forms. *Society and Business Review*, *7*(3), 260–276. doi:10.1108/17465681211271332

Murphy, T. (2008). The case for public-private partnerships in infrastructure. *Canadian Public Administration*, *51*(1), 99–126. doi:10.1111/j.1754-7121.2008.00006.x

Ndandiko, C. (2006). Public private partnerships as modes of procuring public infrastructure and service delivery in developing countries: lessons from Uganda. *International Public Procurement Conference Proceedings*, 693-710.

Neshkova, M. I., & Kostadinova, T. (2012). The Effectiveness of administrative reform in new democracies. *Public Administration Review*, *72*(3), 324–333. doi:10.1111/j.1540-6210.2011.02483.x

Ng, S. T., Wong, Y. M., & Wong, J. M. (2012). Factors influencing the success of PPP at feasibility stage—a tripartite comparison study in Hong Kong. *Habitat International*, *36*(4), 423–432. doi:10.1016/j.habitatint.2012.02.002

Nsasira, R., Basheka, B. C., & Oluka, P. N. (2013). Public Private Partnerships (PPP) and Enhanced Service Delivery in Uganda: Implications from the Energy Sector. *International Journal of Business Administration*, *4*(3), 48–60. doi:10.5430/ijba.v4n3p48

Ogunsanmi, O. E. (2013). Critical success factors (CSF) determining the implementation of public- private partnership projects. *Covenant Journal of Research in the Built Environment*, *1*(2), 41–66.

Olaniyan, O. (2013). *Appraisal of critical success factors (CSFs) for implementation of public- private partnership in Lagos State*. Lagos: Department of Building, University of Lagos.

Osborne, S. P. (2006). The new public governance? *Public Management Review*, *8*(3), 377–388. doi:10.1080/14719030600853022

Osborne, S. P. (2010). *The new public governance*. London: Routledge.

Osborne, S. P., Radnor, Z., & Nasi, G. (2013). A new theory for public service management? Towards a (Public) Service-Dominant Approach. *American Review of Public Administration*, *43*(2), 135–158. doi:10.1177/0275074012466935

Owusu, M. D., & Badu, E. (2009). Determinants of contractors investment finance strategy in Ghana: Conceptual and empirical explanations. *Journal of Financial Management of Property and Construction*, *14*(1), 21–33. doi:10.1108/13664380910942626

Perry, J. L. (2007). Democracy and the New Public Service. *American Review of Public Administration*, *37*(1), 3–16. doi:10.1177/0275074006296091

Petersen, O. H. (2010). Regulation of public-private partnerships: The Danish case. *Public Money and Management*, *30*(3), 175–182. doi:10.1080/09540961003794345

Petersen, O. H. (2011). Public-private partnerships as converging or diverging trends in public management? A comparative analysis of PPP policy and regulation in Denmark and Ireland. *International Public Management Review*, *12*(2), 1–37.

Provan, K. G., & Kenis, P. (2008). Modes of Network Governance: Structure, management, and effectiveness. *Journal of Public Administration: Research and Theory*, *18*(2), 229–252. doi:10.1093/jopart/mum015

Quiggin, J. (2005). Public-private partnerships: Options for improved risk allocation. *The Australian Economic Review*, *38*(4), 445–450. doi:10.1111/j.1467-8462.2005.00388.x

Regan, M., Love, P. E. D., & Smith, J. (2015). Public-Private Partnerships: Capital market conditions and alternative finance mechanisms for Australian infrastructure projects. *Journal of Infrastructure Systems*, *19*(3), 335–342. doi:10.1061/(ASCE)IS.1943-555X.0000136

Robinson, H. S., & Scott, J. (2009). Service delivery and performance monitoring in PFI/PPP projects. *Construction Management and Economics*, *27*(2), 181–197. doi:10.1080/01446190802614163

Robinson, M. (2008). Hybrid states: Globalization and the politics of state capacity. *Political Studies*, *56*(3), 566–583. doi:10.1111/j.1467-9248.2008.00751.x

Sabolová, V., & Tetrevová, L. (2010). *Alternative forms of financing PPP projects*. Paper presented at 6th International Scientific Conference, Vilnius, Lithuania.

Shaik, R. R., & Niketa, N. (2011). Comparative analysis of infrastructure PPP in BRICS nations.*International Conference on Advancements in Information Technology*, *20*, 283-288.

Sharma, C. (2012). Determinants of PPP in infrastructure in developing economies. *Transforming Government: People. Process and Policy*, *6*(2), 149–166.

Shen, L. Y., Platten, A., & Dang, X. (2006). Role of public private partnership to manage risk in public sector project in Hong Kong. *International Journal of Project Management*, *24*(7), 587–594. doi:10.1016/j.ijproman.2006.07.006

Shendy, R., Kaplan, Z., & Mousley, P. (2011). *Towards better infrastructure: Conditions, constraints, and opportunities in financing public-private partnerships*. Washington, DC: The World Bank. doi:10.1596/978-0-8213-8781-8

Shrivastava, V. K. (2011). *Public Private Partnerships in road projects: Critical Success Factors in the Indian context*. Paper presented at the Southern African Transport Conference (SATC).

Siemiatycki, M. (2010). Developing transportation infrastructure through public-private partnerships. *Journal of the American Planning Association*, *76*(1), 43–58. doi:10.1080/01944360903329295

Silvester, H. C., & Aroujo, J. F. (2012). Public Private Partnerships / Private Finance Initiatives in Portugal: Theory, Practice, and results. *Public Performance and Management Review*, *36*(2), 316–339. doi:10.2753/PMR1530-9576360208

Singaravelloo, K. (2010). PPP: The Right Marriage between Local Government and the Private Sector in Malaysia? *International Journal of Institutions and Economics*, *2*(2), 142–166.

Singewar, M., & Deshmukh, S. S. (2016). Analysis of critical success factors for effective implementation of public private partnership in real estate and infrastructural development- A compendium case study. *Imperial Journal of Interdisciplinary Research*, *2*(8), 204–211.

Singewar, M., & Deshmukh, S. S. (2016). Analysis of Critical Success factors for effective implementation of public private partnership in real estate and infrastructural development- A Compendium Case Study. *Imperial Journal of Interdisciplinary Research*, *2*(8), 204–211.

Skietrys, E., Raipa, A., & Bartkus, E. V. (2008). Dimensions of the efficiency of public–private partnership. *Economic Engineering*, *3*, 45.

Soliño, A. S., & Vassallo, J. M. (2009). Using public-private partnerships to expand subways: Madrid-Barajas international airport case study. *Journal of Management Engineering*, *25*(1), 21–28. doi:10.1061/(ASCE)0742-597X(2009)25:1(21)

Steijin, B., Klijn, E.-H., & Edelenbos, J. (2011). Public private partnerships: Added value by organizational form or management? *Public Administration*, *89*(4), 1235–1252. doi:10.1111/j.1467-9299.2010.01877.x

Symth, E., & Edkins, A. (2006). Relationship management in the management of PFI/PPP projects in the UK. *International Journal of Project Management*, *25*(3), 232–240. doi:10.1016/j.ijproman.2006.08.003

Tang, L. Y., Shen, Q., & Cheng, E. W. L. (2010). A review of studies on Public–Private Partnership projects in the construction industry. *International Journal of Project Management*, *28*(7), 683–694. doi:10.1016/j.ijproman.2009.11.009

Taylor-Gooby, P. (2006a). *A further challenge to the welfare state: two paradoxes of trust*. Paper presented at the Conference on —Challenges to the Welfare State at the Minda de Gunzburg Center for European Studies, Harvard University.

Taylor-Gooby, P. (2006b). The Rational Actor Reform Paradigm: Delivering the Goods by Destroying Public Trust? *European Journal of Social Quality*, *6*(2), 121–141. doi:10.3167/ejsq.2006.060207

Tetřevová, L. (2006). Theoretical and Practical Aspects of PPP Projects. *Vadyba/Management, 3–4*(12–13), 105-110.

Toor, S. R., & Ogunlana, S. O. (2008). Problems causing delays in major construction projects in Thailand. *Construction Management and Economics*, *26*(4), 395–408. doi:10.1080/01446190801905406

Trafford, S., & Proctor, T. (2006). Successful joint venture partnerships: Public-private partnerships. *International Journal of Public Sector Management*, *19*(2), 117–129. doi:10.1108/09513550610650392

Tranfied, D., Rowe, A., Smart, P. K., Levene, R., Deasley, P., & Corley, J. (2005). Coordinating for service delivery in public-private partnership and private finance initiative. *Journal of Engineering Manufacture*, *12*(1), 165–175. doi:10.1243/095440505X8037

Valdimarsson, Ó. (2007). *PPP in Iceland from the Viewpoint of the Public Sector.* Paper presented at the FM Conference in Iceland.

van Dijk, M. P. (2008). Public–private partnerships in basic service delivery: Impact on the poor, examples from the water sector in India. *International Journal of Water*, *3*(3/4), 216–234. doi:10.1504/IJW.2008.019495

van Ryzin, G. G. (2007). Pieces of a puzzle: Linking government performance, citizen satisfaction, and trust. *Public Performance and Management Review*, *30*(4), 521–535. doi:10.2753/PMR1530-9576300403

Van Ryzin, G. G. (2011). Outcomes, process, and trust of civil servants. *Journal of Public Administration: Research and Theory*, *21*(4), 745–760. doi:10.1093/jopart/muq092

Vining, A., & Boardman, A. (2008a). Public-private partnerships. Eight rules for governments. *Public Works Management & Policy*, *13*(2), 149–161. doi:10.1177/1087724X08323843

Walker, A. (2007). *Project management in construction* (5th ed.). Oxford, UK: Blackwell Publishing.

Wang, S. Q. (2006). *Lessons Learnt from the PPP Practices in China*. Keynote Speech, Asian Infrastructure Congress, Hong Kong.

Wang, X. H., & Montgomery, V.-W. (2007). When public participation in administration leads to trust: An empirical assessment of managers perceptions. *Public Administration Review*, *67*(2), 265–278. doi:10.1111/j.1540-6210.2007.00712.x

Weber, E. P., & Khademian, A. M. (2008). Wicked problems, knowledge challenges, and collaborative capacity builders in network settings. *Public Administration Review*, *68*(2), 334–349. doi:10.1111/j.1540-6210.2007.00866.x

Weihe, G. (2006). Public-Private Partnerships: Addressing a nebulous concept. Working paper No.16. 10th International Symposium on Public Management, Glasgow, UK.

Weihe, G. (2008). Ordering disorder: On the perplexities of the partnership literature. *The Australian Journal of Public Administration*, *67*(4), 430–442. doi:10.1111/j.1467-8500.2008.00600.x

Westland, J. (2006). *Project Management Life Cycle: A Complete Step-by-step Methodology for Initiating Planning Executing and Closing the Project*. Kogan Page Limited.

Wettenhall, R. (2010). Mixes and partnerships through time. In International Handbook on Public-Private Partnerships. Cheltenham, UK: Edward Elgar.

Xenidis, Y., & Angelides, D. (2005). The financial risks in build-operate-transfer projects. *Construction Management and Economics*, *23*(4), 431–441. doi:10.1080/01446190500041552

Yang, Y., Hou, Y., & Wang, Y. (2013). On the development of public private partnerships in transitional economies; An Explanatory Framework. *The American Society for Public Administration*, *73*(2), 301–310. doi:10.1111/j.1540-6210.2012.02672.x

Zaharioaie, M. (2012). The utility of using public private partnership for local governments. *Journal of Public Administration, Finance and Law*, 17-24.

Zhang, H. (2007). A redefinition of the project risk process: Using vulnerability to open up the event-consequence link. *International Journal of Project Management*, *25*(7), 694–701. doi:10.1016/j.ijproman.2007.02.004

Zhang, L. (2009). *Development of infrastructure sectors in China: status quo and trends*. (Seminar Speech) Revamping PPPs: From "Revisiting and Rethinking" to "Revamping and Revitalizing" PPPs, The University of Hong Kong, Hong Kong, China.

Zhang, X. R. (2005a). Critical success factors for public private partnerships in infrastructure development. *Journal of Construction Engineering and Management*, *131*(1), 3–14. doi:10.1061/(ASCE)0733-9364(2005)131:1(3)

Zimmermann, J., & Eber, W. (2014). Consideration of risk in PPP-projects. *Business. Management in Education*, *12*(1), 30–46.

Zitron, J. (2006). Public private partnership projects: Towards a model of contractor bidding decision making. *Journal of Purchasing and Supply Management*, *12*(2), 53–62. doi:10.1016/j.pursup.2006.04.002

Zou, P., & Fang, D. (2008). A life-cycle risk management framework for PPP infrastructure projects. *Journal of Financial Management of Property and Construction*, *13*(2), 123–142. doi:10.1108/13664380810898131

Section 2

Risk Management Issues and Practices for Success

Chapter 3
Risks and Projects Phases

ABSTRACT

This chapter provides the rational for the importance of developing an effective and efficient replica for risks in PPP arrangement in order to optimize measures to handle them. Various attempts have been made to dig up all the risks in the project phases as an alternative service delivery improvement but to date there has been a lack of proper analogies of risks in the PPP project phases. This is also a lack of clear codification for risk of the project phases in the literature to provide useful benchmark mechanisms to improve a particular phase and to share risk optimally. The aim of this chapter is to develop a conceptual replica to comprehend risks in the project phases, and to determine means to advance risk-free PPP project phase. The different case studies will be examined in an effort to simplify the tasks of creating a risk-free PPP projects. In unearthing the melodrama in handling risks in PPP project phases, it is concluded that there is a lack of proper risk sharing formula that make most PPP projects to fail and a lack of emphasis in designing a less risk prone PPP projects.

Risks are generally deemed acceptable if the possible gains exceed the possible losses. - Rory Burke

INTRODUCTION

The central theme of this chapter is the nature and role of risks in each phase of PPP projects. Perhaps, paradoxically, a good deal of attention is given to the formulation and implementation of a PPP project, for each which will become clear as well proceeds. Most notably because the focus and content PPP projects are deeply engrained with risk that has fundamentally changed the landscape of PPP implementation in the last few years. Three main themes dominate the discussion in this chapter: the selecting, planning and designing phase, the procurement and contractual design choice phase, and the construction/service delivery phase. The importance of this topic for the achievement of successful PPP project cum effective and efficient service delivery should not be underestimated. High value production and quality service consumptions are PPP-driven processes and the conditions and contexts in which projects are incepted, procured and implemented in the contemporary world of rapidly changing wants and

DOI: 10.4018/978-1-5225-2503-5.ch003

needs. It has to be clear from the outset, that, as a general rule, risk management in PPP should not be directed at reaching a point of satisfaction without due consideration of the critical phases of PPP project development. Rather, the central concern should be with inception and development of PPP project process to suit the needs of the parties and prospects of success. As shall be seen these are non-trivial tasks. Even imitation or adaptation far from the technological frontier can require major investment in organizations and capabilities.

Typically, as noted earlier, many projects fail because of choices made in the early stages of development. According to Crompton, Goulding and Pour (2014), a poorly designed project-delivery approach or the wrong decisions about procurement can also lead to delays, higher costs, and diminished returns. Thus, Akintoye and Main (2007) contend that project risk management has to be a core element of project selection, planning, and design, and it has to be continuous across the entire life cycle of the project. Alashwal, Rahman and Beksin (2011) recommends that for each stage of a project, there are important questions that need to be asked on five central areas of forward-looking risk assessment, risk ownership, risk-adjusted process, risk governance and risk culture. On the forward-looking risk assessment, the questions should be which risks is the project facing? What is the potential cost of each of these risks? What are the potential consequences for the project's later stages as a result of design choices made now?. While questions for risk ownership should be which stakeholders are involved and which risks should the different stakeholders own? And what risk-management issues do each of the stakeholders face, and what contribution to risk mitigation can each of them make? The questions that should be asked for risk-adjusted processes are what are the root causes of potential consequences, and through which risk adjustments or new risk processes might they be mitigated by applying life-cycle risk-management principles? On risk governance the questions to ask is how can individual accountability and responsibility for risk assessment and management be established and strengthened across all lines of defense? For the risk culture asks what are the specific desired mind-sets and behaviors of all stakeholders across the life cycle and how can these be ensured. The phases are looked at in turn.

SELECTING, PLANNING AND DESIGNING PROJECTS PHASE

In addressing issues in the phase of PPP project development; there are several likely difficulties that can be faced. The first is the vast range of probable areas where PPP project ideas can be developed from. In terms of individual probable project or the sector or the composition of such projects or the relative contribution of the project or the level of its implementation, or in relation to available resources there are numerous differences between projects. Just like there are differences between the projects inceptions. At one, the great success of a well conceived PPP project arise from proper selection, planning and design; at the other end, it can be observes the continual problems of many unsuccessful PPP projects in predominantly failure to conceive this first phase right (Bennett & Peace, 2006). In between is a vast range of issues and matters to be resolved which will differ from project to project and what is appropriate for one project will not be appropriate for another such that for successful projects. Similarly, the appropriate choice of a project in one sector is quite different from that which is appropriate in another sector. Public sector organizations are adapting workable systems within an evolving projects' probable situation and the derivation of project that can succeed in the end (Eriksson, Dickinson & Khalfan, 2007). A 'one approach fits all' for all projects selection approach clearly will not suffice. Consequently, there is no best approach independent from time, place and the future of the chosen project area. Context is fundamental to all appropriate approach endeavors. Subsequent sections thenceforth analyses project selection *per se*; planning as well as designing the project.

Alderman and Ivory (2007) indicate that a life-cycle risk-management approach involves making decisions using a risk-based perspective. Specifically in the earliest design and planning phases of a project, this may require a conscious effort to identify, assess, and, ideally, quantify the risks the project will be exposed to across its life cycle. This includes reflection on potential adverse circumstances and scenarios (for example, stress testing). In large subway constructions, for instance, the risks of geological obstacles, environmental challenges, and future customer numbers and behaviors can and should be explicitly taken into account as drivers of volatility of project construction and future cash flows. A life-cycle approach demands the alignment of people and management toward a more risk-conscious set of processes. However, it is important to note that each individual project should use a stage-gate approach to ensure that projects do not progress without key deliverables being completed (Esmaeili & Zeephongsekul, 2010). Using predefined risk-register templates enables this to progress smoothly. Private financial discipline should be used in planning, designing, and structuring projects even before private investors are involved, helping to adjust incentives and penalties so that they are matched appropriately—and applied—to each relevant party (Chan, Chan, Fan, Lam & Yeung, 2006).

Selection of Projects

The urges for projects development continue to come in at a rapid pace. For the past few years in particular, countries have seen PPP projects grow more quickly than never had been thought before. Indeed between the 1990s and present, PPP projects have increased three-fold relatives to what ought to have been. Alongside this, countries have seen the continual growth of integrated PPP projects inception and development for many sectors, from service sectors to production sectors. Cooke and Williams (2009) suggests that countries should strive to create a transparent and flawless decision-making process to select the investment that best achieves assigned targets under the global mandate of the sponsor. This is a major challenge. Too often projects are "gold plated" or overdesigned for the commercial opportunity, resulting in too much complexity and a lack of economic viability (Dangerfield, Green and Austin, 2010). Sponsors need to adopt a realistic commercial approach from the outset, making sure the project can meet its defined needs and is designed so that it also meets its target costs. Potential future interface risks would be identified early on in the process, and the required resources and skill set to manage those risks would be factored into any decision taken with respect to alternative project structures (Green, Larsen & Kao, 2008). It should be clear from the outset how any new project fits in to a wider strategy. For example, a project for a new airport should form part of an overall national strategy for transport.

Chen and Chen (2007) remind that it has to be noted that in most cases governments initiate the vast majority of infrastructure projects. This creates natural tension because delivery times for projects typically run beyond the election cycle, for example, meaning that any future payoff might accrue to political opponents. In addition, governments are often reluctant to spend money at the outset, preferring to appear thrifty even if there will be far higher costs later on. Often efforts are hampered by the lack of an overarching infrastructure strategy, but many other factors can lead to individual projects being plagued with problems. These include incorrect forecasts and assumptions (for example, on demographics, demand, prices, revenues, capital expenditure, or operating expenditure), a limited understanding of market dynamics, and lack of willingness to plan for volatility and adverse scenarios (Clamp, Cox & Lupton, 2007). Overestimating revenue and growth potential while underestimating risk results in badly designed projects that deliver lower-than-expected returns or, in the worst case, a project that must be canceled or abandoned after significant up-front investment (Green, Kumaraswamy & Ofori, 2009). Other challenges include poor planning and management of future interface risks, caused by early-stage decisions regarding project structures and design. Crucially, the risk appetite of developers, contractors, and private investors, who are essential in later stages of the project life cycle, is often not taken into account (Barratt, & Oke, 2007).

According to Westland (2006), the purpose of selection of the project is to develop an idea about a potential project. He further describes it in more detail as developing a business opportunity which includes identification of a subject matter or problem which could be further developed into a project. Barrett (2008) contends that identifying business opportunities requires a number of assessments and discussions which should result in creating a project idea. Hong, Chan and Chan (2012) points out that Initial problem description, its scope, time frames and an outline of a plan for activities form the core of project selection process. Westland (2006) augments these are some of the factors which should be determined by the time the proposal is presented to a potential sponsor. Likewise, in the selection process moreover, in the selection phase a project delivery system is chosen as suggested by Cheung and Rowlinson (2011). It establishes relationships between main actors in the project: the owner, the designer and the construction organization. Previous studies show that the choice of procurement system has a great impact of how risks are managed in the construction industry; this indicates that there is a relation between these factors. Holweg, Disney, Holmstrom and Smaros (2005) emphasized there is a correlation between risk response in the PPP arrangement and the PPP project selection process.

In spite of the challenges encountered during the selection of the PPP project, Drew (2005) indicates that not all can be lost if the whole PPP process is laid on the foundation of a transparent process. Bresnen (2009) also proposes that even the partners need to be carefully prepared for a transparent process. For example, the private partner needs to be prepared to make its number, name and itself often to public scrutiny. The recognition and acceptance of this basic tenet should precede all other steps that the partners will take (Drew, 2005). If such transparency is not acceptable, the private partner should walk away from the project. While the public partner is establishing clear-cut goals and projects, the private partner can be preparing by meeting with investors to explain the nature of the PPP for example. As in all PPP development processes, the partners must underwrite the market and determine interest. The public partner should have provided substantial background information during its preparatory phase. The private partner must also identify and assess the opportunity for the project and assess whether it is feasible (Eaton, Akbiyukli & Dickinson, 2006). Increasingly, with the help of legislative authority the private partner submits unsolicited proposals conceptualizing and designing the use of a PPP, which then is implemented with public approval. Holt (2010) shows that all of the selection stage of the PPP project falls under conceptual design, but successes in the end is all about the interface between the public and private partners. A project can go wrong for lots of reasons, for example, a road is being built over contested ground just because there was improper selection of the location of the project, though most may be addressed through force majeure.

Oyegoke, Khalfan, McDermott, Rowlinson and Dickinson (2009) outlines that the stage of the selection of a PPP project comprises a decision making process that starts with a list of the priority Public Sector development projects in the Highway sector and ends with a list of potential highway PPP projects (Wood & Ellis, 2005). These projects will have been prioritized through the planning processes within Government. This stage can be applied by the responsible agencies and at all levels of government i.e. central, provincial, municipal and local. It assumes, and starts with, a public sector development program consisting of a list of highway projects that may be tentatively proposed for a range of implementation modalities under both public, private and IFI (or combinations thereof) funding options. According to Yeung, Chan, Chan and Li (2007), this stage is completed with agreement by the concerned authority that one of more priority highway projects is/are highly suitable for implementation under a PPP modality and therefore are passed to the next stage for feasibility type studies which provide the appropriate levels of due diligence required by Government authorities. This stage includes ensuring proposed PPP projects pass an initial value for money test and are appropriate for funding under the PPP modality. This stage also shows the usefulness of value-for-money (VfM) tests and how VfM can be simplified for use in developing economies, including examples illustrating alternative calculations.

Planning Projects

Planning is crucial for the realization of a successful end of a PPP project. Kohtamaki (2010) illustrates that proper planning through use of state-of-the-art techniques helps in avoidance of common problems such as overdesign, mismatched capacity and demand, or misjudgment of interdependencies with other projects. The project can be evaluated using adverse scenarios; stress tested, and set up with the appropriate monitoring and reporting processes (Murdoch & Hughes, 2008). An economic model that integrates time risk, cost risk, and uncertainties can be deployed to produce a clear business case and range of expected financial returns. In this regard, it is crucial to consider potential private-sector requirements early on (both technical and financial) (Nystrom, 2008). Bresnen (2007) cautions that during the front-end planning there is need to take proper stock of the several key risk levers which must be pulled including:- conceptual design (what you'll ask the contractors to design and build); the procurement model (how you select contractors); contracting model (under what terms the contractors work); and the project-management model (how you will manage the contractors to deliver the project).

Phua (2006) suggests that the developer needs to make an internal assessment of the resources that are required to accomplish the project, including such items as potential staff, assessment of risk, potential deal structures (whether they will work for a fee or be partners in the venture), potential investors, and political and community leadership and working relationships with leaders. This getting-to-know-you stage will ease the subsequent stages in the development process. During the preparatory, or due diligence stage, the developer should familiarize itself with the jurisdiction's plans, approval processes, and length of permitting processes (Grimsey & Lewis, 2005). The developer should assess the public partner's ability to deliver and to commit its resources up front. If the developer decides to continue with the partnership, the developer should assemble a team who brings insight and experience with the public partner. If the developer is new to the community, it would be valuable to find local expertise to assist in the process. The developer needs to be prepared to be an explorer and adapt to what may be discovered (Gunnigan & Eaton, 2006).

Crucially, at this stage, there is need to create a shared vision. This is because any project must start with a vision. Without a vision, the project will most likely fail. The vision is the framework for project goals and serves as the benchmark to ensure the realization of joint objectives (Hodge, 2010). However, it has to be noted that creating a vision is not always easy. It involves building consensus and including all the stakeholders, even those who may be naysayers. By casting a wide net and giving all the stakeholders—including potential partners—an opportunity to help craft the vision, less possibility exists for opposition to a project. Public hearings, charrettes, visioning exercises, and other tools for involving stakeholders in the visioning process should be used to ensure the broadest outreach (El-Gohary, Osman

& El-Diraby, 2006). Involving the media is another key factor for two reasons. First, it helps get the message out about the visioning process, and second, it helps form an alliance with the media, which will be crucial in articulating and publicizing the vision once it is created. Once a vision has been created and shared, it has to be sustained. The rationale is that a vision is not just pretty pictures depicting the ultimate outcome. It involves a strategy for implementation, which includes funding mechanisms (public and private), potential partners (and their responsibilities), and an agenda or time frame for achieving the vision (making the project a reality) (Briscoe & Dainty, 2005). These components are all critical for realizing the vision and ensuring that it gets off the boards and onto the ground. Partners should make a practical analysis of market conditions and demographics to ensure that the vision is neither too grand nor too small. An important component of the vision is specifying the scale of the project or projects that provides people with an understanding of what is going to happen. Moreover, involving the stakeholders will help bring reality to the plans by establishing a collective vision and creating community buy-in for the project (Thomas & Thomas, 2005). The most important component of a vision is ensuring that it can endure the test of time. Most development or redevelopment projects are long term and may span several political administrations. Thus, the vision that is created is not just the whim of the current administration, but represents key community and stakeholder buy-in that will help it endures. A shared vision that is created and embraced by key stakeholders will stand the test of time and will persevere through implementation.

Kumaraswamy, Ling, Anvuur and Rahman (2007) advise that partners must be clear on risks and rewards so as to capture the risk/reward relationship most common in PPP. It has to be remembered that PPP is key to having such a partnership produce tangible, positive results is for each partner to understand and appreciate the nature and scope of the opposite party's potential risks and rewards, as well as its own, so that mutual success is achieved (Burt, Davies, Dawson & Sparks, 2008). Significant obstacles must be overcome and challenges met through joint efforts because the resources and responsibility are distributed differently between the sectors, particularly during project implementation. PPP is built on the mutuality of effort and investment required to accomplish an outcome that is unattainable without such collaboration (Aaltonen, Jaakk & Tuomas, 2008). In the PPP process, they may be affected by changes to quality of life and revenue or tax streams, for example. It's equally important the process of stepping beyond rigorous standard procurement and developer selection procedures should be fraught with the danger of creating real or perceived conflicts of interest for public officials (Freeman, 2010). Often, it is absolutely necessary that state-mandated procedures be followed in selecting the developer for a particular project before a real public/private partnership can be formed.

Beyond a concern for conflicts of interest, the public partner faces an array of rich opportunities for public controversy and bad publicity associated with property acquisition or charges of misuse of public funds and other resources (Bygballe, Jahre & Sward, 2010). The ultimate concern of the public partner is that the developer partner might fail—just drop the project, lose its financing, or even go bankrupt—and leave the community "holding the bag" for substantial additional costs and performance commitments (Maylor, 2005). However, if the selection process for the private partner is conducted properly and appropriate bonding is included in the contract, this outcome will be avoided. Most successful economic development public/private partnerships are the result of a selection process that includes verification of the technical and financial capability of the private partner (Freeman, 2010).

The private partner also has its partners, stockholders, equity investors, and lenders to satisfy (Love, Davis, Ellis & Cheung, 2010). They must believe that their resources are being deployed effectively. Although many of the developer's risks are the same as in a straight private deal—sufficient effective market demand, attracting necessary debt and equity financing, and so on—certain risks are unique to a public/private partnership (Yiu & Cheung, 2007). The counterpoint to the public partner's concerns regarding potential conflicts of interest is the developer's fear of charges based on ignorance of business terms and conditions that are harmful to its reputation and ability to do future deals, for example, that it is taking unfair advantage and "profiting at public expense." Perhaps most risky to the private party is the danger of the process taking far longer than anticipated and becoming a "black hole" for unanticipated costs (Zenonas, Gajzler & Dziadosz, 2012). The fact that "time is money" for the developer is aggravated by the reality that a key public partner can quickly change its position or be voted out of office as a result of bad publicity, leaving the project without a necessary champion before it is fully entitled by public action (Jaskowski & Biruk, 2011). To minimize risk, consultants have created tools for public partners to develop financial and development safeguards that are negotiated and can be included in the development agreement between the public partner and the selected developer.

On the reward side, strong, compelling reasons exist for both public and private partners to take the necessary risks and soldier on to build the partnership and implement the project (Kaplinski, 2008b). Most obvious for the public are the net economic and fiscal benefits—jobs, infrastructure, community wealth and tax base, taxes, fees- that can be produced by joint action to overcome obstacles. Less tangible is the message that the city is on the move—it is progressive in advancing the welfare of its residents (Kaplinski, 2008a). Public officials, who are only human, also seek ego gratification and recognition for their good works. The benefits to the private developer are perhaps the most obvious and readily measured: the deal must be profitable after paying all associated costs of investment of time and resources. However, developers have a reputation to protect and build if their business is to do other deals and continue to prosper, as well as the nonfinancial returns to ego and self-esteem satisfied by a successful project (Pasławski, 2010). Although the risks and rewards of a particular public/private partnership may be more easily measured in the private sector, the public concerns are no less important, and a disciplined accounting of expected rewards and risks, or benefits and costs, will go a long way in demonstrating to key stakeholders and the general public alike that the deal is worth doing and is being made with all relevant factors in mind—that risks are being carefully defined and considered and steps are being taken to offset or mitigate them (Zavadskas, Turskis & Tamošaitien, 2010). Clearly, the objective of this accounting should be to show that the ultimate outcome of the partnership will be a win-win for the public and private partners as a result of their respective investments and risk taking (Matei, 2006). Conversely, if an accounting of risks and rewards fails to show such a positive outcome, good reason exists to reconsider the undertaking.

Chong and Huertand (2006) recommends for the establishment a clear and rational decision making process during the planning stage. This is useful as it enables parties need to articulate and agree upon the process to be followed and the rules of engagement to be used to structure a deal with public and private dimensions as early as possible (Kaplinski, 2010). Agreement on the process helps ensure that partnerships establish effective policies and implement them efficiently and collaboratively. Furthermore, a documented decision-making process increases transparency and facilitates the sharing of information about the project (Bennett & Peace, 2006). At the beginning of the partnership, after a developer has been selected, entities must define the process by which decisions are made, implemented, and reassessed. The most important step is creating a road map for decision making, with a timeline to schedule project implementation. The road map should delineate a plan of action that is maintained throughout the process, particularly during the implementation of entitlements, deal terms, financing, design and planning, and the environmental review phase (Reeves, 2008). The road map formalizes joint action and party commitments to the project, consequently promoting the sharing of information, such as studies and plans, and resulting in more rational decision making. Furthermore, by establishing milestones and deadlines, the partners can assess the project's implementation status and each party's activities (Quiggin, 2005).

Entities within the partnership should also define the relationships for engagement and the various actors' roles in the implementation of the project (Akintan & Morledge, 2013). In many cases, the public partner defines the expectations for private partners, particularly in terms of their role and capacities. If the proposals are clear and accurate, they provide a strong framework by which actors can jointly implement a public/private partnership (Apanavičienė & Rudžianskaitė-Kvaraciejienė, 2010). One tool that many partnerships have used is the memorandum of understanding, which documents (in a succinct and summary fashion) decision-making processes and relationships between partners. Project roles and responsibilities should also be assigned to entity representatives. Project leaders and "go to" people should be targeted to handle specific tasks. To clarify expectations and ensure accountability, partnerships should adopt documentation measures, such as performance standards and clear metrics, for each position (Briscoe & Dainty, 2005). To ensure collaborative decision making, dispute resolution mechanisms should also be incorporated into a contract. A widely supported and collaborative process can be achieved through the inclusion of mechanisms to ensure sufficient and appropriate involvement of stakeholders, such as task force committees, involving input from many actors, and the use of facilitators and intermediaries to build bridges between "cultures." The formalization of the public's role in the process also reduces the likelihood of insurmountable opposition to the partnership and its project (Ross, 2011). Finally, partnerships must create and use mechanisms to allow continuous assessment of the effectiveness of decisions and implementation procedures. To resolve constraints, such as funding source requirements and bottlenecks in the process, partners must have the opportunity to modify the process. Furthermore, to incorporate new information and reassessed goals into the process, parties must allow for incremental "baby step" decision making. To overcome changing conditions, time frames, and conflicts, the process must be inherently flexible.

Alireza, Mohammadreza, Zin, Yahaya and Noor (2013) encourage all the parties to the PPP arrangement to do their work diligently. Cheung, Yiu and Chiu (2009) rationalize that a successful PPP requires all parties to do their homework-at the onset as well as throughout the project. The partners need to understand that they will have to invest time, energy, and resources at all phases of the project. Although due diligence is part of the preparatory stage of a project, all partners must continue to understand all the issues-technical, social, and financial-of a project. By "doing their homework," the partners maintain an understanding of the technical aspects of the project and can anticipate change (Bresnen, 2009). In other words-don't drop out of the process and do stay invested. Public/private partnership projects will fail when both sides do not continue to invest the resources needed to keep the project going. The development process can be complicated and involves many moving parts (Antuchevičiene, Turskis & Zavadskas, 2006). Clearing title for the land, environmental planning and permitting, meeting local land use codes and requirements, proper design and site planning, and complying with design standards and guidelines are just a few of the many details that need to be attended to when completing a project. All the parties need to know the status of each phase and aspect of development. All consultant work needs to be shared—and shared early. Information needs to be presented in a clear and transparent format so that everyone knows what is happening at all phases (Baccarini, 2005).

Choi and Mahadevan (2008) advocate for a secure consistent and coordinated leadership so as to achieve a successful PPP. Any PPP deal needs a champion, whether it is an individual or a small group (Bygballe, Jahre & Sward, 2010). To define clear goals; to build broad constituencies; to bring the right parties around the table; to coordinate process; to bridge private project management with political leadership; to provide stakeholders who are not financially involved but have an interest in, and expectations about, a project, with a forum to express their views; and to keep everyone on point and not let a project languish. Leadership creates positive change. It makes a visible difference. It has to do with creating a vision, motivating others to support it, and implementing it. A good leader is a facilitator, a coach, an orchestra leader, an enabler (Abbasianjahromi & Rajaie, 2012). He or she brings people around the table and helps them move in a given direction. Leadership has to be sustained. Successful leadership persists. It does not grow weary in the middle of a project. It keeps all the parties at the table, coordinating their efforts. Many political leaders have a short lease on life-two years, four years, two terms, maybe longer—and often their successors have other ideas and undo what has been started (Abels, 2007). So, transcending administrations and political change by maximizing opportunities for putting a deal together with one set of public officials makes good sense, as does passing the baton to new leadership in both the public and private sectors, that is, to people who have the same commitment and goals. Just handing off a project will not work (Badenfelt, 2008).

Aldoory and Sha (2007) direct there must be very frequent communication between the partners and all the stakeholders. The communication mode must be incorporate in the design of the PPP arrangement. The more open the communication channels and the more they are used by each partner, the greater the prospects for a successful project outcome and lasting public/private partnership. Regular communication within the partnership assists in the recognition of joint interests and ensures a more efficient decision-making and implementation process (Andersen & Spitzberg, 2010). Communication is essential to the internal dynamics of a complex partnership structure, allowing distribution of information and implementation of compatible efforts. Initially, the partners should communicate overarching project objectives, such as downtown revitalization or increased real estate values, to find common ground within the partnership. After obtaining consensus on project goals, partners should discuss and agree on strategies to reach those objectives. Communication is essential to the public/private partnership process for many reasons, including ensuring a more efficient decision making process by facilitating the exchange of information, ideas, and needs and creating opportunities for public involvement (Bouder, Slavin & Lofstedt, 2009).

A well calculated strategy developed for communication has to be incorporated in the PPP design. According to Jin (2010), a consistent communication with a broad array of actors external to the partnership is integral to ensure widespread support and diverse perspectives within the process. Partners should reach out, listen, and respond to stakeholders and the community, elected and appointed officials, the media, and investors. The partnership should develop a clear and concise concept of the project that can be communicated in a consistent, cohesive voice to these actors (Covello, 2010). The designation of a project spokesperson from the public and private side can help deliver a consistent message about the partnership and its objectives. Leaders can also shepherd the project through the development process by acting as negotiator in securing political and financial support. Finally, the most informed actors, the principals, should be directly involved in communicating partnership objectives (Radeneck, 2008).

A transparent process, achieved through open communication, information sharing, and participation in the decision process, increases the potential for broad support for public/private partnership projects, particularly from non-stakeholders. Community outreach should include public involvement or notification of the project's planning, design, and construction stages through ongoing meetings and news updates (Kasperson & Palmlund, 2005). Sharing information with the public, however, must be timed to occur strategically in order to protect the deal from market overvaluation; for example, a partnership's disclosure of intent to purchase property may affect land prices as well as the outcome of the overall project (Ulmer, Sellnow & Seeger, 2011).

It's very critical to negotiate a fair deal structure in the partnership (Cleland & Gareis, 2006). Fairness" is a value subject to judgment by both sides in any negotiation. Legal documentation provides evidence of the terms that all parties agreed to at closing, but fairness is often determined by subsequent changes in fact. Because we cannot anticipate all future changes, fairness will often remain an elusive goal (Darnall & Preston, 2010). Fairness in negotiating a deal structure means that all parties are reasonably satisfied, at the point of closing, that they will receive the outcomes that were important enough to include in the transaction documentation. In public/private partnerships, it is widely acceptable that the private side, in exchange for taking significant financial risk, will accrue proportionate future financial returns (Eriksen & Jensen, 2010). The public side, in return for providing the infrastructure, entitlements, or other public resources that allow the private activity to advance, will receive sufficient tangible and intangible public benefits—such as improved public infrastructure; increased property, employment, or sales tax base; provision of needed services; clearing of blight; and nontax income and tax revenue generated by the project- that justify the required investment (Engel, Fischer & Galetovic, 2006).

Negotiating a fair deal structure does not begin at the point attorneys begin documenting the transaction (Davies & Eustice, 2005). It is a cumulative process that begins with some of the principles previously outlined. By the time the transaction is documented, a clear understanding of the deal structure should already be in place. Both parties should have already done their homework and evaluated their respective risks and returns. All parties critical to the transaction should already be informed of the evolution of facts as the deal proceeds to closing (Dikmen, Birgonul & Han, 2007). Above all, mutual trust established over time will go a long way in bridging difficult negotiating issues as they invariably arise.

According to Firmenich (2011), some general rules to follow in achieving a fair deal structure include the following: Principals should spend sufficient time preparing or reviewing a detailed term sheet. The term sheet should be circulated and agreed to by all parties before documentation begins. A well-thought-out term sheet will assist in surfacing issues that need to be discussed, and it allows legal counsel to reasonably determine the intent of the parties. Do not let legal counsel or the documentation process drive the outcome. Only the principals retain the shared vision, understand the risks they are willing to take, and generally are able to keep the transaction on track when the inevitable unforeseen conditions arise (Barlish, De Marco & Thaheem, 2013). Transactions fail because the principals either ignore or abdicate their responsibility for supervising the negotiation. When possible, build in objective measures of the expected outcomes that can be used to determine the ultimate fairness of the transaction. For example, asking the private partner to spell out the expected time frames of future development and the consequences if conditions change significantly is reasonable. The same is true for public partner commitments (Drew, 2005). Both sides need to hire competent legal and technical counsel. Allow sufficient time for final negotiations and documentation. If you are faced with an immovable deadline, forced compromises may result in lasting resentment by one or both parties. On the other hand, too much time can also result in an unsatisfactory outcome and will usually mean larger legal bills. Understand the long-term nature of the partnership because the public sector is not going away anytime soon, and private developers, even those with short- to intermediate-term investment horizons, are still creating assets in the built environment that should last for generations (Eaton, Akbiyukli & Dickinson, 2006). The difference in time horizons may require compromise. Understand that compromise is a necessary requirement for achieving a fair transaction. It is not a sign of weakness. Principals are the only parties that can keep the ultimate objectives in mind and know when compromise is appropriate.

Dikmen and Birgonol (2006) opine mutual trust needs to be built among the partners especially during the design stage. Trust is one of the overarching values to be realized from the beginning and throughout the public/private partnership process. To endure, partnerships require a foundation of trust in each partner's commitment to the project and its objectives. Given the complex public/private partnership process and structure, trust is required between the multiple actors and entities to enable shared decision making and taking of financial risks. Partners must also ensure that other stakeholders, such as financial investors, as well as the public are dedicated to and trust the project and the partnership (Enshassi, Mohamed & Abushaban, 2009). Trust is tangible and can be earned through work and commitment to the project. Building trust incrementally through small efforts within the partnership creates a record of small successes that support bigger strides. In other words, success breeds confidence, and confidence breeds trust. Parties begin to build trust in each other's interests, capacity, and diligence toward the project during the selection process. Many approaches exist for selecting appropriate private partners that provide opportunities to verify their qualifications. The Request for Qualifications (RFQ) is submitted by the public partner to evaluate references, track records, and resource capacity. The RFQ provides the public sector with the ability to choose a partner in which it can trust and also helps narrow the list of competitors, particularly if the public partner chooses to invite development proposals by issuing a Request for Proposals (RFP).

After partner selection, trust is reinforced through each partner's realization of expected responsibilities. Reasonable performance schedules for deliverables help document the commitments of parties and ensure consistency in the implementation of the project. Partners can communicate more effectively by building personal relationships with each other. Formal and informal forms of communication between entities create opportunities to build a more open and trusting relationship (Fischer, 2010). Parties must act honestly and in good faith and work under the assumption that the other partners are doing the same. The practice of reciprocity also increases the co- operative nature of the partnership. Finally, to overcome misperceptions and differences impeding the emergence of trust, partners should work to understand the perspective and needs of actors involved in the process (Glasbergen, 2011). Building trust with other stakeholders and the public requires a high degree of transparency and the realization of promised objectives (Ho, 2006b). Although parties may feel compelled to overpromise to secure support, good faith and reliability may be tarnished by lack of follow-through. Overall, partners must understand that people rely upon trust to protect their interests. By pursuing mutual goals, trust can emerge among partners if the process includes mechanisms to encourage honest communication and dedication to the project (Lam, Wang, Lee & Tsang, 2007). Because change is likely and reinvention becomes necessary, trust underlies the partnership's ability to stray from the prescribed path and yet continue to collaborate to realize mutual project objective.

Designing Projects

Designing projects is the second most important step in the selecting, planning and designing projects phase of a PPP project development. It is also relatively longer than the others. It essentially consists of three sequential stages for more convenient phase completion and project delivery. It forms part of the planning stage of a PPP project development. Boussabaine (2007) designates that in the first step, project organization usually the SPV starts to be formulated. In the process of formulation, the main actors in the project and their roles are defined along with competences which are assigned to each position in particular (Bennet & Cusick, 2007). After appointing the project team, a project brief is written which in detail describes the scope of the project and its objectives. For example, in a construction project, first the needs of the stakeholders must being identified and then the design team makes initial sketches of each idea separately (Lambrigger, Shevchenko & Wüthrich, 2009). It helps to identify potential risks associated with proposed solutions. As a result of this examination, all identified ideas are ranked and the most feasible one is chosen for further development (Westland, 2006). Further on, in the planning phase, for example in a construction project still, a site investigation and constructability analysis should be undertaken. A number of potential sites should be examined in respect to soil conditions, topography, location and price. A constructability analysis determines whether a proposed structure is easy to build and what effect will it have on schedule, budget or safety. In a planning phase, it is vital to determine whether potential investment is financially feasible. Thus the cost estimator should prepare a preliminary budget of a project where all types of possible costs and the price per unit or activity are determined (ModuKumshe, Badiya Yusuf Magaji & Bani, 2015).

When all options in the feasibility study are analyzed, the project team chooses the best alternatives and proceeds to the next step in the selecting, planning and designing projects phase which is the design process. All assumptions made in previous stages are put into practice. In other words, schematic drawings drawn up under planning phase are developed into actual detail plans (Ogunsanmi, Salako & Ajayi, 2011). Every technical aspect such as structure calculation or accessory planning is developed by a small specialized group of engineers. As a result of the whole design process, a clear vision of the investment emerges. This is followed by the last activity in the planning and design phase which is development of a contract document. The contract document includes technical specifications, up-front documents and drawings. Its format can be based on standards issued by various institutions such as FIDIC, which is a standard widely used in international projects. This document sets form as well as instructions and invitation to tender. Established tendering processes enable the project team to proceed to the next stage which is contractor selection (Quiggin, 2005).

At this stage, Rafele, Hillson and Grimaldi (2005) advice that it is important to take note of risk occurrences with keen interest. For example in a construction project, Raz and Hillson (2005) encourage paying particular attention to the five main stages of a construction project: feasibility, design, tendering, construction and handling and maintenance. Sachs, Tiong and Wang (2007) aver different types of risk arise at different stages in construction and indicate that because of the low level of certainty, higher level would normally occur at the outset of a project. Tanaka, Ishida, Tsutsumi and Okamoto (2005) reminds that it is impossible to study risk management without understanding the perceptions of project Coordinators about risk and the risk management process. It's important therefore understand and appreciate that risks connected to the design and production be subjected to risk management (Thomas, Kalidindi & Ganesh, 2006). Sadka (2007) suggests that particular attention must be keenly paid the each in each design stage of the PPP project as illustrated in Table 1.

PROCUREMENT AND CONTRACTUAL DESIGN CHOICE PHASE

Stanley and Hensher (2008) re-echo that public procurers, such as governments and their respective ministries, as well as public-private collaborations such as PPP units, developers, and contractors are the main stakeholders for this stage of an infrastructure project. However, Anvuur and Kumaraswamy (2007) reveal that often they fail to select the optimal risk-return ownership structure ahead of the procurement

Table 1. Risks identified at each design stage

Operations	Risk Identified
Need Assessment Planning & Budget	i)Lack of adequate needs assessment i) Poor procurement planning ii) Failure to budget realistically iii) Procurements not aligned with the overall investment decision making process in department iv) Interference of high-level officials
Choice of procedure	i) Lack of procurement strategy for the use of non-competitive procedures ii) Abuse of non-competitive procedures on the basis of legal exceptions through - Contract splitting on the basis of low monetary value contracts - Abuse of extreme urgency
Time frame for preparation of bid	i) A time frame that is not consistently applied for all bidders ii) A time frame that is not sufficient for ensuring a level playing field
Invitation to bid	i) Information on the procurement opportunity not provided in a Consistent manner. ii) Absence of public notice for the invitation to bid iii) Lack of competition or insure cases collusive bidding that leads to inadequate prices
Submission & opening of tender	i) Bid opening procedure flaws ii) Deviations from the correct bid opening procedure
Verification and post qualification analysis	i) Familiarity with bidder in time, manifesting personal interest. ii) Errors or omissions throughout the evaluation in favour of certain bidders
Award	i) Conflict of interest and corruption in evaluation process - Approval process ii) Lack of access to records on the procedure

Source: (OECD, 2007)

stage, making it difficult to adjust or reassign risk or responsibility once the project has commenced. Most strikingly, Sahm (2008) points out that the risk appetite of private players is frequently neglected or poorly understood and there is limited transparency of risk cost, risk ownership, and risk-return trade-offs. Sarmento (2010) shows procurers frequently select the wrong strategy, disregarding or misjudging the ability of private-sector players to control certain risks. It is extremely complex and costly to reverse a tender process once launched, as the discovered by Teo, Ling and Chong (2005). Van Wyk and Akintoye (2007) reveals that a failure to allocate risk to the right parties and to anticipate potential problems—such as sourcing bottlenecks—causes cost overrun and significant time delays. Nonetheless, Westland (2006) explains that a life-cycle risk management approach can help to mitigate these significant risks. Vining and Boardman (2008b) though encourage that there should be an early focus on optimal risk-ownership allocation, including a clear knowledge of alternatives, and early application of risk management before any procurement decision is taken. Zhang (2005c) recommends that funding and financing sources should be aligned early on so that future means of funding support, such as tolls, taxes, or fares, are matched with the proposed financing, such as bank loans, bond proceeds, or equity investments. Yang, Hou and Wang (2013) proposes that the risk profile of the funding source needs to be appropriate for the proposed finance. Specifically, Vining and Boardman (2008a) calls on stakeholders to identify risks and value drivers, such as delays or increases in material prices, from the outset and decide who will be responsible for each of these. This provides a mechanism to drive contractor behavior and ensure ongoing accountability. Yescomb (2007) insinuates its vital to ensure that required expertise in planning, structuring, and so on is brought in early on, and that due diligence is conducted on contractors before selection. The project owner's ability to manage the contract must be assessed and strengthened if necessary. Critically Yang and Yang (2010) intimates this phase adores a deeper consideration of the procurement and its transition.

Traditional Procurement Versus Partnering Procurement

According to Zitron (2006), procurement of a contractual nature has of recent taken on two different dimensions. These dimensions are traditional procurement strategies (design-bid-build) and collaborative/partnering approach to procurement. Zhang (2005b) shows a procurement system is an organizational system that assigns specific responsibilities and authorizes to people and organizations, and defines the relationships of the various elements in the construction of a project. According to Zou and Fang (2008), the choice of a procurement route is one of the many important decisions that construction clients have to make. Moreover, he argues that it is important for clients to objectively assess and prioritize their requirements in order to enable a rational comparison of alternative procurement routes. The choice of the route which best matches the clients' requirements can then be made based on relative advantages of the alternatives, against the criteria defined by the client (Zhang, 2005a).

In spite of the routes though, the performance of the construction industry has largely remained poor (Zimmermann & Eber, 2014). It appears as though the poor performance and the dissatisfaction of clients arise from poorly structured procurement systems, the fragmentation of the industry (that is differing professions or actors coming together) and the adversarial contractual cultures within the industry (Sanchez & Tijuana-Ensenada, 2005). Morledge, Smith and Kashiwagi (2006) aver the traditional design-led approaches, which occurs largely as a natural development following the rise of the architectural profession throughout the seventeenth and eighteenth centuries in the UK are to blame for the adversarial problems in the industry. They argue that, although, the traditional procurement method held sway for more than 150 years, by the early 1960s problems arising from the separation of design and construction functions, often evidenced by the difficulty of apportioning responsibility for defects in completed buildings, led to the development of what have been called 'integrated procurement systems (Sanda & Anigbogu, 2016) generally based upon a design and build approach.

As a result of government pressure to improve predictability and reduction in construction delays, the use of management oriented procurement strategies came on board especially in the 1970s (Morledge, Smith & Kashiwagi, 2006). Cartlidge (2010) shows that later on the interest for management oriented procurement strategies surged on when compulsory competitive tendering (CCT) was introduced in the public sector. He continues to say that the new tendering system spread to the private sector, that design and build procurement began to see a rise in popularity as clients' perceived this as strategy by which to transfer some risk to the contractor.

In the traditional procurement strategies, Cartlidge (2010) reveals that it involves employers or their agents designing or at least specifying in detail the work required prior to competitive tenders being invited from group of construction contractors. Morledge, Smith and Kashiwagi (2006) suggest that the strategy is seen as the least risky approach due to the fact that there is a level of certainty about design, cost and duration inherent in the strategy if it is properly implemented. The implication of this is that in order to assure low risk, the design has to be completed before competitive tenders are invited and before the main construction contract is allocated. This means that the strategy will be relatively slow or time consuming. It has been argued that the strategy may fail if any attempt is made to appoint a contractor for the work before the design is complete. They further suggest that such action will probably result in many post-contract changes which could delay the progress of the works and increase costs. Different variants of the traditional system have been developed over the years to correct this problem. It is possible to have an accelerated traditional procurement strategy where some level of design overlaps construction. Another way to achieve this is to implement a two-stage process, or by negotiation.

Awodele and Ogunsemi (2008) conclude that partnering is best considered as a set of collaborative processes. Processes which seek to emphasize the importance of common goals and raise questions such as how such goals are agreed upon, at what level are they specified and how are they articulated (Samson, Reneke & Wiecek, 2009). Essentially, partnering is a set of collaborative processes rather than simply a form of a relationship (Xu, Yeung, Chan, Chan, Wang and Ke, 2010). It is a co-operative arrangement based on mutual objectives and increased efficiency through shared resources, open communications and continuous improvement (Zou, Wang and Fang, 2008). Most importantly, it is a long-term commitment between two or more organizations for the purposes of achieving specific business objectives by maximizing the effectiveness of each participant's resources (Kwah, Chih & Ibbs, 2009). This requires changing traditional relationships to fit within a shared culture, disregarding organizational boundaries (Meunier & Quinet, 2010). Saussier Staropoli and Yvrande-Billon (2009) contend that the relationship must be based on commitment that is the commitment must come from top management since a jointly-developed partnership charter is not a contract but a symbol of commitment. It must also be based on equity that is all participants' interests are considered in creating mutual goals and this is to satisfy each participant's requirements for a successful project by utilizing win/win thinking (Zou, Zhang & Wang, 2007). It must also be based on trust because teamwork is not possible where there is cynicism about the motives of others. Sears, Sears and Clough (2008) indicate that through the development of personal relationships and communication about each participant's risks and goals, there is a better level of understanding. Wang, Li, Deng, Li and Cai (2007) stress that with understanding comes trust and with trust comes the possibility for a synergistic relationship. Lastly, Xenidis and Angelides (2005) recommend that the relationship must be based on the development of mutual goals/objectives: at a partnering workshop the participants identify all respective goals for the project in which their interests overlap. These jointly-developed and mutually agreed goals of each party limit escalation of costs and require review periods for contracts (Dada, 2010).

From the proceeding premises, Makovsek (2013) argue that procurement strategies such as Alliancing, Prime Contracting, Joint Venture and Public Private Partnership (PPP)/Private Finance Initiative (PFI) (although they do not have the same legal connotations) are al contracting relationships that are based on partnering principles that are currently being used in one form or another worldwide. Table 2 presents the differences between traditional and collaborative project procurement systems.

A shift from traditional procurement to the collaborative systems is justified from the benefits of the latter as narrated by Chan, Chen, Messner and Chua (2005). These benefits include:- reduction in costs and time of project implementation, establishment of favorable and less adversarial relationships, risk sharing, operational cost savings, increased implementation speed, construction projects cost savings, quality improvement, access to skills, experience and new technology, improved design, increased understanding of parties, increased customer satisfaction, enhanced economic growth of a nation, facilitate creative and innovative solutions, true costing and true value, enhanced facility maintenance, improved return on resources, increased revenue generation for national development, improved administration, improved financing options and reduced risk exposure etc.

Table 2. Differences between traditional and collaborative procurement system

Type of Issue	Traditional System	Collaborative System
Atmosphere.	Win-lose attitude. Adversarial problem solving. Formal, contractual relations. Frequent contract claims.	Equal partner attitude. Join problem solving. Cooperative, teamwork environment. Few contract claims.
Relationship.	Project-by-project contracts. Independent project teams. Risks transferred.	Long –term contracts. Joint project teams. Risks shared.
Barriers.	Continuous improvement discouraged through short term contracts. Only essential information shared. Limited cost discussions due to competitive advantage.	Continuous improvement required, or at least encouraged. All useful information shared. Cost and profits freely discussed.

Source: (Kloppenborg, 2009)

Procurement Process Under PPP Projects

The second most important stage in the procurement and contractual design choice phase is the procurement process. In this stage, the procurement process consists of many steps. The first step is procurement planning which according to appropriation law, no government agency can spend until the budget is appropriated by the legislature and apportioned by the central budget office. However, since PPP procurement is a long and time-consuming process, contract planning should begin as soon as the PPP project is identified, preferably well in advance of the fiscal year in which contract award is necessary. According to Anvuur, Kumaraswamy and Mahesh (2011), this can best be done by forming a team consisting of all those who will be responsible for significant aspects of the procurement, such as contracting, fiscal, legal, and technical personnel; coordinating with and securing the concurrence of user departments in all planning; consulting requirements and logistics personnel who determine type, quality, quantity, and delivery requirements; and establishing standard acquisition plan formats, if desired, suitable to agency needs. Rakic and Radjenovic (2011) argue that the purpose of planning is to ensure that the procurement agents meet the agency's needs in the most effective, economical, and timely manner. Kwak, Chih and Ibbs (2009) recommend that knowledge gained from prior acquisitions be used to further refine requirements and acquisition strategies.

Although the procurement planning should start well in advance of the fiscal year in which contract award is necessary, the real procurement action will not commence until the user agency prepares and forwards a procurement request (PR) to the central procurement office. According to Zitron (2006), the purpose of a PR is to provide the procurement professional (or contract specialist or contracting officer) with the information and approvals necessary for initiating procurement. When preparing the PR, user departments should consult with the procurement staff (Marques, 2008a). The more the user department consults with procurement professionals, the more precise the document will be. A procurement that starts with a defective PR is likely to be troublesome at some point in the process. For example, if a single source acquisition is initiated without justification and approvals, the action may later be protested and the entire process disrupted and delayed. Other consequences of a deficient PR might include: need to cancel a solicitation because of improper approvals or lack of funds, failure to order an economic quantity and failure to include price-related evaluation factors in the solicitation.

Chiu and Bosher (2005) contends that it is recommendable to do a market research before developing new requirements documents for an acquisition by user agencies, before soliciting offers for acquisitions with an estimated value in excess of the simplified acquisition threshold, and before soliciting offers for acquisitions with an estimated value less than the simplified acquisition threshold when adequate information is not available and the circumstances justify its cost (El-Sayegh, 2008). The extent of market research and analysis will vary depending on the urgency, value, and complexity of the proposed acquisition (Zhang & AbouRisk, 2006).

In preparing the requirements documents, the public partner may select from existing requirements documents, modify or combine existing requirements documents, or create new requirements documents to meet agency needs. To demonstrate that an item has achieved commercial market acceptance, the criteria in the solicitation should reflect the minimum need of the agency; relate to an item's performance and intended use, not an off error's capability; and include consideration of items supplied satisfactorily under recent or current contracts for the same or similar items. Ankrah, Proverbs and Debrah (2009) remind that requirements documents include the specifications or statements of work and related elements of the PR. The procurement professional may accept requirements documents proposed by the requiring activities "as is" or recommend improvements. According to Thai (2007), a good specification contains the following elements: identifies a minimum requirement; allows for maximum competition (competitive bids); identifies the test methods to be used to verify compliance with the requirement; contributes to obtaining best value at the lowest possible cost using a fair, equitable, and transparent (easy for the public to see and understand) contract award process.

Another important step in the procurement process is creating an evaluation team and procedure and developing evaluation criteria. The goal of the procurement is to achieve the "best value" for the user agency in terms of performance, delivery time, and cost while ensuring that all firms submitting offers are treated in a fair and equitable manner (Marques, 2008b). The discussion in this section deals primarily with solicitations for competitive proposals, rather than sealed bidding. The procedures are much simpler in sealed bidding, where there is a public bid opening, determination of lowest responsive, responsible bidder, and award on that basis.

PPP Tendering

There are three major steps in PPP tendering process. These are prequalification, evaluation and award. According to Zhang (2005a), there are some methods which can be applied for supplier prequalification and other ones that can be used in the final awarding. Wang and Dai (2010) classifies four commonly used prequalification methods: binary simple scoring and multi-attribute methods. These methods are used also for assessing tenders of pre-qualified bidders. As regards the bid evaluation, Wang and Dai (2010) reports some methods from practice: lowest price or shortest period, Kepnoe-Tregoe method and Least Present Value of Revenues (LPVR). According to the first case, the awarded concessionaire is the one asking for the lowest price for carrying out the project or the shortest concession period. This is an approach similar to that used in traditional procurement, but it is strongly criticized by many scholar for not taking in account non-price factors in the project. Kepnoe-Tregoe technique (Torta, 2005) is based on the distinction between must and want criteria. The former are "on-off" criteria: all proposals not satisfying all musts are rejected. The remaining bids are evaluated on want criteria: a committee chooses the sponsor best meeting these requirements. The limit of this method is the discretionary power of the decision makers in distinguishing must and wants factors. The LPVR concept consists in awarding the bidder with the lowest price and letting her operate the concession until the budget value of the project (previously decided by the public client) is obtained (To & Ozawa, 2007).

In the simple scoring, each criterion is assigned a maximum achievable score and each bid is assigned a score ranging from 0 to the maximum achievable for each criterion. The awarded bid is the one with the highest sum of scores on all criteria. According the NPV method, the project is awarded to the bidder with the lowest NPV of the overall required toll during the concession (Costantino, Pellegrino& Sciancalepore, 2011). NPV can be used together with scoring method for the qualitative evaluation of the bid or after the exclusion of bids violating mandatory requirements (binary method). Instead, in the multi-attribute analysis, criteria are grouped in packages and sub-packages, each of which having its own weight. The bid with the best weighted sum score is awarded. As regards the two envelope method, technical proposal seals are firstly opened and bid are ranked against non-price criteria. Then economical price envelopes are open: the best technical-ranked bid within the Governmental budget is awarded. The choice of the method is influenced by the complexity of the project: binary, simple-scoring and two-envelope methods well suits to small-sized and simple projects, while NPV is a valid choice for projects with proven technologies and, finally, Kepner-Tregoe analysis better fits to complex projects (Doni, 2007).

As regards the application of such techniques, Kepner-Tregoe is generally adopted in Hong Kong BOT projects (Zhang, 2005b), while NPV and multi-attribute analysis are used in PFI projects in the United Kingdom (Kwah, Chih, & Ibbs, 2009). Simple scoring technique is adopted in some Italian PPP projects, like, for instance, the Brescia-Milano highway project described by Torta (2005). According to a survey of Zhang (2005a), among these, NPV and multi-attribute analysis are the most used and the most recommended methods. Table 3 lists the described techniques by practitioners for prequalification of bidders and bid evaluation.

Besides the methods used by practitioners, some other proposals can be found in the literature. Rudzianskaite, Apanaviciene and Butauskas (2010) suggest an evaluation procedure based on TOPSIS (Technique for Order Performance by Similarity to Ideal Solution): even if the procedure is addressed to the choice among different projects, it could be applied to the evaluation of different bids for the same project. In addition to this, Costantino, Pellegrino and Sciancalepore (2011) propose a technique based on evaluating different bids according to different stakeholders' perspective: the convenience of each of them is evaluated by means of an appropriate indicator. Finally, Zhang (2009) proposes the adoption of

Table 3. Methods for bidder pre-qualification and bid evaluations used by contracting authorities

	Significant Methods
Prequalification	• Binary method • Simple scoring • Multi-attribute methods
Bid evaluation	• Simple scoring • NPV • Multi-attribute analysis • Two envelope method • NPV+simple scoring • Binary method + NPV • Lowest price • Shortest concession period • Kepnoe-Tregoe technique • Least Present Value of Revenues

Source: (Wang & Dai, 2010)

a fuzzy logic system for his best value concessionaire selection, based on four groups of criteria defined by the same author and illustrated in the following section.

According to Carbonara, Gunnigan, Pellegrino and Sciancalepore (2011), many authors have proposed different set of criteria for choosing the best among the candidate sponsors for a PPP project. Also in this case, some authors focused on prequalification criteria, while many else proposed criteria to be satisfied for the final awarding. These are illustrated in Table 4.

Table 4. Criteria for bid evaluations

	Significant Criteria	Selected Literature
Financial and economical criteria	• Sound financial analysis • Reasonable source and structure of funds • Innovation of financing method • Net present value •Tariff/toll setting up and adjustment mechanism • Ability to address commercial risk (e.g., supply and demand risks) • Minimal financial risks to the client • Internal rate of return • Financial strength of the participants in the project company • Financial guarantee • Total investment schedule • Concession period •Strong financial commitments from shareholders • Pay-Back Period • Profitability Index	Zhang (2005a), Rudzianskaite, Apanaviciene & Butauskas (2010
Technical criteria	• Qualifications and experiences of key design and construction personnel • Experience in similar projects •Conforming to client's requirements • Competencies of designer/sub-designers • Contractor/subcontractors •Conforming to design requirements • Construction programs and abilities to meet them •Design and construction quality control schemes • Use of advanced technologies • Maintainability • Design life • Design standard • Quality management and assurance systems	Zhang (2005a), Wang, Deng, Li & Cai (2007)
Safety, Health, and Environmental Criteria	•Qualifications/experience of relevant personnel •Management system of safety, health and environment •Conformance to laws and regulations •Construction/demolition waste disposal • Control of air and water pollution • Past environmental performance • Protection of items of cultural/archeological values •Management safety accountability • Noise reduction and dust reduction	Wang, Deng, Li & Cai (2007), Zhang (2005a), Rudzianskaite, Apanaviciene & Butauskas (2010)
Social Criteria	• Importance of the project for public transport	Rudzianskaite, Apanaviciene & Butauskas (2010)
Managerial Criteria	• Project management skills •Constitution of the management, their qualification and experience •Coordination system within the consortium • Success rate of cooperation among private consortium • Leadership and allocation of responsibilities in the consortium •Effective project controlling system • Working relationship among participants	Zhang (2005a), Wang, Deng, Li & Cai (2007)

Source: (Carbonara, Gunnigan, Pellegrino & Sciancalepore, 2011)

As regards the prequalification, Zhang (2005b) proposes 11 requirements to meet. Some of them are financial, like the financial report of companies taking part to the consortium, used sources and debt/equity ratio. Other ones are concerned with the meeting of legal requirements, like details of pending or threatened proceedings. Another important subset of criteria is that of the experience requirements: in particular past similar work done by competitors, their current workload, their advisors' experience, their experience in managing PPP projects (Andres & Guasch, 2008). Finally, other prequalification criteria are the management structure of the consortium, the technical, operational and financial capabilities, quality, health and safety requirements and meeting and presentation of consortia. While the prequalification phase is simply based on the qualifications and the capabilities of the candidates, the awarding phase aims at assessing the specific features of the offers.

Zhang (2005a) has found 83 criteria for the private partner selection. He divided them in four categories: financial (26), technical (26), health, safety and environmental (15), managerial (16). The author interviewed public practitioners, private practitioners and academics and found that the most important criteria are the financial and the technical one for all of them. No significant differences could be found among the assessment of the different interviewed groups. A similar but more synthetic criteria classification is that proposed by Wang, Li, Deng, Li and Cai (2007): they proposed 18 criteria for the private partner, whose five are about the financial issues, four determine the ability to design, building, managing and operating, four are about health, safety and environment issues and the remaining are classified as "other factors". Finally, Rudzianskaite, Apanaviciene and Butauskas (2010) propose a set of seven sustainability indices regarding road projects: four of them are economical (Net Present Value, Internal Rate of Return, Pay-Back Period, Profitability Index), two of them are environmental (noise reduction and dust reduction) while the last one is a social factor (importance of the project for public transport).

Kwah, Chih and Ibbs (2009) point out that a well structured tendering process is the base for minimizing tendering costs and encouraging competition. Meunier and Quinet (2010) counsel contracting authorities should design opportunely the tendering process, in order to maximize their outcome. In accomplishing this, it is important to keep in mind three important facts (Saussier, Staropoli & Yvrande-Billon, 2009). First is the procedure to follow in the tender as different phases can form the PPP tendering process, but some of them can be missing in some cases. Secondly, there are different awarding methods used in real projects. Lastly, due to the complexity of such projects, most of the cited awarding methods are assessing different factors: consequently, it is important to provide a collection of the used evaluation criteria.

There is a wide literature comparing negotiation with auction as exclusive tendering procedure: nevertheless, these contributions do not express a clear preference of a procedure over the other one (Saussier, Staropoli & Yvrande-Billon, 2009). Saussier, Saussier, Staropoli and Yvrande-Billon (2009) state that in PPP, a final negotiation phase after the tender evaluation is useful because it allows joining the flexibility needed in such complex project with the rigor given by the tendering mechanism. In order to provide contracting authorities guidelines to follow for designing PPP tenders, Doni (2007) compares three kinds of procedures: the negotiation, the auction and the competitive negotiation procedures. In absence of collusion among one bidder and the public agent, the competitive negotiation gives a higher expected value to the Government than other methods and negotiation is preferable to competitive auction, especially if the public negotiation power is high and the bidder is quite reliable. In such a situation, competitive tendering can work better than negotiation only if the suppliers' market is widely competitive. Otherwise, if there is a strong probability of having a corrupt public agent, auction determines a better value for Government. The power of the negotiation phase is affirmed also by Torta (2005), who underlines that, if negotiation phase had been used the BOT project for the Milano-Brescia highway in Italy; better final conditions could have been obtained by the public counterpart.

Wang and Dai (2010) identify five different kinds of procedures that can be used in PPP tenders. These procedures are open competitive tendering, invited tendering, registered lists, project-specific prequalification and short listing and negotiated tendering. Among these, open competitive tendering is the most used consisting of the phases of request for prequalification, prequalification, invitation to tenders, tender evaluation and short listing, negotiation with shortlisted tenders and selection of best tender and award. To and Ozawa (2007) explain the aims of each of these phases in tendering. Prequalification of tenders aims at reducing the number of interested tenders to a shortlist, which consists only of reputable and experienced tenders, which are able to take over project risks. In this phase also unnecessary tendering costs of weaker bidders are avoided. The evaluation tenders stage consists in the selection of one or more among qualified bidders. Tenders on the shortlist are invited to submit detailed proposals that are evaluated in accordance with the predefined evaluation criteria. Negotiation with preferred tender stage consists in the negotiation prior to the final awarding with one or a few preferred tenders. At this stage, provisions in agreements are carefully reviewed. Once the agreement is signed, a contract award notice will be published and the contract is implemented.

Kwah, Chih and Ibbs (2009) provide a highlight of the procurement process in PPP projects as illustrated in Figure 1.

Figure 1. PPP Procurement Process
Source: (Kwah, Chih & Ibbs, 2009)

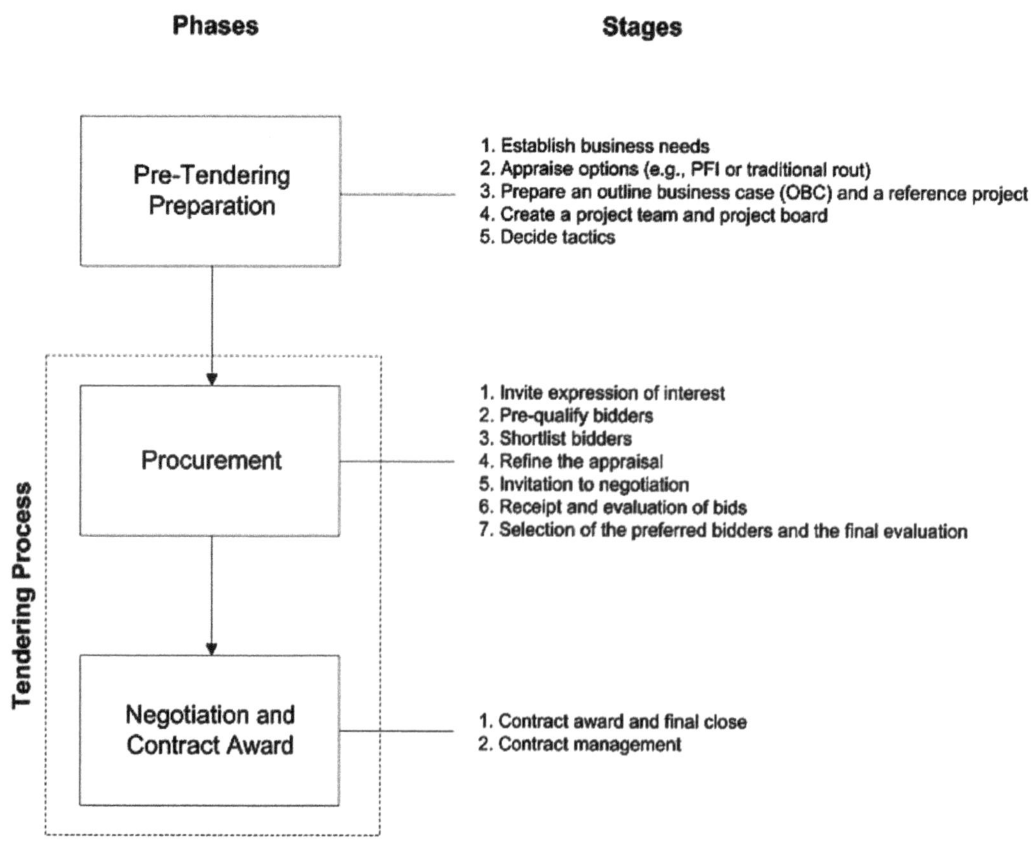

CONSTRUCTION AND SERVICE DELIVERY PHASE

At this phase, the principal stakeholders are the public partners, financiers and the contractor (usually SPV). They are the ones concerned with monitoring of the project as well as responsible for on-time, on-budget, and on-quality delivery and financing. AlSalman and Sillars (2013) reveal that problems often arise because contractors either fail to meet their contracts, resulting in cost overruns, delays, and defects, or are only able to perform their contractual obligations at the cost of significantly reduced profitability of their business. Steijin, Klijn and Edelenbos (2011) suggests that poor original planning and performance management of resources and cost is one of the key drivers of this failure, and this is compounded in many cases by a failure to identify potential issues early in the process. Moreover, according to Chan, Lam, Chan, Cheung and Ke (2010), there is often a focus on the management of individual contracts, which means that the portfolio effects of multiple contracts at the enterprise level are overlooked. Further, Marques (2008a) shows that there is non correlation between contractual obligations and transparency about a contractor's ability to deliver. Zou, Zhang and Wang (2006) contends that management of the relationships between clients, suppliers, and subcontractors can be haphazard, and often this comes back to poor contractor selection and management in the early phases. A consequence can be cost and budget overruns, and these can have a significant impact on a broader economy (Delmon, 2009). This section looks at how to remedy this situation by considering those to be done in the project mobilization stage, project operation stage and project close out and termination phase.

Project Mobilization Phase

Carrillo, Robinson, Foale, Anumba and Bouchlaghem (2008) indicates that in between choosing contractor and beginning of construction there is a number of activities which need to be considered. Essentially, effective conduct of these activities requires a life-cycle approach that can alleviate many of negative issues which may arise in the process. Chinyio and Gameson (2009) explain that owners need to design appropriate metrics and processes to measure contractor performance. This should be translated into a proper documentation and log system for tracking progress that allows the owner to get the information they need to manage the contractor effectively (Nguyen & Ogunlana, 2005). This could include a detailed monthly schedule, with measureable key performance indicators (KPIs) linked to the contract. Toor and Ogunlana (2008) suggests that financial risk should be managed and an incentive system established through milestone payments and daily contractor-compliance monitoring. Trafford and Proctor (2006) recommends that professional standards of information storage and flow should be ensured through clear rules on how information should be handled and the interaction required and expected between owner and supplier. According to (Adams, Alistair & Wu, 2006), any slippage from contractual obligations can be planned for within an overall portfolio of obligations and contracts. Cheung and Yiu (2006) advices that often it is helpful to designate a dedicated project risk manager and team with overarching risk responsibility. For each package or area of a project, clear risk owners need to be identified, and daily site meetings should be held to assess progress against targets, slippage, and potential problems (Osipova & Eriksson, 2013). Jui-Sheng and Pramudawardhani (2015) assert that it is in the contractor's responsibility to comply fully with the terms of the agreement so as to take the project on the right track. Moreover, detail schedule, initially drawn up in the planning phase, is to be closely monitored by both parties. The contractor further needs to plan employment and other resource utilities over time (Ismail & Harris, 2014). Generally, during this stage, the key risks for the sponsor or developer are related to contractual default, claims, keeping public political stakeholders aligned, and monitoring for any mismanagement by the contractor (Cheung, E2009). The interface with the contractor is therefore the critical element. However, this phase is all about mitigating risks, and the ability to influence the magnitude of these risks is smaller than during planning (Mert & Chan, 2012).

Project Operation Phase

Andonova (2010) states this is the least complicated phase because there is a steady-state system where good operational practices can address many of the issues. In this phase of a project, asset owners and financiers are the stakeholders insofar as this relates to operation and maintenance (O&M) contractor monitoring, while O&M contractors are responsible for ensuring on-time, on-budget, and on-quality service delivery and financing (Liu & Wilkinson, 2011). In reality, they often fail to meet contractually agreed-upon KPIs for service quality or availability, resulting in delays and increased costs. This can be because incorrect design specifications do not meet contractors' requirements or because of poor forecasting around service load, maintenance cycles, or operating expenses. An inability to adjust to a changed commercial environment through changes in contract terms can also be a factor.

Ng, Wong and Wong (2012) maintains that project owners can reduce and better manage these risks by outsourcing O&M monitoring to avoid in-house restructuring and to allow for the replacement of poorly performing contractors. A design or construction interface with the O&M contractor should be planned and managed early on and the long-term implications of today's design choices evaluated (Raisbeck, Duffield & Xu, 2010). Cooper, Grey, Raymond and Walker (2005) recommend that state-of-the-art forecasting techniques should be applied and KPIs planned under adverse scenarios, including stress testing. Ongoing monitoring and reporting should be established, and the project should allow for operational flexibility by focusing on KPIs rather than operational structure.

According to Jefferies and McGeorge (2008), during the operation phase, there are three key activities in addition to the construction itself: monitor and control, resource management, and documentation and management. Monitor and control covers supervision of, among others, time, cost and quality (Raisbeck & Tang, 2013). The project manager is usually the person who undertakes this management process to keep track of undergoing activities. Koubatis and Schönberger (2005) opine that time, cost and quality are key aspects of each project and hence managing them is an important activity. Time management is used to log actual time spent for execution of certain tasks. It also helps to allocate resources more effectively and control schedule of performing works (Westland, 2006).

Singewar and Deshmukh (2016) propose that the actual schedule and work progress is compared to the schedule drawn up in previous phases. If any discrepancies are detected, a person responsible should take an appropriate action in order to bring the project back into conformance (Crompton, Goulding & Pour, 2014). Keeping track of the time aspect makes it possible to manage other key issues, finances and quality. Cost control is used to record all actual expenses within the project and gives control over a budget and out-of-pocket expenditures (Bygballe, Jahre & Sward, 2010). Whereas quality monitoring is performed in order to deliver what was promised to the client (Westland, 2006), it also controls whether the work performed is in compliance with technical requirements stated in tender documentation (Abbasianjahromi & Rajaie, 2012).

Grimsey and Lewis (2005) make obvious that undertaking the second activity, resource management, results in better project performance. For example, personnel supervision consists of ensuring that workers perform their tasks in a right manner and comply with officially set working hours. Other resources, such as materials or equipment need to be tracked along with personnel. Any irregularity in these matters may negatively impact the schedule, budget or quality, causing delays or cost overruns (Angerer & Hammerschmid, 2005). According to Wang, Li, Deng, Li and Cai (2007), document management is the last activity in the operation phase, but its importance should not be ignored. It treats communication within the project and grandness of other documents. As in previous examples, proper management of this matter will make the project proceed in a timely, cost-effective and quality assurance manner (Yang, Hou & Wang, 2013).

Project Close-Out and Termination Phase

Vidal, Marle and Bocquet (2011) point out that most PPP projects end up at the execution phase where the final product is handed over after being accepted by the client. Performing a project summary requires additional resources, time and money, which investors tend to prefer to spend on new investments instead (Westland, 2006). However, project close-out and termination is important, among others, from a legal perspective (Shrivastava, 2011). For example, before installation works can be considered as completed, there are still activities which must take place. The main ones are final clean up, inspections, handover to the owner and project closure. Westland (2006) suggests the final procedure in the PPP project is to review the project completion. In this step the overall project assessment is performed (Maseko, 2014). It gives possibility to draw conclusions for next projects to improve their performance. All initially planned activities such as budget, schedule or scope are compared with the completed activities to assess how the product was delivered in comparison to the plan (Antoniou, Aretoulis, Konstantinidis & Kalfakakou, 2013). Such a review can be performed some time after the project handover in order to be able to assess all benefits (Westland, 2006).

CONCLUSION

Risks in each phases of a PPP project can never be exhaustive but attempts can be made as in the preceding pages of this chapter. The effectiveness of any attempt to undertake a comprehensive understanding of risks in the PPP project phases depends on an appropriate matching of demand for handling the risks with its antecedent's solutions. Neglect of the grasps of risks in the phases generally does not work for the better course of having a risk-free PPP project and the major issue becomes the decisive stance for risk managers. If partners cannot identify benefits to having a risk-free PPP projects by a fuller understanding of risks in the project phases then little of substance is likely to happen. Thus, the first function of this chapter is not to produce a list of risks in PPP project *per se* but rather to build the capacity of the reader to appreciate the essence of a deeper knowledge of risks in PPP project phases. Furthermore, it is important that the understanding of the risk should be appropriate in order to develop workable solutions to deride their effects. Failure to do so may as a severe brake on a PPP project success. The chapter therefore, helped to appreciate risks at the three most major phases of PPP projects, those are selecting, planning and designing projects phase, procurement and contractual design choice phase and construction/service delivery phase.

REFERENCES

Aaltonen, K., Jaakko, K., & Tuomas, O. (2008). Stakeholder salience in global projects. *International Journal of Project Management, 26*(5), 509–516. doi:10.1016/j.ijproman.2008.05.004

Abbasianjahromi, H., & Rajaie, H. (2012). Developing a project portfolio selection model for contractor firms considering the risk factor. *Journal of Civil Engineering and Management, 18*(6), 879–889. doi :10.3846/13923730.2012.734856

Abels, G. (2007). Citizen involvement in public policy-making: Does it improve democratic legitimacy and accountability? The case of PTA. *Interdisciplinary Information Sciences, 13*(1), 103–116. doi:10.4036/iis.2007.103

Adams, J., Alistair, Y., & Wu, Z. H. (2006). Public private partnerships in China-system, constraints and future prospects. *International Journal of Public Sector Management, 19*(4), 384–396. doi:10.1108/09513550610669202

Akintan, O. A., & Morledge, R. (2013). Improving the collaboration between main contractors and subcontractors within traditional construction procurement. *Journal of Construction Engineering.*

Akintoye, A., & Main, J. (2007). Collaborative relationships in construction: The UK contractors perception. *Engineering, Construction, and Architectural Management, 14*(6), 597–617. doi:10.1108/09699980710829049

Alashwal, A. M., Rahman, H. A., & Beksin, A. M. (2011). Knowledge sharing in the fragmented construction industry: On the hindsight. *Academic Journals Scientific Research And Essays, 6*(7), 1530–1536.

Alderman, N., & Ivory, C. (2007). Partnering in major contracts: Paradox and metaphor. *International Journal of Project Management, 25*(4), 386–393. doi:10.1016/j.ijproman.2007.01.002

Aldoory, L., & Sha, B. L. (2007). The situational theory of publics: Practical applications, methodological challenges, and theoretical horizons. In The future of excellence in public relations and communication management: Challenges for the next generation. Mahwah, NJ: Lawrence Erlbaum.

Alireza, V., Mohammadreza, Y., Zin, R. M., Yahaya, N., & Noor, N. M. (2013). An enhanced multi-objective optimization approach for risk allocation in public–private partnership projects: A case study of Malaysia. *Canadian Journal of Civil Engineering, 41*(2), 164–177. doi:10.1139/cjce-2013-0342

AlSalman, A., & Sillars, D. (2013). *Modeling the effects of sub-optimal risk allocation in the construction industry.* Paper presented at the Engineering Project Organization Conference.

Andersen, P. A., & Spitzberg, B. H. (2010). Myths and maxims of risk and crisis communication. In Handbook of risk and crisis communication. New York: Routledge.

Andonova, L. B. (2010). Public-private partnerships for the earth: Politics and patterns of hybrid authority in the multilateral system. *Global Environmental Politics, 10*(2), 25–53. doi:10.1162/glep.2010.10.2.25

Andres, L., & Guasch, J. L. (2008). Negotiating and Renegotiating PPPs and Concessions. In G. Schwartz, A. Corbacho, & K. Funke (Eds.), *Public Investment and Public-Private Partnership: Addressing Infrastructure Challenges and Managing Fiscal Risks*. International Monetary Fund. doi:10.1057/9780230593992_13

Angerer, D. J., & Hammerschmid, G. (2005). Public private partnership between euphoria and disillusionment. Recent experiences from Austria and implications for countries in transformation. *Romanian Journal of Political Science.*, *5*(1), 129–159.

Ankrah, N. A., Proverbs, D., & Debrah, Y. (2009). Factors influencing the culture of a construction project organization; An empirical investigation. *Engineering, Construction, and Architectural Management*, *16*(1), 26–47. doi:10.1108/09699980910927877

Antoniou, F., Aretoulis, G. N., Konstantinidis, D., & Kalfakakou, G. P. (2013). Complexity in the evaluation of contract types employed for the construction of highway projects. *Procedia: Social and Behavioral Sciences*, *74*(29), 448–458. doi:10.1016/j.sbspro.2013.03.048

Antuchevičiene, J., Turskis, Z., & Zavadskas, E. K. (2006). Modeling renewal of construction objects applying methods of the game theory. *Ukio Technologinis ir Ekonominis Vystymas, 12*(4), 263-268.

Anvuur, A., & Kumaraswamy, M. (2007). Conceptual model of partnering and alliancing. *Journal of Construction Engineering and Management, 133*(3), 225–234. doi:10.1061/(ASCE)0733-9364(2007)133:3(225)

Anvuur, A. M., Kumaraswamy, M. M., & Mahesh, G. (2011). Building Relationally Integrated Value Networks (RIVANS). *Engineering, Construction, and Architectural Management*, *18*(1), 102–120. doi:10.1108/09699981111098711

Apanavičienė, R., & Rudžianskaitė-Kvaraciejienė, R. (2010). *Analysis of evaluation methodologies for public-private partnership (PPP) projects in infrastructure construction.* Paper presented at the 10th international conference on modern building materials, structures and techniques, Vilnus, Lithuania.

Awodele, O. A., Ogunsemi, D. R., & Olabode, J. B. R. (2008). *Private participation in infrastructure (PPI) development in developing economies- The Nigerian experience.* Paper presented at (COBRA) The Construction and Building Research conference of the Royal Institution of Chartered Surveyors, Dublin, Ireland.

Baccarini, D. (2005). *Understanding project cost contingency–A survey.* Paper presented at the Queensland University of Technology (QUT) Research Week International Conference.

Badenfelt, U. (2008). The selection of sharing ratios in target cost contracts. *Engineering, Construction, and Architectural Management*, *15*(1), 54–65. doi:10.1108/09699980810842061

Barlish, K., De Marco, A., & Thaheem, M. J. (2013). Construction risk taxonomy: An international convergence of academic and industry perspectives. *American Journal of Applied Sciences*, *10*(7), 706–713. doi:10.3844/ajassp.2013.706.713

Barratt, M., & Oke, A. (2007). Antecedents of supply chain visibility in retail supply chains: A resource-based theory perspective. *Journal of Operations Management*, *25*(6), 1217–1233. doi:10.1016/j.jom.2007.01.003

Barrett, P. (2008). *Revaluing construction*. Oxford, UK: Blackwell.

Bennet, C., & Cusick, K. (2007). *Risk Appetite: Practical Issues for the Global Financial Services Industry*. Paper presented to the Institute of Actuaries of Australia Biennial.

Bennett, J., & Peace, S. (2006). *Partnering in the construction industry; A code of practice for strategic collaborative working*. Oxford, UK: Butterworth-Heinemann.

Bouder, F., Slavin, D., & Lofstedt, R. E. (2009). *The tolerability of risk: A new framework for risk management*. London: Earthscan.

Boussabaine, A. (2007). *Cost planning of PFI and PPP building projects*. London: Taylor &Francis.

Bresnen, M. (2007). Deconstructing partnering in project based organization; Seven pillars, seven paradoxes and seven deadly sins. *International Journal of Project Management*, *25*(4), 365–374. doi:10.1016/j.ijproman.2007.01.007

Bresnen, M. (2009). Living the dream? Understanding partnering as emergent practice. *Construction Management and Economics*, *27*(10), 923–933. doi:10.1080/01446190902974145

Briscoe, G., & Dainty, A. (2005). Construction supply chain integration: An elusive goal, *Supply Chain Management. International Journal (Toronto, Ont.)*, *10*(4), 319–326.

Burt, S., Davies, K., Dawson, J., & Sparks, L. (2008). Categorizing patterns and processes in retail grocery internationalization. *Journal of Retailing and Consumer Services*, *15*(2), 78–92. doi:10.1016/j.jretconser.2007.05.008

Bygballe, L. E., Jahre, M., & Sward, A. (2010). Partnering relationships in construction: A literature review. *Journal of Purchasing and Supply Management*, *16*(4), 239–253. doi:10.1016/j.pursup.2010.08.002

Carbonara, N., Gunnigan, L., Pellegrino, R., & Sciancalepore, F. (2011). Tendering Procedures in PPP: A Literature Review. In Public private partnerships in Transport: Trends & Theory. Rome: COST Action TU1001.

Carrillo, P., Robinson, H., Foale, P., Anumba, C., & Bouchlaghem, D. (2008). Participation, barriers and opportunities in PFI: The United Kingdom experience. *Journal of Management Engineering*, *24*(3), 138–145. doi:10.1061/(ASCE)0742-597X(2008)24:3(138)

Cartlidge, D. (2010). *Quantity surveyor's pocket book. Elsevier*. Oxford, UK: Butterworth- Heinemann.

Chan, A. P. C., Chan, D. W. M., Fan, L. C. N., Lam, P. T. I., & Yeung, J. F. Y. (2006). Partnering for construction excellence - A reality or myth? *Building and Environment*, *41*(12), 1924–1933. doi:10.1016/j.buildenv.2005.06.026

Chan, A. P. C., Lam, P. T. I., Chan, D. W. M., Cheung, E., & Ke, Y. (2010). Potential obstacles to successful implementation of public private partnerships in Beijing and the Hong Kong Special Administrative Region. *Journal of Management Engineering*, *26*(1), 30–40. doi:10.1061/(ASCE)0742-597X(2010)26:1(30)

Chan, W. T., Chen, C., Messner, J. I., & Chua, D. K. H. (2005). Interface management for Chinas build–operate–transfer projects. *Journal of Construction Engineering and Management*, *131*(6), 645–655. doi:10.1061/(ASCE)0733-9364(2005)131:6(645)

Chen, W. T., & Chen, T. T. (2007). Critical success factors for construction partnering in Taiwan. *International Journal of Project Management*, *25*(5), 475–484. doi:10.1016/j.ijproman.2006.12.003

Cheung, E. (2009). *Developing a best practice framework for implementing Public Private Partnerships (PPP) in Hong Kong* (Unpublished doctoral dissertation). Queensland University of Technology.

Cheung, S. O., & Yiu, T. W. (2006). Are construction disputes inevitable? *Engineering Management, 53*(3), 456–470.

Cheung, S. O., Yiu, T. W., & Chiu, O. K. (2009). The aggressive-cooperative drivers of construction contracting. *International Journal of Project Management, 27*(7), 727–735. doi:10.1016/j.ijproman.2008.09.001

Cheung, Y. K. F., & Rowlinson, S. (2011). Supply chain sustainability: A relationship management approach. *International Journal of Managing Projects in Business, 4*(3), 480–497. doi:10.1108/17538371111144184

Chinyio, E., & Gameson, R. (2009). Private finance initiative in use. In *Policy, Finance, & Management for Public- Private Partnerships, Innovation in the Built Environment*. London: Wiley-Blackwell.

Choi, H., & Mahadevan, S. (2008). Construction project risk assessment using existing database and project-specific information. *Journal of Construction Engineering and Management, 134*(11), 894–903. doi:10.1061/(ASCE)0733-9364(2008)134:11(894)

Chong, E. F., & Huertand, S. S. (2006). Auctions, ex post competition and prices: The efficiency of public-private partnerships. *Annals of Public and Cooperative Economics, 77*(4), 521–554. doi:10.1111/j.1467-8292.2006.00318.x

Clamp, H., Cox, S., & Lupton, S. (2007). *Which contract? Choosing the appropriate building contract* (4th ed.). London: RIBA Publishing.

Cleland, D. I., & Gareis, R. (2006). *Global project management handbook: Planning, organizing, and controlling international projects* (2nd ed.). New York: McGraw- Hill.

Cooke, B., & Williams, P. (2009). *Construction planning, programming and control* (3rd ed.). London: Blackwell Publishing.

Cooper, D. F., Grey, S., Raymond, G., & Walker, P. (2005). *Project risk management guidelines: managing risk in large projects and complex procurements*. Chichester, UK: Wiley.

Costantino, N., Pellegrino, R., & Sciancalepore, F. (2011). Evaluation of different tolling systems for a transportation PPP project. In K. V. Thai (Ed.), *Towards New Horizons in Public Procurement*. Boca Raton, FL: PrAcademics Press.

Covello, V. T. (2010). Strategies for overcoming challenges to effective risk communication. In Handbook of risk and crisis communication. New York: Routledge.

Crompton, L., Goulding, J. S., & Pour, R. F. (2014). Construction partnering: Moving towards the rationalization for a dominant paradigm. Alam Cipta. *International Journal of Sustainable Tropical Design Research and Practice, 7*(1), 57–78.

Dada, J. O. (2010). Strategies for mitigating risk in construction projects. *Risk Management in Construction. Proceedings of the 40th annual general meeting/ conference of the Nigerian Institute of Building*.

Dangerfield, B., Green, S., & Austin, S. (2010). Understanding construction competitiveness: The contribution of system dynamics, construction innovation. *Information Processing & Management, 10*(4), 408–420.

Darnall, R., & Preston, J. M. (2010). *Project management from simple to complex*. London: Flat World Knowledge, Inc.

Davies, P., & Eustice, K. (2005). *Delivering the PPP promise: A review of PPP issues and activity*. London: PricewaterhouseCoopers.

Delmon, J. (2009). Private sector investment in infrastructure: Project finance, PPP projects and risk (2nd ed.). New York: The World Bank and Kluwer Law International.

Dikmen, I., & Birgonol, N. T. (2006). An analytic hierarchy process based model for risk and opportunities assessment of international construction project. *Canadian Journal of Civil Engineering, 33*(1), 58–68. doi:10.1139/l05-087

Dikmen, I., Birgonul, N. T., & Han, S. (2007). Using fuzzy risk assessment to rate cost overrun risk in international construction projects. *International Journal of Project Management, 25*(5), 494–505. doi:10.1016/j.ijproman.2006.12.002

Doni, N. (2007). *A comparison of alternative procedures for the selection of the private partner in PPP projects*. Working Paper Università degli Studi di Firenze.

Drew, J. (2005). Public Private Partnerships – Opportunities and Challenges. *Proceedings of the Conference on Public Private Partnerships – Opportunities and Challenges*.

Eaton, D., Akbiyukli, R., & Dickinson, M. (2006). An evaluation of the stimulants and impediments to innovation within PFI/PPP projects. *Construction Innovation, 6*(2), 63–77. doi:10.1108/14714170610710668

El-Gohary, N. M., Osman, I. I., & El-Diraby, T. E. (2006). Stakeholder management for public private partnerships. *International Journal of Project Management, 24*(7), 595–604. doi:10.1016/j.ijproman.2006.07.009

Engel, E., Fischer, R., & Galetovic, A. (2006). *Renegotiation without Holdup: Anticipating spending and infrastructure concessions*. Cowles Foundation, Discussion Paper No. 1567.

Eriksen, K. S., & Jensen, S. (2010). The cost of second best pricing and the value of risk premium. *Research in Transportation Economics, 30*(1), 29–37. doi:10.1016/j.retrec.2010.10.005

Eriksson, P. E., Dickinson, M., & Khalfan, M. M. A. (2007). The Influence of partnering and procurement on subcontractor involvement and innovation. *Facilities, 25*(5/6), 203–214. doi:10.1108/02632770710742174

Esmaeili, M., & Zeephongsekul, P. (2010). Seller-buyer models of supply chain management with an asymmetric information structure. *International Journal of Production Economics, 123*(1), 146–154. doi:10.1016/j.ijpe.2009.07.016

Firmenich, J. (2011). *Identification of parameters for a quantitative risk allocation model with systematic review*. Paper presented at the Sixth International Structural Engineering and Construction Conference: Modern Methods and Advances in Structural Engineering and Construction, Zurich, Switzerland. doi:10.3850/978-981-08-7920-4_S3-I003-cd

Fischer, K., Leidel, K., Riemann, A., & Wilhelm Alfen, H. (2010). An integrated risk management system (IRMS) for PPP projects. *Journal of Financial Management of Property and Construction*, *15*(3), 260–282. doi:10.1108/13664381011087515

Freeman, R. E. (2010). *Strategic management: a stakeholder approach*. Cambridge, UK: Cambridge University Press. doi:10.1017/CBO9781139192675

Glasbergen P. (2011). Understanding partnerships for sustainable development analytically: the ladder of partnership activity as a methodological tool. *Environmental Policy and Governance, 21*, 1-13.

Green, S., Kumaraswamy, M., & Ofori, G. (2009). *All change in construction: A comparative analysis of construction industry reform in the UK*. Hong Kong: Innovative Construction Research Centre, University of Reading.

Green, S. D., Larsen, G. D., & Kao, C. C. (2008). Competitive strategy revisited: Contested concepts and dynamic capabilities. *Construction Management and Economics*, *26*(1), 63–78. doi:10.1080/01446190701656174

Grimsey, D., & Lewis, M. K. (2005). Are public private partnerships value for money? Evaluating alternative approaches and comparing academic and practitioner views. *Accounting Forum*, *29*(4), 345–378. doi:10.1016/j.accfor.2005.01.001

Ho, S. P. (2006b). Model for financial re-negotiation in public-private partnership projects and its policy implications: Game theoretic view. *Journal of Construction Engineering and Management*, *132*(7), 678–688. doi:10.1061/(ASCE)0733-9364(2006)132:7(678)

Hodge, G. A. (2010). Reviewing public-private partnerships: some thoughts on evaluation, 81– 112. In G. Hodge, C. Greve, & A. Boardman (Eds.), *International Handbook on Public-Private Partnerships*. London: Edward Elgar Cheltenham. doi:10.4337/9781849804691.00012

Holt, G. (2010). Contractor Selection Innovation: Examination of two decades' published research. *Construction Innovation. Information Processing & Management*, *10*(3), 304–328.

Holweg, M., Disney, S., Holmstrom, J., & Smaros, J. (2005). Supply chain collaboration: Making sense of the strategy continuum. *European Management Journal*, *23*(2), 170–181. doi:10.1016/j.emj.2005.02.008

Hong, Y., Chan, W. M., & Chan, P. C. (2012). Exploring the applicability of construction partnering in Mainland China: A qualitative study. *Facilities*, *30*(13/14), 401–414. doi:10.1108/02632771211270603

Ismail, S., & Harris, F. A. (2014). *Challenges in implementing public private partnership (PPP) in Malaysia*. Paper presented at the International Conference on Accounting Studies 2014, Kuala Lumpur, Malaysia.

Jaskowski, P., & Biruk, S. (2011). The method for improving stability of construction project schedules through buffer allocation. *Technological and Economic Development of Economy*, *17*(3), 429–444. doi:10.3846/20294913.2011.580587

Jefferies, M., & McGeorge, D. (2008). Public–private partnerships: A critical review of risk management in Australian social infrastructure projects. *Journal of Construction Procurement*, *14*(1), 66–80.

Jin, Y. (2010). Making sense sensibly in crisis communication: How publics crisis appraisals influence their negative emotions, coping strategy preferences, and crisis response acceptance. *Communication Research*, *37*(4), 522–552. doi:10.1177/0093650210368256

Jui-Sheng, C., & Pramudawardhani, D. (2015). Cross-country comparisons of key drivers, critical success factors and risk allocation for public-private partnership projects. *International Journal of Project Management*, *33*(5), 1136–1150. doi:10.1016/j.ijproman.2014.12.003

Kaplinski, O. (2008a). Development and usefulness of planning techniques and decision making foundations on the example of construction enterprises in Poland. *Technological and Economic Development of Economy*, *14*(4), 492–502. doi:10.3846/1392-8619.2008.14.492-502

Kaplinski, O. (2008b). Usefulness and credibility of scoring methods in construction industry. *Journal of Civil Engineering and Management*, *14*(1), 21–28. doi:10.3846/1392-3730.2008.14.21-28

Kaplinski, O. (2010). Risk analysis of construction projects: from risk identification to contingency timetable. In *Advances and trends in structural engineering, mechanics and computation*. CRS Press.

Kasperson, R. E., & Palmlund, I. (2005). Evaluating risk communication. In The social contours of risk, volume 1: Publics, risk communication and the social amplification of risk. London: Earthscan.

Kloppenborg, T.J. (2009). *Project Management A Contemporary Approach*. International student edition. South-Western Cengage learning.

Kohtamaki, M. (2010). Relationship governance and learning in partnerships. *The Learning Organization*, *17*(1), 47–57. doi:10.1108/09696471011008233

Koubatis, A., & Schönberger, J. Y. (2005). Risk management of complex critical systems. *International Journal of Critical Infrastructure*, *1*(2/3), 195–215. doi:10.1504/IJCIS.2005.006119

Kumaraswamy, M., Ling, F. Y. Y., Anvuur, A. M., & Rahman, M. M. (2007). Targeting relationally integrated teams for sustainable PPPS. *Engineering, Construction, and Architectural Management*, *14*(6), 581–596. doi:10.1108/09699980710829030

Kwah, Y. H., Chih, Y.-Y., & Ibbs, C. W. (2009). Towards a comprehensive understanding of public private partnerships for infrastructure development. *California Management Review*, *51*(2), 51–78. doi:10.2307/41166480

Lam, K. C., Wang, D., Lee, P. T. K., & Tsang, Y. T. (2007). Modeling risk allocation decision in construction contracts. *International Journal of Project Management*, *25*(5), 485–493. doi:10.1016/j.ijproman.2006.11.005

Lambrigger, D.D., Shevchenko, P.V., & Wüthrich, M.V. (2009). The quantification of operational risk using internal data, relevant external data and expert opinions. *Journal of Operational Risk, 2*(3).

Liu, T., & Wilkinson, S. (2011). Adopting innovative procurement techniques: Obstacles and drivers for adopting Public Private Partnerships in New Zealand. *Construction Innovation: Information, Process Management, 11*(4), 452–469.

Love, P., Davis, P., Ellis, J., & Cheung, S. O. (2010). Dispute causation: Identification of pathogenic influences in construction. *Engineering, Construction, and Architectural Management, 17*(4), 404–423. doi:10.1108/09699981011056592

Makovsek, D. (2013). Public-private partnerships, traditionally financed projects, and their price. *Journal of Transport Economics and Policy, 47*(1), 143–155.

Marques, R. (2008a). Comparing private and public performance of Portuguese water services. *Water Policy, 10*(1), 25–42. doi:10.2166/wp.2007.033

Marques, R. (2008b). The yardstick competition regulatory model: Discussing the Portuguese experience. Water Science and Technology. *Water Supply, 8*(5), 541–549. doi:10.2166/ws.2008.108

Maseko, M. (2014). *Analysis of critical success factors for public-private partnerships in infrastructure development in South Africa.* Paper presented at the 6th International Platinum Conference, 'Platinum–Metal for the Future, The Southern African Institute of Mining and Metallurgy.

Matei, L. (2006). Empirical approaches of the public-private partnership in the services of public utility. *Theoretical and Applicative Economics, 10*(505), 3–14.

Maylor, H. (2005). *Project Management.* Edinburgh, UK: Pearson Education.

Mert, A., & Chan, S. (2012). The politics of partnerships for sustainable development. In Public-private partnerships for sustainable development. emergence, influence and legitimacy. Cheltenham, UK: Edward Elgar.

Meunier, D., & Quinet, E. (2010). Tips and pitfalls in PPP design. *Research in Transportation Economics, 30*(1), 126–138. doi:10.1016/j.retrec.2010.10.013

ModuKumshe, H., Badiya Yusuf Magaji, B.Y., & Bani, L.M. (2015). Public-Private Partnership and Nigeria's infrastructural development: A Panacea for Economic Growth. *International Journal of Humanities Social Sciences and Education, 2*(10), 87–98.

Morledge, R., Smith, A., & Kashiwagi, D. T. (2006). *Risk in building procurement.* Oxford, UK: Blackwell Publishing.

Murdoch, J., & Hughes, W. (2008). *Construction Contracts; Law and Management* (4th ed.). London: Taylor & Francis.

Ng, S. T., Wong, Y. M., & Wong, J. M. (2012). Factors influencing the success of PPP at feasibility stage—a tripartite comparison study in Hong Kong. *Habitat International, 36*(4), 423–432. doi:10.1016/j.habitatint.2012.02.002

Nguyen, L. D., & Ogunlana, S. O. (2005). Modeling the dynamics of an infrastructure project. *Computer-Aided Civil and Infrastructure Engineering*, *20*(4), 265–279. doi:10.1111/j.1467-8667.2005.00392

Nystrom, J. (2008). A quasi-experimental evaluation of partnering. *Construction Management and Economics*, *26*(5), 531–541. doi:10.1080/01446190802036144

OECD. (2007). *Integrity in public procurement good practice from A-Z*. London: OECD Organizations for Economic Co-operation and Development.

Ogunsanmi, O. E., Salako, O. A., & Ajayi, O. M. (2011). Risks classification model for design and build projects. *Journal of Engineering, Project, and Production Management*, *1*(1), 46–60.

Osipova, E., & Eriksson, P. E. (2013). Balancing control and flexibility in joint risk management: Lessons learned from two construction projects. *International Journal of Project Management*, *31*(3), 391–399. doi:10.1016/j.ijproman.2012.09.007

Oyegoke, A., Khalfan, M., McDermott, P., Rowlinson, S., & Dickinson, M. (2009). Construction project procurement routes; an in-depth critique. *International Journal of Managing Projects in Business*, *2*(3), 338–354. doi:10.1108/17538370910971018

Pasławski, J. (2010). Risk management using flexibility in construction engineering. *Proc. of the 10th International Conference "Modern Building Materials, Structures and Techniques"*, 489–492.

Phua, F. T. T. (2006). When is construction partnering likely to happen? An empirical examination of the role institutional norms. *Construction Management and Economics*, *24*(6), 615–624. doi:10.1080/01446190500521256

Quiggin, J. (2005). Public-private partnerships: Options for improved risk allocation. *The Australian Economic Review*, *38*(4), 445–450. doi:10.1111/j.1467-8462.2005.00388.x

Radeneck, A. (2008). A sketch-plan for construction of built environment theory. *Building Research and Information*, *36*(3), 269–279. doi:10.1080/09613210801928115

Rafele, C., Hillson, D. A., & Grimaldi, S. (2005). Understanding project risk exposure using the two-dimensional risk breakdown matrix.*Proceedings of the PMI Global Congress 2005 EMEA*.

Raisbeck, P., Duffield, C., & Xu, M. (2010). Comparative performance of PPPs and traditional procurement in Australia. *Construction Management and Economics*, *28*(4), 345–359. doi:10.1080/01446190903582731

Raisbeck, P., & Tang, L. C. (2013). Identifying design development factors in Australian PPP projects using an AHP framework. *Construction Management and Economics*, *31*(1), 20–39. doi:10.1080/01446193.2012.729133

Rakic, B., & Radjenovic, T. (2011). Public-private partnerships as an instrument of new public management. *Facta Universitatis Series: Economics and Organization*, *8*(2), 207–220.

Raz, T., & Hillson, D. (2005). A comparative review of risk management standards. *Risk Management: An International Journal*, *8*(1), 61–76.

Reeves, E. (2008). The practice of contracting in public private partnerships: Transaction costs and relational contracting in the Irish schools sector. *Public Administration*, *86*(4), 969–986. doi:10.1111/j.1467-9299.2008.00743.x

Ross, A. (2011). Supply chain management in an uncertain economic climate: A UK perspective. *Construction Innovation: Information, Process. Management*, *11*(1), 5–13.

Rudzianskaite-Kvaraciejiene, R., Apanaviciene, R., & Butauskas, A. (2010). Evaluation of road investment project effectiveness. *Inzinerine Ekonomika-Engineering Economics*, *21*(4), 368–376.

Sachs, T., Tiong, R. L. K., & Wang, S. Q. (2007). Analysis of political risks and opportunities in public private partnerships PPP in China and selected Asian Countries—Survey results. *Chinese Management Studies*, *1*(2), 126–148. doi:10.1108/17506140710758026

Sadka, E. (2007). Public-private partnerships: A public economics perspective. *CESifo Economic Studies*, *53*(3), 466–490. doi:10.1093/cesifo/ifm013

Sahm, C. (2008). *How much does risk tolerance change?* Finance and Economics Discussion Series, Federal Reserve Board.

Samson, S., Reneke, J. A., & Wiecek, M. M. (2009). A review of different perspectives on uncertainty and risk and an alternative modeling paradigm. *Reliability Engineering & System Safety*, *94*(2), 558–567. doi:10.1016/j.ress.2008.06.004

Sanchez, P. M., & Tijuana-Ensenada, C. (2005). Neural-Risk Assessment System for Construction Projects. *Journal of Construction Engineering and Management*, *103*, 78–83.

Sanda, Y. N., & Anigbogu, N. A. (2016). A conceptual framework for managing risks in public private partnership in Housing Estate Development in Nigeria. *International Journal of Regional Development*, *3*(1), 50–63. doi:10.5296/ijrd.v3i1.8144

Sarmento, J. M. (2010). Do public-private partnerships create value for money for the public sector? The Portuguese experience. *OECD Journal on Budgeting, 1*.

Saussier, S., Staropoli, C., & Yvrande-Billon, A. (2009). Public–private agreements, institutions, and competition: When economic theory meets facts. *Review of Industrial Organization*, *35*(1-2), 1–18. doi:10.1007/s11151-009-9226-z

Sears, S. K., Sears, G. A., & Clough, R. H. (2008). *Construction Project Management, a practical guide to field construction management* (5th ed.). John Wiley & Sons, Inc.

Shrivastava, V. K. (2011). *Public Private Partnerships in road projects: Critical Success Factors in the Indian context*. Paper presented at the Southern African Transport Conference (SATC).

Singewar, M., & Deshmukh, S. S. (2016). Analysis of critical success factors for effective implementation of public private partnership in real estate and infrastructural development- A Compendium Case Study. *Imperial Journal of Interdisciplinary Research*, *2*(8), 204–211.

Stanley, J., & Hensher, D. A. (2008). Delivering partnerships for route bus services: A Melbourne case study. *Transportation Research Part A, Policy and Practice*, *42*(10), 1295–1301. doi:10.1016/j.tra.2008.05.006

Steijin, B., Klijn, E.-H., & Edelenbos, J. (2011). Public private partnerships: Added value by organizational form or management? *Public Administration*, *89*(4), 1235–1252. doi:10.1111/j.1467-9299.2010.01877.x

Tanaka, D. F., Ishida, H., Tsutsumi, M., & Okamoto, N. (2005). Private finance for road projects in developing countries: Improving transparency through VFM risk assessment. *Journal of the Eastern Asia Society for Transportation Studies*, (6): 3899–3914.

Teo, E. A. L., Ling, F. Y. Y., & Chong, A. F. W. (2005). Framework for project managers to manage construction safety. *International Journal of Project Management*, *23*(4), 329–341. doi:10.1016/j.ijproman.2004.09.001

Thai, K. V. (2007). *Introduction to public procurement* (2nd ed.). Herndon, VA: National Institute of Governmental Purchasing, Inc.

Thomas, A. V., Kalidindi, S. N., & Ganesh, L. S. (2006). Modeling and assessment of critical risks in BOT road projects. *Construction Management and Economics*, *24*(4), 407–424. doi:10.1080/01446190500435275

Thomas, A. V., Kalidindi, S. N., & Ganesh, L. S. (2006). Modeling and assessment of critical risks in BOT road projects. *Construction Management and Economics*, *24*(4), 407–424. doi:10.1080/01446190500435275

Thomas, G., & Thomas, M. (2005). *Construction partnering & integrated team working*. Oxford, UK: Blackwell Publishing Ltd. doi:10.1002/9780470759660

To, N. T., & Ozawa, K. (2007). Evaluation of procurement systems for BOT infrastructures in Asian countries. *Proceedings of the International Symposium on Social Management.*

Torta, F. (2005). The Concession Through a Bid – The New Brescia – Milan Highway: A Case Study. *Research in Transportation Economics*, *15*, 135–143. doi:10.1016/S0739-8859(05)15011-2

Trafford, S., & Proctor, T. (2006). Successful joint venture partnerships: Public Private partnerships. *International Journal of Public Sector Management*, *19*(2), 117–129. doi:10.1108/09513550610650392

Ulmer, R. R., Sellnow, T. L., & Seeger, M. W. (2011). *Effective crisis communication: Moving from crisis to opportunity* (2nd ed.). Thousand Oaks, CA: Sage Publications.

van Wyk, R., & Akintoye, A. (2007). Project risk management practice: The case of a South African utility company. *International Journal of Project Management*, *23*, 584–590.

Vidal, L. A., Marle, F., & Bocquet, J. C. (2011). Measuring project complexity using the analytic hierarchy process. *International Journal of Project Management*, *29*(6), 718–727. doi:10.1016/j.ijproman.2010.07.005

Vining, A., & Boardman, A. (2008a). Public-private partnerships. Eight rules for governments. *Public Works Management & Policy*, *13*(2), 149–161. doi:10.1177/1087724X08323843

Vining, A., & Boardman, A. (2008b). Public-private partnerships in Canada: Theory and evidence. *Canadian Public Administration*, *51*(1), 9–44. doi:10.1111/j.1754-7121.2008.00003.x

Wang, D., & Dai, D. (2010). Research on the concessionaire selection for Build- Operate- Transfer projects.*Proceedings of International Conference on Management and Service Science (MASS)*. doi:10.1109/ICMSS.2010.5575990

Wang, W.-X., Li, Q.-M., Deng, X.-P., Li, L.-H., & Cai, Y. (2007). Selecting optimal private-sector partner in infrastructure projects under PPP model.*Proceedings of International Conference on Management Science and Engineering (ICMSE 2007)*.

Westland, J. (2006). *Project management life cycle: A complete step-by-step methodology for initiating planning executing and closing the project*. Kogan Page Limited.

Wood, G., & Ellis, R. (2005). Main contractor experiences of partnering relationships on UK construction projects. *Construction Management and Economics*, *23*(3), 317–325. doi:10.1080/0144619042000287714

Xenidis, Y., & Angelides, D. (2005). The financial risks in build-operate-transfer projects. *Construction Management and Economics*, *23*(4), 431–441. doi:10.1080/01446190500041552

Xu, Y., Yeung, J. F. Y., Chan, A. P. C., Chan, D. W. M., Wang, S. Q., & Ke, Y. (2010). Developing a risk assessment model for PPP projects in ChinaA fuzzy synthetic evaluation approach. *Automation in Construction*, *19*(7), 929–943. doi:10.1016/j.autcon.2010.06.006

Yang, J.-B., Yang, C.-C., & Kao, C.-K. (2010). Evaluating schedule delay causes for private participating public construction works under the Build-Operate-Transfer model. *International Journal of Project Management*, *28*(6), 569–579. doi:10.1016/j.ijproman.2009.10.005

Yang, Y., Hou, Y., & Wang, Y. (2013). On the Development of Public Private Partnerships in Transitional Economies; An Explanatory Framework. *The American Society for Public Administration*, *73*(2), 301–310. doi:10.1111/j.1540-6210.2012.02672.x

Yescombe, E. R. (2007). *Public-Private Partnerships: Principles of Policy and Finance*. Oxford, UK: Butterworth-Heinemann. doi:10.1016/B978-075068054-7.50025-3

Yeung, J. F. Y., Chan, A. P. C., Chan, D. W. M., & Li, L. K. (2007). Development of a Partnering Performance Index (PPI) for construction projects in Hong Kong: A Delphi Study. *Construction Management and Economics*, *25*(12), 1219–1237. doi:10.1080/01446190701598673

Yiu, K. T. W., & Cheung, S. O. (2007). Behavioral transition: A framework for construction conflict-tension relationships. *Engineering Management*, *54*(3), 498–505.

Zavadskas, E. K., Turskis, Z., & Tamošaitien, X. J. (2010). Risk assessment of construction projects. *Journal of Civil Engineering and Management*, *16*(1), 33–46. doi:10.3846/jcem.2010.03

Zenonas, T., Gajzler, M., & Dziadosz, A. (2012). Reliability, risk management, and contingency of construction processes and projects. *Journal of Civil Engineering and Management*, *18*(2), 290–298. doi:10.3846/13923730.2012.672931

Zhang, X. (2005a). Criteria for selecting the private-sector partner in public– private partnerships. *Journal of Construction Engineering and Management, 131*(6), 631–644. doi:10.1061/(ASCE)0733-9364(2005)131:6(631)

Zhang, X. (2005b). Critical success factors for public–private partnerships in infrastructure development. *Journal of Construction Engineering and Management, 131*(1), 71–80. doi:10.1061/(ASCE)0733-9364(2005)131:1(71)

Zhang, X. (2009). Best value concessionaire selection through a fuzzy logic system. *Expert Systems with Applications, 36*(4), 7519–7527. doi:10.1016/j.eswa.2008.09.039

Zhang, X., & AbouRisk, S. S. (2006). Relational concession in infrastructure development through public-private partnerships. *Proceedings of the CIB W89 International Conference on Building Education and Research.*

Zhang, X. Q. (2005c). Paving the Way for Public–Private Partnerships in Infrastructure Development. *Journal of Construction Engineering and Management, 131*(1), 71–80. doi:10.1061/(ASCE)0733-9364(2005)131:1(71)

Zimmermann, J., & Eber, W. (2014). Consideration of risk in PPP-projects. *Business. Management in Education, 12*(1), 30–46.

Zitron, J. (2006). Public-private partnership projects: Towards a model of contractor bidding decision-making. *Journal of Purchasing and Supply Management, 12*(2), 53–62. doi:10.1016/j.pursup.2006.04.002

Zou, P., & Fang, D. (2008). A life-cycle risk management framework for PPP infrastructure projects. *Journal of Financial Management of Property and Construction, 13*(2), 123–142. doi:10.1108/13664380810898131

Zou, P., Zhang, G., & Wang, J.-Y. (2006). *Identifying key risks in construction projects: Life cycle and stakeholder perspectives.* Sydney: Faculty of Build Environment, University of New South Wales.

Zou, P., Zhang, G., & Wang, J.-Y. (2007). Understanding the key risks in construction projects in China. *International Journal of Project Management, 25*(6), 601–614. doi:10.1016/j.ijproman.2007.03.001

Zou, P. X. W., Wang, S., & Fang, D. (2008). A life-cycle risk management framework for PPP infrastructure projects. *Journal of Financial Management of Property and Construction, 13*(2), 123-142.

Chapter 4
Risk Sharing in a Partnership

ABSTRACT

Risk sharing is an activity which integrates recognition of risk, awareness of a party's capability, risk assessment, and developing strategies to accept and own the risk using managerial resources. Some traditional risk sharing philosophy is focused on taking risk of a lesser costs to the risk taker. Proper risk sharing, on the other hand, focuses on taking and acceptable risk within the capacity of the party to manage. Objective of proper risk sharing is to reduce the possibility the risk taker would not perform the part of the bargain. It may refer to numerous types of measures a partner would undertake to ensure the risk taken does not prevent the partner from performing part of the bargain. The chapter describes the different steps in risk sharing process which methods are used in the different steps, and provides some examples for risk acceptance and risk sharing that can be pursued by a partner.

Don't be afraid to take a big step when one is indicated. You can't cross a chasm in two small steps. - David Lloyd George

INTRODUCTION

There is a growing literature on risk in PPP studies and practices but there is little agreement on what the term means. What causes it as well as its effects on PPP projects is hardly known. Three distinct views on risks can be conveniently distinguished as follows: contractual perspectives which deals with internal and external unforeseen occurrences that tend to derail contractual obligations in the PPP projects and focuses on real execution of the contract as agreed; construction perspective that emphasizes actual implementation of the PPP project and actualizing PPP agreements and inscribed in paper; and operational perspectives which is concerned with the rivalries between implementers and beneficiaries and a power struggle the parties often engage in that derails the PPP project implementation process. Given the diversity of thinking on the issues, it is not surprising that the academic and policy debates on risks in PPPs become so convoluted and emotional. There is also little sign of consensus being reached over practical guidelines for policy makers. The inconclusive state of academic and policy debates means

DOI: 10.4018/978-1-5225-2503-5.ch004

that the concept of risk remains somewhat elusive particularly at the PPPs-level. Furthermore, the connection between public and private level PPPs still seems vague and there appear to be contradictory views in its policy implications. Against this backdrop, this chapter assesses the concept of risk and risk management to enhance a better understanding of the concepts and apply them to the world of PPPs. The main concern of the chapter is to uncover the innermost 'egg-shell' of risk rather than gleaning from the periphery. It aims at a broader and detailed understanding of risk so no iota of doubt remains in the mind. This would act as a benchmark for a fuller grasps of the different risk-topics discussed in the proceeding chapters. Nonetheless, suffice to note that different risk situations present quite different hazards so different modes of safety control and risk management need to be devised. In a public private partnership arrangement, an inverse relationship is found between the accepted norms of handling risks than what is done in practice. Quite sizeable methodologies have been developed over the years, to handle risk in public private partnership.

The chapter begins by examining risk and risk management separately. It then applies the concept of strategy, notably, in the context of appreciating an important distinguishing feature of this book from other works on risk management in PPPs. Emanating from this understanding, the chapter proceeds to chart out and analyze a roadmap for effective risk management. This shall be handled in manner of assessment, designing the risk sharing networks, and implementation. Having highlighted the roadmap, the chapter focuses on those necessary conditions which must be in existence for proper risk sharing to take place. Then it goes on to discuss appropriate conditions in the glow of strong capabilities of the public partners, good capabilities of the private partner, and sustained private partners' commitment. These are intended to improve a better understanding of the central thesis of this book. A conclusion will close the chapter in the end as references consulted will also be listed down.

RISK: BASIC CONCEPTS

Mere entry into a PPP arrangement which is perfectly of a contractual nature, suggests a range of risks that must be dealt with (Alderman & Ivory, 2007). A contract is a risky business in that whatever has been agreed on must be executed as agreed and even to the letter. Unfortunately, unforeseen future occurrences often derail the execution of obligations as inscribed in the contract (Loizou & French, 2012). Hence, like any other form of contract, PPP is bound to fall a victim to risks. Moreover, parties to a PPP arrangement often times tend to ignore risk and enter into a contract with all the imperfections embodied in the contracts in form of uncountable risks (Assaf & Al-Hejji, 2006). While the parties may be contended of having entered into such an agreement to leverage their interests, the tendency of under looking the crucial importance of digging deep in all those risks contained in the project, is the epitome of failure of the agreement they would enter into (Aldoory, Kim, & Tindall, 2010). Somewhat the parties' emphases have tended to shy away from the critical issues which would affect the actual implementation of the PPP arrangement.

In spite of this differing indifference, notions of risk and risk management are real in a PPP arrangement (Ammar, Berman & Sataporn, 2007). Their manifestations are seen in the failure of hundreds of PPP projects that have either stalled or remained incomplete. This shows that the reality of risk and how best to manage it underpinned by a common sharing framework between parties to a PPP arrangement, which is practically lacking in most PPP is very worrying. For this reason, the capabilities to management risk must be demonstrated by both parties to the PPP arrangement (Bloomfield, 2006). The devastating effects of risk are very real especially when they occur. And this is probably why the idea of PPP has its origin, to pool risks so that parties are able to share in equal proportion as they strive to attain a goal. Furthermore, Kolhatkar and Dutta (2013) argue that the presence of some PPPs failures is an indication of risks. They continue to argue that this should provide a significant look out for answers by the parties. Each parties has a role to play in ensuring that the risk does not in any way hammer in negative connotations as to make the PPP arrangement to collapse on its weight (Carbonara, Costantino & Pellegrino, 2013).

In line of related praise, McKim (2005) suggests that while some parties do take risk for granted, that they enter into a PPP arrangement would mean nothing. He argues that the most important determinant of a successful PPP is the complete way in which risk is handled. Smith, Merna and Jobling (2006) go on to propose a new approach, a generalized but concretized one, and offer insights into effectiveness and efficiency of risk management as a most noble tool to ensure PPP projects succeeds. Others suggest that the limited and inadequate resources coupled with high incidences of risks occurrences in the public sector are to blame. Palermo (2014) argues that service delivery in the public sector is affected by various risks occurring in different forms and types which can constrain the course of effective and efficient service delivery. According to Bock and Trück (2011), some partners neglect this critical reality making it difficult for a PPP project to succeed.

Shen, Platten and Deng (2006) calls for proper risk management in a PPP arrangement is simple and for all purpose very relevant and consistent. It highlights the relevance of risk-free atmosphere for PPP project to thrive. It also emphasizes the need to have a contractual commitment bound to be successful. It takes into consideration the best outcome which can be derived from a risk-free PPP project's implementation. Berg (2010) translates these ideas into another level by suggesting that parties and key stakeholders in a PPP arrangement must be brought on board to identify and develop measures to overcome them. These have to have the gut to sit, deliberate and make concrete decisions in a manner that would lead to the enjoyment of the quality of services desired by the beneficiaries (Bracey & Moldovan, 2006). This is particularly pertinent in today's ever changing demands due to technological advancement and globalization. In the midst of failing quality service delivery, it would the defining tool for the seemingly serious barriers of lack of finance and risks existence, a PPP arrangement can better be accelerated and progressively increased through a well designed risk management strategy. Quiggin (2005) links the performance of a PPP arrangement to raising the level of awareness about all kinds of risk through proper management. It's through proper risk management that the parties that adhered to the empirically agreed obligations to be fulfilled by each of them to see the successful end of the arrangement. This last point is particular important for consensus purpose among the parties. It raises their levels of awareness and the possible role-play they can engage themselves in.

This leads directly to the issue of defining the key precepts of this book: risk, risk management, and strategy. Defining these notions necessary for a fuller grasps of the content of this work, gives a directing link to appreciate the existence of risk, how it can act as a bottleneck in achieving a PPP project end goals as well as the medium of outdoing these risks. A concise definition of these notions can be gleaned from the following sub-sections. In each of them, however, some explanations shall be provided. This is intended to raise a conscious awareness of the concept in its fuller. It is based detailed analysis, but more vitally on their relations to the thesis of this book and the quality of the outcome expected of it. At the practical levels, examples and illustrations shall dismember the notions to meet the test of an understanding of the common person.

Risk

The definition of a risk as "an uncertainty which if it occurs would affect one or more objectives" also allows inclusion of opportunities as well as threats within the risk process, since an opportunity is simply an uncertainty with a positive effect on an objective. In the same way that the typical tactical risk process can be extended to deal with strategic risks by focusing on strategic objectives (Lenfle & Loch, 2010), the threat-based process can also be modified to address opportunities by including upside risk (Loch, de Meyer, & Pich, 2006). Risk is a permanent element in every decision-making process, including design and planning decisions. Risk, which may be difficult to deal with, is inherent in every human endeavor (De Bakker, Boonstra & Wortmann, 2010). As such, it is important to understand the nature of risk if an informed decision is to be made, particularly in the case of PPP projects that require different parties to work together towards a common goal, each with varying targets and objectives. It is essential to understand these risk factors if their possible gains and possible losses are to be evaluated and appropriate decisions on what to do about them are made.

Like exposure to unknown occurrences, more happenings which unfortunately is constant is risk and can act as a spur to upset any planned move (Olsson, 2008). In most instances, risk causes that which is totally under desired most times leading to inefficiency and ineffectiveness on whatever had been planned for (Sanchez, Robert, Bourgault & Pellerin, 2009). Planned activities are usually littered with risks which are not only the originator of inefficiency and unprofitable activity outcomes but also crowd out that which would have been achieved (Perminova, Gustafsson & Wikström, 2008). Furthermore, there is often a lack of effective understanding of risk. In this vein, one might conclude that a detailed analogy of risk is necessary tool to prevent failure of planned activities (Petit, 2012). It would therefore be appropriate in this context given the complexity of PPP arrangement, to have a strong urge to understand and have knowledge on the risks likely to infest PPP arrangements. This would act as a set up to design amiable strategies to overcome them. Risk can be decomposed into basic elements of threat, vulnerability, impact, and likelihood of occurrence (Sanchez, Robert & Pellerin, 2008). Risk can also be considered from technical and project perspectives. Today risk is generally increasing due to the challenges of globalization, technological complexity, increased technical and process interdependencies, and other factors (van Opstal 2007).

Risk is a concept endowed with lots of confusing definitions as each and every one who attempts it tends to narrow the definition either to an aspect or a subsequent effect (Roumboutsos & Anagnostopoulos, 2008). Vasvári (2015) puts it plainly that the definition of risk varies by theory, such as in the technical, economic, psychological and sociological approaches. According to van Mieghem (2010), the concept of risk varies according to viewpoint, attitudes and experience of an individual and thus risk has a different meaning to different people. Engineers, designers, and contractors view risk from the technological perspective, lenders and developers tend to view it from economical and financial side, and health professionals, environmentalists, chemical engineers take a safety and environmental perspective (Abednego & Ogunlana, 2006). Risk is, therefore, generally seen as an abstract concept whose measurement is very difficult (Goh & Abdul-Rahman, 2013). For instance, in everyday language, risk refers to an exposure to a chance of loss or damage. For example, it's not uncommon to hear exclamations as; this is a very risky venture to do! You risk losing lots of money in this investment! Why engage in risky business? From the givens, it's prudent to assert that risk arise from hazards and exposure. It does not exist if exposure to hazard does not or will not occur. For instance, for those who are disadvantaged to experience flood during every rainy season, would equate living in the mountain a luxury since the inhabitants up there do not have to worry about their properties whenever it rains. In most cases, the interpretation of risk as an undesirable possible consequence of uncertainty suggests that risk is a combination of two factors: the probability that an adverse event or hazard will occur and the consequences of the adverse event (Acharya, Dai Lee & Man Im, 2006). This seems to suggest that risk is the likelihood of something going wrong and uncertainty meaning that 'the outcome of a course of action is indeterminate or subject to doubt'. Risk, therefore, involves the possibility of placing some 'calculable probability' on a future event occurring (Broadbent, Gill & Laughlin, 2008).

Traditionally, risk was viewed as an agent of damages, dangers and negativity such that when it occur it affects for example, the project negatively (Zou, Zhang & Wang, 2007). However, recent researches tend to emphasize the two-edged nature of risk such as threats and challenges on one hand or opportunities and threats on the other (Girmscheid, 2006). In other words, the impact of risk is not necessary negative; it can also bring positive influence or some profitable results on the project objectives. Whatever, the theory though, a better definition of risk can be derived from its roots. Etymologically, the term risk is derived from the Italian word, "*risicare*" which means "to dare" (Monteiro, 2010). In this sense, risk is a choice, not fate. It follows from this origin that risk is not an option, but something one is exposed to in everyday life. Nonetheless, the most important thing is that each time it occurs, there must be gain control over it. Seen in the Chinese context, risk is *wei ji* which combines the meanings of "danger" and "opportunity". This confirms the interchangeable nature of risk between threat and opportunity.

To date, no universally accepted definition of risk is unanimously accepted by all specialists in the field. There is anyhow some commonly used definition of risks which presents themselves as possibility of obtaining favorable or unfavorable results in future action expressed in terms of probabilities (Aven, 2010). One such definition is that risk is a possible future event whose production could cause some losses (Zwikael & Saleh, 2007). This means risk can be a threat that an event or action can caused to affect in a negative manner the capacity of an organization or individual to achieve planned goals. From this definition, it can be concluded that risk can give rise to probability, consequences, threats, and loss, negative or positive outcomes. It appears then risk is a problem (situation, event etc) which has not yet occurred, but can occur in the future, threatening the achievement of agreed outcomes (Barlish, De Marco & Thaheem, 2013). Viewed in this context, Turnbaughs (2005) intimates that risk is the uncertainty in obtaining expected results and should be treated as a combination of probability and impact.

Amongst, the numerous definitions of risk, two of them are worth mention in this context. According to Loosemore, Raftery, Reilly and Higgon (2006), risk is a possible future event, the occurrence and consequences of which are uncertain, but which could affect the company's ability to achieve its project objectives. This definition brings in another dimension of risk that is a happening likely to occur in the future. This means much as risk is dangerous and perhaps has some opportunities, those dangers and opportunities does not occur in neither the present nor the past, but that which is yet to come. Situating it in a practical reality, Krześ-Dobieszewska (2014) defines risk as any factor, event or influence that threatens the successful completion of a project in terms of time, cost or quality. This means risk is a probability of occurrence and magnitude of the consequences for loss or gain, that is, risk is equal to the probability of occurrence multiplied by the consequences. This distinction has also moved into management literature, although public private partnership may rest on a conceptual conflation of risk and uncertainty.

Again in the field of management, risk is also unclearly defined. As contemplated in line with Nisar (2007) assertion, the different definitions of the concept of risk in management field include common elements that are generic in terms of content. Fischer (2010) takes risk as the chance of an event occurring that has a negative effect on the achievement of goals. While Goh, and Abdul-Rahman (2013) asserts risk can be defined as the positive and/or negative effect of uncertainty that influences the accomplishment of organizational goals. To Kolhatkar and Dutta (2013) risk is a factor that threatens the achievement of organizational goals. In general, according to Ke, Wang & Chan (2013), risk is some kind of event, activity or failure to perform an activity, which will likely occur in the future, and if it does, this will generally have a negative, but in some cases a positive effect on the achievement of the given organization's goals. From these definitions, the understanding of risk in the management field is that it is a probability of all such elements and events occurring that may have an adverse effect on the operation of a budgetary institution, as given in most risk management guidelines (Girmscheid, 2006).

The understanding of what risk is and is not informs the perception of organization towards risk and determines place of risk management in such organizations (Ling & Hoi, 2006). In spite of this though, the most certain thing about risk is that it is an effect of uncertainty on objectives. Here risk is understood as an event which can, if it occurs, act as a threat and impact overall success of delivery, in this case public private partnership (Marques & Berg, 2011). Simply put, risk is a potential event, either internal or external to a PPP arrangement that, if it occurs, may cause the arrangement to fail to meet one or more of its objectives. Essentially, it can be inferred that risk is an undesirable event (for example, failure to perform an activity, error, deficiency, irregularity, damage, loss) that may potentially occur. The impact(s) of such occurrence may pose some kind of a threat, varying in degree, to achieving organizational goals, the operation and activities of the organization. However, Loosemore, Raftery, Reilly and Higgon (2006) warns that the interpretation of risk as a potential event (with a negative effect) is mixed with the notions of "impact" and "probability" which are required for determining its degree.

In general terms, risk is part of any human effort (Goh & Abdul-Rahman, 2013). It comes in any situation whether at home or at work. What seems constant is that any human activity is exposed to risk of different levels and degrees. Hence, the most serious effects of risk on, for example, PPP project objectives as follows: failure to keep within cost estimate, failure to achieve the required estimation time and failure to achieve the required quality and operational requirements. Nisar (2007) affirms that these unexpected events that when they occur will affect the project objectives represent the project risks. Tahir (2007) advices that they are to be systematically managed if at all the project are to reap any success.

Risks which have not been identified and managed are undoubtedly unchecked threats to a project's objectives, which in turn may lead to considerable overruns in cost and scheduling (Almarri & Blackwell, 2014). For this reason, a systematic approach must be taken to manage risks throughout the development of a project (Ogbu, 2013). Despite numerous risk management processes proposed in the literature (Loosemore et al., 2006), there has been failures in all sorts of ways in managing risks in public private partnership. It has to be restated time and again that risk management is the process of identifying, analyzing and responding to the risks the organization faces and is exposed to. The costs of implementing this system depend on the methods used to manage unexpected events. Risk management process is an ongoing one and the results are embodied in the decisions taken on accepting, reducing or eliminating risks that affect the achievement of objectives (Pohle & Girmscheid, 2007). The aim is to optimize the organization's exposure to risk in order to prevent losses, avoid threats and exploit opportunities.

In this respect, designing and implementing a risk management process at corporate level, is appropriate and necessary due to uncertainties of threats in achieving organizational goals. The implementation of this concept leads to certain changes within the organization, whose effects should be materialized through a better use of available funds and obtaining levels of profitability planned (Sanda & Anigbogu, 2016), namely: risk management requires modifications in leadership style, the organization's management would be forced besides the consequences treatment measures of events that occurred, to devise and implement adequate internal control devices to limit or eliminate the possibility of risks manifestation. Implementing these control devices should enable the organization to master, within acceptable limits, risks and to achieve the objectives. Risk management ensures the efficient and effective achievement of objectives, mastering threats the organization deals with, allows to hierarchy risks based on materialization probability, of impact magnitude and costs posed by mitigating or limiting unwanted effects (Teller, Kock & Gemünden, 2014). Risk management requires a healthy internal control system; designing and implementing adequate internal controls and ensuring their operation require a reasonable assurance that objectives will be achieved (Smith. Merna & Jobbling, 2006). Enhancing and strengthening the internal/management control system is indispensable without designing and implementing appropriate risk management.

Risk Management

Risk management as a technical discipline has become a standard area of business practice in recent years (Rohmeyer & Ben-Zvi, 2010). It was driven initially by recognition that an increasingly complex business world was ill-protected against threats from both within the organization and the outside world. However, as the practice becomes embedded in corporate culture, the drivers and facilitators of its growth are changing (Marques & Berg, 2011). Put simply, they are shifting from the direct task of responding to threats to the secondary aims of meeting the expectations of powerful parties.

Gao, Sung and Zhang (2013) contend that among the deliverables that risk management exude will be developing business and operations strategies and plans with the need to address risks as one of the key focuses and effectively identifying the key risks in an organization's business, operations, activities and structure; having the ability to assist the business/operations' owners on their risks, as well as having suggestions or recommendations for ways to manage and treat those risks using appropriate risk controls and risk mitigants. Kim and Vonortas (2014) aver risk management aid in having effective processes to identify all significant risks in the organization as well as providing reasonable assurance that all risks are correctly assessed, scored, measured and prioritized by the risk-owners in the organization. Ali (2005) argues that risk management helps in implementing risk management processes that ensure the management's responses to risks are appropriate and in conformance to the organization's policies and having risk reports for the key risks that managers and directors need to know, address and monitor.

Tahir (2007) briefly describe five-step risk management process as starting with obtaining the mandate and commitment of the risk management team to drive the risk management project. The second step is for the team to design the risk management framework. The third step is to get this framework to be implemented by the relevant risk-owners who normally are the business and support departments in the organization. However, the risk management journey does not stop when the implementation stage is completed because the fourth step is to monitor and review the implementation of the framework. Finally, the fifth step is the continuous improvement of the framework. Past studies enlist requirements in each of the five process-steps in the risk management process. In the process-step 1 which is about mandate and commitment, Nisar (2007) argues that risk management requires sustained and strong commitment by the PMC and management of SPV, as well as rigorous and strategic planning. He stresses that management must communicate the benefits of risk management to all stakeholders and also articulate and endorse the risk management policy. Omwenga and Nasieku (2016) add that management should define the risk management performance indicators that align with organizational performance, ensure that the necessary resources are allocated for risk management, and ensure the regulatory and legal compliance.

The process-step 2 of the risk management process is concerned with the design of the risk management framework. For proper design of such a framework, Jin, Zhang and Yang (2012) recommend that there has to be a correct understanding of the organization and its environment. Wibowo and Mohamed (2010) suggest that there should be integration of risk management policy into the organizational (business and operational processes). Adnan (2008) implores stating the roles of everyone involved in the risk management process. Ibrahim, Price and Dainty (2006) capitalize on the importance of analysis and explanation of the available resources especially people and infrastructure in the risk management process. Smith, Merna and Jobbling (2006) emphasize production of risk management report produced out of a clearly well established internal and external communication and reporting mechanism. They report should indicate the type and deliverables. Loosemore and Cheung (2015) highly recommend for obtaining management endorsement for the risk management framework (RMF) as well as get approval of the SPV board/management. Helbing (2013) proposes announcement and dissemination of the RMF for the organization-wide use/guide.

In process-step 3 of the risk management process is the implementation of the RMF. Koubatis and Schönberger (2005) indicate that this process calls for the development of a plan of implementation of the RMF; implementation of RMF; implementation of risk scoping for the organization's risk landscape; and implementation of the risk management process. Related to this is the monitoring and review of the framework implementation which forms process-step 4 of the risk management process. According to Loosemore, Raftery, Reilly and Higgon (2006), in this step there is need to measure progress periodically against risk management plan and time-line. Lehtiranta (2013) augment by articulating the review is to see if the risk management policy, RMF, and risk management plan are still efficacious (relevant and appropriate). Ng and Loosemore (2007) stress when reviewing, submit regular reports on all the organization's risks, the risk management progress with the risk management plan. Girmscheid (2006) advocates for stating how well the risk management policy and framework are being followed/adhered to. While assessing or reviewing the effectiveness of the risk management process; De Bakker, K., Boonstra and Wortmann (2010) advice for looking at the adequacy of risk control and risk mitigants. In complement, Beckers, Chiara, Flesch, Maly, Silva and Stegemann (2013) add that the assessment or review must look at how inherent risks are identified, and how residual risks are treated.

The last process-step 5 is about continuous improvement of the framework. It is a step based on the reviews in process-step 4 in which management decisions can be made on how the risk management policy, RMF, and risk management plan can be further improved/enhanced (Carbonara, Costantino, Gunnigan & Pellegrino, 2015). Zenonas, Gajzler and Dziadosz (2012) opine such decisions will lead to improvement in the organization's risk management. Sanda, and Anigbogu (2016) designate that the continuous reviews should also inculcate better risk management culture and awareness in the organization's environment since it is one of the most important cornerstone or building blocks for the overall risk management programme. The focus for the continual risk management improvement, so Zou, Zhang and Wang (2007) advice requires meeting the organization's resilience, good and effective governance for responsible and accountable functions that are necessary in the organization.

Asenova (2010) notes the main internal driver for risk management in public private partnership is greater commitment from the parties. It's important to note that the parties are inputs to implementing partnership wide risk management process successfully. Usually parties have bought in, but are in turn driving their managers to master and implement good risk management practice (Cooper, Grey, Raymond

& Walker, 2005). Next on the list, although given considerably less prominence, is the greater complexity that partnerships are experiencing in the project implementation. Advanced business practices, globalised markets and technological change are multiplying the threats partners face, as well as making those threats harder to identify and track (Looseore & Zou, 2005). The move towards financing from the public to the private sector means there's a lot more financing from private partners, and there's less many financing from the public sector. Certainly, there are economic risks, regulatory risks and reputational risks like sweatshops (Arena, Arnaboldi & Azzone, 2010). If you're taking the opportunity to reduce your cost base and drive down your sourcing costs then you end up having to manage other people's risk, so you need some strengthened procurement function that can audit and evaluate the suppliers.

External factors to strengthen risk management in public private partnership are usually from outside the partnership. They are usually not direct threats such as terrorism, political uncertainty or natural weather events that top the list, but the increased focus of regulators on corporate practices (Thomas, Kalidindi & Ganesh, 2006). Regulators have been a powerful force driving the risk management agenda in recent years, and compliance will continue to play an important role in the function. Regulation is certainly playing a part in driving risk management forward. Also governments, and not just politicians but civil servants, seem to be getting on board quickly with risk management (Spikin, 2013). This all adds to a growing awareness of the concept. Next—although by some distance—come demands from investors for greater disclosure and accountability. More vocal shareholders have become a fixture for many companies and, recognizing the importance of risk management for overall corporate reputation, they are increasing their scrutiny of risk practices. In response, companies are strengthening disclosure to investors (something they are also being required to do from a regulatory perspective) and are starting to include more comprehensive treatment of risk management in their annual reports.

Systematic management of risks at all levels of PPP arrangement is a vital pre-condition for a successful outcome of a PPP project. Managing risk helps to develop a concretized plan of action how the PPP project should be executed and implemented. Risk management is the bedrock of any success of a PPP project, so asserts Bovaird (2010). As a PPP project is conceived and moves into a more complex activities such like feasibility study, design, procurement, execution/implementation, completion and use, it becomes necessary that risk management mechanisms must be deployed in all these activities. Equally, important are that the parties to the PPP arrangement must be well conversant of the existences of the risks at each stage of the activities PPP project is required to undergo before an outcome is realized (Bracey & Moldovan, 2006). There are many ways of approaching risk management but one of them seems to be very typical to make it succeeds: concise and precise identification of all the risks that are embedded in every stage of the activities carried out in a PPP arrangement. This entails a deeper survey of all those areas where potential risks can be emanates from. It for that reason needs benchmarking against compromising occurrences to identify the real risks with the potential of disadvantaging the success of the PPP project. This would also guide the steps to be undertaken to reach the end of the tunnel. Other efforts might embrace situation the PPP project within its context be they social, political or economic (Campbell, 2005). Obtaining assistance of experts in the situation would be a noble cause to embrace as would requisite information to make sound decisions for the final entry into the agreement, and actualization of the agreement through execution and implementation of the PPP project.

In a world of rapidly changing technologies and globalization, comprehensive and systematic risk management is critical for garnering success for PPP arrangement (Broadbent, Gill & Laughlin, 2008). For example, in developing countries known with technological capabilities that lag behind but with high consumption needs, managing risk in a PPP project should not be left to chances. Instead, a first call should be on the best way of utilizing the scarce resources without any semblance of risk interfering with them. Activities must be direct at creating situations where risks cannot find an avenue to raise their ugly 'heads'. Risk management is therefore a component of modern management, has become a main concern for the modern world and one of the "key mechanisms" of economic development, a complex process that includes a series of activities meant to alleviate the impact of risk over business and planed or foreseen results. Risk management in an organization means to determine what risks that should be avoided and what risks should be accepted as they are. Cienfuegos (2011) intimates risk management should generally be understood as a process which aims at providing a structured way of identifying and analyzing potential risks, and devising and implementing responses to reduce their impact, and monitoring the effectiveness of actions that have been undertaken. It is formal process which risk factor will identified, analysis, and address systematically so that losses can be minimized (Lewens, 2007). The risk management process is a systematic application of management policies, procedures and practices to the activities of communicating and consulting, establishing the context, identifying, analyzing, evaluating, treating, monitoring and reviewing risk. Risk management is a proactive decision-making process, which involves accepting a known risk and/or taking steps to mitigate the impact and likelihood of the occurrence of risks, to minimize the threats and maximize the opportunities (Loosemore, Raftery, Reilly & Higgon, 2006). Risk management may mean different to different stakeholders. To the public sector, risk management refers to the identification, assessment and evaluation of what risks are to be retained and transferred, and to formulate strategies on how risks are to be mitigated. To the SPV consortium that is responsible for the construction and operation, risk management refers to the assessment and evaluation of the risks that are allocated to them so that risks are priced in such what that the cost of managing them can be properly recovered (Ameyaw & Chan, (2013). To the financiers who are responsible for funding the project, risk management means that the identification, assessment and evaluation of risks that are pertained to loan default, and formulation of the risk mitigation strategies, usually in terms of the interest rates charged over the loans, restrictions to the borrowers to safeguard themselves against the risks. In general, risk management is the broad activity of planning and decision-making designed to deal with the occurrence of hazards or risks (MacGillivray, Hamilton, Strutt & Pollard, (2006a). Risks include both unlikely but high-impact disruption risks, as well as more common volatility in demand, internal processing, and supply (MacGillivray, Pollard, Hamilton & Bradshaw, 2006b).

According to Akintoye (2006), as the idea of PPP progresses on, it becomes more and more desirable that systematic risk management must take center stage. This is the only way in which early detection of risks can be made. It can also encourage PPP stakeholders to identify, analyze, quantify and respond to the risks, as well as to take measures to introduce risk mitigation policies (Cankar & Petkovšek, 2013). It is a scheme that promotes greater actions and stimulates creating linkages to curb risks in a PPP arrangement. Following the principles of management, lots of potential measures to cure the menace of risk in PPP can be developed. To appreciate those principles, requires an understanding of the concept of management.

Management is the coordination of human and capital resources to achieve specific organizational outcomes (Jones & George, 2008). This coordination aims at getting things done effectively through imposition of an order over chaos on the assumption that managers attempt to put things in order through others. Choudhry and Iqbal (2013) opines that management is generally understood as the process of planning, coordinating, organizing, and controlling the efforts of organizational members and of using other organizational resources to achieve stated goals. This definition portrays management as a scientific way of doing things. Management here is taken as the process of interaction in terms of planning, organization, leading, and controlling in a PPP arrangement. It involves parties who perform the acts of managing risk in the arrangement. It further extends to the interaction between the human and technology applied in the PPP project implementation (Cleden, 2009).

According to Kamiya, Kamiya, Shi, Schmit and Rosenberg (2007), risk management is the identification, assessment and prioritization of risk. They argue that risk management is followed by coordinated and economical application of resources to minimize. Monitor and control the probability and/impact of unfortunate events or to maximize the realization of opportunities. Keçi (2005) defines risk management as the process of understanding and managing risks that an entity is inevitably subject to in attempting to achieve its objectives. Risk is for that reason an intervention in economic and behavioral risk dynamics so that the value of the organization is enhanced. Fischer (2010) avers risk management is a systematic method of using a firm's resources – physical, financial, and human capital – to realize certain objectives concerning pure loss exposures. To him, risk management includes the identification and analysis of risks; and the decision to either accept or mitigate the exposure to such when compared to the potential impact on the achievement of the organization's objectives. It's about understanding the nature of such events and practices and, where they represent threats, making positive plans to mitigate them. Its main objective is to assure uncertainty does not deflect the endeavor from the business goals.

Klemetti (2006) claims that risk management follows prioritization process in which risks with the greatest loss (or impact) and the greatest probability of occurring are handled first, and risks with lower probability of occurrence and lower loss are handled in descending order. It encompasses the actions parties take to minimize the uncertainty of expected results and to reduce volatility. It embraces any set of actions taken by individuals or corporations in an effort to alter the risk arising from their primary lines of business. To attain its objectives risk management must be glued to principles (Malmgren, 2010) such as creating and protecting value, that is resources expended to mitigate risk should be less than the consequence of inaction, be an integral part of organizational processes, be part of the decision making process, explicitly address uncertainty and assumptions, be a systematic, structured and timely process, be based on the best available information, and be tailored. Lam (2003) adds that risk management must take human and cultural factors into account; be transparent and inclusive; be dynamic, iterative and responsive to change; be capable of continual improvement and enhancement; and be continually or periodically re-assessed.

In a PPP arrangement, risk management is no exception in cases are to be reaped. The main challenge in a PPP arrangement is losses due to risk occurrence (Bloomfield, 2006). Indeed, there are instances where the ability of the partners in a PPP arrangement well may be jeopardized simply because risk has been made to capture all stages of activities. For example, if a private party fails to reach a financial closure on a deal, the public party will have to start the procurement process over again such that it will need to invest more time energy in securing a new provider. This is a risk by its very nature. Some losses will have to be registered in this case. More so, the private party will lose financially and its reputation will suffer, which could affect its future ability to win contracts in the PPP type or other arrangements (Demirag, Khadaroo, & Stapleton, 2011). In this scenario, the public partner can mitigate this risk by selecting only reputable team from the list of bidders. Again this is risky and likely to produce a number of other risks which may be very unhealthy for a proposed PPP arrangement. For instance, if risks are not mitigated by the public sector, the business and investment community may lose confidence in the government.

In the given circumstance of risk occurrences in a PPP arrangement, McElhinney & Proctor (2005) suggest that increasing commitment to an effective course of action for risk management is very critical. This comes as a result of managerial motivation, social pressures, organizational inertia and political forces. Lam, Wang, Lee and Tsang (2007) articulates that adopting a systematic risk management approach will protect the organization and adds value to the organization. Andres and Guasch (2008) concludes by asserting, such an approach support achievement of organization's objectives by providing a framework that ensures a consistent and controlled approach; improving decision making, planning and prioritization of threats to the business; contributing to the more efficient allocation and use of capital and resources; reducing volatility in the non-essential areas of the business; protecting and enhancing assets and organization image; developing and supporting people and knowledge base; and optimizing operational efficiency within the business. How to make this is reality forms the basis of the next sub section.

Risk management cannot remove all risks from project; it is not synonymous with insurance (Duckert, 2010). Its principle aim is to ensure that risks are managed efficiently. The client and his project manager must recognize that certain risks will remain to be carried by the client. This residual risk must be allowed for in the client's estimate of time and cost. Risk management system must be practical, reasonable and cost effective (Flanagan, Norman & Chapman, 2006). Risk management need not be complicated nor require the collection of vast amounts of data. It is a matter of judgment, common sense, analysis, and experience and a willing or gut to assure the risk. Carbonara, Costatino, Pellegrino and Sciancalepore (2011) reported that, PPP projects have more inherent risks than the traditional method of procurement due to the involvement of many stakeholders with varied interests in addition to the economic, political, social and cultural conditions where the projects are to be undertaken, which are the traditional sources of risk. These PPP related risks need to be studied and managed. Hence, risk management is a necessary condition for a successful PPP projects which have been adjudged to be riskier than the traditionally procured projects (Moosa, 2007). This understanding has triggered numerous researches in the area of risk management.

Risk management is characterized by the establishment and implementation of concrete activities and actions of identification and risk assessment leading to determine the risk level and by this act to implement adequate internal control devices to limit the probability of the risk occurring or the consequences if the risk materializes (Nisar, 2007). The process must be coherent, integrated to the objectives, activities and operations carried out within the organization. The staff within the organization, regardless of the current hierarchical level, should be aware of the importance of risk management to achieve planned results and to form necessary skills in order to perform monitoring and control based on principles of efficiency and effectiveness (Cooper, Grey, Raymond & Walker, 2005). The functional structures responsible within the organization have the task to identify and analyze regularly the risks related to their activities, to propose and substantiate appropriate measures in order to limit the possible consequences of risks and ensure approval by decision makers within the organization (Awodele, Ogunlana & Motawa, 2010). It is therefore recommendable that any organization needs to manage its risks, because in many cases the occurrence of risks can have serious consequences upon the activities, sometimes these consequences jeopardizing the very existence of the organization. After all the complexity of risks and their increase has led organizations' management to understand that it is better to manage a risk than to cover a loss. Based on this requirement, many organizations have proceeded to implement risk management, developing specific strategies that have defined the organization's behavior towards risk and risk management arrangements.

Risk management is a preventive attitude on the elimination or limitation of damages, if any possibility of a risk materializing, namely a process of identifying, analyzing and responding to potential risks of an organization (Mouraviev, 2012a). In these conditions, the role of risk management is to help understand the risks the organization is exposed to, so that they can be managed. This role varies depending on when the analysis is done, as follows: - if the risk assessment is conducted before the risk materialization, the goal is to avoid the occurrence of this event; if the risk assessment is carried out after the risk has materialized; the goal is to ensure the development of the activities and the organization's activities continuity (Ogbu, 2013). The advantage of implementing the risk management system within the organization is to ensure economic efficiency. To achieve this requirement, the organization's management has the responsibility to make known the risks they face and manage them properly, in order to avoid consequences for their materialization (Ke, Wang & Chan, 2010a).

Risk management is the responsibility of the organization's management, and the central objective of this process aims the risks management so that resources to be used efficiently and effectively in order to maximize profit and minimize threats, while safeguarding the interests of employees and customers (Shen, Platten & Deng, 2006). In this respect, Ahmadi and Heybati (2009) suggest that the entity's management must act in the following directions: - establishing the definition of risk that is widely accepted and understood across the organization and also the types of risk; assessing current risks and monitoring potential sources of internal and external risks; establishing clear responsibilities on each hierarchical level and per employee concerning the implementation of risk management process; developing an adequate information system for the management on risks and risk assessment system; setting tolerance in taking risks and limits of exposure in accordance with it; permanent analysis of achievements and poor results in risk management and continuous improvement of risk management process; - ensuring an adequate level of knowledge and skills of employees in accordance with the requirements followed by the implementation of the risk management process.

According to Kishk and Ukaga (2008), effective management of risky projects demands rapid and realistic prediction about the future expectation and the alternative courses of action of positive decision making. It requires flexible attitudes and procedures. So far, as indicated by Edwards and Bowen (2005) risk management is most frequently used in private sector projects.' The public sector should follow their example. It is urgent for politicians and government to notice this issue, and to examine current procedures used in the planning and implementation of projects, because some of these are causing unnecessary delay, avoidable cost overrun, and poor performance. To ensure an efficient risk management is necessary to create certain organizational structures appropriate for the policies and strategies of the organization. In this respect, the organization should adopt appropriate policies regarding the organization plan, in order to effectively monitor each risk or category of risk and in an integrated manner, the whole risks system accompanying activities (Bedell, 2007). Policies and strategies that may be adopted regarding the organization plan are related to: - establishing and developing its own system of rules and procedures that, implemented, to ensure avoiding or minimizing risks; establishing appropriate functional structure based on a clear concept, which should ensure appropriate departments in order to contribute at identifying and monitoring risks (Hodge & Greve, 2005b). Given that risk can be identified, evaluated and limited, but never completely eliminated, the organization must develop both general policies and specific policies to limit exposure.

Dooley, Lupton and O'Sullivan (2005) contend that in the world of today it has become increasingly more imperative for corporate managers to monitor and manage risk in all aspects. A good risk management means avoiding or minimizing loss, and also treating opportunities in a favorable manner. Risk management is necessary because organizations face uncertainty and the biggest challenge of the leadership is to determine what level of risk it is prepared to accept to achieve its mission, in order to add value to activities and to achieve planned goals (Gjerdrum, 2008). Risk management is an essential component of the organization's success and must become an intrinsic part of its functioning (Atkinson, 2005). It must be closely related to corporate governance and internal control, but also connected with performance management.

Delmon (2009) suggested that the impact of risks in implementing a public private partnership project is usually significant. Referring to risk management, he presented an initial framework methodology for implementing internal controls, built-in policies, rules, procedures and regulations that have been used by various organizations to secure control over how to run the plan and meet objectives. Risk management within the organizations was created on the concept of internal controls, but the focus was particularly on risk management (Matei, 2006). This was not intended to replace internal controls, but incorporating basic concepts of internal control in this process. Thus, between risk management and internal control was preserved a strong connection interrelated with common concepts and elements.

A good risk management framework must have an internal control with clear objectives (Awodele, 2012). The main objectives of internal control/management system are to ensure the efficiency and effectiveness of activities, the reality of reporting and regulations compliance in the field (Carbonara, Costantino, & Pellegrino, 2013). The internal control/management system is developed and monitored in order to implement by the organization's management, which is responsible for designing adequate internal control devices in order to ensure limitation of significant risks and keeping them within acceptable limits, aiming to give the security that the organization's objectives will be met (Sanda & Anigbogu, 2016).. Hillson (2006) suggests that risk management system should be structured on components of internal control/management. It has to be structured in accordance with five elements, whose implementation ensures that the tools/internal control devices exist and function as intended. These components have been defined as: the control environment specific to the organization is the one that sets the foundations of internal controls system, influencing the control awareness of employees and represents the basis for other components; risk assessment is carried out by management, is performed at both corporate and activity level and includes identifying and analyzing risks that affect the achievement of objectives (Kuzmina, 2010). In general, risk assessment involves determining the level of importance of the risk, assessing the probability that the risk to occur and determining the way to manage it; - control activities are policies and procedures to ensure that management's provisions are respected (Carbonara, Costantino & Pellegrino, 2013). By this, it is ensured that all necessary measures are taken in order to manage risks and achieve the objectives set by management; information and communication helps other components through proper communication to employees of their responsibilities with regard to internal control and provision of relevant, reliable, comparable and understandable information so that they could perform their duties and tasks; and monitoring implies the verification made by the management of the implementation means of internal controls it demanded, or by responsible pursuing if internal controls imposed by it work and if they are sufficient so that activities or actions to take place as planned (Aquila, 2006).

The objective of a risk management framework must be an integrated one (Too & Weaver, 2014). An integrated risk management is the process conducted by the Board, management and others, applied in setting strategy and across the organization, designed to identify potential events that may affect the entity and to manage risk within the risk appetite to provide a reasonable assurance regarding the achievement of organizational objectives (Grimsey & Lewis, 2005). From the content of this definition it follows some essential elements, characteristic to the integrated risk management, as follows: the process is conducted permanently throughout the organization, being circumscribed to other activities;

the purpose is to manage risks associated with objectives and to secure expected results through their implementation; within the process is involved the whole staff, regardless of the hierarchical level; the approach starts from the strategic goals rather than from operational objectives; the process is applied to the entire organization and not functional structures (Hemming, 2006).

It's important to note that the general objective of integrated risk management is to effectively manage uncertainties, risks and opportunities. The need for risk management stems from the fact that uncertainty is a reality and the reaction to uncertainty is a constant concern (Atkinson, Crawford & Ward, 2006). Risk management involves establishing actions to respond to risk and to implement adequate internal control devices, with which to limit the possibility of occurrence or consequences of risk, if it would materialize (Ibem, 2010). In order to ensure efficiency in achieving objectives, the process must be coherent and convergent, integrated to objectives, activities and operations carried out within the organization. Also, regardless of the staff's hierarchical level, it should be aware of the importance of risk management has in achieving its own objectives and thus to form the necessary skills to perform monitoring and control based on principles of efficiency and effectiveness (Ho, 2006). In order to ensure the success of this approach and to achieve an effective risk management, within the organization it needs to create a culture of risk, namely developing a risk management philosophy specific to the organization and management, and awareness of risk's negative effects at all levels of the organization. From the above it is found that the need for internal control/management is determined by the existence of threats or opportunities in carrying out planned activities or actions with negative consequences in the organization (Yilmaz & Flouris, 2010). This requires the establishment and implementation of certain internal control devices in order to prevent or limit the risks (Klemetti, 2006). Also, the need for risk management stems from the fact that risk is everywhere, in everything we want to achieve. It cannot be removed; any action to eliminate risk can lead to the emergence of new risks, uncontrolled, which may affect too much greater extent the organization. In these conditions, the risk needs to be minimized, process that can be achieved by establishing and implementing adequate internal controls (Kolhatkar & Dutta, 2013).

Risk management should be based on the best available information. Public private partnership has rich data sources that are fostered by open channels of communication, allowing the highest level of information to be conveyed effectively to stakeholders (Kutsch & Hall, 2010). Risk management should be tailored to the whole of public private partnership, its components, and all of its business units, work with risk management procedures that are tailored to meet their specific needs (Cooper, Grey, Raymond & Walker, 2005). Risk management should take human and cultural factors into account: Consultation on the development and implementation of risk management ensures policies; frameworks and practices in public private partnership reflect the diversity of activities of the parties, their staff and their clients. Risk management should be transparent and inclusive (Mahendra, Jayeshkumar, Pitroda & Bhavsar, 2013). Risk management in public private partnership involves the engagement of internal and external stakeholders through respectful acknowledgement of their contribution to the communication & consultation and monitoring & reviewing processes (Delmon, 2010). Risk management should be dynamic, iterative and responsive to change (Pawar, Jain & Patil, 2015): Risk management in public private partnership responds to the changing needs of the parties, their staff and their clients by continually self-assessing, monitoring and reviewing business processes. Risk management should facilitate continual improvement of the organization. In public private partnership the identification and application of controls and treatments as a result of robust risk assessments, including refinement, leads to improved business practices and increased maturity of the risk management process (Delmon & Delmon, 2012).

Strategy

An attractive strategy is viewed by implementers of PPP projects as a shortcut method for success of the project (Heybati, Roodposhti, Nikoomaram & Ahmadi, 2011). For the same reasons that both parties are expected perform their parts of the obligation, it is necessary that they ought to design an appropriate strategy. Moreover, a strategy acts as pointer to the attainment of an objective that had been set before. Because of its relevance, a strategy provides a clear formula of managing risk.

Derived from two Greek words "strato" (army) and "agein" (leading), strategy is a combination of these two Greek words, "strategos" which means the art of troop leader, office of general, command or generalship (Porter, 2008). It is a term that cut across all field of study and taken as an orientation of a business approach setting a competitive moves designed to generate successful outcome. Those organizations which are not fully prepared are unable to make good use of any strategy to achieve their goals. To the extent that commonly found problems can easily come on board is not a myth in such a situation. An improperly designed strategy does not aid any success. Instead it only promotes weaknesses and contributes to a lack of inward concentration in the execution of programs designed to achieve a goal (Yuan, Zeng, Skibniewski & Li, 2009). A poorly conceived strategy is cumbersome to ensure that a success has to be discarded.

A strategy for an effective and efficient risk management requires definition of the pattern in the organization's important decisions and actions (Grant, 2010). This must consist of a few key areas or things by which the organization is distinguished from others. It must enables determination of the basic long-term goals of an organization. It must also prescribe the adoption of a course of action and the allocation of resources necessary for carrying out these goals. It concerns the basic long-term goals of an organization and the adoption of courses of action and the allocation of resources necessary for carrying out these goals (Adams, 2008).

Porter (2008) proclaims that a strategy is a system of finding, formulating and developing a doctrine that will ensure long-term success if followed faithfully. A strategy is therefore understood as a purposeful action, a plan, a ploy, a pattern, a position, and a perspective. According to Wang, Walker and Redmond (2007), a strategy is a management game plan for strengthening the organization's competitive position, satisfying customers, and achieving performance targets. It is also a broad formula for how an organization is going to compete, what its goals should be, and what policies will be needed to carry out those goals. A good strategy calls for a combination of the ends (goals) for which the organization is striving and the means (policies) by which it is seeking to get there. Its purpose is to set direction, focus effort, define or clarify the organization, and provide consistency or guidance in response to the environment (Avazkhah & Mohebbi, 2010). It involves setting goals, determining actions to achieve the goals, and mobilizing resources to execute the actions. It describes how the ends (goals) will be achieved by the means (resources). It can be planned (intended) or can be observed as a pattern of activity (emergent) as the organization adapts to its environment or competes. It includes processes of formulation and implementation. A strategy is guided by the underlying principles of creating a "unique and valuable [market] position", making trade-offs by choosing "what not to do", and creating "fit" by aligning organization activities with one another to support the chosen strategy. However, Porter (2008) advices that in the formulation of competitive strategy three key elements of an organization must be taken into consideration. These are the organization's strength and weaknesses, personal values of the key implementers, and the industry opportunities and threats.

According to Renn (2006), risk management strategy is dressed up on the distinction between complexity, uncertainty, and ambiguity in managing risk as a whole. It's the strategy that makes it possible to design generic strategies of risk management to be applied to classes of risks, thus simplifying the risk management process (Ghoddousi & Hosseini, 2012). Apart from the strategy, a good RMF must have a clear vision (Hallowell & Gambatese, 2009). Wysocki (2009) reveals that defining the vision and business benefits is the realm of strategy, whereas projects, programmes and their deliverables describe the tactics by which the strategy is achieved. Hillson (2006) presents the relationship between the elements of project-based business as shown in Figure 1.

Figure 1 shows that project (and programme) sits between the strategic and tactical levels, since they are defined in relation to the strategic vision, and they in turn define the requirement for projects. Brewer and Strahorn (2012) claim objectives are also used to measure the value of project deliverables. Smyth, Gustafsson and Ganskau (2010) show that many projects fail because of disconnect between strategic vision and tactical project deliverables, often as a result of poorly defined project/programme objectives. Ŝkrtić and Horvatin (2014) confirm the space between the two levels of strategy and tactics requires careful and proactive management if a projects are to succeed in delivering the required benefits to the business. Hillson (2006) indicates that this is precisely the area occupied by project/programme objectives that businesses are most at risk. He continues to say all business activity is undertaken in an environment of uncertainty, arising from a range of sources including, technical issues, commercial restraints, management issues and external dependencies.

According to Iacob (2014), those organizations which are successful do not however, avoid uncertainty because they recognize the relationship between risk and reward. After all, "zero risk" projects do not exist and indeed is not desirable since the available benefits of risk are determined to a large extent by the degree of risk an organization is prepared to confront (Loosemore, Raftery, Reilly & Higgon, 2006). Risk arises when uncertainty has the potential to affect objectives (Zhang, 2007). It is any uncertainty event or set of circumstances that, should it occur, would have an effect on one or more objectives (Zou, Zhang & Wang, 2007). Keçi (2015a) claims there are uncertainties that cannot affect objectives, which

Figure 1. Elements of project-based business
Source: (Hillson, 2006)

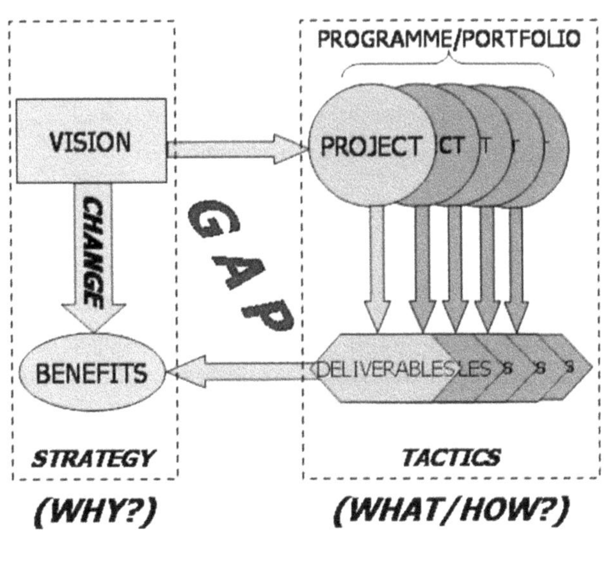

are therefore not risks. Nonetheless, Akintoye (2008) points out that it is this relationship between risk, uncertainty and objectives that makes risk management such an important contributor to both project success and business benefits.

Hillson (2006) provides that project objectives link between the overall and the projects which are established to implement that vision. They also define the acceptance criteria for project deliverables which provide the capability to realize business benefits (Aloini, Dulmin & Mininno, 2007). Bain (2010) contends project objectives are however affected by the uncertain environment within which projects and business are undertaken, resulting in a level of risk exposure. Risk management exists to address this risk exposure, leading to an acceptable and manageable level of risk (Hillson, 2006). This increases the chance of meeting project objectives, which in turn maximizes the likelihood of achieving the required benefits (Cleden, 2009). As a result, there is a clear link between risk management and business performance. According to Hillson (2006), effective risk management should lead to realized business benefits.

A ROADMAP FOR EFFECTIVE RISK SHARING

The specific context, nature and prevalence of risky occurrences will vary between the different activities unto which the performance of a programme undergoes to achieve an objective (Cretu, Stewart, & Berends, 2011). Yet, evidence suggests that many organizations ends up not sharing risks as would have best been taken (Nielsen, 2006). Evidence also suggests that the management of risk sharing needed a coherent approach with clear roadmaps to follow (Perera, Dhanasinghe & Rameezdeen, 2009). It requires an extremely complex, interactive and demanding process (Hillson & Murray-Webster, 2011). It involves a range of overlapping activities including data collection, assessing performance of the sharing process and existing policies, designing a new policy framework, implementing the new policy framework, coordinating policies, monitoring the results, refining the policy framework and capacity building (Gupta & Sharma, 2015). Experiences of developed countries with good PPP success stories offer insights on these activities, which can be represented a stylized road map for other PPP arrangements in other countries.

For simplicity, the processing of sharing risk strategy can be represented as a cycle of three interrelated phases: assessing existing risk sharing performance and the policy framework; designing a new risk sharing policy framework; and implementing the new policy framework (Ahmed, Kayis & Amornsawadwatana, 2007). Each organization will differ in the time taken to accomplish each of these phases and the phases may overlap with each other but none of them can be left out if an organization is to put in place a sustainable risk sharing strategy (Loizou & French, 2012). The key issues under the three phases will be highlighted in the following sub sections.

Assessment of Risk Sharing

A diagnostic assessment is the starting point for developing an acceptable risk sharing strategy (Chapman & Ward, 2008). Its purpose is to collect information and to analyze existing risk sharing strategy and the standard measurement that had been developed and agreed upon (Mauelshagen, Smith, Schiller, Denyer, Rocks & Pollard, 2014). This type of exercise is increasingly referred to an effective risk sharing strategy in policy circles. In essence, it is a benchmarking exercise which compares important aspect of an organization's risk sharing attempts including the strength and weaknesses of those measures.

There are important elements that must be considered while considering the handling of risk sharing. Risk sharing at the PPP arrangement is being increasingly conducted on behalf of both parties (Wei & Ren, 2015). Some are conducted from the economic view point, others from business strategy perspective and some from a combine economics/business strategy, still others are considered from the public value view. Assessment of risk sharing seeks to provide a detailed picture of all-level positioning and performance of an organization as well as the policy, internal and external factors that affect past organizational performance (Shahzad & Safvi, 2010). They also attempt to provide an assessment of future organizational prospects, opportunities and threats on the horizon and suggestions on how to overcome them (Deng, Hua & Li, 2008). Copious studies on risk sharing tend to very in what they cover depending on the purpose at hand and the complexity of the challenges faced by an organization. Bearing this in mind, a typical risk sharing strategy should concentrate on a number of issues that forms a constitute elements for its successful sharing formulae.

According to Jacobson and Choi (2008) risk sharing strategy involves the review of initial conditions for developing an effective risk handling tools. This requires deriving those deserving conditions bearing in mind the places in which the risks are to be handled. Ramiah and Reich (2006) opine an examination of the development, acceptance and structure or the risk sharing philosophy positions the organization as quite important. Essia and Yusuf (2013) puts forward that a detailed the retailed high level strive for overcoming risks clusters as well as those free of local value chains and positioning in the global market. Furthermore, an assessment of risk sharing strategy promotes better take of the critical roles of the parties involved.

Fan, Li and Zhang (2015) suggests that an evaluation of the adequacy of risk sharing strategy and other intervening factors involves in supporting innovative and self-directing skills development. Ahmad, Bhattacharya, Vinella and Xiao (2014) state an assessment of the internal and external links that could interfere in the process would chain achievement of designed objectives disproportionately. In the same vein, Xiao and Yang (2009) suggests that an assessment of risk sharing opportunities and threats on achievement of an objective and the detailed evaluation of such options for the transforming of the organizations function into satisfactory one would be very central. This may be a valuable into the common vision and strategy. Comprehensive assessment of risk sharing is not one-off exercise which can be done once in awhile or so (Gan, Sethi & Yan, 2005). For example, in the wake of intense globalization blessed by 'compassion' of technological advancement have very far-reaching and unpredictable effects on the achievement of an organization's objectives. Thus, assessment of risk sharing strategy need to be conducted (and updated on regular intervals) to take account of new statistical information on organizational performance and changing internal and external circumstances affecting the organization. In this regard, it is relatively cost-effective to develop strong local capabilities within the organization to conduct and update such assessments (by involving internal personnel).

Trafford and Proctor (2006) equate assessment of risk sharing strategy to comparisons of the capabilities of organization to best practice levels. This is useful to indicate critical gaps in an organization's capabilities in developing a workable strategy. For example, a comparing the traditional way of assessing risk sharing with those of the current ways of assessing risks. Such a comparison could aid in revealing weaknesses in the ability to design new risk sharing strategy (Jing & Besharov, 2014). This enables proper management of the process of risk sharing strategy development. Similarly, an evaluation of large and small organizations especially in the developing countries might show up differences in capabilities to maintain the course of handling the risk. Zinn and Taylor-Gooby (2006) claim that it is not easy to benchmark organizational capabilities in handling risk sharing- a proper evaluation can be extremely intensive in information and skills. However, it is possible to devise shortcuts that yield useful results. One is to define the essential technical functions performed by an organization and give each subjective ranking indicating levels of competence. The basic assumption is that organizations that perform these essential functions will also perform well on the larger spectrum of technological activity. It allows for a 'quick and cheap' method of benchmarking that gives plausible rankings. The average capability score can be aggregated in various ways, for instance by the parties with a PPP arrangement (Kwak, Chih & Ibbs, 2009). The scores can also be related to performance in terms of growth, profitability a well shared risks. The results are of obvious interest to promoters and implementers of risk sharing strategy.

A recent study uses this approach to assess the capability of an organization to handle risks. It entails calculating an acceptable index for each of organizations based on two board categories of service functions: delivery and linkages with other producers/suppliers (Zitron, 2006). The former category, delivery is captured by some technical functions, ranging from process sharing tasks like quality management (measured by internal reject) to production/consumption (like quality products, improving existing products and introducing new products). Linkages are captured by transferring risks from one party to another within a framework of a mutual agreement. Each of the measures to do such a transfer ought to be in the interest of the parties, lest the effort would collapse. It is therefore, necessary to show the relation between the average capabilities of the organization and the outcome of the risk sharing matrix.

One of the criticisms that are levied against risk sharing strategy is that it often sit-on shelves. Collecting dust rather than being implemented has been the cause of action of any party involved in the PPP projects (Chiu & Bosher, 2005). Experience suggests that the most widely used risk sharing strategy have the following common features: a) they are tailored to an audience of busy policy markers (that is they are relatively short and completely written); b) they are practically oriented and have a high policy content; and c) theirs findings are communicated to key stakeholders who can influence good policy making (El-Gohary, Osman & El-Diraby, 2006). These stakeholders not only include politician, friends. Indeed, a regular dialogue involving committed and influential leaders drawn from the different groups of stakeholder dialogue (Aaltonen, Jaakko & Tuomas, 2008). This helps in the process of reforming existent policies and institution that handle something as insulting. In turn, the proceedings of these stakeholder dialogues need to be disseminated to society at large via the media to encourage greater awareness of the devastation effect of risk sharing process (Olander, 2007). This requires an understanding of the vision for improving future competitiveness and acceptance of. This aids acceptance of requisite measures for the success of the risk sharing matrix (Morsink, Hofman & Lovett, 2011). Other time, such a nominal dialogue takes place ground in a dialogue form evolving external threat such as steadily increasing

Designing the Sharing Framework

Having undertaken a comprehensive assessment and initiated a conscious move to make good use of the strategy, the next major challenge is to define a common vision and a workable strategy to realize the mission. The rationale for working together on a common approach is based on the recognition that there are shared returns to the participating parties from collectively acting together (Harris, 2010). There could be various induced design distortions, inherent framework imperfections and framework failures that impede implementation of the framework. These shared returns manifest themselves at the level of an improved design stages.

Arriving at a common vision and strategy is itself quite a different process. The need for an overarching vision to guide an organization operation arises because some organization can adopt many possible strategies. The section on 'core elements of partnership strategy' has already outlined some of the elements of best practices, for example, for PPP strategy. These need to be tailor-made to suit individual PPP arrangement goals, environmental circumstances and practical implementation process and it may be practically hard to withstand whatever shortfalls might come in. it is hard to generalize beyond this but the following issues might be relevant to developing a common vision and strategy for a good risk sharing framework.

Awareness of the opportunities and external threats faced by the parties could be misleading. According to Andonova (2010), new opportunities may include new avenues and new measures for designing the strategy while threats could encompass rapid technological progress, increased handling measures, stringent implementation compliance and setting our means to overcome the possible constraints. Diab, Naser and Varma (2012) contend that there must be appropriate objectives for the framework. These can range from diversification of the best mode possible to ensure compliance. AlSalman and Sillars (2013) argues that such activities must have a backward and forward linkages dimensions for increasing opportunities to reap lots of benefits in the implementation process.

A good sharing framework must have a time horizon for achieving set objectives. Several possible time frames are possible for the validity of the vision and implementation of the strategy including short term (under three years), medium term (5-10 years) or long term (more than 10 years). It is not unusual to combine short-and long-term elements within the same strategy. Kuppusamy (2010) advices that a deliberate move must be made to have it clear the desired roles that the framework ought to perform. These can range from an entirely internally-driven approach to the influence of external forces. Kuzmina (2010) cautions the choice might reflect many things- external pressures, location and environmental circumstances and action plans. Abdul-Rahman, Wang and Lee (2013) highlight the framework interventions require promoting those actions which can improve the implementation processes and outcomes. The diagnostic assessment of the strategy in a given circumstance would indicate the main the strength and weaknesses of the framework. The relevant remedies (a mixture of incentives and regulatory actions) would stem from this. There must be a clear selection procedure for a special promotion measures. The strategic question in this case is the identification of factors responsible for achievements to be realized (Ashley, Diekmann & Molenaar, 2006). The greatest potential for dynamic implementation or execution depends on how well the externalities that might constraints the framework are handled. This issue is probably one of the most contentious in designing a good risk sharing framework. Two important consideration that can inform the designing of the framework include short verses long-term comparative advantage and the depth of the parties' capabilities to intervene at the, for example, PPP levels (Apanavičienė & Rudžianskaitė-Kvaraciejienė, 2010).

A framework, however, well-designed it could be, if it does not have resources for implementation is as good as nothing. Financial resources must be available and adequate to meet the cost of different policies and more importantly the technical resources (economic, legal, management and engineering) to design, implement and monitor the implementation of the framework (Bennett & Iossa, 2006). It goes without saying that a risk sharing strategy has to be tailed to suit financial and technical resource availability (Benta, Podean & Mircean, 2011). Both are likely to be in short supply to the public partner and it the partner must rely on the private partner to bridge the gaps.

In some PPP arrangements, for example, some partners may have different frameworks for their vision statement and their implementation strategy while others combined them in a single integrated document (Hodge & Greve, 2007). The differences are not simply a matter of presentation but reveal attitudes to long-term strategy formulation. Each approach has its own merits and the final choice is a matter of judgment. In the former approach, the visions sets the long-term perspective (for example, next thirty years) for the economic and social transformation of the project while the strategy can be updated at regular events within this timeframe to reflect changing external events, domestic economic circumstances and developmental achievements. The PPP projects' aspirations must be well defined but yet there is a degree of flexibility on how to achieve this strategy can be altered at particular intervals (Hoppe & Schmitz, 2013). In the latter approach, the common vision and implementation strategy might be expressed with the same timeframe (for example, the medium term) and can be readily disseminated as one document (Hwang, Zhao & Gay, 2013). The long-term implementation direction is not well known and may cause some uncertainty in the private party's perception and strategy (Jacobson & Choi, 2008). Moreover, there is a strong potential role for the parties (including third parties) in shaping the vision and the strategy at regular intervals.

Implementation

Implementing a strategically designed framework for enhancing risk sharing often poses particular challenges for many partnerships and it is most often at this stage that efforts tend to falter (Loosemore & Cheung, 2015). In this vein, the two main issues that need to be addressed at the implementation stage are:- coordination of the different parts of the strategy agenda and responsible parties and continuers monitoring of the strategy itself. The issue of coordination arises because most parties are not structured for effectively implementing a risk sharing strategy (Morse, 2010). In the case of the public partner, for instance, the responsibilities and functions that affected implementing risk sharing strategy are scattered over an array of the stages in the PPP processes: conception, identification, feasibility, procurement, implementation and operationalization (Lehtiranta, 2013). These often have different objectives and do not communicate with each other on a regular and intimate basis. Turf battles as to the achievement of the tenets of each of these stages are commonplace. Yet proper implementation of the strategy would require having in place measures that are flexible enough to ease implementation process. This assumes that identification of the right and applicable measures must take greater prominence of the actions to be undertaken (Kapsali, 2011). Similarly, the private partner, for example, might lack the experience and the capability to work with the public partner in implementing the strategy. An important step in strategy implementation is therefore to set up an agency that can cut across competing interests and coordinate the public partner and private partner concerned. There is no one prescribed form for a successful coordination and implementation agency, the most commonness in practice is the Special Purpose Vehicle (SPV). Such an organization can be either ad hoc (such as a semi-permanent company for example, for construction purpose only) or a formally organized entity (such as to complete the entire stages of a PPP project- from inception to operation) (Vajdić, & Damnjanović, 2011). These bodies may include a combination of experts, consultants, representatives of the credit institutions, public partner, and private partner. A leading party- the one who takes the highest risk is often responsible for the SPV. In some cases, though, this might prove impracticable especially if the part who took the highest risk does not have the capacity to manage the SPV for example, a public partner lacking requisite management skills. Whatever their form, the basis missions of the SPV is to ensure that the goals of the risk sharing strategy are adhered to, the plans and activities are implemented according to a strict timetable, the results are monitored and plans and activities are altered in the light of performance, and new plans and activities are devised as necessary.

NECESSARY CONDITIONS FOR RISK SHARING SUCCESS

A well-managed risk sharing strategy is clearly a necessary, but not sufficient, condition for PPP success both in the developed and developing world. Even the best managed risk sharing strategies can fail due to a variety of factors and for example, the developing world especially contains examples of failures as well as successes (Brandao & Saraiva, 2008). Three groups of factors can be readily identified (Camilleri, 2011). One group of factors relates to the external shocks (for example, a sudden increase in demands for quality products, international financial crunches, and a sharp increase in production needs) that are outside events that are beyond the control of partners. These events are very disruptive to the management of a risk sharing strategy and there is often little one can do to mitigate their effects. Another group of factors relates to party's size, geographical location and resource base. The presence of counter examples makes it hard to generalize about the relevance of these influences on risk sharing strategy and performance management (Clayton, 2013). However, geographically isolated parties may be at a disadvantage compared with those close to major markets, tiny parties might lack the stimulus of a large domestic market and be less attractive to PPP, and natural resources and skill-poor partners mat find they have fewer options for engaging in PPPs (de Bettignies & Ross, 2009). The design of a coherent risk sharing strategy needs to take these influences into account and develop long-term implementation remedies (Dewatripont & Legros, 2005). The final group is internal to the public sector and within the scope of decision making within that realm. These consist of stability, marked performance, public partner capabilities, public partner commitment and relations with the private sector.

Strong Public Partner's Capabilities

While there is a theoretical case for public partner action to enhance risk sharing strategy, in practice the public partner may lack the requisite skills and information to formulate, implement and monitor such strategies (Amekudzi & Morallos, 2008). Undertaking a comprehensively detailed risk sharing strategies (involving carefully designed targeting, tools, and implementation schemes) demands a host of socio-economic, management, technological and information technology skills that are in short supply in many public sector organizations (Farlam, 2005). In part, this may be due to employment of personnel who lacks requisite skills and no further staff development programs. It would seems the problem lies with the typical focus on hiring and giving them free-range-management skills than being given opportunities to continuously develop in their professions.

Lack of requisite capacity, poor workmanship development programs and lack of financial resources also reduce the public partner's capacity to undertake risk sharing strategies. Inadequacies of finances are often in excess at the expense of design a proper risk sharing strategy (Drew, 2005). Key decisions makers on the side of the public partner are sometimes switched from the right path of pursing correct measures which should be undertaken to overcome the challenges in designing an appropriate risk sharing strategy. In this vein, partnerships cannot assume any higher achievements at all. Instead, ganging up with the private partner becomes something inevitable to do (Farquharson, de Mästle, Yescombe & Encinas, 2011). It's perhaps through this effort that somehow the public partner can take a course in ensuring that a risk sharing strategy takes a direction of reaping some benefits for the public partner as well (Krishnan, Miller & Sedatole, 2011). Requisite skills and adequate financial resources are 'a scarce public sector resource' and can take many decades and millions of intervention in acquisition campaign to realize them. Consequently, risk sharing among partners can easily hit a snag where these issues are not improperly considered.

Good Private Partner Capabilities

Sound performance of the public partner can be enhanced with the involvement of the private partner. The coming into play of the private partner assists in the implementation of risk sharing strategy while the absence of private partners is itself a crisis that ends up being a hindrance (Ling & Hoi, 2006). Difficulties in obtaining finances, sudden shock in the management realm, collapses in the measures to implement a project and failure to maximally utilize the available skills resources often contributes to failure in the management of risk sharing strategy (Reeves & Ryan, 2007). This is rarely a case whenever the private partner comes into play.

Owing in part to their very nature, -profit maximization at the least cost-, the private partner tends to concerns itself not with public good. It is more concerned with doing more which will increase its profit at the least costs, even if, for example, it requires doing more than the usual, say for instance to produce a very high quality goods that customers need (Sears, Sears & Clough, 2008). However, in case of any inadequate commitment by the private partner the resultant effect would often be disastrous. For example, it would limit the seriousness of the risk sharing strategy and this backsliding will automatically affect partners' engagement even at a later time. Lack of commitment by the private partner has frequently led to reversal of achievement of risk sharing strategy.

Sustained Partners' Commitment

Designing and implementing a risk sharing strategy is not a one-off event. It requires good partners' capabilities and relations with each other (Liu & Wilkinson, 2014). Experiences have shown those countries which have had a long period of inward-looking policies for example, most developing countries like Uganda, Burkina Faso, and Malaysia are sometimes characterized by a tiny private sector with limited investment experience (Nsasira, Basheka & Oluka, 2013). Such an 'infant private sector' is unlikely to have the requisite technological and managerial capabilities to respond quickly to a call to risk sharing through PPP, for example. More so, they are not exposure to any external environment which would have perhaps made them relevant to the complexity of risk sharing. Similarly, a government with a 'socialist overhang' is likely to regard the private sector with suspicion, particularly multinational affiliates, and may not seek their participation in a PPP venture, for instance. Even then engaging them in matters that appeals most to PPP- that is risk sharing. Yet as proclaimed by Teo, Ling and Chong (2005) a significant loss would occur if the private sector were not actively involved in the development discourse, particularly risk sharing for to be viable PPP arrangement.

It is important that the public partner has to consciously deal with five major factors which are critical to ensuring that involving the private sector in any risk sharing initiative remained sustainable. Alongside the effective handling of risk, designing and developing a risk sharing strategy together with the private sector appear to have the best chance of enhancing their long-term relationship. As this issue largely relate to the very core of the existence of their relationship. Ogbu (2013) provides some interesting thoughts on risk sharing issues among the public and private partners. These thoughts underlie the implementation programs which may also be relevant to the success of the risk sharing strategy. His ideas include: the intertwining public partners' personnel with those of the private partner composed of those with a common, coherent vision of what needs to be done; the presence at the top of the SPV a manager with a vision of the goals of the partnership rather than an administrator unable to lift sights beyond the next day or an authoritarian preoccupied with defeating the next challenge to the status quo;

a comprehensive plan of action involving radical transformation of risk identification, to be done periodically and regularly; and the will and the ability to appeal to the different stakeholders and especially the employees of the public as well as private partners though all means of communication, including media, by passing vested interest in risk sharing.

CONCLUSION

There is an active debate on how fast risk sharing strategy can be developed within an empirical thrust of systematic analogy of risky situation. Gradual design and development of risk sharing strategy may be justified on financial grounds in large developing economies with long history of poor services delivery amidst inadequate financial resources. Awodele, Ogunsemi and Olabode (2008) suggest remedying the situation by the use of a core of potentially competitive designs, well thought out with application of planned tools. Developed countries, for example, USA or France might be cases in point. Otherwise, without those there would be most disadvantageous as for typical developing economy. Regardless of measures put in place, all those that act as constraints in the risk sharing processes should be eliminated immediately and be followed by staged reductions in the process. This way, the final risk sharing format will be agreeable to both parties. Another priority is for the parties to ensure that each of them should play an active role in designing as well as implementing the risk sharing strategy. Actionable suggestions may include: developing a specialized risk sharing capability within parties, inviting experts and consultants to guide in the process of designing and implementing the strategy. How parties come to realize the benefits of this forms the subject matter discussed in the next chapter.

REFERENCES

Aaltonen, K., Jaakko, K., & Tuomas, O. (2008). Stakeholder salience in global projects. *International Journal of Project Management*, *26*(5), 509–516. doi:10.1016/j.ijproman.2008.05.004

Abbasianjahromi, H., & Rajaie, H. (2012). Developing a project portfolio selection model for contractor firms considering the risk factor. *Journal of Civil Engineering and Management*, *18*(6), 879–889. doi:10.3846/13923730.2012.734856

Abdul-Rahman, H., Wang, C., & Lee, Y. L. (2013). Design and pilot run of fuzzy synthetic model (FSM) for risk evaluation in civil engineering. *Journal of Civil Engineering and Management*, *19*(2), 217–238. doi:10.3846/13923730.2012.743926

Acharya, N. K., Dai Lee, Y., & Man Im, H. (2006). Conflicting factors in construction projects: Korean perspective. *Engineering, Construction, and Architectural Management*, *13*(6), 543–566. doi:10.1108/09699980610712364

Adams, F. K. (2008). Construction contract risk management: A study of practices in the United Kingdom. *Coastal Engineering*, *50*(1), 22–33.

Adnan, H. (2008). *Risk management in design and build on construction projects in Malaysia.* ICCBT 2008-B-(04), 39-50.

Ahmad, E., Bhattacharya, A., Vinella, A., & Xiao, K. (2014). *Involving the Private Sector and PPPs in Financing Public Investments: Some opportunities and challenges.* Asia Research Centre Working Paper 67. Retrieved from www.lse.ac.uk/collections/AsiaResearchCentre

Ahmadi, M., & Heybati, F. (2009). *Risk management in public private partnership in infrastructure projects.* Paper presented at the International Conference on Financing System, Tehran, Iran.

Ahmed, A., Kayis, B., & Amornsawadwatana, S. (2007). A review of techniques for risk management in projects. *Benchmark International Journal, 14*(1), 22–36. doi:10.1108/14635770710730919

Akintoye, A. (2006). Public private partnerships for sustainable development of Infrastructure in developing countries. *Proceedings of International Conference on the Built Environment.*

Akintoye, A. (2008). Project risk management practice: The case of a South African utility company. *International Journal of Project Management, 26*(2), 149–163. doi:10.1016/j.ijproman.2007.03.011

Alderman, N., & Ivory, C. (2007). Partnering in major contracts: Paradox and metaphor. *International Journal of Project Management, 25*(4), 386–393. doi:10.1016/j.ijproman.2007.01.002

Aldoory, L., Kim, J.-N., & Tindall, N. (2010). The influence of perceived shared risk in crisis communication: Elaborating the situational theory of publics. *Public Relations Review, 36*(2), 134–140. doi:10.1016/j.pubrev.2009.12.002

Ali, R. (2005). The application of risk management in infrastructure construction projects. *Coastal Engineering, 47*(8), 20–27.

Almarri, K., & Blackwell, P. (2014). Improving risk sharing and investment appraisal for PPP procurement success in large green projects. *Procedia: Social and Behavioral Sciences, 119*, 847–856. doi:10.1016/j.sbspro.2014.03.095

Aloini, D., Dulmin, R., & Mininno, V. (2007). Risk management in ERP project introduction: Review of the literature. *Information & Management, 44*(6), 547–567. doi:10.1016/j.im.2007.05.004

AlSalman, A., & Sillars, D. (2013). *Modeling the effects of sub-optimal risk allocation in the construction industry.* Paper presented at the Engineering Project Organization Conference.

Amekudzi, A., & Morallos, D. (2008). The state of the practice of value for money analysis in comparing public private partnerships to traditional procurements. *Public Works Management & Policy, 13*(2), 114–125. doi:10.1177/1087724X08326176

Ameyaw, E.E., & Chan, A.P.C. (2013). Identifying public-private partnership (PPP) risks in managing water supply projects in Ghana. *Journal of Facilities Management, 11*(2), 152–182. 10.1108/14725961311314651

Ammar, A., Berman, K., & Sataporn, A. (2007). A review of techniques for risk management in projects. *Benchmarking: An International Journal, 14*(1), 22–36. doi:10.1108/14635770710730919

Andonova, L. B. (2010). Public-private partnerships for the earth: Politics and patterns of hybrid authority in the multilateral system. *Global Environmental Politics, 10*(2), 25–53. doi:10.1162/glep.2010.10.2.25

Apanavičienė, R., & Rudžianskaitė-Kvaraciejienė, R. (2010). *Analysis of evaluation methodologies for public-private partnership (PPP) projects in infrastructure construction.* Paper presented at the 10th international conference on modern building materials, structures and techniques, Vilnus, Lithuania.

Aquila, A. (2006). Best practices in risk management for firms. *Accounting Today, 20*(16), 8–21.

Arena, M., Arnaboldi, M., & Azzone, G. (2010). The organizational dynamics of enterprise risk management. *Accounting, Organizations and Society, 35*(7), 659–675. doi:10.1016/j.aos.2010.07.003

Asenova, D. (2010). *Risk management in private finance initiative projects: The role of financial services providers.* Saarbrücken: Lambert Academic Publishing.

Ashley, D. B., Diekmann, J. E., & Molenaar, K. R. (2006). *Guide to risk assessment and allocation for highway construction management.* Retrieved from http://international.fhwa.dot.gov/riskassess/pl06032.pdf

Assaf, S., & Al-Hejji, S. (2006). Causes of delay in large construction projects. *International Journal of Project Management, 24*(4), 349–357. doi:10.1016/j.ijproman.2005.11.010

Atkinson, A. A. (2005). Risk management and Monte Carlo simulation: An illustration and cautionary tale. *CMA Management, 79*(9), 36–40.

Atkinson, R., Crawford, L., & Ward, S. (2006). Fundamental uncertainties in projects and the scope of project management. *International Journal of Project Management, 24*(8), 687–698. doi:10.1016/j.ijproman.2006.09.011

Avazkhah, H., & Mohebbi, A. (2010). *Project risk management.* Tehran: KianRayanehSabz.

Aven, T. (2010). On how to define, understand and describe risk. *Reliability Engineering & System Safety, 95*(6), 623–631. doi:10.1016/j.ress.2010.01.011

Awodele, O. A. (2012). *Framework for managing risk in privately financed market projects in Nigeria.* Retrieved from http://www.ros.hw.ac.uk/...am/10399/2571/1/

Awodele, O. A., Ogunlana, S. O., & Motawa, I. (2010) Understanding and managing risks necessary condition for success and sustainability of privately financed market projects in Nigeria.*Proceedings of ARCOM Doctoral Researcher Workshop on Sustainability Strategies in the UK Construction Industry at University of Wolverhampton on 25th June.*

Awodele, O. A., Ogunsemi, D. R., & Olabode, J. B. R. (2008). *Private Participation in Infrastructure (PPI) development in developing economies- The Nigerian experience.* Paper presented at (COBRA) The Construction and Building Research conference of the Royal Institution of Chartered Surveyors, Dublin, Ireland.

Bain, R. (2010). *Project finance international.* London: Thomson Reuters.

Barlish, K., De Marco, A., & Thaheem, M. J. (2013). Construction risk taxonomy: An international convergence of academic and industry perspectives. *American Journal of Applied Sciences, 10*(7), 706–713. doi:10.3844/ajassp.2013.706.713

Beckers, F., Chiara, N., Flesch, A., Maly, J., Silva, E., & Stegemann, W. (2013). *A risk- management approach to a successful infrastructure project Initiation, financing, and execution*. McKinsey Working Papers on Risk, Number 52, 4-10.

Bedell, D. (2007). Taking risk beyond regulation. *Global Finance, 21*(6), 58–60.

Bennett, J., & Iossa, E. (2006). Building and managing facilities for public services. *Journal of Public Economics, 90*(10-11), 2143–2160. doi:10.1016/j.jpubeco.2006.04.001

Benta, D., Podean, I. M., & Mircean, C. (2011). On best practices for risk management in complex projects. *Informatica Economica, 15*(2), 142–152.

Berg, H.-P. (2010). Risk management: Procedures, methods and experiences. *RT&T, 1*(2), 79–95.

Bloomfield, P. (2006). The challenging business of long-term public-private partnerships: Reflections on local experience. *Public Administration Review, 66*(3), 400–411. doi:10.1111/j.1540-6210.2006.00597.x

Bock, K., & Trück, S. (2011). Assessing uncertainty and risk in public sector investment projects. *Technology and Investment, 2*(02), 105–123. doi:10.4236/ti.2011.22011

Bovaird, T. (2010). A brief intellectual history of the public-private partnership movement. In *International Handbook on Public Private Partnership*. London: Edward Elgar Publishing. doi:10.4337/9781849804691.00010

Bracey, N., & Moldovan, S. (2006). *Public-private partnerships: Risks to the public and private sector.* Paper presented at the 6th Global Conference on Business and Economics.

Brandao, L. E. T., & Saraiva, E. (2008). The option value of government guarantees in infrastructure projects. *Construction Management and Economics, 26*(11), 1171–1180. doi:10.1080/01446190802428051

Brewer, G., & Strahorn, S. (2012). Trust and the project management body of knowledge. *Engineering, Construction, and Architectural Management, 19*(3), 286–305. doi:10.1108/09699981211219616

Broadbent, J., Gill, J., & Laughlin, R. (2008). Identifying and controlling risk: The problem of uncertainty in the private finance initiative in the UKs National Health Service. *Critical Perspectives on Accounting, 19*(1), 40–78. doi:10.1016/j.cpa.2006.04.006

Camilleri, E. (2011). *Project Success: Critical Factors and Behaviors*. Surrey, UK: Gower Publishing Limited.

Campbell, S. (2005). Determining overall risk. *Journal of Risk Research, 8*(7-8), 569–581. doi:10.1080/13669870500118329

Cankar, S. S., & Petkovšek, V. (2013). Private and public sector innovation and the importance of cross-sector collaboration. *Journal of Applied Business Research, 29*(6), 197–1606.

Carbonara, N., Costantino, N., Gunnigan, L., & Pellegrino, R. (2015). Risk Management in Motorway PPP Projects: Empirical-based Guidelines. *Transport Reviews, 35*(2), 1–12. doi:10.1080/01441647.2015.1012696

Carbonara, N., Costantino, N., & Pellegrino, R. (2013). A three-layer theoretical framework for analyzing public private partnerships: The Italian case. *Organization, Technology and Management International Journal (Toronto, Ont.)*, *6*(2), 799–810.

Chapman, C., & Ward, S. (2008). Developing and implementing a balanced incentive and risk sharing contract. *Construction Management and Economics*, *26*(6), 659–669. doi:10.1080/01446190802014760

Chiu, T., & Bosher, C. (2005). Risk sharing in various public private partnerships arrangements for the provision of water and wastewater services. *Proc., Conf. on Public Private Partnerships—Opportunities and Challenges*, 11–21.

Choudhry, R. M., & Iqbal, K. (2013). Identification of risk management system in construction industry in Pakistan. *Journal of Management Engineering*, *29*(1), 42–49. doi:10.1061/(ASCE)ME.1943-5479.0000122

Cienfuegos, I. (2011). Risk Management Policy in Dutch Municipalities: Understanding the process, identifying its strengths and visualizing the possible improvements. *Revista Enfoques. Ciencia Política y Administración Pública*, *8*(14), 155–176.

Clayton, U. (2013). *Improving the outcomes of public private partnerships*. Sydney, Australia: Academic Press.

Cleden, D. (2009). *Managing project uncertainty*. Abingdon, UK: Ashgate Publishing Group.

Cooper, D., Grey, S., Raymond, G., & Walker, P. (2005). *Project Risk Management Guidelines: Managing Risk in Large Projects and Complex Procurements*. Chichester, UK: John Wiley & Sons Ltd.

Cretu, O., Stewart, R. B., & Berends, T. (2011). *Risk management for design and construction (RSMeans)*. Hoboken, NJ: John Wiley & Sons.

De Bakker, K., Boonstra, A., & Wortmann, H. (2010). Does risk management contribute to IT project success? A meta-analysis of empirical evidence. *International Journal of Project Management*, *28*(5), 493–503. doi:10.1016/j.ijproman.2009.07.002

de Bettignies, J.-E., & Ross, T. W. (2009). Public-Private Partnerships and the Privatization of Financing: An Incomplete Contracts Approach. *International Journal of Industrial Organization*, *27*(3), 358–368. doi:10.1016/j.ijindorg.2008.10.004

Delmon, J. (2009). *Private sector investment in infrastructure project finance - PPP projects and risks* (2nd ed.). Austin, TX: Wolters Kluwer.

Demirag, I., Khadaroo, I., Stapleton, P., & Stevenson, C. (2011). Risks and the financing of PPP: Perspectives from the financiers. *The British Accounting Review*, *43*(4), 294–310. doi:10.1016/j.bar.2011.08.006

Deng,, X., Hua, & Li, Q. (2008). Research on the approach of PPP project risk-sharing. *Construction Economics*, *12*, 62–64.

Dewatripont, M., & Legros, P. (2005). Public-private partnerships: Contract design and risk transfer. *EIB Papers*, *10*(1), 120–121.

Diab, M. F., Naser, K., & Varma, A. (2012). *Using risk assessment to improve highway construction project performance*. Paper presented at the 48th ASC Annual International Conference Proceedings. Retrieved from https://www.researchgate.net/profile/Khaled_Nassar6/publication/266055014_Using_Risk_Assessment_to_Improve_Highway_Construction_Project_Performance/links/54b7b5180cf24eb34f6ed082.pdf

Dooley, L., Lupton, G., & OSullivan, D. (2005). Multiple project management: A modern competitive necessity. *Journal of Manufacturing Technology Management*, *16*(5), 466–482. doi:10.1108/17410380510600464

Drew, J. (2005). Public private partnerships – Opportunities and challenges. *Proceedings of the Conference on Public Private Partnerships – Opportunities and Challenges.*

Duckert, G. H. (2010). *Practical Enterprise Risk Management-A business process approach.* New York: John Wiley & Sons. doi:10.1002/9781118269060

Edwards, P. J., & Bowen, P. A. (2005). *Risk Management in Project Organizations.* Oxford, UK: Butterworth-Heinemann.

El-Gohary, N. M., Osman, I. I., & El-Diraby, T. E. (2006). Stakeholder management for public private partnerships. *International Journal of Project Management*, *24*(7), 595–604. doi:10.1016/j.ijproman.2006.07.009

Essia, U., & Yusuf, A. (2013). Public-private-partnership and sustainable development of infrastructures in Nigeria. *Advances in Management & Applied Economics*, *3*(6), 113–127.

Fan, Z., Li, Y., & Zhang, Y. (2015). Generating project risk response strategies based on CBR: A case study. *Expert Systems with Applications*, *42*(6), 2870–2883. doi:10.1016/j.eswa.2014.11.034

Farlam, P. (2005). *Working together: Assessing public-private partnerships in Africa.* South African Institute of International Affairs, NEPAD Policy Focus Series.

Farquharson, E., de Mästle, C., Yescombe, E. R., & Encinas, J. (2011). *How to engage with the private sector in public-private partnerships in emerging markets.* Washington, DC: World Bank. doi:10.1596/978-0-8213-7863-2

Fischer, K., Leidel, K., Riemann, A., & Wilhelm Alfen, H. (2010). An integrated risk management system (IRMS) for PPP projects. *Journal of Financial Management of Property and Construction*, *15*(3), 260–282. doi:10.1108/13664381011087515

Flanagan, R., Norman, G., & Chapman, R. (2006). *Risk management and construction* (2nd ed.). Oxford, UK: Blackwell Publication.

Gan, X. H., Sethi, S. P., & Yan, H. M. (2005). Risk sharing and information revelation mechanism of a one-manufacturer and one-retailer supply chain facing an integrated competitor. *Production and Operations Management*, *14*, 80–89. doi:10.1111/j.1937-5956.2005.tb00011.x

Gao, S. S., Sung, M. C., & Zhang, J. (2013). Risk management capability building in SMEs: A social capital perspective. *International Small Business Journal*, *31*(6), 677–700. doi:10.1177/0266242611431094

Ghoddousi, P., & Hosseini, M. R. (2012). A survey of the factors affecting the productivity of construction projects in Iran. *Technological and Economic Development of Economy, 18*(1), 99–116. doi:10.3846/20294913.2012.661203

Girmscheid, G. (2006). *Holistic probabilistic risk management process model for project- oriented Enterprises*. Zürich: Eigenverlag IBB, ETH Zürich.

Gjerdrum, D. (2008). Risk management continues to gain international focus. *Professional Safety, 53*(12), 50–52.

Goh, C. A., & Abdul-Rahman, H. (2013). The identification and management of major risks in the Malaysian construction industry. *Journal of Construction in Developing Countries, 18*(1), 19–32.

Grant, R. M. (2010). *Contemporary strategy analysis* (7th ed.). New York: John Wiley & Sons.

Grimsey, D., & Lewis, M. K. (2005). Are public private partnerships value for money? Evaluating alternative approaches and comparing academic and practitioner views. *Accounting Forum, 29*(4), 345–378. doi:10.1016/j.accfor.2005.01.001

Gupta, D., & Sharma, M. (2015). Risk management in construction projects of developing countries. *Journal of Civil Engineering and Environmental Technology, 2*(14), 24–26.

Hallowell, M. R., & Gambatese, J. A. (2009). Construction safety risk mitigation. *Journal of Construction Engineering and Management, 135*(12), 1316–1323. doi:10.1061/(ASCE)CO.1943-7862.0000107

Harris, F. (2010). A historical overview of stakeholder management. In Construction stakeholder management. Chichester, UK: Blackwell Publishing Ltd.

Hemming, R. (2006). *Public Private partnerships, Government Guarantees, and Fiscal Risk*. Washington, DC: International Monetary Fund.

Heybati, F., Roodposhti, F. R., Nikoomaram, H., & Ahmadi, M. (2011). Developing a model for Iran about the relationship between economic freedom indices and public private partnerships. *African Journal of Business Management, 5*(9), 3511–3522.

Hillson, D. (2006). *Integrated Risk management as a framework for organizational success*. Retrieved from http://www.risk-doctor.com/pdf-files/adv13.pdf

Hillson, D., & Murray-Webster, R. (2011). Using risk appetite and risk attitude to support appropriate risk taking: A new taxonomy and model. *Journal of Project, Program, and Portfolio Management, 2*(1), 29–46.

Ho, P. H. K. (2006). Development of public–private partnerships (PPPs) in China. *Surveyors Times, 15*(10).

Hodge, G., & Greve, C. (2005b). *The challenges of public private partnerships: Learning from International Experience*. Cheltenham, UK: Edward Elgar Publications. doi:10.4337/9781845428082

Hodge, G. A., & Greve, C. (2007). Public–private partnerships: An international performance review. *Public Administration Review, 67*(3), 545–558. doi:10.1111/j.1540-6210.2007.00736.x

Hoppe, E. & Schmitz, P. (2013). Public-Private partnerships versus traditional procurement: Innovation incentives and information gathering. *The RAND Journal of Economics*, *44*, 56-74.

Hwang, B.-G., Zhao, X., & Gay, M. J. S. (2013). Public private partnership projects in Singapore: Factors, critical risks and preferred risk allocation from the perspective of contractors. *International Journal of Project Management*, *31*(3), 424–433. doi:10.1016/j.ijproman.2012.08.003

Iacob, V. S. (2014). Risk management and evaluation and qualitative method within the projects. *ECO-FORUM*, *3*(1), 60–67.

Ibem, E. (2010). An assessment of the role of Government agencies in public private partnerships in housing delivery in Nigeria. *Journal of Construction in Developing Countries*, *15*(2), 23-48.

Ibrahim, A. D., Price, A. D. F., & Dainty, A. R. J. (2006). The analysis and allocation of risks in public private partnerships in infrastructure projects in Nigeria. *Journal of Financial Management of Property and Construction*, *11*(3), 149–163. doi:10.1108/13664380680001086

Jacobson, C., & Choi, S. O. (2008). Success factors: Public works and public-private partnerships City of Manhattan Beach, Manhattan Beach, California, USA. *International Journal of Public Sector Management*, *2*(6), 637–657. doi:10.1108/09513550810896514

Jin, X.-H., Zhang, G., & Yang, R. J. (2012). Factor analysis of partners commitment to risk management in public-private partnership projects. *Construction Innovation*, *12*(3), 297–316. doi:10.1108/14714171211244550

Jones, G. R., & George, J. M. (2008). *Contemporary management* (11th ed.). London: McGraw- Hill.

Kamiya, S., Shi, P., Schmit, J., & Rosenberg, M. (2007). *Risk Management Terms*. Madison, WI: University of Wisconsin.

Kapsali, M. (2011). Systems thinking in innovation project management: A match that works. *International Journal of Project Management*, *29*(4), 396–407. doi:10.1016/j.ijproman.2011.01.003

Ke, Y. J., Wang, S. Q., & Chan, A. P. C. (2010a). Risk allocation in public-private partnership infrastructure projects: Comparative study. *Journal of Infrastructure Systems*, *16*(4), 343–351. doi:10.1061/(ASCE)IS.1943-555X.0000030

Keçi, J. (2015a). Public private partnership for infrastructure projects: Mapping the key risks, *International Journal of Social, Behavioral, Educational, Economic. Business and Industrial Engineering*, *9*(9), 3085–3095.

Keçi, J. (2015b). *Practices, barriers and challenges of risk management implementation in Albanian construction industry. In Urban Planning and Civil Engineering* (pp. 175–187). Athens: ATINER.

Kim, Y., & Vonortas, N. S. (2014). Managing risk in the formative years: Evidence from young enterprises in Europe. *Technovation*, *34*(8), 454–465. doi:10.1016/j.technovation.2014.05.004

Kishk, M., & Ukaga, C. (2008). The impact of effective risk management on project success. *Procs 24th Annual ARCOM Conference*, 799-808.

Klemetti, A. (2006). *Risk Management in Construction Project Networks*. Helsinki: University of Technology, Laboratory Industrial management.

Kolhatkar, M., & Dutta, A. B. (2013). Study of risk in construction projects. *Global Research Analysis International*, *2*(9), 104–107.

Koubatis, A., & Schönberger, J. Y. (2005). Risk management of complex critical systems. *International Journal of Critical Infrastructure*, *1*(2/3), 195–215. doi:10.1504/IJCIS.2005.006119

Krishnan, R., Miller, F., & Sedatole, K. (2011). The use of collaborative interfirm contracts in the presence of task and demand uncertainty. *Contemporary Accounting Research*, *28*(4), 1397–1422. doi:10.1111/j.1911-3846.2011.01124.x

Krześ-Dobieszewska, J. (2014). Managing public- private partnership market in the times of economic crisis. *Oeconomia Copernicana*, *5*(2), 63–74. doi:10.12775/OeC.2014.014

Kuppusamy, S. (2010). PPP: The right marriage between local government and the private sector in Malaysia. *International Journal of Institutions and Economics*, *2*(2), 142–166.

Kutsch, E., & Hall, M. (2010). Deliberate ignorance in project risk management. *International Journal of Project Management*, *28*(3), 245–255. doi:10.1016/j.ijproman.2009.05.003

Kuzmina, J. (2010). Risk management for sustainable growth. *Management and Sustainable Development*, *2*, 26–37.

Kwak, Y. H., Chih, Y., & Ibbs, C. W. (2009). Towards a comprehensive understanding of PPPs for infrastructure development. *California Management Review*, *51*(2), 51–78. doi:10.2307/41166480

Lam, K. C., Wang, D., Lee, P. T. K., & Tsang, Y. T. (2007). Modeling risk allocation decision in construction contracts. *International Journal of Project Management*, *25*(5), 485–493. doi:10.1016/j.ijproman.2006.11.005

Lehtiranta, L. (2013). Collaborative risk management processes: A constructive case study. *Engineering Project Organization Journal*, *3*(4), 198–212. doi:10.1080/21573727.2013.832671

Lenfle, S., & Loch, C. (2010). Lost roots: How project management came to emphasize control over flexibility and novelty. *California Management*, *53*(1), 32–55. doi:10.1525/cmr.2010.53.1.32

Lewens, T. (2007). *Risk: Philosophical Perspectives*. Routledge.

Ling, F. Y. Y., & Hoi, L. (2006). Risk faced by Singapore Firms when undertaking Construction Projects in India. *International Journal of Project Management*, *24*(3), 261–270. doi:10.1016/j.ijproman.2005.11.003

Liu, T., & Wilkinson, S. (2014). Large-scale public venue development and the application of public-private partnerships. *International Journal of Project Management*, *32*(1), 88–100. doi:10.1016/j.ijproman.2013.01.003

Loch, C., de Meyer, A., & Pich, M. T. (2006). *Managing the unknown: A new approach to managing high uncertainty and risk in projects*. Hoboken, NJ: John Wiley & Sons, Inc. doi:10.1002/9780470172377

Loizou, P., & French, N. (2012). Risk and uncertainty in development: A critical evaluation of using the Monte Carlo simulation method as a decision tool in real estate development projects. *Journal of Property Investment & Finance*, *30*(2), 198–210. doi:10.1108/14635781211206922

Loosemore, M., & Cheung, E. (2015). Implementing systems thinking to manage risk in public private partnership projects. *International Journal of Project Management*, *33*(6), 1325–1334. doi:10.1016/j.ijproman.2015.02.005

Loosemore, M., Raftery, J., Reilly, C., & Higgon, D. (2006). *Risk management in projects* (2nd ed.). Oxon, UK: Taylor and Francis.

Loosemore, M., & Zou, P. X. W. (2005). *Risk and opportunity management systems for property development and facility management companies*. Paper presented at International Symposium on Advancement of Construction Management and Real Estate, Hangzhou, China.

MacGillivray, B. H., Hamilton, P. D., Strutt, J. E., & Pollard, S. J. T. (2006a). Risk analysis strategies in the water utility sector: An inventory of applications for better and more credible decision making. *Critical Reviews in Environmental Science and Technology*, *3*(6), 85–139. doi:10.1080/10643380500531171

MacGillivray, B. H., Pollard, S. J. T., Hamilton, P. D., & Bradshaw, R. A. (2006b). Benchmarking risk management within the international water utility sector. Part II: A survey of eight water utilities. *Journal of Risk Research*, *10*(1), 105–123. doi:10.1080/13669870601011191

Mahendra, P. A., Jayeshkumar, J. R., Pitroda, R., & Bhavsar, J. J. (2013). A study of risk management techniques for construction projects in developing countries. *International Journal of Innovative Technology and Exploring Engineering*, *3*(5), 139–142.

Marques, R. C., & Berg, S. (2011). Risks, contracts, and private-sector participation in Infrastructure. *Journal of Construction Engineering and Management*, *137*(11), 925–932. doi:10.1061/(ASCE)CO.1943-7862.0000347

Matei, L. (2006). Empirical approaches of the public-private partnership in the services of public utility. *Theoretical and Applicative Economics*, *10*(505), 3–14.

Mauelshagen, C., Smith, M., Schiller, F., Denyer, D., Rocks, S., & Pollard, S. (2014). Effective risk governance for environmental policy making: A knowledge management perspective. *Environmental Science & Policy*, *41*, 23–32. doi:10.1016/j.envsci.2014.04.014

McKim, R. A. (2005). Risk Management – back to basics. *Coastal Engineering*, *34*(12), 7–12.

Monteiro, R. S. (2010). Risk management. In International Handbook on Public-Private Partnerships. Oxford, UK: Willey-Blackwell.

Moosa, I. A. (2007). *Operational risk management*. Basingstoke, UK: Palgrave Macmillan. doi:10.1057/9780230591486

Morse, R. S. (2010). Integrative public leadership: Catalyzing collaboration to create public value. *The Leadership Quarterly*, *21*(2), 231–245. doi:10.1016/j.leaqua.2010.01.004

Morsink, K., Hofman, P. S., & Lovett, J. C. (2011). Multi-stakeholder partnerships for transfer of environmentally-sound technologies. *Energy Policy*, *39*(1), 1–5. doi:10.1016/j.enpol.2010.09.043

Mouraviev, N. (2012a). Risk management in public-private partnerships and research agenda for transitional countries. *International Journal of Management and Business Studies*, *2*(2), 37–41.

Ng, A., & Loosemore, A. M. (2007). Risk allocation in the private provision of public infrastructure. *International Journal of Project Management*, *25*(1), 66–76. doi:10.1016/j.ijproman.2006.06.005

Nielsen, K. R. (2006). Risk Management: Lessons from Six Continents. *Journal of Management Engineering*, *22*(2), 61–67. doi:10.1061/(ASCE)0742-597X(2006)22:2(61)

Nisar, T. M. (2007). Risk Management in Public-Private Partnership Contracts. *Public Organization Review*, *7*(1), 1–20. doi:10.1007/s11115-006-0020-1

Nsasira, R., Basheka, B. C., & Oluka, P. N. (2013). Public Private Partnerships (PPP) and Enhanced Service Delivery in Uganda: Implications from the Energy Sector. *International Journal of Business Administration*, *4*(3), 48–60. doi:10.5430/ijba.v4n3p48

Ogbu, C. P. (2013). Risk management practices of multinational and indigenous construction companies in Nigeria: A comparative analysis. *Journal of Research in National Development*, *9*(2), 315–324.

Olander, S. (2007). Stakeholder impact analysis in construction project management. *Construction Management and Economics*, *25*(3), 277–287. doi:10.1080/01446190600879125

Olsson, R. (2008). Risk management in a multi-project environment: An approach to manage portfolio risks. *International Journal of Quality & Reliability Management*, *25*(1), 60–71. doi:10.1108/02656710810843586

Omwenga, L. K., & Nasieku, T. (2016). Factors that influence risk management of public private partnerships in Kenya's transport sector. *International Journal of Social Science and Information Technology*, *II*(VII), 702–722.

Palermo, T. (2014). Accountability and expertise in public sector risk management: A case study. *Financial Accountability & Management, 30*(3).

Pawar, C. S., Jain, S. S., & Patil, J. R. (2015). Risk management in infrastructure projects in India. *International Journal of Innovative Research in Advanced Engineering*, *4*(2), 172–176.

Perera, B., Dhanasinghe, I., & Rameezdeen, R. (2009). Risk management in road construction: The case of Sri Lanka. *International Journal of Strategic Property Management.*, *13*(2), 87–102. doi:10.3846/1648-715X.2009.13.87-102

Perminova, O., Gustafsson, M., & Wikström, K. (2008). Defining uncertainty in projects: A new perspective. *International Journal of Project Management*, *26*(1), 73–79. doi:10.1016/j.ijproman.2007.08.005

Petit, Y. (2012). Project portfolios in dynamic environments: Organizing for uncertainty. *International Journal of Project Management*, *30*(5), 539–553. doi:10.1016/j.ijproman.2011.11.007

Pohle, T., & Girmscheid, G. (2007). *Risk Management in PPP Maintenance Projects of Communal Street Networks.* Paper presented at CIB World Building Congress 2007, No: CIB2007-122.

Porter, M. E. (2008). *Competitive strategy: Techniques for analyzing industries and competitors.* New York: Simon and Schuster.

Quiggin, J. (2005). Public-private partnerships: Options for improved risk allocation. *The Australian Economic Review*, *38*(4), 445–450. doi:10.1111/j.1467-8462.2005.00388.x

Ramiah, I., & Reich, M. (2006). Building effective public-private partnerships: Experiences and lessons from the African Comprehensive HIV/AIDS Partnerships ACHAP. *Social Science & Medicine*, *63*(2), 397–408. doi:10.1016/j.socscimed.2006.01.007 PMID:16487640

Reeves, I., & Ryan, J. (2007). Piloting public private partnerships: Expensive Lessons from Irelands Schools sector. *Public Money and Management*, *27*(5), 331–338. doi:10.1111/j.1467-9302.2007.00604.x

Rohmeyer, P., & Ben-Zvi, T. (2010). Risk management decision making in service design. *MCIS 2010 Proceedings.* Retrieved from http://aisel.aisnet.org/mcis2010/73

Roumboutsos, A., & Anagnostopoulos, K. (2008). Public Private Partnership projects in Greece: Risk ranking and preferred risk allocation. *Construction Management and Economics*, *26*(7), 751–763. doi:10.1080/01446190802140086

Sanchez, H., Robert, B., Bourgault, M., & Pellerin, R. (2009). Risk management applied to projects, programs, and portfolios. *International Journal of Managing Projects in Business*, *2*(1), 14–35. doi:10.1108/17538370910930491

Sanchez, H., Robert, B., & Pellerin, R. (2008). A project portfolio risk-opportunity identification framework. *Project Management Journal*, *39*(3), 97–109. doi:10.1002/pmj.20072

Sanda, Y. N., & Anigbogu, N. A. (2016). A conceptual framework for managing risks in public private partnership in Housing Estate Development in Nigeria. *International Journal of Regional Development*, *3*(1), 50–63. doi:10.5296/ijrd.v3i1.8144

Sears, S. K., Sears, G. A., & Clough, R. H. (2008). *Construction Project Management, a practical guide to field construction management* (5th ed.). John Wiley & Sons, Inc.

Shahzad, B., & Safvi, S. A. (2010). Risk mitigation and management scheme based on risk priority. *Global Journal of Computer Science and Technology*, *10*(4), 108–113.

Shen, L., Platten, A., & Deng, X. P. (2006). Role of public private partnerships to manage risks in public sector projects in Hong Kong. *International Journal of Project Management*, *24*(7), 587–594. doi:10.1016/j.ijproman.2006.07.006

Ŝkrtić, M. M., & Horvatin, K. (2014). Project Risk Management: Comparative analysis of methods for project risks assessment. *Collegium Antropologicum*, *38*(Suppl. 1), 125–134.

Smith, N. J., Merna, T., & Jobbling, P. (2006). *Managing Risk in Construction Projects* (2nd ed.). Oxford, UK: Blackwell Publishing.

Smyth, H., Gustafsson, M., & Ganskau, E. (2010). The value of trust in project business. *International Journal of Project Management*, *28*(2), 117–129. doi:10.1016/j.ijproman.2009.11.007

Spikin, I. C. (2013). Risk Management theory: The integrated perspective and its application in the public sector. *Estado, Gobierno. Gestión Pública, 21*, 89–126.

Tahir, M. (2007). Risk management in public-private partnership contracts. *Public Organization Review, 7*(6), 1–19.

Teller, J., & Kock, A. (2013). An empirical investigation on how portfolio risk management influences project portfolio success. *International Journal of Project Management, 31*(6), 817–829. doi:10.1016/j.ijproman.2012.11.012

Teller, J., Kock, A., & Gemünden, H. G. (2014). Risk management in project portfolios is more than managing project risks: A contingency perspective on risk Management. *Project Management Journal, 45*(4), 67–80. doi:10.1002/pmj.21431

Teo, E. A. L., Ling, F. Y. Y., & Chong, A. F. W. (2005). Framework for project managers to manage construction safety. *International Journal of Project Management, 23*(4), 329–341. doi:10.1016/j.ijproman.2004.09.001

Too, E. G., & Weaver, P. (2014). The management of project management: A conceptual framework for project governance. *International Journal of Project Management, 32*(8), 1382–1394. doi:10.1016/j.ijproman.2013.07.006

Trafford, S., & Proctor, T. (2006). Successful joint venture partnerships: Public-private partnerships. *International Journal of Public Sector Management, 19*(2), 117–129. doi:10.1108/09513550610650392

Turnbaughs, L. (2005). Risk Management on large capital projects. *Journal of Professional Issues in Engineering Education and Practice, 131*(4), 275–280. doi:10.1061/(ASCE)1052-3928(2005)131:4(275)

Vajdić, N., & Damnjanović, I. (2011). *Risk management in public-private partnership road projects using the real options theory*. Paper presented at the International Symposium Engineering Management and Competitiveness 2011 (EMC2011), Zrenjanin, Serbia. Retrieved from http://www.tfzr.uns.ac.rs/emc/emc2011/Files/B%2005.pdf

van Mieghem, J. A. (2010). Risk management and operational hedging: an overview. In Handbook of Integrated Risk Management in Global Supply Chains. Hoboken, NJ: John Wiley & Sons, Inc.

van Opstal, D. (2007). *The resilient economy: Integrating competitiveness and security*. Retrieved from http://www.compete.org/publications/idea/2/risk-and-resilience/

Vasvári, T. (2015). Risk, risk perception, and risk management. *Public Finance Quarterly*, 1.

Wang, C., Walker, E. A., & Redmond, J. L. (2007). Explaining the lack of strategic planning in SMEs: The importance of owner motivation. *International Journal of Organizational Behavior, 12*(1), 1–16.

Wei, Z., & Ren, X. (2015). Research on risk-sharing of public-private partnership projects. *Management & Engineering, 21*, 1838–5745.

Wibowo, A., & Mohamed, S. (2010). Risk criticality and allocation in privatized water supply projects in Indonesia. *International Journal of Project Management, 28*(5), 504–513. doi:10.1016/j.ijproman.2009.08.003

Wysocki, R. K. (2009). *Effective project management: traditional, agile, extreme*. Indianapolis, IN: John Wiley & Sons.

Xiao, T., & Yang, D. (2009). Risk sharing and information revelation mechanism of a one manufacturer and one-retailer supply chain facing an integrated competitor. *European Journal of Operational Research, 196*(3), 1076–1085. doi:10.1016/j.ejor.2008.05.004

Yilmaz, A. K., & Flouris, T. (2010). Managing corporate sustainability: Risk management process based perspective. *African Journal of Business Management, 4*(2), 162–171.

Yuan, J. F., Zeng, Y. J., Skibniewski, M. J., & Li, Q. M. (2009). Selection of performance objectives and key performance indicators in public private partnership projects to achieve value for money. *Construction Management and Economics, 27*(3), 253–270. doi:10.1080/01446190902748705

Zenonas, T., Gajzler, M., & Dziadosz, A. (2012). Reliability, Risk Management, and Contingency of Construction Processes and Projects. *Journal of Civil Engineering and Management, 18*(2), 290–298. doi:10.3846/13923730.2012.672931

Zhang, H. (2007). A redefinition of the project risk process: Using vulnerability to open up the event-consequence link. *International Journal of Project Management, 25*(7), 694–701. doi:10.1016/j.ijproman.2007.02.004

Zinn, J. O., & Taylor-Gooby, P. (2006). Risk as an interdisciplinary research area. In P. Taylor-Gooby & J. Zinn (Eds.), Risk in social science (pp. 20-53). Oxford, UK: Oxford University Press.

Zitron, J. (2006). Public-private partnership projects: Towards a model of contractor bidding decision-making. *Journal of Purchasing and Supply Management, 12*(2), 53–62. doi:10.1016/j.pursup.2006.04.002

Zou, P., Zhang, G., & Wang, J.-Y. (2007). Understanding the key risks in construction projects in China. *International Journal of Project Management, 25*(6), 601–614. doi:10.1016/j.ijproman.2007.03.001

Zwikael, O., & Saleh, A. (2007). Planning effort as an effective risk management tool. *Journal of Operations Management, 25*(4), 755–767. doi:10.1016/j.jom.2006.12.001

Chapter 5
Risk in a Partnership

ABSTRACT

Each partner has an enormous obligation in the management of risks in any PPP arrangement. The partner must ensure that concerted efforts are exerted that risks are specifically specified in their natures and where they fall. The partners thus have to comprehensively get to the knowledge of the nature and kind of the risk and where they hit most. Literature review is used to identify all forms of risks in a PPP arrangement, and their effects, and their probable solutions. These are then explored through deeper systematic reviews of case studies of implemented PPP projects and those on-going ones implemented and being implemented in various countries. Risk issues in PPP relate to typology, perspectives of parties and criteria. The findings show that effective identification and comprehension of risk in PPP will increase the likelihood that intended purpose is achieved in PPP especially when the boundaries for risk taking is well established.

If you do not actively attack the risks, they will actively attack you. - Tom Gib

INTRODUCTION

In most PPP projects, risks of small, medium and large magnitudes make up the majority of the failures and account for the highest proportion of stalled/incomplete PPP projects. These risks that are intentionally unattended to are made able to rare their ugly faces and continue to survive to destroy a PPP project. In order to become less harmful, these risks must be consciously handled and comprehensively 'disbanded' from the PPP processes. These approaches can be particularly difficult to achieve for a successful PPP projects in both developed and developing economies. However, it's helpful to have a complete understanding of what these risks are which would act as a benchmark for properly managing them. This chapter identifies risks from a worldwide experience with examples and illustration from both the developed and developing world. These objectives can be particular helpful, now that many governments world over have taken to PPP by storm. In particular, this chapter focuses on classifying risks in a partnership by advancing them on terms of development phase, construction phase and operation

DOI: 10.4018/978-1-5225-2503-5.ch005

phase. The section on "approaches of risk management practice" describes the different approaches and their roles in the PPP cycle. The sub section on 'qualitative approach' describes the qualitative nature of risk and how this can be compensated. Quantitative risk approach is a sub section that makes most successful projects admirable. The sub section on "qualitative versus quantitative approach" outlines those that can be done and achieved by using the combined approach of qualitative and quantitative. The final section on "Integrated risk management" summarizes the process of secure risk management taken within the realm of an integral structure. It defines the term to make it clearer to be understood. This will then be followed by discussions on the principles of Integrated Risk Management (IRM) before taking on a deeper understanding of the critical success factors responsible for a smooth management or risks in PPP. This is chapter that must be well understood if risks are to properly managed because no one cam management something which such a one does not know of. There shall where applicable be detailed presentation of the different possible risks that can be experience in a PPP. The presentation shall be accompanied with deeper and detailed illustrations and some relevant examples will be provided as well. This is believed to act as a pace setter for the rest of the remaining chapters. In the end though there shall be a conclusion to the chapter, but as usual references for furthering readings shall also be included in the chapter.

RISK CLASSIFICATION IN A PARTNERSHIP

The term risk encompasses a heterogeneous group of unusual occurrences, ranging from a single event producing devastating effect at a single point to sophisticated events in complex projects, for example, PPP that requires specialized treatment. What is, or is not, a risk is usually defined by the number of those who handle it and definitions vary between actors and implementers. Jin and Doloi (2007) warn that risk is one of the biggest and most fascinating challenges of all times for humanity, because of its presence in all fields. Within the general complex PPP projects a number of risks can be identified: with no particular exception to any stage. In most instances, little efforts have been made to know and understand these risks such that in the end their devastating effects cannot be gauged. Failure to recognize the prevalence of risk in a partnership, caution Yongjian, ShouQing and Chan (2009) can lead to a distorted classification and inability to file proper solution(s). This section aids in that direction by discussing the typology of risk, risk factors as risk categories in a partnership.

Typology of Risk

According to Checherita and Gifford (2007), typology of risk in a partnership can be classified into two: common risks and PPP-specific risks. Common risks can arise in any road infrastructure investment, irrespective of the structure of ownership, financing or operation. Common risks can be classified according to the phase of the project lifetime in i) risks arising during the design-construction phase; ii) operational risks, and iii) permanent or indirect risk. A synthesis of the typology of common risk includes the adequate risk allocation between the government and the private partner. This is presented in Table 1 inclusive of the recommendations regarding contractual design and other measures that the public authority could implement in order to mitigate its risk, as well as the overall risk associated with the project.

Table 1. A typology of common risks in a PPP arrangement

Category of risk	How does it arise?	Who should bear it?	How can the government/public authority mitigate the risk?
		I. Design-construction phase	
		I.1. Technical risks	
1. Design fault	Technical Innovation; New travel demand tools; Errors in the tender specification	The party in charge of design; The public partner for tender specification	Conduct extensive simulations of the impact; Choose a well-experienced technical advisor if the public authority retains the design.
2. Cost and schedule overruns	Within construction consortium's control (inefficient construction practices, technologies, management) Within public partner control or other levels of government, directly affecting the contract - changes of legal and contractual framework; - failure or delay in land acquisition; - failure or delay in granting necessary project approvals and permissions. Outside either party's responsibility	Private partner Public partner See indirect risks	Select a single contractor for both construction and operation of the project; Design a comprehensive tender specification to be able to select a well experienced constructor-operator with adequate financial backing and good track record; Negotiate a fixed-price construction contract, include penalties for delays (penalties should be proportional to the shortfall, e.g. penalty per day or week of delay); Can combine it with bonuses for early completion. Conduct if possible an ex-ante research study on public attitude on the project, as well as political support. Have a legal opinion on the necessary changes in legislation, from an experienced law firm (to take into account successful experience in other jurisdictions).
3. Project completion risks (availability risk)	Defects in construction, quality shortfalls within construction consortium control or due to poor management in relation with subcontractors Within public partner's control (technical specification in the tender) Outside either party's responsibility	Private partner Public partner See indirect risks	Select a single contractor for both construction and operation of the project; Stipulate clear quality standards and penalties for quality shortfalls to be included in the contract; Require the private partner to provide insurance-backed guarantees for project completion.
	I.2. Economic and financial risks (for both construction and implementation phases)		
4. Financial parameters of the contract	- Inflation rate (costs indexation) - Interest rate - Exchange rate	Third party insurers (Risk transferred by the private partner to insurers/hedge funds/banks; premiums to be borne by end users)	Public entity can facilitate access of private consortium to international insurers, if necessary (e.g. multilateral financial institutions in case of developing countries), without extending public guarantees.

continued on following page

Table 1. Continued

Category of risk	How does it arise?	Who should bear it?	How can the government/public authority mitigate the risk?
5. Counterparty financial risks	Capacity of the contractual partners to uphold their financial commitments; Procurement risks	Private partner (consortium members)	Good tender specification for consortium selection; pre-selection criteria Require insurance-backed guarantees
		II. Operation phase	
6. Operating cost overruns and maintenance delays; Maintenancequality.	Within the private partner' control	Private partner (operator)	Specify in the contract: - firm and clear maintenance requirements; - clear expansion obligations or benchmarks that trigger expansion obligation (e.g. congestion levels) - penalties for quality shortfalls in maintenance.
		Revenue risks:	
7. Demand risk	Variability in the traffic volume (economic growth; tourism; urban development etc.) Price elasticity of demand Alternative road capacity (competing facilities, development of adjacent roads)	Private partner (operator) Public partner	First best: Let the private company to bear the risk of demand, both upward and downward variability, without granting revenue guarantees (test the market first by advertising the contract tender with no demand guarantee). - Introduce a contract design to limit the demand risk, such as: • flexible NPV plus strict quality standards and non-performance penalties, or • fixed-term contract plus a given extension period if the level of demand is below an agreed breakeven point specified in the contract; - Offer a balanced non-competing clause Second best: After trying the first option and no private interest is expressed, grant an upfront subsidy or a demand guarantee for the downsize risk, limited to a strictly enforceable period (e.g. 3 years, to vary according to the project's attractiveness). Collaborate with the private consortium in adequate demand modeling; finance or co-finance experienced consulting firm; Introduce dynamic toll pricing - Vary toll levels according to travel peaks on the toll roads and congestion in the free lanes/nearby free roads; vary tolls during the day and direction of traffic and by day of week. Let the private partner absorb the downside risk of price elasticity of demand. As regards the upside risk, correlate the level of tolls with congestion levels and the noncompeting clause. Clearly stipulate in the contract noncompeting clause and restrictions on alternative road capacity; Link this clause with congestion limits and expansion obligation; Need to strike a balance between the project's objectives and the long-term sustainability of the public transportation in the region.

continued on following page

Table 1. Continued

Category of risk	How does it arise?	Who should bear it?	How can the government/public authority mitigate the risk?
8. Price risk	Acceptable toll levels: - Political pressures: government breach of the terms of contract - Demand structure variability (e.g. lower proportion of trucks than estimated leading to a lower weighted average tariff)	Public partner/government Private partner	Conduct sensitivity studies on toll road support among the public; Develop a PPP marketing strategy; adopt a "quality enhancement" policy oriented towards attentiveness to users' suggestions; Encourage the development of auxiliary facilities along the toll road.
9. Collection enforcement risk	Natural disasters Political events affecting the contract indirectly (wars, political embargo, strikes) Exceptional political events affecting the contract directly, such as expropriation, nationalization of private consortium assets	Insurance companies (Private partner to transfer the risk to insurers) Public and private partner for risks not covered by insurance Insurance companies Public partner for risks not covered by insurance	Public entity can facilitate access of private consortium to international insurers, if necessary (e.g. multilateral financial institutions in case of developing countries), without extending public guarantees. Stipulate firmly and clearly in the contract cases of force majeure for: - transfer of the project into public operation; - cases/ thresholds for renegotiation (e.g. toll levels) in case the profitability of the project is affected.
11. Macroeconomic risks	Economic/financial/ balance of payment/currency crises Real output crises (severe energy shortage)	Insurance companies (Private partner to transfer the risk to insurers) Private partner for risks not covered by	Stipulate firmly and clearly in the contract cases for: - transfer of the project into public operation; - cases/ thresholds for renegotiation (e.g. toll levels) in case the profitability of the project is affected
12. Legal and institutional risks	Changes in the general legal framework (taxes, environmental standards) Institutional changes; legal recourse by third parties on noncommercial matters; conflicts between jurisdictions	Private company Public partner Private partner (seek insurance coverage for the sub sovereign risk)	The contract can specify clearly the trigger clauses for renegotiation (e.g. toll levels) in case the profitability of the project is affected Ensure compatibility of PPP legislation with current legislation (contract legal advisory if necessary) Strengthen the institutional framework in advance

Source: (Adopted from Checherita & Gifford, 2007)

At the design-construction phases, Table 1 indicates a number of risks. These risks whether in the form of technical or economic-financial risks or not, do affect the outcome of the project. In a PPP project, technical risks in the design and operation phase should be borne by the party responsible for the risk-generating factors, usually the private partner. If the public authority retains the project design, then any risks stemming from this phase should be borne by the public party (Tahir, 2007). However, generally technical risks can be classified into the categories of design fault risk, costs and schedule overruns, and project completion/project availability risk. The design default risk can arise when untested technical innovations are specified in the tender documents or an existing technology is proposed for a new application (for example, new location). Usually insufficient engineering and design work in the preliminary stages of the project can induce risks in all subsequent phases, in terms of compatibility, performance, and demand risk (Renn, 2006). Cost and schedule overruns can have different sources: internal to the project, external or a combination of the two (Adams, Alistair & Wu, 2006). Inefficient construction practices, management practices resulting in bad coordination with suppliers, delays in administrative approvals, land acquisition, geological conditions, default on the part of suppliers (Chan, Yeung, Yu, Wang & Ke, 2011). The occurrence of such risks will impact the financial terms during the operating phase, as well. According to Monteiro (2010), project completion/project availability risk consists in the private partner's failure to meet performance criteria at completion (quality shortfall and other defects in construction). Loosemore (2007) claims this risk stems primarily from the constructor's practices in the area of engineering and management (coordination with suppliers, poor allocation of resources, poor coordination and control over project components). Unforeseen risks related to conditions of the work site – climatic and subsoil conditions – can also play a role, but in this case, quality risk can be traded against cost or schedule overruns (Li, Akintoye, Edwards & Hardcastle, 2005b).

Morledge, Smith and Kashiwagi (2006) make a case that the economic-financial risks relate to the financial arrangements for project evaluation, design and construction, as well as for the phase of operation/implementation. Smith, Merna and Jobling (2006) demonstrates that such risks consist first and foremost of the set of parameters exogenous to the project, which are used in setting up the financial contract: (i) inflation rate risk - inherent for long-term construction projects, where prices are not firm for the whole period, but include an indexation clause to a relevant economic parameter, such as producer price index; (ii) interest rate risk – when the project is financed through variable-rate loans; (iii) exchange rate risk – when costs and revenues are expressed in different currencies. Bing, Akintoye, Edwards and Hardcastle (2005a) insinuate economic-financial risks relate to the capacity of the contractual partners to adhere to their financial commitments. This counterparty risk can stem from various causes, such as misevaluation of the financial position of the contractual partner (the constructor in the case of a road project), the chosen subcontractors (e.g. procurement risks), or the companies providing the project's financing, insurance and reinsurance. Essentially, Akbiyikli, Eaton and Turner (2006) proposes that it's recommendable to transfer economic-financial risks to the third parties, such as hedging funds, and banks. Cheung, Chan and Kajewski (2009a) suggest that the premiums for bearing these risks must be paid by the private consortium and transferred to end-users, i.e. toll-road users.

During the project's operation phase, risks relate to the period when the project generates revenue, but also continue to incur costs. Such risks can be classified as revenue risk; operating cost risks and financial risks (Daube, Vollrath and Alfen, 2007). The last two categories of risks are similar to those encountered in the design construction phase, but relate to the actual "functioning" of the project: The revenue risk is often the most important risk a project confronts. This category includes a pure "demand" risk or traffic volume risk, a price risk related to toll setting conditions, and an enforcement risk stemming from technological and regulatory risks in toll collection (Hodge & Greve, 2007). Teo, Ling and Chong (2005) shows that the demand risk is particularly strong in the case of newly built transportation facilities, where the absence of historical data complicates demand estimates. Zou, Zhang and Wang (2007) recommend that a PPP contract should provide for an adequate balance regarding restrictions on competing facilities or development of adjacent roads, so that neither the project, nor the long-term sustainability of transportation development is endangered. Tang, Shen and Cheng (2010) claims revenue risk can also arise from price risk or unexpected changes in the level of tolls, including fixing the tolls when the contract provides differently. Political opposition to increasing the level of tolls to the agreed contractual levels will affect the profitability of the contract. Price risk can also arise from the composition of demand (Shaoul, 2005b). A high variability in the nature of demand structure (for example, a lower proportion of trucks than initially estimated) induces a corresponding variability in the weighted average tariff, and in revenue. Sarmento (2010) states that enforcement risk arises from technology risks in automatic toll collection systems, as well as the risk of legal and regulatory disputes over revenue collection or, more generally, any regulatory issues that could prevent the project from becoming operational in full and on time. New technologies can significantly improve the profitability of the project, but also adversely impact the functioning of other projects that use obsolete technology (Adnan, Jusoff & Salim, 2008).

At the operation phase also, Acharya, Dai Lee and Man Im (2006) claim that there are indirect risk related to the project's environment. These risks are residual, not pertaining specifically to either party in the contract, and can be classified in three categories: risk of force majeure; macroeconomic risks, and legal risks. The risk of force majeure includes risks such as natural disasters, but also political risks such as riots, strikes (outside the two contractual parties), embargoes on supplies, etc (Akintan & Morledge, 2013). Alireza, Mohammadreza, Zin, Yahaya and Noor (2013) recommends that the risks of force majeure should be transferred to insurance companies, if the risk is insurable, otherwise it should be mostly borne by the public sector. Macroeconomic risks include indirect risks related to the overall stance of the economy, such as balance of payment crises, currency crises, severe economic downturns, and other economic and financial disturbances (Mouraviev, 2012a). Legal risks include changes in the general legal framework such as corporate laws, tax laws, environmental standards, and changes in the judicial system, especially regarding arbitration-related clauses (Goh & Abdul-Rahman, 2013). English and Baxter (2010) propose that risks arising from legal changes that are not determined by the public partner of the contract should be borne by the private consortium (as opposed to risks determined by changes in the legal or contractual framework that affect directly the private partner, which must be borne by the government).

PPP-specific risks are risks that stem from a particular relationship between private and public entities whose economic interests are distinctly bundled in the project (Demirag & Khadaroo, 2008). They are not specifically related to the infrastructure investment project. For such risks, the government usually retains residual ownership, while the financing-operation is mainly transferred to the private sector; (2) the parties have different objectives to maximize (satisfy); and (3) the parties have different prospects for risk diversification. PPP-specific risks can be categorized into three major groups: (i) fiscal risks, (ii) residual value risks, and (iii) bidding risk (Demirag, Khadaroo, Stapleton & Stevenson, 2011).

Fiscal risks occur as a result of government solicits for funds from the private sector to close financial gaps that exists between infrastructure needs and available public funds (Burke & Demirag, 2013). These risks are usually of two categories: contingent liability-related risk and fiscal investment risks. Contingent liability risk is the variability in fiscal expenditure induced by future uncertain events under the use of government guarantees (Costello, 2013). It is an indirect risk, with the fiscal variability being triggered by factors related to the project to which the guarantee is extended. Under a PPP framework, it is easier for the government to justify moving public investment off the budget, and public debt off the government balance sheet, in spite of still bearing the explicit or implicit fiscal risk resulting from residual asset ownership (Chung, 2009). Moreover, the partnership behind this type of arrangement can justify provision of government guarantees more easily than within traditional financing or complete contracting-out (Chung, Hensher & Rose, 2010). Hence, resorting to guarantees to secure private financing can expose the government to hidden and often higher costs than traditional financing (Christ, Sedatole & Towry, 2012). Fiscal risks and budget management can be complicated by such contingent liabilities due to lack of transparency. While this risk is most likely higher in developing countries, where problems of fiscal transparency and accounting are more pervasive, there are concerns in some developed countries as well (Chao & Liou, 2007). On the other hand, fiscal investment or fiscal management risk is that large upfront payments from the private partner to the government can have two impacts on government debt ratings. In principle, a prevalent impact, stemming for the time value of money – a dollar received today is worth more than a dollar tomorrow – would be an upgrading of the government fiscal position and risk outlook. However, there is a need to match investment decisions made today with long-term sustainability of public transportation (the government will not receive any revenues from the project during the entire duration of the concession). If this matching is not achieved, then this type of arrangement is likely to have a negative impact on the risk's assessment. Conversely, it will view negatively "the use of proceeds for short-term operating needs of the government" (Boardman & Vining, 2012). The credit ratings assigned to government debt and to the project itself can influence the financial parameters of the project in case of refinancing, hence impacting on the overall risk of the project.

Residual value risk is another category of PPP-specific risk. This risk relates to the future price of an asset (Broadbent, Gill & Laughlin, 2008). Barlish, De Marco and Thaheem (2013) retorts that it is specific to concession or leasing contracts, in which the road infrastructure assets is returned to the government after (a long period of) private operation. It relates to the gradual payment of concession fees as opposed to an upfront lump sum. For example, payment for toll road project is unique in that its economic value grows over time; thereby permitting increasing credit stability the longer it has been operating.

The third category of PPP-specific risk is the bidding risk - winner's curse or opportunistic renegotiation risk. This risk arises from the bidder's evaluation of other risks involved in the project. Bidding risk can be of two categories: the winner's curse and opportunistic behavior. The winner's curse risk arises in a competitive bidding, when a private firm makes a much better offer than any other competitor, based on its evaluation of the project (Badenfelt, 2008). It can result from insufficient experience of the bidder, poor risk assessment, or simply from high confidence in the project's potential (Antuchevičiene, Turskis & Zavadskas, 2006). Hence, the winner may actually end up paying more than the project is worth, or in any case, more than if he had bid more conservatively. The risk of opportunistic behavior is premised by Antón, Rodríguez and López (2011) as arising from any relationship involving competitive bidding. This is because of the fact that the government may be still be having the asset ownership and consequently, it has an interest in the project/bears at least a residual risk (as opposed to asset privatization). Also the project usually involves a complex risk bearing and institutional arrangement. Above all, the private partner's involvement in the project is usually longer and bigger stake involved in a PPP framework than under traditional financing.

Risk Factors in a Partnership

PPP projects are deeply associated with various sorts of risks (Aldoory, Kim & Tindall, 2010). These risks usually occur at three levels: macro, meso and micro levels. At the macro level, the risk are said to be at ecological level as the focus is on the PPP at the national or country level variables. Risks at the macro levels are associated with political and legal conditions (Singh & Kalidindi, 2006), economic conditions

(Thomas, Kalidindi & Ganesh, 2006), and social conditions (Ayeni, 2005). At the meso level, the risk are said to be at project level and represent the PPP implementation problem such as project demand/usage (McCann, Aranda-Mena & Edwards, 2014), location (Banerjee, Oetzel & Ranganathan, 2006), design and construction and technology (Gupta, Trivedi & Kansal, 2013). The micro level of PPP present risks between the contradictions in the public and private sector in contract management. Chan, Yeung, Yu, Wang and Ke (2011) highly encourage generation of risk categories according to these levels in order to take full responsibility of handling them. It is healthy, therefore, as advice by Chen and Partington (2006) to have a preliminary checklist of potential risk. Such a list can be generated from the existing risk factors in all the levels, that is, macro, meso and micro. Table 2 shows a probable checklist of risks involved in a PPP project which can be classified as macro, meso and micro level risks.

From Table 2 it can be asserted that there are a number of risk factors in PPPs. Conditions that can propel risk to occur, therefore, can be gleaned from the following facts: for example, newer projects are more prone to risks as they are different from the other projects. Older projects are likelihood of success

Table 2. Checklist of public private partnership risk factors

Risk Level	Risk	Risk Factors
Macro	Political and government policy unstable government Expropriation and nationalization Corruption Macroeconomic performance Poor financial market Inflation and interest rate fluctuation Exchange rate fluctuation Influential economic evens Legal Hard currency not transferability Currency exchange unavailable	Legislation change Change in tax regulation Social Social corruption Shortage of society voluntary Traditional public opposition Industrial Sector specified Industrial regulatory change Labor/material unavailable Natural Force majeure
Meso	Project selection Project demand Land acquisition Residual risk Project finance Project investment attraction Finance cost Design Design deficiency Construction Construction cost overrun	Construction time delay Delay material supply Design alteration risk Poor quality Technological Geographic conditions Operation Operation cost overrun Income under-performance Low productivity Maintenance
Micro	Public risk Higher project cost Private company capability Private monopoly risk Private inefficiency risk Private Risk Approval and permit risks Tort liability risks Publicly accountability Staff Crisis Reliability and creditworthiness of government	Both Contract variation Organization and co-ordination risk Little experience Inadequate distribution of responsibilities and authorities Laborious political decision-making process Difference in working method and know-how Power struggle No enough commitment

Sources: Reviewed literature.

against risks because there are similar projects has been done before. Management stability means the whole management shares the same goal or objective for any project (Andi, 2006). Therefore, it will be beneficial to achieve the project objectives with much ease. If the management is unstable then it can lead to affect the project objectives. If the staff for any project is sufficiently experienced and with different expertise the likelihood of quality, cost and other objectives can be achieved is higher with less cause of risk (Lam, Wang, Lee & Tsang, 2007). For larger teams of any project there are more chances of occurrence of problem because of mis-communication. If the project is available with a good amount of resources then the response to the problem will be good. Because if the project is available with greater amount of resources than it can deal with different risks with ease. If the project schedule is highly compressed there are more chances of occurrence of risks in projects. When more time is available for the project, then it can be coped up by reducing risk impact on the project. If the project is highly complex there are more chances for the occurrence of problem in the project.

Aside from the existence of risk factors at the macro, meso and micro levels, they are as well embedded in the phases of a PPP project: those are development, construction and operation phases (Chinyio & Gameson, 2009). Each of these phases has their own sets or risks. In the development phase, the main risk is rejection by the host government. The risk is usually high though usually involves small losses and are always borne primarily by the sponsors. Examples of the most common risks at the development stage include: technology risk, credit risk, bid risk, expropriation risk and force majeure risk. At the construction phase, the main risk is failure to complete the project with accepting performance and within an acceptable time frame and budget (Liu & Wilkinson, 2011). Consequently, any interruption because of risk might result in the delay of the projected cash flow and thus delay the scheduled payment of loans. Although the risks mainly fall on the sponsors, they in turn hedge the risks by purchasing insurance or surety bond and require guarantees from the contractors and subcontractors in the form of predetermined agreement. The risks involved in this phase are high and involves potentially significant losses (Rohmeyer & Zvi, 2009). Examples of the most common risks in the construction phase include: - completion risk, cost overrun risk and performance risk. At the operation phase, the most common risks include: operation cost overrun risk, sponsor performance risk, liability risk, equity resale risk, and off-take risk. There are also other risks involved in the phases such as interest rate risk and exchange rate risk.

Aven (2010) suggests that it is better to define and describe a particular risk so as to have a proper understanding for findings solutions unto it. For example, past studies (Cooper, Grey, Raymond, & Walker, 2005) have identified and listed risks associated with PPP projects in different infrastructure sectors as presented in Table 3.

According to Zinn and Taylor-Gooby (2006), risks need to be properly interpreted for ease of finding sustainable solutions to them. Various past studies have provided easier means of interpreting risks in a PPP projects as presented in Table 4.

Risk Categories in Stages of PPP Projects

Different stages of a PPP project have varied categories of risks. Risks in the PPP project stages have been categorized into four main areas: - Site risk; design, construction and commissioning risk, financial risk; and operating risk.

According to Jin (2010a), site risk is a risk category that the project land will be unavailable or unable to be used at the required time, in the manner or at the cost anticipated, or that the site will gener-

Table 3. List of risks associated with PPP projects in different infrastructure sectors

Sector	Sector-Specific Risk
All sectors	Force majeure risk Political risks (change in law and regulation; revoke; expropriation) Financial risks (inflation; interest rate; exchange rate and convertibility) Competition risk Environmental risk (increasing consciousness in society) Land acquisition and compensation risk Construction risks (cost overrun; delay; quality) Operation risk (operator inability; output quantity and quality; production regularity) Condition of facility Supply risk (shortage; quality) Off-take risk (quantity; pay in time) Documentation/contractual risk (conflict and arbitration; applied law)
Power	Repayment of external debt Restriction on imported equipment and raw materials Fluctuating demand of power generated Problem in bill collection Illegal connection to transmission system (power theft) Transmission failure Lowered tariffs due to competition Specification not being fulfilled, resulting in refusal of power purchase by state utility Power plant location (inadequate transport facilities) Environmental dispute Fluctuation of cost and availability of fuel/coal Construction delay Prolonged downtime during operation Liquidated damages or termination of Power Purchase Agreement (output and quality do not meet off-taker's requirement) Government's restrictions on profitability (rate of return) and tariff levels
Transport (road)	Inadequate traffic volume (inadequate traffic forecasts or subsequent deviation) Competing routes (particularly free or underpriced ones) Restrictions on toll level and increase Cost overruns (because of size and scope, particularly if project crosses a hilly region) Construction delays (land acquisition; unexpected technical difficulty) Long land acquisition period Right-of-way disputes (e.g., archaeological mines) Necessitating measures to minimize the impact of construction on traveling public Delay in other projects connecting to this road Income streams are usually in local currency (exchange rate and convertibility risk)
Transport (tunnel and bridge)	Geological risks for immersed tunnel Safety at work and disturbances to surface traffic in municipal areas Health risks of compressed air Stability of seabed for submerged tunnel Traffic accidents and fire breakouts for tunnels during operation Restrictions to harbor navigation and air traffic flight path for bridge Hydrological opposition from ferry workers and fishermen Bad weather conditions Competition from ferries and airlines
Transport (rail)	Long land acquisition period Complex relocation of existing utilities Uncoordinated attempt in various districts Controlled fare levels Complexity of getting design approvals Competition from road transportation Environmental dispute Taxation Expensive rolling stock and control systems
Transport (airport and port)	Competition from other airports Regional or international trade prosperity Tourism business prosperity Political stability and spending pattern Integration with other connecting facilities Inadequate adjoining land for expansion Throughput capacity affected by breakdown of equipment, labor disputes, and extreme weather conditions for port Economic and trade conditions Changes in tariff regulations and quotas Political risk
Process plant	Take-or-pay agreement with gas producer Leakage of pipe Nonpayment and pilferage Controlled tariffs Fast changing environmental regulations for waste treatment (rising concerns and advancing technology making improvements possible)
Telecommunication	Most competitive sector High research and development costs Restrictions by incumbent operator for new entrants to access to established network Addition cost and problem in integrating with existing network including technological incompatibility Bureaucracy in licensing

continued in next column

Table 3. Continued

Source: Reviewed literature in reference

Table 4. Interpretation of each risk factor associated with PPP Projects

s/no	Risk Factors	Description	Source
1	Government corruption	The behavior of the corruption of government officials will increase the cost of keeping the relationships between the government and the project company. Meanwhile, it will increase the risk of contract breaking by the government.	Warburton and Baker(2005); Maslyukivska and Sohail (2007); Zou, Wang & Fang (2008)
2	Government intervention	Government officials intervene in the project operations directly, which will affect the autonomy of private investors' decision making.	Warburton and Baker(2005); Shen, Platten & Deng (2006); Ng and Loosemore (2007); Medda (2007)
3	Nationalization/ expropriation	Central or local government seizes the projects.	Li, Akintoye, Edwards, & Hardcastle (2005; Ng and Loosemore (2007); Estache, Juan & Trujillo (2007); Medda (2007)
4	Public credit	The rejection of government to implement the responsibilities agreed in the contract, which brings direct or indirect damages.	Li, Akintoye, Edwards, & Hardcastle (2005); Ng and Loosemore (2007); Li, Akintoye, Edwards, & Hardcastle (2005)
5	Third-party delay/ violation	Apart from government or private investors, other project participants do not implement the responsibilities agreed in the contract or project delay.	Li, Akintoye, Edwards, & Hardcastle (2005
6	Political/public opposition	For various reasons leading to the public interest being unprotected and damaged, which, as a consequence, causes political and even public opposition to the risk of the project construction.	Li, Akintoye, Edwards, & Hardcastle (2005); Estache, Juan & Trujillo (2007); Zou, Wang & Fang (2008)
7	Imperfect law and supervision system	The damage arising from the current PPP legislation which is low level, low effectiveness, conflict bearing, and poor operability.	Shen, Platten & Deng (2006); Maslyukivska and Sohail (2007)
8	Legislation change	Change of law and regulations and other government macroscopic economic policies will cause the increase in project costs and decrease in revenue, etc.	Shen, Platten & Deng (2006); Li, Akintoye, Edwards, & Hardcastle (2005); Maslyukivska and Sohail (2007); Ng and Loosemore (2007); Estache, Juan & Trujillo (2007)
9	Interest rate fluctuation	The loss of PPP projects arising from the uncertainties of the interest rate volatility.	Estache, Juan & Trujillo (2007); Li, Akintoye, Edwards, & Hardcastle (2005); Ng and Loosemore (2007); Medda (2007): Zou, Wang & Fang (2008)
10	Foreign exchange fluctuation	The risk of the variability of foreign currencies exchange and the foreign currencies exchangeability risk.	Ng and Loosemore (2007); Estache, Juan & Trujillo (2007); Medda (2007); Zou, Wang & Fang (2008)
11	Inflation	The increase of the price level of the commodities, the decrease of purchasing power of currencies, which cause the increase of cost and other consequence.	Zou, Wang & Fang (2008); Li, Akintoye, Edwards, & Hardcastle (2005); Shen, Platten & Deng (2006)
12	Poor public decision-making process	Non-standardized procedures, bureaucracy, lacking of PPP project experience and ability, insufficient preparation and information asymmetry, leading to poor decision making.	Li, Akintoye, Edwards, & Hardcastle (2005)
13	Land acquisition	The increase in project cost and extension of project duration caused by the difficulty of acquiring the rights of the land. The cost and time for land acquisition exceeds the original plans.	Li, Akintoye, Edwards, & Hardcastle (2005); Estache, Juan & Trujillo (2007);

continued on following page

Table 4. Continued

s/no	Risk Factors	Description	Source
14	Delay in project approvals and permits	Complicated procedures are required for project approval with high cost and long time. Upon approval, it is very difficult to precede business adjustments regarding the project scope and nature.	Li, Akintoye, Edwards, & Hardcastle (2005); Estache, Juan & Trujillo (2007); Ng & Loosemore (2007)
15	Conflicting or imperfect contract	The risk of the contract with inaccuracy, vagueness, inflexibility, inconsistency, inequitable risk-sharing, unclear division of responsibility, etc.	Li, Akintoye, Edwards, & Hardcastle (2005); Shen, Platten & Deng (2006)
16	Financing risk	The risk arising from the irrational financing structure, unsound financial market, and difficulty in financing.	Li, Akintoye, Edwards, & Hardcastle (2005); Shen, Platten & Deng (2006)
17	Project/operation changes	Poor constructability in design phase, design error or vagueness, standards and contracts variation, owners' variation leading to the project, or operation changes.	Grimsey Warburton & Baker (2005)
18	Completion risk	Project delay and cost overrun, etc., which cause insufficient cash flow and inability to pay off debts on time.	Estache, Juan & Trujillo (2007); Ng & Loosemore (2007)
19	Material/ labor non-availability	Loss because of delay in raw materials, resources, machines and equipment, or energy supply.	Ng & Loosemore (2007); Li, Akintoye, Edwards, & Hardcastle (2005); Shen, Platten & Deng (2006); Estache, Juan & Trujillo (2007)
20	Unproven engineering techniques	The techniques adopted are immature and cannot fulfill the standards and requirements as expected, or the techniques are of poor applicability which makes private investors to reinvest for the technology improvement.	Estache, Juan & Trujillo (2007); Ng & Loosemore (2007);
21	Unforeseen weather/ geotechnical conditions	Because of the project site's bad natural conditions, for example, climate condition, special geographical environment, and poor site conditions, etc.	Ng & Loosemore (2007); Li, Akintoye, Edwards, & Hardcastle (2005);
22	Operation cost overrun	Government raises the standard of the products or services leading to the cost overrun by the noncommercial factors such as increase in interest rates, exchange rates or force majeure, or poor operation management.	Ng & Loosemore (2007); Li, Akintoye, Edwards, & Hardcastle (2005); Estache, Juan & Trujillo (2007); Shen, Platten & Deng (2006)
23	Market competition (uniqueness)	An actual market competition of the existing project caused by the new project or rebuild project of government or other investors.	Maslyukivska & Sohail (2007); Zou, Wang & Fang (2008)
24	Change in market demand	Apart from the risk from arising from market competition, factors attributed to macroeconomics, social environment, change in population, adjustment of laws, and regulations leading to the change in market demand.	Li, Akintoye, Edwards, & Hardcastle (2005)
25	Price change	Price of PPP products or services are too high, too low, or inflexible to adjust, leading to the revenue of the project company lower than expected.	Ng & Loosemore (2007)
26	Expense payment risk	Infrastructure of the project or the process of the service provision is affected by other factors which prevents the timely payment of the client's (or government's) fees.	Shen, Platten & Deng (2006); Ng & Loosemore (2007)
27	Lack of supporting infrastructure	The risks generated by the unavailability of the supporting facilities of the project.	Ng & Loosemore (2007); Shen, Platten & Deng (2006)
28	Residual risk	Investors overuse the resources like equipment or other technical conditions, etc., which cause insufficient materials and equipment with depreciation at the end of the concession period. As a consequence, it affects the continuous operation of the projects.	Li, Akintoye, Edwards, & Hardcastle (2005); Ng & Loosemore (2007)

continued on following page

Table 4. Continued

s/no	Risk Factors	Description	Source
29	Inadequate competition for tender	The risk includes unfair, nontransparent tendering process, incomplete tender information, insufficient number of tenders, vicious market competition, and bidding lowest price to win the tenders.	Maslyukivska & Sohail (2007)
30	Inability of concessionaire	The insufficient ability of the concessionaire leading to low productivity of project construction and operation.	Ng & Loosemore (2007); Estache, Juan & Trujillo (2007) (2007)
31	Force majeure	Before signing contract, the contract party cannot control or prevent reasonably. When the events happen, the situation cannot be escaped or conquered, such as a worker strike, or other unforeseen items that are not "natural" risks.	Li, Akintoye, Edwards, & Hardcastle (2005); Ng & Loosemore (2007); Estache, Juan & Trujillo (2007)
32	Organization and coordination risk	Because of the insufficient coordination ability of project company, the cost of communication among project participants' increases and conflicts occurs.	Li, Akintoye, Edwards, & Hardcastle (2005); Ng & Loosemore (2007); Shen, Platten & Deng (2006);
33	Change in tax regulation	The change in tax regulation of central or local government.	Li, Akintoye, Edwards, & Hardcastle (2005); Ng & Loosemore (2007); Estache, Juan & Trujillo (2007); Medda (2007)
34	Environment risk	Because of the increasing requirement of the government or social organization regarding the environment protection, risk generated from the project cost increase, delay in work schedule, or other loss.	Li, Akintoye, Edwards, & Hardcastle (2005); Maslyukivska & Sohail (2007)

ate unanticipated liabilities. Thus, risks included into this category are: land acquisition risk, landsite unsuitability risk and environmental risk. Table 5 presents categories of site risks and their distribution.

Design, construction and commissioning risk is the risk that the design, construction or commissioning of the facility or certain elements of each of these processes, are carried out in a way which results in adverse cost and/or project delivery consequences. Jefferies and McGeorge (2008) indicates risks such

Table 5. Site risk categories and their distribution

Type of Risk	Impact of Risk	Public	Private
Land acquisition delay and costs overrun	Delay and costs increase due to unclear and then prolonged land acquisition process	+	
Land acquisition can't be performed entirely	Unable to acquire project land site due to difficult land acquisition process	+	
Complex resettlement process	Costs overrun and delay due to a complicated resettlement process	+	
Unforeseen difficulties of site conditions	Delay due to uncertainty of ground conditions		+
Damaged of arte-facts and antiquates in the site			+
Demolition			+
Fail in keeping site safety			+
Unusual weather claim			+
Contamination/ Pollution to the site environment			+

Source: (Yongjian, ShouQing & Chan, 2009).

as planning risk, design risk, completion risk, cost overrun risk and commissioning risk are included in this category of risk. Table 6 shows this category of risk and their distribution in a PPP arrangement.

Financial risks are those risks related to financial viability aspects of the project. There are a number of risks involved in this category including financial risk, financial parameter risk, financial structure risk and insurance risk (Carpintero & Petersen, 2015). Table 7 presents risks categorized as financial risk as their distribution.

Operating risk is the risk that the process for delivering the contracted services- or an element of that process (including the inputs within or as part of that process) - will be effected in a way that prevents the Project company from delivering the contracted services according to the agreed specifications and/ or within the projected costs (Koubatis & Schönberger, 2005). In this category, the risks included are maintenance risk, latent defect risk, technology risk, utilities risk and resource or input risk, and industrial relations risk. The distribution of these risks is presented in Table 8.

Table 6. Design, construction and commissioning risk categories and their distribution

Type of Risk	Impact of Risk	Public	Private
Cost increase due planning issues			+
Design brief risk	Time and cost overruns due to unclear/ incomplete design brief		+
Additional design works required by operator			
Delay in completing construction works and returning site access			+
Construction cost increase			+
Design faults	Technical commissioning leads to discovery of design faults		+
Commissioning risk	Incorrect time/cost estimates of technical commissioning		+

Source: (Yongjian, ShouQing and Chan, 2009).

Table 7. Financial risks and their distribution

Type of Risk	Impact of Risk	Public	Private
Fail to achieve financial close	Inability to achieve financial close due to market uncertainty		+
Financial structure risk	Inefficiency due to in-optimal project's capital structure		+
Foreign exchange rate risk	Foreign exchange rate risk		+
Inflation rate risk	Increase of inflation rate used for estimating life-cycle costs		+
Interest rate risk	(non extreme) fluctuation of loan interest rate		+
(non extreme) fluctuation of loan interest rate Insurance	cover for a certain risk is no longer available from reputable insurers in the market		+
Insurance risk (2)	Substantial increases in rates at which insurance premiums are calculated		+

Source: (Yongjian, ShouQing and Chan, 2009).

Table 8. Operating risk categories and their distribution

Type of Risk	Impact of Risk	Public	Private
Availability of facilities			+
Non-performance of services			+
Poor performance of services			+
Industrial action (1)	Industrial actions (strike, lockout, go slow, etc) by operator staff		+
Industrial action (2)	Industrial actions (strike, lockout, go slow, etc) by subcontractor or supplier		+
O&M cost overrun risk	Mis-estimation of O& M costs		+
Estimation of life cycle expenditure is incorrect			+
Increase in energy costs - due to inefficient plant			+
Irregular availability of required utilities			+
Shortfall of input quantity	Raw water deficit due to reasons under public sector control	+	
Decrease of input quality	Declining water quality due to reasons under public sector control	+	
Uncertainty of input continuity		+	
Shortfall of output quantity			+
Decrease of output quality			+

Source: (Yongjian, ShouQing and Chan, 2009).

Chiu and Bosher (2005) opined that much of the risk of PPP projects comes from the complexity of the arrangement itself in terms of documentation, financing, taxation, technical details, and sub-agreements involved in a major infrastructure venture, while the nature of the risk changes over the duration of the projects. It would seems, the taxonomy of risk sources and their respective control requirements should have a consistent basis for the development of a proactive PPP risk management strategies (Hwang, Zhao & Gay, 2013). Accordingly, this will be suitable for a vigorous and complex PPP relationship as suggested by Xu, Yeung, Chan, Chan, Wang and Ke (2010). For ease of risk management in a PPP project, Renn (2006) proposes that risk should be classified into four distinct categories: simple risk problems, complex risk problems, risk problems due to high unresolved uncertainty, and risk problems due to interpretative and normative ambiguity. This classification is captured in Table 9.

Table 9 provides a summary of the four risk strategies as classified by Renn (2006). The Table also lists the instruments and tools that are most appropriate for the respective strategy. Again it should be emphasized that the list of strategies and instruments is not exhaustive and can be amended if the case requires it.

Jin (2010a) avers simple risks problems are a class that requires hardly any deviation from traditional decision making. Data is provided by statistical analysis, goals are determined by law or statutory requirements and the role of risk management is to ensure that all risk reduction measures are implemented and enforced. Traditional risk-risk comparisons (or risk-risk trade-offs), risk-benefit analysis and cost-effectiveness studies are the instruments of choice for finding the most appropriate risk reduction measures. Additionally, risk managers can rely on best practice and, in cases of low impact, on trial and error. It should be noted, however, that simple risks should not be equated with small or negligible risks (Zahari-

Table 9. Risk characteristics and their implications for risk management

Knowledge Characterization	Management Strategy	Appropriate Instruments	Stakeholder Participation
1 'Simple' risk problems	Routine-based: (tolerability/ acceptability judgment) (risk reduction)	Applying 'traditional' decision-making • Risk-benefit analysis • Risk-risk trade-offs • Trial and error • Technical standards • Economic incentives • Education, labeling, information • Voluntary agreements	Instrumental discourse
2 Complexity induced risk problems	Risk-informed: (risk agent and causal chain)	Characterizing the available evidence • Expert consensus seeking tools: o Delphi or consensus conferencing o Meta analysis o Scenario construction, etc. • Results fed into routine operation	Epistemological discourse
	Robustness focused: (risk absorbing system)	Improving buffer capacity of risk target through: • Additional safety factors • Redundancy and diversity in designing safety devices • Improving coping capacity • Establishing high reliability organizations	
3 Uncertainty induced risk problems	Precaution based: (risk agent)	Using hazard characteristics such as persistence, ubiquity etc. as proxies for risk estimates Tools include: • Containment • ALARA (as low as reasonably achievable) and ALARP (as low as reasonably possible) • BACT (best available control technology), etc.	Reflective discourse
	Resilience focused: (risk absorbing system)	Improving capability to cope with surprises • Diversity of means to accomplish desired benefits • Avoiding high vulnerability • Allowing for flexible responses • Preparedness for adaptation	
4 Ambiguity induced risk problems	Discourse based:	Application of conflict resolution methods for reaching consensus or tolerance for risk evaluation results and management option selection • Integration of stakeholder involvement in reaching closure • Emphasis on communication and social discourse	Participative discourse

Source: (Renn, 2006).

oaie, 2012). The major issues here are that the potential negative consequences are obvious, the values that are applied are non-controversial and the remaining uncertainties low. Examples are car accidents, known food and health risks, regularly reoccurring natural disasters or safety devices for high buildings.

Complex risk problems are class whose major input for risk management is provided by the scientific characterization of the risk (Loizou & French, 2012). Complex risk problems are often associated with major scientific dissent about complex dose-effect relationships or the alleged effectiveness of measures to decrease vulnerabilities (for complexity refers to both the risk agent and its causal connections and the risk absorbing system and its vulnerabilities). The objective for resolving complexity is to receive a complete and balanced set of risk and concern assessment results that fall within the legitimate range of plural truth claims. In a situation where there is no complete data the major challenge is to define the factual base for making risk management or risk regulatory decisions (Osipova & Eriksson, 2011). So the main emphasis is on improving the reliability and validity of the results that are produced in the risk appraisal phase. Risk and concern assessors as well as managers need to make sure that all relevant knowledge claims are selected, processed and evaluated. They may not get a single answer but they might be able to get a better overview on the issues of scientific controversy. If these efforts lead to an acknowledgment of wide margins of uncertainty, the management tools of the uncertainty strategy should be applied (Chong, Huet, Saussier & Steiner, 2006). If input variables to decision-making can be properly defined and affirmed, risk characterization and evaluation can be done on the basis of risk-benefit balancing and normative standard setting.

According to Ameyaw and Chan (2015) for the risk problems due to high unresolved uncertainty, if there is a high degree of remaining uncertainties, risk management needs to incorporate hazard criteria (which are comparatively easy to determine), including aspects such as reversibility, persistence, and ubiquity, and select management options empowering society to deal even with worst case scenarios (such as containment of hazardous activities, close monitoring of risk-bearing activities, securing reversibility of decisions in case risks turn out to be higher than expected). The management of risks characterized by multiple and high uncertainties should be guided by the precautionary approach (Spikin, 2013). Since high unresolved uncertainty implies that the (true) dimensions of the risks are not (yet) known, one should pursue a cautious strategy that allows learning by restricted errors. The main management philosophy for this risk class is to allow small steps in implementation (containment approach) that enable risk managers to stop or even reverse the process as new knowledge is produced or the negative side effects become visible. The primary thrust of precaution is to avoid irreversibility (Demirag, Khadaroo & Stapleton, 2011).

Steijin, Klijn and Edelenbos (2011) suggests that for risk problems due to interpretative and normative ambiguity: If risk information is interpreted differently by different stakeholders in society – that is, there are different viewpoints about the relevance, meaning and implications of factual explanations and predictions for deciding about the tolerability of a risk as well as management actions – and if the values and priorities of what should be protected or reduced are subject to intense controversy, risk management needs to address the causes for these conflicting views (Khanom, 2010). Tiwari (2007) recommends that risk managers should thus initiate a broader societal discourse to enable participative decision making. These discursive measures are aimed at finding appropriate conflict resolution mechanisms capable of reducing the ambiguity to a manageable number of options that can be further assessed and evaluated (Chiu & Bosher, 2005). The main effort of risk management is hence the organization of a suitable discourse combined with the assurance that all stakeholders and public groups can question and critique the framing of the issue as well as each element of the entire risk chain.

Adams, Alistair and Wu (2006) in their study of the system, constraints and future prospects of PPP in China, discovered that typical risks reported from the PPP literature can be classified into two major categories: systematic/country risks and specific project risk. The systematic/country risks are related to objective market environment, and they are always beyond control of the private investors. According to Kobbeltvedt, Brun, Johansen and Eid (2005) systematic risks include political risk (Sottilotta,

2013), economic risks, legal risks, social risks and nature risks. The specific project risks arise from the various nature of a project or from the events in the immediate micro-environment. Examples of specific risk, as given by Alaszewski (2005) consist of construction risks, operations risks, market risks, relationship risks and other specific project risks. Details on both the systematic and specific project risks are presented in Table 10.

In a nutshell, there are huge risk classification schemes for possible risks in PPP projects as each author and institutions apply the classification depending on specific areas of their concern in a PPP arrangement. Loosemore (2007) avers some authors classify risk according to the features of the PPP contracts. Li, Akintoye, Edwards and Hardcastle (2005) on their part, classifies risks into three levels: a macro level with exogenous risk occurring outside the project; the meso level for risks occurring within the boundaries of the project; and micro level risks due to inherent differences between the private and public entity. Greiling (2009) asserts that there is no standard method of categorization. Marques and Berg (2011) proposes that whatever classification scheme is applied, a whole-life-cycle assessment needs to be made and risks of the project itself as well as exogenous risks should be identified. Jin and Doloi (2007) caution there is need to deal with perceived risk from a certain point of view, because every party will have its own interpretation and estimation of the risk.

RISK PERSPECTIVES OF PARTIES

Given that most PPP projects are initiated for the good of the citizens, the largest and single most partner is the public partner (Pattberg, Biermann, Chan & Mert, 2012). This partner makes up more than half of

Table 10. Systematic and special project risk descriptions

s/no	Risk	Risk Description
	Systematic risk category	
1	Political risk group	Government corruption, government intervention, nationalization/expropriation, public credit, poor public decision-making process
2	Economic risk group	Interest rate fluctuation, foreign exchange fluctuation, inflation, financing risk
3	Legal risk group	Legislation change, imperfect law and supervision system, change in tax regulation
4	Social risk group	Political/public opposition
5	Natural risk group	Force majeure, unforeseen weather/geotechnical conditions, environment risk
	Specific project risk category	
6	Construction risk group	Completion risk, material/labor nonavailability, unproven engineering techniques
7	Operation risk group	Project/operation changes, operation cost overrun, price change, expense payment risk
8	Market risk group	Market competition, change in market demand
9	Relationship risk group	Third-party delay/violation, organization and coordination risk, inability of the concessionaire
10	Other risks	Land acquisition, delay in project approvals and permits, conflicting or imperfect contract, lack of supporting infrastructure, residual risk, inadequate competition for tender

Source: (Chan, Yeung, Yu, Wang and Ke, 2011).

the parties involved in a PPP arrangement, who tend to be active and most important participants (Regan, Love & Smith, 2015). The remaining portion of the parties is split between the private partners and the creditors (Dewatripont & Legros, 2005). Each of them has different perspectives on PPP projects. The perspectives are considered in turn of public partner, private partner and creditors.

Public Partner

According to Callan and Davies (2013), the public partner tends to engage more at the preliminary stages of PPP project development. While it is a common perception that PPP projects are 'implemented', perhaps by the private partners solely, it is the public partner that initiative the projects. At the earlier stages of PPP project development, therefore, the public partner tends to dominate the processes of developing a PPP project, for example, apart from initiating a PPP project, the public partner can also carry out a feasibility study of the proposed project. When the actual positions of the public partner in a PPP arrangement are taken into account, it becomes apparent that the majority of PPP projects are initiated by the public sector (Galilea & Medda, 2007).

Risk is the defining moment in which the public partner moves to take on a PPP arrangement. In essence, it is risk that compels the public partner to enter into an agreement with the private partner to provide infrastructure and/or services. Because of this, Conley and Dukkipati (2012) claim, the public partner forms the risk and supply side of the PPP arrangement. The public partner comprises of the government, local self-government unit, and regional investment funds (Delmon, 2011). These entities bring into an agreement: financial capital, mostly cash, assets, especially real estate; municipalities often own lands and buildings, attractive for investors (Fischer, 2010).

The involvement of public partner signalizes that obtaining PPP arrangement would be easier, shorter to reduce financial burden on the public sector (Krześ-Dobieszewska, 2014). In a circumstance of entering into a PPP arrangement as the only option, it becomes the responsibility of the public partner to get well allocated in order to make PPP projects attractive. If this is not done, the project would over burden the public finance like in a traditional procurement. Therefore, the main criteria of choosing PPP model should be its efficiency, so called "value for money" (vfm). The public partner on the conceptual stage should evaluate if the project is profitable for public finances and end-users, or if it represents its vfm comparing to alternative methods of making an investment. The public partner cannot only think about "here and now" they should analyze the influence of PPP projects on the budget in 10-15 years. That postulate is idealistic, taking into account the fact that big investment projects are connected with political voting cycles, which are of much shorter time horizon (Krześ-Dobieszewska, 2014).

Martimort and Pouyet (2006) specify that in PPP arrangement, the public partner would opt to retain or transfer a risk when the difference of total costs between private partner and itself is within or exceeding a predetermined level. This is because it is assumed that if risk management performance discrepancy is too huge, joint management would not reduce the total costs further below the costs individual management would incur. Otherwise, public partner may decide to manage that risk jointly with private partner, either equally or unequally, by assuming that joint management would reduce the total costs below the costs either partner would incur when managing the risk individually (Rossi & Civitillo, 2014).

According to Mahalingam (2010), in a PPP arrangement, risk is perceived from the public sector's view as 'any event which jeopardizes the quality or quantity of service that they have contracted for', and from the private sector's view as 'thought of any event which causes the cash flow profile of the project to depart from the base case and jeopardize the debt servicing ability of the project or its ability to generate a dividend stream for shareholders' (Silvester & Aroujo, 2012). It is critical for government to understand that while it is sub-optimal for the public sector to retain inappropriate risks, it is also sub-optimal to transfer inappropriate risk to the private sector (Farquharson, de Mästle, Yescombe & Encinas, 2011). This is because transfer of risks to the private sector comes at a price though it is one of the key VFM drivers in a public private partnership transaction (Hayford, 2006).

Acar, Guo and Yang (2008) claims that although PPP is often taken as a great relief to the public authority because it can sometimes moves projects off the government balance sheet, the arrangement is treated by the public partner as an element of creative accounting and nobody is interested increasing the project efficiency. The public partner views PPP as bringing in no extra money but constitutes elements of creating accounting and none of the public partner is interested in increasing the project efficiency. Furthermore, institutions responsible for public debts are much better at identifying the actual liabilities which PPP brings (Zhang & Chen, 2012). For a PPP to successfully meet its target there must be stringent rules put in place and the public partner must have greater stake in the making of such rules.

Private Partner

There is a general consensus that the performance of the private partner is important for the PPP project to achieve its objectives (Hamizah, Sasmita, Harianto & Pallu, 2014). From the risk perspective, the private partner forms the risk and demand side of the PPP arrangements (Brown, 2007). According to Jiménez and Pasquero (2005), the private partner provides a number of other benefits to the PPP. Private partner due to its financial capabilities can adapt to changing demand patterns, production patterns and investment conditions. This increases PPP project flexibility. Bult-Spiering and Dewulf (2006) aver the private partner has a reasonable propensity to acquire technological capabilities and develop new product and processes and can this contribute to national technological development and competitiveness. In a PPP project, the private partner can be an important vehicle for generating income and employment and so contribute to gross domestic product (GDP), economic growth and reductions in unemployment. Mouraviev and Kakabadse (2012) claim the private partner in a PPP arrangement provides a setting in which assets and skills can be accumulated. This can lead to better economic opportunities for the individuals who acquire the skills, and for the PPP project beneficiaries they help to support. PPP arrangement also acts as an avenue through which the private partner can decrease income inequality. It does so largely by increasing economic participation among those in the lower half of the income distribution. Velotti, Botti and Vesci (2012) cautions though neither SPV nor its partners (publics, private and creditors) are likely to be the poorest of the poor, and so promoting private partner performance in PPPs to achieve equity objectives is not necessarily as direct methods like income transfers. The social benefits of private partner participation in a PPP, while analytically separable, are closely linked to economic benefits.

Kahwajian, Baba, Amudi and Wanos (2014) notes that private partners in a PPP are private entities which are mostly companies, big corporations or consortiums able to manage financial, technological and organizational challenges connected with big investment projects. Dada (2010) shows that besides cash and fixed assets they bring to the project, they can also provide long term loans. Ismail and Harris (2014) points to the fact that, for example, in infrastructural investments- like in energy sector or road construction- 10 to 15 per cent funds come from contribution from partners, the remaining 85-90 per cent usually from long-term bank loans, long-term bonds, as a bond holder; bonds issued by companies are cheaper form of getting capital than obtaining investment loan. Dacin, Oliver and Roy (2007) intimate the recession time is often very attractive for private sector to involve in public investments. These investments allow to survive difficult times regarding a decline in orders on the private investment market. The private party more agrees to compromise and to hold down the expectations to the level of profit, in order to gain certain and stable source of revenues, which is a public investment contract. So, from that perspective, the public-private partnership seems to be very attractive – and at adequate arrangement with public partner, provides the source of profit not only stable, but also long-term (Darnall & Preston, 2010). The entry of private partner in public PPP is a chance for authentic stabilization, gaining the perspective of economic safety, necessary in building a long-term strategy. It should be emphasized that a prerequisite for effective usage of advantages which public private partnership projects generate to private partner are solid basis and realistic expectations. The private partner must have a financial and organizational capability to complete and manage investment, which guarantees capital return after longer time and on moderate level. Therefore, PPP is not an instrument of dynamic expansion, but of stabilization and strengthening position (Krześ-Dobieszewska, 2014).

Creditors

The financial and technical contributions of creditors to PPP project engagement suggest that it is clearly in the interest of the PPP project to thrive (Akbiyikli, Eaton & Turner, 2006). But this alone would not necessarily mean that creditors cannot actively intervene by conditions to support the implementation of PPP project. The more pressing argument that favors the development of conditions in support of such PPP projects is a strong PPP project sector, and particularly the implementation processes cannot be possible without some form of support from the creditors (Alonso-Conde, Brown & Rojo-Suarez, (2007). This argument rests on the observation that most PPP projects suffer completion deficiencies because of inadequate finances. It holds that failures routinely occur that systematically undermine PPP project implementation, and that many PPP project requirements are those of a 'substantially adequate' finances. Accordingly, PPP projects need diverse sources of finances including, most importantly, from the creditors.

Creditors form the risks and financial institution of the PPP arrangement. They are the ones that make a PPP project to happen because PPPs are long term contract with long term capital return (Bloomfield, 2006). Akintoye and Chinyio (2005) declares a typical project covers an investment phase (or construction phase), which lasts 2-5 years, and an operational phase lasting 20-30 years. The investment phase demands significant financial funds for the provision of which the private partner is responsible (from the point of view of the public entity, private partner's ability to bear the investment costs is a main reason of application the public private partnership model). These funds usually come from loans provided by financial institutions (Hodge, 2010). The repayment of a loan takes place during an operational phase from the private partner remuneration in the form of "availability fees" from the public partner or from user's fees. The features of such a credit resemble the features of mortgage loan for home buyer or builder– the equity contribution (about 20%) and the credit period (20-30 years) are similar. However, the amount of credit is substantially different – the property value is several hundreds of thousands of euro, the public private partnership project value reaches a few hundred million dollars. In many countries, granting a credit in such difficult times is not a tempting perspective for commercial banks, especially when the collateral are the future revenues coming from charges of service users. The best example is motorway tolls for drivers (Vining & Boardman, 2008b). The level of these revenues, resulting from the demand for services, is highly uncertain in the perspective of the next decades. Many factors may change: the economy, behavior and preferences of potential users (e.g. increase of alternative means of transport popularity), the construction of competitive roads, rails and air networks. The number of variables which influence the profitability of investment and the economic risk is large. The risk aversion among banks has caused an increase in credit margins, which effected higher costs of raising capital (Vining & Boardman, 2008a). Furthermore, due to unsuccessful financial operations, some banks have problems with their liquidity.

Broadbent and Laughlin (2005) decry difficulties in obtaining funds from the commercial banks for long-term projects. For example, most commercial banks demand flexibility from lenders, especially in terms of the right to increase interest rates. Such situation has certainly been going on for sometimes, and the current situations seem to portray a signal from the market for banks to return to pre-financial crisis offers. Consequently, very few borrowers are willing to obtain loan of flexible interest rates. According to Vining and Boardman (2008b), short-term, consumptive and commercial credits are dominant; they are less hazardous and generate high revenues for banks. In most cases therefore, PPP arrangement often prefers loans from international financial institutions (IFI) rather than commercial banks. Yescombe (2007) argues that much as IFIs also provides commercial terms to their loans, such conditions are favorable and ensures that is continuous lending otherwise there would be no reason to borrow from them if the same terms could be obtained elsewhere. In addition, IFIs also provide advisory services on the loans they extend. They also provide solutions to minimize project economic risks by various kinds of public sector commitment, for example, credit guarantees or investment profitability guarantee (if private partner gets no profit caused by lower demand for services, the public party covers with subsidies all not earned revenues) (Broadbent, Gill & Laughlin, 2008). It should be taken into consideration that bearing economic risk by the public sector as a result of obtaining credits from creditors implies that the registration of PPP assets on the public partner's balance sheet and the public sector liability. For the creditors, the terms and conditions of the loans to be extended much be equitable to the interest and with minimal chances of loss occurring.

RISK CRITERIA

In making choices of the risk to undertake the principal parties- the public and private partners can either use three different approaches: normative, descriptive, and normative and descriptive approaches vis-à-vis other approaches (Delmon, 2009). Basically, both normative and descriptive approaches provide some reasonable criterions when making choices under risk although most risk takers often do not behave according to the rules suggested by normative approach (Cheng, Chiang & Tang, 2007). In brief, though, this section describes the basic rules and concepts to make decision in a risky situation. Its content indicates that before trying to manage more complex project, there is need to manage risk in a systematic way. Typically, a peculiar risk management system is needed to be developed to analyze the risk as well as to quantify it and deal with it.

Normative Approach

Interest in normative approach to choose risk is based on some rules. These rules are there to guide the processes of choosing risk using normative approach. The rules are grouped into two: the expected value rule and the expected utility rule. According to Dixon, Pottinger and Jordan (2005), statistical decision theory suggests that the expected value (EV) is the best rule for choice under risk. Under this rule, McKim (2005) shows that the most important crucial factor that must be analyzed is the probability distribution. Jeffares, Sullivan and Bovaird (2009) reveal that if the factor is not realistic then the complete analysis will give the wrong information. Furthermore, Muller and Turner (2005) contend people's decision-making in the risk environment is not always consisting with the theory of EV. This is because the principal objection to using EV maximization is that it ignores the attitude to risk (Yuan, Skibniewski, Li, & Zheng, 2010). Osipova and Eriksson (2013) postulate that, when approaching risky choices, people do not simply use the face value rule of outcomes (such as expected value). Rather, they use some psychological value of these outcomes, which can be termed the utility of outcomes. While choosing risk using the EV theory, Tserng, Russell, Hsu and Lin (2012) recommend the following steps to be taken. First, consider the different options available. Secondly, estimate the value of each option. Third, estimate the probability distribution of each option. Fourth multiply the value of each option by its respective probability. Fifth sum the EV of each option. And lastly, sixth, select the option with the maximum EV.

Meanwhile, the expected utility rule is a simple transformation of the expected value rule. It is still a summation of probabilities times their respective values, except that the values are subjective values called utilities, rather than the actual monetary values (Ngoma, Mundia, & Kaliba, 2014). According to Mashamba (2009) the utility function is depicted in the form of a curve with the utility scale on the vertical axis and expected outcomes on the horizontal axis. There are several methods applied to the assessment of a person's utility function, such as the von Neumann-Morgenstern (NM), the Ramsey method, and direct measurement (Dadzie & Acquah, 2012). The NM is considered to be the most effective approach. Mukela (2007) asserts that there are two major steps in NM. The first step in deriving a utility function by the NM method is to determine two monetary outcomes values as reference points. For convenience look at the most favorable and least favorable monetary outcomes in a decision situation. It's from there that values should be assigned to these two reference points. Since utility is an ordinal rather than a cardinal concept, these utility values are arbitrary, for which due to the need for convenience, again these references utility may be assign the values of 0 and 1. In the second step, assign the utility values for all the other monetary outcomes lying between these two reference points. The utility values determined by the NM method are based on the concept certainty equivalent. It assumes that the decision-maker has to choose between two strategies.

The reason that the normative approach appear to center most on expected value rule and the expected utility rule, is that they both foster inter-partner learning and taking advantage of making the right choice for the risk to take. Thus the normative approach therefore, appears to be advantageous while taking a risk choice approach.

Descriptive Approach

Tang, Shen and Cheng (2010) squabbles that sometimes, in many situations, the amount of data required for making a rational choice may be overwhelming. In such circumstances, it's only the prospect theory that can well explain the situation (van Mieghem, 2010). Prospect theory provides a boulevard the choice of the risk management approach must accounts for paradoxes exhibited earlier in any attempt to make such a choice. According to proponents of prospect theory (Smith, Merna & Jobling, 2006), this is a theory that accounts for the pattern of risky choice in a complex environment. Prospect theory assists in making risky choices into three main functions. First, a value function that plays the role of a utility function. Second, a decision weights function that plays the role of probabilities. And last the editing function. Chao and Liou (2007) aver that the uncertain prospects are characterized by the value function and the decision weights and summed in a similar way to expected utility.

According to Ashley, Diekmann and Molenaar (2006), in a descriptive approach, value function can have three characteristics. First, it defines values as deviations from a certain reference point. Secondly, both gains and losses diminish in value, suggesting that people are more sensitive to changes around the reference point. Third, it is steeper for losses than for gains, reflecting the assumption that people are more sensitive to losing a certain amount than to gaining the same amount. A major aspect of the value function is therefore the reference point. Much as many points can play the role of a reference point, Abednego and Ogunlana (2006) proposed that the asset position also plays the role of adoption level, hence implying an almost instantaneous adjustment to a new asset position. Thus, wealth does not matter much, for example, because if a person wins 1 million, he/she will immediately adapt to this new wealth and respond in a risk-averse manner to the gambles in Situation 1 and respond in a risk-seeking manner in situation 2. Abbasianjahromi and Rajaie (2012) argue that changes in wealth are a more important determinant of risky choice than the absolute value of wealth. That is, within a very wide range of options, a millionaire and a poor person would respond in a similar way to the gambles in the situations just described. An important feature of prospect theory is the editing rule. Given a choice between risky alternatives, decision-makers edit the choice problem until they arrive at a simple choice between edited alternatives that can be compared in either the domain of gains or the domain of losses.

Normative and Descriptive Vis-À-Vis Other Approaches

Statistical basis for decision-making in a risky situation is advocated for by the normative approach (Abdul-Rahman, Wang & Lee, 2013). For example, when there are large samples of repeated events. Expected values provide the soundest summary statistic for choice under risk. Ahmed, Kayis and Amornsawadwatana (2007) conclude that in the expected value formula, the most likely outcome gets the highest weight, and the least likely outcome gets the lowest weight. Furthermore Gauthier and Ika (2012) indicate that utility theory proposes that the subjective value of outcomes can be calculated, and, following Matei (2006) suggestion, subjective probabilities are entered instead of objective ones. Erstwhile, Sanda and Anigbogu (2016) articulate that the descriptive approach stems from the studies that people do not always follow the normative rules toward risky choice. Instead, descriptive approach uses decision weights rather than opportunities. It also suggests that decision-maker edit the choice until the other alternatives can be compared in terms of gains or losses. However, Xiao and Zhang (2011) shows that evidences abound to prove that there is a growing incompatibility of the two approaches. For example, Ai and Brockett (2008) contend that the normative approach tells people what they should do, whereas the descriptive approach is an attempt to get an account of what people actually do. Several experts' studies (Ali & Mohammad, 2010) all the same suggest that only through developing normative, descriptive and perspective models of choice could improvements in decision-making be achieved. This has led to advices being given to undertake risky choice criteria which are neither normative nor descriptive, as propagated by Ammar, Berman and Sataporn (2007). Reasons advanced for such a direction indicate that sometimes it's unrealistic to use one rule of thumb toward risk decision because of the contradiction between normative and descriptive approaches.

In addition to the normative or descriptive approach, though, some other rules that can be used includes: Mean-Variance (M-V) criterion, certainty equivalence, risk premium, and risk adjusted discount rate: Net Present Value (NPV). The M-V criterion is based on the fact that a basic characteristic of risk is volatility which is measured by the variance of the distribution. It is the expected value of the squared deviations from the expected return. Jin and Zhang (2010) argue that indeed, the concept of variance is the cornerstone in the M-V approach to the analysis of decision under uncertainty. This approach suggests that, in choosing among risky alternatives, people should consider both the expected return and the variance of the probability distribution over the possible outcomes. The criteria suggest that, if two alternatives have the same variance, then people should choose the one with higher expected return (Kim & Kim, 2005). If, on the other hand, the two alternatives have the same expected return, people should choose the one with lower variance (Lubis & Majid, 2013).

The certainty equivalence approach is premised on the conception that as utility values can be compared to the rate offered on risk-free investment while choosing between a risk one and a safe one, a risky alternative utility value can be interpreted as its "certainty equivalent" rate of return to an investor. That is, the certainty equivalent rate of a risky alternative is the rate that risk-free investments would need to offer with certainty to be considered equally as attractive as the risky alternative (Jin, 2011). If, in other words, an individual is offered a choice to decide between a project with certain net present value, NPV, and the other with expected net present value, ENPV, that are equal, the one with uncertainty must offer higher return for compensation for risk bearing (Kefallinos, Lambrou & Sykas, 2009).

According to Antuchevičiene, Turskis and Zavadskas (2006), a discount rate reflect the investor's time value of money and the rate of return the property must earn to justify the investment. But Demirag, Dubnick and Khadaroo (2005) avow some projects are almost risk free, such as the case of a tenant prepared to sign a long term lease on a building at the early design stage, whereas a project which is considered risky to attract a premium to the discount rate. Vidal, Marle and Bocquet (2011) illustrates that the risk premium is usually added to the risk free discount rate in order to compensate for the risk taking. In other words, though investor can put his money in a risk free security, the riskier investment provides an attractive premium for the investor to be willing to bear the risk. There is no formula which derives an appropriate risk premium; each investor has to decide how much risk he/she wants to take and what premium is appropriate for him/her to assume the risk.

A risk-adjusted discount rate: NPV rule is one way of taking risks into account in investment appraisal. Zitron (2006) insists that a real discount rate used in the calculation of net present value of a project may be viewed as composed of three parts: a time value of money, a risk premium and an adjustment for inflation. Carbonara, Costantino and Pellegrino (2013) maintains that the risk premium is added to reflect the investor's view of the degree of sensitivity of the project to risk factors. The size of the premium depends on the degree of risk associated with project and the investor's attitude toward risk. The greater the risk is; the greater the premium (Coulson, 2005). Boateng, Chen and Ogunlana (2012) re-echo that the decision rule based on the discount rate is that always choose the project with positive NPV since it provides net profit, taking into account opportunity cost of capital and the risk of the project.

CONCLUSION

Partnerships have on many occasions been initiated and entered into in order to benefit intended parties/beneficiaries. Partnerships between the public sector and the private sector are naturally wary of arrangement that would appear to direct resources in terms of finance, energy and time to that which does not pay at all. These are some priorities in partnership-based interventions that systematically favor particular course of action, for example, provision of quality public services to the public and citizenry.

None of these, however, are immune to the devastating effects of risk. Yet, it left unattended to, the very purpose for which such an arrangement was entered into would become meaningless. Strong system of shared understanding and development network of cooperation in understanding and finding solutions to risk in a partnership is therefore critical for such an arrangement to reap the true benefits of its formation. This was the purpose of this chapter since any form of partnership is bound to be exposed to a variety of risks. This chapter therefore explored the principal PPP risks and highlighted how they are understood. It noted that given that PPP is a world-wide thing, it brings along with it risks which both the public sector and the private sector, including the users of public goods and services, need to address and manage. Two obligations in the risk in a partnership can easily be comprehended. First, the requirement for a risk understanding in PPP arrangements; the risks should be identified, analyzed and probably priced (Ameyaw & Chan, 2013). Secondly, PPP procurement methods are associated with many pitfalls, uncertainties and risks (Shen, Platten & Deng, 2006) to the governments and the private sectors (Tworek, 2010). These set the boundaries for taking risks in a PPP arrangement, which forms the basis of the next chapter.

REFERENCES

Abbasianjahromi, H., & Rajaie, H. (2012). Developing a project portfolio selection model for contractor firms considering the risk factor. *Journal of Civil Engineering and Management*, *18*(6), 879–889. doi:10.3846/13923730.2012.734856

Abdul-Rahman, H., Wang, C., & Lee, Y. L. (2013). Design and pilot run of fuzzy synthetic model (FSM) for risk evaluation in civil engineering. *Journal of Civil Engineering and Management*, *19*(2), 217–238. doi:10.3846/13923730.2012.743926

Abednego, M. P., & Ogunlana, S. O. (2006). Good project governance for proper risk allocation in the public-private partnership in Indonesia. *International Journal of Project Management*, *24*(7), 622–634. doi:10.1016/j.ijproman.2006.07.010

Acar, M., Guo, C., & Yang, K. (2008). Accountability when hierarchical authority is absent: Views from public-private partnerships practitioners. *American Review of Public Administration*, *38*(1), 3–23. doi:10.1177/0275074007299481

Acharya, N. K., Dai Lee, Y., & Man Im, H. (2006). Conflicting factors in construction projects: Korean perspective. *Engineering, Construction, and Architectural Management*, *13*(6), 543–566. doi:10.1108/09699980610712364

Adams, J., Alistair, Y., & Wu, Z. H. (2006). Public private partnerships in China-system, constraints and future prospects. *International Journal of Public Sector Management*, *19*(4), 384–396. doi:10.1108/09513550610669202

Adnan, H., Jusoff, K., & Salim, M. K. (2008). The Malaysian construction industrys risk management in design and build. *Modern Applied Science*, *2*(5), 27. doi:10.5539/mas.v2n5p27

Ahmed, A., Kayis, B., & Amornsawadwatana, S. (2007). A review of techniques for risk management in projects. *Benchmark International Journal*, *14*(1), 22–36. doi:10.1108/14635770710730919

Ai, J., & Brockett, P. L. (2008). Enterprise risk management. In E. Melnick & B. Everitt (Eds.), *Encyclopedia of Quantitative Risk Analysis and Assessment*. London: John Wiley & Sons Ltd. doi:10.1002/9780470061596.risk0047

Akbiyikli, R., Eaton, D., & Turner, A. L. (2006). Project finance and the private finance initiative (PFI). *The Journal of Structured Finance*, *12*(2), 65–75. doi:10.3905/jsf.2006.644162

Akintan, O. A., & Morledge, R. (2013). Improving the collaboration between main contractors and subcontractors within traditional construction procurement. *Journal of Construction Engineering,* 1-11. 10.1155/2013/281236

Akintoye, A., & Chinyio, E. (2005). Private Finance Initiative in the healthcare sector: Trends and risk assessment. *Engineering, Construction, and Architectural Management*, *12*(6), 601–616. doi:10.1108/09699980510634155

Alaszewski, A. (2005). Risk communication: Identifying the importance of social context. *Health Risk & Society*, *7*(2), 101–105. doi:10.1080/13698570500148905

Aldoory, L., Kim, J.-N., & Tindall, N. (2010). The influence of perceived shared risk in crisis communication: Elaborating the situational theory of publics. *Public Relations Review*, *36*(2), 134–140. doi:10.1016/j.pubrev.2009.12.002

Ali, M., & Mohammad, K. (2010). Selecting appropriate project delivering system: Fuzzy approach with risk analysis. *Journal of Construction Engineering and Management*, *136*(8), 923–930. doi:10.1061/(ASCE)CO.1943-7862.0000190

Alireza, V., Mohammadreza, Y., Zin, R. M., Yahaya, N., & Noor, N. M. (2013). An enhanced multi-objective optimization approach for risk allocation in public–private partnership projects: A case study of Malaysia. *Canadian Journal of Civil Engineering*, *41*(2), 164–177. doi:10.1139/cjce-2013-0342

Alonso-Conde, A. B., Brown, C., & Rojo-Suarez, J. (2007). Public private partnerships: Incentives, risk transfer and real options. *Review of Financial Economics*, *16*(4), 335–349. doi:10.1016/j.rfe.2007.03.002

Ameyaw, E.E., & Chan, A.P.C. (2013).Identifying public-private partnership (PPP) risks in managing water supply projects in Ghana. *Journal of Facilities Management, 11*(2), 152–182..10.1108/14725961311314651

Ameyaw, E. E., & Chan, A. P. C. (2015). Evaluation and ranking of risk factors in public–private partnership water supply projects in developing countries using fuzzy synthetic evaluation approach. *Expert Systems with Applications*, *42*(12), 5102–5116. doi:10.1016/j.eswa.2015.02.041

Ammar, A., Berman, K., & Sataporn, A. (2007). A review of techniques for risk management in projects. *Benchmarking: An International Journal*, *14*(1), 22–36. doi:10.1108/14635770710730919

Andi, P. (2006). The importance and allocation of risks in Indonesian construction projects. *Construction Management and Economics*, *24*(1), 69–80. doi:10.1080/01446190500310338

Antón, A. J. M., Rodríguez, G. S., & López, A. (2011). Financial risks in construction projects. *African Journal of Business Management*, *5*(31), 12325–12328.

Antuchevičiene, J., Turskis, Z., & Zavadskas, E. K. (2006). Modelling renewal of construction objects applying methods of the game theory. *Ukio Technologinis ir Ekonominis Vystymas, 12*(4), 263-268.

Ashley, D. B., Diekmann, J. E., & Molenaar, K. R. (2006). *Guide to Risk Assessment and Allocation for Highway Construction Management.* Retrieved from http://international.fhwa.dot.gov/riskassess/pl06032.pdf

Aven, T. (2010). On how to define, understand and describe risk. *Reliability Engineering & System Safety*, *95*(6), 623–631. doi:10.1016/j.ress.2010.01.011

Awodele, O. A., Dada, S. O., & Ogunsemi, D. R. (2007). Effect of risk on contractors performance in oil producing areas of Ondo State Nigeria. *Proceedings of the International Conference Theme: Towards Sustainable Built Natural Environment.*

Ayeni, K. (2005). Risk identification and management in BOT Project Implementation. *Proceedings of BOT Awareness Seminar, Abuja Investment and Property Development Company.*

Badenfelt, U. (2008). The selection of sharing ratios in target cost contracts. *Engineering, Construction, and Architectural Management*, *15*(1), 54–65. doi:10.1108/09699980810842061

Banerjee, S. G., Oetzel, J. M., & Ranganathan, R. (2006). Private provision of infrastructure in emerging markets: Do institutions matter? *Development Policy Review*, *24*(2), 175–202. doi:10.1111/j.1467-7679.2006.00321.x

Barlish, K., De Marco, A., & Thaheem, M. J. (2013). Construction Risk Taxonomy: An International Convergence of Academic and Industry Perspectives. *American Journal of Applied Sciences*, *10*(7), 706–713. doi:10.3844/ajassp.2013.706.713

Bing, L., Akintoye, A., Edwards, P., & Hardcastle, C. (2005a). Perceptions of positive and negative factors influencing the attractiveness of PPP procurement for construction projects in the UK – Findings from a questionnaire survey. *Engineering, Construction, and Architectural Management*, *12*(2), 125–148. doi:10.1108/09699980510584485

Bloomfield, P. (2006). The challenging business of long-term public-private partnerships: Reflections on local experience. *Public Administration Review*, *66*(3), 400–411. doi:10.1111/j.1540-6210.2006.00597.x

Boardman, A. E., & Vining, A. R. (2012). The political economy of public-private partnerships and analysis of their social value. *Annals of Public and Cooperative Economics*, *83*(2), 117–141. doi:10.1111/j.1467-8292.2012.00457.x

Boateng, P., Chen, Z., & Ogunlana, S. (2012). A conceptual system dynamic model to describe the impacts of critical weather conditions in megaproject construction. *Journal of Construction Project Management and Innovation*, *2*(1), 208–224.

Broadbent, J., Gill, J., & Laughlin, R. (2008). Identifying and controlling risk: The problem of uncertainty in the private finance initiative in the UKs National Health Service. *Critical Perspectives on Accounting*, *19*(1), 40–78. doi:10.1016/j.cpa.2006.04.006

Broadbent, J., & Laughlin, R. (2005). The Role of PPP in the UK Governments modernization agenda. *Financial Accountability and Management*, *21*(1), 75–97. doi:10.1111/j.0267-4424.2005.00210.x

Brown, K. (2007). Are public–private transactions the future of infrastructure finance? *Public Works Management & Policy*, *12*(1), 320–324. doi:10.1177/1087724X07303680

Bult-Spiering, M., & Dewulf, G. (2006). *Strategic issues in public–private partnerships. An international perspective*. London: Blackwell Publishing. doi:10.1002/9780470759653

Burke, R., & Demirag, I. (2013). Changing Perceptions on PPP Games: Demand risk in Irish Roads. *Critical Perspectives on Accounting*. doi:10.1016/j.cpa.2013.11.002

Callan, M., & Davies, R. (2013). *When business meets aid: analyzing public-private partnerships for international development*. Development Policy Centre Discussion Paper 28, Crawford School of Public Policy, The Australian National University, Canberra.

Carbonara, N., Costantino, N., & Pellegrino, R. (2013). A three-layer theoretical framework for analyzing public private partnerships: The Italian case. *Organization, Technology and Management International Journal (Toronto, Ont.)*, *6*(2), 799–810.

Carpintero, S., & Petersen, O. H. (2015). Bundling and Unbundling in Public-Private Partnerships: Implications for Risk Sharing in Urban Transport Projects. *Project Management Journal*, *46*(4), 35–46. doi:10.1002/pmj.21508

Chan, A. P. C., Yeung, J. F. Y., Yu, C. C. P., Wang, S. Q., & Ke, Y. (2011). Empirical study of risk assessment and allocation of public-private partnership projects in China. *Journal of Management Engineering*, *27*(3), 136–148. doi:10.1061/(ASCE)ME.1943-5479.0000049

Chao, L. C., & Liou, C. N. (2007). Risk-minimizing approach to bid-cutting limit determination. *Construction Management and Economics*, *25*(8), 835–843. doi:10.1080/01446190701393018

Checherita, C., & Gifford, J. (2007). *Risk Sharing in Public-Private Partnerships: General Considerations and an Evaluation of the U.S. Practice in Road Transportation*. Paper submitted to the 11th World Conference on Transportation Research (WCTR), Berkeley, CA.

Chen, P., & Partington, D. (2006). Three conceptual levels of construction project management work. *International Journal of Project Management*, *24*(1), 412–421. doi:10.1016/j.ijproman.2006.02.009

Cheng, E. W. L., Chiang, Y. H., & Tang, B. S. (2007). Alternative approach to credit scoring by DEA: Evaluating borrowers with respect to PPP projects. *Building and Environment*, *42*(4), 1752–1760. doi:10.1016/j.buildenv.2006.02.012

Cheung, E., Chan, A. P. C., & Kajewski, S. (2009a). Enhancing value for money in public private partnership projects: Findings from a survey conducted in Hong Kong, Australia compared to findings from previous research in the United Kingdom. *Journal of Financial Management of Property and Construction*, *14*(1), 7–20. doi:10.1108/13664380910942617

Chinyio, E., & Gameson, R. (2009). Private finance initiative in use. In *Policy, Finance, & Management for Public- Private Partnerships, Innovation in the Built Environment*. London: Wiley-Blackwell.

Chiu, T., & Bosher, C. (2005). Risk sharing in various public private partnerships arrangements for the provision of water and wastewater services. *Proceeding of the Conference on Public Private Partnerships—Opportunities and Challenges*, 11–21.

Chong, E., Huet, F., Saussier, S., & Steiner, F. (2006). Public-private partnerships and prices: Evidence from water distribution in France. *Review of Industrial Organization, 29*(1-2), 149–169. doi:10.1007/s11151-006-9106-8

Christ, M. H., Sedatole, K. L., & Towry, K. L. (2012). Sticks and Carrots: The Effect of contract frame on effort in incomplete contracts. *Accounting Review, 87*(6), 1913–1938. doi:10.2308/accr-50219

Chung, D. (2009). Private Provision of Road Infrastructure: Unveiling the Inconvenient Truth in New South Wales, Australia. *Road and Transport Research, 18*(1), 68–85.

Chung, D., Hensher, D. A., & Rose, J. M. (2010). Toward the betterment of risk allocation: Investigating risk perceptions of Australian stakeholder groups to public-private- partnership Tollroad Projects. *Research in Transportation Economics, 30*(1), 43–58. doi:10.1016/j.retrec.2010.10.007

Conley, H., & Dukkipati, U. (2012). *Leading from behind in public-private partnerships: An assessment of European engagement with the private sector in development.* Centre for Strategic and International Studies. Retrieved from http://csis.org/publication/leading-behind-public-private-partnerships

Cooper, D. F., Grey, S., Raymond, G., & Walker, P. (2005). *Project risk management guidelines: managing risk in large projects and complex procurements.* Chichester, UK: Wiley.

Costello, A. M. (2013). Mitigating incentive conflicts in inter-firm relationships: Evidence from long-term supply contracts. *Journal of Accounting and Economics, 56*(1), 19–39. doi:10.1016/j.jacceco.2013.02.001

Coulson, A. (2005). A plague on all your partnerships: Theory and practice in regeneration. *International Journal of Public Sector Management, 18*(2), 151–163. doi:10.1108/09513550510584973

Dacin, M. T., Oliver, C., & Roy, J.-P. (2007). The legitimacy of strategic alliances: An institutional perspective. *Strategic Management Journal, 28*(2), 169–187. doi:10.1002/smj.577

Dada, J. O. (2010). *Strategies for mitigating risk in construction projects.* Paper presented the 40th Annual General Meeting/Conference of the Nigerian Institute of Builders.

Dadzie, S. K. N., & Acquah, H. (2012). Attitudes toward risk and coping responses: The Case of food crop farmers at Agona Duakwa in Agona East District of Ghana. *International Journal of Agriculture and Forestry, 2*(2), 29–37. doi:10.5923/j.ijaf.20120202.06

Darnall, R., & Preston, J. M. (2010). *Project Management from Simple to Complex.* Flat World Knowledge.

Daube, D., Vollrath, S., & Alfen, H. W. (2007). A comparison of Project Finance and the Forfeiting Model as financing forms for PPP projects in Germany. *International Journal of Project Management, 26*(4), 376–387. doi:10.1016/j.ijproman.2007.07.001

Delmon, J. (2009). *Private sector investment in infrastructure project finance - PPP projects and risks* (2nd ed.). Austin, TX: Wolters Kluwer.

Delmon, J. (2011). *Public-Private Partnership Projects in Infrastructure: An Essential Guide for Policymakers.* New York: Cambridge University Press.

Demirag, I., Dubnick, M., & Khadaroo, I. (2005). A framework for examining accountability and value for money (VFM) in the UK's private finance initiative (PFI). In I. Demirag (Ed.), *Corporate Social Responsibility, Accountability and Governance: Global Perspectives*. Sheffield, UK: Greenleaf Publishing. doi:10.9774/GLEAF.978-1-909493-55-1_7

Demirag, I., & Khadaroo, I. (2008). Accountability and value for money in private finance initiative contracts. *Financial Accountability & Management*, *24*(4), 455–478. doi:10.1111/j.1468-0408.2008.00462.x

Demirag, I., Khadaroo, I., Stapleton, P., & Stevenson, C. (2011). Risks and the Financing of PPP: Perspectives from the Financiers. *The British Accounting Review*, *43*(4), 294–310. doi:10.1016/j.bar.2011.08.006

Dewatripont, M., & Legros, P. (2005). Public-private partnerships: Contract design and risk transfer. *EIB Papers*, *10*(1), 120–121.

Dixon, T., Pottinger, G., & Jordan, A. (2005). Lessons from the private finance initiative in the UK: Benefits, problems and critical success factors. *Journal of Property Investment & Finance*, *23*(5), 412–423. doi:10.1108/14635780510616016

English, L., & Baxter, J. (2010). The changing nature of contracting and trust in public-private partnerships: The Case of Victorian PPP prisons. *Abacus*, *46*(3), 289–319. doi:10.1111/j.1467-6281.2010.00320.x

Estache, A., Juan, E., & Trujillo, L. (2007). *Public-private partnerships in transport*. Policy Research Working Paper 4436, The World Bank.

Farquharson, E., de Mästle, C., Yescombe, E. R., & Encinas, J. (2011). *How to engage with the private sector in public-private partnerships in emerging markets*. Washington, DC: World Bank. doi:10.1596/978-0-8213-7863-2

Fischer, K., Leidel, K., Riemann, A., & Wilhelm Alfen, H. (2010). An integrated risk management system (IRMS) for PPP projects. *Journal of Financial Management of Property and Construction*, *15*(3), 260–282. doi:10.1108/13664381011087515

Galilea, P., & Medda, F. (2007). *Influence of foreign private investors and multilateral lenders on the success of public private partnerships in transport*. Paper presented at the Second international conference on funding transport infrastructure, Leuven, Belgium.

Gauthier, J. B., & Ika, L. A. (2012). Foundations of project management research: An explicit and six-facet ontological framework. *Project Management Journal*, *43*(5), 5–23. doi:10.1002/pmj.21288

Goh, C. A., & Abdul-Rahman, H. (2013). The identification and management of major risks in the Malaysian construction industry. *Journal of Construction in Developing Countries*, *18*(1), 19–32.

Greiling, D. (2009). Public-Private Partnerships – A driver for efficient public services or just an example of wishful thinking. *Journal for Public and Nonprofit Services*, (Supplement 37), 108–125.

Gupta, A. K., Trivedi, M. K., & Kansal, R. (2013). Risk variation assessment of Indian road PPP projects. *International Journal of Science. Environmental Technology*, *2*(5), 1017–1026.

Hamizah, S., Sasmita, S. A., Harianto, T., & Pallu, S. A. (2014). Private involvement in sustainable management of Indonesia Port; Need and strategy with PPP scheme. *Journal of Procedia Environmental Science*, *20*, 187–196. doi:10.1016/j.proenv.2014.03.025

Hayford, G. J. (2006). *Successfully allocating risk and negotiating a PPP contract.* Paper presented at the 6th Annual National public Private Partnership Summit: Which way now for Australia's PPP Market? Sydney, Australia.

Hodge, G. A. (2010). Reviewing public-private partnerships: some thoughts on evaluation, 81– 112. In G. Hodge, C. Greve, & A. Boardman (Eds.), *International Handbook on Public-Private Partnerships.* London: Edward Elgar Cheltenham. doi:10.4337/9781849804691.00012

Hodge, G. A., & Greve, C. (2007). Public–private partnerships: An international performance review. *Public Administration Review*, *67*(3), 545–558. doi:10.1111/j.1540-6210.2007.00736.x

Hwang, B.-G., Zhao, X., & Gay, M. J. S. (2013). Public private partnership projects in Singapore: Factors, critical risks and preferred risk allocation from the perspective of contractors. *International Journal of Project Management*, *31*(3), 424–433. doi:10.1016/j.ijproman.2012.08.003

Ismail, S., & Harris, F. A. (2014). Challenges in implementing public private partnership (PPP) in Malaysia. *Procedia: Social and Behavioral Sciences*, *164*, 5–10. doi:10.1016/j.sbspro.2014.11.044

Jeffares, S., Sullivan, H., & Bovaird, T. (2009). *Beyond the contract - The challenge of evaluating the performance(s) of public-private partnerships*. Paper for the annual conference of International Research Society for Public Management, (IRSPM), Copenhagen, Denmark.

Jefferies, M., & McGeorge, D. (2008). Public–private partnerships: A critical review of risk management in Australian social infrastructure projects. *Journal of Construction Procurement*, *14*(1), 66–80.

Jiménez, A., & Pasquero, J. (2005). Explaining the endurance of a permanently challenged public-private partnership: A stakeholder approach. *Management Research: The Journal of the Iberoamerican Academy of Management*, *3*(1), 49–61.

Jin, X. (2011). Model for efficient risk allocation in privately financed public infrastructure projects using neuro-fuzzy techniques. *Journal of Construction Engineering and Management*, *137*(11), 1003–1014. doi:10.1061/(ASCE)CO.1943-7862.0000365

Jin, X., & Doloi, H. (2008). Interpreting risk allocation mechanism in public-private partnership projects: An empirical study in a transaction cost economic perspective. *Construction Management and Economics*, *26*(7), 707–721. doi:10.1080/01446190801998682

Jin, X.-H. (2010a). Allocating risks in public-private partnerships using a transaction cost economics approach: A case study. *The Australasian Journal of Construction Economics and Building*, *9*(1), 19–26. doi:10.5130/ajceb.v9i1.3011

Jin, X. H. (2010b). Determinants of efficient risk allocation in privately financed public infrastructure projects in Australia. *Journal of Construction Engineering and Management*, *136*(2), 138–150. doi:10.1061/(ASCE)CO.1943-7862.0000118

Jin, X. H., & Zhang, G. (2010). Modeling optimal risk allocation in PPP projects using artificial neural networks. *International Journal of Project Management*, 1–13.

Kahwajian, A., Baba, S., Amudi, O., & Wanos, M. (2014). Identification of critical success factors (CSFs) for public private partnership (PPP) construction projects in Syria. *Jordan Journal of Civil Engineering*, *8*(4), 393–405.

Kefallinos, D., Lambrou, M., & Sykas, E. (2009). An extended risk assessment model for secure E-Government. *International Journal of Electronic Government Research*, *5*(2), 72–92. doi:10.4018/jegr.2009040105

Khanom, A. N. (2010). Conceptual issues in defining public private partnership (PPP). *International Review of Business Research Papers*, *6*(2), 150–163.

Kim, S.-G., & Kim, J.-J. (2005). A risk threshold calculation methodology for the construction projects applying value at risk. *Journal of Construction Engineering and Management*, *120*, 665–670.

Kobbeltvedt, T., Brun, W., Johansen, B. H., & Eid, J. (2005). Risk as feelings or risk and feelings? A cross-lagged panel analysis. *Journal of Risk Research*, *8*(5), 417–437. doi:10.1080/1366987042000315519

Koubatis, A., & Schönberger, J. Y. (2005). Risk management of complex critical systems. *International Journal of Critical Infrastructure*, *1*(2/3), 195–215. doi:10.1504/IJCIS.2005.006119

Krześ-Dobieszewska, J. (2014). Managing public – private partnership market in the times of economic crisis. *Oeconomia Copernicana*, *5*(2), 63–74. doi:10.12775/OeC.2014.014

Lam, K. C., Wang, D., Lee, T. K., & Tsang, Y. T. (2007). Modeling risk allocation decision in construction contracts. *International Journal of Project Management*, *25*(5), 485–493. doi:10.1016/j.ijproman.2006.11.005

Li, B., Akintoye, A., Edwards, P. J., & Hardcastle, C. (2005b). The allocation of risk in PPP/PFI construction projects in the UK. *International Journal of Project Management*, *23*(1), 25–35. doi:10.1016/j.ijproman.2004.04.006

Liu, T., & Wilkinson, S. (2011). Adopting innovative procurement techniques: Obstacles and drivers for adopting Public Private Partnerships in New Zealand. *Construction Innovation: Information, Process Management*, *11*(4), 452–469.

Loizou, P., & French, N. (2012). Risk and uncertainty in development: A critical evaluation of using the Monte Carlo simulation method as a decision tool in real estate development projects. *Journal of Property Investment & Finance*, *30*(2), 198–210. doi:10.1108/14635781211206922

Loosemore, A. N. M. (2007). Risk allocation in the private provision of public infrastructure. *International Journal of Project Management*, *25*(1), 66–76. doi:10.1016/j.ijproman.2006.06.005

Lubis, H.-a., & Majid, N. N. (2013). Developing a standardized assessment for PPP Infrastructure Project. *Proceedings of the Eastern Asia Society for Transportation Studies*, *9*, 345–378.

Mahalingam, A. (2010). PPP experiences in Indian Cities; Barriers, enablers and the way forward. *Journal of Construction Engineering and Management*, *136*(4), 419–429. doi:10.1061/(ASCE)CO.1943-7862.0000130

Marques, R. C., & Berg, S. (2011). Risks, contracts, and public-sector participation in infrastructure. *Journal of Construction Engineering and Management*, *137*(11), 925–932. doi:10.1061/(ASCE)CO.1943-7862.0000347

Martimort, D., & Pouyet, J. (2006). *Build it or not: Normative and positive theories of public private partnerships*. Centre for Economic Policy Research. Discussion Paper DP5610.

Mashamba, S. (2009). *Developments in the Zambian construction industry and the expected roles of our construction schools*. Lusaka, Zambia: National Council for Construction.

Maslyukivska, O., & Sohail, M. (2007). European infrastructure procurement through PPP. *Proc., Institution of Civil Engineers: Management Procurement and Law*, *160*(4), 159–167.

Matei, L. (2006). Empirical approaches of the public-private partnership in the services of public utility. *Theoretical and Applicative Economics*, *10*(505), 3–14.

McCann, S., Aranda-Mena, G., & Edwards, P. J. (2014). Delivering value-for-money in the operating phase of public private partnership: Interview findings. *International Public Management Review*, *15*(2), 91–110.

McKim, R. A. (2005). Risk Management – back to basics. *Coastal Engineering*, *34*(12), 7–12.

Medda, F. (2007). A game theory approach for the allocation of risks in transport public private partnerships. *International Journal of Project Management*, *25*(3), 213–218. doi:10.1016/j.ijproman.2006.06.003

Monteiro, R. S. (2010). Risk management. In International Handbook on Public-Private Partnerships. Oxford, UK: Willey- Blackwell.

Morledge, R., Smith, A., & Kashiwagi, D. T. (2006). *Risk in building procurement*. Oxford, UK: Blackwell.

Mouraviev, N. (2012a). Risk management in public-private partnerships and research agenda for transitional countries. *International Journal of Management & Business Studies*, *2*(2), 27–41.

Mouraviev, N., & Kakabadse, N. (2012). Conceptualizing public–private partnerships: A critical appraisal of approaches to meanings and forms. *Society and Business Review*, *7*(3), 260–276. doi:10.1108/17465681211271332

Mukela, M. (2007). *The significant other: A case of public-private partnership in Zambia, lessons learned in the infrastructure reform process*. Lusaka, Zambia: Zambia Printers.

Muller, R., & Turner, R. (2005). The impact of principal-agent relationship and contract type on communication between project owner and manager. *International Journal of Project Management*, *23*(5), 398–403. doi:10.1016/j.ijproman.2005.03.001

Ng, A., & Loosemore, A. M. (2007). Risk allocation in the private provision of public infrastructure. *International Journal of Project Management*, *25*(1), 66–76. doi:10.1016/j.ijproman.2006.06.005

Ngoma, S., Mundia, M., & Kaliba, C. (2014). Benefits, constraints and risks in infrastructure development via public-private partnerships in Zambia. *Journal of Construction in Developing Countries*, *19*(1), 15–33.

Osipova, E., & Eriksson, P. E. (2011). How procurement options influence risk management in construction projects. *Construction Management and Economics*, *29*(11), 1149–1158. doi:10.1080/01446193.2011.639379

Osipova, E., & Eriksson, P. E. (2013). Balancing control and flexibility in joint risk management: Lessons learned from two construction projects. *International Journal of Project Management*, *31*(3), 391–399. doi:10.1016/j.ijproman.2012.09.007

Pattberg, P., Biermann, F., Chan, S., & Mert, A. (2012). *Public-private partnerships for sustainable development: emergence, influence and legitimacy*. Cheltenham, UK: Edward Elgar. doi:10.4337/9781849809313

Regan, M., Love, P. E. D., & Smith, J. (2015). Public-Private Partnerships: Capital market conditions and alternative finance mechanisms for Australian infrastructure projects. *Journal of Infrastructure Systems*, *19*(3), 335–342. doi:10.1061/(ASCE)IS.1943-555X.0000136

Renn, O. (2006). *Risk Governance: Towards an integrative approach*. Geneva: International Risk Governance Council.

Rohmeyer, P., & Zvi, T. B. (2009). Risk management decision making in ICT for development. *Proceedings of the Second Annual SIG GlobDev Workshop*.

Rossi, M., & Civitillo, R. (2014). Public private partnership: A general overview in Italy. *Journal of Social and Behavioral Science*, *109*, 140–149.

Sanda, Y. N., & Anigbogu, N. A. (2016). A Conceptual Framework for Managing Risks in Public Private Partnership Projects in Housing Estate Development in Nigeria. *International Journal of Regional Development*, *3*(1), 50–63. doi:10.5296/ijrd.v3i1.8144

Sarmento, J. M. (2010). Do public-private partnerships create value for money for the public sector? The Portuguese Experience. *OECD Journal on Budgeting*, *1*(1), 1–28. doi:10.1787/budget-10-5km8xx3fgws5

Shaoul, J. (2005b). A critical financial analysis of the Private Finance Initiative: Selecting a financial method or allocating wealth. *Critical Perspectives on Accounting*, *16*(4), 441–471. doi:10.1016/j.cpa.2003.06.001

Shen, L., Platten, A., & Deng, X. P. (2006). Role of public private partnerships to manage risks in public sector projects in Hong Kong. *International Journal of Project Management*, *24*(7), 587–594. doi:10.1016/j.ijproman.2006.07.006

Silvester, H. C., & Aroujo, J. F. (2012). Public private partnerships / private finance initiatives in Portugal: Theory, practice, and results. *Public Performance and Management Review*, *36*(2), 316–339. doi:10.2753/PMR1530-9576360208

Singh, L. B., & Kalidindi, S. N. (2006). Traffic revenue risk management through annuity model of PPP road projects in India. *International Journal of Project Management*, *24*(7), 605–613. doi:10.1016/j.ijproman.2006.07.008

Smith, N. J., Merna, T., & Jobling, P. (2006). *Managing risk in construction projects*. Oxford, UK: Blackwell.

Sottilotta, C.E. (2013). *Political Risk: Concepts, Definitions, Challenges*. LUISS School of Government, SOG-WP6/2013.

Spikin, I. C. (2013). Risk Management theory: The integrated perspective and its application in the public sector. *Estado, Gobierno. Gestión Pública*, *21*, 89–126.

Steijn, B. E. H., Klijn, J., & Edelenbos, J. (2011). Public Private Partnerships: Added value by organizational form or management? *Public Administration*, *89*(4), 1235–1252. doi:10.1111/j.1467-9299.2010.01877.x

Tahir, M. (2007). Risk management in public-private partnership contracts. *Public Organization Review*, *7*(6), 1–19.

Tang, L. Y., Shen, Q., & Cheng, E. W. L. (2010). A review of studies on Public–Private Partnership projects in the construction industry. *International Journal of Project Management*, *28*(7), 683–694. doi:10.1016/j.ijproman.2009.11.009

Teo, E. A. L., Ling, F. Y. Y., & Chong, A. F. W. (2005). Framework for project managers to manage construction safety. *International Journal of Project Management*, *23*(4), 329–341. doi:10.1016/j.ijproman.2004.09.001

Thomas, A. V., Kalidindi, S. N., & Ganesh, L. S. (2006). Modeling and assessment of critical risks in BOT road projects. *Construction Management and Economics*, *24*(4), 407–424. doi:10.1080/01446190500435275

Tiwari, R. (2007). The early phases of innovation: Opportunities and challenges in public-private partnership. *Asia Pacific Tech Monitor*, *24*(1), 32–37.

Tserng, H., Russell, J., Hsu, C., & Lin, C. (2012). Analyzing the role of national PPP units in promoting PPPs: Using new institutional economics and a case study. *Journal of Construction Engineering and Management*, *138*(2), 242–249. doi:10.1061/(ASCE)CO.1943-7862.0000398

Tworek, P. (2010). Methods of risk identification in companies' investment projects. *5th International Scientific Conference "Managing and Modelling of Financial Risks"*. VŠB-Technická Univerzita Ostrava.

van Mieghem, J. A. (2010). Risk management and operational hedging: an overview. In *Handbook of Integrated Risk Management in Global Supply Chains*. Hoboken, NJ: John Wiley & Sons, Inc.

Velotti, L., Botti, A., & Vesci, M. (2012). Public-private partnerships and network governance. What are the challenges? *Public Performance & Management Review*, *36*(2), 340–365. doi:10.2753/PMR1530-9576360209

Vidal, L. A., Marle, F., & Bocquet, J. C. (2011). Measuring project complexity using the analytic hierarchy process. *International Journal of Project Management*, *29*(6), 718–727. doi:10.1016/j.ijproman.2010.07.005

Vining, A., & Boardman, A. (2008a). Public-private partnerships. Eight rules for governments. *Public Works Management & Policy*, *13*(2), 149–161. doi:10.1177/1087724X08323843

Vining, A., & Boardman, A. (2008b). Public-private partnerships in Canada: Theory and evidence. *Canadian Public Administration*, *51*(1), 9–44. doi:10.1111/j.1754-7121.2008.00003.x

Warburton, W., & Baker, G. (2005). Integrity systems and local government. *Australian Journal of Public Administration*, *64*(2), 62–68. doi:10.1111/j.1467-8500.2005.00441.x

Xiao, H. J., & Zhang, G. (2011). Modeling optimal risk allocation in PPP projects using artificial neural networks. *International Journal of Project Management*, *29*(5), 591–603. doi:10.1016/j.ijproman.2010.07.011

Xu, Y., Yeung, J. F., Chan, A. P. C., Chan, D. W. M., Wang, S. Q., & Ke, Y. (2010). Developing a risk assessment model for PPP projects in China- A fuzzy synthetic evaluation approach. *Automation in Construction*, *19*(7), 929–943. doi:10.1016/j.autcon.2010.06.006

Yescombe, E. R. (2007). *Public-Private Partnerships: Principles of Policy and Finance*. Oxford, UK: Butterworth-Heinemann. doi:10.1016/B978-075068054-7.50025-3

Yongjian, K., ShouQing, W., & Chan, A.P.C. (2009). Preferred risk allocation in China's Public Private Partnership (PPP) Projects. *Journal of Project Management*, *28*, 482–492.

Yuan, J., Skibniewski, M. J., Li, Q., & Zheng, L. (2010). Performance objectives selection model in public-private partnership projects based on the perspective of stakeholders. *Journal of Management Engineering*, *26*(2), 89–104. doi:10.1061/(ASCE)ME.1943-5479.0000011

Zaharioaie, M. (2012). The utility of using public private partnership for local governments. *Journal of Public Administration, Finance and Law,* 17-24.

Zhang, X., & Chen, S. (2012). A systematic framework for Infrastructure development through public private partnerships. *International Association of Traffic and Social Science Research*, *36*, 88–97.

Zinn, J. O., & Taylor-Gooby, P. (2006). Risk as an interdisciplinary research area. In P. Taylor-Gooby & J. Zinn (Eds.), Risk in social science (pp. 20-53). Oxford, UK: Oxford University Press.

Zitron, J. (2006). Public private partnership projects: Towards a model of contractor bidding decision making. *Journal of Purchasing and Supply Management*, *12*(2), 53–62. doi:10.1016/j.pursup.2006.04.002

Zou, P. X. W., Wang, S., & Fang, D. (2008). A life-cycle risk management framework for PPP infrastructure projects. *Journal of Financial Management of Property and Construction, 13*(2), 123-142.

Chapter 6
Establishing Boundaries for Risk Taking

ABSTRACT

In this chapter, a model for risk taking tool directed towards and tailored specifically for establishing risk boundaries. The goal of the chapter is to cover the particular threats pertinent to the risk context and provide an interface between the broader philosophy of risk raking frameworks and the risk attitude perception, thus aiding in the successful and secure risk taking. The model incorporates a wide range of factors concerning risk returns and risk responses, assembled into a checklist to ensure properly manageable risks are taken by the parties. It is concluded that this is the starting point for a systematic risk management in PPPs.

Knowing our risks provides opportunities to manage and improve our chances of success. - Roger VanScoy

INTRODUCTION

Partners in the world of PPPs are increasingly looking for best-practices in risk taking and sharing. Renewed confidence in a well taken and shared risk has led many partners that feared to enter into PPP arrangement to be open towards engaging in such like projects. The public sector is opening up as it associate with the private sector in finding the most cost-effective, economical and quality-production in the provision of goods and services dearly wanted by the public and the effects of such engagement has been applauded in several successful areas. Of course, in actual practice objectives to attract risk taking and risk sharing differ by the partner and the effects of such a stand many not always be similar. Increased risk awareness and risk preparedness have led to a rapid growth in risk management in PPPs over the years. Urges for risk management across different countries and amongst different parents increased as an equal percentage of the increase in the number of PPPs projects world over. However, while most countries and partners alike are attracted to PPPs and know their very proper way to working, others have been less successful in implementing a good PPP, even though they had all resources

DOI: 10.4018/978-1-5225-2503-5.ch006

required for a successful implementation of a PPP project. Intensified search for what has gone wrong in stalled project, uncompleted projects, and 'projects-well-conceived-but-die-a-still-birth' has led many governments and partners to look for benchmarks of the causes towards re-shaping the trends PPP projects should undertake. Countries and partners are forced to be more open to one another about their conceived PPP arrangements where it is difficult to build a barrier that 'ride' away causes of constraints.

While for some countries and partners there is concern about the improper inception and poor conduct of feasibility study on a proposed PPP project, there is a shift in other countries and the thinking of other partners towards the unpredictable position of risk. The term risk usually refer to unpredictable occurrence which can happens in the future and has all the potential of failing achievement of a particular goal or objective. It always has a negative linkages and spillover effects for an arrangement, such like PPP entered into by the public partner on the one hand and the private partner on the other. It would seems appropriate that countries and partners that have had successful PPP projects based on application of clearly defined measures to tackle risks; need to continue to upgrade to a level of risk-free PPP projects, or by targeting higher value-added risk management strategies. Those countries and partners that have not made some convincing moves towards PPP and even those other ones that have strides but along the way, outcomes of the efforts is not pleasing as it ought to be, much more is needed to have a clear boundary of the risks to be managed.

With frequent risk occurrences limiting performance and implementation of PPP arrangement, this chapter will look at what areas of concern ought to be taken up seriously by the public as well as private partners. Relying on technocrats does not guarantee (and most times prevent) the successful implementation of PPP arrangement. Countries and partners of a PPP arrangement ought to review whether the agreed PPP arrangement has positive spillover leading to success as initially designed in terms of growth and achievement of intended objectives. Theoretical developments (Velotti, Botti & Vesci, 2012) and empirical evidences (Akintoye, 2006) show that the success development and implementation of PPP projects is dependent on properly established boundaries of risk taking and risk sharing. The encouragement of linkages between PPP project development and PPP project implementation may also be important in developing a successful PPP arrangement, for example, through a linkage programme or in cluster risk taking and risk sharing.

Countries and partners wanting to have a risk-free PPP projects as part of achieving the very purpose of service delivery intentions will therefore have to think of strategies towards attracting precise risk taking and risk sharing, advancing solid risk taking and risk sharing, and encouraging linkages between risk taking and risk sharing (Cankar & Petkovšek, 2013). Some countries and to some extent some partners want risk taking and risk sharing more than others and may try harder accordingly. Countries and partners can base their risk taking and risk sharing strategy on establishing the boundaries of risk (attitude, return and response) taking into account all the elements that makes them which are only partially understood by most parties (Zitron, 2006). This chapter helps to classify such established boundaries into more concrete building blocks. The literature frequently regards establishment of the boundaries of a particular subject matter of a risk as examples of efficient move towards a PPP risk-free project. Here we find interesting discoveries.

The structure of this chapter is as follows. The next section discusses the nature of risk attitude in theory and practice. These discussions shall caption the areas of risk loving, risk aversion, and risk neutral. We will then discuss the need to have some returns in the risk management process. As part of pre-defined purpose of this sub section, risk and return has been classified into risk appetite, risk capacity and risk appetite versus risk return. We subsequently, discuss risk response on the basis of the classification in terms of risk avoidance, risk retention and risk reduction. We conclude the chapter with appropriate conclusion that can take us to the safe landing onto the proceeding chapter.

RISK ATTITUDE

Risk attitude is the organization's or individual's view/perspective of the perceived qualitative and quantitative value that may be gained in comparison to the related potential loss or losses (Hillson & Murray-Webster, 2005). For example, many people who place their memory at risk in gambling perceive that the small (quantifiable) average financial loss combined with the qualitative excitement benefits is a net gain. According to Wang and Yuan (2011), risk attitude is different from one partner to another, as each partner needs to overcome the extra cost of risk taking and risk sharing under different circumstances in a PPP arrangement. The difference is termed an ownership acceptance (Han, Diekmann & Ock, 2005) as shown in tangible and intangible PPP arrangement (Brewer & Strahorn, 2012). The studies reviewed in large measure (Sulaiman, 2012) show that risk attitude are major determinants of handling risk and finding solutions unto it. The distinctiveness and the superiority of the partners in taking and sharing risks are determined by the risk attitude held by the partner (Wang, Keller & Siegrist, 2011). Having a positive risk attitude create an ambient atmosphere in which the partner can come in to take or share the risk with all its skills, new technologies, and management strategies (Hillson & Murray-Webster, 2007). However, in practice the benefits of having a positive risk attitude may some way be scaled back when the responsible risk taker and share decide to back ground (Alexopoulos, Kavadi, Bakoyannis & Papantonopoulos, 2009). A risk attitude can also lead to less desirable or undesirable outcomes such as disputation of who is more placed to take the risk as well as rising conflict about the nature and the sharing formula between the parties (Bonin, Dohmen, Falk, Huffman & Sunde, 2007). This can lead to crowing-out of the action plan for the risk taking or an erosion of the stand upon which the parties ought to base themselves for handling and treating the risk (Lima, Barnett & Vala, 2005).

Simply taking or sharing a risk does not mean a partner has a positive risk attitude (Au & Chan, 2005). In order to identify that a partner has been successful in taking and sharing risk, it seems necessary to rely at least partly on models that explains more sophisticated partnerships especially those that determines either ownership or profit distribution (or both) (Aibinu & Odeyinka, 2006). French, Sutton, Kinmonth & Marteau (2006) shows that risk attitude is affected by the motives of the partners which is either public value or profit correspondingly to ownership and profit distribution in a PPP project. For example, according to Bennet and Cusick (2007) partnership is tethered on 'source of origination'. Shahzad and Safvi (2010) opine that the source of origination indicates the form of partnership in which there is a "lockstep" and "eat what you kill" attitude. Coispeau and Luo (2015) stress lockstep involves new partners joining the partnership with a certain number of "points". They continue to argue that as time passes, the new partners accrue additional points, until they reach a set maximum sometimes referred to as a plateau. Krane, Olsson and Rolstadås (2012) suggests that the length of time it takes to reach the maximum is often used to describe the company (so, for example, one could say that one firm has a "seven-year lockstep" and another has a "ten-year lockstep" depending on the length of time it takes to reach a maximum equity). The lockstep form of partnership usually instigates a positive risk attitude in the partners. This because the partners who weight risk against rewards and could possibly concludes that much as the risk is there, the rewards can compensates due to the longer period of the partnership (Aramvareekul & Seider, 2006).

Banaji (2007) maintains that the "eat-what-you-kill" form of partnership risk attitude is rarely, if ever, seen outside of law firms. The principle is simply that each partner receives a share of the partnership profits up to a certain amount, with any additional profits being distributed to the partner who was responsible for the organization of the work that generated the profits (Oyegoke, Khalfan, McDermott & Dickinson, 2008). This kind of attitude built a culture in which the partner who is presumed to benefit the more must take and share the most burden of the risk (Peng, Miao & Xiao, 2013). Such attitude affects the manner in which consideration for risk taking and sharing ought to be based.

The principle purpose for which partners enter into PPP agreement actually determines the 'source of origination' of the partnership (Cox, 2008). In turn, this dictates the kinds of attitude each of the partner will have towards the arrangement. According to Silvester and Arauyo (2012), the public partner provides, among others accountability/transparency, institutional and regulatory framework, all in an attempt to provide favorable environment for a successful PPP. This means therefore, the public partner's risk attitude is tethered on the preservation of a favorable environment so that PPP could thrive. The implication here is that the public partner cannot have a negative risk attitude in a PPP arrangement since its interest is to preserve a favorable environment so that PPP projects, for example, can thrive without any brave of hindrances (Pasławski, 2010). Ibem (2010) on the other hand declares that the private partner provides technical expertise, managerial skills and financial capacity among others. Here again the risk attitude of a private partner is a positive one. This is because the private partner would not want to make losses. It would there forth strive a little harder to ensure that resources it brings forth into the partnership do not go to waste. However, Cankar and Petkovšek (2013) remind that risk attitude of the partners in a PPP arrangement is influenced by a number of factors such as the characteristics (composition, aim and objectives, the roles of the partners) of PPPs and the political, economic, socio-cultural, technological and other contextual situations within the operational area of the PPPs. Every partner ought not to be influenced negatively in terms of the attitude each takes about the risks in the arrangement. The belief behind this argument is provided by Pessoa (2006) who acclaims the collaboration between the partners is based on the principles of comparative advantages because PPP recognizes that there are some activities that the public partner does best and others, where the private partner has more to offer. El-Sayegh (2008) reiterates that the overall aim of PPP is to structure the relationship between the public and public partners in such as way that the risks associated with the specification, delivery and regulation of public services are allocated to the best party able to manage them. This calls for a part to which a risk has been assigned and taken to have a positive attitude towards the risk so as to be able to handle it amicably.

Choudhry and Iqbal (2013) propose that partners ought to remind themselves constantly their attitude on risks should be informed by the very tenets upon which they entered into the agreement. One critical and most important issues for such a reminder, as put forward by Aaltonen and Sivonen (2009) is that though PPPs are defined as partnerships, some aspects of PPPs show that it doesn't sit within the traditional norms of partnerships where the two partners work together in achieving the same goals and where the profits as well as risks are shared. Hiren (2010) professes the relationship is more of that of a principal and an agent where information asymmetry and opportunism are present. This implies that the partners must have clear in their minds the kind of risks they are about to delve themselves into lest a PPP project might die a still-birth. Since the relationship is more of a principal-agent nature, it is probable risk attitude of the partners must be centered on three main philosophical viewpoints on how the principal and agent can later on interact in order to achieve the best outcome for the principal (Bäckstrand, 2012). In this way, Jayasudha, Vidivelli and Surjith (2014) recommend there must be competition between the parties; this should be followed by integration and finally providing incentives. The competition aspects, as proclaimed by Owusu and Badu (2009) is supposed to be based on the establishing whether a partner will be in a position to take the risk or to mutually share the risks amongst the parties themselves. The integration aspect invites the parties to appreciate the share each of them is to take. But the taking of the risk does not mean its handling should exclusively rest with the party that had taken. Sometimes integrating the handling process of the risk might do wonders that could have perhaps been left entirely in the hand of only one party (Chan, Chan, Lam, Yeung & Chan, 2011). It would therefore appear noble to integrate risk taking and sharing for optimal results. Provision of incentives aspect acts as mirror upon which the parties can gauge through the benefits they will derive from taking or sharing the risks. To achieve all these, Hwang, Zhao and Gay (2013) recast there are three most important conditions that can make partners to have a positive attitude towards risks in a PPP arrangement. These are reducing information asymmetry through competition and monitoring; providing incentives through tariff policy, penalties and risk and reward assignments; and providing credible commitments through enforcement of contracts.

In addition partners ought to take upon themselves that each of them must be credible partners. This is because designing a partnership in the world of imperfect competition is not an easy task. Papajohn, Cui and Bayraktar (2011) postulate it will always require information asymmetry between the principal and the agent. Bäckstrand, Campe, Chan, Mert and Schäferhoff (2012) opines that information asymmetry and opportunism are the core issues in a principal agent relationship which further leads to two problems of adverse selection and moral hazard of the risk handling. Adverse selection problem is associated with the partners taking or sharing risk with one who is not most suitable and moral hazard deals with partners not taking and sharing the 'right' risks.

Choice of the risk to take and/or share highly depends on the attitude that the partner has built about the project. Usually, the taking or sharing of a risk is 'chained' onto some other benefits which are presumed to be achieved at a future date. In their work about risk allocation in the private provision of public infrastructure, Ng and Loosemore (2007) rate risk always goes hand in hand with rewards. In spite of this, Hayford (2013) warns that the premium that gives the basic judgments of whether one should bear the risk is quite different among individuals. For that reason, Diallo and Thuillier (2005) attest the attitude toward risk choice is based on each individual's risk preference. Such preference is presented in Figure 1.

Figure 1. Risk preference choices
Source: (Diallo and Thuiller, 2005)

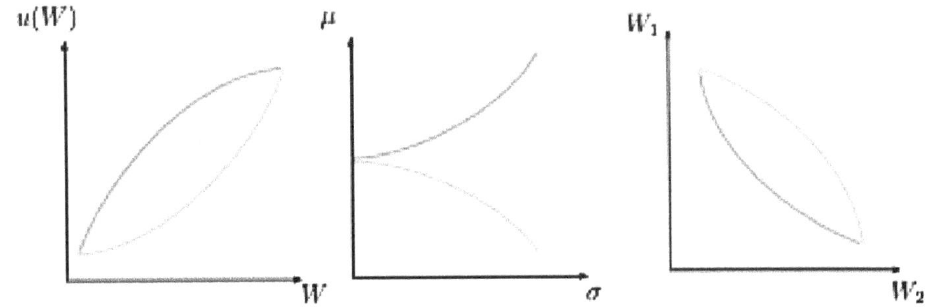

**For a more accurate representation of this figure, please see the electronic version.*

From Figure 1: risk aversion (red) contrasted to risk neutrality (yellow) and risk loving (orange) in different settings. Left graph: A risk averse utility function is concave (from below), while a risk loving utility function is convex. Middle graph: In standard deviation-expected value space, risk averse indifference curves are upward sloped. Right graph: With fixed probabilities of two alternative states 1 and 2, risk averse indifference curves over pairs of state-contingent outcomes are convex.

Whatever, the preferences of the risk choices it must be based on some utility function as illustrated in Figure 2.

Following sub section will therefore explain the three preference choices of risk each in turn beginning with risk loving, followed by risk averse and risk neutral.

RISK LOVING

A crucial question that should be at the forefront of partners concerned with implementation of a PPP arrangement is how each of them can be linked to risks involved in the arrangement (Andi, 2006). Depending on the pre-conditions (presence of partners' capabilities; endowments of production factors such as labor, natural resources and capital; small or large economy, e.t.c…) and ideologies regarding the degree of partner's interventions, a partner can define an entry into the agreement, for example, in terms of loving or cold of risk (Jin & Doloi, 2008). The partner can then decide whether it has the capacity and capability of taking and/or sharing the risk in an efficient and effective way of achieving this and what outcome of a PPP arrangement is needed, if it had such a choice (Ke, Wang & Chan, 2010a). Any of the partners has to ensure that the arrangement is specific to it and another party and that they have agreed to operate on shared understandings of mutual benefits, rather than relying primarily on written contracts (Ibrahim, Price & Dainty, 2006). Such a relationship Yuan, Skibniewski and Li (2008) argue has important benefits for choosing rick, since it implies a commitment to deal with unforeseen contingencies, rather than seeking to rely on rigorous interpretation of contractual terms. It invokes the spirit of risk loving such that the disadvantages of partnership being inflexible cannot normally dispose of the partners' interest without the consent of the fellow partners (Sciulli, 2008).

Figure 2. Risk utility function and risk preference
Source: (Grable, 2008)

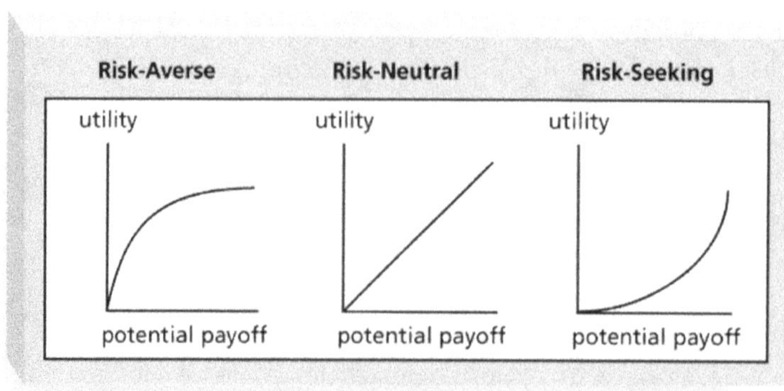

Concina (2014) articulates that risk loving goes in the opposite direction: the certainty equivalent of a risk lover is always higher than the expected. Thus, the risk premium is negative and represents the maximum amount of money that the person is willing to give in order to maintain the risky activity. Santoso, Joewono, Wibowo, Sinaga and Santosa (2012) intimate that for risk lovers, the absolute value of the risk premium represents the maximum amount that they are ready to lose when choosing between a risky activity and its expected value. They prefer to maintain the risk activity rather than accept its expected value: risk is a positive characteristic (Vajdić, 2011).

According to Tadayon, Jaafar and Nasri (2012), risk loving sometimes referred to as risk-seeking is when one accepts the bet even when the guaranteed payment is more than the agreed sum. Beh (2010) postulates a risk-seeker or risk lover is a person who has a preference for risk. For example, a risk-seeking who is a gambler would prefer to gamble even though the gamble and the sure thing have some expected value. Inekwe (2015) recaps though a risk-seeking behavior can be observed in the negative domain especially for prospect theory value functions, where the functions are convex and not concave. In the meantime, a risk loving partner can use risk loving as its long term strategy in ensuring PPP succeeds, but provided both parties engage with complex negotiation and special challenges that must be navigated unto agreement (Ding, Hartog & Sun, 2010). Mwaguni and Busienei (2014) advice that for a partner to be a good risk-lover, the parties must negotiates overarching goals, levels of give-and-take, areas of responsibility, lines of authority and succession, and how success is evaluated and distributed, and often a variety of other factors. Implementation of the terms and conditions of the PPP contract would require trust and pragmatism on the part of the partners on top of having in place a written agreement enforceable by civil law. This again entails risk loving because essentially it cannot be expected that everything can be written in the initial partnership agreement, thereby quality governance and clear communication are CSFs in the long run (Zhong, Chew, Set, Zhang, Xue, Sham, Ebstein & Israel, 2009). Risk loving also makes it possible to provide information to the outsiders about formally partnered entities to be made public, such as through a press release, a newspaper ad, or public records laws. Where risk-loving is none existence such could be possible.

In an ideal situation, risk loving would stand to amplify mutual interests and accelerate success. In a non ideal situation though, risk loving may turn out to be problematic (Dohmen, Falk, Huffman, Sunde, Schupp & Wagner, 2011). For example, when a politician partner with a company to advance his/her interests in exchange for some benefits, a conflict of interest results, even if there may be risk-loving. In such circumstances, the surest outcome is the suffering of the public good. In some quarters this could be technically legal, but such practice is broadly viewed negatively or as corruption with all its negative impacts (Ainamo, 2005). Where there is a dishonest risk-loving, Bryde and Robinson (2005) cautions partners may be exposed to greater personal liability than they would had it been there was risk-loving amongst themselves.

There are a variety of strategies based on risk-loving implying different degrees of implementation measures which can be suitably applied for PPP projects to succeed (Matei, 2006). First, partners need to address the challenge of taking risks at face value. In general, all PPP projects suffer from uncertainty of knowledge about the risks involved in them. But the private partners are naturally at a disadvantage with regard to information on the PPP potential projects muted by the public partner (Selsky & Parker, 2005). To speed up the PPP projects implementation processes, the pubic partner may want to intervene by offerings modest information that proposed potential PPP project would entails. This is the only basis upon which the private partner and even the public partner can get to know about all possible risks in a PPP arrangement, and it's such knowledge that would make them take on the risk by its horn. Second, partners need to address the divergence in interest between themselves and the public good. A private partner, for example, can intervene in the PPP arrangement for skills and technologies, where PPP project failures are most likely and gear the development of technologies and skills more towards the needs of the arrangement. But this can only be possible of the private partner is a risk-seeker/risk-lover (Voelker, Permana, Sachs & Tiong, 2008). Related to this, a public partner may want to intervene in acquiring enough land for the PPP projects, but such a decision can only be effective if the public partner has an affectionate love for all the risks involved.

There is, however, less agreement on the optimal degree of risk taking and risk sharing when it comes to risk-loving by the parties (Smyth, 2008). It is therefore possible to define four probable indications of risk-loving by any of the partners: i) active receptive acceptance of all sorts of risk in a PPP arrangement, ii) open-door strategy with selected intervention to improve risk acceptance conditions, iii) strategic targeting of primary and prime risks, and iv) devising of immediate sustainable intervention. It can be argued that while options i and iv may not be sufficient to exploit opportunities for full-scale risk-loving, the optimum for any partner will be near the second approach and only if their capabilities develop, and a more strategic and targeted approach may produce better results (Firsova, 2011).

A choice for risk loving needs to be followed by adequate implementation (Gbadegesin & Aluko, 2014). Partners that can follow risk-loving measures consistently and respond in a flexible way to demands by potential creditors/ financiers are most successful (Mouraview, Kabadse & Robinson, 2012). The conviction to love any kinds of risks in a PPP arrangement is generally seen as providing all the necessary information and permits within which the PPP contract is to implemented and mutually executed by all the parties. The implementation of action plans derived out of risk loving over time is also important. Uncertainty deters PPP projects progress, and hence consistent follow up risk loving measures must be adhered to. Much as Grossman (2012) suggests that the importance of risk loving may also vary with the different partners, it is only helpful that the love be turned into something meaningful for the success of the PPP contract.

Finally, in the emerging context of numerous PPPs initiations, new modes of developing risk loving must be inculcated into the minds of the architectures and implementers of PPP projects. All other measures adopted for PPP project to succeed must have some components of measures designed to keep risk loving active and rolling (Obermann, 2007). This begs the question how much scope still exists in the acceptance of risks by the parties to a PPP arrangement and in all the processes and stages of PPPs in particular, putting aside the question whether partners want to treat risks differently at all (Koontz & Thomas, 2012). There are three categories of possible course of action in this respect: those actions that specifically target proper risk identification and are still possible at least to some extent (for example, during initiation, inception and feasibility stages of the PPP project); those that target post-feasibility study stages of PPP processes but are disallowed or will be disallowed completely (ignored and left out as unimportant); and those that target all the processes of PPP projects but have special effects on the implementation processes itself (Bostrom, French & Gotllieb, 2008). Hence, there is still some scope (for example, i and iii) for a successful PPP projects, although PPP contract agreements do limit a number of options (category ii). The latter may not be serious as PPP projects covers less than half of the whole PPP project processes ranging from inception to completion and subsequent handover to the public partner. In addition, risk loving deals with positive actions but not passive actions. It is more a question of whether a partner desires or is able to conduct a proactive risk handling processes.

Risk Aversion/Reduction

Overviews of risk attitude handling usually address either acceptance conditions or rejection or reduction attempt linkages, but not all at the same time. While the inclusion of all such actions inevitably entails a loss of detail, there is a gain in regarding handling of risk as integrated and running through the entire risk handling processes. Risk aversion provides another framework for handling risk in a manner that does not make it destructive (Bohnenblust, Holthausen, & Merz, 2008). Risk aversion is a kind of human behavior commonest amongst consumers and investors in which when exposed to uncertainty, one attempt to reduce that uncertainty. Coudert and Gex (2007) state that risk aversion relates to the reluctance of a person to accept a bargain with an uncertain payoff rather than another bargain with a more certain, but possibly lower, expected payoff. For example, a risk-averse investor might choose to put his or her money into a bank account with a low but guaranteed interest rate, rather than into a stock that may have high expected returns, but also involves a chance of losing value. Curiously, a person is said to be: risk-averse (or risk-avoiding) - if he or she would accept a certain payment (certainty equivalent) of less than say $50 (for example, $40), rather than taking the gamble and possibly receiving nothing.

Bohnenblust, Holthausen and Merz (2008) claim that a broadly accepted and precise definition of risk aversion has to date proved elusive. This is because the understanding of the term differs considerably depending on the given discipline and viewpoint, for example, engineering versus humanities and social sciences. Bohnenblust, Holthausen and Merz (2008) suggest that only decision-making theory and utility theory have established a clear, unequivocal, albeit somewhat abstract and restricted definition of the term. This understanding often fails to be positioned within a clear conceptual framework, which normative theory affords it. Risk aversion has been defined as a phenomenon that is empirically observable in many situations and has a theoretical basis which weighs possible incidents with serious consequences more heavily than the associated expected damage value (Epanchin-Niell & Hastings, 2010). This definition implies that the certainty equivalent for a risky activity is lower than its expected value (CE<EV). Provan, Huang and Milward (2009) portrays the difference between the expected value and the certainty equivalents is called the risk premium (RP=EV-CE). The risk premium is positive in the context of risk-averse behavior; it is the maximum amount of money that an individual accepts they might lose in order to avoid risk (Guiso & Paiella, 2008). Risk aversion in the project management is a system, for that probability, loss of process or project mandatory avoidance counter measures (Provan & Kenis, 2008). In wide terms risk aversion means losing profit opportunities, which is a kind of negative and preventive measures (Acar & Göc, 2011).

In agreement with earlier scholars, Bohnenblust, Holthausen and Merz (2008) declare that there two different ways to account for risk aversion: explicit methods in which risk aversion is quantifiably and comprehensively documented; and implicit methods, which take indirect and latent account of aversion in risk decisions. Marcelino-Sádaba, Pérez-Ezcurdia, Echeverría Lazcano and Villanueva (2014) clarify that risk aversion can be looked at from two perspectives: individual risk aversion and risk aversion in the public sector. The individual risk aversion perspective looks at risk aversion as an inherent characteristic of the human race. Individuals are identified as risk-averse, when they prefer a sure value, for example their own capital assets- over an equally large, but unsure expected value, for example the expected values of the capital assets in a lottery draw. Poba-Nzaou, Raymond and Fabi (2014) states that often this is intuitive, but it can also be a rational response, as humans generally have a diminishing marginal utility for wealth.

Erstwhile, Forlani, Parthasarathy and Keaveney (2008) demonstrate that risk aversion in the public sector is somewhat confusion. This is because the society is sometimes faced with similar, though mostly complex decisions. For example, the state may be able to fund rehabilitation efforts without any great difficulty following minor incident causing minor material and human damage. Hiebl (2013) suggests that for incidents with a rather low impact, provisions for the management of such an incident are often already in place, for example, the contingency plans of the emergency services. Gao, Sung and Zhang (2013) reecho incidents which cause major damage are more difficult to manage. This is because it can be observed in practice that such incidents are weighted more heavily. The risk conversion and acceptability curve approaches to risk aversion consider this fact (Fan, Li & Zhang, 2015).

For a successful risk aversion, Blavatskyy (2008) highlights some conditions must be present. These conditions includes:- various damage indicators must be individually suited to different types of risk, especially in relation to mapping the damage, and the same function cannot be universally applied to all risks. In risk aversion, Kraeussl, Lucas and Siegmann (2010) recommends that prior to the implementation of the risk aversion instrument, decision-makers should primarily concern themselves with its impact if planning phase takes particular account of major damage (that is their budget for no-damage case). Wuerth and Schumacher (2011) recommend further and add that an important basis for any decision is therefore information concerning the impact on the planning of measures, with or without risk aversion. Coudert and Gex (2007) argue that there are a number of variables which influence the size of the aversion function. For example, the aversion function tends to be greater, the higher the value of the given direct and consequential damage. According to Guiso and Paiella (2008), the aversion function must always be linked to a clearly defined damage indicator (for example, fatalities). Al-Ajmi (2011) writes that if there is a need to adequately show the scale of indirect and consequential damage by means of an aversion function, no standard or correct aversion function exists which is appropriate to use in all fields of operation.

There are many reasons why partners decide to do risk aversion in a particular instance. Following Cheng's (2010) study, partners do risk aversion because they are neither sure of the outcome of the risk left unattended nor have it clear the benefits attained for handling the risk. In his study, De Dreu and Bikker (2012) assumes that risk whatever its nature have a negative and positive outcomes and that its proper for the partners to have it clear the magnitude of the negativity and positivity of the risk. This would enable taking appropriate action resonate with the outcome of the risk. Hallahan, Faff and McKenzie (2005), thus, analyze the risk aversion framework of risk handing as well as all associated factors that affects risk handling as something that can be used and applied simultaneously.

The determinants of risk aversion can be divided into personal attempt specifically relating to personal conviction, and more general strategies. Personal conviction has been an important determinant of risk aversion. Private partner, often in the form of SPVs, has promoted and targeted the risk aversion as a way of handling risk by providing general information and undertaking matchmaking activities to reduce risks. Roszkowski and Grable (2005) show that risk aversion is significantly and positively related with PPP project success, though less so applied in many countries. Risk aversion promotion addresses a situation where a risk can easily go out of hand. However, continues adaption can be expensive and expenses vary considerably by PPP projects. While partners often lack the skills and experience to facilitate risk aversion and used to screen and approve measures to tackle risks, are often more in touch with risky situation (Weber, Weber & Nosić, 2013). With sufficient awareness of the risk, the partner can help itself get off the dangerous impact of risks when appropriate step is taken. This is frequently called a one-stop shop, where one partner deals with screening, approval of and obtaining permits for the partner.

Partners can also take special consideration into the adoption of risk aversion attitude by taking it as a probable condition for the handling of risk. Grable and Roszkowski (2008) were reviewing a number of studies; found that risk aversion significantly influences risk handling. Experience, however, suggest that incentives to risk aversion are mostly low for the public partners whose interest is always to provide public good undeterred by risk occurrences (Chan, Chan, Lam & Chan, 2010b). Kourtidis, Sević and Chatzoglou (2011) profess that risk aversion plays decisive role once the fundamentals are sufficiently understood. Less evidence is available on the effects of risk aversion on the success of a PPP project (Koleczko, 2012). Risk aversion measures implicitly lower the devastating effects of risks (Koonce, McAnally & Mercer, 2005). They provide partners some discretionary powers during the PPP arrangement process, which could foster implementation if monitored properly. They can also be used as part of the wider risk handling strategy to stimulate certain risks handling policy (Roszkowski & Davey, 2010).

Other risk aversion perception towards a PPP arrangement includes the formulation of reduction procedures and rules on risk handling. Reduction procedures can form a significant barrier to risk handling, especially in developing countries (Gattig & Hendrickx, 2007). Public partners' organizations, for example, are sometimes unaware that certain regulations can be streamlined without losing its regulatory powers. This can be the result of the past when public sector often relied on screening of new investment projects rather than facilitating. Competition amongst partners on reduction procedures (especially if they put risk handling at a disadvantage) towards PPP project investment should eventually lead to convergence of procedures toward best-practice, so that the partners do not distinguish between the basis of reduction procedures.

Risk Neutral

Factors affecting risk taking can be crucial in determining whether a project can succeed or not. Sometimes the investor may decide to avoid the risk completely or transfer it to another party. In some instances, though an investor may be left with no option than to remain neutral in the circumstance of an occurrence of risk. A significant of investors for sure may prefer being neutral in a risky situation. Risk neutral preferences are neither risk averse nor risk seeking (Adams, 2008b). Ashuri, Kashani, Molenaar, Lee and Lu (2012) state that; the decisions of a risk neutral party are not affected by the drgree of uncertainty in a set of outcomes. This means a risk neutral party is indifferent between choices with equal expected payoffs even if one choice is riskier. For example, if offered either \$50 or a 50 per cent chance each of \$100 and \$0, a risk neutral party would have no preference. In contrast, a risk averse person would prefer the first offer, while a risk seeking person would prefer the second. Constantinides, Jackwerth and Perrakis (2008) declare that a person is said to be risk-neutral, if he or she is indifferent between the bet and a certain \$50 payment.

According to Cheng (2010), risk neutral indicates a situation where the partner is uncomfortable with uncertainty in the long term so prepared to take whatever short=term actions are necessary to deliver a certain long-term outcome. Ashuri, Kashani, Molenaar, Lee and Lu (2013) assert that a risk-neutral organization values gains and losses by their dollar vale no matter how large the gain or loss is. For example, a loss of \$1 million is equally as bad as a gain of \$1 million is good. Usually, the risk neutral organization evaluates alternative decisions using expected monetary value, calculated by multiplying the value of each possible result by its probability of occurring and adding the probability-weighted values of all possible results. This is equivalent to applying a linear utility function. Generally, Chan, Lam, Chan, and Wong (2010a) attests that if the value of a decision calculated this way is not large enough the organization will not do it.

RISK AND RETURN

This section reviews key areas of risk taking and other factors determining the response of the partners to risk management in the PPP arrangement. Factors in this case would affect risk taking and risk sharing whether each of the partners benefits or not. Rakic and Radjenovic (2011) argue that risk sharing and risk taking are important factors for which PPP has been adopted as an instrument of new public management. Akbiyikli, Eaton and Turner (2006) describe the importance of these factors on the basis of risks and returns. They define these concepts as a close to ideal situation, under which PPP arrangement can ably succeed. In line with Maskin and Tirole (2008), these concepts herein are related to the ability to capture a good understanding of the risk return trade off.

The following graphic (Figure 3) illustrates the relationship between risk capacity, risk appetite, risk tolerance and risk limits. The red vertical line represents risk capacity. This is the absolute maximum amount of risk that the public private partnership can take at this point in time, regardless of the opportunity that is available. The blue line represents risk appetite and the purple line represents risk limits (Sahm, 2008). The risk limits line is below the risk appetite line for all risk and return points. This is because risk appetite is the sum total of the P3 risk limits plus a buffer (risk tolerance) for prudence. Risk tolerance is represented by the green (middle) line.

Figure 3. Risk and return: the relationship
Source: Goldstein and McElligott, 2014

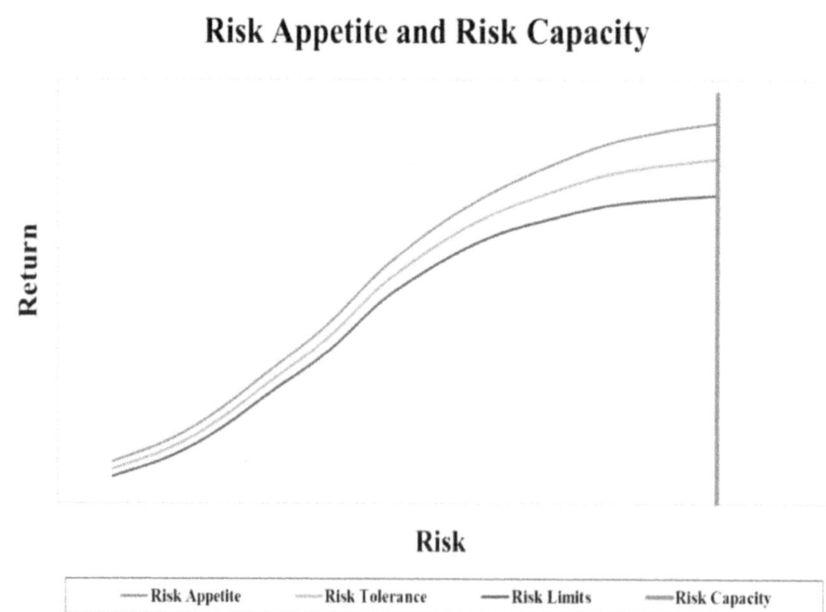

**For a more accurate representation of this figure, please see the electronic version.*

The risk return trade off in Figure 3 illustrates that the strategic goals of a public private partnership cannot be achieved without taking risk. The amount of risk that a public private partnership can take is expected to be commensurate with the return available up to a maximum of amount of risk that the public private procurement can bear at any one time (Weber, Weber & Nosić, 2013). It is the duty of the PMC to consider what represents an acceptable and an unacceptable risk in the context of the public private partnership strategy.

Risk Target

According to Rohmeyer and Zvi (2009), a risk target is a desired level of risk that the organization believes is optimal to meet its objectives. This often can be some level within the risk tolerance boundaries, possibly depicted along a risk/reward curve. Bailey and Kinerson (2005) postulate that implicit in the risk tolerance and risk target concepts are reviews to determine the suitability, adequacy and effectiveness in operating within the boundaries at the desired target levels. Monitoring changes from the expected outcomes is vital for risk tolerance statements to be meaningful. Unexpected or unacceptable deviations should trigger further analysis and action, including escalation to senior management (Wiguna & Scott, 2006). As with appetite, an organization's risk tolerance generally is driven by its objectives and stakeholder expectations, ranging from value protection (generally lower tolerance levels) to value creation (generally higher tolerance levels) (Dey, 2009). Tolerances are also highly dependent on how well capitalized or financed the organization is (Skorupka, 2008).

Risk Capacity

Yescombe (2013) recommends that an organization should not define risk appetite without considering its risk capacity. Risk capacity is the amount of risk an organization can actually bear. An organization's board and management may have a high-risk appetite but not have enough capacity to handle a risk's potential volatility or impact (Ojo & Ogunsemi, 2009). Conversely, the risk capacity may be high but the company may decide based on strategy, management objectives and stakeholder expectations to adopt a lower risk appetite (Rojas & Kell, 2008).

Risk Appetite

Risk appetite is derived from the combination of risk exposure and risk capacity (Serrador & Turner, 2015). It is not a concept but a realistic approach that can protect an organization from loss through inefficiency (Domokos., Nyéki, Jakovác, Németh & Hatvani, 2015). Hillson and Murray-Webster (2011) claims that implementation of an effective risk management in PPP is incomplete without determining and defining the partner's risk appetite and risk tolerance. In fact, according to risk management studies, likes those of Kobbeltvedt, Brun, Johansen and Eid (2005), Roszkowski and Grable (2005) and Roszkowski and Davey (2010), risk appetite management is one of seven essential attributes of an effective risk management framework and an essential part of any risk-mature organization. According to Althaus (2005), risk maturity is determined by the degree of understanding and accountability of five factors: defining acceptable boundaries, calculating and articulating tolerance, developing risk portfolio views, making risk and reward trade-offs in daily management, and attacking gaps between perceived and actual risks. Klos, Weber and Weber (2005) advocate that a clearly-expressed risk appetite and tolerance statements help protect organizations against solely pursuing single, narrow goals without considering potential consequences as they pursue rewards for an "appropriate" level of risk. Blais and Weber (2006) warn that what is appropriate and acceptable for on organization may be unacceptable to another, as their attitudes toward risk necessarily range along a continuum from risk taking to risk averse.

Moeller (2007) minces no word in asserting that risk appetite is an extremely ambiguously defined concept. The basis of this assertion is that risk appetite is often considered in different context giving different interpretations. For example, in the literature, risk appetite is sometimes associated with risk tolerance, risk willingness or risk attitude (Chapman, 2007; Hopkin, 2010). Whatever association, the concept of risk appetite is clearly a tendency to take risks (propensity to take risk) and the tendency to risk control (propensity to exercise control). Moreover, these two concepts cannot be analyzed in isolation from each other (Coter, & Chen, 2006). Consequently, there are numerous sources providing formal definitions of risk appetite, as compiled by researchers from the University of Wisconsin-Madison (Kamiya, Shi, Schmit & Rosenberg, 2007). Examples of the risk appetite definitions they found include: The level of aggregate risk that a company can undertake and successfully manage over an extended period of time; a company's ability and/or willingness to absorb declines in the value of an asset, liability, trade, transaction, or portfolio; and the broad-based amount of risk a company or other entity is willing to accept in pursuit of its mission or vision (Vlaev, Chater & Stewart, 2009).There are three levels of risk appetite. The corporate risk appetite is the overall amount of risk judged appropriate for a public private partnership partner to tolerate, which should be agreed at board level. Delegated risk appetite is the risk appetite agreed on different levels of the public private partnership arrangement (Tanaka, Ishida, Tsutsumi & Okamoto, 2005). The project risk appetite is attached to the projects that fall outside of day-to-day business operations of the public private partnership arrangement. The approach to determining risk appetite for particular risk groups makes it easier to define the acceptable level of risk exposure, both in value and frequency.

The definition of risk appetite is also valid from the risk management efficiency point of view. For instance, Cienfuegos (2011) contends that the PPP arrangement may focus on protection of more risky areas while maximizing the resources to secure less risky areas. Also, it obtains greater clarity in the indication of the benefits of risk management, which is a valid argument in a better understanding of risk management and the need for expenses on it. Determination of risk appetite is also important for partners of a PPP arrangement, as it makes its activities more transparent (Abednego & Ogunlana, 2006). Accordingly, it ensures the cohesion of the decisions concerning the approved risk bearing capacity. Risk bearing capacity means the risk that a PPP arrangement may take with respect to the implemented risk control mechanisms. It should be underlined, that risk capacity is not always synonymous to risk appetite. If the risk bearing capacity is slightly higher or similar to the risk appetite, the public private partnership arrangement represents the balanced (neutral) approach to risk. If the risk appetite is greatly exceeding the risk bearing capacity, the PPP arrangement represents the aggressive attitude to risk and is often called a risk taker (Roumboutsos & Anagnostopoulos, 2008). In a contrary situation, the PPP arrangement manifests its risk aversion. Assuming that the public private partnership arrangement tends to continuously improve the relations with its stakeholders (as it helps to increase the value maximization), the partners' risk preferences should also be taken into account. In this context, the role of risk appetite is also valid. If risk appetite is set correctly, then it can be a subject of deeper consideration in terms of combination of risk preferences of particular partner (Sachs, Tiong & Wang, 2007).

According to Grimsey and Lewis (2005), risk Appetite is the aggregate level and types of risk a PPP partner is willing to assume within its risk capacity to achieve its strategic objectives and business plan.

It is normally provided in form of a statement which is the formal articulation of an entity's willingness to take on certain risks and avoid or minimize other risks in the pursuit of its strategic objectives. Risk capacity is the maximum amount of risk which the public private partnership is technically able to assume before breaching one or more of its capital base, liquidity, and borrowing capacity, reputational and regulatory constraints (Roszkowski, Davey, & Grable, 2005). Setting risk appetite without taking into account the risk capacity of the entity may have serious consequences. This therefore calls on the partners to understand and appreciate how their risk capacities can impact on their performances. Risk capacity may be easy to quantify in terms of capital or required funding but it is more challenging to consider the point at which a PPP's reputation is beyond repair.

Tanaka, Ishida, Tsutsumi and Okamoto (2005) associate risk appetite with the maximum risk exposure that the PPP is able to accept in achieving its goals. It is related to the amount of risk that a partner is prepared to accept, tolerate or be exposed to at any point in time. This means risk appetite is an acceptable level of risk and so called residual risk. It is usually discussed relating to the investment decisions of the investors. Zhang (2005a, 2005b) reveals that an investor considers his or her risk appetite when selecting from a range of investment options presenting different risk/return trade-offs. The challenge for an individual investor is to determine which point on this risk/return tradeoff provides either: the lowest level of volatility to meet financial needs and goals, the highest return given the investor's tolerance for risk, or some intermediate point that maximizes utility (Zou, Wang & Fang, 2008). At a very basic level, this is not unlike the challenges a corporation faces when making decisions about its business.

English (2006) claims that many individual investors are aware of the need to understand their own risk appetite, yet most make decisions that affect the risk profile of their wealth and income only infrequently. Corporations need to make these decisions more regularly. In the case of the public private partnership arrangement, decisions affecting the risk profile of its business are made daily. As a result, managing and profiting from calculated risks is a core skill for many public private partnership arrangements (Hanoch, Johnson & Wilke, 2006). Although these PPP arrangements are in the business of risk, defining a PPP-wide risk appetite can be complicated in practice. For example, Cleland and Gareis (2006) contend that much like the basic risk/return trade-off decisions presented to the individual investor, the common thread across risk appetitive is the need for the company to decide on the appropriate amount of risk it can accept in order to enhance the PPP's value over a given time frame.

There are conditions which need to be taken into consideration when defining risk appetite. First, the 'total risk exposure' of the organization must be known. According to Cienfuegos (2012), 'total risk exposure' is the total value of risks in financial terms that have been identified in the risk portfolio. This enables knowledge of the total VaR (Value at Risk) for the organization in relation to its risk appetite. Secondly, risk exposure is to be considered in terms of potential financial loss from all risk types that could impact the ability of the organization to remain sustainable. Thirdly, risk exposure should be lower than the risk capacity. If risk exposure exceeds risk capacity, there is a possibility the organization will experience difficulties in absorbing the risks it is faced with and is likely to spend more to bring disruptions under control. Fourthly, while the considering risks capacity attention ought to be paid to the ability and expertise for managing the risks. This should embody the understanding of the different risk types across the business, an embedded risk framework, a positive risk culture (attitudes), and a fit-for-purpose risk infrastructure.

Risk appetite is best handled using risk appetite framework (RAF). It is an overall approach, including policies, controls and systems, through which risk appetite is established, communicated and monitored (Dikmen & Birgonol, 2006). The RAF demonstrates the implicit link between risk appetite and strategy.

In doing so, it defines the risk limits and tolerances around those limits (Cleden, 2009). The RAF also clarifies the action required in the event of a breach of risk limits and risk tolerance. Finally, it specifies the roles and responsibilities of the officers that are responsible for the implementation of the RAF.

One way in which the perceived deficiencies within RAS may be addressed is by providing industry with a generic checklist setting out the expected content of the statement and against which the Supervisor would be able to tick off whether these requirements have been met. Camilleri (2011) argues that it is improper to advocate such an approach as it implies that public private partnership design RAF and Risk Appetite Statements (RAS) in response to regulatory requirements. The risk appetite of a PPP must express the strategy of that PPP through desirable and undesirable risk exposures (Zimmermann & Eber, 2014). A generic list that is provided as a response to regulation is unlikely to achieve this. A further risk is that companies would create boilerplate statements without due consideration to the real risks facing their PPP. According to Sulaiman (2012), the strategy and risk appetite of a PPP are interlinked. Risk appetite is as much about enabling a public private partnership to take on calculated risks in pursuit of long term strategy as it is about placing constraints on activities (Helm, 2010). In that sense the RAS allows an institution to demonstrate to stakeholders that achievement of results stem from deliberate strategy and risk allocation as opposed to happenstance. Public private partnership should view a risk appetite statement as a positive and dynamic document

Exposure to risk is an inevitable part of doing business. What differentiates a successful business from one that is not is the ability to take on calculated risks in order to realize strategic goals (Baccarini, 2005). The goals achieved and the risks undertaken to achieve them should be demonstrable to stakeholders. The RAS enables the PPP to demonstrate that the achievement of its strategic goals has not been the result of luck (Ali & Mohammad, 2010). Setting a risk appetite is not about elimination of all risks; rather it is about embracing risks in areas in which management has the appropriate skills, knowledge and experience to take advantage of the opportunities presented, whilst limiting risks in other areas (Dikmen & Birgonol, 2007). When considered with strategy this explains why a public private partnership 'does' and 'does not' do what they do.

A clearly defined risk appetite provides the directors, management and staff with a framework which facilitates the identification and management of both risks and opportunities. Clear and concise strategic objectives should underpin the RAS (Meidute & Paliulis, 2011). Even though this implies that risk appetite and strategy are interlinked, it is clear that one does not lead the other; risk appetite and strategic planning occur and evolve in parallel (Ammar, Berman & Sataporn, 2007). An effective risk appetite statement is empowering in that it enables the decisive accumulation of risk in line with the strategic objectives of the public private partnership while giving the board and management confidence to avoid risks that are not in keeping with the strategic objectives (Ho, 2006a).

A clear RAS is a necessary condition for an effective RAF but it is not sufficient on its own. An effective RAF is often best evidenced through an assessment of the culture, in particular the risk culture, of the public private partnership. risk culture is the norms of behavior for individuals and groups within a public private partnership that determine the collective ability to identify and understand, openly discuss and act on the public private partnerships current and future risk (Ho, 2006b). A public private partnership with a strong risk culture is one where employees, management and the board clearly understand what risks should be accepted and what risks should be minimized or avoided (Barlish, De Marco & Thaheem, 2013). There should be no confusion as to where the limits and tolerances lie (Karim, 2011). Communication is encouraged regarding risk accumulation and risk measurement. The desired culture is enforced through behavior from management and directors as well as the use of incentives and sanctions (Ogbu, 2013). The extent to which the risk appetite of the public private partnership is evidenced by the behavior of individuals in that public private partnership is a key factor in reinforcing risk culture (El-Sayegh, 2008). Rewarding employees and management for achieving goals that were attained by breaching risk limits undermines the effectiveness of the RAF. When assessing the RAF of a public private partnership one should question 'whether the end justifies the means' (Aven, 2010).

According to Hillson & Murray-Webster (2012), in designing a risk appetite statement, look at the following: - Risk Capacities: Does the PPP understand the current limits to its risk capacity? Desirable Risks: What risks does the public private partnership wish to actively take? Strategically, this is why the PPP exists. How does the PPP optimize these risks in order to generate a return? Undesirable Risks: What risks does the PPP wish to avoid? Strategically, what does the PPP not do? Unavoidable Risks: How are these risks managed? Inter linkages: How do risks identified influence other risks? Risk timelines: Is consideration given to the risks that may materialize over short, medium and longer term horizons? What information, controls and systems do the board, executive management, line management and employees actually require in assessing the nature of risks and how they relate to on-going strategic choices? Incentives and Compensation: How are the strategic choices and attendant risks linked to incentives and compensation? Culturally does the public private partnership reward the attainment of risk adjusted return or simple return? Escalation and mitigation: How are risks that are outside of risk appetite identified, communicated and mitigated? Brevity and Clarity: Is it possible to communicate the appetite concisely in an understandable form?

Appetite for risk must be measurable and the type of measurement depends on the level of governance at which risk is considered (i.e. strategic, tactical or operational) (Raz & Hillson, 2005). At the strategic level, appetite for risk should focus on risks that may shape the PPP arrangement's competitive advantages. The key point of reference should be the shareholders value creation. At the tactical level, the appetite for risk relates to the risks normally associated with the implementation of already established PPP arrangement's strategy (Cheung, Chan & Kajewski, 2009a, 2009b). Here, the recommended way to measure risk appetite is the establishment of the Key Risk Indicators (KRI). At the operational level, the appetite for risk is a set of recommendations on the procedure in the event of specific threats, without having to consult with the senior management. At this level, as a measure of risk appetite Key Control Indicators (KCI) are suggested.

Rezakhani (2012) postulates essential attributes of an effective risk appetite encompasses risk appetite-based approach, process management, risk appetite management, uncovering risks, performance management, business resiliency and sustainability. Sanda and Anigbogu (2016) opines the common methods of expressing risk appetite includes:- setting boundary on a probability and impact-grid, economic capital measured/balance sheet based expression, changes in credit rating (headroom before a potential downgrade), profit and loss measures (for example, tolerable level of annual loss), value-bases measures (based on probability of ruin or default), limits/targets or thresholds for key indicators, and qualitative statement, for example, zero tolerance for regulatory breaches or loss of life.

RISK RESPONSE

Risk response, also called risk treatment is a choice in relation to an identified risk which can be categorized broadly as the decision whether to avoid the risk or accept it (Turnbaughs, 2005). It is an appropriate steps taken or procedures implemented upon discovery of an unacceptably high degree of exposure to one or more risk. It is the fourth stage of risk management in which there is establishment of a strategy to mitigate the potential threats and maximize the potential opportunities (Loosemore, Raftery, Reilly & Higgon, 2006). Wang and Dai (2009) recommends that the selection of risk response must be appropriate to the significance of the risk; it must be cost effective and realistic with regard to the timing of the project and it also must be agreed upon by other involved parties.

Wason (2006) avers risk response measurement include risk estimation, analysis and evaluation. On the basis of evaluation of risk factor, Xu, Yeung, Chan, Chan, Wang and Ke (2010) argues that it's determined how to eliminate or reduce risk about certain factor. For example, before the happening of an accident, it is necessary to reduce the accident frequency and minimize the losses due to accidents. Dallas (2006) articulates that risk response is an important step for risk management, based on several considerations, for each risk factor that one can choose risk measurements from different angles. For example, the purpose of risk management, risk decision factors, relevant cost alternative, risk management ability and various related parts are involved certain policy, laws and regulations. According to the result of risk identification, risk assessment and then the nature of specific risks potential impact risk responses are planned. Later on, the basis of these response plans, the implementation of plans to deal with risk and to avoid or reduce losses is analyzed for better results (Keith, 2011). Risk response measures include five parts, such as risk retention, risk reduction, risk transfer, risk avoidance and insurance (Perminova, Gustafsson & Wikstrom, 2008).

Having defined the characteristics of a good risk response, consideration can be given to the specifics of developing such responses (Wishnu & Pradono, 2011). Sangsomboom and Yan (2014) proposes that a two-stage approach should be followed, first defining the appropriate strategy for dealing with a particular risk, then designing tactics to implement the chosen strategy. Finally, before accepting a risk response Flyvbjerg (2006) advocates for testing of the response against seven criteria. These criteria are appropriate; affordable; actionable; achievable; assessed; agreed; and allocated and accepted (Hulett, 2011).

In the appropriate criteria, it is important that the correct level of response must be determined based on the "size" of the risk. This ranges from a crisis where the project cannot proceed without the risk being addressed, through to a "do nothing" response for minor risks. Ashok and Birajdar (2015) advice that it is important not to spend inordinate amount of time or effort developing inappropriate responses for minor risks, but also not to spend too little time considering how to respond to key risks. Buertey, Abeere-Inga and Kumi (2013) argue that the affordable criteria advocates the cost-effectiveness of responses must be determined, so that the amount of time, effort and money spent on addressing the risk does not exceed the available budget or the degree of risk exposure. Each risk response should have an agreed budget. Waghmare and Pimplikar (2012) suggests that in the actionable criteria, an active window should be determined, defining the time within which responses need to be completed in order to address the risk. Some risks require immediate action, while others can safely be left until later. Latief, Pallu, Adisasmita, Aly and Suyuti (2014) postulate that with the achievable criteria, there is no point in describing responses which are not realistically achievable or feasible, either technically or within the scope of the respondent's capacity and responsibility. Lam, Wang, Lee and Tsang (2007) states in the assessed criteria, all proposed responses must work! The effectiveness of a response is best determined by making a "post-response risk assessment" of the size of the risk assuming effective implementation of the response. Van Gestel and Voets (2012) compliment that in the agreed criteria, the consensus and commitment of stakeholders should be obtained before agreeing responses. Oyewobi, Ibrahim, and Ganiyu (2012) intimates that in the allocated and accepted criteria each response should be owned and accepted to ensure a single point of responsibility and accountability for implementing the response.

After careful subjection of the risks to these criteria, it is wiser to again consider the various alternative strategies available when planning risk responses (Artto, Kujala, Dietrich & Martinsuo, 2008). Apparently, Atkinson, Crawford and Ward (2006) propose appropriate strategies includes avoid, that is seeking to eliminate uncertainty, transfer, that is seeking to transfer ownership and/or liability to a third party, mitigate, that is seeking to reduce the size of the risk exposure to below an acceptable threshold, and accept, that is recognizing residual risks and devising responses to control and monitor them. Sanderson (2012) highly recommends that it is extremely important to determine the appropriate strategy first, then to design responses to implement the chosen strategy. According to Thomas and Mullaly (2007), this avoids the "scatter-gun" approach. Where a number of alternative responses may be proposed, some of which may negate the effect of others. Determining strategy first, Zhai, Xin and Cheng (2009) claims will ensure that responses are aiming for the same goal, and avoid nugatory effort. There is no single "best" response strategy, and each risk must be considered on its own merits. Young and Jordan (2008) caution some risks may require a combination of strategies and multiple responses, whereas, others may need only one strategy with a single response.

Artto, Kujala, Dietrich and Martinsuo (2008) aver strategy selection should be driven by consideration of the type and nature of the risk, manageability and amenability to reduction or control, the degree of severity of impact, available resources and cost-effectiveness. Aubry, Hobbs and Thuillier (2007)) also recommends that avoidance strategies should be considered as the first option, since it is clearly best to remove risk completely if possible. Eskerod and Riis (2009) contend that transfer should be investigated second, although the scope of this is often limited. Garrido, Ruotolo, Ribeiro and Naked (2011) advice the third choice is risk mitigation, seeking to reduce risk exposure, leaving acceptance as the last resort for residual risk which cannot be addressed by any other strategy. Having selected the appropriate strategy, attention can then be given to development of tactical responses which target individual risks and aim to realize the strategy. Öztaş and Ökmen (2005) argue that there are six typical risk responses strategies which are retention, reduction, control, sharing, transfer and avoidance. Specific responses for risk avoidance and retention are discussed in the following sections, the rests are discussed elsewhere.

Risk Utility/Tolerance

A good risk response strategy must be backed up with an acceptable risk utility/risk tolerance. The supposed to be affected party must derive some utility from the risk so as to be able to tolerate it. Ogunsanmi, Salako and Ajayi (2011) note that elements such as feelings, dread, knowledge, trust, optimism, overconfidence make perceived risk differ from the objective risk as by empirical and experimental research include the so-called certainty effect. This has the potentials of over-stating or under-stating the probability associated with a possible event, even when it is known and no estimates needed. This is a manifestation that risk tolerance varies according to the context in which the risk is occurring. For example, people may appreciate risk in their leisure activities but flee from it when making financial decisions. Therefore, people's actual attitude to financial risk, for instance, must therefore be measured explicitly in the financial context. Ajayi, Ogunsanmi, Salako and Mafimidiwo (2012) contend that even in the financial context people may exhibit different attitude to risk depending on how they framed their assets and their choices.

Risk tolerance is generally referred to as the "the maximum amount of uncertainty someone is willing to accept when making a financial decision" (Grable, 2008). Roszkowksi and Davey (2013) claim there are two major different viewpoints in conceptualizing and understanding risk tolerance. The first considers risk tolerance to be influenced by not only personal characteristics but also situational factors which induce risk tolerance to change overtime (van de Venter, et. al., 2012). The other defines risk tolerance as a stable trait that does not change significantly (van de Venter, et. al., 2012). Regarding the first point of view, inter-temporal studies highlight the less stable view of risk tolerance. For example, Hoffman, Post and Pennings (2013), in their study of the influence of the Global Financial Crisis (GFC) in 2007-2009 on investor perceptions, found that risk tolerance decreased during the GFC. Interestingly, the change was found to be temporary because risk tolerance quickly recovered when the market improved. Conversely, risk tolerance has been found to be relatively stable in a number of studies. For instance, Roszkowski and Davey (2010) examined the changes of both financial risk tolerance and risk perception after the GFC using the *FinaMetrica* risk profiling system. In addition to a significant change in financial risk perception, they found just a small change in risk tolerance. Similarly, a recent study by Gerrans, Faff and Hartnett (2013) also provided supporting evidence for a fairly stable feature of risk tolerance, even after the GFC. Notably, Van de Venter et al. (2012) employed the *FinaMetrica* risk profiling system to examine the longitudinal annual change of financial risk tolerance and found only a small annual change in risk tolerance. Van de Venter et al. (2012) also examined if changes in demographic and situational factors including age, marital status, number of dependants, level of education, income level, wealth, location, financial planner services, market expectations, and index values could explain changes in financial risk tolerance. They found only two factors: number of dependants and financial planner services explained changes in risk tolerance, suggesting that although many demographic and situational factors have been found to associate with financial risk tolerance in the prior literature, changes in them do not necessarily translate to changes in financial risk tolerance. More importantly, based on their findings, Roszkowski and Davey (2010) and Van de Venter et al. (2012) combined two different viewpoints of financial risk tolerance discussed above by suggesting that (1) financial risk tolerance is generally considered as a personal trait but it can change over time and (2) the change in financial risk tolerance is driven by external factors.

Decisions on risk tolerance are determined by the outcomes risk parties have in their "mental account" (Itzhak & Hirshleifer, 2012). The basis of this assertion is that people tend to code, categorize and evaluate economic outcomes depending on the "mental account" involved, that are on whether assets come either from current income, current wealth or future income and on the needs an account is set for (Harrison, 2007). Zhang (2006) indicates that accounts are largely non-fungible and behavior for each account is different. A mental account, according to Sachse, Jungermann and Belting (2012), is subject to several biases. For example, the so called "house money effect" predicts that investors will be more likely to purchase risky stocks after having experienced a gain. Since they don't yet consider the profit to be their own, they are willing to take more risk with it. On the other hand every time a mental count realizes a loss, individuals may either exhibit higher risk aversion or be encouraged to take greater risks in the hope of being able to recover the initial amount ("break even" effect). In other words, opportunities allowing individuals to break even may become more appealing. Overcoming these biases may help investors profit more over the long term (Chen, Kök & Tong, 2013).

Suffice to note that different organizations and people have different tolerances for risk. This is an indication that the risk utility or risk tolerance is the amount of satisfaction or pleasure received payoff. For example, utility rises at a decreasing rate for people who are risk-averse; those who are risk-seeking have a higher tolerance for risk and their satisfaction increases when more payoffs is at stake. Karim (2011) intimates the risk-neutral approach achieves a balance between risk and payoff.

Risk Avoidance

Risk avoidance refers to the risk has not yet occurred, take the initiative to give up or refuse to implement may lead to risk loss (Seyed, Seyrafianpour & Ebrahimnejad, 2010). From the perspective of risk management, risk avoidance is refusing to take risks; it is one of the ways to eliminate the risk. Although the construction project can't eliminate all risks, but by the method of risk aversion, to a certain risk, eliminate before it occurrences, so it reduce the opportunity of risk or reduce causes of damage (Walton & Bellhouse, 2012). Risk avoidance is a refusal to accept the risk, or action taken to ensure that the risk is not going to happen (Minassian & Jergeas, 2009).

According to Abbasianjahromi and Rajaie (2012), risk avoidance is the elimination of hazards, activities and exposures that can negatively affect an organization's assets (Cruz, Cano & Cruz, 2006). Whereas risk management aims to control the damages and financial consequences of threatening events, risk avoidance seeks to avoid compromising events entirely. While the complete elimination of all risk is rarely possible, a risk avoidance strategy is designed to deflect as many threats as possible in order to avoid the costly and disruptive consequences of a damaging event. A risk avoidance methodology attempts to minimize vulnerabilities which can pose a threat. Risk avoidance and mitigation can be achieved through policy and procedure, training and education and technology implementations. While the complete elimination of all risk is rarely possible, a risk avoidance strategy is designed to deflect as many threats as possible in order to avoid the costly and disruptive consequences of a damaging event. A risk avoidance methodology attempts to minimize vulnerabilities which can pose a threat. Risk avoidance and mitigation can be achieved through policy and procedure, training and education and technology implementations.

Risk avoidance is not performing any activity that may carry risk. For example, suppose an investor wants to buy stock in an oil company, but oil prices have been falling significantly over the past few months. There is political risk associated with the production of oil and credit risk associated with the oil company. She assesses the risks associated with the oil industry and decides to avoid taking a stake in the company. This is known as risk avoidance. On the one hand, risk reduction deals with mitigating potential losses. For example, suppose an investor is invested in oil stocks. There is political risk associated with the production of oil, and the stocks have a high level of unsystematic risk. He can reduce his risk by diversifying his portfolio by buying stocks in other industries, such as retail or airlines. Suppose the investor diversifies his portfolio and invests in various sectors of the market. However, he currently faces systematic risk due to an economic downturn. The investor may reduce his risk through a hedge. For example, the investor can protect his long positions and reduce his risk by buying put options for his long positions. He is protected from a potential drop in his portfolio value because he is able to sell his stocks at a predetermined price within a specified period. The investor who avoids the risk forfeits any potential gains the oil stock may have. On the other hand, the investor who reduces his risk still has potential gains. If the stock market goes higher, his long positions will appreciate in value. However, if his positions decrease in value, he is protected by his put options.

Risk avoidance means that by looking at alternatives in the project, many risks can be eliminated. If major changes are required in the project in order to avoid risks, Wiguna and Scott (2006) suggest applying known and well developed strategies instead of new ones, even if new ones may appear to be more cost efficient. In this way, the risks can be avoided and work can proceed smoothly because strategy is less stressful to the users. Mubin and Mannan (2013) recommends that if the risk is classified as bringing negative consequences to the whole project, it is of importance to review the project's aim. In order words, if the risk has significant impact on the project, the best solution is to avoid it by changing the scope of the project or, worst scenario, cancel it. There are many potential risks that a project can be exposed to, and which can impact success (Mubin & Mubin, 2008).This is why risk management is required in the early stages of a project instead of dealing with the damage after the occurrence of the risk (Kuppusamy, 2010).

In general, the following several ways, usually risk avoidance strategy should be considered: i) the probability of risk events happening a lot of loss in big projects and the consequences; ii) the probability of the loss is not large but when the risk of incident loss is severe; and iii) risk aversion objectively don't must for projects but just need for the better set up of project. Turnbaughs (2005) reminds that the risk avoidance strategy seeks to eliminate uncertainty. This can be achieved by two types of response: direct and indirect. Patrick, Shouqing and Dongping (2008) argues that where risk arises from lack of knowledge (epistemic uncertainty), it can be tackled directly. To eliminate uncertainty, therefore, Pasławski (2010) recommends the following actions:-clarifying requirements, defining objectives, obtaining information, improving communication, and undertaking research, prototyping or development and acquiring expertise (via training or recruitment). Cagno, Caron and Mancini (2007) state that; an alternative avoidance response might be devised to target the cause of the risk, where this is identified. Removing the source (or breaking the causal chain) can make it impossible for the risk to occur, thus eliminating the uncertainty. Indirect avoidance responses involve doing the project in a different way, which can also eliminate much of the uncertainty by making any impact irrelevant to the project.

Noble and Jones (2006) intimate that it may also be possible to "design out" certain types of risk in the early stages of a project, by making strategic project decisions, which preclude certain risky possibilities. To the extent that risk avoidance means the employer and/or the contractor (via for example procedures such as ECI) investigating the risks pre-contract or as part of a two stage contract and this results in avoiding a risk through, for example, changing the design, then avoidance is important. If, however, it simply means that a potential risk is avoided by the employer transferring it to the contractor with no analysis or consideration of appropriate allocation then this is inappropriate and likely to be costly. In short, investigation, and acceptance that both parties have a vested interest in avoiding, or at least reducing risk, is the right approach. To avoid risk by ignoring it or transferring it without analysis is generally not sensible.

Risk Retention

When a risk cannot be transferred or avoided, the best solution is to retain the risk. In this case the risk must be controlled; in order to minimize the impact of its occurrence (Tingting & Wilkinson, 2011). Retention can also be an option when other solution is uneconomical (Wibowo & Mohamed, 2010). Risk retention involves acknowledging that a particular risk situation exists and making a conscious decision to accept the associated level of risk, without engaging in any special efforts to control it (Smith, Merna & Jobling, 2006). Risk reduction is an approach used to bring the probability and impact of the risk down below an acceptable threshold and risk sharing is principally achieved through a contractual mechanism to develop a sense of collective responsibility among the project stakeholders (Loosemore, Raftery, Reilly & Higgon, 2006). Dallas (2006) suggests that one of the key principles of PPP is for the public sector to retain only those risks that pertain to its core business of service delivery, with all risks relating to the design, construction and management of a facility, from which the services are delivered, allocated to the private sector contractor.

CONCLUSION

We began this chapter by saying that partners in both developed and developing worlds are increasingly looking for best-practice ways towards risk taking in a PPP arrangement. Whilst risk taking bring positive effects (risk free project implementation), it can also bring negative effects. Moreover, the positive effects are not automatic any PPP projects and depend on the measures undertaken and put in place. Which measures are important in which project depends on the specific project characteristics, the objectives of the project and the derived risk taking-strategy intended for success in implementation and outcomes there off. On the basis of this chapter, we discussed risk attitude in terms of risk loving, risk aversion/reduction, and risk neutral. We then proceeded to discuss risk and return where we looked at risk target, risk capacity and risk appetite. This then introduced us to risk response where we considered and discussed risk utility/risk tolerance, risk avoidance and risk retention. The chapter provided needed information to formulate appropriate risk management framework which is the basis and content of the proceeding chapter.

REFERENCES

Aaltonen, K., & Sivonen, R. (2009). Response strategies to stake-holder pressures in global projects. *International Journal of Project Management*, *27*(2), 131–141. doi:10.1016/j.ijproman.2008.09.007

Abbasianjahromi, H., & Rajaie, H. (2012). Developing a project portfolio selection model for contractor firms considering the risk factor. *Journal of Civil Engineering and Management*, *18*(6), 879–889. doi :10.3846/13923730.2012.734856

Abednego, M. P., & Ogunlana, S. O. (2006). Good project governance for proper risk allocation in public–private partnerships in Indonesia. *International Journal of Project Management*, *24*(7), 622–634. doi:10.1016/j.ijproman.2006.07.010

Acar, E., & Göc, Y. (2011). Prediction of risk perception by owners psychological traits in small building contractors. *Construction Management and Economics*, *29*(8), 841–852. doi:10.1080/01446193.2011.611521

Adams, F. K. (2008b). Risk perception and Bayesian analysis of international construction contract risks: The case of payment delays in a developing economy. *International Journal of Project Management*, *26*(2), 138–148. doi:10.1016/j.ijproman.2007.05.007

Aibinu, A. A., & Odeyinka, H. A. (2006). Construction delays and their causative factors in Nigeria. *Journal of Construction Engineering and Management*, *132*(7), 667–677. doi:10.1061/(ASCE)0733-9364(2006)132:7(667)

Ainamo, A. (2005). Co-evolution of knowledge management processes: Drawing on project experience in a global engineering consulting firm. *Research in Management Consulting*, *5*, 107–129.

Ajayi, O. M., Ogunsanmi, O. E., Salako, O. A., & Mafimidiwo, B. A. (2012). Impact of risk on performance of design and build projects in Lagos State, Nigeria.*Proceedings of 4th West Africa Built Environmental Research (WABER) Conference,*203-215.

Akbiyikli, R., Eaton, D., & Turner, A. L. (2006). Project finance and the private finance initiative (PFI). *The Journal of Structured Finance*, *12*(2), 65–75. doi:10.3905/jsf.2006.644162

Akintoye, A. (2006). Public private partnerships for sustainable development of Infrastructure in developing countries. *Proceedings of International Conference on the Built Environment*.

Al-Ajmi, J. Y. (2011). Risk tolerance of individual investors in an emerging market. *Journal of Risk and Identification*, *2*, 101–112.

Alexopoulos, E. C., Kavadi, Z., Bakoyannis, G., & Papantonopoulos, S. (2009). Subjective risk assessment and perception in the Greek and English Bakery industries. *Journal of Environmental and Public Health*, *2*, 1–8. doi:10.1155/2009/891754 PMID:20041018

Ali, M., & Mohammad, K. (2010). Selecting appropriate project delivering system: Fuzzy approach with risk analysis. *Journal of Construction Engineering and Management*, *136*(8), 923–930. doi:10.1061/(ASCE)CO.1943-7862.0000190

Althaus, C. E. (2005). A disciplinary perspective on the epistemological status of risk. *Risk Analysis*, *25*(3), 567–588. doi:10.1111/j.1539-6924.2005.00625.x PMID:16022691

Ammar, A., Berman, K., & Sataporn, A. (2007). A review of techniques for risk management in projects. *Benchmarking: An International Journal*, *14*(1), 22–36. doi:10.1108/14635770710730919

Aramvareekul, P., & Seider, D. J. (2006). Cost-time-risk diagram: Project planning and management. *Coastal Engineering*, *48*(11), 12–18.

Artto, K. A., Kujala, J., Dietrich, P., & Martinsuo, M. (2008). What is project strategy? *International Journal of Project Management*, *26*(1), 4–12. doi:10.1016/j.ijproman.2007.07.006

Ashok, Y. A., & Birajdar, B. V. (2015). Risk analysis and management for public-private partnership infrastructure projects in India. *International Research Journal of Engineering and Technology*, *2*(4), 1549–1551.

Ashuri, B., Kashani, H., Molenaar, K., Lee, S., & Lu, J. (2012). Risk-neutral pricing approach for evaluating BOT highway projects with government minimum revenue guarantee options. *Journal of Construction Engineering and Management*, *10*(4), 545–557. doi:10.1061/(ASCE)CO.1943-7862.0000447

Atkinson, R., Crawford, L. H., & Ward, S. (2006). Fundamental uncertainties in projects and the scope of project management. *International Journal of Project Management*, *24*(8), 687–698. doi:10.1016/j.ijproman.2006.09.011

Au, M. C. Y., & Chan, E. H. W. (2005). *Attitudes of contractors and employers towards transfer of a time-related risk in construction contracts*. ASCE Construction Research Congress 2005. doi:10.1061/40754(183)68

Aubry, M., Hobbs, B., & Thuillier, D. (2007). A new framework for understanding organizational project management through the PMO. *International Journal of Project Management*, *25*(4), 328–336. doi:10.1016/j.ijproman.2007.01.004

Aven, T. (2010). On how to define, understand and describe risk. *Reliability Engineering & System Safety*, *95*(6), 623–631. doi:10.1016/j.ress.2010.01.011

Baccarini, D. (2005). *Understanding project cost contingency–A survey*. Paper presented at the Queensland University of Technology (QUT) Research Week International Conference.

Bäckstrand, K. (2012). Are partnerships for sustainable development democratic and legitimate? In P. Pattberg, F. Biermann, S. Chan, & A. Mert (Eds.), *Public-private partnerships for sustainable development: emergence, influence and legitimacy*. Cheltenham, UK: Edward Elgar. doi:10.4337/9781849809313.00018

Bäckstrand, K., Campe, S., Chan, S., Mert, A., & Schäferhoff, M. (2012). Transnational public– private partnerships. In F. Biermann & P. Pattberg (Eds.), Global environmental governance reconsidered (pp. 123–148). Academic Press.

Bailey, J. J., & Kinerson, C. (2005). Regret avoidance and risk tolerance. *Financial Counseling and Planning*, *16*(1), 23–28.

Banaji, J. (2007). Islam, the Mediterranean and the rise of capitalism. *Historical Materialism*, *15*(1), 47–54. doi:10.1163/156920607X171591

Barlish, K., De Marco, A., & Thaheem, M. J. (2013). Construction risk taxonomy: An international convergence of academic and industry perspectives. *American Journal of Applied Sciences*, *10*(7), 706–713. doi:10.3844/ajassp.2013.706.713

Beh, L. (2010). Development and distortion of Malaysian public-private partnerships patronage, privatized profits and pitfalls. *The Australian Journal of Public Administration*, *69*(S1), S74–S84. doi:10.1111/j.1467-8500.2009.00655.x

Bennet, C., & Cusick, K. (2007). *Risk Appetite: Practical Issues for the Global Financial Services Industry*. Paper presented to the Institute of Actuaries of Australia Biennial Convention, Christchurch, New Zealand.

Blais, A.-R., & Weber, E. U. (2006). A domain-specific risk-taking (DOSPERT) scale for adult populations. *Judgment and Decision Making*, *1*, 33–47.

Blavatskyy, P. R. (2008). *Risk Aversion*. IEW – Working Papers, iewwp370, Institute for Empirical Research in Economics – University of Zurich.

Bohnenblust, H., Holthausen, N., & Merz, H. A. (2008). *Risk aversion – Development of instruments to assess the risks and safety associated with natural and technological hazards. In Management summary. Implementation of the Swiss Natural Hazards Strategy: Project B 2.1* (p. 18). Bern: Federal Office for Civil Protection FOCP.

Bonin, H., Dohmen, T., Falk, A., Huffman, D., & Sunde, U. (2007). Cross-sectional earnings risk and occupational sorting: The role of risk attitudes. *Labour Economics*, *14*(6), 926–937. doi:10.1016/j.labeco.2007.06.007

Bostrom, A., French, S. P., & Gotllieb, S. J. (2008). *Risk Assessment Modeling and Decision Support*. Berlin: Springer Publishing. doi:10.1007/978-3-540-71158-2

Brewer, G., & Strahorn, S. (2012). Trust and the project management body of knowledge. *Engineering, Construction, and Architectural Management*, *19*(3), 286–305. doi:10.1108/09699981211219616

Bryde, D. J., & Robinson, L. (2005). Client versus contractor perspectives on project success criteria. *International Journal of Project Management*, *23*(8), 622–629. doi:10.1016/j.ijproman.2005.05.003

Buertey, J. I. T., Abeere-Inga, E., & Kumi, T. A. (2013). The financial impact of risk factors affecting project cost contingency: Evidential reasoning method. *Journal of Engineering, Project, and Production Management*, *3*(2), 65–73.

Cagno, E., Caron, F., & Mancini, M. (2007). A multi-dimensional analysis of major risks in complex projects. *Risk Management*, *9*(1), 1–18. doi:10.1057/palgrave.rm.8250014

Camilleri, E. (2011). *Project Success: Critical Factors and Behaviors*. Surrey, UK: Gower Publishing Limited.

Cankar, S. S., & Petkovšek, V. (2013). Private and public sector innovation and the importance of cross-sector collaboration. *Journal of Applied Business Research*, *29*(6), 197–1606.

Chan, D. W. M., Chan, A. P. C., Lam, P. T. I., & Chan, J. H. L. (2010b). Exploring the key risks and risk mitigation measures for guaranteed maximum price and target cost contracts in construction. *Constitutional Law Journal (Newark, N.J.)*, *26*(5), 364–378.

Chan, D. W. M., Chan, A. P. C., Lam, P. T. I., Yeung, J. F. Y., & Chan, J. H. L. (2011). Risk ranking and analysis in target cost contracts: Empirical evidence from the construction industry. *International Journal of Project Management*, *29*(6), 751–763. doi:10.1016/j.ijproman.2010.08.003

Chan, D.W.M., Lam, P.T.I., Chan, A.P.C., & Wong, J.M.W. (2010a). Achieving better performance through target cost contracts – the tale of an underground railway station modification project. *Facilities, 28*(5/6), 261-277.

Chapman, R. J. (2007). *Simple Tools and Techniques for Enterprise Risk Management*. Hoboken, NJ: John Wiley &Sons.

Chen, L., Kök, A. G., & Tong, J. D. (2013). The effect of payment schemes on inventory decisions. *Management Science*, *59*(2), 436–451. doi:10.1287/mnsc.1120.1638

Cheng, K. C. (2010). *A new framework to estimate the risk-neutral probability density functions embedded in options prices*. IMF Working Papers, 10/181, International Monetary Fund.

Cheung, E., Chan, A. P. C., & Kajewski, S. (2009a). Enhancing value for money in public private partnership projects: Findings from a survey conducted in Hong Kong, Australia compared to findings from previous research in the United Kingdom. *Journal of Financial Management of Property and Construction*, *14*(1), 7–20. doi:10.1108/13664380910942617

Cheung, E., Chan, A. P. C., & Kajewski, S. (2009b). Reasons for implementing public private partnership projects: Perspectives from Hong Kong, Australian and British practitioners. *Journal of Property Investment & Finance*, *27*(1), 81–95. doi:10.1108/14635780910926685

Choudhry, R. M., & Iqbal, K. (2013). Identification of risk management system in construction industry in Pakistan. *Journal of Management Engineering*, *29*(1), 42–49. doi:10.1061/(ASCE)ME.1943-5479.0000122

Cienfuegos, I. (2011). Risk management policy in Dutch Municipalities: Understanding the process, identifying its strengths and visualizing the possible improvements. *Revista Enfoques. Ciencia Política y Administración Pública*, *VIII*(14), 155–176.

Cienfuegos, I. (2012). Decision theory and risk management in public organizations: A literature review. *Revista de Gestión Pública*, *1*, 101–126.

Cleden, D. (2009). *Managing project uncertainty*. Abingdon, UK: Ashgate Publishing Group.

Cleland, D. I., & Gareis, R. (2006). *Global Project Management Handbook: Planning, Organizing, and Controlling International Projects* (2nd ed.). New York: McGraw- Hill.

Coispeau, O., & Luo, S. (2015). *Mergers and acquisitions and partnerships in China*. Singapore: World Scientific. doi:10.1142/9411

Concina, L. (2014). *Risk attitude & economics*. Number 2014-01 of *Les Regards*, Foundation for an industrial safety culture, Toulouse, France. Freely available at: http://www.foncsi.org/

Constantinides, G. M., Jackwerth, J. C., & Perrakis, S. (2008). Option pricing: Real and risk- neutral distributions. In Handbooks in OR & MS (Vol. 15). London: Elsevier B.V.

Coter, J. E., & Chen, Y. J. (2006). Do investment risk tolerance attitudes predict portfolio risk? *Journal of Business and Psychology*, *20*(3), 369–381. doi:10.1007/s10869-005-9010-5

Coudert, V., & Gex, M. (2007). *Does risk aversion drive financial crises? Testing the predictive power of empirical indicators*. Working Papers, 2007-02, CEPII Research Center.

Cox, L. A. T. (2008). Whats Wrong with Risk Matrices? *Risk Analysis*, *28*(2), 497–512. doi:10.1111/j.1539-6924.2008.01030.x PMID:18419665

Cruz, M. P., Cano, A., & Cruz, E. (2006). Downside risks in construction projects developed by civil services: The case study of Spain. *Journal of Construction Engineering and Management*, *132*(8), 844–852. doi:10.1061/(ASCE)0733-9364(2006)132:8(844)

Dallas, M. (2006). *Value and risk management; a guide to best practice*. Oxford, UK: Blackwell Publication.

De Dreu, J., & Bikker, J. A. (2012). Investor sophistication and risk taking. *Journal of Banking & Finance*, *36*(7), 2145–2156. doi:10.1016/j.jbankfin.2012.03.023

Dey, P. K. (2009). Managing risks of large scale construction projects. *Coastal Engineering*, *51*(6), 23–27.

Diallo, A., & Thuillier, D. (2005). The success of international development projects, trust and communication: An African perspective. *International Journal of Project Management*, *23*(3), 237–252. doi:10.1016/j.ijproman.2004.10.002

Dikmen, I., & Birgonol, N. T. (2006). An analytic hierarchy process based model for risk and opportunities assessment of international construction project. *Canadian Journal of Civil Engineering*, *33*(1), 58–68. doi:10.1139/l05-087

Dikmen, I., Birgonul, N. T., & Han, S. (2007). Using fuzzy risk assessment to rate cost overrun risk in international construction projects. *International Journal of Project Management*, *25*(5), 494–505. doi:10.1016/j.ijproman.2006.12.002

Ding, X., Hartog, & Sun, Y. (2010). *Can we measure individual risk attitudes in a survey?* The Institute for the Study of Labor (IZA) Discussion Paper No. 4807.

Dohmen, T., Falk, A., Huffman, D., Sunde, U., Schupp, J., & Wagner, G. G. (2011). Individual risk attitudes: Measurement, determinants, and behavioral consequences. *Journal of the European Economic Association*, *9*(3), 522–550. doi:10.1111/j.1542-4774.2011.01015.x

Domokos, L., Nyéki, M., Jakovác, K., Németh, E., & Hatvani, C. (2015). Risk analysis and risk management in the public sector and in public auditing. *Public Finance Quarterly*, *1*, 7–28.

El-Sayegh, S. M. (2008). Risk assessment and allocation in the UAE construction industry. *International Journal of Project Management*, *26*(4), 431–438. doi:10.1016/j.ijproman.2007.07.004

English, L. M. (2006). Public private partnerships in Australia: An overview of their nature, purpose, incidence and oversight. *The University of New South Wales Law Journal*, *29*(3), 250–262.

Epanchin-Niell, R. S., & Hastings, A. (2010). Controlling established invaders: Integrating economics and spread dynamics to determine optimal management. *Ecology Letters*, *13*(4), 528–541. doi:10.1111/j.1461-0248.2010.01440.x PMID:20455926

Eskerod, P., & Riis, E. (2009). Project management models as value creators. *Project Management Journal*, *40*(1), 4–18. doi:10.1002/pmj.20098

Fan, Z., Li, Y., & Zhang, Y. (2015). Generating project risk response strategies based on CBR: A case study. *Expert Systems with Applications*, *42*(6), 2870–2883. doi:10.1016/j.eswa.2014.11.034

Firsova, A. (2011). The possibility of using public-private partnerships in investment process of innovation activity. *Resursy, Informatsiya, Snabzhenie Konkurentsiya*, *2*, 563–566.

Flyvbjerg, B. (2006). From Noble Price to project management: Getting risk right. *Project Management Journal*, *37*(3), 5–15.

Forlani, D., Parthasarathy, M., & Keaveney, S. M. (2008). Managerial risk perceptions of international entry-mode strategies: The interaction effect of control and capability. *International Marketing Review*, *25*(3), 292–311. doi:10.1108/02651330810877225

French, D. P., Sutton, S., Kinmonth, A. L., & Marteau, T. M. (2006). Assessing perceptions of risks due to multiple hazards. *Journal of Risk Research*, *9*(6), 657–682. doi:10.1080/13669870600813837

Gao, S. S., Sung, M. C., & Zhang, J. (2013). Risk management capability building in SMEs: A social capital perspective. *International Small Business Journal*, *31*(6), 677–700. doi:10.1177/0266242611431094

Garrido, M. C., Ruotolo, M. C. A., Ribeiro, F. M. L., & Naked, H. A. (2011). Risk identification techniques knowledge and application in the Brazilian construction. *Journal of Civil Engineering and Construction Technology*, *2*(11), 242–252.

Garrison, S. T., & Gutter, M. S. (2010). Gender differences in financial socialization and willingness to take financial risks. *Journal of Financial Counseling and Planning*, *21*(2), 60–72.

Gattig, A., & Hendrickx, L. (2007). Judgmental discounting and environmental risk perception: Dimensional similarities, domain differences, and implications for sustainability. *The Journal of Social Issues*, *63*(1), 21–40. doi:10.1111/j.1540-4560.2007.00494.x

Gbadegesin, J. T., & Aluko, B. T. (2014). Public private partnerships/private finance initiatives for financing infrastructure in public tertiary institutions in Nigeria. *Built Environment Project and Asset Management*, *4*(2), 199–215. doi:10.1108/BEPAM-04-2013-0010

Goldstein, R., & McElligott, J. (2014). *Risk appetite: A discussion paper*. Bank of Ireland.

Grable, J. E. (2008). Risk tolerance. In Advances in consumer financial behavior research. New York: Springer.

Grimsey, D., & Lewis, M. K. (2005). Are public private partnerships value for money? Evaluating alternative approaches and comparing academic and practitioner views. *Accounting Forum*, *29*(4), 345–378. doi:10.1016/j.accfor.2005.01.001

Grossman, S. A. (2012). Introduction: The emerging role of partnership governance. *Public Performance & Management Review*, *35*, 575–577. doi:10.2753/PMR1530-9576350400

Guiso, L., & Paiella, M. (2008). Risk aversion, wealth and background risk. *Journal of the European Economic Association*, *6*(6), 1109–1150. doi:10.1162/JEEA.2008.6.6.1109

Hallahan, T. A., Faff, R. W., & McKenzie, M. D. (2005). An empirical investigation of personal financial risk tolerance. *Financial Services Review*, *13*, 57–78.

Han, S. H., Diekmann, J. E., & Ock, J. H. (2005). Contractors risk attitudes in the selection of international construction projects. *Journal of Construction Engineering and Management*, *131*(3), 283–292. doi:10.1061/(ASCE)0733-9364(2005)131:3(283)

Hanoch, Y., Johnson, J. G., & Wilke, A. (2006). Domain specificity in experimental measures and participant recruitment: An application to risk-taking behavior. *Psychological Science*, *17*(4), 300–304. doi:10.1111/j.1467-9280.2006.01702.x PMID:16623686

Harrison, G. W. (2007). House money effects in public good experiments. *Experimental Economics*, *10*(4), 429–437. doi:10.1007/s10683-006-9145-x

Hayford, O. (2013). *Improving the outcomes of public private partnerships*. Sydney, Australia: Clayton UTZ.

Helm, D. (2010). Infrastructure and infrastructure finance: The role of the government and the private sector in the current world. *EIB Papers, 15*(2), 8-27.

Hiebl, M. R. W. (2013). Risk aversion in family firms: What do we really know? *The Journal of Risk Finance*, *14*(1), 49–70. doi:10.1108/15265941311288103

Hillson, D., & Murray-Webster, R. (2005). *Understanding and managing risk attitude*. London: Gower.

Hillson, D., & Murray-Webster, R. (2007). *Understanding and managing risk attitude* (2nd ed.). Aldershot, UK: Gower Publishing Ltd.

Hillson, D., & Murray-Webster, R. (2011). Using risk appetite and risk attitude to support appropriate risk taking: A new taxonomy and model. *Journal of Project, Program, and Portfolio Management*, *2*(1), 29–46.

Hillson, D., & Murray-Webster, R. (2012). A short guide to risk appetite. Farnham.

Hiren, M. M. (2010). A case study on risk analysis in Infrastructure Highway Projects in India. *The IUP Journal of Financial Risk Management*, *2*, 1–27.

Ho, P. H. (2006a). Development of Public Private Partnerships (PPP) in China. *Surveyors Times, 15*(10).

Ho, S. P. (2006b). Model for financial re-negotiation in public-private partnership projects and its policy implications: Game theoretic view. *Journal of Construction Engineering and Management*, *132*(7), 678–688. doi:10.1061/(ASCE)0733-9364(2006)132:7(678)

Hoffmann, A. O. I., Post, T., & Pennings, J. M. E. (2013). Individual investor perceptions and behavior during the financial crisis. *Journal of Banking & Finance*, *37*(1), 60–74. doi:10.1016/j.jbankfin.2012.08.007

Hopkin, P. (2010). *Fundaments of risk management*. London: Kogan Page, IRM.

Hulett, D. T. (2011). Integrated cost-schedule risk analysis using risk drivers and prioritizing risks. In *Proceeding of 8th Annual PMICOS Scheduling Conference*.

Hwang, B.-G., Zhao, X., & Gay, M. J. S. (2013). Public private partnership projects in Singapore: Factors, critical risks and preferred risk allocation from the perspective of contractors. *International Journal of Project Management*, *31*(3), 424–433. doi:10.1016/j.ijproman.2012.08.003

Ibem, E. (2010). An assessment of the role of Government agencies in public private partnerships in housing delivery in Nigeria. *Journal of Construction in Developing Countries, 15*(2), 23-48.

Ibrahim, A. D., Price, A. D. F., & Dainty, A. R. J. (2006). The analysis and allocation of risks in public private partnerships in infrastructure projects in Nigeria. *Journal of Financial Management of Property and Construction*, *11*(3), 149–163. doi:10.1108/13664380680001086

Inekwe, M. (2015). Public private partnership and infrastructural development In Nigeria Polytechnics: The Federal Polytechnic, Idah Experience. *International Journal of Research Development*, *9*(1), 20–33.

Itzhak, B.-D., & Hirshleifer, D. (2012). Are investors really reluctant to realize their losses? Trading responses to past returns and the disposition effect. *Review of Financial Studies*, *25*(8), 2485–2532. doi:10.1093/rfs/hhs077

Jayasudha, K., Vidivelli, B., & Surjith, E. R. G. (2014). Risk assessment and management in construction projects. *International Journal of Scientific & Engineering Research*, *5*(8), 387–396.

Jin, X. H., & Doloi, H. (2008). Interpreting risk allocation mechanism in public-private partnership projects: An empirical study in a transaction cost economics perspective. *Construction Management and Economics*, *26*(7), 707–721. doi:10.1080/01446190801998682

Kamiya, S., Shi, P., Schmit, J., & Rosenberg, M. (2007). *Risk management terms*. University of Wisconsin–Madison.

Karim, N. A. A. (2011). Risk allocation in public-private partnership (PPP) projects: A review of risk factors. *Journal of Sustainable Construction. Engineering and Technology*, *2*(2), 8–16.

Ke, Y., Wang, S. Q., & Chan, A. P. C. (2010, December). Risk allocation in public-private partnership infrastructure projects: Comparative study. *Journal of Infrastructure Systems*, *16*(4), 343–351. doi:10.1061/(ASCE)IS.1943-555X.0000030

Keith, R. M. (2011). A risk based approach to contingency estimating in highway project development. American Society of Civil Engineers, 786-795.

Klos, A., Weber, E. U., & Weber, M. (2005). Investment decisions and time horizon: Risk perception and risk behavior in repeated gambles. *Management Science*, *51*(12), 1777–1790. doi:10.1287/mnsc.1050.0429

Kobbeltvedt, T., Brun, W., Johansen, B. H., & Eid, J. (2005). Risk as feelings or risk and feelings? A cross-lagged panel analysis. *Journal of Risk Research*, *8*(5), 417–437. doi:10.1080/1366987042000315519

Koleczko, K. (2012). Risk and uncertainty in project management decision-making. *Public Infrastructure Bulletin*, *1*(8), 76–83.

Koonce, L., McAnally, M. L., & Mercer, M. (2005). How do investors judge the risk of financial items? *Accounting Review*, *80*(1), 221–241. doi:10.2308/accr.2005.80.1.221

Koontz, T. M., & Thomas, C. W. (2012). Measuring the performance of public-private partnerships: A systematic method for distinguishing outputs from outcomes. *Public Performance & Management Review*, *35*(4), 769–786. doi:10.2753/PMR1530-9576350410

Kourtidis, D., Sević, Z., & Chatzoglou, P. (2011). Investors trading activity: A behavioral perspective and empirical results. *Journal of Socio-Economics*, *40*(5), 548–557. doi:10.1016/j.socec.2011.04.008

Kraeussl, R., Lucas, A., & Siegmann, A. (2010), Risk Aversion under Preference Uncertainty. Tinbergen Institute Discussion Papers 10-117/2/DSF 4, Tinbergen Institute.

Krane, H. P., Olsson, N. O. E., & Rolstadås, A. (2012). How project manager-project owner interaction can work within and influence project risk management. *Project Management Journal*, *43*(2), 54–67. doi:10.1002/pmj.20284

Kuppusamy, S. (2010). PPP: The right marriage between local government and the private sector in Malaysia. *International Journal of Institutions and Economics*, *2*(2), 142–166.

Lam, K. C., Wang, D., Lee, P. T. K., & Tsang, Y. T. (2007). Modeling risk allocation decision in construction contracts. *International Journal of Project Management*, *25*(5), 485–493. doi:10.1016/j.ijproman.2006.11.005

Latief, R. U., Pallu, S., Adisasmita, S. A., Aly, S. H., & Suyuti, A. (2014). Risk response preferences on public private partnership (PPP) in Indonesia airport infrastructure development. *International Journal of Application or Innovation in Engineering & Management*, *3*(8), 120–124.

Lima, M. L., Barnett, J., & Vala, J. (2005). Risk perception and technological development at a societal level. *Risk Analysis*, *25*(5), 1229–1239. doi:10.1111/j.1539-6924.2005.00664.x PMID:16297227

Loosemore, M., Raftery, J., Reilly, C., & Higgon, D. (2006). Risk Management in Projects (2nd ed.). Oxon, UK: Taylor and Francis.

Marcelino-Sádaba, S., Pérez-Ezcurdia, A., Echeverría Lazcano, A. M., & Villanueva, P. (2014). Project risk management methodology for small firms. *International Journal of Project Management*, *32*(2), 327–340. doi:10.1016/j.ijproman.2013.05.009

Maskin, E., & Tirole, J. (2008). Public-private partnerships and government spending limits. *International Journal of Industrial Organization*, *26*(2), 412–420. doi:10.1016/j.ijindorg.2007.05.004

Matei, L. (2006). Empirical approaches of the public-private partnership in the services of public utility. *Theoretical and Applicative Economics*, *10*(505), 3–14.

Meidute, I., & Paliulis, N. K. (2011). Feasibility study of public-private partnership. *International Journal of Strategic Property Management*, *16*(5), 257–274. doi:10.3846/1648715X.2011.617860

Minassian, V. K., & Jergeas, G. F. (2009). A prototype risk analysis for determining contingency using approximate reasoning method. *Coastal Engineering*, *51*(1), 26–33.

Moeller, R. A. (2007). *COSO Enterprise risk management*. Hoboken, NJ: Wiley & Sons.

Mouraview, N., Kabadse, N., & Robinson, I. (2012). Concessionary nature of public-private partnerships in Russia and Kazakhstan: A critical review. *International Journal of Public Administration*, *35*(6), 1–11.

Mubin, S., & Mannan, A. (2013). Innovative approach to risk analysis and management of oil and gas sector Engineering, Procurement and Construction (EPC) contracts from a contractor's perspective. *Journal of Business & Economics*, *5*(2), 149–170.

Mubin, S., & Mubin, G. (2008). Risk analysis for construction and operation of gas pipeline projects in Pakistan. *Pakistan Journal of Engineering & Applied Sciences*, *2*, 23–37.

Mwaguni, H. J., & Busienei, P. K. (2014). Effect of public-private partnership on the provision of quality services; a case of the grain terminal at the port of Mombasa, Kenya. *Journal of International Academic Research for Multidisciplinary*, *2*(5), 609–643.

Ng, A., & Loosemore, M. (2007). Risk allocation in the private provision of public infrastructure. *International Journal of Project Management*, *25*(1), 66–76. doi:10.1016/j.ijproman.2006.06.005

Noble, G., & Jones, R. (2006). The role of boundary-spanning managers in the establishment of partnerships. *Public Administration*, *84*(4), 891–917. doi:10.1111/j.1467-9299.2006.00617.x

Obermann, G. (2007). The role of the state as a guarantor of public services – Transaction cost issues and empirical evidence. *Annals of Public and Cooperative Economics*, *78*(3), 475–500. doi:10.1111/j.1467-8292.2007.00343.x

Ogbu, C. P. (2013). Risk management practices of multinational and indigenous construction companies in Nigeria: A comparative analysis. *Journal of Research in National Development*, *9*(2), 315–324.

Ogunsanmi, O. E., Salako, O. A., & Ajayi, O. M. (2011). Risks classification model for design and build projects. *Journal of Engineering, Project, and Production Management*, *1*(1), 46–60.

Ojo, A. S., & Ogunsemi, D. R. (2009). Assessment of contractor's understanding of risk management in Seychelles construction industry.*Proceeding of RICS COBRA Research Conference*.

Owusu, M. D., & Badu, E. (2009). Determinants of contractors investment finance strategy in Ghana: Conceptual and empirical explanations. *Journal of Financial Management of Property and Construction*, *14*(1), 21–33. doi:10.1108/13664380910942626

Oyegoke, A. S., Khalfan, M. M. A., McDermott, P., & Dickinson, M. (2008). Managing risk and uncertainty in an agile construction environment: Application of agile building specialist model. *International Journal of Agile System Management*, *3*(3–4), 248–262. doi:10.1504/IJASM.2008.021212

Oyewobi, L. O., Ibrahim, A. D., & Ganiyu, B. O. (2012). Evaluating the impact of risk on contractor's tender figures in Northern Nigeria. *Journal of Engineering, Project, and Production Management*, *2*(1), 2–13.

Öztaş, A., & Ökmen, Ö. (2005). Judgmental risk analysis process development in construction projects. *Building and Environment*, *40*(9), 1244–1254. doi:10.1016/j.buildenv.2004.10.013

Papajohn, D., Cui, Q., & Bayraktar, M. E. (2011). Public-private partnerships in US transportation: Research overview and a path forward. *Journal of Management Engineering*, *27*(3), 126–135. doi:10.1061/(ASCE)ME.1943-5479.0000050

Pasławski, J. (2010). Risk management using flexibility in construction engineering. *Proceedings of the 10th International Conference "Modern Building Materials, Structures and Techniques"*, 489–492.

Patrick, X. W., Shouqing, W., & Dongping, F. (2008). A life-cycle risk management framework for PPP infrastructure projects. *Journal of Financial Management of Property and Construction*, *13*(2), 123–142. doi:10.1108/13664380810898131

Peng, J., Miao, D., & Xiao, W. (2013). Why are gainers more risk seeking. *Judgment and Decision Making*, *8*(2), 150–160.

Perminova, O., Gustafsson, M., & Wikstrom, K. (2008). Defining uncertainty in projects- a new perspective. *Journal of Project Management*, *26*(1), 73–78. doi:10.1016/j.ijproman.2007.08.005

Pessoa, A. (2006). *Public private partnerships in developing countries: Prospects and drawbacks*. Faculdade de Economia do Porto.

Poba-Nzaou, P., Raymond, L., & Fabi, B. (2014). Risk of adopting mission-critical OSS applications: An interpretive case study. *International Journal of Operations & Production Management*, *34*(4), 477–512. doi:10.1108/IJOPM-03-2012-0117

Provan, K. G., Huang, K., & Milward, B. H. (2009). The evolution of structural embeddedness and organizational social outcomes in a centrally governed health and human service network. *Journal of Public Administration: Research and Theory*, *19*(4), 873–893. doi:10.1093/jopart/mun036

Provan, K. G., & Kenis, P. (2008). Modes of network governance: Structure, management, and effectiveness. *Journal of Public Administration: Research and Theory*, *18*(2), 229–252. doi:10.1093/jopart/mum015

Rakic, B., & Radjenovic, T. (2011). Public-private partnerships as an instrument of new public management. *Facta Universitatis Series: Economics and Organization*, *8*(2), 207–220.

Raz, T., & Hillson, D. (2005). A comparative review of risk management standards. *Risk Management: An International Journal*, *8*(1), 61–76.

Rezakhani, P. (2012). Fuzzy MCDM model for risk factor selection in construction projects. *Engineering Journal, 16*(5).

Risk Aversion. (2015, May 30). Retrieved from https://en.wikipedia.org/wiki/Risk_aversion

Rohmeyer, P., & Zvi, T. B. (2009). Risk management decision making in ICT for development. *Proceedings of the Second Annual SIG GlobDev Workshop.*

Roszkowski, M. J., & Davey, G. (2010). Risk perception and risk tolerance changes attributable to the 2008 economic crisis: A subtle but critical difference. *Journal of Financial Service Professionals*, *64*(4), 42–53.

Roszkowski, M. J., Davey, G., & Grable, J. E. (2005). Insights from psychology and psychometrics on measuring risk tolerance. *Journal of Financial Planning*, *18*, 66–77.

Roszkowski, M. J., & Grable, J. (2005). Estimating risk tolerance: The degree of accuracy and the paramorphic representations of the estimate. *Journal of Financial Counseling and Planning*, *16*(2), 29–47.

Roumboutsos, A., & Anagnostopoulos, K. P. (2008). Public-private partnership projects in Greece: Risk ranking and preferred risk allocation. *Construction Management and Economics*, *26*(7), 751–763. doi:10.1080/01446190802140086

Sachs, T., Tiong, R. L. K., & Wang, S. Q. (2007). Analysis of political risks and opportunities in public private partnerships PPP in China and selected Asian Countries—Survey results. *Chinese Management Studies*, *1*(2), 126–148. doi:10.1108/17506140710758026

Sachse, K., Jungermann, H., & Belting, J. M. (2012). Investment risk – the perspective of individual investors. *Journal of Economic Psychology*, *33*(3), 437–447. doi:10.1016/j.joep.2011.12.006

Sahm, C. (2008). *How much does risk tolerance change?* Finance and Economics Discussion Series, Federal Reserve Board.

Sanda, Y. N., & Anigbogu, N. A. (2016). A Conceptual framework for managing risks in public private partnership projects in housing estate development in Nigeria. *International Journal of Regional Development*, *3*(1), 50–63. doi:10.5296/ijrd.v3i1.8144

Sanderson, J. (2012). Risk, uncertainty and governance in megaprojects: A critical discussion of alternative explanations. *International Journal of Project Management*, *30*(4), 432–443. doi:10.1016/j.ijproman.2011.11.002

Santoso, D. S., Joewono, T. B., Wibowo, A., Sinaga, H. P. A., & Santosa, W. (2012). Public- private partnerships for Tollway construction and operation: Risk assessment and allocation from the perspective of investors. *Journal of Construction in Developing Countries*, *17*(2), 45–66.

Sciulli, N. (2008). Public private partnerships: An exploratory study in health care. *Asian Review of Accounting*, *16*(1), 21–38. doi:10.1108/13217340810872454

Selsky, J. W., & Parker, B. (2005). Cross-sector partnerships to address social issues: Challenges to theory and practice. *Journal of Management*, *31*(6), 849–873. doi:10.1177/0149206305279601

Serrador, P., & Turner, R. (2015). The relationship between project success and project efficiency. *Project Management Journal*, *46*(1), 30–39. doi:10.1002/pmj.21468

Seyed, M. M., Seyrafianpour, H., & Ebrahimnejad, S. (2010). Risk identification and assessment for build-operate-transfer projects: A fuzzy multi attribute decision making model. *Expert Systems with Applications*, *37*(1), 575–586. doi:10.1016/j.eswa.2009.05.037

Shahzad, B., & Safvi, S. A. (2010). Risk mitigation and management scheme based on risk priority. *Global Journal of Computer Science and Technology*, *10*(4), 108–113.

Shen, L. Y., Platten, A., & Deng, X. P. (2006). Role of public private partnerships to manage risks in public sector projects in Hong Kong. *International Journal of Project Management*, *24*(7), 587–594. doi:10.1016/j.ijproman.2006.07.006

Silvester, H. C., & Aroujo, J. F. (2012). Public private partnerships/private finance initiatives in Portugal: Theory, practice and results. *Public Performance and Management Review*, *36*(2), 316–339. doi:10.2753/PMR1530-9576360208

Smith, N. J., Merna, T., & Jobling, P. (2006). *Managing risk in construction projects*. Oxford, UK: Blackwell.

Smyth, H. (2008). The credibility gap in stakeholder management: Ethics and evidence of relationship management. *Construction Management and Economics*, *26*(6), 633–643. doi:10.1080/01446190801905414

Soane, E., & Chmiel, N. (2005). Are risk preferences consistent? The influence of decision domain and personality. *Personality and Individual Differences*, *38*(8), 1781–1791. doi:10.1016/j.paid.2004.10.005

Sulaiman, E. K. (2012). An empirical analysis of financial risk tolerance and demographic features of individual investors. *Procedia Economics and Finance*, *2*(0), 109–115. doi:10.1016/S2212-5671(12)00070-6

Tadayon, M., Jaafar, M., & Nasri, E. (2012). An assessment of risk identification in large construction projects in Iran. *Journal of Construction in Developing Countries*, (Supp. 1), 57–69.

Tanaka, D. F., Ishida, H., Tsutsumi, M., & Okamoto, N. (2005). Private finance for road projects in developing countries: Improving transparency through VFM risk assessment. *Journal of the Eastern Asia Society for Transportation Studies*, (6), 3899–3914.

Thomas, J., & Mullaly, M. (2007). Understanding the value of project management: First steps on an international investigation in search of value. *Project Management Journal*, *38*(3), 74–89. doi:10.1002/pmj.20007

Tingting, L., & Wilkinson, S. (2011). Adopting innovative procurement techniques-obstacles and drivers for adopting public private partnerships in New Zealand. *Construction Innovation-Information, Process Management*, *11*(4), 452–469.

Turnbaughs, L. (2005). Risk management on large capital projects. *Journal of Professional Issues in Engineering Education and Practice*, (October), 274–280.

Vajdić, N. (2011). *Risk management in public-private partnership road projects using the real options theory*. Paper presented at International Symposium Engineering Management and Competitiveness 2011 (EMC2011), Zrenjanin, Serbia.

Van Gestel, K., & Voets, J. (2012). How governance of complex PPPs affects performance. *Public Administration Quarterly*, *36*(2), 140–188.

Velotti, L., Botti, A., & Vesci, M. (2012). Public-private partnerships and network governance. What are the challenges? *Public Performance & Management Review*, *36*(2), 340–365. doi:10.2753/PMR1530-9576360209

Vlaev, I., Chater, N., & Stewart, N. (2009). Dimensionality of risk perception: Factors affecting consumer understanding and evaluation of financial risk. *Journal of Behavioral Finance*, *10*(3), 158–181. doi:10.1080/15427560903167720

Voelker, C., Permana, A., Sachs, T., & Tiong, R. (2008). Political risk perception in Indonesia power projects. *Journal of Financial Management of Property and Construction*, *13*(1), 18–34. doi:10.1108/13664380810882057

Waghmare.A.P., & Pimplikar.S.S. (2012). Risk analysis in feasibility study of road construction project: Case Study construction of the four laning of Amravati –Talegaon Section Nh- 6. *International Journal of Engineering Research and Applications*, *2*(3), 3166-3169.

Walton, J., & Bellhouse, J. (2012). Risk avoidance, transfer, acceptance or management. *BuildLaw*, *16*, 1–29.

Wang, J., & Yuan, H. (2011). Factors affecting contractors risk attitudes in construction projects: Case study from China. *International Journal of Project Management*, *29*(2), 209–219. doi:10.1016/j.ijproman.2010.02.006

Wang, M., Keller, C., & Siegrist, M. (2011). The less you know, the more you are afraid of - a survey on risk perceptions of investment products. *Journal of Behavioral Finance*, *12*(1), 9–19. doi:10.1080/15427560.2011.548760

Wang, W., & Dai, D. (2009). Risk allocation mechanism for Public-Private Partnership (PPP) projects. *Proceedings of International Conference on Management and Service Science (MASS 2009)*. doi:10.1109/ICMSS.2009.5305514

Wason, S. (2006). *Risk management fundamentals, insurance core principle 18A*. Paper presented at the International Association of Insurance Supervisors.

Weber, M., Weber, E. U., & Nosić, A. (2013). Who takes risks when and why: Determinants of changes in investor risk taking. *Review of Finance*, *17*(3), 847–883. doi:10.1093/rof/rfs024

Wibowo, A., & Mohamed, S. (2010). Risk criticality and allocation in privatized water supply projects in Indonesia. *International Journal of Project Management*, *28*(5), 504–513. doi:10.1016/j.ijproman.2009.08.003

Wiguna, I. P. A., & Scott, S. (2006). Relating risk to project performance in Indonesian building contracts. *Construction Management and Economics*, *24*(11), 1125–1135. doi:10.1080/01446190600799760

Wishnu, B. O., & Pradono, P. (2011). Risk Treats in creative funding scheme for infrastructure projects in Indonesia: Cileunyi-Sumedang Toll road project case. *Journal of Civil Engineering and Architecture*, *5*(1), 89–96.

Wuerth, A. M., & Schumacher, J. M. (2011). Risk aversion for no smooth utility functions. *Journal of Mathematical Economics*, *47*(2), 109–128. doi:10.1016/j.jmateco.2010.10.003

Xu, Y., Yeung, J. F. Y., Chan, A. P. C., Chan, D. W. M., Wang, S. Q., & Ke, Y. (2010). Developing a risk assessment model for PPP projects in ChinaA fuzzy synthetic evaluation approach. *Automation in Construction*, *19*(7), 929–943. doi:10.1016/j.autcon.2010.06.006

Yescombe, E. R. (2013). *Principles of Project Finance*. London: Academic Press.

Young, R., & Jordan, E. (2008). Top management support: Mantra or necessity? *International Journal of Project Management*, *26*(7), 713–725. doi:10.1016/j.ijproman.2008.06.001

Yuan, J., Skibniewski, M. J., & Li, Q. (2008). *Managing the performance of public private partnership projects to achieve value for money: Key performance indicators selection*. Paper presented at the International Conference on Multi-national Construction Projects, Shanghai, China.

Zhai, L., Xin, Y., & Cheng, C. (2009). Understanding the value of project management from a stakeholders perspective: Case study of mega-project management. *Project Management Journal*, *40*(1), 99–109. doi:10.1002/pmj.20099

Zhang, X. (2006). Public clients best value perspectives of public-private partnerships in infrastructure development. *Journal of Construction Engineering and Management*, *132*(2), 107–114. doi:10.1061/(ASCE)0733-9364(2006)132:2(107)

Zhang, X. Q. (2005a). Critical success factors for public-private partnerships in infrastructure development. *Journal of Construction Engineering and Management*, *131*(1), 3–14. doi:10.1061/(ASCE)0733-9364(2005)131:1(3)

Zhang, X. Q. (2005b). Paving the way for public–private partnerships in infrastructure development. *Journal of Construction Engineering and Management*, *131*(1), 71–80. doi:10.1061/(ASCE)0733-9364(2005)131:1(71)

Zhong, S., Chew, S. H., Set, E., Zhang, J., Xue, H., Sham, P. C., & Israel, S. et al. (2009). The heritability of attitude toward economic risk. *Twin Research and Human Genetics*, *12*(01), 103–107. doi:10.1375/twin.12.1.103 PMID:19210185

Zimmermann, J., & Eber, W. (2014). Consideration of risk in PPP-projects. *Business. Management in Education*, *12*(1), 30–46.

Zitron, J. (2006). Public-private partnership projects: Towards a model of contractor bidding decision-making. *Journal of Purchasing and Supply Management*, *12*(2), 53–62. doi:10.1016/j.pursup.2006.04.002

Zou, P. X. W., Wang, S., & Fang, D. (2008). A life-cycle risk management framework for PPP infrastructure projects. *Journal of Financial Management of Property and Construction, 13*(2), 123-142.

Chapter 7
Risk Management Framework

ABSTRACT

This chapter examines the adoption of a formal risk management strategy framework in a PPP arrangement. The chapter shows the relevance of risk management as an PPP project management tool. The chapter also reveals how the use of risk management is dependent on relational skills, knowledge of the PPP project activities and experience. Risk management can therefore be seen as both a context-dependent devices and as a technique abstracted from the context. The paper discusses how managing risk can be dealt with in risk's complexity, addressing the expectation of multiple PPP actors and external stakeholders. It is concluded that a good risk management framework must be derived from the risk fundamentals through a clear processes and above all be monitored on a regular basis. This requires proper planning to ensure sustainability of the framework with an inclusion of the varied stakeholders.

Good risk management fosters vigilance in times of calm and instills discipline in times of crisis. - Dr. Michael Ong

INTRODUCTION

If there were full information about the praiseworthiness of PPP arrangements and other collaborations, risk management programs would probably not exist. All PPP projects would be implemented without any hurdles in the sense that nothing would debar the achievement of its objectives and service delivery without doubt is very superb. Likewise, there would probably be no need for private finances since borrowing and financing from the private sector would form a portfolio of undesired for development purposes. Moreover, the vision of a development attempts without the inclusion of the private sector may be contemplated in the context of the full consequences of the ongoing urge and craze for PPP projects. PPP arrangement is already replacing the traditional form of infrastructural development and service delivery provision (Armistead & Pettigrew, 2008). Although it is normally assumed that the public sector has all required resources and obligations to deliver quality goods and services, the reality is that the public sector is now sort of all required resources and cannot therefore provide quality goods

DOI: 10.4018/978-1-5225-2503-5.ch007

and services. Scarcity of resources amidst rising ever changing demands for quality services is already undermining the role of the public sector in infrastructural development and service delivery provision (Chen, 2010). It is thus possible that inclusion of the private sector in the development processes could ultimately mean just that, lending direct involvement of private sector organizations and cutting out a deal with the public sector in form of PPP (Gazley & Brudney, 2007).

Risk currently plays an important role in devastating the course of PPP initiation and implementation because of lack of full information on the management framework standings of the partners (Aldoory & Sha, 2007). The public partner normally has more information about PPP project risk standings than the private partner and consequently there is asymmetry of information. In the real world of information asymmetry, which is most acute in developing countries, the public partner do not only exploit but leave the private partner in the cold in some cases. As PPP project progresses on, essentially 'swimming' in risks, both partners may not have the same understanding of outdoing the risks. In the process of a framework for countering such, they should allocate resources to develop a framework which is most efficient and ensures that risks can be appropriately handled. However, it is rational for the partners to panic if they suspect a PPP project is unsound, implementation process is inherently unstable and must be gripped to protect the PPP project and to cause stability in the implementation process. This implementation challenge, combined with the risk of fraudulent misuse of the PPP project itself, necessitates the formulation of a promising risk management framework (RMF). The first step in developing a promising framework for a successful PPP is therefore to ensure that both partners understood and respectively agree on a workable RMF. Thus the RMF ought to be seriously taken as the art and science of identifying, analyzing, and responding to risk throughout the life of a PPP project and in the best interests of meeting its objectives. Berg (2010) cautions that; RMF should not be overlooked for any PPP projects. This is because it helps to improve PPP project success by helping to select good projects, determining project scope, and developing realistic estimates. Bolvin, Farret and Salvi (2007) reminds that though crisis management has higher visibility due to the obvious danger to the success of the PPP project, its only proper RMF that can help a PPP project have a fewer problems to begin with.

The remainder of this chapter is structured into 4 other sections. The section on 'Risk management fundamentals' discusses the importance of risk estimation in promoting the developing of an effective RMF. Risk mitigation as well as risk transfer/allocation, as means of correcting the deficit of risk exposure, are examined under this section. Risk identification, assessment and analysis are explored in the section on 'Risk management processes. The section on 'Risk control and monitoring' focuses into detail risk control and risk monitoring. It also discusses risk auditing and reporting. Conclusion is offered in the last section.

RISK MANAGEMENT FUNDAMENTALS

In order to obtain their objectives, partners must be prepared to take risks and face uncertainties. Evidently, there are no shortages of risks and uncertainties to challenge a PPP partners' ability to manage risks (Gupta & Sharma, 2015). New technologies, globalization, and innovations in products and service delivery processes will influence even more complex and dynamic decision making environment for an effective risk management (Flanagan, Norman & Chapman, 2006). At their basic level, risk and uncertainty are fundamentally multifunctional and multidisciplinary concepts, applicable in PPP arrangement as much as in implementation. Additionally, risk and uncertainty involves concepts from other disciplines which may not necessarily be related to PPP project management. According to Nisar (2007) an effective risk management must conform to some framework. Wason (2006) provides such a framework as illustrated in Figure 1.

Risk Estimation

Risk estimation is the process of trying to determine the significance of the risk (Buertey, Abeere-Inga & Kumi, 2012).It is a quantitative assessment of a future endeavor's likely cost or outcome. It's used to forecast a project's cost, size, resources, effort, or duration. According to Ali (2005), risk estimation serves three main purposes:-it helps the organization determine whether the risks are so significant, or cannot be managed, that the project should not be undertaken; where the project risks can be accepted and managed, it helps set priorities for addressing them; and in cases where there is no specific legislation, or other appropriate guidance to serve as a benchmark for managing the activities giving rise to the risk. Thus Ahmed, Kayis and Amornsawadwatana (2007) certify that risk estimation can also be helpful in deciding whether or not precautions are adequate.

Risk estimation (or estimating) is the process of finding an estimate, or approximation, which is a value that is usable for some purpose even if input data may be incomplete, uncertain, or unstable (Alonso-Conde, Brown & Rojo-Suarez, 2007). The value is nonetheless usable because it is derived from the best information available (Cretu, Stewart & Berends, 2011). Typically, risk estimation involves "using the value of a statistic derived from a sample to estimate the value of a corresponding population parameter" (Finucane & Holup, 2006).The sample provides information that can be projected, through various formal or informal processes, to determine a range most likely to describe the missing information. An estimate that turns out to be incorrect will be an overestimate if the estimate exceeded the

Figure 1. Risk management framework (Wason, 2006)
Source: IAIS ICP 18A: Risk Management Fundamentals

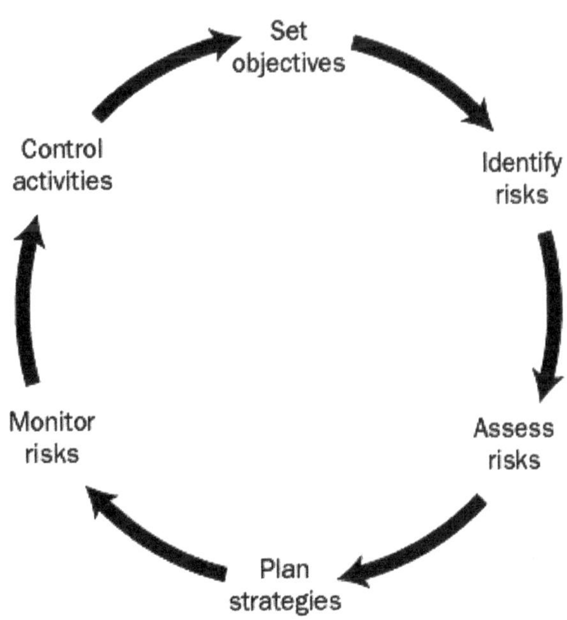

actual result and an underestimate if the estimate fell short of the actual result (MacGillivray, Hamilton, Strutt & Pollard, 2006).

Too and Weaver (2014) indicate that risk estimation can include both qualitative and quantitative assessments of the likelihood and consequence of the risk. The balance between qualitative and quantitative analysis will vary from project to project and will have to be determined by the availability of data and the need to remain cost-effective (Mahendra, Jayeshkumar, Pitroda & Bhavsar, 2013). For example, for most exploration activities, particularly in the early stages of exploration, it will not be cost-effective to conduct quantitative analysis and it will add little or no value to the effective management of the project. It is much more sensible and productive to restrict effort to a simple qualitative approach. In later stages of exploration, however, where the scope of activities that gives rise to risk and the potential consequences are likely to be more serious, it may make sense to adopt a quantitative analysis.

In practice, today there are a number of techniques which are used in risk estimation. These include: - expert judgment, analogy, decomposition and statistical (or parametric) methods. According to Pluess, Groso and Meyer (2013) expert judgment is based on brainstorming of one or more experts which have experience with similar projects; a consensus mechanism then produces the estimates. Rao and Ranade (2013) state that analogy estimation is one of the techniques used in risk estimation which is based on comparing previous, similar activities, analyzing the most relevant project and service attributes, and trying to figure out the new project's effort and cost values through estimator experience. As with expert judgment, this technique requires skilled people who can properly understand and see relationships and implicitly evaluate qualitative and quantitative figures to determine possible clusters of projects. According to Sarmento and Renneboog (2014), decomposition is a top-down estimation technique that tries to make a granular list of initially planned tasks. The more granular the tasks associated with a certain requirement in a work breakdown structure (WBS), the closer the planned effort is with its final value, thereby reducing the mean relative error and possible slippage in project deliverables. Jorion (2006) states that; statistical (parametric) models are a set of related mathematical equations in which you define alternative scenarios by changing the assumed values of a set of fixed coefficients (parameters).

Takashima, Yagi and Takamori (2010) recommend to have in a place a "to do" list for making a case and improving risk estimates. Avazkhah and Mohebbi (2010) aver as a first step to determine the informative goal and establish the proper process to gather, verify, and validate data before their storage in the historical data. The second step is the analysis, bringing valuable information for the decision making process. Abednego and Ogunlana (2006) advice that own data should be collected on a regular basis and at the right level of granularity. Menches and Hanna (2006) intimate that estimation models based on multiple regression analysis are more effective than using a single independent variable. Matei (2006) cautions that; reporting isn't second-level process because the decision-making process comes from information, not from single data. Ökmen and Öztas (2010) assert that report presentation can dramatically change the way the original data would suggest to take a certain action. Rakic and Radenović (2014) counsels risk estimation should be viewed as cause-effect logic. He continues to argue that what is forecast for a certain phenomenon will affect other processes. Hence, without clarifying the series of links, the risk is to over-or underestimate more than expected. Singaravelloo (2010) advocates that target a risk estimation accuracy in line with organization's needs.

In PPP project management, risk is the measure of the probability and consequence of not achieving a defined project goal. It is of common opinion that most people agree that risk involves a notion of uncertainty (Donahue & Zeckhauser, 2011). Yet, when considering risk, the consequences or damage associated with the event occurring must also be taken into account. To evaluate risk is not always a simple task, since the probability of occurrence and the consequence of occurrence are usually not directly measurable parameters and must be estimated by judgment, statistical, or other procedures. In broad terms, as either the probability or consequence increases, so does the risk. Both the probability and consequence must be considered in risk management (Kerzner, 2009).

According to Lawrence (2007) any estimate, by definition, is imprecise and carries financial risks, the cost implications of which are reflected in the application of contingency to an estimate and in assigning an accuracy range to that estimate. He thinks that excessive statistical terminology in literature only adds to the confusion and lack of understanding of the correct calculation and application of contingency. For example, in a PPP infrastructure projects, the cost estimator or designer prepares an estimate based on the scope of work supplied to him/her at the initial stage. Any items not picked up by the estimator or omitted from the scope of works will remain as potential risks to the project cost outcome (Macário, 2010). Similarly, clearly defined items of work will carry less risk than ill-defined or loosely defined items of work. If the scope itself is revised at a later date in the project lifecycle, then according to Lawrence (2007) a separate estimate needs to be prepared for the revised scope to account for the cost variations due to the new uncertainty and associated risks. Contingency and management reserves, terms excellently explained by Lawrence (2007), are not funds for scope changes. As the design evolves and project progresses, the less risk and uncertainty there is in successive estimates of the project as more and more 'unknowns' become 'knowns' i.e. the uncertainty (or ranges of cost outcomes) is reduced and therefore the associated risks. Figure 2 presents the reduction of risk ranges.

Figure 2 suggests that how well developed the scope is for a project at the time of developing the estimate for budgeting purposes is paramount in the forecasting process. If no cost estimates are prepared for budgeting purposes and project budgets are allocated based on 'guesstimate' of quantities and subjective assessment then the allocated budget could be extremely misleading and often difficult to defend, as will be explained through the case studies in this paper. Subjective assessments are opinions and judgment based on historical data and experience/knowledge in a specific area.

Figure 2. Reducing risk reduces the range and the contingency requirement
Source: (Lawrence, 2007)

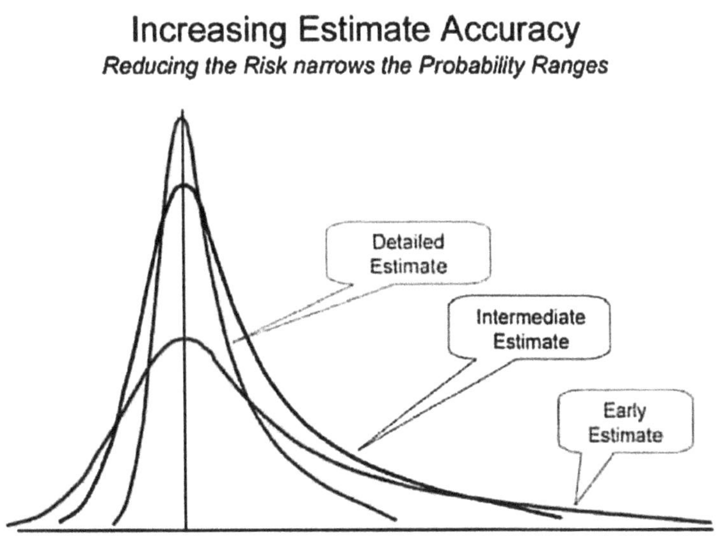

Risk Mitigation

The downside aspect of risk, namely those risks that pose a threat to the realization of the PPP objectives, is of concern. There is therefore a need to seek solutions to the effects or the occurrence of these risks. Examination of the strategies suggested by Ammar, Berman and Sataporn (2007) for risks that have negative impacts suggest that avoidance, transfer or mitigation could be used. Mistarihi, Al Refai, Al Qaid, and Qeed (2012) suggest mitigating, avoiding, transferring, sharing or retaining as responses to risks.

Mitigating risk involves two basic strategies: reducing the likelihood that the event will occur and/or reducing the impact that the adverse event would have on the project (Krause, 2014). Finally, in some cases a conscious decision is made to accept the risk of an event occurring. For instance, a risk such as an earthquake or flood may be retained by the project owner as the magnitude of the risk is too big and the probability of it occurring is low. It worth noting that the more effort given to risk response before the project begins the better the chances of minimizing project surprises (Antuchevičiene, Turskis & Zavadskas, 2006). Appreciation of the project's risk profile, allocation of risk to the appropriate parties best able to manage it and the choice of risk response provides the basis for selecting the most appropriate procurement strategy.

Risk mitigation involves two steps identifying the various activities, or steps; to reduce the probability and/or impact of an adverse risk and creation of a contingency Plan to deal with the risk should it occur (Emirullah & Azam, 2014). Taking early steps to reduce the probability of an adverse risk occurring may be more effective and less costly than repairing the damage after a risk has occurred. However, some risk mitigation options may simply be too costly in time or money to consider. Mitigation activities should be documented in the Risk Register, and reviewed on a regular basis. They include identification of potential failure points for each risk mitigation solution, for each failure point, document the event that would raise a "flag" indicating that the event or factor has occurred or reached a critical condition, and for each failure point, provide alternatives for correcting the failure (Asenova & Beck, 2010). This strategy involves taking those actions that eliminate any chances of risk materializing. This would involve eliminating sources of risk such as adoption of another design, or alternative the work procedures so as to avoid the consequence of the risks. Such a strategy is implemented when the consequences of the risk is so severe that no party is found to be suitable for taking the risk. The implementation of this strategy may generate other risks which will require the formulation of appropriate risk treatment options (Apanavičienė & Rudžianskaitė-Kvaraciejienė, 2010). Table 1 shows the mitigation strategies judged suitable for the identified key risks by the panel of experts. Only for the key risk due to force majeure events the panel does not identify a suitable mitigation strategy, scoring Government indemnities as neutral.

According to Bedell (2007), there are three traditional ways of risk mitigation: point estimates, range estimates and what-if scenarios. Point estimates, which are the easiest, use the most likely values for the uncertain variables. But this could give misleading estimates. Range estimates typically show a range of outcomes such as: the best case, the worst case and the most likely case, but not the probability of any of these outcomes. What-if scenarios are typically about exploring the effect of controllable things and are usually based on range estimates. What is the worst case? This form of analysis can be time consuming, and results in a great deal of data. Tan and Makwasha (2010) inform of the pros & cons of sensitivity analysis for considering uncertainty. Sensitivity analyses test if 'designed' or intended changes in key variables (inputs) have considerable impact on project cost. Sensitivity analysis has its drawbacks which they elaborate further.

Table 1. Suitable mitigation strategies for key risks

Risk Category	Risk Mitigation Strategy
Financial Closure Risk (Project Finance)	**Provision for Alternate Promoter/Lender**
Construction risks Cost overrun	_ Additional capital _ Contingency fund _ Fixed price (lump sum) contracts _ Guaranteed Maximum Price agreement _ Escrow account to complete the project
Revenue risks Demand/usage risk	_ Revenue sharing mechanism _ Revenue distribution mechanism
Financial risks Interest rates increase Inflation Debt servicing risk	_ Interest rate guarantee, futures, options and swaps _ Adjust concession price; debt guarantee _ Inflation caps/floors _ Flexible price formula to meet traffic revenue deficiencies _ Debt reserve accounts
Regulatory/political risks Changes in legislation	_ Compensation from Government _ Government assurances _ Extension of concession _ Compensation clauses from Government

Source: (Pellegrino, Vajdic & Carbonara, 2013)

Risk Transfer and Allocation

Risk transfer shifts and reallocates, along with ownership, from one party to another third party, without changing the total amount of risk or reducing the criticality of risk sources (Smith, Merna and Jobling, 2006). A fundamental principle is that risks associated with the implementation and delivery of services should be allocated to the party best able to manage the risk in a cost-effective manner (Yongjian, ShouQing & Chan, 2009). However, Roumboutsos and Anagnostopoulos (2008) found that there are risks that the private sector is reluctant to absorb from the public sector. Examples include inflation rate, exchange rate, interest rate fluctuation, and delays in project approvals and permits.

Abednego and Ogunlana (2006) recommend that risk factors have to be determined before the risk being allocated, they have to anticipate the risk so it will be more organize and prepared. Basically, the purpose of the mapping is to get the ranking of factors that are considered in the risk allocation of the PPP project (Ibrahim, Price & Dainty, 2006). Risk allocation should be clearly communicated and understood between the collaborating parties. Both public and private sectors therefore must pay particular attention to the procurement process to ensure equitable risk allocation (Ke, Wang & Chan, 2011). Li, Akintoye, Edwards and Hardcastle (2005b) argue that since risk allocation refers to a primary measure of assignment between the public and private sector, it is important that risk allocation is clearly communicated and understood between the parties. An equitable risk allocation and management is important to the project success of a PPP project within a rather long concession period (Zhang, 2005a; Li, Akintoye, Edwards & Hardcastle, 2005a). For example, Governments would state their preference as to how the project risks should be shared in the invitation of tendering, while private investors would assess their capability of taking these risks and then propose a bidding price. The contract negotiation would thereafter probably focus on the risk allocation scheme. A general principle is that each risk should be allocated to the party best able to manage it and at the least cost (Cooper, Grey, Raymond & Walker, 2005). In other words, an optimal risk allocation is not to pass all risks to the private sector, but to seek a solution minimizing both the total management costs of the public and private sectors. Sometimes, the partner from which the risk emanates and thus who is considered to be best able to control it, may not actually be able to control the risk in the most efficient way and at the lowest cost (Medda, 2007).

A number of academic researchers have provided solutions to achieve equitable risk allocation schemes. Among them, a questionnaire survey is the most common research technique used. For instance, Li, Akintoye, Edwards and Hardcastle (2005b) developed a preferred risk allocation scheme for PPP projects in the UK and Roumboutsos and Anagnostopoulos (2008) and Ke, Wang and Chan (2010a) conducted a similar survey using the same questionnaire in Greece and China, respectively, and then compared the findings to those in the UK. A case study is another popular technique for exploring a suitable risk allocation scheme for PPP projects, such as Abednego and Ogunlana (2006) and Ng and Loosemore (2007). Recent researchers have developed more complicated and vigorous methods in the risk allocation arena, such as game theory (Medda, 2007), the fuzzy synthetic allocation model (Xu, Chan & Yeung, 2010; Jin & Doloi, 2009; Ke, Wang & Chan, 2010b), theoretical framework based on transaction cost economics (Jin and Doloi, 2008; Jin, 2010a) and the neuro-fuzzy decision support system (Jin, 2010b).

Carbonara, Costantino, Pellegrino and Sciancalepore (2011) contend that the realization of the objectives through PPP projects implies huge risks that have to be properly allocated and managed by both of the involved parties. Adequate allocation of risk in PPP projects is a crucial factor in their success and it is widely accepted that risk should be allocated to the party best able to manage that risk. That is, "the goal is not to maximize, but optimize risk transfer" (Carbonara, Costantino, Pellegrino & Sciancalepore (2011, p. 1). A possible way to manage and alleviate risk is through incorporating flexibility into PPP contracts by adding special clauses that can diminish risk by, for instance, modifying the order and time of activities. The Real Option approach can be used to model this contractual flexibility. It can be applied both to mitigating risk and to evaluating managerial flexibility, which increases the value of the project by enabling project managers to change their decisions depending on the project's future performance. Jin and Doloi (2008) conducted an empirical study in a transaction cost economic perspective to interpret the risk allocation mechanism. Multiple linear regressions were used to develop models to determine the causal relationship between explanatory and response variables of an operationalized theoretical framework for risk allocation in PPP projects. They recommended that non-probability-based analytical techniques and consideration of the nonlinear relationship should be applied in future research.

An efficient risk allocation is crucial for a sound management of PPP projects. Risk allocation in infrastructure projects between the public and private sector is considered to be another crucial issue in the management of PPP projects (Marques & Berg, 2011). The main principle regarding risk allocation in PPP projects is that the agent that should bear the risk is best able to influence and control the risky outcome (Loosemore, Raftery, Reilly & Higgon, 2006; Medda, 2007). More specifically, Liu and Wilkinson (2014) argue that the government should retain the risks that are beyond the control of the private sector. However, in some cases risks are allocated to parties without the knowledge, resources and capabilities to manage them effectively. Ng and Loosemore (2007) argue that there is considerable evidence to suggest that risk transfer is often handled poorly between parties to many PPP projects and that these types of problems are common in PPP projects. An inadequate risk allocation is supposed to have a relevant impact in project performance. Ke, Wang and Chan, (2013) carried out an empirical analysis to evaluate the correlation between risk misallocation and project performance. It was found that there was a significant negative relationship between project performance and the degree of risk misallocation. The smaller the degree was, the more successful the project would be. A risk management approach for partnerships.

Lam, Wang, Lee and Tsang (2007) provide fruitful insights of risk allocation. They identify seven key risk allocation criteria. The criteria are:- ability of the party to foresee the risk; ability of the party to assess the possible magnitude of the consequences of the risk; ability of the party to control the chance of the risk occurring; ability of the party to manage the risk in case it occurs; ability of the party to sustain the consequences if the risk occurs; whether the party will benefit from bearing the risk; and whether the premium charged by the risk-receiving party is considered reasonable and acceptable for the owner. Although the above criteria are quite detailed and may be helpful in partnership design and contract preparation, often the focus in the risk allocation discussion shifts to the links between risk management and the private partner performance incentives.

With regard to how risks are allocated, it is argued that perhaps the most challenging feature of public private partnership for contractors is the need to understand fully the risk allocation mandated under the public private partnership agreement between the project company and the government (Cook, 2007). This view calls attention to the first and foremost challenge for parties – the need to identify the risks that each partner is going to accept in a partnership. Parties may not fully realize the nature and range of risks they may be exposed to, and how difficult and costly dealing with each risk may be. However, risk management tools may be available. As an example, Cook suggests using insurance coverage, such as surety bonds, for a number of project situations to offset a private company for some unaddressed risks in an original PPP contract (Cook, 2007). In line with Cook's proposal is a suggestion that those risks that are foreseeable and can be insured shall be handled by insurance as much as possible (Wang, 2006). Jin and Zhang (2011) advocate a notion that risks should be insured whenever possible and should be allocated through negotiations between parties. However, getting insurance depends on willingness of an insurer to accept a particular risk, which in turn depends on how high a risk is priced (Medda, 2007). Thus, buying insurance may be possible, although it may be pricey for a private company and, ultimately, for the government and citizens.

Bing, Akintoye, Edwards and Hardcastle (2005a, 2005b) argue that the allocation of public private partnership risks between the public sector and private sector is not always obvious. A number of studies have examined how risk is allocated in practice. In their paper examining the lessons learned from pilot public private partnership projects in Ireland, which is also one of the few published studies covering public private partnership financing risk; Reeves and Ryan (2007) describe the complex allocation process in the schools' sector. Complexity arose firstly because some risks, such as statutory planning approval and business risks are shared. Secondly, risk allocation may be re-negotiated part way through the contract, as was the case for information technology obsolescence, which was allocated to the private sector for the first three years only. Thirdly, the allocation of finance risks may be dependent on performance. Although the private sector is responsible for raising all required finance, in the event of SPV default the public sector becomes liable for the senior debt payments (Reeves & Ryan, 2007).

Several studies have examined how risks ought to be allocated (Wibowo & Mohamed, 2010). Bing, Akintoye, Edwards and Hardcastle (2005b) argue that most macro-level risks – for example: political, legal, social and economic risks – and other risks which are 'exogenous' to the project should be borne by the public sector, but that project related risks should be allocated to the private sector. However, these authors recognize that a high risk premium may lead the public sector to reschedule risks by sharing or retaining more of them to reduce the contract price. Shen, Platten and Deng (2006) argue that an 'effective' risk allocation occurs if: site acquisition, and legal and policy risks are allocated to the public sector; design and construction, operation and industrial action risk are allocated to the private sector; and development, market, financial and force majeure risks are shared between the two partners. Abednego and Ogunlana (2006) argue that because parties involved in public private partnership projects have different perceptions of risks, good project governance systems are essential for proper risk allocation and ultimately for the projects' success – inadequate specification of requirements and improper allocation of responsibilities among the contracting parties are the main problems faced by the public sector. Risks are considered only when they materialize, and solutions are sought in response to the threats posed to minimize losses. The contracting parties are satisfied with risk allocation so long as its consequences are minimized. Moreover, the risk management strategy adopted is geared towards problem-solving rather than taking preventive actions (Abednego & Ogunlana, 2006). Unlike traditional procurement option that maximum risk transfer is practiced, the public private partnership approach follows the principle of optimal risk allocation in allocating risks. The principle of optimal risk allocation principle suggests that risks should only be taken by the parties who are in the best position to control them, taken into account the public interest (Hayford, 2006). There is a cost for managing the risk. The party who is at the best position to manage the risks should be able to do it at the least cost. With the private party being assigned the risks that it is capable of managing them, it can manage the risks at a lower cost than the public sector. If, however, the private party is assigned the risks that are beyond their control, it will either refuse to take the risk, or to charge a higher premium to reimburse the extra risk. This will escalate the overall cost of the public private partnership approach. Karim (2011) recommends that when determining the lists of risks to be transferred to the private sector, the public sector client should also consider the private party's capability and resources to cope with the risk and the risk appetite of the private party in taking the risk. In general, the public sector client should only transfer those risks that it has not been managing well in the past, or that it has little experience in managing. It should retain those risks that it can manage well in the past and those risks it is in a more informed position to control than the private sector (Singh, 2011). There are some risks that should be taken by neither party and these should be shared between the parties. These include risks that neither party is in a better position to control the risks, e.g. force majeure risk; risks that are beyond the control of either party, e.g. movements in general price levels, or exchange rates; and risks that may be difficult to identify in advance or their consequences is difficult to measure.

Allocation of risks can be achieved by evaluating the capabilities of both parties and their previous experience with respect to the identified project risks. Alternatively, the public sector client can rely on a standardized risk allocation matrix which states its preference on how risks are to be allocated between parties (Jin, 2011). This matrix is constructed based on the risk management information obtained from previous public private partnership projects. It identifies the common types of risks to be retained and transferred in previous public private partnership projects (Xiao & Zhang, 2011). The advantage of using the list is that it simplifies the tender process and minimizes bid costs. The risk allocation method suggested in the matrix only represents the preferred position of the public sector client. It does not represent the final risk allocation position. The private party would assess the public sector client's preferred list of risk allocation and indicate their willingness to accept or not. Very often, the private sector will be given the opportunity to negotiate with the public sector client on the ownership of certain risks. The negotiations will continue until both parties agree on how risks are to be allocated. However, evidence from projects worldwide shows that risks are not managed properly (Chan, Lam, Chan, Cheung & Ke, 2011). The complexity of arrangements and incomplete contracting nature of PPP projects have led to increased risk exposure for all the parties involved (Marques & Berg, 2011). A perception that privatization involves transfer of all risks to the private sector is still prevalent in many countries (Papajohn, Cui & Bayraktar, 2011). It is thus critical for government to understand that it is sub-optimal for them to either retain or transfer inappropriate risks (Chan, Lam, Wen, Ameyaw, Wang & Ke, 2015) because transfer of risks to the private sector comes at a price (Hayford, 2006) and improper allocation of risks among stakeholders may lead to higher than necessary prices (Bing, Akintoye, Edwards & Hardcastle, 2005b).

Optimal risk allocation seeks to minimize the risks to the project by allocating particular risks to the party in the best position to control them (Hayford, 2006; Kangari, 1995). This is based on the principle that the party in the greatest position of control or possessing the best capability of management with respect to a particular risk has the best opportunity to reduce the likelihood of the risk eventuation and to control the consequences of the risk if it materializes, and thus should assume it (Rahman & Kumaraswamy, 2002; Thomas, Kalidindi, & Ananthanarayanan, 2003). However, the capability-based principle of risk allocation has its own shortcomings. It has been recently argued that in order to achieve optimal risk allocation, apart from appropriate capability of risk management, a risk should be borne by the party who presents willingness or commitment (Abednego & Ogunlana, 2006; Jin, 2011; Loosemore, Raftery, Reilly & Higgon, 2006).

Karim (2011) argues that a conceptual model for an effective risk allocation in PPP comprise of five constructs: - environmental uncertainty, risk management commitment, risk management capability, risk allocation strategy and risk management performance. In consideration of these constructs, Li, Akintoye, Edwards and Hardcastle (2005b) recommends the process of risk allocation should combine a systematic risk-management approach with the principle of risk sharing. Under the proposed framework, the public sector sponsor identifies the risks attached to the project in a risk register, sets out the risks relevant to each stage of the project, the likelihood of occurrence for each risk event and an estimate of the financial consequences (Ng & Loosemore, 2007). The analysis helps the public client establish the type and quantum of risks that it seeks to transfer to the private sector. Shen, Platten and Deng (2006) found that the public sector partner should retain site availability and political risks. Relationship risks, force majeure risks, and the risks of legislation changes should be shared by both private and public sectors. The majority of the remaining project risks, especially those at the meso risk level (i.e. directly associated with the project itself), should be allocated to the private sector partner.

RISK MANAGEMENT PROCESSES

Risk management process involves maximizing opportunity, namely increasing the probability and impact of positive events, and decreasing the probability and impact of adverse events (Nisar, 2007). While risk management framework (RMF) may be described as the glue that holds the organization together in pursuit of its objectives, risk management process provides the resilience (Badenfelt, 2008). Risk management process is a formal and orderly process of systematically identifying, analyzing, and responding to risks throughout the lifecycle of a project in order to obtain the optimum degree of risk elimination, mitigation and/or control. Sarvari, Valipuor, Yahaya and Noor (2014) states that risk management process is an important and integral element of risk management. All managers (and indeed all human beings) manage risk either consciously or unconsciously, but rarely systematically. Managing risk is a forward-thinking act in which individuals or groups take a look at the future of a particular process or endeavor to identify, in a responsible manner, the downsides or upsides of actions or inactions. This enables balanced thinking to be achieved, which provides a framework to facilitate more effective decision-making.

Risk management process as put forward by Maylor, Vidgen and Carver (2008) is a progression involving risk management planning, risk identification, risk assessment, risk analysis, risk response, risk monitoring and risk communication. Lehtiranta (2013) suggests that risk management processes in a PPP arrangement are threefold: identifying risk factors; analyzing their effect; and responding to risk. Bon-Gang, Xianbo and Ping (2014) assert that risk management should be approached as an iterative process, and not in the discrete phases of identification, evaluation and control. They argue that the identification of risks should be followed by a search for solutions that can ameliorate or eliminate these risks. Boussabaine (2007) suggests that the risk management process should follow five consecutive steps: identification of risk, risk assessment and analysis, risk mitigation, namely the development of risk reduction and reaction to threats; implementation of risk management plans; and the review and correction of risk assessment.

Klemetti (2006) maintains risk management processes undergo six stages. First, there is risk Management Planning (RMP), that is, deciding how to approach, plan, and execute the risk management activities for a project. Secondly, risk Identification that is determining which risks might affect the project and documenting their characteristics. Thirdly, qualitative risk analysis, that is prioritizing risks for subsequent further analysis or action by assessing and combining their probability of occurrence and impact. Fourth stage is quantitative risk analysis that is numerically analyzing the effect on the overall project objectives of identified risks. Fifth, risk response planning that is developing options and actions to enhance opportunities and to reduce threats to project objectives. Sixth, risk monitoring and control that is tracking identified risks, monitoring residual risks, identifying new risks, executing risk response plans, and evaluating their effectiveness throughout the project life cycle. In addition, it should be noted that communication and consultation are important considerations at each step of the risk management process (Bouder, Slavin & Lofstedt, 2009). Effective communication can help ensure that those responsible for implementing risk management and stakeholders understand the basis on which decisions are made and why particular actions are required (Peng, Cui, Lu and Huang, 2014). Since stakeholders have a significant impact on the decisions made, it is important that their perceptions of both risks and benefits be identified and documented and that the underlying reasons for them are understood and addressed appropriately.

Risk Identification

Risk identification is a process for uncovering any risks that could potentially affect a process (Ibem, 2010). This step is of considerable importance as other processes such as risk analysis and response can only be undertaken on the potential risks that have been identified. Risk identification is a simple but difficult task as there are no absolute procedures that may be used to identify risks in a project (Ameyaw & Chan, 2013). Managers often rely heavily on their experience and on the insight of other key personnel involved in the process. Depending on the process documentation available and the nature of the process, a variety of considerations may prompt risk discovery. Regarding risk, Kendrick (2009) notes that managers need to focus on the interface between the consultant and the client, between departments of the client organization, between phases or tasks of a client process, or between geographic areas. Azar, Zangoueinezhad, Elahi and Moghbel (2013) further suggest that the project schedule should clearly show dependencies between tasks in order to help pinpoint risk-prone areas. Alternatively, managers may use process maps that show interfaces between processes or tasks. Flanagan, Norman and Chapman (2006) compared attempts at risk identification in projects with multiple layers of planning, complex vertical and horizontal interactions.

According to Ahmed, Kayis and Amornsawadwatana (2007), in order to choose the appropriate technique for identifying risk, practitioners should consider several factors, such as the organization's objectives. In addition, Mousavi, Tavakkoli-Moghaddam, Azaron, Mojtahedi and Hashemi (2011) recommends the use of tools and techniques such as documentation reviews, information gathering techniques, checklist analysis, assumptions analysis and diagramming techniques. In order to allocate the risk, risk management is the key factor to provide a better risk allocation. There are four logical process of risk management which is identification of risks, analysis of the implications, respond to minimize risk and allocate appropriate contingencies (Smith, Merna & Jobling, 2006). Jutte (2014) reported that many of project identification teams are overloaded with work thereby creating a project dynamics where only negative risks matter. It is therefore important to also take time to consider opportunities as well because there are chances identifying opportunities with high pay-off that do not require a big investment in time or resources. The identified risks, especially those that require further actions are penciled down for assessment and analysis which Klemetti (2006) referred to as risk estimation.

To reiterate, risk management is the critical part of PPP management as 'unmanaged or unmitigated risks are one of the primary causes of project failure' (Dey, 2010). The risk management process aims to identify and assess risks in order to enable the risks to be clearly understood and managed effectively (Loizou & French, 2012). The term 'risk management' has multiple meanings. Many use this term synonymously with risk identification. For many others, it is synonymous to risk analysis, risk monitoring and /or risk control. In fact, these all are the phases of risk management. It is the process concerted with identifying, analyzing and responding to uncertainty throughout the project life cycle'.

The general consensus in current literature, available in the field of risk management, incorporates four steps in the process of risk management (Ali, 2005). These are risk identification, risk analysis, risk response planning and risk monitoring and control (Choi, Chung & Lee, 2010). Risk identification is a process of identifying risks that shall help further in analyzing, monitoring and controlling risks. For example, for a construction project, risk identification consists of defining which risks most likely affect the project and documenting characteristics of each. Risk identification process is to be performed on regular basis throughout the project and should address both internal and external risks (Turnbaughs, 2005). A large number of techniques exist for risk identification, such as, brainstorming and workshops, checklist and prompt techniques like cause effect diagram, influence diagrams etc (Ibrahim, Price & Dainty, 2006).

Risk identification entails risk analysis which is an evaluation process of uncertainty associated with occurrence of internal and external risks, as well as consequences of occurrence of these risks on the basis of best available information (Jin, 2011). Certain risks affect the project performance negligibly. Such risks can be very well ignored and their impact on project need not be quantified. While certain risks have potential to adversely affect the project objectives to large extent. These risks are to be quantified. Risks analysis can be subjective as well as objective. Risk analysis involves the Qualitative is and quantitative assessment of the identified risks. Project management has to estimate the probability of occurrence of the risks as well as their potential consequences. The risk management database can then be updated with the new information (Schatteman, 2008). Qualitative risk analysis is to determine the likelihood and potential effect of identified risks on project objectives. It helps in prioritizing risks for further attention. Techniques like Fault tree analysis, Event tree analysis, and Sensitivity analysis and probability impact grid are used for qualitative risk analysis (Ammar, Berman & Sataporn, 2007).

Risk identification is the first step of the risk management process. In order to manage risk, an organization needs to know what risks it faces. This helps to determine the risks that might affect the project and document their characteristics. The identification of risk can be separated into initial and continuous risk identification. Initial identification is for new projects or activity within an organization for which the risks have not been identified (Roumboutsos & Anagnostopoulos, 2008). Continuous risk identification is for ongoing project in order to identify new risks which did not previously arise, changes in existing risks in the course of the project, or risks which did exist ceasing to be relevant to the organization (Sanda & Anigbogu, 2016). Implementation of the risk management should start with risk identification at the feasibility stage, followed by risk assessment and risk treatment. However these processes should be carried out continuously throughout the project. During the project any event that may have a detrimental effect on achieving the objectives of the project would be considered as a risk (Seyed, Seyrafianpour & Ebrahimnejad, 2010). For example, during the option appraisal stage, any events that would affect the net present value of a particular option would be considered as a risk; during the procurement stage, any event that has an adverse impact on chosen procurement option in delivering the value for money would be considered a risk; during the construction stage, any event that would have a detrimental impact on the time, cost and quality of the project would be considered as risks.

Risk identification is a cyclical process and should be continued throughout the project. No matter how rigorous the risk identification process is carried out, it is inevitable that some risks will arise as the project proceeds (Wang & Dai, 2009). Different risk identification techniques should be employed at different stages of a project. Before the project commences, proactive risk identification techniques should be employed. These involve imagining potential future events that would affect the achievement of the project objectives (Chowdhury, Chen & Tiong, 2011). As the project proceeds, some unpredictable events which have an adverse effect on the project objectives would arise. Reactive risk identification techniques which involve identification of risks after actual losses have occurred should be employed (Tahir, 2007).

Common methods for risk identification include brainstorming and workshops, focus group session, checklists, flowcharts, questionnaires, scenario building (Sarmento & Renneboog, 2014). Barlow, Roehrich and Wright (2013) identified three additional approaches to identify the upside risks as well. They are SWOT analysis, constraints and assumption analysis and force field analysis. No one method is better than the others. A combination of techniques can be used if it is appropriate. People who are involved in the risk identification process should have experience in a public private partnership project (Medda, 2007). Usually they are the stakeholders representing the public sector clients and the private sector. Those who are involved in the identification process should be engaged in a public private partnership project before. External consultants representing the stakeholders may be necessary in some circumstances, depending on the type of identification methods and the kind of expertise involved (Zou, Wang & Fang, 2008).

A checklist consists of a list of risks that are identified from previous public private partnership projects. It is often considered as an idea elicitation aid which helps to generate ideas about potential risks for the current project, particularly at the beginning of the risk identification process (Cretu, Stewart & Berends, 2011). Based on the checklist, stakeholders can base on their experience and judgment to evaluate the applicability of the risks included the checklist to the current project. They should exclude any risks that are not applicable to the current project and include those risks that have been missed out in the checklist (Xu, Yeung, Chan, Chan, Wang & Ke, 2010). Because of its simplicity in nature, the checklist approach is the most common risk identification approach in the construction.

The brainstorming process is originally a problem solving method borrowed from business management. It involves redefining the problem, generating ideas, finding possible solutions, developing selected feasible solutions and conducting evaluation (Chung, Hensher & Rose, 2010). The brainstorming is considered to be a risk workshop in which all major project stakeholders together identify the risks that are going to affect the project and their corresponding impacts (Kwak, Chih & Ibbs, 2009). One of the advantages of gathering the project stakeholders together is that it can produce a much larger quantity of useful information in less time and can take advantage of group thinking.

Risks identified are recorded in a risk register, which is part of the Risk Management Plan for regular review and reporting of risks (Choudhry & Iqbal, 2012). A risk register should provide a full description of the risks including source, risk owner, likelihood of occurrence, impact, and timeframe of the risk, proposed mitigation strategies and the time these strategies are to be taken. While at this stage, only the risks and their description are available other information will become available in the subsequent stages of the risk management (Zarco-Jasso, 2005). In preparing a risk register for a public private partnership project, it may be relied on a template Risk Register. However, the public sector client should carefully assess the suitability of the template Risk Register against the current project and should also involve its external advisors and members of the risk management team in preparing the Risk Register.

A typically brainstorming group consists of between 10 and 15 people. These people are preferably those who will be involved in risk quantification and for managing risks in the construction and the operation stages of the project. Examples are core service operational managers, project managers, technical consultants such as architects and design engineers, financial and legal advisers. The brainstorming should be served by a facilitator, who is responsible for managing the risk identification process (Meidute & Paliulis, 2011). He should be an independent and experienced person with no interest in the decision outcome. Before the brainstorming begins, the facilitator should brief the stakeholders the purpose of the brainstorming, the expected outcome and what constitutes a risk in the current project. Since these people are of different background, they may have different understanding on what constitutes a risk. The facilitator should ensure that each of them clearly understands the definition of risk before the brainstorming process begins (Maski & Tirole, 2008). The facilitator will then ask the project stakeholders to list out his or her ideas regarding the potential risks in the current project on a paper anonymously. He will conduct open discussion on the risks regarding their applicability and categorization.

Once identified, risks are then categorized. Risks of similar nature are grouped under the same risk category. There is no standard method of categorization. Some classify the risks according to the parties who will be responsible for managing the risks (Avanesov, 2009). Examples of the risk categories are site risk, design, construction and commissioning risk, sponsor and financial risk, operating risk, market risk, network and interface risk, industrial relations, legislative and government policy, force majeure, and asset ownership. Other classifies the risks according to their own classification system. For instance, Li, Akintoye, Edwards and Hardcastle (2005a) proposed a meta-classification of risk which divides the risks into macro level, meso level and micro level. The macro level of risks refers to risks that are external to the project itself. The meso level of risks refers to the risks and their consequences which occur within the project. The micro level of risks refers to risks that are found in the stakeholder relationships formed in the procurement process. They differ from the meso level of risks in that they are party-related rather than project related (Aven, 2010). With this meta-classification, it is claimed that risks could be considered in terms of the nature of their relationship to projects (Li, Akintoye, Edwards & Hardcastle, 2005a).

No matter which categorization system is adopted, the selected categorization should enable a better understanding about the risks, how the risks are allocated between parties and what actions should be taken for managing the risks (Boardman, Poschmann & Vining, 2005). It is likely that a large number of risks may be identified in a particular project. These risks will not all be independent of each other; rather they will typically form natural groupings. All risks, once identified, should be assigned to an owner. It is not enough to only identify a risk, but it should also be made clear who is responsible for that risk (Lam, Wang, Lee & Tsang, 2007). The identification process should not focus only on events that will affect the projects negatively, but should also include those events that will positively influence project outcome since modern risk approaches also focus on opportunities. Jutte (2014) reported that many of project identification teams are overloaded with work thereby creating a project dynamics where only negative risks matter (Baccarini, 2005). It is therefore important to also take time to consider opportunities as well because there are chances identifying opportunities with high pay-off that do not require a big investment in time or resources (Cano & Cruz, 2002).

Quite a number of risk identification techniques and tools are available to be explored by the identification team (Li, 2008). These methods include document review (review of project documents); information gathering (brainstorming, Delphi technique, interviewing, root cause analysis, SWOT (strength, weakness, opportunities and threats) analysis; checklist analysis; assumption analysis; and diagram techniques (cause-and-effect diagrams, process flow charts and influence diagrams) in order to identify the interrelationships between activities, risks, consequences and responses (Olsson, 2008). The risks associated with service provision public private partnerships, for example, maintenance of communal street networks need to be captured in a structured form. To capture such risks or risk groups an empirical research approach with literature review and partially structured qualitative interviews and workshops was chosen (Tallman, 2010).

The risk groups have been related to the classified according to the main causes of risks, such as political, contractual and operational Risk identification occurs throughout each phase of project development: planning, scoping, design/plans, specifications, and estimate (engineer's estimate), and construction (Jayasudha, Vidivelli & Surjith, 2014). As projects evolve through project development, the risk profile evolves and understanding grows. Therefore, previously identified risks may change and new risks may be identified throughout the life of the project. The first and most important input is a defined project. In order to fully understand and assess the risks that our projects are exposed to, we must first ensure there is a mutual understanding of the project under evaluation (Tanaka, Ishida, Tsutsumi & Okamoto, 2005). This means that in order to focus on the risks and uncertainties our project will face, we must first define the project in terms of context, scope, schedule, and estimate, commensurate with the level of project development at the time of risk analysis (Lenfle & Loch, 2010). Progressive elaboration should not be confused with scope creep. Projects tend to develop in small steps. This incremental process of project development is sometimes termed "progressive elaboration." Progressive elaboration means developing in steps, and continuing by increments. For example, the project scope will be broadly described early in the project and made more explicit and detailed as the project team develops a better and more complete understanding of the objectives and deliverables

The project team, sometimes in collaboration with cost risk experts and subject matter experts, identify as many risks as possible that may affect project objectives. State the assumptions for risk identification and analysis, and delineate thresholds for risks (Teller & Kock, 2013). For example, a project team may want to describe risks with impacts below $100,000 or less than two weeks as minor. By doing so, we do not spend excessive amounts of time on risks that do not significantly impact our ability to meet project objectives. Focus must be directed toward risks that can significantly impact the project (Kwan & Leung. 2011). Assumptions and thresholds for risk assessment are project-specific and are influenced by the size and complexity of the project and project environment, and the owners' tolerance for risk. There are a wide variety of techniques used for risk identification. Some common techniques are provided below.

Documentation Reviews: Peer-level reviews of project documentation, studies, reports, preliminary plans, estimates, and schedules are a common and early method to help identify risks that may affect project objectives. Information gathering: brainstorming – Formal and informal brainstorming sessions with project team members, specialty groups, stakeholders, and regulatory agency representatives is a technique for risk identification (Campbell & Currie 2006). This technique can be scaled for use on the simplest to the most complex projects. This technique can also be tailored to specific areas of interest for the project risk; for example, if a Project Manager is most concerned about geotech conditions, a brainstorming session on geotech can be convened. Lessons learned database – Searching for lessons learned using key words in the Lessons Learned Database that are relevant to your project can provide an abundance of information on projects that may have faced similar risks (Lee & Chun, 2009). Other Methods and techniques include: questionnaires and surveys; interviews, checklists, and examination of the work breakdown structure for the project with appropriate specialty groups; and asking "what if" questions (Wood, 2005).

Risk Assessment

Risk assessment is the determination of quantitative or qualitative estimate of risk related to a well-defined situation and a recognized threat (also called hazard) (Diab, Naser & Varma, 2012).Risk assessment is a complex stage, regardless of the activity associated with it, because, beyond any statistical and mathematical calculations, implies a certain vision and an attempt to predict the future, to assess possible dangers, attacks and threats which could face an economic entity including the actions of those involved in its activities (Adams, Alistair & Wu, 2006). In principle, risk assessment is a systematic process to identify and compare that to consider the organization's key assets, threats and vulnerabilities that can occur, the likelihood and consequences and protective measures that can be counteracted. This activity is often the most complex of the risk management process because of such factors as: opportunities and threats can interact in ways that cannot be anticipated (for example, behind the initial schedule may force consideration of a new strategy that ultimately leads to decrease the time allocated to project); a single risk can have multiple effects: additional costs, delays, penalties, reducing the quality of results; events which are opportunities for a person or organization (cost savings) may be threats to other (reducing profits); and mathematical techniques used to quantify the risk may provide a time accuracy and safety unfounded (Molenaar, 2005).

Risk assessment is a critical step in achieving and defining the PPP project risk management. Under these conditions, the concerns for developing the best methods in this field are varied. Both at practical and theoretical level, in PPP project, but also in other activities, are numerous qualitative, semi-quantitative and quantitative methods which try to estimate individual components of risk for a result to better reflect the reality. However, in currently, there is now a universally accepted method, able to predict and assess all events and actions carry risks (Andi, 2006). According to Chan, Yeung, JYu, Wang and Ke, (2011), an acceptable risk is a risk that is understood and tolerated usually because the cost or difficulty of implementing an effective countermeasure for the associated vulnerability exceeds the expectation of loss. For Chiu and Bosher (2005), if the risk estimate R i = p (L i) {\displaystyle R_{i}=p(L_{i})\,\!}

R i = p (L i) {\displaystyle R_{i}=p(L_{i})\,\!} takes into account information on the number of individuals exposed, it is termed a "population risk" and is in units of expected increased cases per a time period. If the risk estimate does not take into account the number of individuals exposed, it is termed an "individual risk" and is in units of incidence rate per a time period. Population risks are of more use for cost/benefit analysis; individual risks are of more use for evaluating whether risks to individuals are "acceptable" (El-Sayegh, 2008).

Essentially, risk assessment includes variations, such as risk as the type and severity of response, with or without a probabilistic context (Jin & Doloi, 2008). Jin and Doloi (2009) insinuate that risk assessment consists of an objective evaluation of risk in which assumptions and uncertainties are clearly considered and presented. However, Medda (2007) warns that part of the difficulty in risk management is that both the quantities by which risk assessment is concerned – potential loss and probability of occurrence – can be very difficult to measure. The chance of error in measuring these two concepts is high. Risk with a large potential loss and a low probability of occurrence, is often treated differently from one with a low potential loss and a high likelihood of occurrence. In theory, both are of near equal priority, but in practice it can be very difficult to manage when faced with the scarcity of resources, especially time, in which to conduct the risk management process. This is because risk assessment is not only concern with managing risk occurrences but also impacts.

Jin and Doloi (2008) articulate that risk assessments are typically guided by two questions: which party is better able to control the occurrence of the risk (risk frequency)? And which party is better positioned to manage the outcome of the risk, or control its ultimate cost (consequence severity)? Although PPP practitioners are usually aware of the distinction between occurrence and impact, in practice, risks are often allocated along the principle of occurrence. For example, because the private sector has no influence over a change in law, this risk is usually fully retained by the public agency (Hodge & Greve, 2005a, 2005b). Or, because the public agency has no control over cost overruns during construction, this risk is typically fully borne by the private party. Maximizing VFM, however, requires that public private partnership practitioners also consider the extent to which parties may face incentives to influence the total impact of the risk (Meier O'Toole, 2007). Even if a party is not able to prevent a risk from materializing, it may still assume the risk if it has control over the ultimate cost.

The identified risks, especially those that require further actions are penciled down for assessment and analysis which Klemetti (2006) referred to as risk estimation. The estimating stage focuses on calculating the degree of uncertainty associated with risks by combining the likelihood of the risk being realized and of the impact if the risk realized. The estimation stage therefore deals with determining the probability of occurrence and severity of impact of each identified risks, prioritizing risks for further attention, grouping risks into categories to identify hot spots of risk exposure or common causes and analyzing the combined effect of risk on objectives using statistical models (Hillson, 2006). Since different risks have different impacts on project objectives, the risk manager or management team needs to prioritize the identified risks for further action.

In risk prioritization, the organization determines which combinations of probability and impact result in a classification of high risk (red condition), moderate risks (yellow condition) and low risks (green condition) (Loosemore, Raftery, Reilly & Higgon, 2006). Prioritizing risks serves as guide to risk response because it points out the risk that requires much attention and those that can just be kept under watch by the organization. The highest priority risks should be given regular attention at the highest level of organization. Risk analysis refers to the assessment on the likeliness of risk occurrence, its consequence, the time at which the risks will occur and the duration (Li, Akintoye, Edwards & Hardcastle, 2005). It also informs decisions on how best to manage risks, by drawing attention to risks factors which require particularly careful monitoring and management, and enabling suitable risk management measures to be implemented. With the implementation of risk assessment, decision makers are informed about how to prioritize the resources in the light of limited resources (Dallas, 2006).

The basic principle of risk assessment is to determine the value of a risk based on its probability and consequence (Kefallinos, Lambrou & Sykas, 2009). Probability refers to the likelihood of the occurrence of a risk. It is represented by a number which lies between zero and one inclusive. If the probability of a risk is said to be zero, it suggests that its occurrence is impossible. On the other hand, if the probability of a risk is said to be one, it suggests that we are certain about the occurrence of such risk. The consequence of risk measures the difference between the base cost of the component and the expected outcome if the risk eventuates (Sharma, 2007). Yuan, Skibniewski and Zheng (2010) give a highlight of five steps that ought to strictly follow while carrying out risk assessment. Step one is the establishment of the context of the risk. This step requires understanding the operating context and the environment of the risk. In the second step is the identification of the risks/hazards. This can best be achieved through identification of the internal and external risks/hazards that poses threat. The third step is the analysis of the risk which is achieved through systematic analysis of various contributing and leading factors, for example, extend of the exposure, multiple exposures. The fourth step requires evaluation and prioritization of the risks. This is achieved through characterization and prioritization in the list of risks for further action. In the fifth and last step, there is real tackling of the risks. This step requires identification of the range of options to tackle risk and implementation of the best choice using available resources (Hillson, 2006).

There are two major ways in which risk assessment can be carried out: quantitative and qualitative. According to Iacob (2014), quantitative Risk assessment (QuRA) is an objective risk assessment tool used to project threat impacts. It provides an estimate of the magnitude of consequences for each identified budget threat. It systematically determines the likelihood of threats occurring and evaluates the cost of the occurrence. Hsu and Sandford (2007) contend QuRA sets out to define; measure; predict and provide a confidence level of likelihood and occurrence of threat impacts. It is derived using a range of values rather than a single value. QRA makes an estimate to be within a range of possible costs from a range of possible values; meaning the cost will fall within the estimated range. It requires calculations of two components of risk (R): the magnitude of the potential loss (L), and the probability (p) that the loss will occur. Qualitative risk assessment (QlRA) methods can be used to identify assets to be detailed and bear a simple and rapid assessment. In this case, a single person or team can gather information. This assessment is used often when numerical data are inadequate or unavailable, resources are limited (budget or expertise) and time allowed is reduced. Like any risk assessment, the quality begins with obtaining information on risk factors, followed by risk classification in terms like "acceptable" or "unacceptable" or classifications such as "low", "medium", "high". Once seen as risk for assets with a high risk will take mitigation measures, while the remainder will be subject to further examination by semi quantitative or quantitative methods. These measures are based on a hierarchy of business activities and their associated risks. According to Rot (2008), qualitative assessment does not require determining the likelihood of data, only estimates of potential losses.

In risk assessment, analysis and statistical calculations reported in frequency of occurrence of risks are designed to determine the likelihood of their occurrence. If there is relevant and reliable data available, subjective estimates may be used. To avoid confusion caused by subjectivism in the risk assessment can be consulted experts. Benefits of risk assessment phase are reflected in: provides the possibility to take comparisons with historical data or risk level in the field, can risk aggregation of several activities to provide a value for total risk, the knowledge level of uncertainty associated with results tracked and whether to be made when the decision risks. The value of a risk is then given by = Probability x Consequence. Depending on the availability of data and the stages at which the risk assessment is performed, there are different approaches to determine the value of a risk: qualitative, semi-quantitative and qualitative approaches (Stern, & Arias, 2011). Qualitative approach are mostly employed at the early stage of the project in which information do not permit a valid quantification process. It is also used when past data regarding the risk is not available. In the qualitative approach, the significance of the risk can be determined by constructing a matrix which shows the degree of significance according to the risk's consequences and its likelihood of occurrence (Klemetti, 2006).

The quantitative approach to risk assessment also determines the value of a risk by multiplying its probability and consequence (Sachs & Tiong, 2009). It differs from the previous two approaches in that specific numbers are assigned to represent the probability and consequence of a risk. There are two approaches in estimating the probability of a risk: simple and advanced valuation techniques. The simple valuation technique involves a subjective assessment of the probability of a risk, while the advanced valuation technique estimates the probability of a risk by construction of probability distributions (Barlish, De Marco & Thaheem, 2013). The advantage of the simple valuation technique is that it is easier to construct and interpret than advanced valuation technique. However, for risks that are expected to have a serious impact on the project, advanced probability technique is preferred. The use of either method depends on the availability of data and the significance of a risk (Shen, Platten, & Deng, 2006).

With the simple probability valuation technique, a group of project stakeholders will be appointed to assign a number which represent their best estimates on the each risk's likelihood of occurrence (Ammar, Berman & Sataporn, 2007). The number is assigned based on the project stakeholders' judgment, which are formed as a result of their past experience, and data from previous projects (Ke, Wang & Chan, 2013). Data on previous projects can be obtained from sources such as: past records; relevant experience; industry practice and experience; published literature; test marketing and market research; experiments and prototypes; economic, engineering or other models; specialist and expert judgments. There are two approaches to elicit subjective probabilities of the project stakeholders: direct and indirect methods. The direct method involves asking them to assign a number to indicate their judgment on the chances of risk materializing (Khadaroo, 2014). This approach assumes that the selected project stakeholders are a rational decision maker and are well aware of the rudiments of probability. Based on their knowledge and experience, they will assign a number from 0 to 1 indicating the chance of risk materializing. The greater the number, the greater the chance he believes that the risk will materialize. The indirect method involves asking the project stakeholders a series of questions (Chan, Yeung, Yu, Wang & Ke, 2011). The questions are designed in such a way that it is possible to impute the subjective probability from the answers given by them.

Risk assessment techniques at the option appraisal stage: Risk Premium provides a single value for the expected impact of all risks (Roumboutsos & Anagnostopoulos, 2008). Instead of calculating the value of a risk based on its probability and consequence, the value of a risk is determined based on the base cost, e.g. 20% of the base cost. Assessment of risk using risk premium is particularly useful at the early stage of a project in which there is insufficient information for estimating the likelihood of risk occurrence (Zou, Zhang & Wang, 2007). Risk premium only gives a very rough estimate on the impact of the risks on the project outcome (Azari,Mousavi, Mousavi & Hosseini, 2011). Expected Monetary Value (EMV) is similar to risk premium in that the expected value of all risks, rather than individual risk is determined. In this approach, the probability of the consequence a risk under a number of scenarios, rather than one scenario, will be considered. The number of scenarios to be considered can be ranged from two scenarios – best and worst scenarios must equal one. The expected monetary value is thus given by the summation of the consequence multiplied by its associated probabilities in each scenario (Wang, & Yuan, 2011). Sensitivity Analysis is used to test the vulnerability of options to unavoidable future uncertainties. Given the likely range of values that key variables may take in the presence of uncertainties, the way in which the conclusions may alter will be considered (Hayford & Partner, 2006). This is particularly useful at the option appraisal stage for understanding how uncertainties affect the choice between options (Menches & Hanna, 2006). Very often, the advantage of the preferred option will be eroded in light of the uncertainties. The use of sensitivity analysis can test the robustness of the appraisal conclusions. This also provides value information on whether a proposal should proceed or not in spite of the risk. A switching value will be calculated which shows how a variable would have to fall or rise to make it not worthwhile in undertaking an option (Awodele, Ogunlana & Motawa, 2010).

At the business case stage, quantitative analysis of each individual risk is required during the construction of the infrastructure in which the value of risk is one of the components of the PSC (Ayeni, 2005). However, it may not be possible to quantify every risk because of the lack of data and/or the difficulties in quantifying the consequence. In addition, the availability of time and resources also affect the choice of approaches (Nguyen & Ogunlana, 2005). In general, approach that gives reliable result should be employed to assess risks that have a serious impact on the project. Quantitative approach with advanced probability technique should be used to assess risks which are classified as 'Extreme' and 'High' significance in the qualitative or semi-quantitative approaches (El-Sayegh, 2008).

At the procurement stage, the value for money will hinge on the level and cost of risk transferred to the private sector. The risk assessment carried out at the business case stage is based on the public sector client's preferred risk allocation (Dikmen, I., Birgonul, Anac, Tah & Aouad, 2008). The private sector may negotiate with the public sector client on the allocation of certain risks. In addition, new information regarding the risk will have changed the value of the risk. This may also affect the results of the value for money assessment. Before the award of the contract, final value for money assessment should be performed to ensure that the modifications made to the allocation of risk after negotiations with the private sector also deliver value for money (Xiao & Zhang, 2011). This necessitates quantification of the transferred and retained risks again to ensure that value for money is delivered for the finalized allocation of risks.

Risk Analysis

Identification and classification of risk is usually followed by risk analysis, that is, the possibility and the consequences of each risk factor are examined in order to establish the level of risk of our project. Normally, risk analysis determines which risk factors would potentially have a greater impact on our project and, therefore, must be managed by the entrepreneur with particular care. Mubin and Mannan (2013) claims the most important task of risk management is to analyze risk to provide an integral solution to decision-maker. Raja (2015) proposes that a simple method for considering project risks would be to analyze any risk independent of others, with no attempt to estimate the probability of occurrence of that risk. The estimated effects of each risk could then be accumulated to provide total project outcome values. According to Maniar (2010) assert another approach, though more complex, greater realism and confidence can be achieved by applying probabilities to risks and considering the inter-dependencies between the risks. The two most useful techniques for doing so are sensitivity analysis and probability analysis, as we will discuss later. De Marco and Thaheem (2014) avers the essence of risk analysis is that it attempts to capture all feasible options and to analyze various outcomes. By giving specific weighted number to each option, decision-maker is able to quantify risk and respond to it. Firmansyah, Veronika, and Trigunarsyah (2006) propose that the choice of a risk analysis technique to be used should be based on following factors: - type and size of project, information available, cost of the analysis and the time available to carry it out and experience of the analyst. Berg (2010) warns that the application of any risk analysis technique requires that the uncertain data can be given a range of different values. For example, if the duration and costs for specific activities are uncertain, use a range of values within which the decision maker believes they are likely to lie.

In the risk analysis stage, managers try to estimate the overall magnitude of the risk, and the expected losses. Typically, the risk event drivers and their impact drivers are determined at this stage. Any risk event that cannot be justified through probability of occurrence and impact is automatically dropped from the risk register. Broadly speaking, risks can be analyzed either qualitatively or quantitatively, depending on the purpose, required degree of detail, and the data and resources available for analysis. However, Bagui and Ghosh (2011) articulate that risk analysis has three kinds of methods to determine the level of risk for the organization. These methods are qualitative, quantitative and semi-quantitative. In the qualitative risk analysis, risks are subjectively estimated and ranked in a descriptive manner.

Iloiu and Csiminga (2009) describe qualitative risk analysis as the process of prioritizing risks for subsequent further analysis or action by assessing and combining their probability and impact. Qualitative estimation can be used for the following purposes: as an initial screening activity to identify risks that require more detailed estimation; when it provides sufficient information for decision making; or where available data or resources are insufficient for a quantitative estimation (Apanavičienė & Rudžianskaitė-Kvaraciejienė, 2010). Because of such analysis, risks can be rated, for example, as high, moderate, or low. Qualitative risk analysis is usually a rapid and cost-effective means of establishing priorities for risk response planning, and lays the foundation for quantitative risk analysis. As in risk identification, reviews of process documentation, past experiences or lessons learned from previous projects can be good sources of the information needed to prioritize the identified risks. This enables an update to be made to the risk register (Ajayi & Isah, 2014). Risks are listed in terms of their probability and impact in matrix form, which the project manager can use to focus attention on those risks with high significance to the project where responses can lead to better project outcomes. In the risk register, risks may also be grouped by categories showing the root causes of risks or areas of the project that require particular or urgent attention and those that can be handled later. From this, some risk items will go straight to the response stage, while some may require further analysis, such as quantitative risk analysis.

Qualitative risk analysis assesses the impact and likelihood of the identified risks and develops prioritized lists of these risks for further analysis or direct mitigation (Jin, 2010a). The project team assesses each identified risk for its probability of occurrence and its impact on project objectives. Project teams may elicit assistance from subject matter experts or functional units to assess the risks in their respective fields. Qualitative risk analysis can be used by project teams: As an initial screening or review of project risks (Ling & Hoi, 2006). Qualitative techniques include the definition of risk, the recording of risk details and relationships, and the categorization and prioritization of risks relative to each other Risk identification, results in the generation of a risk register (Agyakwa-Baah, Chileshe & Fugar, 2010). The risk register can be sizeable; it is necessary to evaluate and prioritize the risk events identified in the risk register. Evaluation and prioritization is typically accomplished by the project team and is an iterative process and can take place at various points in project development. In some cases, the project team may enlist help from cost risk experts and subject matter experts to evaluate and prioritize the risks.

Quantitative method is the kind of risk analysis method most often used for decision making in business projects; entrepreneurs base themselves on their judgment, experience and intuition for decision making. It can be used when the level of risk is low and does not warrant the time and resources necessary for making a full analysis. It can also be used when the numerical data available are not adequate for a more quantitative analysis that would serve as the basis for a subsequent and more detailed analysis of the entrepreneur's global risk. Chileshe and Kikwasi (2013) indicate that quantitative risk analysis is performed on risks that have been prioritized through the qualitative risk analysis process as potentially and substantially influencing the project's competing demands. Quantitative risk analysis is the process of numerically analyzing the effect on overall project objectives (Grace, 2010). The evaluation of both consequences and probability are based on data from a variety of sources, for example past project records, collected field data, experimental data (including prototype testing). Quantitative risk analysis is often used when the need to predict with confidence the probability of completing a project on time, on budget, at the agreed-upon scope, and/or the agree-upon quality is critical (Thaheem, 2012).Enshassi, Mohamed and Abu-Mosa (2008) identified some of the quantitative risk analysis tools and techniques currently in use: statistical probability distribution; simple multi-attribute rating technique; expected value technique; sensitivity analysis; decision trees; Bayes' theorem; simulation; utility theory; analytic hierarchy process; fuzzy-set theory; neuro-fuzzy networks; and financial methods.

Risk Control and Monitoring

Risk monitoring and control is a process of identifying, analyzing, and planning for newly arising risks, keeping track of the identified risks and those on the watch list, reanalyzing existing risks, monitoring trigger conditions for contingency plans, monitoring residual risks, and reviewing the execution of risk responses while evaluating their effectiveness (May & Koski, 2013). The purpose of this stage is to determine if: project assumptions are still valid, risks as assessed has changed, proper risk management policies and procedures are being followed. These become necessary so as ensure the successful implementation of the project with a guarantee degree of success. Risk monitoring and control tracks identified risks, monitors residual risks, and identifies new risks—ensuring the execution of risk plans and evaluating their effectiveness in reducing risk. Risk monitoring and control is an ongoing process for the life of the project (Loosemore, Raftery, Reilly & Higgon, 2006). Perhaps the phrase "control is an illusion" is familiar. It requires a blend of qualitative judgments and quantitative measures to determine the "health" of the project. The Project Manager must document the response action by describing the action, the work activities it will affect, and the cost of the response action. Identify the person(s) responsible for successful implementation of the response action (Ogunsanmi, Salako & Ajayi, 2011). Also, consider the time impacts of the response action and how the risk response may affect the overall project and/or other risks. The Project Manager determines appropriate metrics for the project, ensuring they are not burdensome and do not affect behavior. Too often, metrics change behavior to provide better metrics, not better performance (Ogbu, 2013). Set the amounts and conditions for use of the project risk reserves. Establish the final objectives of the project with stakeholders to improve the chances of project success. Confirm endorsement of team members and stakeholders as the project plan evolves. It is therefore apparent that managers responsible for risk monitoring and control try to focus on the proposed processes and responses available for the identified risks. The outputs of the other five stages must be kept under review as things evolve. Changes in the environment, or simply the discovery of better information, may render the original assessment out of date, thereby triggering the need for reassessment (Beisheim, Liese & Vosseler, 2014). Periodic reassessment of risks (re-measurement) and risk audits should be carried out. Risk audits examine and document the effectiveness of risk responses in dealing with identified risks and their root causes, as well as the effectiveness of the risk management process.

Kerzner (2009) argues that risk monitoring and control is not a problem-solving technique but is rather a proactive technique to obtain objective information on the progress to date of reducing risks to acceptable levels. Earned Value Analysis (EVA) or other methods of project variance and trend analysis (for example programme metrics, scheduled performance monitoring and technical performance measurement) could be used to monitor overall performance; deviation from the baseline plan may indicate the potential impact of new threats (Nisar, 2007). It is not generally necessary to begin the whole process over again when this happens unless the change or deviation is particularly profound, though those parts that are directly affected by changing circumstances must be brought up to date.

Risk Control

Risk control does not attempt to remove the source of the risk, but seeks to reduce the risk itself (Marques & Berg, 2011). Risk controls should be determined according to six main hierarchies called 'hierarchy of control'. Where appropriate, Berg (2010) advices that the hierarchy be used in the following order: elimination, substitution, isolation, engineering, administration and personal protective equipment (PPE). The elimination hierarchy of control is the top most measures involving eliminating or removing the risk in its entirety. For example, risk- high levels of manual handling when loading and unloading glassware onto trolleys from shelving; control- store glassware directly onto trolleys hence eliminating the need to unload and load from the shelves. Substitution is a form of control involving substituting a safer process or material for the hazardous process/material identified. Isolation control involves separating the hazard or hazardous work practice from employees other work areas. This may involves sectioning off the area by erecting barriers or by relocating either the hazardous work practice or the "other" employees and their work practice (Parvinen, Kujala, Lillrank and Kouri, 2005). For example, risk- excessive noise emanating from machinery, control- enclosing the machinery or the personnel hence creates an isolating barrier between the hazard and the person by using a barrier.

Engineering controls involves designing and/or adding physical safety features to plant or equipment (Osipova & Eriksson, 2013). It can be done in four aspects. First equipment and workplace design involves the provision of new and/or additional equipment or redesign of a workplace can be used to control identified hazards. For example, risk-animal handling, control- hoists, slide boards. Or risk- a poor clerical workstation design resulting in a risk of injury to the back, neck, shoulder and wrist; control- re-design the workstation to recommend ergonomic specifications for the personnel including the provision of equipment such as slope-boards, document holders, foot stools and ergonomic chairs. Automation fully or partially automating a process removes the need for, or reduces the risk of, performing a hazardous task. For example, risk-manual handling in washing glassware process, control- introduction of an automatic washing system. For example: risk: Chemical fumes given off during cleaning, laboratory, or welding processes, control- construction of a local extraction system to remove the fumes at the source. Guarding in which guards must be provided when there is the potential for people to come into contact with hazardous situations to ensure that no part of the person (including hair, clothing etc) can be caught in the moving part (Arain & Pheng, 2005). There are several different types of guards, movable/

interlocked, fixed, and photoelectric beam. For example, risk- accessible high speed rotating parts on a machine, control- placing appropriate guards to prevent access to the rotating parts.

Administrative control is most effective when used in conjunction with measures mentioned above or as an interim control whilst more effective control measures are developed and implemented. It requires systems to be established or amended in order to control the risk presented (Dwivedi, Papazafeiropoulou, Brinkman & Lal, 2010). Most often it requires the assessment and modification of the task(s) performed. It may include measures such as: amendment or establishment of new policy and procedures. For example, developing documented safe work practices for a hazardous task, or implementing restrictive policy to prevent staff or students from coming in contact with identified hazards. The introduction or review of existing maintenance schedules for plant and equipment, or safe work practices (Doloi, Iyer & Sawhney, 2011). This measure is used to ensure that existing plant, equipment and procedures do not deteriorate to the point where they become hazardous. These types of hazards can include: noise, radiation, heat, chemicals, etc., and can be controlled by introducing elements as simple as job rotation. Providing training and information in safe work practices and other workplace health issues so that personnel can work safely.

Atkinson, Crawford and Ward (2006) reminds that PPE is not a particularly effective control method and should only be used: when all other control measures are impractical; or in conjunction with other more effective, control measures. It is important to select the correct PPE for the hazard identified, and advice should be sought in this regard if you are not sure (Eaton, Akbiyukli & Dickinson, 2006). However, the "Hierarchy of Control" provides a basic guide for controlling hazards in the workplace. Once appropriate controls are identified it is necessary to consult senior management and the staff that will be affected by the changes. This will reduce the possibility of oversights and help to gain the support of the staff in the implementation phase. Caglio and Ditillo (2008) contend that control of risk and management activities can be done through: - the project manager must specify criteria for risk management success, including targets and measures used to assess performance. They further suggest follow up with risk owners regarding the status of completing the risk response actions and the resulting effect; track resource allocation(s) associated with risk response actions.

Risk Monitoring

Mitra (2010) recommends that it's important to carry out risk monitoring because the profile of the identified risks will change, and new risks will emerge as a project proceeds. The purpose of monitoring to monitor the effectiveness of risk treatment measures, to identify any new risks that arise as the project process and formulate the risk treatment measures accordingly. The implementation of these response strategies requires proper monitoring to ensure there is no deviation from the original plan (Geraldi, 2008). Risk monitoring encourages monitoring the project status, looking for trends that can indicate variations (good and bad) in the project execution. Results of the analysis need to be communicated and adjustments made through a change management and/or issue resolution process. The ability to describe the history of the project and how it evolved is essential to developing lessons learned for the future (Oyewobi, Ibrahim & Ganiyu, 2012). Useful hints are bee thorough and tenacious in gathering status update information for risks, monitor status and trends continually (scope, schedule, cost estimates, quality of product, etc.) and address problems and issues immediately; in fact, anticipate and discuss in advance if possible as well as communicate.

Risk monitoring entails commitment of the project team to making effective use of the actionable information that emerges from risk identification and analysis (Bouder, Slavin & Lofstedt, 2009). This aids in developing an appropriate risk response strategy. In this case, according to Dada (2010), risk response strategy is the process of the team determining what, if anything should be done with identified risks significant enough to impact project objectives. It leads to specific actions what will be incorporated into the Project Management Plan (PMP) and work plans and then proactively executed. Later on, the project team can then pursue response actions for threats (avoid, transfer, mitigate, reduce) and opportunities (exploit, share, enhance), or the team can accept the risk event if the response action is not cost-effective. Camilleri (2011) advices the project team should promptly develop and implement response actions following identification and analysis. Risks have a shelf life, and Risk Management Plans (RMPs) can become stale if not monitored and updated regularly. Patanakul (.2015) strongly urged for commitment of the project tea, to making use of information when it is fresh and keeping our PMPs and RMPs up to date so they do not lapse into irrelevance because they have become outdated and obsolete.

Risk monitoring aid the project team to capture the inevitable fact that as a project develops, its risk profile will change. The team would then have to identify the risks and ensure that the response actions are implemented, which changes the nature of the project risk profile and new risks are identified. During risk monitoring the project team identifies risk events. The first time this is accomplished, it constitutes a list of primary risks; as actions are taken, secondary risks can emerge as a result of implementing the treatment response to the primary risk (Sun & Meng, 2009). Where possible, the project team should deal with secondary risks as part of the primary risk response action. When developing the response actions, the project team ought to be vigilant in considering the ramifications of the response actions. Dallas (2000) insinuates that the project team should take measures to include strategies that deal with the primary risk as well as secondary risks and endeavor to minimize or eliminate residual risk as part of risk response efforts.

Dikmen, Birgonul and Han (2007) recommend that the requirements for an effective risk monitoring have to include: project team; record assumptions that underlie judgments and decisions; monitor and document results of implemented risk response actions; upper management and executives; avoid unpleasant surprises; fully inform parties of risks, response actions, and trade-offs; accountability. The Project Manager documents the risk assessment process in such a way that it can be reviewed and examined to learn the reasons particular judgments and decisions were made. Continuous monitoring by the project risk manager and the project team ensures that new and changing risks are detected and managed and that risk response actions are implemented and effective. Risk monitoring continues for the life of the project. Risk monitoring keeps track of the identified risks, residual risks, and new risks (El-Sayegh, 2008). It also monitors the execution of planned strategies for the identified risks and evaluates their effectiveness. Risk monitoring and control continues for the life of the project. The list of project risks changes as the project matures, new risks develop, or anticipated risks disappear. Risk ratings and prioritizations can also change during the project lifecycle.

Regular risk monitoring aids in establishing whether there has been regular meetings during the project execution. Typically, during project execution, risk meetings should be held regularly to update the status of risks in the risk register, and add new risks. Periodic project risk reviews repeat the process of identification, analysis, and response planning. If an unanticipated risk emerges, or a risk's impact is greater than expected, the planned response may not be adequate (Busch & Givens, 2013). Monitoring also determines whether the project management committee (PMC) is performing periodic risk review and updating; risk management policies and procedures are being followed; the remaining contingency reserves for cost and schedule are adequate. And it may involve recommending: alternative risk responses; implementing a contingency plan; taking corrective actions; and changing the project objectives (Swan & Khalfan, 2007).

The monitoring and review process for risk management has to take place on three levels: First, adequacy and effectiveness of internal control have to be monitored, evaluated and reported for every single internal control action (Hans, Dickmann & Ock, 2005). It is extremely important for the evolution of risk management in an organization to communicate and share lessons learned at this level. Second, the general risk profile of the organization and eventual changes in uncertainties have to be monitored to allow an early identification of upcoming risks early enough and to stop internal control on outdated risks. The monitoring process can, if need be, entail the redistribution of resources (Nagaraju, Reddy & Chauduri, 2012). Again it is crucial at this stage to communicate with partners, stakeholders, and the environment in general. Third, the progress of the implementation of risk management itself has to be monitored and fostered.

Risk Auditing and Reporting

Monitoring and control are not complete unless auditing and reporting have occurred (Iossa & Martimort, 2015). Following a review, important developments – such as a change in importance from orange to red – should be communicated through reporting and escalation. Communicating risks to partners and stakeholders also allows the organization that risks are being managed on both sides. While communication and reporting are an ongoing process, reporting on specific risks should primarily be included in existing reporting and communication mechanisms (Sarmento, 2010). An up-to-date version of the risk profile should be available, for example to help auditors. Communication is the lynch-pin of effective project management and risk management. Communication within and among the project team will be crisp, concise, complete, correct, and timely, as will the communication to upper management and executives (Dikmen & Birgonol, 2006). Effectiveness of the risk response actions will be monitored and reported regularly, as indicated previously, at our project meetings; adjustments will be made as needed.

According to Bowlin (2011), the core audit role in PPP includes; giving assurance on the risk management process, giving assurance that risks are correctly evaluated, evaluating risk management process, evaluating the reporting of key risks, reviewing the management of key risks, legitimate internal audit roles with safeguards, facilitating identification and evaluation of risks, coaching management in responding to risks, coordinating public private partnership activities, consolidating reporting on risk, maintaining and developing public private partnership risk management framework, championing establishment of public private partnership risk management, developing public private partnership risk management strategies for parties' approval.The roles audit should not undertake accountability for risk management, implementing risk response on management's behalf, taking decisions on risk responses, management assurance on risk, imposing risk management plan, and setting the risk appetite (Shaoul, 2005b).

On the discretion of the higher management of the Organization, risks should also be reviewed in the context of other major processes and functions that have a bearing on the achievement of expected strategic outcomes/results, such as, monitoring and evaluation, project management, standing committees, requests for extra budgetary funding, and proposals and reports to oversight bodies. The matrix of the main strategic risks facing the Organization can also be reviewed throughout the planning process with the aim of reducing the number of high risk items (Li, Li & Deng, 2008). Organizations have to maintain a state of continuous alertness with regard to changing patterns in their operating environment (societal, political, legal, physical) once the risk profile has been mapped. This constant updating and sharing of what they know, of error reporting, at what they are doing is the essence of organizational situation awareness, which is key to decision making and risk management (Dudkin & Välilä, 2005). There are two reasons for reviewing and reporting risks: measuring the effectiveness in the way the risks are being managed and gaining assurance that the process is working, and monitoring whether the risk profile is changing (Delmon, 2009). In all cases, ensure that reporting and communications are accurate, as complete as possible, and regularly updated to reflect reality to the best of your knowledge. Remember that risk formulation and risk reporting are essential for the understanding of issues at stake.

A key aspect of Risk Management is based upon experience, especially the experience of dealing with risk on prior projects. Thus, the importance of documenting project information and experiences is critical. This documentation allows for capturing lessons learned and eventually feeding these lessons back into each of the five risk phases (Choi & Mahadevan, 2008). Capturing and feeding back lessons learned improves the Risk Management process and makes continuous improvement a precedent that will ultimately strengthen the Risk Management Framework. Review and communicate risks, at least as often as performance is reviewed, to see if: further action is needed; appropriate controls are in place; new uncertainties are emerging; and changes to the PPP project's strategic uncertainties require unit level action (Dixon, Pottinger & Jordan, 2005). Best practice for reviews is to use existing management/staff meetings, not to create new mechanisms. Involve relevant focal points and experts to constructively challenge the unit's risk management.

CONCLUSION

Partners' intervention, in the form of risk management framework and in the provision of measures for a risk-free PPP project, is necessary due to PPP project failures (constraints and challenges of PPP), but a properly designed risk management framework is the key to the evolution of a risk-free PPP and authenticity of quality service delivery. Both partners should be brought into the partnership with a clear view of the frame of the risk management framework, for overcoming subjective bias in the design of the risk management framework wherever possible.

PPP project can only thrive where risk management framework plays a leading role in promoting a risk-free environment, especially risk management fundamentals, although in the course and over time estimation, mitigation and transfer/allocation will become increasingly necessary as the project is initiated and progresses on. Risk management process, as a means of correcting PPP initiation and implementation-induced distortions, is an important ingredient of the symbiotic growth of risk-free PPP project. To sustain the momentum for such a growth, mechanism for proper risk identification must be in place. Pending the development of a proper RMP, risk assessment will remain important for establishing authentic risks to be planned for. Seriously engaged partners will continue to tap into the risk management process by critically analyzing risks in a fully pledged systematic manner. The partners should also develop a concrete control and monitoring mechanism. In other words, both partners should focus on addressing PPP project failures through risk control. As the PPP project failure in realizing the ends declines in importance, both partners should increasingly focus on carrying out risk monitoring. For it is risk auditing and reporting that will be the engine of future PPP project success.

REFERENCES

Abednego, M. P., & Ogunlana, S. O. (2006). Good project governance for proper risk allocation in public-private partnership in Indonesia. *International Journal of Project Management*, *24*(7), 622–634. doi:10.1016/j.ijproman.2006.07.010

Adams, J., Alistair, Y., & Wu, Z. H. (2006). Public private partnerships in China-system, constraints and future prospects. *International Journal of Public Sector Management*, *19*(4), 384–396. doi:10.1108/09513550610669202

Agyakwa-Baah, A., Chileshe, N., & Fugar, F. D. K. (2010). Perceptions to barriers to risk assessment and management practices deployment: Opinion survey findings. *Journal of Construction*, *3*(2), 17–23.

Ahmed, A., Kayis, B., & Amornsawadwatana, S. (2007). A review of techniques for risk management in projects. *Benchmark International Journal*, *14*(1), 22–36. doi:10.1108/14635770710730919

Ajayi, J. R., & Isah, Y. (2014). Impediments to risk assessment techniques in public-private partnership construction projects in Abuja-Nigeria. *Malaysian Journal of Civil Engineering*, *26*(3), 366–381.

Aldoory, L., & Sha, B. L. (2007). The situational theory of publics: Practical applications, methodological challenges, and theoretical horizons. In The future of excellence in public relations and communication management: Challenges for the next generation. Mahwah, NJ: Lawrence Erlbaum.

Ali, R. (2005). The Application of risk management in infrastructural construction projects. *Journal of Cost Engineering*, *47*(8), 20–27.

Alonso-Conde, A. B., Brown, C., & Rojo-Suarez, J. (2007). Public private partnerships: Incentives, risk transfer and real options. *Review of Financial Economics*, *16*(4), 335–349. doi:10.1016/j.rfe.2007.03.002

Ameyaw, E.E., & Chan, A.P.C. (2013). Identifying public-private partnership (PPP) risks in managing water supply projects in Ghana. *Journal of Facilities Management*, *11*(2), 152–182..10.1108/14725961311314651

Ammar, A., Berman, K., & Sataporn, A. (2007). A review of techniques for risk management in projects. *Benchmarking: An International Journal*, *14*(1), 22–36. doi:10.1108/14635770710730919

Andi, P. (2006). The importance and allocation of risks in Indonesian construction projects. *Construction Management and Economics*, *24*(1), 69–80. doi:10.1080/01446190500310338

Antuchevičiene, J., Turskis, Z., & Zavadskas, E. K. (2006). Modelling renewal of construction objects applying methods of the game theory. *Ukio Technologinis ir Ekonominis Vystymas*, *12*(4), 263-268.

Apanavičienė, R., & Rudžianskaitė-Kvaraciejienė, R. (2010). *Analysis of evaluation methodologies for public-private partnership (PPP) projects in infrastructure construction.* Paper presented at the 10th international conference on modern building materials, structures and techniques, Vilnus, Lithuania.

Arain, F. M., & Pheng, L. S. (2005). The potential effects of variation orders on institutional building projects. *Facilities*, *23*(11/12), 496–510. doi:10.1108/02632770510618462

Atkinson, R., Crawford, L., & Ward, S. (2006). Fundamental uncertainties in projects and the scope of project management. *International Journal of Project Management, 24*(8), 687–698. doi:10.1016/j.ijproman.2006.09.011

Avazkhah, H., & Mohebbi, A. (2010). *Project risk management.* Tehran: KianRayanehSabz.

Awodele, O. A., Ogunlana, S. O., & Motawa, I. (2010). Understanding and managing risks necessary condition for success and sustainability of privately financed market projects in Nigeria.*Proceedings of ARCOM Doctoral Researcher Workshop on Sustainability Strategies in the UK Construction Industry at University of Wolverhampton on 25th June.*

Ayeni, K. (2005). Risk identification and management in BOT Project Implementation. *Proceedings of BOT Awareness Seminar, Abuja Investment and Property Development Company.*

Azar, A., Zangoueinezhad, A., Elahi, S., & Moghbel, A. (2013). Assessing and understanding the key risks in a PPP power station projects. *Advances in Management & Applied Economics, 3*(1), 11–33.

Azari, A. R. K., Mousavi, N., Mousavi, S. F., & Hosseini, S. B. (2011). Risk assessment model selection in construction industry. *Expert Systems with Applications, 38*(8), 9105–9111. doi:10.1016/j.eswa.2010.12.110

Badenfelt, U. (2008). The selection of sharing ratios in target cost contracts. *Engineering, Construction, and Architectural Management, 15*(1), 54–65. doi:10.1108/09699980810842061

Bagui, S. K., & Ghosh, A. (2011). Risk Analysis for a BOT Project. *Jordan Journal of Civil Engineering, 5*(3), 330–342.

Barlish, K., De Marco, A., & Thaheem, M. J. (2013). Construction Risk Taxonomy: An International Convergence of Academic and Industry Perspectives. *American Journal of Applied Sciences, 10*(7), 706–713. doi:10.3844/ajassp.2013.706.713

Barlow, J., Roehrich, J., & Wright, S. (2013). Europe sees mixed results from public-private partnerships for building and managing health care facilities and services. *Health Affairs, 32*(1), 146–154. doi:10.1377/hlthaff.2011.1223 PMID:23297282

Bedell, D. (2007). Taking risk beyond regulation. *Global Finance, 21*(6), 58–60.

Beisheim, M., Liese, A., & Vosseler, C. (2014). Who governs partnerships? On the role of boards, donors, partners, and other stakeholders. In Transnational partnerships: effectively providing for sustainable development? London: Palgrave Macmillan.

Berg, H.-P. (2010). Risk management: Procedures, methods and experiences. *RT&T, 1*(2), 79–95.

Bing, L., Akintoye, A., Edwards, P., & Hardcastle, C. (2005a). Perceptions of positive and negative factors influencing the attractiveness of PPP procurement for construction projects in the UK – Findings from a questionnaire survey. *Engineering, Construction, and Architectural Management, 12*(2), 125–148. doi:10.1108/09699980510584485

Bing, L., Akintoye, A., Edwards, P. J., & Hardcastle, C. (2005b). The allocation of risk in PPP construction projects in the UK. *International Journal of Project Management*, *23*(1), 25–35. doi:10.1016/j.ijproman.2004.04.006

Boardman, A. E., Poschmann, F., & Vining, A. (2005). North American infrastructure P3s: examples and lessons learned. In The Challenge Of Public-Private Partnerships: Learning From International Experience. Cheltenham, UK: Edward Elgar Publishing. doi:10.4337/9781845428082.00014

Bolvin, C., Farret, R., & Salvi, O. (2007). Convergence towards integrated risk management: results from the European SHAPE-RISK project and other initiatives.*Proc. ESREL*, 1683-1687.

Bon-Gang, H., Xianbo, Z., & Ping, T. L. (2014). Risk management in small construction projects in Singapore: Status, barriers and impact. *International Journal of Project Management*, *32*(1), 116–124. doi:10.1016/j.ijproman.2013.01.007

Bouder, F., Slavin, D., & Lofstedt, R. E. (2009). *The Tolerability of Risk: A New Framework for Risk Management*. London: Earthscan.

Boussabaine, A. (2007). *Cost planning of PFI and PPP building projects*. London: Taylor &Francis.

Bowlin, K. (2011). Risk-based auditing, strategic prompts, and auditor sensitivity to the strategic risk of fraud. *Accounting Review*, *86*(4), 1231–1253. doi:10.2308/accr-10039

Buertey, J. I. T., Abeere-Inga, E., & Kumi, T. A. (2012). Estimating cost contingency for construction projects: The challenge of systemic and project specific risk. *Journal of Construction Project Management and Innovation*, *2*(1), 166–189.

Busch, N. E., & Givens, A. D. (2013). Achieving resilience in disaster management: The role of public-private partnerships. *Journal of Strategic Security*, *6*(2), 1–19. doi:10.5038/1944-0472.6.2.1

Caglio, A., & Ditillo, A. (2008). A Review and discussion of management control in inter-firm relationships: Achievements and future directions. *Accounting, Organizations and Society, 33*(7–8), 865-898.

Camilleri, E. (2011). *Project Success: Critical Factors and Behaviors*. Surrey, UK: Gower Publishing Limited.

Campbell, S., & Currie, G. (2006). Against Beck: In defense of risk analysis. *Philosophy of the Social Sciences*, *36*(2), 149–172. doi:10.1177/0048393106287209

Carbonara, N., Costantino, N., Pellegrino, R., & Sciancalepore, F. (2011). Risk Management in PPP: Real Option Theory. *Symposium Public Private Partnerships in Transport: Trends & Theory- Research Roadmap* (pp. 1-3). Lisbon: European Cooperation in Science and Technology. Retrieved August 10, 2016, from http://www.ppptransport.eu/index.php?option=com_k2&view=item&task=download&id35

Chan, A. P. C., Lam, P. T. I., Chan, D. W. M. M., Cheung, E., & Ke, Y. (2010). Potential obstacles to successful implementation of public private partnerships in Beijing and the Hong Kong special administrative region. *Journal of Management Engineering*, *1*(30), 30–40. doi:10.1061/(ASCE)0742-597X(2010)26:1(30)

Chan, A. P. C., Lam, P. T. I., Wen, Y., Ameyaw, E. E., Wang, S. Q., & Ke, Y. (2015). Cross- sectional analysis of critical risk factors for PPP water projects in China. *Journal of Infrastructure Systems*, *21*(1), 04014031. doi:10.1061/(ASCE)IS.1943-555X.0000214

Chan, A. P. C., Yeung, J. F. Y., Yu, C. C. P., Wang, S. Q., & Ke, Y. (2011). Empirical study of risk assessment and allocation of public-private partnership projects in China. *Journal of Management Engineering*, *27*(3), 136–148. doi:10.1061/(ASCE)ME.1943-5479.0000049

Chileshe, N., & Kikwasi, G. J. (2013). Perception of barriers to implementing risk assessment and management practices by construction professional in Tanzania. In *Proceedings of the 29th Annual ARCOM Conference*. Reading, UK: Association of Researchers in Construction Management.

Chiu, T., & Bosher, C. (2005). Risk sharing in various public private partnerships arrangements for the provision of water and wastewater services. *Proceedings of the Conference on Public Private Partnerships—Opportunities and Challenges*, 11–21.

Choi, H., & Mahadevan, S. (2008). Construction project risk assessment using existing database and project-specific information. *Journal of Construction Engineering and Management*, *134*(11), 894–903. doi:10.1061/(ASCE)0733-9364(2008)134:11(894)

Choi, J., Chung, J., & Lee, D. J. (2010). Risk perception analysis: Participation in Chinas water PPP market. *International Journal of Project Management*, *28*(6), 580–592. doi:10.1016/j.ijproman.2009.10.010

Chung, D., Hensher, D. A., & Rose, J. M. (2010). Toward the betterment of risk allocation: Investigating risk perceptions of Australian stakeholder groups to public-private- partnership Tollroad Projects. *Research in Transportation Economics*, *30*(1), 43–58. doi:10.1016/j.retrec.2010.10.007

Cook, J. (2007). *U.S. PPP Market on the Upswing: Some Thoughts from Abroad", IP3's Public- Private Partnership Information Series*. Available: http://www.ip3.org/pub/2007_publication_002.htm

Cooper, D., Grey, S., Raymond, G., & Walker, P. (2005). *Project Risk Management Guidelines: Managing Risk in Large Projects and Complex Procurements*. Chichester, UK: John Wiley & Sons Ltd.

Cretu, O., Stewart, R. B., & Berends, T. (2011). *Risk management for design and construction (RSMeans)*. Hoboken, NJ: John Wiley & Sons.

Csiszar, E. N. (2008). Managing risk and uncertainty. *Business and Economic Review*, *55*(1), 3–7.

Dada, J. O. (2010). *Strategies for mitigating risk in construction projects*. Paper presented the 40th Annual General Meeting/Conference of the Nigerian Institute of Builders.

Dallas, M. (2006). *Value and risk management; a guide to best practice*. Oxford, UK: Blackwell Publication.

De Marco, A., & Thaheem, M. J. (2014). Risk analysis in construction projects: A practical selection methodology. *American Journal of Applied Sciences*, *11*(1), 74–84. doi:10.3844/ajassp.2014.74.84

Delmon, J. (2009). *Private sector investment in infrastructure project finance - PPP projects and risks* (2nd ed.). Austin, TX: Wolters Kluwer.

Dey, P. K. (2010). Managing project risk using combined analytic hierarchy process and risk map. *Applied Soft Computing*, *10*(4), 990–1000. doi:10.1016/j.asoc.2010.03.010

Diab, M. F., Naser, K., & Varma, A. (2012). *Using risk assessment to improve highway construction project performance*. Paper presented at the 48th ASC Annual International Conference. Retrieved from https://www.researchgate.net/profile/Khaled_Nassar6/publication/266055014_Using_Ris k_Assessment_to_Improve_Highway_Construction_Project_Performance/links/54b7b51 80cf24eb34f6ed082.pdf

Dikmen, I., & Birgonol, N. T. (2006). An Analytic Hierarchy Process based model for risk and opportunities assessment of international construction project. *Canadian Journal of Civil Engineering*, *33*(1), 58–68. doi:10.1139/l05-087

Dikmen, I., Birgonul, M. T., Anac, C., Tah, J. H. M., & Aouad, G. (2008). Learning from risks: A tool for post-project risk assessment. *Automation in Construction*, *18*(1), 42–50. doi:10.1016/j.autcon.2008.04.008

Dikmen, I., Birgonul, N. T., & Han, S. (2007). Using fuzzy risk assessment to rate cost overrun risk in international construction projects. *International Journal of Project Management*, *25*(5), 494–505. doi:10.1016/j.ijproman.2006.12.002

Dixon, T., Pottinger, G., & Jordan, A. (2005). Lessons from the private finance initiative in the UK: Benefits, problems and critical success factors. *Journal of Property Investment & Finance*, *23*(5), 412–423. doi:10.1108/14635780510616016

Doloi, H., Iyer, K. C., & Sawhney, A. (2011). Structural equation model for assessing impacts of contractors performance on project success. *International Journal of Project Management*, *29*(6), 687–695. doi:10.1016/j.ijproman.2010.05.007

Donahue, J. D., & Zeckhauser, R. J. (2011). *Collaborative governance: Private roles for public goals in turbulent times*. Princeton, NJ: Princeton University Press. doi:10.1515/9781400838103

Dudkin, G., & Välilä, T. (2005). *Transaction Cost in Public-Private Partnership: A First Look at the Evidence. EIB Economic and Financial Report 2005/03*. Luxembourg: European Investment Bank.

Dwivedi, Y. K., Papazafeiropoulou, A., Brinkman, W. P., & Lal, B. (2010). Examining the influence of service quality and secondary influence on the behavioral intention to change internet service provider. *Information Systems Frontiers*, *12*(2), 207–217. doi:10.1007/s10796-008-9074-7

Eaton, D., Akbiyukli, R., & Dickinson, M. (2006). An evaluation of the stimulants and impediments to innovation within PFI/PPP projects. *Construction Innovation*, *6*(2), 63–77. doi:10.1108/14714170610710668

El-Sayegh, S. M. (2008). Risk assessment and allocation in the UAE construction industry. *International Journal of Project Management*, *26*(4), 431–438. doi:10.1016/j.ijproman.2007.07.004

Finucane, M. L., & Holup, J. L. (2006). Risk as value: Combining affect and analysis in risk judgments. *Journal of Risk Research*, *9*(2), 141–164. doi:10.1080/13669870500166930

Firmansyah, B. A., Veronika, A., & Trigunarsyah, B. (2006). *Risk analysis in feasibility study of building construction project: case study - pt. Perusahaan gas Negara Indonesia*. Paper presented at the Tenth East Asia-Pacific Conference on Structural Engineering and Construction, Bangkok, Thailand.

Flanagan, R., Norman, G., & Chapman, R. (2006). *Risk management and construction* (2nd ed.). Oxford, UK: Blackwell Publication.

Geraldi, J. G. (2008). The balance between order and chaos in multi-project firms: A conceptual model. *International Journal of Project Management, 26*(4), 348–356. doi:10.1016/j.ijproman.2007.08.013

Grace, K. O. (2010). An assessment of the Construction Site Risks–related factors. *Risk Management in Construction. Proceedings of the 40th annual general meeting/ conference of the Nigerian Institute of Building.*

Gupta, D., & Sharma, M. (2015). Risk management in construction projects of developing countries. *Journal of Civil Engineering and Environmental Technology, 2*(14), 24–26.

Hans, S. H., Dickmann, J. E., & Ock, J. H. (2005). Contractors risk attitudes in the selection of internal construction projects. *ASCE Journal of Construction Economics and Management, 131*(3), 283–292. doi:10.1061/(ASCE)0733-9364(2005)131:3(283)

Hayford, G. J. (2006). *Successfully allocating risk and negotiating a PPP contract.* Paper presented at the 6th Annual National public Private Partnership Summit: Which way now for Australia's PPP Market? Sydney, Australia.

Hayford, O., & Partner, C. U. (2006). Successfully allocating risk and negotiating a PPP contract. *6th Annual National Public Private Partnerships Summit: Which Way Now for Australia's PPP Market?.*

Hillson, D. (2006). *Integrated Risk management as a framework for organizational success.* Retrieved from http://www.risk-doctor.com/pdf-files/adv13.pdf

Hodge, G., & Greve, C. (2005a). Introduction. In G. Hodge & C. Greve (Eds.), *The Challenge of Public-Private Partnerships: Learning from International Experience.* Cheltenham, UK: Edward Elgar Publishing. doi:10.4337/9781845428082

Hodge, G., & Greve, C. (2005b). *The Challenge of Public-Private Partnerships: Learning from International Experience.* Cheltenham, UK: Edward Elgar Pub. doi:10.4337/9781845428082

Hsu, C., & Sandford, B. A. (2007). The Delphi Technique: Making sense of consensus. *Practical Assessment, Research & Evaluation, 12*(10).

Iacob, V. S. (2014). Risk management and evaluation and qualitative method within the projects. *ECO-FORUM, 3*(1), 60–67.

Ibem, E. (2010). An Assessment of the role of government agencies in public private partnerships in housing delivery in Nigeria. *Journal of Construction in Developing Countries, 15*(2), 23–48.

Ibrahim, A. D., Price, A. D. F., & Dainty, A. R. J. (2006). The analysis and allocation of risks in public private partnerships in infrastructure projects in Nigeria. *Journal of Financial Management of Property and Construction, 11*(3), 149–163. doi:10.1108/13664380680001086

Iloiu, M., & Csiminga, D. (2009). Project risk evaluation methods - sensitivity analysis. *Annals of the University of Petroşani. Economics, 9*(2), 33–38.

Iossa, E., & Martimort, D. (2015). The simple microeconomics of public-private partnerships. *Journal of Public Economic Theory*, *17*(1), 4–48. doi:10.1111/jpet.12114

Jin, X. (2011). Model for efficient risk allocation in privately financed public infrastructure projects using neuro-fuzzy techniques. *Journal of Construction Engineering and Management*, *137*(11), 1003–1014. doi:10.1061/(ASCE)CO.1943-7862.0000365

Jin, X. H. (2010a). Determinants of efficient risk allocation in privately financed public infrastructure projects in Australia. *Journal of Construction Engineering and Management*, *136*(2), 138–150. doi:10.1061/(ASCE)CO.1943-7862.0000118

Jin, X. H. (2010b). Neuro-fuzzy decision support system for efficient risk allocation in public- private partnership infrastructure projects. *Journal of Computing in Civil Engineering*, *24*(6), 525–538. doi:10.1061/(ASCE)CP.1943-5487.0000058

Jin, X. H., & Doloi, H. (2008). Interpreting risk allocation mechanism in public-private partnership projects: An empirical study in a transaction cost economics perspective. *Construction Management and Economics*, *26*(7), 707–721. doi:10.1080/01446190801998682

Jin, X. H., & Doloi, H. (2009). Modeling risk allocation in privately financed infrastructure projects using fuzzy logic. *Computer-Aided Civil and Infrastructure Engineering*, *24*(7), 509–524. doi:10.1111/j.1467-8667.2009.00609.x

Jin, X. H., & Zhang, G. (2011). Modeling optimal risk allocation in PPP projects using artificial neural networks. *International Journal of Project Management*, *29*(5), 591–603. doi:10.1016/j.ijproman.2010.07.011

Jorion, P. (2006). *Value at Risk: The New Benchmark for Managing Financial Risk*. New York: McGraw Hill.

Jutte, B. (2014). *10 Golden Rules of Project Risk Management*. Retrieved from http://www.scrbd.com/

Karim, N. A. A. (2011). Risk allocation in public-private partnership (PPP) projects: A review of risk factors. *Journal of Sustainable Construction Engineering and Technology*, *2*(2), 8–16.

Ke, Y., Wang, S., & Chan, A. (2013). Risk misallocation in public—private partnership in China. *International Public Management Journal*, *16*(3), 438–460. doi:10.1080/10967494.2013.825508

Ke, Y., Wang, S. Q., & Chan, A. P. C. (2011). Equitable risks allocation of projects inside China: Analyses from Delphi survey studies. *Chinese Management Studies*, *5*(3), 298–310. doi:10.1108/17506141111163372

Ke, Y. J., Wang, S. Q., & Chan, A. P. C. (2010a). Risk allocation in public-private partnership infrastructure projects: Comparative study. *Journal of Infrastructure Systems*, *16*(4), 343–351. doi:10.1061/(ASCE)IS.1943-555X.0000030

Ke, Y. J., Wang, S. Q., Chan, A. P. C., & Lam, P. T. I. (2010b). Preferred risk allocation in Chinas public-private partnership (PPP) projects. *International Journal of Project Management*, *28*(5), 482–492. doi:10.1016/j.ijproman.2009.08.007

Kefallinos, D., Lambrou, M., & Sykas, E. (2009). An extended risk assessment model for secure E-Government. *International Journal of Electronic Government Research*, *5*(2), 72–92. doi:10.4018/jegr.2009040105

Kendrick, T. (2009). *Identifying and Managing Project Risk: Essential Tools for Failure- Proofing Your Project* (2nd ed.). New York: AMACOM Div. American Management Association.

Kerzner, H. (2009). *Project management: A systems approach to planning, scheduling, and controlling*. New York: John Wiley & Sons.

Khadaroo, I. (2014). The valuation of risk transfer in UK school Public-Private Partnership contracts. *The British Accounting Review*, *46*(2), 154–165. doi:10.1016/j.bar.2013.12.004

Klemetti, A. (2006). *Risk Management in Construction Project Networks*. Helsinki University of Technology, Laboratory. *Industrial Management (Des Plaines)*.

Krause, T. (2014). A contingency framework on partnership risk. *International Journal of Public Sector Management*, *27*(4), 317–333. doi:10.1108/IJPSM-09-2013-0128

Kwak, Y. H., Chih, Y., & Ibbs, C. W. (2009). Towards a comprehensive understanding of public private partnerships for infrastructure development. *California Management Review*, *51*(2), 51–78. doi:10.2307/41166480

Kwan, T. W., & Leung, H. K. N. (2011). A risk management methodology for project risk dependencies. *IEEE Transactions on Software Engineering*, *37*(5), 635–648. doi:10.1109/TSE.2010.108

Lam, K. C., Wang, D., Lee, P. T. K., & Tsang, Y. T. (2007). Modeling risk allocation decision in construction contracts. *International Journal of Project Management*, *25*(5), 485–493. doi:10.1016/j.ijproman.2006.11.005

Lawrence, G. R. (2007). Use and misuse of capital cost estimate contingency – why deleting it makes projects more expensive, not less. *Pharmaceutical Engineering: The Official Magazine of ISPE, 27*(5). Retrieved from http://apnetworks.com/dmdocuments/2007-09-01-Pharmaceutical%20Engineering-Contingency.pdf

Lee, J., & Chun, J. (2009). Risk response analysis model for construction method using the forced-decision method and binary weighting analysis. *Journal of Asian Architecture and Building Engineering*, *8*(1), 205–212. doi:10.3130/jaabe.8.205

Lenfle, S., & Loch, C. (2010). Lost roots: How project management came to emphasize control over flexibility and novelty. *California Management*, *53*(1), 32–55. doi:10.1525/cmr.2010.53.1.32

Li, B., Akintoye, A., Edwards, P. J., & Hardcastle, C. (2005a). Perceptions of positive and negative factors influencing the attractiveness of PPP/PFI procurement for construction projects in the UK: Findings from a questionnaire survey. *Engineering, Construction, and Architectural Management*, *12*(2), 125–148. doi:10.1108/09699980510584485

Li, B., Akintoye, A., Edwards, P. J., & Hardcastle, C. (2005b). The allocation of Risk in PPP/PFI Construction Projects in the UK. *International Journal of Project Management*, *23*(1), 25–35. doi:10.1016/j.ijproman.2004.04.006

Li, M., Li, Q., & Deng, X. (2008). Transaction Cost Analysis of PPP Risk Share.*Proceedings of 2008 International Conference on Construction and Real Estate Management.*

Li, X. D. (2008). Monte Carlo simulation and a value-at-risk of concessionary project. *Management Research News*, *31*(12), 912–921. doi:10.1108/01409170810920620

Liu, T., & Wilkinson, S. (2014). Large-scale public venue development and the application of public-private partnerships. *International Journal of Project Management*, *32*(1), 88–100. doi:10.1016/j.ijproman.2013.01.003

Loizou, P., & French, N. (2012). Risk and uncertainty in development: A critical evaluation of using the Monte Carlo simulation method as a decision tool in real estate development projects. *Journal of Property Investment & Finance*, *30*(2), 198–210. doi:10.1108/14635781211206922

Loosemore, M., Raftery, J., Reilly, C., & Higgon, D. (2006). *Risk management in projects* (2nd ed.). Oxon, UK: Taylor and Francis.

Macário, R. (2010). Future challenges for transport infrastructure pricing in PPP arrangements. *Research in Transportation Economics*, *30*(1), 145–154. doi:10.1016/j.retrec.2010.10.015

MacGillivray, B. H., Hamilton, P. D., Strutt, J. E., & Pollard, S. J. T. (2006). Risk analysis strategies in the water utility sector: An inventory of applications for better and more credible decision making. *Critical Reviews in Environmental Science and Technology*, *36*(2), 85–139. doi:10.1080/10643380500531171

Mahendra, P. A., Jayeshkumar, J. R., Pitroda, R., & Bhavsar, J. J. (2013). A study of risk management techniques for construction projects in developing countries. *International Journal of Innovative Technology and Exploring Engineering*, *3*(5), 139–142.

Maniar, H. M. (2010). A case study on risk analysis in infrastructure highway projects in India. *The IUP Journal of Financial Risk Management*, *2*, 1–27.

Marques, R. C., & Berg, S. (2011). Risks, contracts, and private-sector participation in Infrastructure. *Journal of Construction Engineering and Management*, *137*(11), 925–932. doi:10.1061/(ASCE)CO.1943-7862.0000347

Matei, L. (2006). Empirical approaches of the public-private partnership in the services of public utility. *Theoretical and Applicative Economics*, *10*(505), 3–14.

May, P. J., & Koski, C. (2013). Addressing public risks: Extreme events and critical infrastructure. *Review of Policy Research.*, *30*(2), 139–159. doi:10.1111/ropr.12012

Maylor, H., Vidgen, R., & Carver, S. (2008). Managerial complexity in project-based operations: A grounded model and its implications for practice. *Project Management Journal*, *39*(1), 15–26. doi:10.1002/pmj.20057

Medda, F. (2007). A game theory approach for the allocation of risks in transport public private partnerships. *International Journal of Project Management*, *25*(3), 213–218. doi:10.1016/j.ijproman.2006.06.003

Meier, K., & OToole, L. J. Jr. (2007). Modeling public management: Empirical analysis of the management-performance nexus. *Public Management Review*, *9*(4), 503–527. doi:10.1080/14719030701726630

Menches, C. L., & Hanna, A. S. (2006). Quantitative measurement of successful performance from the project managers perspective. *Journal of Construction Engineering and Management*, *132*(12), 1284–1293. doi:10.1061/(ASCE)0733-9364(2006)132:12(1284)

Mistarihi, A. M., Al Refai, M. S., Al Qaid, B. A., & Qeed, M. A. (2012). Competency requirements for managing public private partnerships (PPPs): The case of infrastructure projects in Jordan. *International Journal of Business and Management*, *7*(12), 60–73. doi:10.5539/ijbm.v7n12p60

Mitra, A. (2010). Complex project management: An appropriate monitoring / evaluation / course correction methodology. *Journal of Defence Studies*, *4*(1), 33–48.

Molenaar, K. (2005). Programmatic cost risk analysis for highway megaprojects. *Journal of Construction Engineering and Management*, *131*(3), 343–353. doi:10.1061/(ASCE)0733-9364(2005)131:3(343)

Mousavi, S. M., Tavakkoli-Moghaddam, R., Azaron, A., Mojtahedi, S. M. H., & Hashemi, H. (2011). Risk assessment for highway projects using jackknife technique. *Expert Systems with Applications*, *38*(5), 5514–5524. doi:10.1016/j.eswa.2010.10.085

Mubin, S., & Mannan, A. (2013). Innovative approach to risk analysis and management of oil and gas sector Engineering, Procurement and Construction (EPC) contracts from a contractor's perspective. *Journal of Business & Economics*, *5*(2), 149–170.

Ng, A., & Loosemore, M. (2007). Risk allocation in the private provision of public infrastructure. *International Journal of Project Management*, *25*(1), 66–76. doi:10.1016/j.ijproman.2006.06.005

Nguyen, L. D., & Ogunlana, S. O. (2005). Modeling the dynamics of an infrastructure project. *Computer-Aided Civil and Infrastructure Engineering*, *20*(4), 265–279. doi:10.1111/j.1467-8667.2005.00392

Nisar, T. M. (2007). Risk Management in Public-Private Partnership Contracts. *Public Organization Review*, *7*(1), 1–19. doi:10.1007/s11115-006-0020-1

Ogbu, C. P. (2013). Risk management practices of multinational and indigenous construction companies in nigeria: A comparative analysis. *Journal of Research in National Development*, *9*(2), 315–324.

Ogunsanmi, O. E., Salako, O. A., & Ajayi, O. M. (2011). Risks classification model for design and build projects. *Journal of Engineering, Project, and Production Management*, *1*(1), 46–60.

Ökmen, Ö., & Öztas, A. (2010). Construction cost analysis under uncertainty with correlated cost risk analysis mode. *Construction Management and Economics*, *28*(2), 203–212. doi:10.1080/01446190903468923

Olsson, R. (2008). Risk management in a multi-project environment: An approach to manage portfolio risks. *International Journal of Quality & Reliability Management*, *25*(1), 60–71. doi:10.1108/02656710810843586

Osipova, E., & Eriksson, P. E. (2013). Balancing control and flexibility in joint risk management: Lessons learned from two construction projects. *International Journal of Project Management*, *31*(3), 391–399. doi:10.1016/j.ijproman.2012.09.007

Oyewobi, L. O., Ibrahim, A. D., & Ganiyu, B. O. (2012). Evaluating the impact of risk on contractor's tender figures in northern nigeria. *Journal of Engineering, Project, and Production Management*, *2*(1), 2–13.

Papajohn, D., Cui, Q., & Bayraktar, M. E. (2011). Public-private partnerships in US transportation: Research overview and a path forward. *Journal of Management Engineering*, *27*(3), 126–135. doi:10.1061/(ASCE)ME.1943-5479.0000050

Parvinen, P., Kujala, J., Lillrank, P., & Kouri, J. (2005). *Managing process interventions in healthcare: a question of governance.4th International Conference on the Management of Healthcare and Medical Technology*, Aalborg.

Patanakul, P. (2015). Key attributes of effectiveness in managing project portfolio. *International Journal of Project Management*, *33*(5), 1084–1097. doi:10.1016/j.ijproman.2015.01.004

Pellegrino, R., Vajdic, N., & Carbonara, N. (2013). Real option theory for risk mitigation in transport PPPs. Built Environment Project and Asset Management, *3*(2).

Peng, W., Cui, Q., Lu, Y., & Huang, L. (2014). Achieving value for money: an analytic review of studies on public–private partnerships.*Construction Research Congress, Construction in a Global Network*. ASCE. doi:10.1061/9780784413517.122

Pluess, D. N., Groso, A., & Meyer, T. (2013). Expert Judgments in Risk Analysis: A Strategy to Overcome Uncertainties. *Chemical Engineering Transactions*, *31*, 307–312.

Raja, M. A. R. (2015). Risk analysis of infrastructure projects under public private partnerships. *International Journal of Civil Engineering and Technology*, *6*(6), 108–113.

Rakić, B., & Rađenović, T. (2014). Real options methodology in public-private partnership projects valuation. *Economic Annals*, *59*(200), 91–113. doi:10.2298/EKA1400091R

Rao, M., & Ranade, H. W. (2013). *Risk based cost estimation of capital intensive road projects using Monte-Carlo simulation*. Paper presented at the 2013 International Public Works Conference, Darwin, Australia.

Reeves, I., & Ryan, J. (2007). Piloting public private partnerships: Expensive lessons from Irelands Schools sector. *Public Money and Management*, *27*(5), 331–338. doi:10.1111/j.1467-9302.2007.00604.x

Rot, A. (2008). IT Risk Assessment: Quantitative and qualitative approach.*Proceedings of the World Congress on Engineering and Computer Science 2008 WCECS*.

Roumboutsos, A., & Anagnostopoulos, K. (2008). Public Private Partnership projects in Greece: Risk ranking and preferred risk allocation. *Construction Management and Economics*, *26*(7), 751–763. doi:10.1080/01446190802140086

Sachs, T., & Tiong, R. (2009). Quantifying qualitative information on risks: Development of the QQIR method. *Journal of Construction Engineering and Management*, *135*(1), 56–71. doi:10.1061/(ASCE)0733-9364(2009)135:1(56)

Sarmento, J. M. (2010). Do public-private partnerships create value for money for the public sector? The Portuguese Experience. *OECD Journal on Budgeting*, *1*(1), 1–28. doi:10.1787/budget-10-5km8xx3fgws5

Sarmento, J. M., & Renneboog, L. (2014). *Public-Private Partnerships: Risk Allocation and Value for Money*. CentER Discussion Paper Series No. 2014-022; TILEC Discussion Paper No. 2014-017. 10.2139/ssrn.2411450

Sarvari, H., Valipuor, A., Yahaya, A., & Noor, N. M. (2014). risk ranking of Malaysian public private partnership projects. *Applied Mechanics and Materials*, *567*, 613–618. doi:10.4028/www.scientific.net/AMM.567.613

Schatteman, D., Herroelen, W., Van de Vonder, S., & Boone, A. (2008). Methodology for integrated risk management and proactive scheduling of construction projects. *Journal of Construction Engineering and Management*, *134*(November), 885–893. doi:10.1061/(ASCE)0733-9364(2008)134:11(885)

Seyed, M. M., Seyrafianpour, H., & Ebrahimnejad, S. (2010). Risk identification and assessment for build-operate-transfer projects: A fuzzy multi attribute decision making model. *Expert Systems with Applications*, *37*(1), 575–586. doi:10.1016/j.eswa.2009.05.037

Shaoul, J. (2005b). The private finance initiative or public funding of private profit. In The Challenge of Public-Private Partnerships. Cheltenham, UK: Edward Elgar.

Sharma, S. (2007). Exploring best practices in public-private partnership (PPP) in e- Government through select Asian case studies. *The International Information & Library Review*, *39*(3-4), 203–210. doi:10.1080/10572317.2007.10762750

Shen, L., Platten, A., & Deng, X. P. (2006). Role of public private partnerships to manage risks in public sector projects in Hong Kong. *International Journal of Project Management*, *24*(7), 587–594. doi:10.1016/j.ijproman.2006.07.006

Singaravelloo, K. (2010). PPP: The Right Marriage between Local Government and the Private Sector in Malaysia? *International Journal of Institutions and Economics*, *2*(2), 142–166.

Singh, K. P. (2011). Issues and prospects of public private partnership in India. *ZENITH. International Journal of Multidisciplinary Research*, *1*(5), 244–256.

Smith, N. J., Merna, T., & Jobling, P. (2006). *Managing risk in construction projects* (2nd ed.). Oxford, UK: Blackwell Publishing.

Stern, R., & Arias, J. C. (2011). Review of risk management methods. *Business Intelligence Journal*, *4*(1), 59–78.

Sun, M., & Meng, X. (2009). Taxonomy for change causes and effects in construction projects. *International Journal of Project Management*, *27*(6), 560–572. doi:10.1016/j.ijproman.2008.10.005

Swan, W., & Khalfan, M. M. (2007). Mutual objective setting for partnering projects in the public sector. *Engineering, Construction, and Architectural Management*, *14*(2), 119–130. doi:10.1108/09699980710731254

Tahir, M. (2007). Risk management in public-private partnership contracts. *Public Organization Review*, *7*(6), 1–19.

Takashima, R., Yagi, K., & Takamori, H. (2010). Government guarantees and risk sharing in public-private partnerships. *Review of Financial Economics, 19*(2), 78–83. doi:10.1016/j.rfe.2009.10.001

Tallman, R. A. J. W. (2010). Lessons on risk transfer from Canadian public-private partnerships. *Review of Business Research, 10*(4), 194–200.

Tan, F., & Makwasha, T. (2010). Best practice cost estimation in land transport infrastructure. *Australian Transport Research Team Forum 2010 Proceedings*. Retrieved from http://www.atrf.info/papers/2010/2010_Tan_Makwasha.pdf

Tanaka, D. F., Ishida, H., Tsutsumi, M., & Okamoto, N. (2005). Private finance for road projects in developing countries: Improving transparency through VFM risk assessment. *Journal of the Eastern Asia Society for Transportation Studies, 6*, 3899–3914.

Teller, J., & Kock, A. (2013). An empirical investigation on how portfolio risk management influences project portfolio success. *International Journal of Project Management, 31*(6), 817–829. doi:10.1016/j.ijproman.2012.11.012

Thaheem, J. (2012). *A review of quantitative analysis techniques for construction project risk management*. Paper presented at Creative construction conference, Budapest, Hungary.

Too, E. G., & Weaver, P. (2014). The management of project management: A conceptual framework for project governance. *International Journal of Project Management, 32*(8), 1382–1394. doi:10.1016/j.ijproman.2013.07.006

Turnbaughs, L. (2005). Risk management on large capital projects. *Journal of Professional Issues in Engineering Education and Practice*, (October), 274–280.

Wang, J., & Yuan, H. (2011). Factors affecting contractors risk attitudes in construction projects: Case study from China. *International Journal of Project Management, 29*(2), 209–219. doi:10.1016/j.ijproman.2010.02.006

Wang, S. (2006). *Lessons learnt from the PPP practices in China (keynote speech).Asian Infrastructure Congress*, Hong Kong.

Wibowo, A., & Mohamed, S. (2010). Risk criticality and allocation in privatized water supply projects in Indonesia. *International Journal of Project Management, 28*(5), 504–513. doi:10.1016/j.ijproman.2009.08.003

Wood, P. (2005). Risk management off the shelf and into practice. *British Journal of Administrative Management, 45*, 26–27.

Xiao, H. J., & Zhang, G. (2011). Modeling optimal risk allocation in PPP projects using artificial neural networks. *International Journal of Project Management, 29*(5), 591–603. doi:10.1016/j.ijproman.2010.07.011

Xu, Y., Yeung, J. F. Y., Chan, A. P. C., Chan, D. W. M., Wang, S. Q., & Ke, Y. (2010). Developing a risk assessment model for PPP projects in China- A fuzzy synthetic evaluation approach. *Automation in Construction, 19*(7), 929–943. doi:10.1016/j.autcon.2010.06.006

Xu, Y. L., Chan, A. P. C., & Yeung, J. F. Y. (2010). Developing a fuzzy risk allocation model for PPP projects in China. *Journal of Construction Engineering and Management*, *136*(8), 894–903. doi:10.1061/(ASCE)CO.1943-7862.0000189

Yongjian, K., ShouQing, W., & Chan, A. P. C. (2009). Preferred Risk Allocation in China's Public Private Partnership (PPP) Projects. *Journal of Project Management*, *28*, 482–492.

Yuan, J., Skibniewski, M. J., Li, Q., & Zheng, L. (2010). Performance objectives selection model in public-private partnership projects based on the perspective of stakeholders. *Journal of Management Engineering*, *26*(2), 89–104. doi:10.1061/(ASCE)ME.1943-5479.0000011

Zarco-Jasso, H. (2005). Public–private partnerships: A multidimensional model for contracting. *International Journal of Public Policy*, *1*(1/2), 22–40. doi:10.1504/IJPP.2005.007791

Zou, P., Zhang, G., & Wang, J.-Y. (2007). Understanding the key risks in construction projects in China. *International Journal of Project Management*, *25*(6), 601–614. doi:10.1016/j.ijproman.2007.03.001

Section 3

Enticement Actions for Effective Risk Management in Public–Private Partnership

Chapter 8
Risk Management Planning, Sustainability Risks Management, and Risk Stakeholders

ABSTRACT

Concepts in risk management in PPP projects have continuously evolved over the years. Introduction of new concepts, risk management planning, sustainability risk management and risk stakeholders, create a greater understanding of the acceptable workings of PPP projects. This chapter aims to investigate and compare these concepts in academic literatures and to the practices of PPP project implementations as exemplified in numerous PPP projects. This chapter reviews and analyzes information on these concepts. Extant literatures are reviewed and their take on the concepts are compared with the results obtained from the case studies. The chapter found both similarities and differences and also suggests some interesting researches on several key areas that should be emphasized for a better take in having an effective risk management strategy.

Everyone is entitled to his own opinion, but not to his own facts. - Daniel Patrick "Pat" Moynihan

INTRODUCTION

The aim of this chapter is to provide a literature survey and practical hints for PPP developers, partners and implementers in PPP implementation for three interrelated topics: risk management planning, risk sustainability and risk stakeholders. Its main focus is to critically assess the backgrounds of these topics, review practice and provide clues on their importance in the implementation of PPP projects. These topics form the core of PPP arrangement. Risk planning refer to the stance both partners adopt towards the functional mode in which the PPP arrangement ought to operate and the measures to be taken to

DOI: 10.4018/978-1-5225-2503-5.ch008

implement the arrangement. risk sustainability usually attempt to influence the degree of a long lasting nature in which the PPP project is to hold, such as, attainment of the long-term greater good from a program. The term risk stakeholder refers to a set of individuals 'gathered' about a PPP project aiming at influencing the PPP project performance towards a desired objective. As all these topics affect PPP arrangement in one way or the other, boundaries between risk management planning, risk sustainability and risk stakeholders are not always clear. There seems to be a binding 'cord' between them. The nearer one can get to a demarcation line is arguably by referring to partner's own perception of what they aim risk management planning, risk sustainability and risk stakeholders to be plus an underlying body of empirical/practical knowledge hopefully informing such perceptions. The partners' objective is assumed to be the improvement on the successful implementation of PPP projects. This happens when the partners rightfully understand the roles and position in the PPP arrangement and that their actions is taking place a pace preferably faster than in lagging behind in implementing PPP projects. Risk management planning is believed to be the most important contributor to the success of PPP project, its positive link with sustainability, and even its close link with risk stakeholders. It follows that a partner wishing to improve its performance in a PPP arrangement will be well advised to design measures that lead to efficient allocation of resources and equitable share of risks. There is a universal agreement among development practitioners that risk sustainability in PPP project implementation can be a potent means of facilitating the desired objective. However, views differ as the role, the function, the responsibilities and even the nature of involvement of stakeholders in the process. In is not possible or even useful to discuss all these issues in detail in this chapter, but a bird's eye view of alternative perspective can facilitate understanding, including the link between risk management planning, risk sustainability and risk stakeholders.

The following section deals with risk planning in theory and practice while the next section deal with risk sustainability and provide guidance on ways of sustaining risk management in a PPP project. The section on risk stakeholders discusses the dynamics of stakeholders in a PPP arrangement. The final section has a conclusion.

RISK MANAGEMENT PLANNING

According to Firmenich (2012), risk management planning is the systematic process of deciding how to approach, plan, and execute risk management activities throughout the life of a project. It is a process for identifying how to carry out the activities of project risk management (Yuan, Skibniewski & Li, 2008). Bloomfield (2006) argues that the purpose risk management planning is to determine actions to efficiently respond to the identified risks that have a positive and/or negative effect on at least one project objective (such as cost, scope, performance and time). Koppenjan (2005) articulates that risk management planning is intended to maximize the beneficial outcome of the opportunities and minimize or eliminate the consequences of adverse risk events. Akintoye (2006) compliments asserting that risk management planning is a necessary component within the overall project management process. Liu and Zheng. (2008) cites numerous merits of risk management planning to the project management process including:- saving both financial and non-financial resources; increasing the efficiency and stability of activities and operations; reducing legal liability; protecting property and people involved in the project from harm and injury; protecting and strengthening the reputation of your organization and employees; and increasing the likelihood of successful implementation. In addition to these, though Dechev (2015) vies that the risk management planning process should result in developing a feasible and efficient plan for minimizing risk occurrence rate and exploiting available opportunities. Risk management planning should be completed early during the project planning stage since it is crucial to successfully performing the other project management phases (Cankar & Petkovšek, 2013).

Abels (2007) contends that the control function of the risk management system then must serve to manage the potential interaction of such side effects by identification of the boundaries of safe operation for each decision-maker. For this it is necessary to ensure that information about the boundaries will be active as local constraint, visible to the particular decision-maker. When the government enters into a PPP arrangement, it is vital that benefit analyses are carried out, such as return on investment (RoI), access to funding, feasibility of the project, and access to private sector resources such as human expertise and technology, since they form the basis of need for governments (Forrer, Kee, Newcomer & Boyer 2010). Failure to complete proper planning will lead to governments committing to projects with no prospects of success, and may lead to project delays due to lack of funding and resources. A government is a public entity and should act responsibly by planning properly before committing to projects, as society holds only government accountable (even in a PPP arrangement) so far as project and service delivery is concerned.

Process of Risk Management Planning

Suffice to reecho any project will always generate a kind of challenge that makes it hard to find efficient ways to respond to the various threats and uncertainties generated by the challenges. Ayeni (2005) indicates that the threat and uncertainties may jeopardize the successful completion of a project, for example. Makovsek (2013) avers it's the implementation of the risk planning process that lets the manager solve the challenge by planning for potential risk and developing solutions that reduce the likelihood of risk occurrence and mitigate the negative impact of the risks. Rakic and Radenović (2011) advice before starting to implement the project, some efforts must be made as to plan and manage for potential risks. Absent those, there is a likelihood of failure right at the start for the achievement of the objectives as well the goals of the project. Silvester and Aroujo (2012) assert it's important to understand the reason for risk occurrence because it will help to determine the direction to choose. For example, in a project, risk can occur as a result of changing circumstances, updates, and new developments, changes to the constraints (like scope, time and budget), changes to the initial project documentations (like project charter) resulted from further discussions and negotiations with stakeholders; and detailed elaboration and further refinement of the overall project planning process.

A good and sound risk management planning process requires adherence to five most important steps. Velotti, Botti and Vesci (2012) point out that since a project manager of PMC are charged with managing risk on a daily basis, it is important that they take these core risk management planning process steps into deep consideration. It is the only surest way in which the project can run more smoothly and be a positive experience for everyone involved. In conformity to the old adage "Accept the inevitable and turn to your advantage"; Ye (2009) recommends that in being open to those risks that create opportunities, it can make a project smarter, streamlined and more profitable. Accordingly, to deliver a simple and effective risk management planning process, there is needed to follow the same five basic steps (Delmon, 2009). First, identify the risk by uncovering, recognizing and describing risks that might affect the project and its outcomes. Use a number of techniques as discussed before and also prepare a project risk register at this stage. Secondly, analyze the risk by developing an understanding of the nature of the risks and its potential to affect project goals and objectives. Such information should also be captured in the risk register. Thirdly, evaluate or rank the risk by determining the risk magnitude, which is the combination of likelihood and consequence. Apart from adding the risk rankings into the risk register, make decisions about whether the risk is acceptable or whether it is serious enough to warrant treatment. Fourthly, treat the risk, often referred to as risk response planning can be done by assessing the highest ranked risks and setting out a plan to treat or modify these risks as well as enhancing the opportunities. It is important to create risk mitigation strategies, preventive plans and contingency plans at this step. Again add the risk treatment measures for the highest ranking or most serious risks to the project risk register. Fifth and last step is monitor and review the risk by taking the project risk register and using it to monitor, track and review risks.

Adams, Alistair and Wu (2006) argue that partners ought to be reminded from time to time that risk is about uncertainty. It is critical therefore to put a framework around the uncertainty that become an effective way to de-risk the project. From then one, the partners can move with confidence to achieve the project goals. Sharma (2007) calls upon partners to identify and manage a comprehensive list of project risk, unpleasant surprises and barriers. This is only possible through proper risk management planning. In the endeavor, henceforth, risks can be reduced and golden opportunities presenting themselves can be discovered. Soliño and Vassallo (2009) make a case that the risk management process helps to resolve problems when they occur, because those problems have could have been envisaged and plans to treat them could have already been developed and agreed. A sound risk management process, therefore, aids in avoiding impulsive reactions and going into "fire-fighting" mode to rectify problems that could have been anticipated. According to Mert and Chan (2012), this makes for happier, less stressed project teams and stakeholders. The resultant outcome would then be minimization of the impact of project threats and capture of the opportunities that may occur (Ismail & Harris, 2014).

Weihe (2006) claims the process of putting a strategic plan of managing identified threats and exploiting opportunities into action, may take many forms. This depends on the organization culture of performance, history of previous efforts, valuable resources, number of individuals involved in the project, and other factors. Singaravelloo (2010) adds that the implementation can be done in various ways, for example, in a marketing campaign project, approaches that can be used includes:- creating barriers to market entry, establishing competitive pricing, damping, using new unique technology, innovation etc. however, it has to be noted that each of these methods implies a very different set of tools for implementation.

In spite of the methods and tools that can be adopted and use to implement risk management planning process, Babatunde, Opawole and Akinsiku (2012) attributes the success of the overall implementation to three fundamental activities. First, is the acquisition of the correct quantity of resource to be availed and eventually ready for use. Resources can be obtained in a range of way, for example, by purchasing with credit, renting/leasing, sub-contracting, shared management, partnerships, etc. Second, is managing the resource flow with the idea behind as to ensure that the resources are available at appropriate levels, needed placed and at required time. Cheung, Chan and Kajewski (2012) state the flow of the resources should be managed in terms of quantity, location and time. Jacobson and Choi (2008) demonstrate that once the use of resources is optimized the risk management process is likely to generate optimum output. Third, is resource coordination is very critical once resources are acquired an allocated throughout the implementation process. Jefferies (2006) reveals that resource coordination requires development of detailed operational plans and conduct day-to-day oversight of the operations. Ng, Wong and Wong (2012) portrays resource availability as the only way through which risk management initiative can be a driving force to enable the making of a proper decision on the scope of the implementation process.

Singewar and Deshmukh (2016) hypothesize that it's the way of acquisition, use and coordination of resources within the risk management planning process that determines the future of the project effort.

Shrivastava (2011) puts another serious consideration during the implementation process of risk management planning to review the plan. Ogunsanmi (2013) justifies this by showing how very important it is to ensure the plans remains current and efficient. Dada and Oladokun (2012) expresses that regular reviews help find out if the plan provides feasible and effective risk mitigation activities assigned to individuals who are responsible for the implementation process. Trafford and Proctor (2006) counsel throughout the risk management planning process, risk identification should be made to take changing circumstances into consideration when responding to risk. This is because risk management plan should clearly identify what people are responsible for the maintenance.

Most significantly, Kutsch and Hall (2010) stipulate that its common practice of effective risk management planning process to add the outcome of the risk management activities. This is done to ensure that when making decisions on how efficiently the project has been performed and whether the risk management plan has been implemented appropriately. It is important for the PMC to have a report with separate section dedicated to risk management results. It should show which threats have been identified, which opportunities have been exploited and how all this has been managed. According to Kolhatkar and Dutta (2013), the risk register is used as the primary source of information on the identified risks and ways of mitigation.

Risk Management Plan

A risk management plan is a document that a project manager prepares to foresee risks, estimate impacts, and define responses to issues (Abbasianjahromi and Rajaie, 2012). It also contains a risk assessment matrix. Risk management plan identifies and establishes the activities of risk management for the project in the project plan. According to Zaharioaie (2012), a good risk management plan is critical to cutting down on unexpected risks. Abdul-Rahman, Wang and Lee (2013) assert that a strong plan can decrease problems on a project by as much as 80 to 90 per cent. Research has shown that well-designed risk management plans can decrease problems encountered on a project by as much as 90 per cent. Al-Kharashi and Skitmore (2009) reveal that combined with a world-class project management methodology, a good risk management process can be essential in diminishing unexpected project risks.

Before developing a risk management plan, Assaf and Al-Hejji (2006) recommend for identification and evaluation of potential risks and examination of applicable options for risk elimination or at last mitigation. Berg (2010) advocates for three steps to be followed while designing and implementing risk management plan. First is the identification of potential loss exposures because of the need to control and monitor those of exposures to loss. No effective decisions can be made without identification of risks. It's important to identify potential risks that may harm the project. This is done by making a project goals and objectives and then associates every goal and objective with potential threats and uncertainties that may cause a loss. For example, if the project's primary goal is to develop a software product, potential risks surrounding this goal are poor usability, product malfunction, improper functionality; user dissatisfaction etc. second is the evaluation of the risk whose process includes two main components of assessing frequency (the probability of each risk to become real) and estimating severity (the possible effect and cost of risk occurrence to the performing organization). Both of these components ought to be evaluated against their own merits. Third is examination of applicable options for managing those risks. This step requires selection of risk management techniques, such as avoidance, prevention, mitigation, retention and transfer.

A risk management plan sets out the measures to reduce and control risks, the process involved in reduction and control of risks and summarizes the risk management. Risk Management Plan (RMP) describes how a project team will incorporate the risk management process into its Project Management Plan (Bing, Akintoye, Edwards and Hardcastle, 2005a). Particular emphasis should be given to how a project team will respond to risks and monitor and control risk throughout the life of the project. By identifying and analyzing risks, and then responding to risks aggressively and monitoring the effectiveness of the response, project teams can improve the odds of meeting project objectives. A formal project RMP is a detailed plan of action for the management of project risk. Project risk planning involves the thoughtful development, implementation, and monitoring of appropriate risk response strategies. It is the process to: develop and document an organized, comprehensive, and interactive risk management strategy; and determine the methods to be used to execute a risk management strategy and plan for adequate resources. The project RMP may be specific in some areas and general in others. The key to this tool is its scalability. Every project should have a formal RMP, but the level of detail varies with project complexity.

A project RMP gives a summary of the project and outlines the steps of the risk management process and how the Project Manager and project team are approaching them (Chapman, 2007). Depending on the complexity of the project, RMP should include an introduction, a summary, definitions, organization and roles, risk management strategy/approach, risk identification, risk assessment and analysis, risk response actions/allocations, and risk monitoring and control (Carbonara, Costantino, Gunnigan & Pellegrino, 2015). It's important to use a RMP because it explains how a Project Manager and project team manages risk for their project. It provides guidance and requirements, and serves as a communication tool for those who wish to be informed of a project's risk management approach. The plan formalizes the ideas presented during the risk management process and may clarify some of the assumptions the project team has regarding the risk management process. Furthermore, the project RMP is used to determine the risks of a project and how to respond in a manner that is forthright accountable (Cleden, 2009). The project RMP can be referred to regularly and should be updated throughout the life project. A project RMP provides specific guidance for the project team members in all steps of the risk management process for their project. It documents the processes to use throughout the project for identifying, assessing, and managing risk. The formal plan should be developed by the Project Manager early in project development, typically early in scoping. The RMP must be updated during subsequent project development phases.

Risk management will be a directed, focused, and intentional effort for this project. To that end, the following items are to be included in the RMP:-level of risk assessment has been determined; risk management activities are in the project schedule. Risk management activities are included in the appropriate sections of the project schedule, using the appropriate WSDOT Master Deliverables List (MDL) codes (Nisar, 2007). Risk management is an agenda item in regularly scheduled project meetings. Risk management is included as an agenda item in our monthly project meetings and is the number one agenda item each quarter (Cleland & Gareis, 2006). Communication regarding our risk management effort and expectations has been communicated to the project team. During initiate and align, plan the work, and endorse the plan, risk management has been communicated as an item of work for this project. Specifically, it is included in the team mission/assignment and in our roles and responsibilities. Risk will be managed, documented, and reported.

It is the responsibility of the project manager to reviews and maintains RMP throughout the project, to ensure the risk process remains appropriate to deal with the level of risk faced by the project (Didraga, 2013). He/she should aim to manage all foreseeable risks (both opportunities and threats) in a manner which is proactive, effective and appropriate, in order to maximize the likelihood of the project achieving its objectives, while maintaining risk exposure at an acceptable level. "Acceptable risk" is defined as clear definition of how much risk is acceptable to key stakeholders such as the project sponsor, perhaps in terms of how many "high" threats can be present in the project, or maximum acceptable Threat P-I Score and minimum acceptable Opportunity P-I Score, or extent of allowable delay or additional cost (Nielsen, 2006).

The risk process should aim to engage all stakeholders appropriately, creating ownership and buy-in to the project itself and also to risk management actions (Ho, 2006b). Risk-based information has to be communicated to project stakeholders in a timely manner at an appropriate level of detail, to enable project strategy to be modified in the light of current risk exposure (Ogbu, 2013). The risk management process should enable project stakeholders to focus attention on those areas of the project most at risk, by identifying the major risks (both opportunities and threats) potentially able to exert the greatest positive or negative influence on achievement of project objectives.

The risk management process has to cover all activities undertaken during the lifetime of the project. There is therefore, need to clarify whether the risk process is intended to cover internal project risks only, or whether it extends to supplier risks, corporate risks, programme risks, business risks etc (Roumboutsos & Anagnostopoulos, 2008). Also clarify what types of risk are included, for example technical risks, commercial risks, management risks, external risks, etc. Consider using a Risk Breakdown Structure (RBS). Where some sources or types of risk are excluded, state how these will be dealt with if they are identified. Risk assessment should begin early, but there must be enough known about the project to understand what is being assessed (Gunawansa, 2010). This will be to varying levels of detail depending on the point in project development at which the risk assessment is conducted (planning, scoping, design/PS&E); hence, schedule risk assessments at appropriate times.

A formal project RMP is a detailed plan of action for the management of project risk. Project risk planning involves the thoughtful development, implementation, and monitoring of appropriate risk response strategies (Hameed & Woo, 2007). It is the process to: develop and document an organized, comprehensive, and interactive risk management strategy; and determine the methods to be used to execute a risk management strategy and plan for adequate resources. The project RMP may be specific in some areas and general in others. The key to this tool is its scalability. Every project should have a formal RMP, but the level of detail varies with project complexity (Hanna, Thomas & Swanson, 2013). A project RMP gives a summary of the project and outlines the steps of the risk management process and how the Project Manager and project team are approaching them. It must contain introduction, summary, definitions, organization and roles, risk management strategy/approach, risk identification, risk assessment and analysis, risk Response actions/allocations, and risk monitoring and control.

A risk management plan summarizes the proposed risk management approach for the project and is usually included as a section in the project business plan. For larger or complex projects it can be maintained as a separate document (Liu & Wilkinson, 2014). Refer to the risk management plan template for more information. It is dependent upon the establishment of a Risk Register. According to Papajohn, Cui and Bayraktar (2011), at a minimum, the Risk Management Plan should cover: the process which will be used to identify, analyze, evaluate and treat risks both initially and throughout the life of the project, including estimated costing the process for transferring approved risk costing into the project budget the process for transferring risk mitigation strategies into the project Work Breakdown Structure how often the Risk Register will be reviewed, the process for review and who will be involved who will be responsible for which aspects of risk management, how Risk Status will be reported and to whom include as an appendix the initial snapshot of the major risks, current grading, planned mitigation strategies and costing, and who will be responsible for implementing them (Ho, 2006a).

Risk assessment should begin early, but there must be enough known about the project to understand what is being assessed. This will be to varying levels of detail depending on the point in project development at which the risk assessment is conducted (planning, scoping, design/PS&E); hence, schedule risk assessments at appropriate times. Allow time in the schedule for prep activities (Shen, Platten and Deng, 2006). Allow a budget for risk assessment, risk management, and risk response activities. Report on the status of project risk in regularly scheduled project meetings. Process of developing a risk management plan includes; Initial risks must be identified and graded according to likelihood and seriousness very early in the project. This initial risk assessment will form part of the project proposal or project business case for the project. Once the project is approved the Risk Management Plan and Risk Register should be fully developed. In the case of smaller projects the Risk Register may serve both purposes (Pajunen, 2006). There is need to have a fuller knowledge and understanding of the project; knowledge and understanding of the Key Stakeholders, and knowledge and understanding of appropriate types of risk management activities, or where to obtain them.

There is need to have in place documents before you set about developing a risk management plan. Although optional document such as project proposal, project business case, or project business plan are very important to produce a good plan. While preparing a risk management plan, Jasanoff (1986) recommends four steps to be undertaken. First, before risks can be properly managed, they need to be identified. One useful way of doing this is defining categories under which risks might be identified. For example, categories might include Corporate Risks, Business Risks, Project Risks and System Risks. These can be broken down even further into categories such as environmental, economic, human, etc. Another way is to categorize in terms of risks external to the project and those that are internal. For a medium to large project, start by conducting a number of meetings or brainstorming sessions involving (as a minimum) the Project Manager, Project Team members, Steering Committee members and external key stakeholders (Kriześ-Dobieszewska, 2014). It is often advisable to use an outside facilitator for this. Preparation may include an environmental scan, seeking views of key stakeholders etc. One of the most difficult things is ensuring that all major risks are identified. For a small project, the Project Manager may develop the Risk Register perhaps with input from the Project Sponsor/Senior Manager and colleagues, or a small group of key stakeholders. The results of this exercise should be documented in a Risk Register for the project (Kurunmäki & Miller, 2011). For larger projects, if an outside facilitator is used, it would be expected that they would develop the initial documentation.

Second, once the risks have been identified, analyze them by determining how they might affect the success of the project. Risks can result in four types of consequences; benefits are delayed or reduced; timeframes are extended; outlays are advanced or increased; and output quality (fitness for purpose) is reduced (Rafele, Hillson & Grimaldi, 2005). Risks should be analyzed and evaluated in terms of likelihood of occurring and seriousness of impact if they do occur. Firstly, assess the likelihood of the risk occurring and give this a rating of Low (L), Medium (M) or High (H) likelihood. Once the risks have been rate, assess the seriousness of the impact of the risk if it did occur and rate at Low (L), Medium (M) or High (H) seriousness. Using ratings for likelihood and seriousness you can then determine a current grading for each risk that in turn provides a measure of the project risk exposure at the time of the evaluation. Depending upon the size and nature of the project, some choose to use numerical scales for this analysis and evaluation (Reeves & Ryan, 2007). The resulting grades of risk help the project team to focus on treating the most important risks, once evaluated and prioritized, and to mitigate them before the project progresses much further into the manage Phase.

Third, manage or treat the risks according to the grading table produced using the risk matrix. Usually it's very important to begin with risks extreme that has been identified earlier. Where possible use mitigation strategies very early in the project because it reduces the chance that a risk will be realized and/or reduce the seriousness of a risk if it is realized. Other less extreme risks should be continually monitored and have planned mitigation strategies ready to be implemented if appropriate (Roumboutsos & Anagnostopoulos, 2008). These plans need to be recorded on the risk register. There are two broad types of risk mitigation strategies: preventative - planned actions to reduce the likelihood a risk will occur, and the seriousness if it does occur. In other words, what should you do now? Contingency - planned actions to reduce the seriousness of the risk if it does occur. In other words, what should you do if? Once a risk has occurred, recovery actions to allow you to move on should be built into the work breakdown structure for your project. In other words, what should you do when? For each action in the Risk Register, it is necessary to specify: Who will be responsible for implementing each action? When the action must be implemented? What are the costs associated with each action (for larger projects in particular)?

Fourthly, the risk register should be visited fortnightly with re-evaluation of the risks occurring on a monthly basis. If the prevention strategies are being effective, some of the extreme risks should be able to be downgraded fairly soon into the project. Risk status should be reported to the steering committee or project sponsor/senior manager on an agreed regular basis and form part of the project status reporting processes (Zhang, 2005). It's important to remember that risk Management is an iterative process that should be built into the management processes for your project. It is closely linked with your Issues Management processes, as untreated issues may become significant risks (Sachs,Tiong & Wang, 2007). Likewise, it's also important to remember to communicate and consult. Even though you may have done this really well at the beginning and involved your key stakeholders in the identification, analysis and evaluation of risks, it is important to remember to keep the communication going. The communication strategy for your project should build this into the activities.

In the end, risk management plan ought to be approved or endorsed by the steering committee/project sponsor or senior manager, depending upon the size of the project (Zou, Wang & Fang, 2008). Once the risk management plan has been approved, it is important to: add the actions into the project business plan with the appropriately assigned resource(s) add the costs for the actions into the project budget.

Risk Budgeting

According to Baars, Kocourek and van der Lende (2012), the concept of "risk budget" has been used in recent years to provide a lodestar for active management of an investment portfolio. They continue to say that the risk budget is traditionally expressed in terms of tracking error relative to a long-term strategic framework. For example, the risk budget and strategic framework are interrelated such that by adding a risk budget, the strategic benchmark should change. On their part, de Carvalho, Lu and Pierre Moulin (2014) contend that the concept of risk budgeting is not nearly as well defined as value-at-risk. To them, the concept is not only a buzzword but also controversial. However, risk budgeting is a process of measuring and decomposing risk, using the measures in asset-allocation decisions, assigning portfolio managers risk budgets defined in terms of these measures, and using these risk budget in monitoring the asset allocation and portfolio managers (de Carvalho, Lu & Pierre Moulin, 2014). Roncalli (2013) states that the prerequisite for risk budgeting is risk decomposition which involves identifying the various sources of risk, or risk factors, such as equity returns, interest rates, and exchange rates; measuring each factor's, manager's and asset class's contribution to the total risk; comparing ex post realized outcomes to the ex ante risk; and identifying the risks that were taken intentionally, and those taken inadvertently.

Risk decomposition allows a plan sponsor to have a better understanding of the risks being assumed and how they have changed, and to have more informed conversations with the portfolio managers (Roncalli, 2013). Risk budgeting therefore, can be said to be a quantitative endeavor that brings logic and scientific rigor to the portfolio management process that helps one to understand the risks they are taking as they attempt to maximize returns (Peterson, 2006). According to Asness Frazzini and Pedersen (2012), risk budgeting underpins the risk management planning process. Risk budgeting in practical terms, implies the use of quantitative risk modeling in the firm's corporate-level financial planning process. Its main use is to create transparency about how corporate policies influence the firm's expected financial position and its total risk profile. At its most ambitious level, risk budgeting involves describing, in quantitative terms, the trade-off between the costs and benefits associated with a certain risk profile (i.e. "risk optimization") (Berkelaar, Kobor & Tsumagari, 2006).

A necessary first step in risk budgeting is to quantitatively model the firm's cash flows, similar to some of the Cash-Flow-at-Risk approaches that have become popularized in recent years (Berkelaar, Kobor, & Tsumagari, 2006). The purpose of modeling the cash flows using Monte Carlo simulation methodology is to create an idea of how 'risky' the firm's underlying business is in an overall sense, taking into consideration the combined impact on cash flow volatility from the variables identified in the risk universe (Firmenich, 2011). The probability-impact estimates included in the public private partnership risk mapping are thus the basic building blocks of a probability distribution of cash flow concerning some future point in time (Yu, Shen, Kelly & Hunter, 2008). This implies establishing, in a model format, the impact of volumes, prices, exchange rates, and various other risk factors on the aggregate cash flow of the public private partnership. The risk budgeting mindset also involves an analytical consolidation of project risks that are often neglected in the financial planning process (Tserng, Russell, Hsu & Lin, 2012). Some assets and liabilities may not institutionally be a part of the firm, yet the firm bears the risk associated with those assets and liabilities.

It's vital that the partners should have an opportunity to use a similar risk budgeting framework to analyze the composition of risk among active strategies, separate from beta exposure (Maillard, Roncalli & Teiletche, 2010). By integrating the sizing of alpha risk into a total portfolio risk budgeting framework, investors can better understand the role of each exposure in their portfolio (Bruder & Roncalli, 2012). This process will help partners target the appropriate aggregate allocation to active risk and the program. A Decision Framework for Active Portfolio Construction to build a program of active strategies, an investor must make a variety of decisions, including: determining the level of active risk, choosing where to allocate active risk, selecting and sizing active risk exposures. The risk tolerance for alpha volatility may be high (low) for investors with belief (skepticism) in active management as a source of added value to total portfolio returns (Posner, Ryu & Tkachenko, 2009). While these philosophical considerations can shape decisions, the active risk tolerance may instead be driven by structural conditions to earn a certain level of return to meet portfolio objectives. In these cases, expected alpha can help to satisfy a total return requirement not easily achieved through strictly passive market exposures.

The level of total portfolio active risk is often analyzed in terms of tracking error (the volatility of returns due to departures from the strategic benchmark). A more instructive approach to understanding how active strategies contribute to portfolio risk is to integrate active risk into the total portfolio risk budgeting analysis. This approach reveals how much of total portfolio volatility is driven by beta (passive market exposure) and how much is driven by alpha (active manager skill).

SUSTAINABILITY RISKS MANAGEMENT

Sustainability is an organizational commitment to achieving competitive advantage through the strategic and adoption and development of ecologically and socially supportive production processes, products and services and innovative human resource management practices (Smith, 2006). Anderson (2005) avers sustainability risk management requires holistic and systematic integration of ecological, socio-economic and corporate risk factors in the business management. Handley-Schachler and Navare (2010) argue that the risk sustainability value is based on effective governance structures and risk, quality, performance, culture management structures that demonstrate key benefits to the stakeholders and to the partnership over a sustained period of time. Kuzmina (2010) advices that sustainable development is about fulfilling human needs through simultaneous socio-economic and technological progress, it's dependent upon careful attention being paid to the preservation of the resources. He continues to say that in the process an adequate risk management plays an important role and could not be neglected. He urges that evidence allows coming to the conclusion that sustainability risk management could be achieved through consideration of risks, uncertainties, and information and knowledge imperfection. It has to be sounded that the phenomenon of risk plays a ubiquitous role in all PPP activities. It is therefore worth mentioning that each PPP crisis brought about by risk must be carefully managed in a sustainable way.

PPP risk is a foremost concern in today's global service delivery environment. As organizations expand their scopes to include international operations, PPP becomes an increasingly critical function. While outside sources may pose extensive and expansive risks to private partners, the policies and actions of the private partner may pose an even greater risk of transaction or project failure (Pollard & Stephen, 2008). Unlike external risks, which may be entirely or partially uncontrollable by the public partner, the generators of internal supply chain risk generators are almost always within the control of the buying firm. However, while a great deal of attention is paid to external PPP risks, the risks that may arise from internal policies and actions are often largely ignored. Sustainability efforts are also increasing pressure on PPP managers to improve internal sustainability practices and to demand the same from their suppliers (Bäckstrand, 2006).

Characteristics of Sustainability

Sustainability is often characteristics as having three pillars: environmental sustainability, social responsibility and organizational sustainability. According to Evans and Brereton (2007), these characteristics of sustainability is often called triple bottom. Actions in one area invariably have consequences in the other. For these reasons, addressing PPP risk and sustainability collectively makes sense. For example, logistical risks may relate to energy consumption, atmospheric emissions, labor relations, and profitability, among others. Hazardous material use relates to ethics, accidents, governmental regulations, and suppliers. If a firm is discovered to have acted unethically in one country, say, by using bribery to access prime locations, it could result in other states or countries stopping all of that firm's projects to investigate each transaction (Christopher & Gaudenzi, 2015). Clearly, such behavior will impact the firm, its profitability, and the firm's reputation with its customers. Therefore, PPP risks and sustainability risk should be considered collectively in both strategic planning and organizational activity.

Environmental concerns are intricately linked to various aspects of the PPP. Environment sustainability includes: - minimizing an organization's use of nonrenewable resources; minimizing consumption of all forms of energy; minimizing or eliminating effluent discharge; eliminating or minimizing atmospheric and carbon emissions; minimizing landfill deposits; and minimizing hazardous materials use (Dechev, 2015). The concepts of reuse, recycle, rebuild and resale are core to the effectiveness of minimization efforts.

Social responsibility encompasses ethical behavior, gender equity, living wage payment, use of appropriate labor, and labor relations. Ethical behavior spans an array of activities, from truthful financial reporting to abstaining from price fixing activities to prohibiting bribery in any form (Yuan, Skibniewski & Li, 2008). Gender equity relates to treating men and women equally in the workplace, in terms of equal pay and equal advancement opportunities. Regardless of where an organization operates, it is socially responsible to pay employees a living wage. Use of appropriate labor means using private partners that do not employ child or prison labor, continuing problems in the PPP projects. Andersen (2006) encourages promotion of excellent labor relations through allowing employees the freedom of assembly and freedom to unionize and minimizing adversarial relationships with unions. Social responsibility including ethics is a foundational value for many organizations. Violations of ethical standards and social responsibility put firms at significant risk.

Organizational sustainability requires that an organization maintain financial viability while acting with social responsibility and minimal environmental impact (Ajayi & Isah, 2014). This means that profitability will be maintained, customers will be satisfied, and the organization will refrain from activities that will damage its perception by both current and potential customers and suppliers. All of this leads to long term viability.

These characteristics aside, risk sustainability is premised on the concept of risk management culture. A risk management culture can be defined as the prevailing standard for how a risk is handled (Borghesi & Gaudenzi, 2012). Foerstl, Reuter, Hartmann and Blome (2010) propounds that an organization with a strong risk management culture has policies and procedures that require its workforce to go through disciplined risk planning, identification, assessment, and risk responses project phasing. Carrillo, Robinson, Anumba and Bochilaghem (2006) reveal that organizations with a risk management culture do not treat risk management as a separate process, but rather embed the risk process into the whole project planning and control process. Risk then becomes an integral part of the thinking of its core members of staff. In the same way that the quality movement matures to the point that quality assurance and statistical process control processes become institutionalized into the organization rubric, risk assessment tools and response mechanisms become an indistinguishable part of the organization mosaic in a mature organization (Pollard & Stephen, 2008). This is in line with Dallas (2006), who argues for the implementation and review of risk management throughout the entire life cycle of any project. Dallas asserts that this will allow project managers to always be able to answer questions such as whether the risks are acceptable, whether conditions are in place to proceed, whether risks are allocated appropriately, whether risks are under control, what can be learned for the future and whether the business is sustainable.

A number of studies have attempted to identify the benefits that can be expected by those organizations that are implementing a structured approach to risk management (Enshassi, Mohamed & Abu-Mosa, 2008). There are both tangible and intangible benefits to building a risk management culture. The tangible or measurable benefits of risk management include: - better informed and achievable project plans, schedules and budgets; increased likelihood of project meeting targets; proper allocation of risk through the contract; ability to avoid taking on unsound projects; better allocation of contingency to reflect risk; recording metrics to improve future projects; objective comparison of risk exposure of alternatives and identification of best risk owner (Andonova, 2010). Other soft or intangible benefits of risk management include: improved communication; development of a common understanding of project objectives; enhancement of team spirit; focused management attention on genuine threats; facilitates appropriate risk-taking and demonstrates professional approach to customers (Bäckstrand, 2012).

Fischer (2010) proposes that risk sustainability must encompass comprehensive and continuous assessment of risk over the project lifecycle, from preparation till transfer, and to allocate the risks on the long term, the most important thing is that the analysis of the interests of the public party as well as of the private party in how to share risks needs to be fully understood for any organization to have a good risk sustainability. Agyakwa-Baah, Chileshe and Fugar (2010) suggests that it must develop its competence in a number of areas including active training and development in risk planning and management, a strong linkage between organization planning and project planning, particularly between business analysis of threats and opportunities, and analysis of project risks, (in-depth project experience in its industry, capacity to document project experience and learn as an organization and develop workforce of strong functional managers who address product quality as a risk reduction issue.

Strategies for PPP and Sustainability Risks Management

PPPs are focusing on sustainability in very different ways. However, successful sustainability programs methodically address strategic, operational, collaborative, and governance requirements (Aziz, 2007). There is need to address the interaction between PPP partners and the categories of stakeholders in a PPP projects. It is also important to find ways of implementing sustainability risks management that can provide benefits to the PPP arrangement. Strategies for sustainability risks management reflect the change of mindset in risk management over the past decades. PPP partners realized that certain risks are inevitable in order to create value through operations and some risks are indeed offer precious opportunities if effectively exploited and managed. Strategies for sustainability risks management should be made on risk management principles as following: first, a shared product vision in which there is a shared vision for success based upon commonality of purpose, shared ownership, and collective commitment (Jooste, Levitt & Scott, 2011). Secondly, open communications through a free flow of information at and between all program levels through formal, informal, and impromptu communication and consensus-based processes. Third, system perspective in which the project ought to be viewed within the larger systems-level definition, design and development (Pattberg, 2010). Fourth, proactive strategies that involve planning and executing program activities based on anticipating future events. Firth is the systematic and adaptable methodology approach to the program's infrastructure and culture.

Cherevykov (2013) advices that sustainable risks management model should have five strategic road maps. The road map should be that which provides a contextual framework for the PPP project serious about taking on the challenges and opportunities of sustainable PPP project. Delmon (2011) suggests that the road map should follow these phases: strategic management through strategic plan and orientation; management and organization through organizational and infrastructural orientation (includes strategic and cultural dimensions (values and norms, communication, leadership styles and conflicts); framework set up through establishment and framework orientation; report and monitor through internal control orientation; and enterprise sustainability performance.

Beisheim and Liese (2014) decries that the decisions to undertake sustainability is a relatively easy one but implementing it in a way that balances opportunity and risk is significant challenge requiring fundamental business model innovation. Mert and Chan (2012) encourage breakthrough thinking as a necessary condition for incorporating sustainability into every aspect of the PPP implementation model. For example, through collaboration with firms those have upper hands in the use of advanced technologies into sustainable strategies and operations. Beisheim (2012) reminds that sustainability risks management should involves both financial and nonfinancial measurements. For instance, cost reduction can be achieved through improved environmental, health and safety performance (for example, fewer accidents, fines, lost workdays etc) or revenue increases can be achieved through gain in market share due to new environmentally sound products.

Martens (2007) cautions PPP partners cannot dictate the time frames or expectations for managing sustainability alone. This must be done and driven by involving all the stakeholders in the PPP projects. It is critical that the partners together will the all stakeholders to undertake initiative and integrate sustainability into the PPP project. However, Pattberg (2005) warns that sustainability need not be a reactive response to environmental or regulatory threats. Pattberg, Biermann, Chan and Mert (2012) reveals as sustainability develops in the PPP world, partners can move from short-term risk avoidance and regulation compliance to long-term development of quality production and high value service delivery. Morsink, Hofman and Lovett (2011) implore the building up of proactive sustainability risks management initiatives. Such an initiative gives an opportunity for the PPP partners to differentiate themselves as partners for a purpose, ensuring long-term success of the PPP project. The next section discusses the possibility of having such an initiative.

Model of Sustainability Risks Management

Smith (2006) proposes a model for understanding risk and sustainability as indicated in Figure 1. He however notes that "...whilst this addition added the missing dimension of risk it provides little in the way of practical assistance to risk managers" (p.5).

Figure 1. Adding the risk dimension to sustainability
Source: (Smith, 2006)

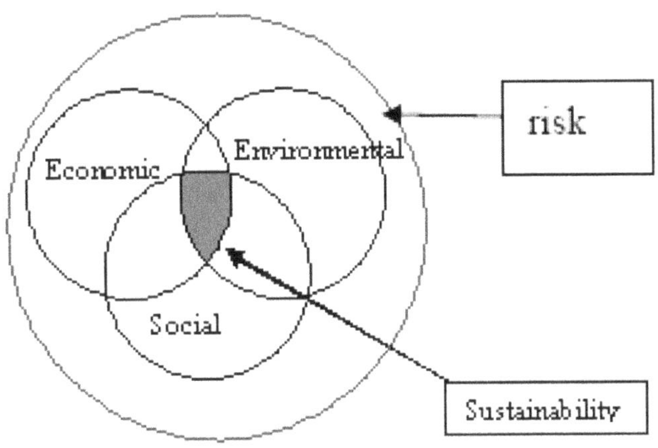

Citing Dyllick and Hockerts, who developed six criteria required for organizational sustainability, Smith (2006) indicates that the advantage of the criteria in Figure 2 is that it is an organizational model for sustainability, however the terminology is confusing, and does not concentrate on the sustainability risk that need to be managed. He recommended that what Risk managers need is a sustainability risk model that can be a useful tool and an aide memoire that takes into account economic, environmental and social issues within an organizational context, and looks at equity, viability and bearability issues.

Yilmaz and Flouris (2010) recommend that a good model must be that which presents a holistic and proactive fresh way to manage PPP-wide sustainability risk. This suggests that the model should go beyond compliance and legal liabilities but integrate risk management based philosophy and culture into core PPP project functions, for example. Glasbergen, Biermann and Mol (2007) argue that sustainability management will only succeed only if PMC teams and the partners recognize that the reforms create value for them.

According to Yilmaz and Flouris (2010), sustainability risks management framework model is a specific management and organization system to manage integration between the PPP goals of creating economic and financial value and the aspects of environmental and social responsibility. It has to be developed as an important mechanism for improving PPP project sustainability performance. It can protect, create and enhance the project values through measurement and management of sustainability threats and opportunities (Glasbergen, 2011). In addition, this can help PPP projects effectively respond to the growing expectations of the stakeholders. Esquer-Peralta (2006) claims that sustainability risk management framework provides guidance to managers on how to establish holistic and systematic sustainability risk management process that generates the risk indicators, risk sources, objectives and reporting systems needed to ensure effective handling of sustainability risks and improved overall organizational performance and value. Epstein (2009) believes that integrating sustainability considerations into existing organizational systems and processes is the most effective way to embed sustainability into organization business rather than creating new systems and processes. The model should enable

Figure 2. Sustainability business case criteria
Source: (Smith, 2006)

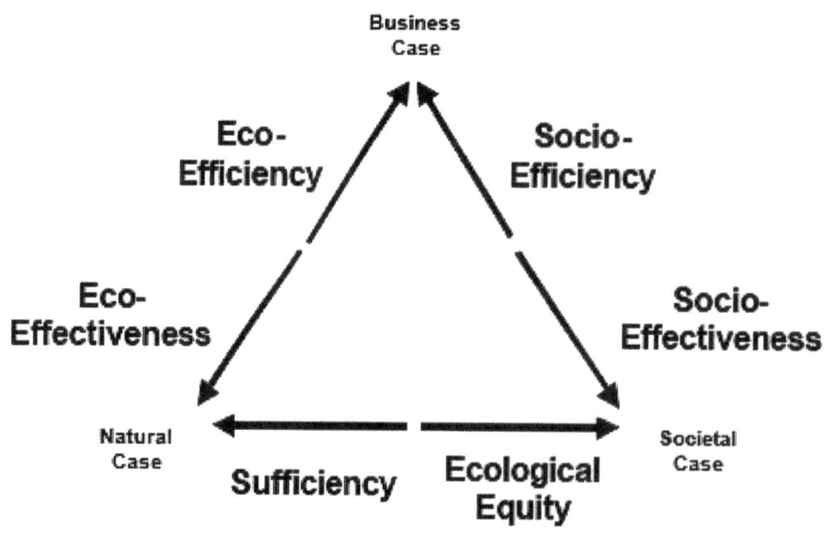

the PPP project to enhance its competitiveness and future orientation while minimizing its operational and maintenance risks (Glasbergen, 2010).

Ofori (2006) shows that sustainability based approach is crucial in today's global business environment. This calls for organizations to incorporate sustainability based approach in their decision-making process and activities in pursuit of the organization's objectives. Yilmaz and Flouris (2010) recommends that the approach must be designed as a process to help following subjects mainly: improving awareness of the necessity for sustainability risk management, promoting innovation and operational efficiency; developing a PPP project specific sustainability risk management model, policy and guideline; integrating sustainable considerations into the decision making process and practices; managing sustainability funds; proactively managing risk and achieve competitive advantages; increasing value and innovative capacities; moving towards sustainable PPP project practices; promoting corporate social investment, citizenship, and social responsibility; increasing financial, social and environmental contributions; and improving corporate reputation.

RISK STAKEHOLDERS

PPP projects especially those of very large natures are multidimensional in terms of cultures, organization and social environment (Bourne, 2009, Aatonen, Jaakko and Tuomas, 2008, Yescombe, 20007, El-Gohary, Osman & El-Diraby, 2006). In these situations, stakeholder management becomes even more pertinent because they are carried out in demanding and unpredictable institutional environments involving a number of diverse actors who are impacted and attempt to impact a project (Aaltonen, Jaakko & Tuomas, 2008). Chinyio and Akintoye (2008) indicate that even from a social perspective, PPP projects in particular should - because of its impact - attempt to serve a vast amount of heterogeneous stakeholders. Given the nature of PPP projects, they do go beyond direct environmental change to the extent of impacting long-term economical and social circumstances as well as the natural environment itself. This causes a need to extend the definition of stakeholders as a whole and thereby merging with the conceptual idea of Corporate Social Responsibility (CSR) (Leiringer, 2006).

Engaging stakeholders in the early stages of a project can help capture potential problems before they occur so that they can be worked through (Aaltonen, Jaakko & Tuomas, 2008). Such problems have the ability, if left unchecked, to derail the construction process at a later stage. Stakeholder engagement is critical for capturing potential project impediments, and implies a willingness to listen, to discuss issues of interest to stakeholders, and, importantly, the organization has to be prepared to consider changing what it aims to achieve and how it operates, as a result of stakeholder engagement. However, the art of handling stakeholders is a challenging issue in the construction sector.

Olander and Landin (2008) argue that a deliberate stakeholder management is able to maximize the value of a PPP project while taking everyone's concerns and needs into consideration. For example, a PPP carried out by a private investor who establishes a SPV, ought to handle external stakeholders well, otherwise managed by the public client. After all, among others, those can be the actual users and their representative unions, landowners and neighbors, local communities, affected businesses, statutory bodies, media, the natural environment and its advocates such as environmentalists, as well as the general public opinion (Eesley & Lenox, 2006). Due to the SPVs impact, they are under supervision by many since they act as financer, executor, and operator. In so doing, the section discusses the vitality of stakeholders, relationships and project politics, and trust and stakeholders' circle.

Vitality of Stakeholders

Literature regarding stakeholder management has increased in popularity in project management journals during the last few years (Littau, Jujagiri & Adlbrecht, 2010). A reason for this interest might be that managers have started to understand that stakeholders can add value to the project, but also threaten its success (Walker & Rowlinson, 2007). Though, when adding PPP to the equation, the research gap increases and few authors have investigated the practitioners' perspective and experiences (Yang, Shen, Drew, & Ho, 2010), which this thesis intends to do. Even so, there is a serious lack of articles discussing important people engagement skills (Achterkamp & Vos, 2008), which are required for a successful stakeholder management (Bourne, 2009).

In order to grasp proper management of stakeholders in a PPP arrangement, it is important to understand who and what really counts (Mitchell, 2013). Freeman (2010) describes stakeholders as any group or individual who can affect or is affected by the achievements of the organization's objectives. According to Atkin and Skitmore (2008), this is a classic definition of stakeholders. While reviewing stakeholder theory in project management literature for a period of 25 years (1984-2009), Littau, Jujagiri & Adlbrecht, 2010) note that there are 22 definitions of stakeholders, but they all origin from three types. Freeman's is one of those, Cleland's individuals and institutions who share a stake or an interest in the project is another, and the third is a mix between those two. A kind of the third type is for example a definition given by Walker and Rowlinson (2007) as "Stakeholders are individuals or groups who have an interest or some aspect of rights or ownership in the project, and can contribute to, or be impacted by, either the work or the outcomes of the project".

Narrowed into different groups, scholars chose to set stakeholders into voluntary and involuntary risk bearers in the project with the commonest being internal and external stakeholders (Harris, 2010; Leung, 2010; Winch, 2010). Typically, internal stakeholders are described as entities with a legal contract to the project and externals as entities with an interest in the project but without a contract (Johnson, Scholes & Whittington, 2007). This would imply that for example the client is seen as an internal stakeholder. Furthermore, Leung (2010) argue that the public client consists of different sub-groups, including for example an environmental bureau, transport and housing bureau, and development bureau. This makes the definition more difficult. To further strengthen the ambiguity of a client definition, it is argued that the concept of the construction (Harris, 2010). In essence, it can be argued that whether a stakeholder is internal or external depends on its proximity to, and activity in the project. Elsewhere, stakeholders have been grouped as primary versus secondary (Littau, Jujagiri & Adlbrecht, 2010). Primary stakeholders have a contractual bond to the project and secondary are those who can affect or can be affected by the project, but might not be essential for the projects' success.

There is a broad array of literature related to the understanding of stakeholders including their identification and management (Olander, 2006). For example, Elmualim (2010) views stakeholders as comprising of those who have power, legitimacy and urgency. Whilst Clegg, Kornberger and Pitsis (2008) are convinced stakeholders also comprises those who are only urgent in their interest and thus may not have direct economical impact on a project outcome. Meanwhile Littau, Jujagiri and Adlbrecht (2010) highlight the process, where identification, classification, analysis, and lastly management of stakeholders are particularized. Bourne (2009) has a slightly different process, which is more commercialized: identify, prioritize, visualize, engage, and monitor. Mitchell (2013) reflects on classification and analysis by examining the stakeholder salience, which is "the degree to which managers give priority to competing stakeholder claims". This is evaluated through power, legitimacy, and urgency (Jones,

Felps & Bigley, 2007). By defining these attributes for each identified stakeholder, they can be classified into seven categories, which are dormant, discretionary, demanding, dominant, dangerous, dependent, and definitive, and a proper management strategy can thereby be chosen. Other authors have discussed legitimacy and urgency, but what Mitchell (2013) adds, is the power and then finally salience. Similar to Mitchell (2013), Bourne (2009) elaborates on power, proximity, and urgency instead. For example, this difference leads to less salience for ministries and other authorities, and stakeholders close to the project become more relevant than the legal authorities. This shows that stakeholder theory is situation adapted and methods should be chosen related to the circumstances and the nature that a project is located in (Yang, Shen, Drew & Ho, 2010).

Beckers, Chiara, Flesch, Maly, Silva and Stegemann (2013) contend that a more comprehensive approach to risk management would address the key issues facing all parties and stakeholders involved in a project throughout its life cycle. Parties and stakeholders to be involved must include project originators and sponsors, the government and public entities tackling both perceived risk and financing gaps (Roome & Wijen, 2006). Andres, Guasch, Andrâes and Andrés (2008) put forward that the extended responsibilities possessed by the private party in a PPP arrangement seem to require a different approach toward external stakeholders. For example, Atkin and Skitmore (2008) argue that construction projects are fairly closed, meaning that the focus is often toward internal stakeholders such as contractors or subcontractors. Managing external stakeholders, however, has been seen as a task for the public officials to deal with, and private parties are perceived as rather narrow-minded in regards to external stakeholder management (de Schepper, Dooms, Haezendonck, 2014).

Suffice to note that stakeholder management concept acknowledges areas such as risks, uncertainties, ethics, empowerment, and sustainability (Atkin & Skitmore, 2008). In order to cope with the PPP specific stakeholder characteristics, the use of a dynamic dual stakeholder management tool is recommended as well as the identification of governance structures that allow the sharing and division of responsibilities between stakeholders (de Schepper, Dooms & Haezendonck, 2014). In respect to a proactive stakeholder management, different strategies can be used in order to cope with contingencies (Tang, Shen & Cheng, 2010). A misjudgment or inadequate selection of a strategy could lead to failure when executing stakeholder management. Morsing and Schultz (2006) deems decision-making as crucial for satisfying stakeholders. Furthermore, Roloff (2008) argues that companies uses two different types of stakeholder theory. These are organization-focused stakeholder management and issue-focused stakeholder management.

Studies have shown that stakeholder management is a key factor for PPP project success (Manowong & Ogunlana, 2010; Atkin & Skitmore, 2008; Jepsen & Eskerod, 2009; Bourne, 2006). Bourne (2009) even argues, "All activities' success or failure, whether they are strategic, operational or tactical, depends on the input, commitment, and support of the stakeholders". In PPP projects, stakeholder management is a decisive factor as well for a projects success or failure. There are several examples of failure in PPP projects due to stakeholder opposition, and therefore understanding and acknowledging stakeholders input is crucial (El-Gohary, Osman & El-Diraby, 2006). For instance, in a PPP project, the private partner through the SPV can help mitigate ideologically driven discussions and thus facilitate stakeholder management. For example, the SPVs are the ones with all contractual relationships as a result they are under supervision by many. This is because they act as different roles in the project. In consequence, proactive stakeholder management contributes and synergizes with proactive risk management as it anticipates and foresees possible social risks and relationship risks (Bing, Akintoye, Edwards & Hardcastle, 2005b; Bourne, 2009). All relationships are created, shaped, and nurtured with communication (Clegg,

Kornberger & Pitsis, 2008; Yang, Shen, Drew & Ho, 2010). Leadership has been identified as vital for a prudent execution of stakeholder management (Elmualim, 2010). This is because all decisions related to stakeholders are built upon personal values and morality (Smyth, 2008).

Proactive stakeholder management contributes and synergizes with proactive risk management as it may anticipates and foresees possible social risks and relationship risks (Bourne, 2009; Bing, Akintoye, Edwards & Hardcastle, 2005b). On PPP projects, those are among others social risks, including public opposition, relationship risks, such as inadequate experience in PPP or differences in working methods between working partners (Bing, Akintoye, Edwards & Hardcastle, 2005b). Management of stakeholders can be conducted by means of traditional risk assessment methods, such as the impact probability-analysis. Conceived in a similar way, the power-interest graph constitutes the bespoken methodology for classifying stakeholder types (Leung, 2010).

From a commercial and managerial perspective, stakeholder management can facilitate successful project execution (Manowong & Ogunlana, 2010; Atkin & Skitmore, 2008; Jepsen & Eskerod, 2009; Bourne & Walker, 2005) in terms of time, costs, and quality. Active stakeholder management has been found to prevent time delays and increased costs that may occur (Harris, 2010). Combining this with the divergent project role that the SPC possesses, it appears necessary to manage stakeholders with due deliberation, especially on infrastructure PPPs (El-Gohary, Osman & El-Diraby, 2006). Cases have shown that projects that a lack of stakeholder management can lead to irreparable damages to a projects' image and its parties involved and can entail detrimental effects on societal benefit. There are for example the Hallandsåsen Tunnel (Olander, 2006), the Berlin Brandenburg International Airport (Germany) (Berg, Deggerich, Hornig & Wassermann, 2012), or the expansion of the west coast line through the city of Lund (Sweden) (Olander & Landin, 2008), which are faced with critics.

Although stakeholder management processes are widely acknowledged, the optimal deployment of resources on stakeholder management activities is contested (Turner, 2006). An important feature in stakeholder management is managing stakeholders' expectations (Atkin & Skitmore, 2008; Bourne & Walker, 2005). Jepsen and Eskerod (2009) argue that the process of detecting these expectations includes an analysis of the stakeholders, which could be time consuming. However, other authors conclude that this process could be well worth the efforts. They also claim that stakeholder management data should be continuously updated through the process in order to cope with, and manage their expectations throughout the project life cycle (Bourne, 2009; Chinyio & Akintoye, 2008). Jepsen and Eskerod (2009) challenge this by stating that a single stakeholder evaluation before the inception of the project may very well last. This initial analysis gives project managers the holistic perspective of the stakeholder environment. Loch and Kavadias (2011) explain the trade-off between effort and gain according to Figure 3. How much resources are worth to spend on a stakeholder analysis? He argues that the challenge is to know when enough is enough.

The entire stakeholder management process is much based on project managers' combination of consciousness and intuitiveness in order to understand stakeholders' expectations and thereby increase their positive input and maximize the project value (Wood, Mukherjee, Bridges & Linkov, 2010; Bourne, 2006; Bourne & Walker, 2005). In essence, experience is an important ingredient in stakeholder management and all decisions taken are therefore often based on instinctiveness, intuitiveness, or prejudices (Sharma, 2013). Even expert decision-makers do not always know how to explain their conclusions (Wood, Mukherjee, Bridges & Linkov, 2010). To conclude, stakeholder management is recognized as a soft skill (Manowong & Ogunlana, 2010; Atkin & Skitmore, 2008; Bourne & Walker, 2005), which is little elaborated in literature (Atkin & Skitmore, 2008).

Figure 3. Optimal resource deployment curve
Source: (Siering & Svensson, 2012)

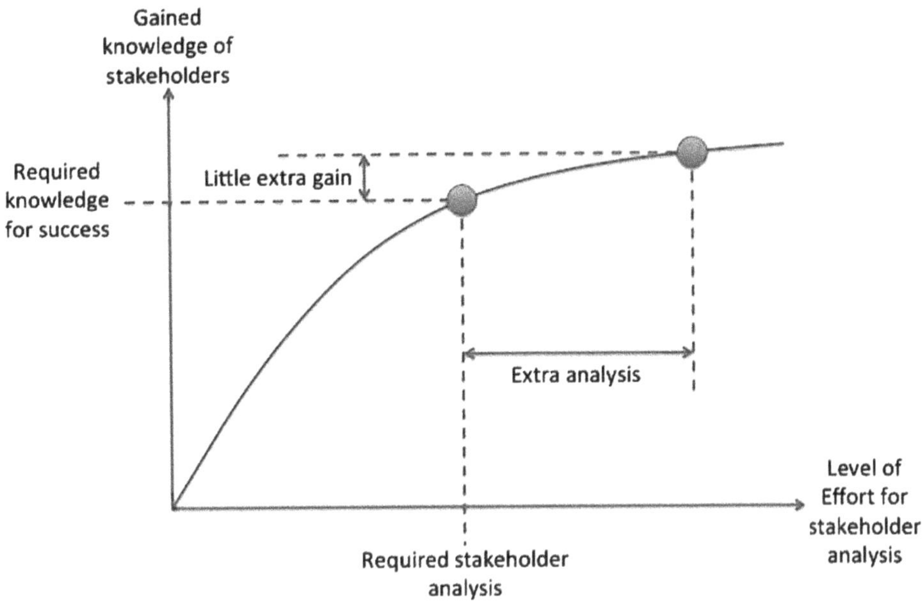

Active participation by key stakeholders should be embraced by all the stakeholders who can potentially influence the project (Yuan, Skibniewski, Li & Zheng, 2010). Project managers should acknowledge the stakeholder management process as an important activity for which adequate resources should be committed (Olander and Landin, 2008). The project manager should have the skill to manage relationships with stakeholders to help raise awareness of the project, thereby making it better prepared to deal with changing stakeholder needs (Vos & Achterkamp, 2006). The ability to respond efficiently and effectively to the difficulties that may arise or issues that need to be resolved is a 'soft skill' that those engaged with the stakeholders should have.

According to Bartkus and Glassman (2008), engaging stakeholders in the early stages of a PPP project can help capture potential problems before they occur so that they can be worked through. Such problems have the ability, if left unchecked, to derail the PPP process at a later stage. Stakeholder engagement is critical for capturing potential project impediments, and implies a willingness to listen, to discuss issues of interest to stakeholders, and, importantly, the organization has to be prepared to consider changing what it aims to achieve and how it operates, as a result of stakeholder engagement (Bourne and Walker, 2005). However, Olander and Atkin (2010) warn that the art of handling stakeholders is challenging issues in the PPP engagement. For example, Shah and Harris (2010) cite factors bringing about these challenges as including effective communication, identifying stakeholder interest, scope and concerns earlier, and building trust, better management of conflicting interest and risk and sense of ownership. It is important, therefore, for PMC and partners to the PPP to have a graphic picture of the composition of stakeholders in the PPP arrangement. This will enable the embrace of the landscape of the several dimensions of the stakeholders groups. Bourne (2006) provides such a graphic picture as illustrated in Figure 4.

From Figure 4 in the circle concept, lines or patterns divide stakeholder groups; the size of a group stands for its interest. Several subdividing lines can visualize a stakeholder group that is heterogeneous

Figure 4. The stakeholder circle
Bourne (2006)

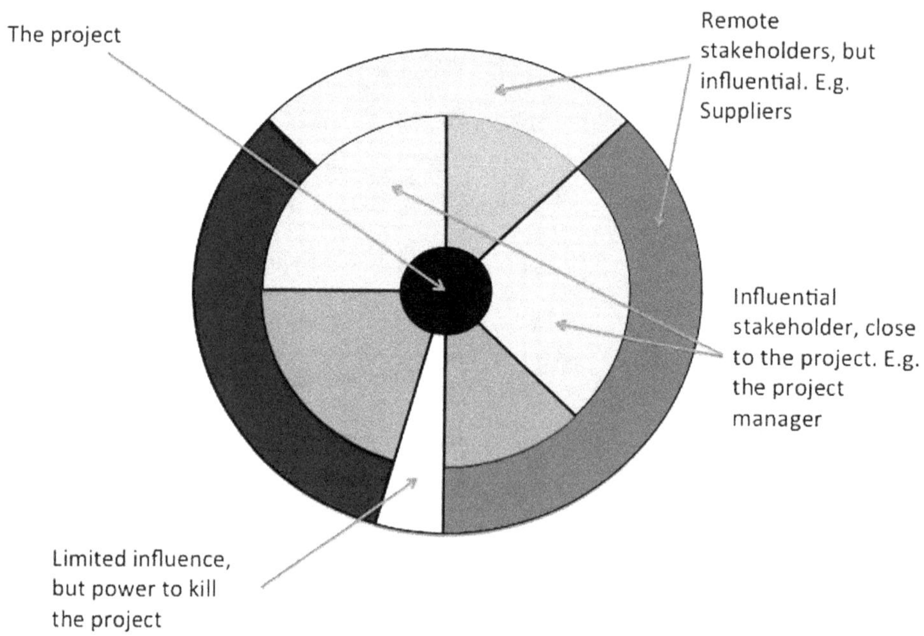

and consists of various individual interests. Their respective direction of influence, for example, upward via senior managers or outwards via external groups can be visualized by specific colors (Bourne & Walker, 2005). Principally, darker colors indicate external stakeholders influence, whereas internal influence shed light. Moreover, the distance of a stakeholder group from the center of the circle indicates how remote or directly a stakeholder exerts influence.

Managing Relationships in a PPP Project

Jepsen and Eskerod (2009) aver most PPP projects consist of individuals and groups with different. This makes PPP project complex in that it has to incorporate the different perspectives of the large number of parties involved (Yescombe, 2007; Bourne, 2009). Related to the importance of understanding stakeholders' expectations, Atkin and Skitmore (2008) contend that managing these diverse interests is a complex task, especially when they are conflicting. Bourne (2009) holds the view that dependent on the stake a stakeholder possesses in a project, they often have diverse perceptions of success and failure. She continues, when adding that their influence or salience is dependent on the power and interest they possess, which is continuously changing, the challenge becomes even more apparent. The prioritization of stakeholders should be exclusive. Mitchell. (2013) as well as Manowong and Ogunlana (2010) propose that certain stakeholders require pertinent devotion and the level of attention should be configured accordingly.

Managing relationships between the different and diverse stakeholders in a PPP project can prove to be very complex and complicated at the same time (van Marrewijk, Clegg, Pitsis & Veenswijk, 2008). According to Kivleniece & Quelin, (2012), this emanates from the fact that the management strategies are context specific, and in terms of stakeholder management, the project managers have to adapt to the stakeholder environment and understand stakeholders' mind-sets toward the project. For example, external stakeholders might try to increase their legitimacy by using media to negatively affect the projects outcome (Aaltonen, Jaakko & Tuomas, 2008). Likewise, Bourne and Walker (2005) argue that project managers have to observe the stakeholder environment actively and constantly by being socially sensible. Many projects, such as large international PPP infrastructure projects are extremely multidimensional in terms of cultures, organizations, and social environments (Bourne, 2009; Aaltonen, Jaakko & Tuomas, 2008; El-Gohary, Osman & El-Diraby, 2006). In addition, stakeholders also share different political risks, and might point out demands for local constraints. Therefore, foreign managers first have to build trust and create good relationships with local employees, and it is essential to study the politics and bureaucracies of local governments (Manowong & Ogunlana, 2010).

In essence, complex projects natures like those of PPPs demand a deliberate stakeholder management (El-Gohary, Osman & El-Diraby, 2006). This is because they are prone to a number of conflicts that requires a good relationship management (Lindgreen & Swaen, 2010). For example, conflicts in construction projects occur mostly because of poor interpersonal skills, inefficient communication, lack of responsiveness and unethical or opportunistic behavior (Frooman, 2005). They are shaped by its legal, political, economical, cultural, social, and technical circumstances (Moura & Teixeira, 2010). It is stated, however, that conflicts are not principally a bad or abnormal phenomenon; it is just a fact of life that managers have to cope with. Moura and Teixeira (2010) contend that stakeholder management is a way to cope with and to prevent these conflicts by proactively managing the relationships. Nonetheless, literature exposes a tendency towards reactive behavioral patterns in the construction industry when relationships are managed (Smyth & Edkins, 2007).

According to Aaltonen, Jaakko and Tuomas (2008), relationships management is one of the most essential ingredients for a successful project. It is fundamental to understand that stakeholder management and relationship management are closely intertwined (Smyth, 2008). Some even consider stakeholder management or stakeholder engagement as the formal procedure of relationship management (Bourne, 2006). In the construction sector, the focus has been toward managing internal relationships. External relationships, however, are considered as being a task that the public client is assigned with (Atkin & Skitmore, 2008). Smyth and Edkins (2007) discuss Gummessons' thirty types of relationships and relate these to the PPP concept. One of these is the relationship to the customers' customer, i.e. the end users, which is seen as a critical success factor. In this respect, SPV managers have to reflect upon what they can do in order to help the clients' users and then take actions. Smyth (2008) contends that all relationships have to be nurtured by the project team. By doing so, social and economical value is added to the project (Smyth, 2008). It is desirable that managers induce a collective behavior among stakeholders in order to reach beneficial results and improve the performance of the project. In respect to this, a proactive management approach is necessary (Smyth, 2008; Atkin & Skitmore, 2008).

According to El-Gohary, Osman and El-Diraby (2006), relationships are much based on shared or non-shared value systems, which determines if a relationship is effective or not. Even though the relationships might be tougher to manage when the value systems are different, it is still possible with various approaches (Moura & Teixeira, 2010). Bourne (2009) proposes three dimensions for a successful relationship management, namely; hard skills referred to as the craft of management, soft skills referred to as the art of leadership, and a third dimension termed as flow. The flow is referred to as the understanding of power structures within and outside the project. Soft skills are essential to cope with hard skills since there are people pursuing the projects and not computers or machines. As Bourne and

Walker (2005) state, there have been many examples of project failure due to misunderstandings and a lack of control over the political process. Therefore, the third dimension becomes fundamental as well.

Clegg, Kornberger and Pitsis (2008) define the process of politics with the process of mobilizing or demobilizing power. Bourne (2006) believes that project managers have to understand these relationships of power and manage them without authority in order to be successful. Furthermore, she concludes that project managers need to understand both formal and informal structures related to the project. Chinyio and Akintoye (2008) avers managing PPP project is not divorce from politics. They are inherently linked since stakeholders who make the bulk of the functioning of a PPP project are political animals. This calls for vigilant on the part of project managers who should have deep reflections on dealing with politics in the course of implementing PPP project. Atkin and Skitmore (2008) advices that such a team should understand and acknowledge the political nature; learn to use appropriate political tactics; understand and accept Wiifm (what's in it for me/them?); level the playing field; learn the art of influencing; develop your negotiation skills and recognize that conflicts are a natural side effect of PPP project management. However, these must be accomplished within the prescient of balancing the power of authority, status and influence as in Figure 5.

Figure 5. Three dimensions of relationship management
Source: (Bourne, 2009)

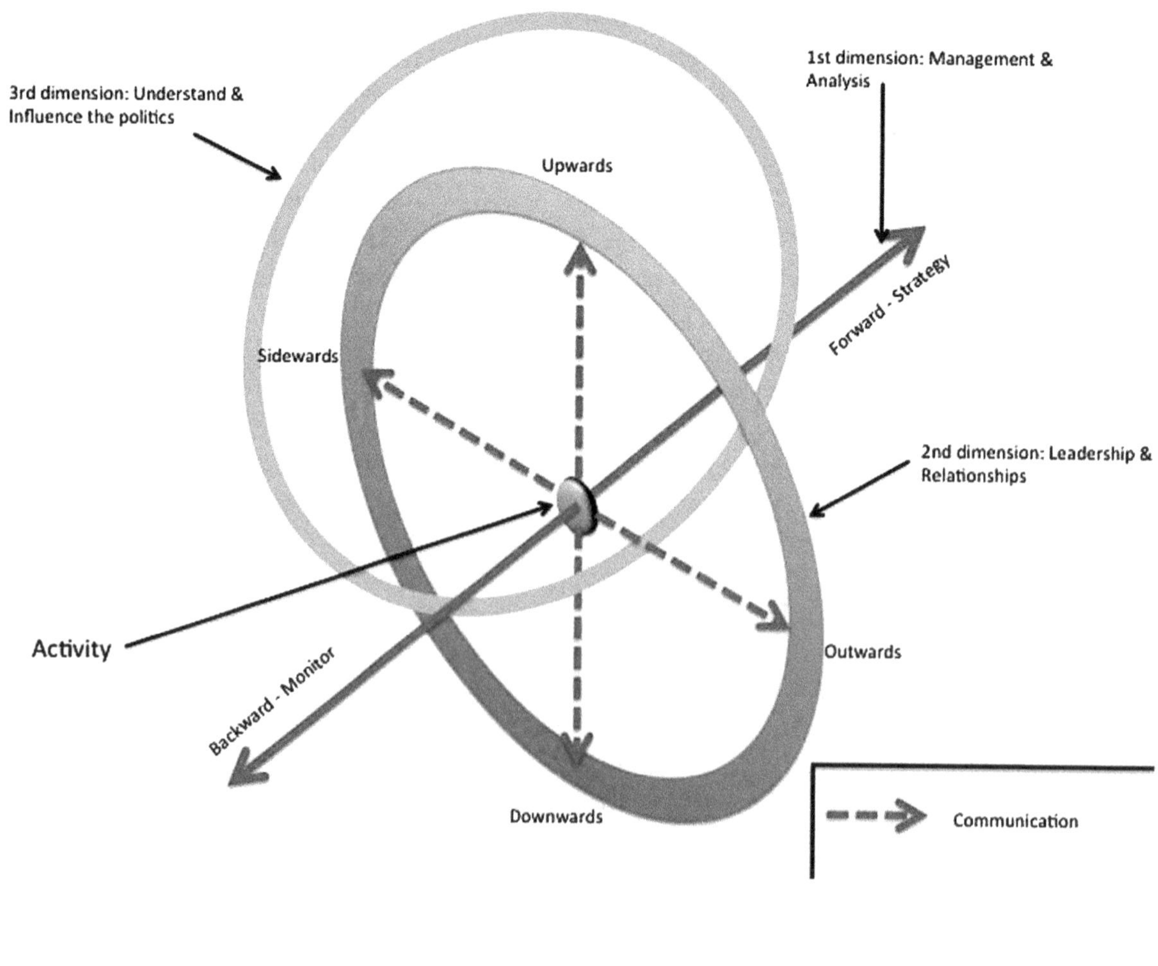

From Figure 5, it is suggested that formal structures are related to hierarchies and other explicit relationships, whereas informal structures are associated to friendships, alliances, and other tacit ties. Bourne (2006) intimates further that personal and social networks are related to the informal structures. Symth and Edkins (2007) claim the informal networks often determine the business networks in a project. They add that some cultures only enter businesses with friends or friends-of-friends, resulting in the informal networks having a colossal power over the project. Consequently, Smyth and Edkins (2007) suggest a greater prioritization for strategic and tactical considerations related to a proactive management of relationships to nurture collaboration between parties, hence increase productivity, and a shift in philosophy from relational contracting to relationship management.

In essence, whether individuals and groups are convinced to follow the project in a desired direction is highly dependent on the project managers' political skills. Clegg, Kornberger and Pitsis (2008) conclude that organizations should be seen as arenas where battles or wars are held between different organizations, departments, individuals, or cultures. In contrast, it is shown that many successful project managers tend to consider their organizations as sensible ecosystems, rather than a battlefield. Pursuing this way, they can easier form project teams, but also partnerships with other branches, customers, and even competitors, who can lead to an organization that follows the market more efficiently Smyth and Edkins (2007) elaborate on the relations between involvement and ability to read the political game. By reflecting on this, project managers can understand their position in the political environment and thereby develop their skills on how to work with pivotal stakeholders.

Building Legitimacy Vis-a-Vis Risk Stakeholders

The legitimacy of risk stakeholders in PPPs can only be build based on trust with the different parties in the projects. It is important to note that when building relationships, trust is a fundamental factor and has shown to improve productivity (Prager & Freese, 2009). Trust can be understood as a psychological state comprising the intention to accept vulnerability based upon positive expectations of the intentions or behavior of another. Smyth and Edkins (2007) draw attention to trust within PPP, where relevant reasons for the importance of trust within these projects are presented. One of these is the long-term nature of the concession agreements, which inherently results in long-term relationships. Positive or negative consequences of trust or lack thereof may cause significant impacts related to that trust could improve productivity. Furthermore, Smyth and Edkins (2007) found that not all, but many of the critical relationships, such as the SPV-Public client relationship, are considered as negative and lack trust and confidence. But there are ways to bridge this and prevent a distrustful environment. For example, informal gatherings, activities and open discussions have shown to increase trust between construction parties (Mika, John & Hannu, 2009).

There are a number of ways in which trust can aid in building risk stakeholders' legitimacy in PPPs. These includes: communication, core values, and corporate social responsibility. Manowong and Ogunlana (2010) advice that it is crucial to establish good communication channels with involved stakeholders, both internal and external by setting clear communication goals, keeping an active involvement, and being persistent. Communication can be seen as an interactive circle including a sender, receiver, message, media, possibly a feedback, and should not be regarded as a one-way process. According to Clegg, Kornberger and Pitsis (2008), communication ought to be seen as an activity to create, shape, and maintain relationships and endorsing mutual understanding. Bourne (2009) suggests that toward external stakeholders, who are little involved in the process, it is important to target the communication with the right information in the right way to the specific stakeholder in mind.

Core values of the PPP must be promoted and communicated robustly. For instance, Clegg, Kornberger and Pitsis (2008) elaborate on a polyphonic environment, which means the presence of many voices, ideas, and perspectives. Smyth (2008) argues in terms of international multidimensional projects, managers must recognize the value of this and not overlook its importance. Everybody needs to be heard, because if someone's voice is ignored its environment becomes less safe and this ultimately serves as a stimulus for the stakeholder to become unpredictable in order to be taken serious. These types of risks and risk management are often related to relationships. Bing, Akintoye, Edwards and Hardcastle, (2005b) suggest some typical samples of micro risks related to relations and PPP projects, such as inadequate experience in PPP, differences in working method and know-how between partners, inadequate distribution of authority in partnerships etc. where the environment in which the PPP exist is sensitive to ethical questions, there is a likelihood of threats to its core values, Elmualim (2010) advices following the rubrics of ethical principles is the way to go. Moreover, individual managers' decisions related stakeholders are built upon a normative foundation of personal values and morality (Smyth, 2008).

Undertaking CSR is one of the superior critical success factors for stakeholder management (Yang, Shen, Drew & Ho, 2010). It demonstrates how PMC and the SPV itself behave towards external groups or individuals who do not have direct access to the PPP project (Porter & Kramer (2006). Since business actions touch on the lives of citizens at many points, it is important that a PPP project must have a clear policy on CSR (Carroll & Shabana, 2010). However, most challenging the idea of CSR, Friedman (2007) claims that social responsibility and business are opposing poles; the only responsibility management held is to make profit for its shareholders. Thus, investing in Stakeholder relations may lead to client or supplier loyalty or improved brand reputation (Leung, 2010). This in turn, leads to positive relationship between stakeholder management and shareholder value wherein effective stakeholder management leads to improved financial performance (Smyth, 2008). In respect to construction, Winch (2010) establishes a new ground as he defines project social responsibility. It comprises to exceed the minimum that is required and determined according to specifications and regulatory consents (Moodley, Smith & Preece, 2008). With respect to PPP projects, Bing, Akintoye, Edwards and Hardcastle (2005) argues that creating value for the society's money is accomplished by a mutually accepted risk allocation scheme, including the mitigation of stakeholder risks. Kumaraswamy and Anvuur (2008) describe that well-performing PPP coalition preliminary rely on collective values and attitudes of individual team members. Top most are listed openness, commitment and joint-decision making, which eventually endorse co-operation and relationships with external parties (Porter & Kramer, 2006).

The purpose of stakeholder management tools is to support decision-making, to share knowledge, to reduce the level of subjectivity and to remain transparent for 'project-outsiders' (Akintoye, Beck & Hardcastle, 2008). Later in the process, it may facilitate understanding of stakeholders' expectations and finally monitors if the process is done effectively (Bourne & Weaver, 2010). Ample stakeholder management tools, methods and techniques exist. More specifically, related terms include: stakeholder analysis; stakeholder mapping; stakeholder risk assessment; power-interest matrix; power-impact grid; influence-interest grid; impact-probability matrix; stakeholder impact index; vested interest index; stakeholder attribute value; stakeholder position value; stakeholder circle; relationship matrices; stakeholder ethical responsibility matrix; stakeholder-commitment matrix; stakeholder review techniques (Bourne & Weaver, 2010; Olander & Atkin, 2010; Manowong & Ogunlana, 2010; Moodley, Smith & Preece, 2008; Olander, 2007).

In building the legitimacy further, it is also important to carry out stakeholder mapping (Arbnor & Bjerke, 2009). According to Bourne and Weaver (2010), stakeholder mapping is compiling a list of stakeholders and consequently to assess and discuss their characteristics. This list finally provides the project team with key information on the stakeholder pool at present. Further, management principles inherently seek to organize, refine and present data in a uniform manner that facilitates a common understanding. Winch (2010) writes that a stakeholder analysis is performed by mapping interests and subsequently identifying potential levers for action. Manowong and Ogunlana (2010) describe plans, such as internal relationship matrices, communication charts and standard communication plans as useful tactics to manage relationships with stakeholders. The importance of clear communication channels is emphasized. In total, it is argued in favor for a greater strategic consideration of proactive behavior towards stakeholders (Manowong & Ogunlana, 2010). Another author states that by means of a stakeholder analysis the unforeseen or uncertainty is evaluated. Hence it may contribute to a contingency plan, functioning as a guiding tool (Harris, 2010). Furthermore, it is added that the outcome of this can be used for an effective conflict management procedures (Shah & Harris, 2010).

In a simplistic manner, stakeholder management tools can help to visualize (Atkin and Skitmore, 2008) what remains tacit in individuals or communities of practice otherwise. As Bourne and Weaver (2010) discuss, information sticks best in human minds if it is reiterated in several modes, including inter-personal discussions, intra-personal reflection and also visualization. Due to the fact that a construction stakeholder landscape is made of complex information, it is best displayed graphically in order to identify effective communication channels. However, even Bourne and Weaver (2010) reflect on their own findings that everything stands or falls on how simple and flexible a tool can eventually be applied. Motivated by this notion, the managerial approach to deploy tools for dealing with stakeholders is confronted with critics. From the practitioners point of view the question raises whether it is worth the effort to list everyone (Jepsen & Eskerod, 2009). In their case study, Jepsen and Eskerod (2009) identify that project teams had difficulties whether to treat a stakeholder as a group or as an individual according to a list. Further they acknowledge that it appeared difficult to keep a stakeholder analysis of a community durable because stakeholders change during the course of a project. Moreover, practitioners stated that vague project boundaries entail a risk when mapping and classifying a limited number of stakeholders (Olander & Landin, 2005).

Finally, the boundary between techniques and tactics on stakeholder management on the one hand, and what is attributed to managing relationships on the other hand, as discussed above, remains opaque. Chinyio and Akintoye (2008) evaluate the existence of those tools by means of operational techniques, such as joint workshops and negotiations. This includes finding trade-offs, making concessions and eventually relying on intuition. Endorsed by several case studies, Chinyio and Akintoye (2008) finally describe stakeholder management as a dialogue-based approach, rather than as a coping strategy. Therefore, the application of tools is not exclusive from relationship management.

Zhang (2005) confers a lot of success factors that contribute to the effective engagement of stakeholders in PPP projects. According to Olander and Landin (2008), effective communication is one of the most common and crucial factors in engaging and managing stakeholders during the planning and project phase. Sutterfield, Friday-Stroud and Shivers-Blackwell (2006) stress that the communication must be effective, regular and planned with community members to ensure project success. Ball, Heafey and King (2007) advice the project manager or stakeholder manager should have excellent negotiation and communication skills to manage the stakeholder expectations and create a positive culture within the organization and for the project.

The need to identify the scope of interest of the various stakeholders was recognized by Mitchel (2013) and Reed (2008). Similarly, Sharma (2008) suggested the key to identifying stakeholders is by developing a comprehensive understanding of who are the stakeholders of the project, what they care about and how they relate to the initiative that the project is trying to launch. Mitchell (2013) highlighted that the opinions and interests of stakeholders can even influence the feasibility phase of the project, including helping improve project planning and design. In addition, identifying stakeholders relative to their interest, power and attitude helps to bring the most salient stakeholders into the decision-making process. Atkin and Skitmore (2008) pointed out that identifying and analyzing stakeholder concerns in the project are indispensable tasks during the participation process in order to arrive at a consensus and avoid project failures. Consequently, stakeholder identification is becoming a critical component of the initial scoping phase and should occur before an engagement plan is formulated and consultation begins (Ball, Heafey & King, 2007)

Trust can be built if the stakeholders are engaged at an early stage of the project (Yang, Shen, Drew & Ho, 2011). Bal, de Lange, Zacher and Van der Heijden (2013) listed "build trust and long term collaborative relationships" as one of the benefits resulting from general stakeholder engagement. Building trust between key internal and external stakeholders is a fundamental prerequisite to meaningful engagement (Jeffery, 2009), as is a focused effort to deepen the level of trust during engagement. It is an even greater step to understand the motivation of the stakeholders, i.e. their thinking, perception, views, cultural, interest, history, political differences, and the willingness of the external stakeholders to engage in the project. Lundy, Gottret & Ashby (2005) stated that to influence positive change and understand why that change has occurred requires long-term, stable relationships capable of evolving to meet new challenges. Trust is the glue that cements these relationships, but develops gradually as partners interact with each other and perceive benefits from the alliance. Building trust between the project manager and the stakeholders helps develop a mutually understanding relationship and enhances the quality of project organization.

Atkin and Skitmore (2008) reported that public participation does not automatically guarantee a mutually agreeable solution, as the interest of various stakeholders vary and are often conflicting. Without thoroughly analyzing and properly managing these various concerns and needs, severe conflicts and controversies can be expected, which may then cause cost and time overruns (Olander, 2007; Olander & Landin, 2005). Conflict is inevitable as each stakeholder group has its own history, character, gender, culture, values, beliefs, and behaviors which influence its actions and motivation (Randeree & Faramawy, 2011). It is suggested that it is better to manage expectations and conflicting interest by not avoiding or postponing the engagement. Generally, conflicts that are observed are due mainly to miscommunication and to the mismanagement of the impacts and concerns of stakeholders (Olander & Landin, 2005).

Engaging stakeholder groups early in relation to strategic decisions and alternatives can help to avoid project opposition and other reputational risks, expensive re-design, and compensation payment according to IFC (2007). They highlighted that there are of course risks to engaging at such an early stage such as project location, uncertain investment of directly engage and during gathering information to develop project concept. Therefore, dialogue and interaction with the stakeholders needs to be carefully handled. Jeffery (2009) explained that organizations can either seek to mitigate risk through the use of stakeholder management, or exploit these new trends to identify and establish new opportunities through the use of meaningful stakeholder engagement. Bal, de Lange, Zacher and Van der Heijden (2013) suggested that risk can be reduced through alignment of mutual interest.

A desire to engage with stakeholders in project decision-making processes is also linked to enhancing the sense of ownership of a project (Mathur, Price & Austin, 2008). The characteristics of successful engagement as highlighted by Shepherd and Bowler (1997) in environmental impact assessments, for instance, have claimed that when citizens' values are incorporated in the project decision making, they develop a sense of ownership of the project. This is considered important for the long-term success and upkeep of a project, and thus incorporates the concern for durability of the project as one of the criteria for its success (Mathu Price & Austin, 2008).

Active participation by key stakeholders should be embraced by all the stakeholders who can potentially influence the project. Project managers should acknowledge the stakeholder management process as an important activity for which adequate resources should be committed (Olander & Landin, 2008). The project manager should have the skill to manage relationships with stakeholders to help raise awareness of the project, thereby making it better prepared to deal with changing stakeholder needs (Bal, de Lange, Zacher and Van der Heijden, 2013). The ability to respond efficiently and effectively to the difficulties that may arise or issues that need to be resolved is a 'soft skill' that those engaged with the stakeholders should have.

Exploring stakeholders' needs and constraints in projects means to investigate stakeholders' areas of interests and list the detailed issues of concern (Freeman et al., 2007). Case studies in Sweden by Olander and Landin (2008) have shown the importance of stakeholder analysis of concerns and needs. The project manager also must clearly identify all types of stakeholders and accommodate their conflicts and needs (Olander & Landin, 2005). Yang, Shen, Ho, Drew and Chan (2009) stated that the stakeholders' commitment, interest and power should be fully assessed so that the project managers can tackle the key problems in the stakeholder management process.

CONCLUSION

This chapter discussed three interrelated topics in risk management: risk management planning, sustainability risk management and risk stakeholders in theory and in practice, with an eye to drawing lessons from theory and experience on conceptual and implementation issues pertaining to these topics, of use for PPP partners and implementers. In brief, the chapter indicated that risk management in PPP is often motivated by stakeholder's involvement in proper planning in a sustainable manner which are currently challenged by alternative views. In practice, risk management in PPP varied between and within projects and were often inconsistent with their alleged objectives. Risk management planning has been an important policy issue, trying to address the problem of PPP failure. Interestingly, it has led to resource-intensive and institutionally demanding needs for sustainability. There is an ongoing controversy on the evidence of active involvement of the stakeholders, yet balance support for the idea that it has led to improved and successful PPPs. The evidence on stakeholders' inclusive involvement is less sanguine. PPP partners often lack the competence required for successful incorporation of the stakeholders in the PPP processes. In the absence of such competence proceeding with risk management in PPP may fail to lead to success. In addition, for some of the PPPs it is arguably more crucial to develop a purposeful planning strategy, sustainability promotion and stakeholders' inclusiveness, including institutional and social capital, thus to enable PPP project succeed. In this context, risk management planning, sustainability risks management and risk stakeholders should all be seen within the broader context of enhancing productivity as well as success. At the theoretical level, the risk management planning should aim at maximizing the net benefits from sustainability principles. In this context, sustainability risk management can be a potent means of addressing problems of PPP project failures, introducing competition and enhancing incentives for productivity. Establishing a framework to promote and encourage involvement of all the stakeholders can be important for the benefits of the PPP project to succeed; as it is a better mean to make those who matter to play their rightful roles. It is important to observe that the road to PPP project productivity and success is not one-way. PPP partners and implementers should exploit the informational benefits from the existence of proper planning and principles of sustainability, to include deeply involves all the stakeholders. Theory and practice suggest there are no panaceas. Risk management planning, sustainability risk management and risk stakeholders should be combined in a way that aims at enhancing innovation and productivity, rather than finding an optimal state. These should be a means to an end. If not properly conceived and implemented, and in the absence of a suitable regulatory framework, their benefits could be severely compromised. Mistakes are bound to occur to derail managing risks in the PPP project.

REFERENCES

Aaltonen, K., Jaakko, K., & Tuomas, O. (2008). Stakeholder salience in global projects. *International Journal of Project Management*, *26*(5), 509–516. doi:10.1016/j.ijproman.2008.05.004

Abbasianjahromi, H., & Rajaie, H. (2012). Developing a project portfolio selection model for contractor firms considering the risk factor. *Journal of Civil Engineering and Management*, *18*(6), 879–889. doi:10.3846/13923730.2012.734856

Abbott, K. W. (2012). Engaging the public and the private in global sustainability governance. *International Affairs*, *88*(3), 543–564. doi:10.1111/j.1468-2346.2012.01088.x

Abdul-Rahman, H., Wang, C., & Lee, Y. L. (2013). Design and pilot run of fuzzy synthetic model (FSM) for risk evaluation in civil engineering. *Journal of Civil Engineering and Management*, *19*(2), 217–238. doi:10.3846/13923730.2012.743926

Adams, J., Alistair, Y., & Wu, Z. H. (2006). Public private partnerships in China-system, constraints and future prospects. *International Journal of Public Sector Management*, *19*(4), 384–396. doi:10.1108/09513550610669202

Ajayi, J. R., & Isah, Y. (2014). Impediments to risk assessment techniques in public-private partnership construction projects in Abuja-Nigeria. *Malaysian Journal of Civil Engineering*, *26*(3), 366–381.

Akintoye, A. (2006). Public private partnerships for sustainable development of Infrastructure in developing countries. *Proceedings of International Conference on the Built Environment.*

Akintoye, A., Beck, M., & Hardcastle, C. (Eds.). (2008). Public-Private Partnerships: Managing risks and opportunities. Chichester, UK: Wiley.

Al-Kharashi, A., & Skitmore, M. (2009). Causes of delays in Saudi Arabian public sector construction projects. *Construction Management and Economics*, *27*(1), 3–23. doi:10.1080/01446190802541457

Anderson, D. (2005). *Corporate survival: The critical importance of sustainability risk management.* New York: iUniverse.com.

Andonova, L. B. (2010). Public-private partnerships for the earth: Politics and patterns of hybrid authority in the multilateral system. *Global Environmental Politics*, *10*(2), 25–53. doi:10.1162/glep.2010.10.2.25

Andres, L., Guasch, J. L., Andrâes, L. & Andrés, L. (2008). *The impact of private sector participation in infrastructure*. Academic Press.

Arbnor, I., & Bjerke, B. (2009). *Methodology for creating business knowledge*. London: SAGE Publications Ltd. doi:10.4135/9780857024473

Asness, C. S., Frazzini, A., & Pedersen, L. H. (2012). Leverage aversion and risk parity. *Financial Analysts Journal*, *68*(1), 47–59. doi:10.2469/faj.v68.n1.1

Assaf, S. A., & Al-Hejji, S. (2006). Causes of delay in large construction projects. *International Journal of Project Management*, *24*(4), 349–357. doi:10.1016/j.ijproman.2005.11.010

Atkin, B., & Skitmore, M. (2008). Stakeholder management in construction. *Construction Management and Economics*, *26*(6), 549–552. doi:10.1080/01446190802142405

Atkin, B., & Skitmore, M. (2008). Stakeholder management in construction. *Construction Management and Economics*, *26*(6), 549–552. doi:10.1080/01446190802142405

Ayeni, K. (2005). Risk identification and management in BOT Project Implementation. *Proceedings of BOT Awareness Seminar, Abuja Investment and Property Development Company.*

Aziz, A. M. A. (2007). Successful delivery of public-private partnerships for infrastructure development. *Journal of Construction Engineering and Management*, *133*(12), 918–931. doi:10.1061/(ASCE)0733-9364(2007)133:12(918)

Baars, J., Kocourek, P., & van der Lende, E. (2012). Integrated approach to ALM, Risk budgeting and alpha. *Multi-Asset Solutions Research Papers*, *2*, 1–13.

Babatunde, S. O., Opawole, A., & Akinsiku, O. E. (2012). Critical success factors in public– private partnership (PPP) on infrastructure delivery in Nigeria. *Journal of Facility Management*, *10*(3), 212–225. doi:10.1108/14725961211246018

Bäckstrand, K. (2006). Multi-stakeholder partnerships for sustainable development: Rethinking legitimacy, accountability and effectiveness. *European Environment*, *16*(5), 290–306. doi:10.1002/eet.425

Bäckstrand, K. (2012). Are partnerships for sustainable development democratic and legitimate? In P. Pattberg, F. Biermann, S. Chan, & A. Mert (Eds.), *Public-private partnerships for sustainable development: emergence, influence and legitimacy*. Cheltenham, UK: Edward Elgar. doi:10.4337/9781849809313.00018

Baharuddin, H., Wilkinson, S., & Costello, S. (2014). Enhancing features of early stakeholder engagement in expressway projects.*Proceedings of the 4th New Zealand Built Environment Research Symposium (NZBERS).*

Bal, P.M., de Lange, A.H., Zacher, H., & Van der Heijden, D.I.J. (2013). A lifespan perspective on psychological contracts and their relations with organizational commitment. *European Journal of Work and Organizational Psychology, 22*(3), 78-86.

Ball, R., Heafey, M., & King, D. (2007). The Private Finance Initiative in the UK: A value for money and economic analysis. *Public Management Review, 9*(2), 289–310. doi:10.1080/14719030701340507

Bartkus, B., & Glassman, M. (2008). Do firms practice what they preach? The relationship between mission statements and stakeholder management. *Journal of Business Ethics, 83*(2), 207–216. doi:10.1007/s10551-007-9612-0

Beckers, F., Chiara, N., Flesch, A., Maly, J., Silva, E., & Stegemann, W. (2013). *A risk- management approach to a successful infrastructure project Initiation, financing, and execution*. McKinsey Working Papers on Risk, Number 52, 4-10.

Beisheim, M. (2012). *Partnerships for sustainable development: why and how Rio+ 20 must improve the framework for multi-stakeholder partnerships. RP 3. Stiftung Wissenschaft und Politik*. German Institute for International and Security Affairs.

Beisheim, M., & Liese, A. (2014). *Transnational partnerships: effectively providing for sustainable development?* London: Palgrave Macmillan. doi:10.1057/9781137359537

Berg, H.-P. (2010). Risk management: Procedures, methods and experiences. *RT&T, 1*(2), 79–95.

Berkelaar, A.B., Kobor, A., & Tsumagari, M. (2006). The sense and nonsense of risk budgeting. *Financial Analysts Journal, 62*(5), 63-75.

Bing, L., Akintoye, A., Edwards, P., & Hardcastle, C. (2005a). Perceptions of positive and negative factors influencing the attractiveness of PPP procurement for construction projects in the UK – Findings from a questionnaire survey. *Engineering, Construction, and Architectural Management, 12*(2), 125–148. doi:10.1108/09699980510584485

Bing, L., Akintoye, A., Edwards, P. J., & Hardcastle, C. (2005b). The allocation of risk in PPP/PFI construction projects in the UK. *International Journal of Project Management, 23*(1), 25–35. doi:10.1016/j.ijproman.2004.04.006

Bloomfield, P. (2006). The challenging business of long-term public-private partnerships: Reflections on local experience. *Public Administration Review, 66*(3), 400–411. doi:10.1111/j.1540-6210.2006.00597.x

Borghesi, A., & Gaudenzi, B. (2012). *Risk management: How to assess, transfer and communicate critical risks*. Milano: Springer.

Bourne, L. (2006). Visualizing stakeholder influence - Two Australian examples. *Project Management Journal, 37*(1), 5–21.

Bourne, L. (2009). *Stakeholder Relationship Management: a maturity model for organizational implementation*. Farnham, UK: Gower.

Bourne, L., & Walker, D. H. T. (2005). Visualizing and mapping stakeholder influence. *Management Decision, 43*(5), 649–660. doi:10.1108/00251740510597680

Bourne, L., & Weaver, P. (Eds.). (2010). Mapping Stakeholders. In Construction stakeholder management. Chichester, UK: Backwell Publishing Ltd.

Bruder, B., & Roncalli, T. (2012). *Managing risk exposures using the risk budgeting approach.* Paper presented at a conference at ESSEC Business School (WG Risk), Paris, France. Retrieved from http://www.thierry-roncalli.com/download/risk-budgeting.pdf

Cankar, S. S., & Petkovšek, V. (2013). Private and public sector innovation and the importance of cross-sector collaboration. *Journal of Applied Business Research, 29*(6), 197–1606.

Carbonara, N., Costantino, N., Gunnigan, L., & Pellegrino, R. (2015). Risk Management in Motorway PPP Projects: Empirical-based Guidelines. *Transport Reviews, 35*(2), 1–12. doi:10.1080/01441647.2015.1012696

Carrillo, P. M., Robinson, H. S., Anumba, C. J., & Bochilaghem, N. M. (2006). A knowledge transfer framework: The PFI context. *Construction Management and Economics, 24*(10), 1045–1056. doi:10.1080/01446190600799224

Carroll, A. B., & Shabana, K. M. (2010). The Business Case for Corporate Social Responsibility: A Review of Concepts, Research and Practice. *International Journal of Management Reviews, 12*(1), 85–105. doi:10.1111/j.1468-2370.2009.00275.x

Chapman, R. J. (2007). *Simple tools and techniques for enterprise risk management.* Hoboken, NJ: John Wiley &Sons.

Cheung, E., Chan, A. P. C., & Kajewski, S. (2012). Factors contributing to successful public private partnership projects, comparing Hong Kong with Australia and the United Kingdom. *Journal of Facility Management, 10*(1), 45–58. doi:10.1108/14725961211200397

Chinyio, E., & Akintoye, A. (2008). Practical approaches for engaging stakeholders: Findings from the UK. *Construction Management and Economics, 26*(6), 591–599. doi:10.1080/01446190802078310

Chinyio, E., & Akintoye, A. (2008). Practical approaches for engaging stakeholders: Findings from the UK. *Construction Management and Economics, 26*(6), 591–599. doi:10.1080/01446190802078310

Christopher, M., & Gaudenzi, B. (2015). Managing risks in sustainable supply chains. *Sinergie Italian Journal of Management, 33*(96), 57–74.

Cleden, D. (2009). *Managing project uncertainty.* Abingdon, UK: Ashgate Publishing Group.

Clegg, S., Kornberger, M., & Pitsis, T. (2008). *Managing & Organizations* (2nd ed.). London: SAGE Publications Ltd.

Cleland, D. I., & Gareis, R. (2006). *Global Project Management Handbook: Planning, Organizing, and Controlling International Projects* (2nd ed.). New York: McGraw- Hill.

Dada, M. O., & Oladokun, M. G. (2012). Analysis of critical success sub-factors for public- private partnership in Nigeria. *Alam-cipta, 5*(2), 13–26.

Dallas, M. (2006). *Value and risk management; a guide to best practice.* Oxford, UK: Blackwell Publication.

de Carvalho, R., Lu, X., & Moulin, P. (2012). Demystifying equity risk–based strategies: A simple alpha plus beta description. *Journal of Portfolio Management, 38*(3), 56–70. doi:10.3905/jpm.2012.38.3.056

de Carvalho, R. L., Lu, X., & Pierre Moulin, P. (2014). An integrated risk-budgeting approach for multi-strategy equity portfolios. *Journal of Asset Management, 15*(1), 24–47. doi:10.1057/jam.2014.11

De Schepper, S., Dooms, M., & Haezendonck, E. (2014). Stakeholder dynamics and responsibilities in Public–Private Partnerships: A mixed experience. *International Journal of Project Management, 32*(7), 1210–1222. doi:10.1016/j.ijproman.2014.01.006

Dechev, D. (2015). Public-private partnership - a new perspective for the transition countries. *Trakia Journal of Sciences, 3*(3), 228–236. doi:10.15547/tjs.2015.03.005

Delmon, J. (2009). *Private sector investment in infrastructure: Project finance, PPP projects and risk.* New York: The World Bank and Kluwer Law International.

Delmon, J. (2011). *Public-private partnership projects in infrastructure: An essential guide for policy-makers.* New York: Cambridge University Press.

Didraga, O. (2013). The role and the effects of risk management in IT projects success. *Informatica Economică, 17*(1), 86–79. doi:10.12948/issn14531305/17.1.2013.08

El-Gohary, N. M., Osman, H., & El-Diraby, T. E. (2006). Stakeholder management for public private partnerships. *International Journal of Project Management, 24*(7), 595–604. doi:10.1016/j.ijproman.2006.07.009

Elmualim, A. (2010). Culture and leadership in stakeholder management. In Construction stakeholder management. Chichester, UK: Backwell Publishing Ltd.

Enshassi, A., Mohamed, S., & Abu-Mosa, J. (2008). Risk Management in building projects in Palestine contractors' perspective. *Emirates Journal for Engineering Research, 13*(1), 29–44.

Epstein, M. J. (2009). *Making sustainability work: Best practices in managing and measuring corporate social, environmental, and economic impacts.* London: Berrett-Koehler Publishers.

Esquer-Peralta, J. (2006). *The Sustainability performance criteria. Sustainability Management Systems (SMS): Sustainable development in relation to different kinds of management systems.* 10th Canadian Pollution Prevention Roundtable, Halifax, Canada. Retrieved from http://www.c2p2online.com/documents/Javier_Esquer-Peralta.pdf

Firmenich, J. (2011). *Identification of parameters for a quantitative risk allocation model with systematic review.* Paper presented at the Sixth International Structural Engineering and Construction Conference: Modern Methods and Advances in Structural Engineering and Construction, Zurich, Switzerland. doi:10.3850/978-981-08-7920-4_S3-I003-cd

Fischer, K., Leidel, K., Riemann, A., & Wilhelm Alfen, H. (2010). An integrated risk management system (IRMS) for PPP projects. *Journal of Financial Management of Property and Construction, 15*(3), 260–282. doi:10.1108/13664381011087515

Foerstl, K., Reuter, C., Hartmann, E., & Blome, C. (2010). Managing supplier sustainability risks in a dynamically changing environment- Sustainable supplier management in the chemical Industry. *Journal of Purchasing and Supply Management*, *16*(2), 118–130. doi:10.1016/j.pursup.2010.03.011

Forrer, J., Kee, J. E., Newcomer, K. E., & Boyer, E. (2010). Public private partnerships and the public accountability question. *Public Administration Review*, *70*(3), 475–484. doi:10.1111/j.1540-6210.2010.02161.x

Freeman, R. E. (2010). *Strategic management: a stakeholder approach*. Cambridge, UK: Cambridge University Press. doi:10.1017/CBO9781139192675

Freeman, R. E., Harrison, J. S., & Wicks, A. C. (2007). *Managing for Stakeholders – Survival, reputation, and success*. Louis Stern Memorial Fund.

Friedman, M. (2007). The Social Responsibility of Business Is to Increase Its Profits. In W. Zimmerli, M. Holzinger, & K. Richter (Eds.), *Corporate Ethics and Corporate Governance*. Berlin: Springer. doi:10.1007/978-3-540-70818-6_14

Frooman, J., & Murrell, A. J. (2005). Stakeholder influence strategies: The roles of structural and demographic determinants. *Business & Society*, *44*(1), 3–31. doi:10.1177/0007650304273434

Glasbergen, P. (2010). Global action networks: Agents for collective action. *Global Environmental Change*, *20*(1), 130–141. doi:10.1016/j.gloenvcha.2009.09.002

Glasbergen, P. (2011). Understanding partnerships for sustainable development analytically: the ladder of partnership activity as a methodological tool. *Environmental Policy and Governance, 21*, 1-13.

Glasbergen, P., Biermann, F., & Mol, A. P. J. (Eds.). (2007). *Partnerships, governance and sustainable development: reflections on theory and practice*. Cheltenham, UK: Edward Elgar. doi:10.4337/9781847208668

Gunawansa, A. (2010). *Is there a need for public private partnership projects in Singapore*? Paper presented at the Construction, Building and Real Estate Research Conference of the Royal Institution of Chartered Surveyors, Paris, France.

Hameed, A., & Woo, S. (2007). Risk importance and allocation in Pakistan construction industry: A contractors perspective. *KSCE Journal of Civil Engineering*, *11*(2), 73–80. doi:10.1007/BF02823850

Handley-Schachler, M., & Navare, J. (2010). Port risk management and public private partnerships: Factors relating to risk allocation and risk sustainability. *World Review of Intermodal Transportation Research*, *3*(1-2), 150–166. doi:10.1504/WRITR.2010.031585

Hanna, A. S., Thomas, G., & Swanson, J. R. (2013). Construction risk identification and allocation: Cooperative approach. *Journal of Construction Engineering and Management*, *139*(9), 1098–1107. doi:10.1061/(ASCE)CO.1943-7862.0000703

Harris, F. (2010). A historical overview of stakeholder management. In Construction stakeholder management. Chichester, UK: Backwell Publishing Ltd.

Ho, H. K. (2006). Development of public private partnerships (PPPs) in China. Surveyors Times, 15(10).

Ho, S. P. (2006b). Model for financial re-negotiation in public-private partnership projects and its policy implications: Game theoretic view. *Journal of Construction Engineering and Management, 132*(7), 678–688. doi:10.1061/(ASCE)0733-9364(2006)132:7(678)

Ika, L. (2009). Project success as a topic in project management journals. *Project Management Journal, 40*(4), 6–10. doi:10.1002/pmj.20137

Ismail, S., & Harris, F. A. (2014). *Challenges in implementing public private partnership (PPP) in Malaysia*. Paper presented at the International Conference on Accounting Studies 2014, Kuala Lumpur, Malaysia.

Jacobson, C., & Choi, S. O. (2008). Success factors: Public works and public– private partnerships. *International Journal of Public Sector Management, 21*(6), 637–657. doi:10.1108/09513550810896514

Jefferies, M. (2006). Critical success factors of public private sector partnerships: A case study of the Sydney SuperDome. *Engineering, Construction, and Architectural Management, 13*(5), 451–462. doi:10.1108/09699980610690738

Jeffery, N. (2009). *Stakeholder Engagement: A road map to meaningful engagement #2 in the Doughty Centre 'How to do Corporate Responsibility' Series*. Retrieved from https://dspace.lib.cranfield.ac.uk

Jepsen, A. L., & Eskerod, P. (2009). Stakeholder analysis in projects: Challenges in using current guidelines in the real world. *International Journal of Project Management, 27*(4), 335–343. doi:10.1016/j.ijproman.2008.04.002

Johnson, G., Scholes, K., & Whittington, R. (Eds.). (2007). *Exploring corporate strategy text & cases*. Pearson Education.

Jones, T. M., Felps, W., & Bigley, G. A. (2007). Ethical theory and stakeholder-related decisions: The role of stakeholder culture. *Academy of Management Review, 32*(1), 137–155. doi:10.5465/AMR.2007.23463924

Jooste, S. F., Levitt, R. E., & Scott, W. R. (2011). Beyond one size fits all: How local conditions shape PPP enabled field development. *Engineering Project Organization Journal, 1*(1), 11–25. doi:10.1080/21573727.2010.549612

Kivleniece, I., & Quelin, B. V. (2012). Creating and capturing value in public-private ties: A private actors perspective. *Academy of Management Review, 37*(2), 272–299. doi:10.5465/amr.2011.0004

Kolhatkar, M., & Dutta, A. B. (2013). Study of risk in construction projects. *Global Research Analysis International, 2*(9), 104–107.

Koppenjan, J. F. M. (2005). The formation of public-private partnerships: Lessons from nine transportation infrastructure projects in the Netherlands. *Public Administration, 83*(1), 135–157. doi:10.1111/j.0033-3298.2005.00441.x

Kriześ-Dobieszewska, J. (2014). Managing public-private partnership market in the times of economic crisis. *Oeconomia Copernicana, 5*(2), 63–73. doi:10.12775/OeC.2014.014

Kumaraswamy, M. M., & Anvuur, A. M. (2008). Selecting sustainable teams for PPP projects. *Building and Environment, 43*(6), 999–1009. doi:10.1016/j.buildenv.2007.02.001

Kurunmäki, L., & Miller, P. (2011). Regulatory Hybrids: Partnerships, Budgeting and Modernizing Government. *Management Accounting Research*, *22*(4), 220–241. doi:10.1016/j.mar.2010.08.004

Kuzmina, J. (2010). Risk management for sustainable growth. *Management and Sustainable Development, 2*, 26-34.

Leiringer, R. (2006). Technological innovation in PPPs: Incentives, opportunities and actions. *Construction Management and Economics*, *24*(3), 301–308. doi:10.1080/01446190500435028

Leung, M. O. P. (2010). Risk and construction stakeholder management. In Construction stakeholder management. Chichester, UK: Blackwell Publishing Ltd.

Lindgreen, A., & Swaen, V. (2010). Corporate social responsibility. *International Journal of Management Reviews*, *12*(1), 1–7. doi:10.1111/j.1468-2370.2009.00277.x

Littau, P., Jujagiri, N. J., & Adlbrecht, G. (2010). 25 years of stakeholder theory in project management literature (1984–2009). *Project Management Journal*, *41*(4), 17–29. doi:10.1002/pmj.20195

Liu, H. Z., & Zheng, M. L. (2008). Analysis on integrated risk response planning in large projects. *Proceedings of the 3rd international conference on product innovation management*, 1-2, 1325-1328.

Liu, T., & Wilkinson, S. (2014). Large-scale public venue development and the application of public-private partnerships. *International Journal of Project Management*, *32*(1), 88–100. doi:10.1016/j.ijproman.2013.01.003

Loch, C., & Kavadias, S. (2011). Implementing Strategy Through Projects. In The Oxford Handbook of Project Management. Oxford, UK: Oxford University Press.

Lundy, M., Gottret, M. V., & Ashby, J. (2005). *Learning alliances: An approach for building multi-stakeholder innovation systems. Institutional learning and change*. ILAC.

Maillard, S., Roncalli, T., & Teiletche, J. (2010). The properties of equally weighted risk contributions portfolios. *Journal of Portfolio Management*, *36*(4), 60–70. doi:10.3905/jpm.2010.36.4.060

Makovsek, D. (2013). Public-private partnerships, traditionally financed projects, and their price. *Journal of Transport Economics and Policy, 47*(1), 143-155.

Manowong, E., & Ogunlana, S. (2010). Strategies and tactics for managing construction stakeholders. In Construction stakeholder management. Chichester, UK: Blackwell Publishing Ltd.

Martens, J. (2007). *Multistakeholder partnerships: future models of multilateralism.* Occasional paper, Friedrich Elbert Stiftung. Retrieved from http://library.fes.de/pdf-files/iez/04244.pdf

Maseko, M. (2014). *Analysis of critical success factors for public-private partnerships in infrastructure development in South Africa*. Paper presented at the 6th International Platinum Conference, 'Platinum–Metal for the Future, The Southern African Institute of Mining and Metallurgy.

Mathur, V. N., Price, A. D. F., & Austin, S. (2008). Conceptualizing stakeholder engagement in the context of sustainability and its assessment. *Construction Management and Economics*, *26*(6), 601–609. doi:10.1080/01446190802061233

McNeil, A., Frey, R., & Embrechts, P. (2006). *Quantitative risk management concepts, techniques and tools*. New York: Princeton University Press.

Mert, A., & Chan, S. (2012). The politics of partnerships for sustainable development. In Public-private partnerships for sustainable development: Emergence, influence and legitimacy. Cheltenham, UK: Edward Elgar.

Mika, G., John, D., & Hannu, S. (2009). Transformational team-building across cultural boundaries. *Team Performance Management*, *15*(5/6), 235–256. doi:10.1108/13527590910983512

Mitchell, R. (2013). Best Practice Stakeholder Engagement. *IAIA13 Conference Proceedings Impact Assessment the Next Generation 33rd Annual Meeting of the International Association for Impact Assessment*. Retrieved from www.iaia.org

Moodley, K., Smith, N., & Preece, C. (2008). Stakeholder matrix for ethical relationships in the construction industry. *Construction Management and Economics*, *26*(6), 625–632. doi:10.1080/01446190801965368

Morsink, K., Hofman, P. S., & Lovett, J. C. (2011). Multi-stakeholder partnerships for transfer of environmentally-sound technologies. *Energy Policy*, *39*(1), 1–5. doi:10.1016/j.enpol.2010.09.043

Moura, H. M., & Teixeira, J. C. (2010). Managing Stakeholder Conflicts. In Construction stakeholder management. Chichester, UK: Backwell Publishing Ltd.

Ng, S. T., Wong, Y. M., & Wong, J. M. (2012). Factors influencing the success of PPP at feasibility stage—a tripartite comparison study in Hong Kong. *Habitat International*, *36*(4), 423–432. doi:10.1016/j.habitatint.2012.02.002

Nielsen, K. R. (2006). Risk Management: Lessons from Six Continents. *Journal of Management Engineering*, *22*(2), 61–67. doi:10.1061/(ASCE)0742-597X(2006)22:2(61)

Nisar, T. M. (2007). Risk Management in Public-Private Partnership Contracts. *Public Organization Review*, *7*(1), 1–20. doi:10.1007/s11115-006-0020-1

Ofori, G. (2006). Attaining sustainability through construction procurement in Singapore. *Proceedings of symposium on sustainability and value through construction procurement*.

Ogbu, C. P. (2013). Risk management practices of multinational and indigenous construction companies in Nigeria: A comparative analysis. *Journal of Research in National Development*, *9*(2), 315–324.

Ogunsanmi, O. E. (2013). Critical success factors (CSF) determining the implementation of public- private partnership projects. *Covenant Journal of Research in the Built Environment*, *1*(2), 41–66.

Olander, S. (2006). *External stakeholder analysis in construction project management*. Lund University.

Olander, S. (2007). Stakeholder impact analysis in construction project management. *Construction Management and Economics*, *25*(3), 277–287. doi:10.1080/01446190600879125

Olander, S., & Atkin, B. L. (Eds.). (2010). Stakeholder Management - The gains and pains. In Construction stakeholder management. Chichester, UK: Backwell Publishing Ltd.

Olander, S., & Landin, A. (2005). Evaluation of stakeholder influence in the implementation of construction projects. *International Journal of Project Management*, *23*(4), 321–328. doi:10.1016/j.ijproman.2005.02.002

Olander, S., & Landin, A. (2008). A comparative study of factors affecting the external stakeholder management process. *Construction Management and Economics*, *26*(6), 553–561. doi:10.1080/01446190701821810

Pajunen, K. (2006). Stakeholder influences in organizational survival. *Journal of Management Studies*, *43*(6), 1261–1288. doi:10.1111/j.1467-6486.2006.00624.x

Papajohn, D., Cui, Q., & Bayraktar, M. E. (2011). Public-private partnerships in US transportation: Research overview and a path forward. *Journal of Management Engineering*, *27*(3), 126–135. doi:10.1061/(ASCE)ME.1943-5479.0000050

Pattberg, P. (2005). What role for private rule-making in global environmental governance? Analyzing the Forest Stewardship Council (FSC). *International Environmental Agreement: Politics, Law and Economics*, *5*(2), 175–189. doi:10.1007/s10784-005-0951-y

Pattberg, P. (2010). Public–private partnerships in global climate governance. *Wiley Interdisciplinary Reviews: Climate Change*, *1*(2), 279–287. doi:10.1002/wcc.38

Pattberg, P., Biermann, F., Chan, S., & Mert, A. (2012). *Public-private partnerships for sustainable development: emergence, influence and legitimacy*. Cheltenham, UK: Edward Elgar. doi:10.4337/9781849809313

Peterson, S. (2006). *Risk budgeting theory and application*. VRS White paper series. Retrieved from http://citeseerx.ist.psu.edu/viewdoc/download?doi=10.1.1.526.8682&rep=rep1&type

Pollard, D., & Stephen, D. W. (2008). *Sustainability, risk and opportunity: A holistic approach*. New York: Global Accounting Alliance.

Porter, M. E., & Kramer, M. R. (2006). The link between competitive advantage and corporate social responsibility. *Harvard Business Review*, *84*, 78–92. PMID:17183795

Posner, P., Ryu, S. K., & Tkachenko, A. (2009). Public-private partnerships: The relevance of budgeting. *OECD Journal on Budgeting*, *1*(1), 1–26. doi:10.1787/budget-v9-art3-en

Prager, K., & Freese, J. (2009). Stakeholder involvement in agri- environmental policy making – Learning from a local and a state-level approach in Germany. *Journal of Environmental Management*, *90*(2), 1154–1167. doi:10.1016/j.jenvman.2008.05.005 PMID:18632199

Rafele, C., Hillson, D. A., & Grimaldi, S. (2005). Understanding project risk exposure using the two-dimensional risk breakdown matrix.*Proceedings of the PMI Global Congress 2005 EMEA*.

Rakic, B., & Radenović, T. (2011). Public-private partnerships as an instrument of new public management. *Facta Universitatis Series: Economics and Organization*, *8*(2), 207–220.

Reed, M. S. (2008). Stakeholder participation for environmental management: A literature review. *Biological Conservation*, *141*(10), 2417–2431. doi:10.1016/j.biocon.2008.07.014

Reeves, I., & Ryan, J. (2007). Piloting public private partnerships: Expensive lessons from Irelands schools sector. *Public Money and Management*, *27*(5), 331–338. doi:10.1111/j.1467-9302.2007.00604.x

Roloff, J. (2008). Learning from multi-stakeholder networks: Issue-focused stakeholder Management. *Journal of Business Ethics*, *82*(1), 233–250. doi:10.1007/s10551-007-9573-3

Roncalli, T. (2013). *Introduction to risk parity and budgeting*. London: Chapman & Hall/CRC Financial Mathematics Series.

Roumboutsos, A., & Anagnostopoulos, K. (2008). Public Private Partnership projects in Greece: Risk ranking and preferred risk allocation. *Construction Management and Economics*, *26*(7), 751–763. doi:10.1080/01446190802140086

Sachs, T., Tiong, R. L. K., & Wang, S. Q. (2007). Analysis of political risks and opportunities in public private partnerships PPP in China and selected Asian Countries—Survey results. *Chinese Management Studies*, *1*(2), 126–148. doi:10.1108/17506140710758026

Shah, N., & Harris, P. T. (Eds.). (2010). Using Change Management to Support Stakeholder Management. Chichester, UK: Blackwell Publishing Ltd.

Sharma, R. (2013). *The Potential of private institutional investors for financing transport infrastructure*. Paper presented at the International Transport Forum, New York, NY. doi:10.1787/2223439X

Sharma, S. (2007). Exploring best practices in public-private partnership (PPP) in e-Government through select Asian case studies. *The International Information & Library Review*, *39*(3-4), 203–210. doi:10.1080/10572317.2007.10762750

Shen, L. Y., Platten, A., & Deng, X. P. (2006). Role of public private partnerships to manage risks in public sector projects in Hong Kong. *International Journal of Project Management*, *24*(7), 587–594. doi:10.1016/j.ijproman.2006.07.006

Shrivastava, V. K. (2011). *Public Private Partnerships in road projects: Critical Success Factors in the Indian context*. Paper presented at the Southern African Transport Conference (SATC).

Siering, J., & Svensson, A. (2012). *Managing external stakeholder relationships in PPP Projects - A multidimensional approach* (Unpublished Master of Science Thesis). Chalmers University of Technology, Gothenburg, Sweden.

Silvester, H. C., & Aroujo, J. F. (2012). Public private partnerships / private finance initiatives in Portugal: Theory, practice, and results. *Public Performance and Management Review*, *36*(2), 316–339. doi:10.2753/PMR1530-9576360208

Singaravelloo, K. (2010). PPP: The Right Marriage between Local Government and the Private Sector in Malaysia? *International Journal of Institutions and Economics*, *2*(2), 142–166.

Singewar, M., & Deshmukh, S. S. (2016). Analysis of critical success factors for effective implementation of public private partnership in real estate and infrastructural development- A Compendium Case Study. *Imperial Journal of Interdisciplinary Research*, *2*(8), 204–211.

Smith, D. (2006). *Understanding risk and sustainability - the future for risk managers.* Retrieved from http://riskmatters.com.au/doc/Understandingriskandsustainability.pdf#page=5&zoom=auto,-12,575

Smyth, H. (2008). The credibility gap in stakeholder management: Ethics and evidence of relationship management. *Construction Management and Economics, 26*(6), 633–643. doi:10.1080/01446190801905414

Smyth, H., & Edkins, A. (2007). Relationship management in the management of PFI/PPP projects in the UK. *International Journal of Project Management, 25*(3), 232–240. doi:10.1016/j.ijproman.2006.08.003

Soliño, A. S., & Vassallo, J. M. (2009). Using public-private partnerships to expand subways: Madrid-Barajas international airport case study. *Journal of Management Engineering, 25*(1), 21–28. doi:10.1061/(ASCE)0742-597X(2009)25:1(21)

Sutterfield, J. S., Friday-Stroud, S. S., & Shivers-Blackwell, S. L. (2006). A case study of project and stakeholder management failures: Lessons learned. *Project Management Quarterly, 37*(5), 26.

Tang, L. Y., Shen, Q., & Cheng, E. W. L. (2010). A review of studies on Public–Private Partnership projects in the construction industry. *International Journal of Project Management, 28*(7), 683–694. doi:10.1016/j.ijproman.2009.11.009

Trafford, S., & Proctor, T. (2006). Successful joint venture partnerships: Public-private partnerships. *International Journal of Public Sector Management, 19*(2), 117–129. doi:10.1108/09513550610650392

Tserng, H., Russell, J., Hsu, C., & Lin, C. (2012). Analyzing the role of national PPP units in promoting PPPs: Using new institutional economics and a case study. *Journal of Construction Engineering and Management, 138*(2), 242–249. doi:10.1061/(ASCE)CO.1943-7862.0000398

Turner, J. R. (2006). Towards a theory of project management: The functions of project management international. *International Journal of Project Management, 24*(3), 187–189. doi:10.1016/j.ijproman.2006.03.001

van Marrewijk, A., Clegg, S. R., Pitsis, T. S., & Veenswijk, M. (2008). Managing public–private megaprojects: Paradoxes, complexity, and project design. *International Journal of Project Management, 26*(6), 591–600. doi:10.1016/j.ijproman.2007.09.007

Velotti, L., Botti, A., & Vesci, M. (2012). Public-private partnerships and network governance. What are the challenges? *Public Performance & Management Review, 36*(2), 340–365. doi:10.2753/PMR1530-9576360209

Vos, J. F., & Achterkamp, M. C. (2006). Stakeholder identification in innovation projects: Going beyond classification. *European Journal of Innovation Management, 9*(2), 161–178. doi:10.1108/14601060610663550

Walker, D., & Rowlinson, S. (2007). *Procurement System: A cross-industry project management perspective*. Abingdon, UK: Taylor & Francis.

Weihe, G. (2006). *Public-Private Partnerships: Addressing a nebulous concept.* Working paper No.16. 10th International Symposium on Public Management, Glasgow, UK.

Winch, G. M. (2010). *Managing construction projects: An information processing approach* (2nd ed.). Oxford, UK: Wiley-Blackwell.

Wood, M., Mukherjee, A., Bridges, T., & Linkov, I. (2010). A Mental Modeling Approach to Study Decision-Making in Dynamic Task Environments. In Construction Stakeholder Management. Chichester, UK: Blackwell Publishing Ltd.

Yang, J., Shen, G., Drew, D., & Ho, M. (2010). Critical success factors for stakeholder management: Construction practitioners perspectives. *Journal of Construction Engineering and Management, 136*(7), 778–786. doi:10.1061/(ASCE)CO.1943-7862.0000180

Yang, J., Shen, G., Drew, D., & Ho, M. (2011). A typology of operational approaches for stakeholder analysis and engagement. *Construction Management and Economics, 29*(2), 145–162. doi:10.1080/01446193.2010.521759

Yang, J., Shen, G. O., Ho, M., Drew, D. S., & Chan, A. P. C. (2009). Exploring critical success factors for stakeholder management in construction projects. *Journal of Civil Engineering and Management, 15*(4), 337–348. doi:10.3846/1392-3730.2009.15.337-348

Ye, S. (2009). Patterns of financing PPP projects. In Policy, finance & management for public private partnerships. West Sussex, UK: Blackwell Publishing.

Yescombe, E. R. (2007). *Public-private partnerships: principles of policy and finance*. Oxford, UK: Butterworth- Heinemann. doi:10.1016/B978-075068054-7.50025-3

Yilmaz, A. K., & Flouris, T. (2010). Managing corporate sustainability: Risk management process based perspective. *African Journal of Business Management, 4*(2), 162–171.

Yu, A. T. W., Shen, Q. P., Kelly, J., & Hunter, K. (2008). Comparative study of the variables in construction project briefing/architectural programming. *Journal of Construction Engineering and Management, 134*(2), 122–138. doi:10.1061/(ASCE)0733-9364(2008)134:2(122)

Yuan, J., Skibniewski, M. J., & Li, Q. (2008). *Managing the performance of public private partnership projects to achieve value for money: Key performance indicators selection*. Paper presented at the International Conference on Multi-national Construction Projects, Shanghai, China.

Yuan, J., Skibniewski, M. J., & Li, Q. (2008). *Managing the performance of public private partnership projects to achieve value for money: Key performance indicators selection*. Paper presented at the International conference on multi-national construction projects "Securing high Performance through Cultural awareness and Dispute Avoidance", Shanghai, China.

Yuan, J., Skibniewski, M. J., Li, Q., & Zheng, L. (2010). Performance objectives selection model in public-private partnership projects based on the perspective of stakeholders. *Journal of Management Engineering, 26*(2), 89–104. doi:10.1061/(ASCE)ME.1943-5479.0000011

Zaharioaie, M. (2012). The utility of using public private partnership for local governments. *Journal of Public Administration, Finance and Law,* 17-24.

Zhang, X. (2005). Critical success factors for public-private partnerships in infrastructure development. *Journal of Construction Engineering and Management*, *131*(1), 3–14. doi:10.1061/(ASCE)0733-9364(2005)131:1(3)

Zou, X. W., Wang, S. Q., & Fang, D. P. (2008). A life-cycle risk management framework for PPP infrastructure projects. *Journal of Financial Management Property Construction*, *13*(2), 123–142. doi:10.1108/13664380810898131

Chapter 9
Keys to Partnership:
Building Effective Risk Management

ABSTRACT

This chapter identifies the key critical pillars for a successful PPP project implementation in order to assist all stakeholders in the process. It also analyses the potential application models of PPP in respect to ingredients, tools and the roles of ICT. The chapter is based on results from a comprehensive analysis of even cases of successful PPP projects that have been implemented in different countries over the years. As a result several keys for an effective risk management have been identified. This can explain why some PPP projects are successful whereas others are not. It is concluded these key pillars must be dearly considered if PPP project is to succeed.

The greatest potential for control tends to exist at the point where action takes place. - Louis A. Allen

INTRODUCTION

The operating environment for a PPP project depends only fully on direct interventions by the respective public and private partners. Many efforts and activities carried out in a PPP arrangement can be as significant as direct policy interventions towards the success of PPP project. And the public and private partners will have some common basic understanding as to the right course of action and activities to perform. In an interrelated PPP project development, actions need not even be directed at a one partner, an action to be performed must be done by all the partners in order to cause attractiveness of such an engagement. PPP success is for those partners who are open and collaborate effectively with each others, for both of active involvement or rather role play is a prerequisite, a marginal activity: the result of a balance of a deeper understanding and convictions they have for the successful outcomes of the PPP engagement. Therefore all the partners should act on this basis. This position at the intersection of a range of actions and activities condition means that assessing the 'success' or 'effectiveness' of the PPP project may also require multiple criteria. A PPP arrangement mist promote, or at least nor hinder, a variety of

DOI: 10.4018/978-1-5225-2503-5.ch009

objectives. The objectives, the weighting of each, and the effects to be expected from them will change as the PPP project develops, as the partners cooperate. This chapter is directed at identifying the keys to partnership and building effective risk management specifically directed to ensure successful PPP project outcomes. It will first examine briefly the evolution of the understanding of the ingredients for a successful PPP risk management. It must then look at the operating environment, building blocks for successful risk partnership and principles and keys to successful PPP risk management which as necessary conditions for the success of PPP engagements. After this background, it will examine the tools that are often used and are available in contractual partnerships. Under this section, risk mapping, risk register and risk matrix will be presented and discussed in details. A section on the transforming risk management will examine the role of ICT and the possibilities available to partners to adopt it. Aspects of information needs and networks for mitigating risk, current ICT best practices and risk communication shall be reflected on, before concluding with an assessment of the best practices to be adopted.

INGREDIENTS FOR A SUCCESSFUL RISK MANAGEMENT

The opening statement to their catchy article entitled 'On best practices for risk management in complex projects' Benta, Podean and Mircean (2011) pronounced, thus: "Risk management shall be proactive, (p.142)". Successful risk management is recognized as an integral part of a good and effective PPP project practices (Smith & Fischbachera, 2009). As the saying goes, *a chain is only as strong as its weakest link.* This adage rings true in many situations. In regard to risk, for example, there are countless points at which various individuals might contribute to the overall strength of an organization's management of risks (Marle & Vidal, 2011). Effective risk management is an interactive process consisting of steps, which when undertaken in sequence, enable continual improvement in decision making (Kwan & Leung, 2011). Mouraviev (2012) portrays effective risk management as a logical and systematic method of establishing the context, identifying, analyzing, treating, monitoring and communicating risks associated with any activity, function or process in a way that will enable organization sot minimize losses and maximize opportunities. Zou, Zhang and Wang (2007) compliment effective risk management is as much about identifying opportunities as avoiding or mitigating losses. Suffice to note that significant hurdles in the operating environment of risk partnerships must be overcome to ensure risk management process can deliver effective and effective PPP project implementation in ways that preserve the public interest. at the fundamental level, the parties must establish open and transparent PPP environment, retain not only sufficient but also correspondingly adequate and fair to retain sufficient expertise in risk and contract management and remain determine to achieve the ends for which the PPP was performed.

Operating Environment of Risk Partnership

An effective risk partnership arrangement demands a favorable environment to ensure that risk hurdles and PPP project implementation constraints are reduced to a bearable level. The operating environment is composed of at least two essential elements: the presence of laws and implementation mechanism (Yang, Hou & Wang, 2013) which could be reduced to legal and institutional frameworks regarding the operation of risk partnership arrangement. The existence of enforceable laws provides assurance to private partners for safeguarding their interests and alleviating risk and at the same time help in curbing opportunistic behavior in risk partnership. A sound legal system also assists in ensuring the efficient operation of risk partnership in accordance with the broader PPP project objectives while the absence of same breeds insolvable disputes (Al-Tmeemy, Abdul-Tahman & Harun, 2011). The implementation mechanisms cover measures put in place to increase the chances of successful implementation of the PP project, one free of risks. Risk frequently occurs in PPP project implementation for either worst or complete curtailment of the project processes. Risk occurrence imposes heavy burden on the partners. A proper implementation mechanism includes the improvement of openness, fairness and transparency in the implementation process; the enforcement of the supervision of operation; and the strengthening of performance, monitoring, evaluation and auditing (Sanda & Anigbogu, 2016).

Next to the implementation mechanisms is the credibility of the public partner. Credibility is very important in attracting private investment. Public partner credibility is enhanced by factors such as availability of political checks and balances, and independent judicial system, and independent regulation (Bryde, 2005). Yang, Hou and Wang (2013) note lack of credibility among participating public partners has been a serious issues in PPP implementation. Ho (2006) demonstrates that some public partners promise more than they can deliver to attract foreign investment, for example. A successful risk partnership requires a strong central administration structure to steer and guide PPP project implementation (Bloomfield, 2006). This underscores the need for good governance as a prerequisite for successful risk partnership. According to Jha and Iyer (2007), good governance is participatory, transparent and accountable and has the following characteristics which have far implications in the performance of risk partnership arrangement.

Closely linked to credibility of the participating public partner is the political environment. Political support is another necessary requirement for a successful risk partnership (Kort & Klijn, 2011). Private partners would always require some sort of immunity from unnecessary political interference. This is due to the fact that the risk partnership contract is closed on a long period of time under which major political changes could occur (McLeod, Doolin & MacDonell, 2012). For example, in an event of change in government, the private partner may face the political risks such as contract expropriation or unilateral termination of the contract. Zaharioaie (2012) opined that, the risk partnerships contract not being under the auspices of the commercial law, can be discretionary modified by the public partner against the public partner. The private partner- the investor, therefore, will be more attracted by investments in stable states from a political point of view (Sharma & Bindall, 2014). This is because the risks that are supported by the state are in most of the cases are the ones that the private operators have little control of, such as political, financial and usage risk (Ongolo, 2006).

In addition, implementation of a set of indicators or matrices is equally important for a successful risk partnership (Beyene, 2014). In order to develop an effective risk partnership, key risk indicators (KRIs) must exist such that risk partnership is a profitable venture to undertake, the private party will be willing to participate and the financiers are willing to lend finances. Hence successful risk partnerships require a strong KRIs and KPIs to support the success of a PPP project (Asress & Kumari, 2016). The KRIs allows better management of risk events by involving attention, a future-oriented focus as a prerequisite to achieve goals. They are cornerstones of an effective risk management, critical part of the risk management process that is why it is very important and necessary to allocate time in order to create set of reliable KRIs. Bostrom, French and Gotllieb (2008) decry concerns that have developed of lately with the problem of risk indicators and how they help to detect and reduce the risk at organizational level. Davis, Finlay, McLenaghen and Wilson (2006) contend that risk indicator provides a forward direction and information about risk, which may, or may not exist and is used as a warning system for future actions. Bryde and Robinson (2005) aver KRIs can be monitored a specific risk and can be undertaken mitigation actions. Coleman (2009) states that KRIs indicators are statistic or measurements that can provide a perspective into an organization's risk position tend to be revised periodically (monthly or quarterly) to alert the organization about the changes that may indicate risks.

KRIs is used by management to show how risky an activity or investment project is (Coleman, 2009). Duckart (2010) believes that building a set of key risk indicators require skill and expertise. This means every person who is responsible with managing a risk must know all the definitions, conversions and standardization that will be used. He cautions that it is not enough to assume that the data are correct, it must be validated. Bostrom, French and Gotllieb (2008) conclude that determination of the risk varies from one organization to another, from one process to another and from one system to another. They recommend that is important to take into account the events with low probability of occurrence, which can be extremely risky. However, they caution that no focus should be placed on the probability of occurrence without considering the consequences as this is a mistake. Beasley, Clune and Hermanson (2005) assert that implementing KRIs is necessary because any business is in continual change. Lam (2006) advices that for a successful implementation of KRIs it must be ensured: the quantification of indicators, the use of standard and methodologies available, the continuous monitoring of progress indicators, the KRIs connection to the business objectives and the correctness of the formula.

According to Tabish and Jha (2012), KRIs need not be confused with KPIs though they are allowed to be implemented by an organization that wants to be effective in its risk management. It is important though to distinguish between them. KPIs indicators tend to focus especially on the historical performance of the organization or its key operations, are important for a successful management. Carbonara, Costantino and Pellegrino (2013) asserts on the other hand, KRIs provides real-time indicators that offer information about emerging risks. To Toor and Ogunlana (2010) KRIs can be the key relationships that locate the emerging risks and opportunities that signals the need to act. Ibem (2010) indicates the difference between KPIs and KRIs are that KPIs tell if goals will be achieved, and KRIs help in understanding changes in risk profile, impact and likelihood to achieve goals. A clearer distinction of these indicators give opportunity to understand what type of question need to be answered through them and how the definition of the indicators will help improve management quality and the clarity of results (Zaharioaie, 2012).

Building Blocks for Successful Risk Partnerships

A successful risk partnership depends on all partners and stakeholders involved with the project (Roig & Soriano, 2015). Ismail (2016) indicates that most times, problematic risk partnership usually result from non-technical challenges that arise in the working relationship. Abdul Aziz (2010) avers lack of executive and project leaderships, insurmountable communication issues, or deficiencies in planning and defined processes can create barriers to collaboration during the risk partnership arrangement. Unfortunately, Abdul Aziz and Kassim (2011) claims that the technology often is the "scapegoat" within an unsuccessful risk partnership. Similarly, if nothing appears broken from a technology perspective, and the operation is apparently running smoothly, the working relationship may be deemed successful when in truth the partnership lacks key building blocks for success (Endut, Akintoye & Kelly, 2006).

For a successful risk partnership, Essia and Yusuf (2013) argue there must be some building blocks. These building blocks create enabling environment for risk informed decision and implementation. Typically, there are eight building blocks for a successful risk partnership. First, commitment from the top leadership can result in to a successful risk partnership. It is important that the "the top" of both the public and private partner organizations must work together. For example, the most senior public partner official must be willing to be actively involved in supporting the concept of risk partnerships, and take an aggressive role in the development of each collaborative venture in the risk partnership arrangement. Beisheim, Liese and Vosseler (2014) show a well informed public partner official can play a critical role in minimizing misperceptions about the value to the public of an effectively developed risk partnership.

Secondly, the risk partnership must be grounded on a statutory foundation. Armistead and Pettigrew (2008) argue that it's equally important that there should be a statutory foundation for the implementation of the risk partnership within the framework arrangement of the PPP. Too often, Batley and Rose (2011) maintain state laws may limit or lack clarity regarding the formation and management of the public and private partners in a risk partnership. Batley (2006) intimates that without this clarity, leaders often view collaborative risk partnerships as risky venture and cannot take advantage of innovative and creative solutions. There has to be a firm regulatory framework to foster collaborative work between the partners.

Thirdly, the existence of a direct public sector involvement is very helpful for a successful risk partnership (Alcock, 2010). It is important that once a risk partnership has been established, the public partner must remain actively involved in the project or program at all levels. It's equally important to keep on-going monitoring of the performance on course as this will bring about assurance of risk partnership success (Dacin, Oliver & Roy, 2007). This monitoring should be done a daily, weekly, monthly, or quarterly basis for different aspect of each partnership (the frequency of is often defined in the PPP project contract) from an outcome basis.

Fourth, put in place a well crafted plan as it will aid in knowing beforehand that which is expected of each partner. Gazley (2010) shows that a carefully developed plan (often done with the assistance of an outside expert in this field) will substantially increase the probability of success of the risk partnership. Jeffares, Sullivan and Bovaird (2009) demonstrates that this plan most often will take the form of an extensive, detailed contract, clearly describing the responsibilities of both the public and private partners. In addition to addressing areas of respective responsibilities, Edelenbos and Klijn (2009) reveal that a good plan or contract will include a clearly defined method of dispute resolution (because not all contingencies can be foreseen).

Fifth, develop an effective communication mode with the stakeholders since risk partnership neither affects the public nor private partner only (Abdel Aziz, 2007). Affected employees, for example, the portions of the public receiving the service, the press, public labor unions and relevant interest groups will all have opinions and, frequently, significant misconceptions about a risk partnerships and its value to all the public. It is important to communicate openly and candidly with these stakeholders to minimize potential resistance to establishing a risk partnership. Ramiah and Reich (2006) urge both parties to develop an effective communication plan. The plan should ensure that the communication management process provides a structured approach to creating and delivering effective information, defining audiences and delivery vehicles. Calabrese (2008) alleges that the process helps ensure accurate and consistent massages are conveyed, by appropriate senders, to necessary audiences, through appropriate channels and vehicles at the right time. A successful implementation will positively affect the work environment and relationship with the financiers, employees and other stakeholders (Aaltonen, Jaakko & Tuomas, 2008). In order to be successful, Doerfel, Lai and Chewning (2010) recommend that good communication strategies should rely on some critical success factors. These factors include:- timely sharing of information, accurate and consistent messages conveyed to key audiences, and realistic messages from trusted sources that set realistic expectations. Most importantly, Abednego and Ogunlana (2006) argue that is critically important that the project develop, organize and prioritize its formal messages and informal communication with a riffle not a shotgun approach. This means aligning messages and sharpening them for specific audiences.

Sixth is the right opportunity that is only a select number of government business problems that are ripe for a true partnership. Cankar and Petkovšek (2013) recommend these should have the right characteristics- uncertainty, high complexity, challenging problems etc. When forming a risk partnership, it is critically important that both parties set and manage reasonable expectations, especially the public partner.

Seventh, choosing the right partner does not always mean the "lowest bid" since it's not always the best choice for selecting a partner (Gupta & Biswas, 2010). It's important to remember that the "best value" in a partner is critical in a long-term relationship. A partner's experience in the specific area of partnership being considered is an important factor in identifying the right partner.

Eight, well-defined management processes will set the right course for the risk partnership to undertake. It is critically important that both the public and private partners agree on key management processes early in the formation of the relationship (Matei, 2006). For example, it is critical that both parties agree on the risk governance and resilient development. This is the surest pathway towards making sustainable risk partnership. It also provides the enabling environment for risk informed partnership and therefore more resilient PPP outcomes.

The risk governance building blocks provide a framework for strengthening the enabling environment for managing and responding to the risk (Quiggin, 2005). It places for example, gender and social dimensions at the centre to the very definition of risk. Risk governance has three components each of which comprise a number of specific opportunities for strengthening which can be applied at all levels of governance (defined as decision making and implementation. The building blacks are interdependent and mutually reinforcing (Rakić & Rađenović, 2014). This shows that strengthening a number of blocks simultaneously can increase mainstreaming successes even though priority building blocks are context specific. Figure 1 presents the risk governance building blocks.

Figure 1. Risk governance building blocks
Source: (Selby & Jiwani, 2016)

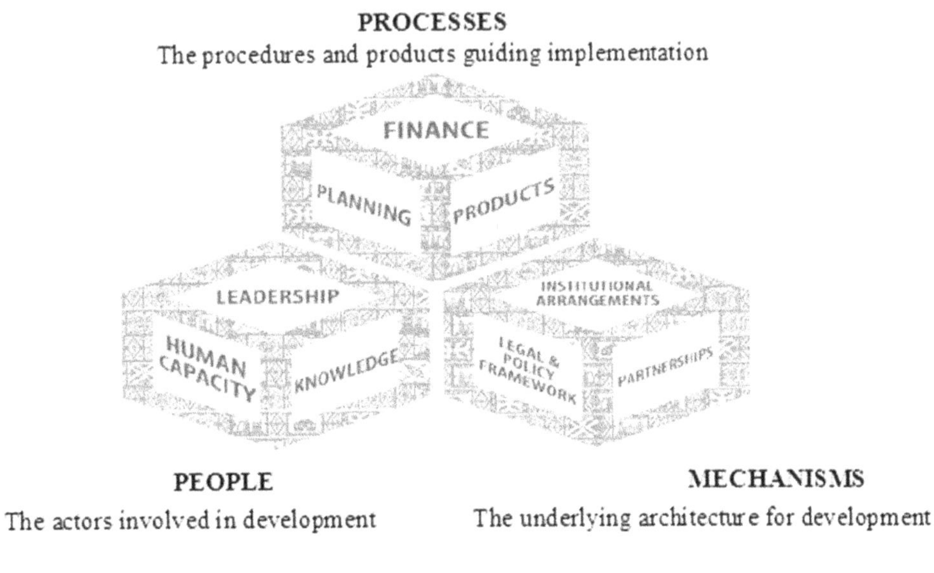

Figure 1. reveals that the building blocks are interdependent and mutually reinforcing. In achieving for example, the goal of risk partnership, the building blocks depend on a sound enabling environment including resources, institutional arrangement, dialogue and communication. The risk governance building blocks can help make sense of these, by breaking them into the three governance components and constituent building blocks as described in details below.

People component of the building block is composed of the actors involved in development. They are at the root of more resilient development outcomes. Strengthening this component to galvanize a change in the way that stakeholders approach risk management means building leadership, skills and knowledge for risk informed development, notably of development actors. Core building blocks for this governance component are:

- Leadership and change agents (Block 1) that is build the political commitment and leadership of key development actors (and specifically practitioners from finance, planning, and key sectors) at all levels to advocate for and inspire a shift in mindset, new ways of thinking, and behavioral change in support of risk informed development.
- Human capacity and awareness (Block 2) that is build risk awareness and in-house capacity of development actors (moving beyond traditional training) for driving and sustaining risk informed development from "within" development practice. This means creating a network of risk partnership focal point specialists or change agents within the planning, finance and sector agencies.
- Knowledge and communication (Block 3) that is build awareness and knowledge of risk management (including the gender and social dimension of risk), for example through risk assessment and risk mapping, and strengthening communication networks, to risk inform local development priorities, planning and budgeting processes.

The mechanisms component of the building block is the underlying architecture for development which is vital to structure the way that people interact and take part in risk management to facilitate a more coordinated and sustainable approach. Enabling risk management within development decision making and implementation involves strengthening the institutional arrangements, networks, roles, responsibilities, and policy framework. Core building blocks for this governance component are:

- Institutional arrangements (Block 4) that is build upon existing arrangement (for example committees/working groups) as far as possible to ensure roles and responsibilities for risk are embedded or mainstreamed within functions of departments, sectors or cross-sectoral fora.
- Partnership and coordination networks (Block 5) that is build partnerships and coordination mechanisms for risk management to increase resources (and support more efficient use of resources) and joint actions of multiple-stakeholders.
- Legal and policy framework (Block 6) that is strengthen legislation, regulations, policies and strategies from a risk perspective and put in place mechanism and capacities for their implementation.

The processes component of the building block is the procedures and products guiding implementation. Risk management must become an integral part of routine development procedures, tools and products for risk informed development activities on the ground (for example projects) and resilient development outcomes. Strengthening routine development processes (for example, planning) and associated products (for example, plans, monitoring an evaluation reports) to facilitate risk management, will ensure that risk informed development is the new norm. Core building for this governance component are:

- Financing processes and allocations (Block 7) that is strengthen allocation of development budget for risk informed development projects and policies alongside the ability to identify, increase and manage funds for risk (including climate finance).
- Planning processes and tools (Block 8) that is embed risk and link bottom-up/top-down development planning processes and procedures (for example, project design, assessment/screening, planning, review, implementation, monitoring and evaluation) and accompanying tools (for example screening guidelines, project templates) as a basis for more risk informed projects and policy implementation.
- Products (Block 9) that is strengthen key development products (such as sector, community development plans, monitoring and evaluation reports) to ensure they address and incorporate risk in support of more resilient outcomes.

Key Principles for a Successful Risk Partnerships

On top of having clearer building blocks for a risk partnership, Zitron (2006) asserts that a successful risk management requires adherence to some key principles. These principles are the general or fundamental doctrines, assumptions or codes of conduct (Aziz, 2007). According to Adams, Alistair and Wu (2006), the principles enjoin the public and private partner as well. The principles enjoin the private partner to do its homework by ensuring that its part of the bargain is articulated in an informed manner; having in place list of activities to be performed with the approval of the public partner; working towards building long-term relationship; expecting no quick benefits; and comply with all the requirements in the risk partnership as to be performed by the private partner.

The public partner is enjoined to work together to create an understanding of the private partner (Trafford & Proctor, 2006). It has to share strategic plans and missions, goals and objectives openly with the private partner. It should allow venues by which the private partner can meet and communicate with the user community in the PPP environment. It has to educate the procurement staffs and understand the impact of all legislations related to public private partnership. The public partner ought not to place unreasonable restrictions on the private partner and should never have unrealistic expectations (Soliño & Vassallo, 2009). Both parties are enjoined by the principles to be inclusive-not exclusive. They must both strive for "win/win" scenarios in all their interactions and dealings. They are further enjoined to expand neutral ground opportunities to communicate. They must identify common interest (for example, project failures or overruns in paper, lesson learned). And above all, the principles enjoin them to take advantage of the risk partnerships for their own good.

Yu, Shen, Kelly and Hunter (2008) argue that there are key ingredients for a successful risk partnership that must obtain in the arrangement. First, there must be political will and government overnight as long-term political support and government commitment to risk partnership is important for business confidence. Ahmad, Bhattacharya, Vinella and Xiao, 2014) reveals that lenders will be reluctant to invest in PPP markets if there is no clear vision on what the government hopes to achieves with PPPs, and if it fails to commit adequate resources to create a sustainable pipeline of PPP deals. Bloomfield (2006) avers that to develop a consistent PPP policy framework and provide guidance/support on PPP matters at the central level, establishing a champion unit is essential.

Secondly standardized contractual and accounting framework improves transparency and efficiency in the PPP process, thereby reducing negotiation time and costs. At the same time Akbiyikli, Eaton and Turner (2006), portray such standardization must also be balanced with enough flexibility in the contract to promote innovation and continuous improvement. Importantly, amidst concerns that PPPs exist to flatter the public finances and "get government spending off the balance sheet", the government must establish credible accounting standards/rules and fully disclose its liabilities in PPPs in order to build stakeholder confidence.

Third, a robust performance measurement and monitoring framework safeguard public interest. In this way the government will clearly identify measurable outcomes and monitor the PPP's performance. Crompton, Goulding and Pour (2014) indicate that this may be challenging in sectors such as healthcare education and sports infrastructure. Bresnen (2007) warns that when fundamental public interest clash with the cost-saving behavior of private firms, costly contractual negotiations and strict monitoring are necessary. The availability of fixed and stable indicators is also problematic in sectors characterized by fast-paced technological process or constantly changing market conditions (Gaffey, 2010).

Alderman and Ivory (2007) suggests that there are three keys to a successful risk partnership process: quality assurance plan, risk mitigation plan and transition plan. Quality assurance (QA) plan serves as a guideline for the overall working relationship for both parties. It is a standard practice for a public partner to place a quality assurance process either before a project award or within a specified timeframe after award. The private partner should have full awareness and potential input into the established QA guidelines to insure that both parties have clarity on what is expected from a delivery standpoint. Risk mitigation plan needs to be jointly developed for both parties to lower risk reduction for the SPV. Transition planning is critical in a risk partnership that involves the outsourcing of managed services. These plans include: staffing transition plan- Alashwal, Rahman and Beksin (2011) indicates that of there is an incumbent, the private partner must have a transition plan in place for managing the project from the incumbent- for new staff, organizational structure etc. And business process transition plan in which the private partner should still have a transition plan form current state to new operations telling the customer 'how' they are implementing or deploying their proposed solution.

Bygballe, Jahre and Sward (2010) counsel that for risk partnership to remain sustainable and relevant in the post-crisis environment, there has to be in place credible and practical measures. These measures must be aimed to improve the legal, financial, regulatory and policy framework to support risk partnership markets. The measures must include developing mechanisms to refinance risk sharing between the public partner and the private partner, facilitation measures to maximize competition for debt finance (for example by holding a funding competition after the selection of the preferred bidder) and public partner-supported debt or credit guarantee finance models.

CONTRACTUAL PARTNERSHIP: THE TOOLS

The type of contract gives rise to a different level of contractual partnership (Kumaraswamy, Ling, Anvuur & Rahman, 2007). In PPP, the most common contractual relationships exist in the form of time and materials (T&M), firm fixed price (FFP), performance based, shared-in-service savings, and collaborative partnership. Under the T&M contractual relationship, the public partner has the most control during the term of the relationship (Love, Davis, Ellis & Cheung. 2010). There are no performance-based measured outcomes; thus, performance thresholds have not been identified, and there are no reporting mechanisms for performance. Under the FFM contractual relationship, the public partner has less control and must define the deliverable for the private partner. Outcomes are identifies as "deliverables", and typically not in the form of metrics- nor they are measured during the course of the contract. According to Murdoch and Hughes (2008), there is a desired "to-be" state in mind, but uncertainty regarding "how" to reach those outcomes is assumed by the private partner. Performance based contractual relationship is actually a marriage between T&M and FFM with joint solution design meetings and mutually agreed upon service level agreements (SLAs). Nystrom (2008) indicate performance thresholds and reporting mechanisms are jointly established between the public partner and the private partner, there are stated objectives and outcomes by the public partner, and performance is measured on a predetermined and consistent basis. Under the shared-in-services savings contractual relationship, the public partner relinquishes control to the private partner. The private partner has the most control and the public partner should justify this arrangement by knowing their total cost of ownership of doing this business before outsourcing. Under collaborative partnerships, there is a non-legal working relationship that often occur between the public and private partners to meet a common objective or goal (Rakic & Radjenovic, 2011). Primarily goodwill gestures, collaborative partnerships are often used to provide knowledge exchange or collective leverage resources for a specified goal (Oyegoke, Khalfan, McDermott, Rowlinson & Dickinson, 2009).

The contractual agreement between the public and private partner in the PPP arrangement is a concession that lies at the heart of PPP transaction structure. Because of this contractual nature, there a number of tools that can be used to guide and direct the process of implementation of the PPP project. For the purpose of this book, only three of those tools are looked at: risk mapping, risk register and risk matrix as discussed and presented in the three sections which follows.

Risk Mapping

A risk map is a graphical depiction of a select number of a PPP's risks designed to illustrate the impact or significance of risk on one axis, and the likelihood or frequency on the other axis (Phua, 2006). Many types and variations of risk maps exist. For example, the axes can vary (impact and likelihood on different axes), the scales can vary, and some are even three-dimensional. According to Philip, Bratvold and Bickel (2014), in addition to identifying a PPP's "show-stopper" risks, there are numerous benefits to risk mapping. On a stand-alone basis, the risk profile is an effective communications tool particularly for members of senior management and board members. As the old expression goes, a picture is worth a thousand words. The risk map prioritizes risks by their placement on the profile and reveals which threats require management's time and company resources (Hofmann, 2007). This may entail reallocation of time and resources from controlled threats to those that require immediate attention. Different mapping techniques, depending on the methodology, have varying benefits. Methodologies utilizing facilitation build consensus and bring the senior management team together. However, the most important benefit for the facilitation method is a drastic reduction in decision-making cycles. Decision time is often reduced from months to weeks or from weeks to days. Complying with corporate governance requirements, improving the allocation of resources, and eliminating the "silo" mentality are among the potential benefits of devising a risk map (Bon-Gang, Xianbo & Ping, 2014). Decision-making is also optimized—a decision made by one department or division might be the correct decision when considered in isolation, but when considered in the context of the company as a whole, that decision may not be optimal.

The risk mapping process is part of a systematic, comprehensive methodology to identify, prioritize, and quantify (at a macro level) risks to an organization. Other methods of capturing information include structured interviews, surveys (written and electronic) or a combination of these. Individual client characteristics and needs dictate the appropriate method of data collection. Further risk profiling process can be done by highlighting major elements such as the workshop, scope, team composition, time horizon, scenario development and categorization, tolerance boundary, profile development, action plan, process and technology transfer, and quantification and modeling (Bracey & Moldovan, 2006). According to Gupta and Biswas (2010.), the profiling process entails a highly interactive workshop with one or two trained facilitators to guide the team through the process. The workshop can last from one to two days. Experience has shown that workshops lasting one and one-half days, including an overnight break, achieve the best result. In most cases, the role of the facilitator is not that of a functional or content expert, but that of a process manager keeping the team on track and goal-oriented. In certain cases where specific expertise is required, functional or subject matter experts can supplement the team. The scope of the exercise is determined at the beginning of the analysis to specify the areas of the business considered. The scope provides the parameters for the analysis (Weihe, 2006). Scope is often defined as identifying, prioritizing, and understanding risks and impediments to achieving corporate and strategic objectives (Zhang, 2005b). The scope can be as broad or as narrow as desired; however, a balance exists between the breadth of scope and the value of information derived from the risk mapping process.

The composition of the SPV's team is critical to the success of the profiling process. The team should consist of senior level specialists and management staffs who possess the experience, expertise, and institutional knowledge necessary to perform a thorough analysis of the areas addressed in the process (Baccarini, 2005). Most teams contain six to ten individuals. The scope of the risk profile should determine who comprises the team. For a narrower scope, such as the risks specific to a particular division or operating unit, the team would consist of the senior members of the division's management team (Brench, Beckers, Heinrich & von Hirschhausen, 2005). Or, if the scope were limited to a specific area such as ecommerce, the team composition would consist of senior representatives from appropriate functional areas and the divisions most likely affected. Most importantly, the team must represent the institutional knowledge of the organization and the seniority to implement the actions agreed upon by the group.

It is through the facilitation process, the team undertakes controlled brainstorming to identify potential risks. Once identified, risks or scenarios are thoroughly discussed to gain consensus and develop written descriptions of the scenarios (Camilleri, 2011). Each scenario is comprised of "vulnerability", a "trigger", and a "consequence". Vulnerability is an inherent, potential threat or weakness, offset by any controls or mitigating factors. Triggers cause consequences. Consequences are expressed in terms of the nature and the magnitude of the loss(s) resulting from the vulnerability and trigger. The second step in this phase of the process is to categorize scenarios in terms of "impact" and "likelihood" (Cheung, Chan & Kajewski, 2009b). The team defines both impact and likelihood in terms relevant to the organization. For example, in qualitative terms, the four impact categories are often defined in descending order as catastrophic, critical, significant, and marginal. Likelihood categories, of which there are six, are defined in qualitative terms on a scale from "almost impossible" to "very high" (Boardman & Vining, 2012). Both scales can also be defined in company-specific quantitative terms, and the team can elect to use either the qualitative definitions and/or the quantitative definitions.

Roszkowski and Davey (2010) contend that the critical issue tolerance boundary, a stepped line on the profile, separates those risks that are currently tolerable and those that are intolerable. Business risks above and to the right of the boundary line are considered intolerable and require immediate management attention. Those threats below and to the left of the boundary are currently considered tolerable. This boundary varies depending on the risk appetite of the organization. Prior to plotting business risks on the profile, the team determines the tolerance boundary line (Vlaev, Chater & Stewart, 2009). The final step in developing the profile is the placement of the business risks onto the risk map based on their impact and likelihood categorizations (Kobbeltvedt, Brun, Johansen & Eid, 2005). It is important to note that the ultimate value of the risk profile does not lie in determining the precise impact or likelihood level of a particular threat, but it is the placement of that threat relative to the placement of other threats that determines its value (Coter & Chen, 2006). Business threats that lie above the tolerance boundary require immediate attention by the team. It is important to develop specific action plans to reduce either the potential impact or likelihood, or both (Soane & Chmiel, 2005). The team also develops success measurements; target completion dates, and assigns responsibility for each action to team members. The purpose of the action plan is to move each intolerable risk (above the tolerance boundary line) into the tolerable zone. Upon completion of the risk mapping/profiling exercise, it is important that the process and technology be integrated into the firm's operations (De Marco & Thaheem, 2014). This allows updates and future profiling to be performed by public private partnership management.

The degree of detail necessary to analyze a particular risk varies from one risk to the next. If a team consensus can be achieved, then significant detail is not required. Some business risks and actions plans will require more detailed examination and quantification than can be achieved in the profiling facilitation workshop (Krane, Olsson & Rolstadås, 2012). Profiling acts as a filtering mechanism to determine which risks, if any, require special or detailed quantification. However, experience demonstrates that the vast majority of risks and action plans can be successfully addressed within the workshops allotted time. For risks requiring additional analysis, it's better to utilize sophisticated quantification and modeling techniques (Scandizzo, 2005). Risk mapping is an excellent tool for identifying, assessing and prioritizing key business risks. Yet, there can be unrealized value in the risk mapping process that could significantly enhance the ability of an organization to generate new economic value. Risk mapping techniques can be used to test existing strategies in the context of unrealized/under-realized risks and opportunities (such as e-commerce), or to support a new strategic development process (Hillson, Grimaldi & Rafele, 2006).

Risk mapping can be better achieved if there is a proper risk tracking (Alzahrani & Boussabaine, 2014). According to Ibrahim, Price and Dainty (2006), risk tacking is a measure of the risk in an investment portfolio that is due to active management decisions made by the portfolio manager. It indicates how closely a portfolio follows the index to which it is benchmarked. For example, the best measure is the standard deviation of the difference between the portfolio and index returns. Wibowo and Mohamed (2010) contend that tracking error is measured historically is called 'realized' or 'ex-post' tracking error. If a model is used to predict tracking error, it is called 'ex-ante' tracking error. Ex-post tracking error is more useful for reporting performance, whereas ex-ante tracking error is generally used by portfolio managers to control risk. Smith, Merna and Jobling (2006) reveals that various types of ex-ante tracking error models exist, from simple equity models which use beta as a primary determinant to more complicated multi-factor fixed income models. In a factor model of a portfolio, the non-systematic risk (that is the standard deviations of the individuals) is called "tracking error" in the investment field.

Risk Register

Avazkhah and Mohebbi (2010) aver a risk register records details of all the risks identified at the beginning and during the life of the project. It grades the risk in terms of likelihood of occurring and seriousness of impact on the project. It also captures the initial plans for mitigating each high level risk, the costs and responsibilities of the prescribed mitigation strategies, and subsequent results (Ajayi & Isah, 2014). A risk register usually includes a unique identifier for each risk, a description of each risk and how it will affect the project, an assessment of the likelihood it will occur and the possible seriousness/impact if it does occur (low, medium, high), a grading of each risk according to a risk assessment table, who is responsible for managing the risk an outline of proposed mitigation actions (preventative and contingency) in larger projects, costing for each mitigation strategy. Chileshe and Kikwasi (2013) provides that a risk register should be kept throughout the project, and will change regularly as existing risks are re-graded in the light of the effectiveness of the mitigation strategy and new risks are identified. In smaller projects the risk register is often used as the risk management plan (Enshassi, Mohamed & Abu-Mosa, 2008).

Dey (2009) shows that a risk register is developed to provide a useful tool for managing and reducing the risks identified before and during the project document risk mitigation strategies being pursued in response to the identified risks and their grading in terms of likelihood and seriousness. Joshua (2010) expresses that a risk register provides the PMC/senior management with a documented framework from which risk status can be reported upon ensure the communication of risk management issues to key stakeholders provide a mechanism for seeking and acting on feedback to encourage the involvement of the key stakeholders identify the mitigation actions required for implementation of the plan and associated costing.

According to Figueiredo and Kitson (2009), a risk register is first constructed at the risk identification stage. It is updated as more information is collected regarding each identified risk (…). At the risk monitoring and review stage, a risk register should contain the following information of each identified risk: risk category - the risk category in which the identified risk belongs to, for example, construction risk, site risk; a description of the risk - full description of the risk including source, what it could affect and the potential scope of the impact; risk likelihood - the probability of the risk occurring; risk consequence - the impact of the risk, usually in monetary value, if it occurs; initial risk rating - the priority of the risk, such as low, high and extreme; existing controls - the list of measures that are proposed to mitigate the risk; adequacy of existing controls - the effectiveness of the proposed measures in mitigating the risk; timeframe - the length of time the risk is expected to affect the project, or over what stage of the project the risk is applicable; date reviewed - date of last risk review; and date action taken - date when action was taken to mitigate the risk (Miller, 2006).

A risk register is essential to achieve the noted purpose of the risk management framework and combines risk assessment, risk treatment and risk response into one comprehensive tool (Hambly, Fice & Hambly, 2009). A well-developed risk register is very important for the agency to have prior to executing a Comprehensive Agreement (CA) to ensure proper risk allocation is achieved, which helps inform whether the project brings the best value (de Brito & Branco, 2006). Create the initial risk register, which begins as a simple list of project specific risks categorized under subheadings (Ke, Wang & Chan, 2011). The risk register should be revisited as often as necessary in consultation with the project team and identified project manager. The initial risk assessment is qualitative and subsequently updated with quantified values as more project data becomes available. The risk register is used to record these risk assessments (Ling & Hoi, 2006). The risk register and risk assessment inform the risk management plan, which is a detailed plan of action for the management of project risk. This plan should include the levels of contingency to maintain for a project in order to reflect its risk exposure.

Risk Matrix

Risk matrix is a matrix that is used during risk assessment to define the various levels of risk as the product of the harm probability categories and harm severity categories. It is a simple mechanism to increase visibility of risks and assist management decision making. Berg (2010b) states that risk matrix is a systematic overview of the ranked risks facing an organization. It can be used to depict the organization's risk universe as a whole or for entity-or category specific risks. It is usually constructed after the allocation of risk to represent the risk profile of the project. It helps to identify the public and private partners' preferred allocation of risks agreed by both parties together with the proposed risk treatment options, and other information including a description of each risk, its magnitude and likelihood of occurrence. This provides an immediate view of the project's risk profile. It is also an important document to be submitted to the relevant agency for approval of the public private partnership option. The risk matrix is a useful tool for managing risk during the different lifecycle of a public private partnership project. During both pre-tender and tender phases, the risk matrix can assist the public sector client to define relevant project risks and its proposed allocation.

According to Hillsona, Grimaldi and Rafele (2006) during negotiations the matrix can work as a checklist to ensure all risks are addressed. After the contract has been signed, the matrix can be a useful summary of the risk allocation effected by the contract. The value and usefulness of the risk matrix is directly related to the way the risks are treated. The construction of a risk matrix is aided by the Risk Breakdown Structure (RBS). Agyakwa-Baah, Chileshe and Fugar (2010) state that RBS is a recognizable useful tool for structuring the risk process which has been included in several risk standards and guidelines. It is defined in a similar terms to the Work Breakdown Structure (WBS) as a source-oriented grouping of project risks that organizes and defines the total risk exposure of the project. According to Tiwari (2007), each descending level of the RBS represents an increasingly detailed definition of sources of risks to the project. The RBS is therefore a hierarchical structure of potential risk resources, which can be an invaluable aid to understanding the risk faced by the project. It can act as a framework to structure and guide the risk management process, in the same way the WBS can structure and guide the project management process because it scopes and defines the work of the project (Hillsona, Grimaldi & Rafele, 2006).

The combined use of WBS and RBS can be used to generate a matrix structure, which allows the project team to manage the risk at a level of detail appropriate to the specific business context (Inekwe, 2015). To produce such a combined framework, risk analysis is first performed identifying and classifying risks using the RBS, either directly or to support other methods of identification such as brainstorming or interviews. The lowest levels of the RBS are then linked to the WPs in the WBS, producing a two dimensional matrix. Obviously, a link is created only if a particular risk can affect a specific WP. A WBS – RBS matrix is generated by the "Risk Breakdown Matrix" (RBM) (Rafele, Hillson & Grimaldi, 2005), for every RBM cell containing risks, the value of each risk is calculated using two components: the probability of occurrence (P) and the degree of impact (M). Probability is related to the presence of a risk in the RBS, and impact refers to the effect of that risk in the WBS. The calculation of the value of each risk can be determined in various ways, depending on the availability of data, as follows (Mwaguni & Busienei, 2014): using an " ordinal scale " approach, the degree of impact (M) and the index of occurrence (P) are assessed using descriptive labels (De Bettignies & Ross, 2009): for instance, very low, low, medium, high, and very high; using a " cardinal scale " approach, both the degree of impact and the index of occurrence are divided into classes, distinguished with numerical values included in dimensionless preset scales (Kobbeltvedt, Brun, Johansen & Eid, 2005); using a " quantitative approach ", in which the degree of impact is related to the parameter directly influenced by the risk (e.g. time delay, increase of costs or other), whereas the probability of occurrence is usually described as a percentage (from 1 to 99 per cent).

The interconnection between the Work Breakdown Structure (WBS) of a project and its RBS is a useful technique to associate risks to the activities of a project Zhong, Chew, Set, Zhang, Xue, Sham, Ebstein & Israel, 2009). The WBS uses a hierarchical structure to define the major tasks, minor tasks and work packages (WPs) necessary to reach the final objectives of a project, while the RBS classifies project risks using a hierarchical system of sources of risk (Hampton, Baldwin & Holt, 2012). Both WBS and RBS commonly have three or four levels of increasing detail. There are evident analogies between WBS and RBS: WBS constitutes the basic framework for the management of a project; likewise, RBS can be used as a tool to structure the risk management process (Javed, Lam & Zou, 2013). Kim and Kim (2005) claim that the highest RBM matrix is defined by the intersection of the first levels of the WBS and RBS. This identifies the macro areas of risks in a project, because it crosses the main tasks or "aggregated deliverables" with generic types of risk (Kim & Kim, 2005). This first level of generic analysis therefore only allows identification of areas of risk within the main sectors of the project. The next level of the WBS defines the main deliverables of the project (Mistarihi, Al Refai, Al Qaid & Qeed, 2012) and if they are crossed with the second level of RBS, the possible vulnerability and criticality of each deliverable is exposed. At this level, an ordinal scale could be used, with descriptive categories of impact and probability of occurrence. If the detail of WBS and RBS is increased further, a more precise analysis of the risk can be undertaken, using the cardinal scale approach, or if the economic or time impacts are known, a quantitative analysis becomes possible (Al-Kharashi & Skitmore, 2009).

In spite of the numerous benefits that a risk matrix presents, it has to be noted that there are several problematic mathematical features making it harder to assess risks (Philip, Bratvold & Bickel, 2014). Some of these problematic mathematical features include: poor resolution, errors, suboptimal resource allocation and ambiguous inputs and outputs (Hubbard & Seiersen, *2016*). For the poor resolution feature, for example, typical risk matrices can correctly and unambiguously compare only a small fraction (for example less than 10 per cent) of randomly selected pairs of hazards. They can assign identical ratings to quantitatively very different risks ("range compression"). For the errors feature, for example, risk matrices can mistakenly assign higher qualitative ratings to quantitatively smaller risks. For risks with negatively correlated frequencies and severities, they can be "worse than useless", leading to worse-than-random decisions. For the ambiguous inputs and outputs, for example, categorizations of severity cannot be made objectively for uncertain consequences. Inputs to risk matrices (for example, frequency and severity categorizations) and resulting outputs (that is risk ratings) require subjective interpretation, and different users may obtain opposite ratings of the same quantitative risks. These limitations suggest that risk matrices should be used with caution, and only with careful explanations of embedded judgments.

In the PPP project, for example, Greiling (2009) reiterates it should be noted that to improve the risks allocation mechanisms there are several risks matrix can be constructed according to the nature of the projects in each sector. Table 1 provides an example of such a matrix.

Table 1 shows the nature of each risk and which actor (public, private partner) fully supports it, if not shared, and how much it is shared between different actors. Nevertheless, in general, the public sector is the most qualified to identify those risks that are repetitive and usually encountered in similar projects including those directly and indirectly related to the time management, cost and quality of the construction. But the best way to risk allocation is largely based on the nature of the project and will

Table 1. General risk matrix of PPP construction projects

Allocation	Similarities
Public sector	- Site risk (land acquisition-related) - Political risk - Currency inconvertibility and Non transferability - Expropriation - Discriminatory and Specific Change of Law (incl. Tax) - Regulatory consent - Authority's default - Operational risk - Input quantity, quality and continuity - Revenue risk - Tariff adjustment breach - Network connectivity risk - Competing route & connectivity
Private sector	- Site risk (ground conditions-related) - Design, construction and commissioning - Operating risks - Output quantity and quality - Political risk - General Change of Law - Revenue risk - General Change of Law - Financial risks - Sponsor risks - PC, Contractor's Default
Shared	- Force Major risk - Interface risk - Disparity of the quality of the works

Source: (Hoffman, 2007)

depend in particular its technical characteristics and uncertainties that may affect the construction or operation phases. It is necessary that the analysis requires the public partner gives special attention to the extent that the risk matrix is the dashboard to find the balance of the project during the competitive dialogue and reflect on the various safeguards and including insurance mechanisms to cover or not a particulars risk. After the identification and allocation of risks recorded in the different types of PPP construction projects, it is then to select, among all identified risks, significant risks in terms of cost and time to integrate its impacts in the overall final costs. These risks are generally analyzed according to the period during which they are likely to occur: design risk, construction and operation. They are temporary (related to a phase) or permanent (Hofmann, 2007).

TRANSFORMING RISK MANAGEMENT: THE ROLE OF ICT

It is not uncommon for PPPs to incorporate technology to explore new ways of producing high quality goods and services. For example, SPV often establish an advisory board, stakeholder group or governance body which includes private partner representatives. These groups may be formed to assist with strategic planning, to provide on-going expertise and guidance, or to target specific issues or projects. These bodies may be standing committees or they may be task forces, convened for short term, tactical purpose. No matter what the title or structure of these entities, they create an environment to foster collaboration and partnerships. These collaborative efforts provide an open forum for both public and private partner to exchange ideas and promote the interest of the technology community and government to provide better services and meet new citizen demands.

Obermann (2007) reminds that we live in a fast paced world where technology is everywhere, so much so that it often goes unnoticed, that is until something goes wrong. Bonnafous (2010) explains that technology solutions are assumed as an enabler, for example, one can go online to shop, renew a license, pay bills, and even complain about a pothole or a noisy plane. Given that the public expects the same customer service and responsiveness from government as they have grown accustomed to from the private sector, it is ICT that can easily make this possible. Basic elements of ICT have become expected and essentially mandatory resources in developed nations while many parts of the globe remain virtually isolated (Avgerou, 2008; Roberts 2008).

According to Ökmen and Öztas (2010), governments world over have the difficult task of protecting the interest of their public while at the same time meeting the diverse demands of the citizen using the very least of resources at their disposal. Singh and Khan (2015) give you an idea about how citizens' expectations continue to rise as they demand more and better government services at lower costs. Moreover, Ogbu (2013) decries the high quality goods and services demanded by the citizens at the same time. There is nothing more but the confidence of the citizens in their governments and leaders has for the first time run too high hinging on the quality of services, for example. The continual challenge to deliver services within the existing government services faster and cheaper as well as make use of them to create new services has seen the incorporation of the use of ICT in all government actions. Thus ICT has become a new role for government to enhance social and economic progress and foster prosperity for its citizens. This section deals with the central position of ICT in managing risk in a PPP arrangement.

Information Needs and Networks for Mitigating Risk

As presented before, access to information is identified as one of the key enablers of enhancing risk management in a PPP arrangement. So far, various formal and informal networks are being used by partners to get PPP-related information for managing PPP risk, both before and after the risk have occurred. But the applicability as well as the coverage of these sources remain limited and have different effects across PPP projects. Suffice to note that information technology (IT) has become a powerful tool to enable enhanced service delivery in both the public and private sectors. Acharya, Dai Lee and Man Im (2006) claims that getting IT right is becoming more critical than ever for governments in meeting the demands of citizens, businesses, and employees who are expecting the same high level of services they are receiving from commercial venture. Akintoye (2008) demonstrates that IT's utility, and how it is managed, can dramatically impact efficiency, effectiveness, and citizen-centric focus of government services and programs, including PPPs.

In the 21st Century, there is hardly anyone who doubts the power of IT. This is because technology acts not only as the enabler to create better, faster services to the citizens, it also acts as a facilitator between the public and private partners, for example. Aldoory, Kim & Tindall (2010) illustrates further by asserting that while a rapidly changing technology environment requires new thinking and innovative approaches, government and private sector leaders are strengthening their cooperation and collaboration to reap the benefits of these emerging technologies and innovations. Much as effective public-private sector collaboration is often born out of necessity, IT comes in to make the collaboration real and successful (Alonso-Conde, Brown & Rojo-Suarez, 2007). For example, worldwide, countries have witnessed unprecedented urge as well as adoption of PPP as a new mode of service delivery. In these unprecedented urges and adoptions, technology has actually facilitated numerous PPP arrangements through improved communication and provision of methods for meeting impending challenges.

In order to provide information about PPP (for instance, financing capacity, required materials) or about the PPP project in general, knowledge of the specific data about the PPP project is a prerequisite. Lack of information increases the risk and uncertainty that the partners face on a day-to-day basis. Information can play an important role in mitigating PPP risks. Girmscheid (2006) contends that given the advances made by technology today, it is imperative to leverage it to look at different indicators in context of the risk data being collated for a PPP project. If the SPV is already using a risk management system, for example, then it has its risk and control assessment data, issue data, and can combine existing control system with ICT effectively.

Goldstein and Naor (200) aver technology enables the measurement of different risk categories, metrics, and even occurrences. ICT is not only for risks, it can also be used for asset classes, objectives, controls, processes, business entities, etc. Greiling (2009) states one can define thresholds which represent rising and dropping indicators, both critical and non-critical. Reporting and dashboards enabled by ICT make it easy to see critical areas for analyses, thresholds-breached or otherwise. Too and Weaver (2014) shows ICT can be used to create a comprehensive story when PPP thresholds escalate. Automating PPP to give it longer lives, track remedial action when PPP is escalated, track follow ups- are some of the options available when technology is harnessed.

Solana (2014) demonstrates that using ICT also makes it easier to explain to financiers the actions performed, and the situations that mandated them, since it leaves an audit trail which reveals these details clearly. Risk management strategies can also be realized for specific measurable, relevant and timely actions and responsibilities (Smith, Merna & Jobling, 2006). Smith (2006) advices towards this objective, it is essential to understand PPP standards and measurement specifications. Furthermore, it is essential to determine the PPP project analytics providers and the metrics consumers through various tools and resources. Shrivastava. (2011) claims that one of the biggest benefits of leveraging ICT to management PPP is that it does away with manual efforts, which can be time consuming and cumbersome. ICT supports manual and automated data collation methods, enables easy definitions of thresholds, and track issues and actions for breaches. It provides a single interface to define KRIs and KPIs and risk appetite. It is possible to track metrics for causes, consequences and risks and these are easily accessible to employees engaged in the implementation of PPP project.

According to Rohmeyer and Zvi (2009), ICT are necessary to improve access to vital services and to ultimately support efforts to improve economic conditions in developing regions. For example, access to information resources provides substantial benefits in the public and private sectors of regions with low standards of living. Success in achieving any benefit from ICT investment in any development enterprise will be directly affected by the resiliency of the ICT systems and services, including technical and non-technical domains. ICT plays a substantial role in global development. For example, cleverly (2009) claims ICT can make developing countries to gain rapid advances and perhaps "leapfrog" the developed world in some respects. ICT has the potential to improve access to service delivery information in addition to increase in richness as a result of social networking (Cleverly, 2009). ICT can enable participation in all sorts of interactive pursuits; for example, it can be used against environmental and other resource challenges. Paredes (2009) recognized ICT as an important vehicle for the achievement of sustainable development in order to promote national improvements in efficiency and equity in the Dominican Republic. Pade (2006) noted that ICTs contribute significantly in supporting and promoting rural development and stressed the important role of knowledge sharing in rural development efforts, including the promise of participation in national, regional, and global communities. The author also suggested that the success of ICT projects could be diminished by factors that affect deployment and usage. Avgerou (2008) reviewed Information Systems research on intended benefits of ICT for development initiatives, including an examination of project failures. This included process, interaction, and expectation failures, respectively. Fuchs (2006) also described sustainability in the ICT development context, highlighting ecological, technological, economic, political, and cultural sustainability. Avgerou (2008) noted theories of the strategic importance of ICT in organizations have been extended to the development context. Boateng, Heeks, Molla and Hinson (2008) examined the diffusion of e-Commerce into development contexts and identified economic, socio-cultural, and legal impacts.

Designing and setting up ICT is critical to a successful PPP outcomes. While potential advantages of creating an effective set of ICT has been highlighted, it is equally important to set the design elements and protocols for their proper communication and flow within the sphere of PPP implementation. Proper ICT use is deemed to be efficient indicator of not just the potential risk handler to the PPP project but also an effective mean to reap success. It is believed that harnessing technology and leveraging it will only enhance PPP project risk management approach and complement existing risk identification methods so as to yield significant benefits.

ICT Best Practices

Tremendous successful progress has been registered in the use of ICT in government programs (Hanna & Knight, 2011) including PPPs. In many cases, the public and private collaboration have been in the forefront of many of these trends (McManus, Seville, Brunsdon & Vargo, 2007). Madon (2005) suggests that best practices which can be adopted while using ICT are many but commonest among them are: well-developed PPP technology plans aligned with the goal of the public partner. There has to be directive from the public partner to demonstrate saving from technology investments. There has to be emphasis on the PPP view and the governance model it has adopted in respect to the ICT policy. There has to be more ICT investment oversight by the partners with greater emphasis on accountability, measuring value and performance. There ought to be adaptation of consolidation and shared services for IT services with a focus on cost control and/or reduction of duplication. There has to be a stronger business discipline introduced and nurtured which can track the project and resources consumed. Innocenti (2015) recommends a stronger influence of PPP architecture in defining a framework for business processes, IT investments and procurement decisions. The growing understanding of citizens, clients and customers needs especially their experience in the marketplace need to be enhanced. There has to be a continued growing trend of more outsourcing to bring in varieties of goods and services. Most importantly, because of the changing ICT workforce demographics, there is need for recruitment, retention and retaining issues which must be attended to in order to overcome the challenges of aging ICT workforce with legacy skills sets.

According to Week (2009), it is vital to build a culture of resiliency to support ICT development and operations. The success of any implementation will be limited if the new system is not reliable. Weeks and Benade (2007) explained the importance of building a culture of resiliency awareness, and offered guidance on how to do so. Similarly, McManus (2007) described a resilience management process that included identifying the need to build awareness of resilience issues, selecting organization-critical components, completion of a self-assessment of vulnerabilities, identification of key vulnerabilities, and what was characterized as increasing adaptive capacity. According to Dalberg, Angelvik, Elvekrok and Fossbert (2006), this is represented by a continuum that sought to move the organization away from functional silos to mature and integrated leadership, management, and governance structures. A high level mapping of strategic concerns was also provided in Pade (2006) that identified domains of sustainability in development initiatives as socio-cultural, institutional, economic, political, and technological.

Achieving technical resiliency is required to enable success in ICT development enterprises (Armitage, 2006). Radhakrishnan, Mark and Powell (2008) presented a model of key performance indicators for IT Service management that may be directly applied to the ICT context. They identified the concept of high availability service management (HASM) to prioritize resiliency within the IT service management domain through the use of Six Sigma and other quality methods. HASM emphasizes system event and incident management as well as high quality infrastructure, architecture and design towards the objective of building sustainable systems (Sakurai, 2007).

ICT development efforts should be guided by formalized planning that takes proactive and reactive viewpoints with respect to risk management (McNaughton, Ray & Lewis, 2010). Effective ICT should not simply follow the traditional definition of resilience (i.e. ability to rebound or bounce back from an incident) but to block the effects of incidents as well (i.e. repel). Weeks (2009) explained the importance of including both proactive and reactive postures in the resiliency model. Resilience in the broad sense suggests an ability to withstand events, system attacks, physical disruption, and other possible incidents. Organizations should adopt a comprehensive scope of planning. Pade (2006) identified domains of sustainability in development initiatives as socio-cultural, institutional, economic, political, and technological, and planning activities should take a similarly broad perspective.

It is important to establish pre- and post-implementation governance structures. Governance considerations vary across the implementation lifecycle (Kefallinos, Lambrou & Sykas, 2009). The organizations and individuals involved in planning, design, and deployment in many cases will often not be involved in the ongoing operations of the ICT (Fitzsimmons & Fitzsimmons, 2008). Therefore it is import to identify governance structures that will oversee funding, internal controls, and reporting from pre and post perspectives. Operational ICT should include structures to include accountability to maintain the resiliency management program (Lapão, 2011). The responsibility of local managers and technicians must extend beyond basic service provisioning and emphasize the importance of delivering high quality, reliable, and dependable service.

Risk Communication

Risk communication is the exchange of risk-specific information with the emphasis on creating understanding between the sender and the receiver (Cooper & Faseruk, 2011). Effective risk communication is one of the most important factors contributing to the success of a PPP project (Fassin, 2009). Communication is further on said to be one of the most important critical success factors for dealing with risks during the implementation of projects and for corporations' readiness of risk management (Yaraghi & Langhe, 2011). Risk communication is a complex cross-disciplinary academic field related to core values of the targeted audiences (Pandey & Garnett, 2006). It can be explained as a combination of external and internal communication where the prior refers to communication related to PPP project marketing, and the latter refers to written and interpersonal communication (Cooper & Faseruk, 2011). Ramsing (2009, p.347) defines it as "...the personal interaction in a project between managers, management, project team members, project stakeholders or other individuals...of importance to the project". Aligned with this definition, it is the project manager's responsibility to obtain a good internal communication within the project which can also be described as a way to implement the strategic visions of the project (Pop & Dumitrascu, 2013).

Problems for risk communicators involve how to reach the intended audience, how to make the risk comprehensible and relatable to other risks, how to pay appropriate respect to the audience's values related to the risk, how to predict the audience's response to the communication, etc (Baker, & Cameron, 2008). A main goal of risk communication is to improve collective and individual decision making (Crawford & Helm, 2009). Risk communication is somewhat related to crisis communication. It requires collaboration and interaction between the project owner and project management which is essential in both project-and risk management (Krane, Olsson & Rolstadås, 2012). Kwan and Leung (2011) proved that well-functioning communication channels between the involved stakeholders are a necessity to reach project success. According to Ruch and Welch (2012), the level of commitment and how clear management is in their expectations also plays an extensive role regarding internal communication and how significant it will be. Krane, Olsson and Rolstadås (2012) contend that the different perceptions that could occur between the level, or the strategic level, and the project level, the operational level is relevant to understand related progress of the project.

Intuitively, the literatures confirm communication as a prerequisite for successful project management and project risk management to align (Leung & Isaacs, 2008). It has to be said, however, that communications with multiple stakeholders such as in a PPP project is more difficult to manage. As Thamhain (2013) found, the project owner's primary interest lies on the result of the project and in receiving the benefits, whereas the project management prioritize to deliver the result on time and within budget. Cervone (2006) emphasizes the perceptions of a successful project and the expectations on the outcome are hence not always aligned. Varied priorities is said to increase the need for high collaboration, trust and strong communication between the owner and management (Artto, Kujala, Dietrich & Martinsuo, 2008). Besner and Hobbs (2013) confirm this argument by emphasizing the importance of human interactions between decision-makers and managers to reach project success. Varied stakeholders interest (Besner & Hobbs, 2012b), and poor communication (Doloi, 2009) are however not only factors which could negatively affect the project's risk management and/or outcome. Besner and Hobbs (2012a) identify the perceptions regarding risks of a poor producing project are also different between senior managers and project managers. According to Thamhain (2013), this in the long run implicates that if a project is not performing satisfactory it is likely that the top management will hold the project manager responsible. Marle and Vidal (2011) assert even though it might be risks and events that are not possible to control

Avgerou (2008) calls for PMC to provide timely and accurate information to all stakeholders. The information prepared by the PMC must be in a variety of ways to meet the needs of PPP project shareholders who should also receive feedback from these stakeholders (Thamhain, 2013). Risk communication includes general communication between PMC but is more encompassing. It utilizes the WBS for a framework, it is customer focused, it's limited in time, it is product focused with the end in mind, and it involves all levels of the SPV. It is therefore important to communicate through reporting and escalation. This is because communicating risks to partners and stakeholders allows the organization that risks are being managed on both sides. While communication and reporting are an ongoing process, reporting on specific risks should primarily be included in existing reporting and communication mechanisms (Marle & Vidal, 2011). An up-to-date version of the risk profile should be available, for example to help auditors.

There are two reasons for reviewing and reporting risks: measuring the effectiveness in the way the risks are being managed and gaining assurance that the process is working, and monitoring whether the risk profile is changing (Krane, Olsson & Rolstadås, 2012). In all cases, ensure that reporting and communications are accurate, as complete as possible, and regularly updated to reflect reality to the best of your knowledge. Remember that risk formulation and risk reporting are essential for the understanding of issues at stake. Doloi (2009) suggests that on a frequent basis, risks should also be reviewed in the context of other major processes and functions that have a bearing on the achievement of expected strategic outcomes/results, such as, monitoring and evaluation, project management, standing committees, requests for extra budgetary funding, and proposals and reports to oversight bodies. The matrix of the main strategic risks facing the Organization can also be reviewed throughout the planning process with the aim of reducing the number of high risk items (Besner & Hobbs, 2013). Organizations have to maintain a state of continuous alertness with regard to changing patterns in their operating environment (societal, political, legal, physical) once the risk profile has been mapped. This constant updating and sharing of what they know, of error reporting, at what they are doing is the essence of organizational situation awareness, which is key to decision making and risk management (Crawford & Helm, 2009).

CONCLUSION

If the problem is to change the menace of failed and/or stalled PPP projects due to risks, in both developed and developing world, then little is known about how it is done. There can be no presumption that one type of corrective tool from the basic to the most complex, will work better than another, from inception of the PPP project to completion. And if the public partner has additional objectives, whether for a quality-led production and/or service delivery, it becomes even less possible to make general prescriptions. The risk that PPP project decision-makers may be less able to respond to risks or other risks related matters, because of lack of experience or lack of full awareness of the alternatives suggests that all efforts and measures needed to be stronger than ever thought of. In practical terms, this may require more effort (which may be a practical difficulty in this prescription: the decision-makers and implementers of PPP projects are in need of training). In actual terms, this may mean greater potential for conflict with the increasingly rigid citizens' demands for high value goods and quality services, specific difficulty of identifying authentic courses of action to take. There is, however, more scope than is sometimes recognized for all sorts of efforts.

There is probably a sequence of corrective tools that is more effective than any single tool, as partners' potentials to perform their part of the bargain evolve, and also as the implementation demands of the PPP project changes. The sequence of the most recent PPP project successes suggest that it is one from mere partnerships to concrete partnerships, but there are examples of SPVs that were successfully implemented on the basis of ingredients for a successful risk management to permit the application of the tools in a contractual relationship. This is of particular interest to those partners where full information about the PPP project is blurred. Although it may be inappropriate to emphasize in this closing chapter, the use of ICT in risk management is not an end in itself but a tool, either for identification of the information needs and ICT best practices that assists in risk communication. Once these are done, the success of risk management in a PPP becomes non-negotiable.

REFERENCES

Aaltonen, K., Jaakko, K., & Tuomas, O. (2008). Stakeholder salience in global projects. *International Journal of Project Management*, *26*(5), 509–516. doi:10.1016/j.ijproman.2008.05.004

Abdel Aziz, A. (2007). Successful delivery of public-private partnerships for infrastructure development. *Journal of Construction Engineering and Management*, *133*(12), 918–931. doi:10.1061/(ASCE)0733-9364(2007)133:12(918)

Abdul Aziz, A. R. (2010). Housing private public partnership: Perspective from the government agencies. *Proceedings: 4th NAPREC Conference*. Retrieved from http://www.inspen.gov.my/inspen/

Abdul Aziz, A. R., & Kassim, P. S. J. (2011). Objectives, success and failure factors of housing public-private partnerships in Malaysia. *Habitat International*, *35*(1), 150–157. doi:10.1016/j.habitatint.2010.06.005

Abednego, M. P., & Ogunlana, S. O. (2006). Good project governance for proper risk allocation in the public-private partnership in Indonesia. *International Journal of Project Management*, *24*(7), 622–634. doi:10.1016/j.ijproman.2006.07.010

Adams, J., Alistair, Y., & Wu, Z. H. (2006). Public private partnerships in China-system, constraints and future prospects. *International Journal of Public Sector Management*, *19*(4), 384–396. doi:10.1108/09513550610669202

Agyakwa-Baah, A., Chileshe, N., & Fugar, F. D. K. (2010). Perceptions to barriers to risk assessment and management practices deployment: Opinion survey findings. *Journal of Construction*, *3*(2), 17–23.

Ahmad, E., Bhattacharya, A., Vinella, A., & Xiao, K. (2014). *Involving the Private Sector and PPPs in Financing Public Investments: Some opportunities and challenges*. Asia Research Centre Working Paper 67. Retrieved from www.lse.ac.uk/collections/AsiaResearchCentre

Ajayi, J. R., & Isah, Y. (2014). Impediments to risk assessment techniques in public-private partnership construction projects in Abuja-Nigeria. *Malaysian Journal of Civil Engineering*, *26*(3), 366–381.

Akbiyikli, R., Eaton, D., & Turner, A. L. (2006). Project finance and the private finance initiative (PFI). *The Journal of Structured Finance*, *12*(2), 65–75. doi:10.3905/jsf.2006.644162

Al-Kharashi, A., & Skitmore, M. (2009). Causes of delays in Saudi Arabian public sector construction projects. *Construction Management and Economics*, *27*(1), 3–23. doi:10.1080/01446190802541457

Al-Tmeemy, S. M. H. M., Abdul-Tahman, H., & Harun, Z. (2011). Future criteria for success of building projects in Malaysia. *International Journal of Project Management*, *29*(3), 337–348. doi:10.1016/j.ijproman.2010.03.003

Alashwal, A. M., Rahman, H. A., & Beksin, A. M. (2011). Knowledge sharing in the fragmented construction industry: On the hindsight. *Academic Journals Scientific Research and Essays*, *6*(7), 1530–1536.

Alcock, P. (2010). A strategic unity: Defining the third sector in the UK. *Voluntary Sector Review*, *1*(1), 5–24. doi:10.1332/204080510X496984

Alderman, N., & Ivory, C. (2007). Partnering in major contracts: Paradox and metaphor. *International Journal of Project Management*, *25*(4), 386–393. doi:10.1016/j.ijproman.2007.01.002

Alonso-Conde, A. B., Brown, C., & Rojo-Suarez, J. (2007). Public private partnerships: Incentives, risk transfer and real options. *Review of Financial Economics*, *16*(4), 335–349. doi:10.1016/j.rfe.2007.03.002

Alzahrani, S., & Boussabaine, H. (2014). Risk mapping in public private partnership projects. *Proceedings of the Second International Conference on Advances in Social Science, Economics and Management Study- SEM 2014*. doi:10.15224/ 978-1-63248-007-1-86

Armistead, C., & Pettigrew, P. (2008). Partnerships in the provision of services by multi- agencies: Four dimensions of service leadership and service quality. *Service Business*, *2*(1), 17–32. doi:10.1007/s11628-006-0017-4

Artto, K., Kujala, J., Dietrich, P., & Martinsuo, M. (2008). What is project strategy? *International Journal of Project Management*, *26*(1), 4–12. doi:10.1016/j.ijproman.2007.07.006

Asress, N. S., & Kumari, T. (2016). Assessing the roles of public private partnership in Ethiopian urban local governance. *International Journal of Applied Research*, *2*(1), 595–599.

Avazkhah, H., & Mohebbi, A. (2010). *Project risk management*. Tehran: KianRayanehSabz.

Avgerou, C. (2008). Information systems in developing countries: A critical research review. *Journal of Information Technology*, *23*(3), 133–146. doi:10.1057/palgrave.jit.2000136

Aziz, A. M. A. (2007). Successful delivery of public-private partnerships for infrastructure development. *Journal of Construction Engineering and Management*, *133*(12), 918–931. doi:10.1061/(ASCE)0733-9364(2007)133:12(918)

Baccarini, D. (2005). *Understanding project cost contingency–A survey*. Paper presented at the Queensland University of Technology (QUT) Research Week International Conference.

Baker, M. J., & Cameron, E. (2008). Critical success factors in destination marketing. *Tourism and Hospitality Research*, *8*(2), 79–97. doi:10.1057/thr.2008.9

Batley, R. (2006). Engaged or divorced? Cross-service findings on government relations with non-state service-providers. *Public Administration and Development*, *26*(3), 241–251. doi:10.1002/pad.422

Batley, R., & Rose, P. (2011). Analyzing collaboration between non-governmental service providers and governments. *Public Administration and Development*, *31*(4), 230–239. doi:10.1002/pad.613

Beasley, M. S., Clune, R., & Hermanson, D. R. (2005). Enterprise risk management: An empirical analysis of factors associated with the extent of implementation. *Journal of Accounting and Public Policy*, *24*(6), 521–531. doi:10.1016/j.jaccpubpol.2005.10.001

Beisheim, M., Liese, A., & Vosseler, C. (2014). Who governs partnerships? On the role of boards, donors, partners, and other stakeholders. In M. Beisheim & A. Liese (Eds.), *Transnational partnerships: effectively providing for sustainable development?* (pp. 107–127). Palgrave Macmillan. doi:10.1057/9781137359537_6

Belassi, W., & Tukel, O. I. (1996). A new framework for determining critical success/failure factors in projects. *International Journal of Project Management, 14*(3), 141–151. doi:10.1016/0263-7863(95)00064-X

Benta, D., Podean, I. M., & Mircean, C. (2011). On best practices for risk management in complex projects. *Informatica Economica, 15*(2), 142–152.

Berg, H.-P. (2010b). Risk management: Procedures, methods and experiences. *RT&T, 1*(2), 79–95.

Besner, C., & Hobbs, B. (2012a). An empirical identification of project management toolsets and a comparison among project types. *Project Management Journal, 43*(5), 24–46. doi:10.1002/pmj.21292

Besner, C., & Hobbs, B. (2012b). The paradox of risk management; A project management practice perspective. *International Journal of Managing Projects in business, 5*(2), 230- 247.

Besner, C., & Hobbs, B. (2013). Contextualized project management practice: A cluster analysis of practices and best practices. *Project Management Journal, 44*(1), 17–34. doi:10.1002/pmj.21291

Beyene, T. T. (2014). Factors for Implementing Public-Private Partnership (PPP) in the Development Process: Stakeholders' Perspective from Ethiopia. *International Journal of Science and Research, 3*(3), 792–797.

Bloomfield, P. (2006). The challenging business of long-term public–private partnerships: Reflection on local experience. *Public Administration Review, 66*(3), 400–411. doi:10.1111/j.1540-6210.2006.00597.x

Boardman, A. E., & Vining, A. R. (2012). The political economy of public-private partnerships and analysis of their social value. *Annals of Public and Cooperative Economics, 83*(2), 117–141. doi:10.1111/j.1467-8292.2012.00457.x

Boateng, R., Heeks, R., Molla, A., & Hinson, R. (2008). E-commerce and socio-economic development: Conceptualizing the link. *Internet Research, 18*(5), 562–594. doi:10.1108/10662240810912783

Bon-Gang, H., Xianbo, Z., & Ping, T. L. (2014). Risk management in small construction projects in Singapore: Status, barriers and impact. *International Journal of Project Management, 32*(1), 116–124. doi:10.1016/j.ijproman.2013.01.007

Bonnafous, A. (2010). Programming, optimal pricing and partnership contract for infrastructures in PPPs. *Research in Transportation Economics, 30*(1), 15–22. doi:10.1016/j.retrec.2010.10.003

Bostrom, A., French, S. P., & Gotllieb, S. J. (2008). *Risk assessment modeling and decision support.* Berlin: Springer Publishing. doi:10.1007/978-3-540-71158-2

Bracey, N., & Moldovan, S. (2006). *Public-private partnerships: Risks to the public and private sector.* Paper presented at the 6th Global Conference on Business and Economics.

Brench, A., Beckers, T., Heinrich, M., & von Hirschhausen, C. (2005). Public-Private Partnerships in New EU Member Countries of Central and Eastern Europe. *European Investment Bank, 10*, 2.

Bresnen, M. (2007). Deconstructing partnering in project based organization; Seven pillars, seven paradoxes and seven deadly sins. *International Journal of Project Management, 25*(4), 365–374. doi:10.1016/j.ijproman.2007.01.007

Bryde, D. J. (2005). Methods for managing different perspectives of project success. *British Journal of Management, 16*(2), 119–131. doi:10.1111/j.1467-8551.2005.00438.x

Bryde, D. J., & Robinson, L. (2005). Client versus contractor perspectives on project success criteria. *International Journal of Project Management, 23*(8), 622–629. doi:10.1016/j.ijproman.2005.05.003

Bygballe, L. E., Jahre, M., & Sward, A. (2010). Partnering relationships in construction: A literature review. *Journal of Purchasing and Supply Management, 16*(4), 239–253. doi:10.1016/j.pursup.2010.08.002

Calabrese, D. (2008). *Strategic communication for privatization, public-private partnerships, and private participation in infrastructure projects.* World Bank Working Paper, No.139. Retrieved from http://siteresources.worldbank.org/EXTDEVCOMMENG/Resources/StrategicCommun

Camilleri, E. (2011). *Project Success: Critical Factors and Behaviors.* Surrey, UK: Gower Publishing Limited.

Cankar, S. S., & Petkovšek, V. (2013). Private and public sector innovation and the importance of cross-sector collaboration. *Journal of Applied Business Research, 29*(6), 197–1606.

Carbonara, N., Costantino, N., & Pellegrino, R. (2013). A three-layer theoretical framework for analyzing public private partnerships: The Italian case. *Organization, Technology and Management International Journal (Toronto, Ont.), 6*(2), 799–810.

Cervone, F. H. (2006). Project risk management. *OCLC Systems & Services: International Digital Library Perspectives, 22*(4), 256–262. doi:10.1108/10650750610706970

Cheung, E., Chan, A. P. C., & Kajewski, S. (2009b). Reasons for implementing public private partnership projects: Perspectives from Hong Kong, Australian and British practitioners. *Journal of Property Investment & Finance, 27*(1), 81–95. doi:10.1108/14635780910926685

Chileshe, N., & Kikwasi, G. J. (2013). Perception of barriers to implementing risk assessment and management practices by construction professional in Tanzania.*Proceedings of the 29th Annual ARCOM Conference*, 1137-1146.

Cleverly, M. (2009). Emerging Markets: How ICT advances might help developing nations. *Communications of the ACM, 52*(9).

Coleman, L. (2009). *Risk strategies – Dialing up optimum firm risk.* Burlington, MA: Gower e- Book Publishing.

Cooper, T., & Faseruk, A. (2011). Strategic risk, risk perception and risk behavior: Meta-analysis. *Journal of Financial Management and Analysis, 24*(2), 20–29.

Coter, J. E., & Chen, Y. J. (2006). Do investment risk tolerance attitudes predict portfolio risk? *Journal of Business and Psychology, 20*(3), 369–381. doi:10.1007/s10869-005-9010-5

Crawford, L. H., & Helm, J. (2009). Government and governance: The value of project management in the public sector. *Project Management Journal, 40*(1), 73–87. doi:10.1002/pmj.20107

Crompton, L., Goulding, J. S., & Pour, R. F. (2014). Construction partnering: Moving towards the rationalization for a dominant paradigm. Alam Cipta. *International Journal of Sustainable Tropical Design Research and Practice*, *7*(1), 57–78.

Dacin, M. T., Oliver, C., & Roy, J.-P. (2007). The legitimacy of strategic alliances: An institutional perspective. *Strategic Management Journal*, *28*(2), 169–187. doi:10.1002/smj.577

Davies, J., Finlay, M., McLenaghen, T., & Wilson, D. (2006). *Key risk indicators – Their role in operational risk management and measurement*. Retrieved from http://citeseerx.ist.psu.edu/viewdoc/download?doi=10.1.1.457.893&rep=rep1&type=pdf

De Bettignies, J. E., & Ross, T. W. (2009). Public Private Partnerships and the Privatization of Financing: An Incomplete Contracts Approach. *International Journal of Industrial Organization*, *27*(3), 358–368. doi:10.1016/j.ijindorg.2008.10.004

de Brito, J., & Branco, F. A. (2006). Bridge management policy using cost analysis. *Journal of Civil Engineering*, *244*, 92–98.

De Marco, A., & Thaheem, M. J. (2014). Risk analysis in construction projects: A practical selection methodology. *American Journal of Applied Sciences*, *11*(1), 74–84. doi:10.3844/ajassp.2014.74.84

Dey, P. K. (2009). Managing risks of large scale construction projects. *Coastal Engineering*, *51*(6), 23–27.

Doerfel, M. L., Lai, C.-H., & Chewning, L. V. (2010). The evolutionary role of inter- organizational communication: Modeling social capital in disaster contexts. *Human Communication Research*, *36*(2), 125–162. doi:10.1111/j.1468-2958.2010.01371.x

Duckert, G. H. (2010). *Practical Enterprise Risk Management-A business process approach*. New York: John Wiley & Sons. doi:10.1002/9781118269060

Edelenbos, J., & Klijn, E.-H. (2009). Project versus process management in public private partnership: Relation between management style and outcomes. *International Public Management Journal*, *12*(3), 310–331. doi:10.1080/10967490903094350

Endut, I. R., Akintoye, A., & Kelly, J. (2006). *Relationship between duration and cost of Malaysian construction projects*. Paper presented at International Conference in the Built Environment in the 21st Century, Kuala Lumpur, Malaysia.

Enshassi, A., Mohamed, S., & Abu-Mosa, J. (2008). Risk Management in building projects in Palestine contractors' perspective. *Emirates Journal for Engineering Research*, *13*(1), 29–44.

Essia, U., & Yusuf, A. (2013). Public-private-partnership and sustainable development of infrastructures in Nigeria. *Advances in Management & Applied Economics*, *3*(6), 113–127.

Fassin, Y. (2009). The stakeholder model refined. *Journal of Business Ethics*, *84*(1), 113–135. doi:10.1007/s10551-008-9677-4

Figueiredo, F., & Kitson, B. (2009). Defining risk and contingency for pipeline projects. *AACE International Transactions*, *8*(1), 1–10.

Gaffey, D. W. (2010). Outsourcing infrastructure: Expanding the use of public-private partnerships n the United States. *Public Contract Law Journal*, *39*, 351–360.

Gauthier, J. B., & Ika, L. A. (2012). Foundations of project management research: An explicit and six-facet ontological framework. *Project Management Journal*, *43*(5), 5–23. doi:10.1002/pmj.21288

Gazley, B. (2010). Linking collaborative capacity to performance measurement in Government- Nonprofit Partnerships. *Nonprofit and Voluntary Sector Quarterly*, *39*(4), 653–673. doi:10.1177/0899764009360823

Girmscheid, G. (2006). *Holistic Probabilistic Risk Management Process Model for Project- Oriented Enterprises*. Zürich: Eigenverlag IBB, ETH Zürich.

Goldstein, S. M., & Naor, M. (2005). Linking publicness to operations management practices: A study of quality management practices in hospitals. *Journal of Operations Management*, *23*(2), 209–228. doi:10.1016/j.jom.2004.07.007

Gomes, C., Yasin, M. M., & Small, M. H. (2012). Discerning interrelationships among the knowledge, competencies, and roles of project managers in the planning and implementation of public sector projects. *International Journal of Public Administration*, *35*(5), 315–328. doi:10.1080/01900692.2012.655461

Greiling, D. (2009). Public-Private Partnerships – A driver for efficient public services or just an example of wishful thinking. *Journal for Public and Nonprofit Services*, (Supplement 37), 108–125.

Gupta, O., & Biswas, N. (2010). Public private partnership: Indian economy. *SCMS Journal of Indian Management*, *7*, 44–53.

Hampton, G., Baldwin, A. N., & Holt, G. (2012). Project delays and cost: Stakeholder perceptions of traditional v. PPP procurement. *Journal of Financial Management of Property and Construction*, *17*(1), 73–91. doi:10.1108/13664381211211055

Hanna, N. K., & Knight, P. T. (2011). *Seeking transformation through information technology*. New York: Springer. doi:10.1007/978-1-4614-0353-1

Hanna, S., & Rowley, J. (2008). An analysis of terminology use in place branding. *Place Branding and Public Diplomacy*, *4*(1), 61–75. doi:10.1057/palgrave.pb.6000084

Hanna, S., & Rowley, J. (2011). Towards a strategic place brand-management model. *Journal of Marketing Management*, *27*(5-6), 458–476. doi:10.1080/02672571003683797

Hillson, D. A., Grimaldi, S., & Rafele, C. (2006). Managing project risk using a cross risk breakdown matrix. *Risk Management*, *8*(1), 61–76. doi:10.1057/palgrave.rm.8250004

Ho, P. H. (2006). Development of Public Private Partnerships (PPP) in China. *Surveyors Times, 15*(10).

Hofmann, B. (2007). Public procurement and PPP. *Real Estate Investment in Germany Review*, *10*(2), 229–250. doi:10.1007/978-3-540-72179-6_10

Hubbard, D. W., & Seiersen, R. (2016). *How to measure anything in Cybersecurity risk*. London: Wiley. doi:10.1002/9781119162315

Ibem, E. (2010). An assessment of the role of Government agencies in public private partnerships in housing delivery in Nigeria. *Journal of Construction in Developing Countries*, *15*(2), 23–48.

Ibrahim, A. D., Price, A. D. F., & Dainty, A. R. J. (2006). The analysis and allocation of risks in public private partnerships in infrastructure projects in Nigeria. *Journal of Financial Management of Property and Construction*, *11*(3), 149–163. doi:10.1108/13664380680001086

Inekwe, M. (2015). Public private partnership and infrastructural development In Nigeria Polytechnics: The Federal Polytechnic, Idah Experience. *International Journal of Research Development*, *9*(1), 20–33.

Innocenti, E.B. (2015). *Public-Private Partnerships in e-Government guide*. Paper presented during the two day workshop "PPPs in e-Government" held, Kyiv, Ukraine.

Ismail, S. (2013). Factors attracting the use of public private partnership in Malaysia. *Journal of Construction in Developing Countries*, *18*(1), 95–108.

Javed, A. A., Lam, P. T. L., & Zou, P. X. W. (2013). Output-based specifications for PPP projects: Lessons for facilities management from Australia. *Journal of Facilities Management*, *11*(1), 5–30. doi:10.1108/14725961311301448

Jeffares, S., Sullivan, H., & Bovaird, T. (2009). *Beyond the contract - The challenge of evaluating the performance(s) of public-private partnerships*. Paper for the annual conference of International Research Society for Public Management, (IRSPM), Copenhagen, Denmark.

Jha, K. N., & Iyer, K. C. (2007). Commitment, coordination, competence and the iron triangle. *International Journal of Project Management*, *25*(5), 527–540. doi:10.1016/j.ijproman.2006.11.009

Joshua, O. D. (2010). Stratage for mitigating risk in construction projects. Risk Management in Construction. *Proceedings of the 40th annual general meeting/conference of the Nigerian Institute of Building*.

Ke, Y., Wang, S. Q., & Chan, A. P. C. (2011). Equitable risks allocation of projects inside China: Analyses from Delphi survey studies. *Chinese Management Studies*, *5*(3), 298–310. doi:10.1108/17506141111163372

Kefallinos, D., Lambrou, M., & Sykas, E. (2009). An extended risk assessment model for secure E-Government. *International Journal of Electronic Government Research*, *5*(2), 72–92. doi:10.4018/jegr.2009040105

Kim, S.-G., & Kim, J.-J. (2005). A risk threshold calculation methodology for the construction projects applying value at risk. *Journal of Construction Engineering and Management*, *120*, 665–670.

Kobbeltvedt, T., Brun, W., Johansen, B. H., & Eid, J. (2005). Risk as feelings or risk and feelings? A cross-lagged panel analysis. *Journal of Risk Research*, *8*(5), 417–437. doi:10.1080/1366987042000315519

Kort, M., & Klijn, E.-H. (2011). Public–private partnerships in urban regeneration projects: Organizational form or managerial capacity? *Public Administration Review*, *71*(4), 618–626. doi:10.1111/j.1540-6210.2011.02393.x

Krane, H. P., Olsson, N. O. E., & Rolstadås, A. (2012). How Project Manager-Project Owner Interaction Can Work Within and Influence Project Risk Management. *Project Management Journal*, *43*(2), 54–67. doi:10.1002/pmj.20284

Kumaraswamy, M., Ling, F. Y. Y., Anvuur, A. M., & Rahman, M. M. (2007). Targeting relationally integrated teams for sustainable PPPS. *Engineering, Construction, and Architectural Management*, *14*(6), 581–596. doi:10.1108/09699980710829030

Kwan, T. W., & Leung, H. K. N. (2011). A risk management methodology for project risk dependencies. *IEEE Transactions on Software Engineering*, *37*(5), 635–648. doi:10.1109/TSE.2010.108

Lam, J. (2006). Managing risk across the enterprise: Challenges and benefits. In Risk Management: A Modern Perspective. Burlington: Elsevier.

Lapão, L. V. (2011). Organizational challenges and barriers to implementing IT governance in a Hospital. *Electronic Journal of Information Systems Evaluation*, *14*, 37–45.

Leung, F., & Isaacs, F. (2008). Risk management in public sector research: Approach and lessons learned at a national research organization. *R & D Management*, *38*(5), 510–519. doi:10.1111/j.1467-9310.2008.00529.x

Ling, F. Y. Y., & Hoi, L. (2006). Risk faced by Singapore firms when undertaking construction projects in India. *International Journal of Project Management*, *24*(3), 261–270. doi:10.1016/j.ijproman.2005.11.003

Marle, F., & Vidal, L. A. (2011). Project risk management processes: Improving coordination using a clustering approach. *Research in Engineering Design*, *22*(3), 189–206. doi:10.1007/s00163-011-0106-9

Matei, L. (2006). Empirical approaches of the public-private partnership in the services of public utility. *Theoretical and Applicative Economics*, *10*(505), 3–14.

McLeod, L., Doolin, B., & MacDonell, S. G. (2012). A perspective-based understanding of project success. *Project Management Journal*, *43*(5), 68–86. doi:10.1002/pmj.21290

McNaughton, B., Ray, P., & Lewis, L. (2010). Designing an evaluation framework for IT service management. *Information & Management*, *47*(4), 219–225. doi:10.1016/j.im.2010.02.003

Miller, G. (2006). Time and cost risk analysis. *Journal of Civil Engineering*, *64*, 1149–1155.

Mistarihi, A. M., Al Refai, M. S., Al Qaid, B. A., & Qeed, M. A. (2012). Competency requirements for managing public private partnerships (PPPs): The case of infrastructure projects in Jordan. *International Journal of Business and Management*, *7*(12), 60–73. doi:10.5539/ijbm.v7n12p60

Mouraviev, N. (2012). Risk management in public-private partnerships and research agenda for transitional countries. *International Journal of Management & Business Studies*, *2*(2), 27–41.

Müller, R., & Jugdev, K. (2012). Critical success factors in projects: Pinto, Slevin, and Prescott – the elucidation of project success. *International Journal of Managing Projects in Business*, *5*(4), 757–775. doi:10.1108/17538371211269040

Murdoch, J., & Hughes, W. (2008). *Construction Contracts; Law and Management* (4th ed.). London: Taylor & Francis.

Mwaguni, H. J., & Busienei, P. K. (2014). Effect of public-private partnership on the provision of quality services; a case of the grain terminal at the port of Mombasa, Kenya. *Journal of International Academic Research for Multidisciplinary*, *2*(5), 609–643.

Nystrom, J. (2008). A quasi-experimental evaluation of partnering. *Construction Management and Economics*, *26*(5), 531–541. doi:10.1080/01446190802036144

Ogbu, C. P. (2013). Risk management practices of multinational and indigenous construction companies in Nigeria: A comparative analysis. *Journal of Research in National Development*, *9*(2), 315–324.

Ökmen, Ö., & Öztas, A. (2010). Construction cost analysis under uncertainty with correlated cost risk analysis mode. *Construction Management and Economics*, *28*(2), 203–212. doi:10.1080/01446190903468923

Ongolo, D. O. (2006). *Public private partnerships (PPP): Practice and regulatory policy in Kenya*. Paper presented at the Institute of Economic Affairs, Kenya.

Oyegoke, A., Khalfan, M., McDermott, P., Rowlinson, S., & Dickinson, M. (2009). Construction project procurement routes; an in-depth critique. *International Journal of Managing Projects in Business*, *2*(3), 338–354. doi:10.1108/17538370910971018

Pade, C., Mallinson, B., & Sewry, D. (2006). An exploration of the categories associated with ict project sustainability in rural areas of developing countries: A case study of the Dwesa Project. *ACM Proceedings of SAICSIT*, 100 –106.

Pandey, S. K., & Garnett, J. L. (2006). Exploring public sector communication performance: Testing a model and drawing implications. *Public Administration Review*, *66*(1), 37–51. doi:10.1111/j.1540-6210.2006.00554.x

Paredes, S. (2009). *The social and economic impact from broadband implementation in Dajabón Dominican Republic* (Master's Thesis). Stevens Institute of Technology.

Philip, T., Bratvold, R., & Bickel, J. E. (2014). The risk of using risk matrices. *SPE Economics and Management*, *6*(2), 56–66. doi:10.2118/166269-PA

Phua, F. T. T. (2006). When is construction partnering likely to happen? An empirical examination of the role institutional norms. *Construction Management and Economics*, *24*(6), 615–624. doi:10.1080/01446190500521256

Quiggin, J. (2005). Public-private partnerships: Options for improved risk allocation. *The Australian Economic Review*, *38*(4), 445–450. doi:10.1111/j.1467-8462.2005.00388.x

Radhakrishnan, R., Mark, K., & Powell, B. (2008). IT service management for high availability. *IBM Systems Journal*, *47*(4), 549–561. doi:10.1147/SJ.2008.5386521

Rafele, C., Hillson, D. A., & Grimaldi, S. (2005). Understanding Project Risk exposure using the Two-Dimensional Risk Breakdown Matrix.*Proceedings of the PMI Global Congress 2005 EMEA*.

Rakić, B., & Rađenović, T. (2014). Real options methodology in public-private partnership projects valuation. *Economic Annals*, *59*(200), 91–113. doi:10.2298/EKA1400091R

Rakic, B., & Radjenovic, T. (2011). Public-private partnerships as an instrument of new public management. *Facta Universitatis Series: Economics and Organization*, *8*(2), 207–220.

Ramsing, L. (2009). Project communication in a strategic internal perspective. *Corporate Communications: An International Journal*, *14*(3), 345–357. doi:10.1108/13563280910980113

Rohmeyer, P., & Zvi, T. B. (2009). Risk management decision making in ICT for development. *Proceedings of the Second Annual SIG GlobDev Workshop*.

Roig, J., & Soriano, J. M. (2015). Public-private partnerships for real estate projects: Current framework and new trends. *Regional and Sectoral Economic Studies*, *15*(1), 35–44.

Roszkowski, M. J., & Davey, G. (2010). Risk perception and risk tolerance changes attributable to the 2008 economic crisis: A subtle but critical difference. *Journal of Financial Service Professionals*, *64*(4), 42–53.

Ruck, K., & Welch, M. (2012). Valuing internal communication; management and employee perspectives. *Public Relations Review*, *38*(2), 294–302. doi:10.1016/j.pubrev.2011.12.016

Sakurai, A. (2007). Achieving integrated IT service management. *Fujitsu Scientific and Technical Journal*, *43*(3), 345–353.

Sanda, Y. N., & Anigbogu, N. A. (2016). A conceptual framework for managing risks in public private partnership projects in housing estate development in Nigeria. *International Journal of Regional Development*, *3*(1), 50–63. doi:10.5296/ijrd.v3i1.8144

Scandizzo, S. (2005). Risk mapping and key performance indicators in operational risk management. *Economic Notes*, *34*(2), 231–256. doi:10.1111/j.0391-5026.2005.00150.x

Selby, S., & Jiwani, M. (2016). *Risk governance: Building blocks for resilient development in the Pacific, UNDP Policy Brief, October, 2016*. Retrieved from http://reliefweb.int/sites/reliefweb.int/files/resources/PRRP%20Risk%20Governance- Policy%20Brief.pdf

Sharma, M. R., & Bindal, A. (2014). Public-private partnership. *International Journal of Research*, *1*(7), 1270–1274.

Shrivastava, V. K. (2011). *Public Private Partnerships in road projects: Critical Success Factors in the Indian context*. Paper presented at the Southern African Transport Conference (SATC).

Singh, G., & Khan, S. (2015). The role of public private partnership (PPP) in building society. *Management Studies and Economic Systems*, *2*(2), 103–110. doi:10.12816/0019396

Smith, D. (2006). *Understanding risk and sustainability - the future for risk managers*. Retrieved from http://riskmatters.com.au/doc/Understandingriskandsustainability.pdf#page=5&zoom=auto,-12,575

Smith, D., & Fischbachera, M. (2009). The changing nature of risk and risk management: The challenge of borders, uncertainty and resilience. *Risk Management*, *11*(1), 1–12. doi:10.1057/rm.2009.1

Smith, N. J., Merna, T., & Jobling, P. (2006). *Managing risk in construction projects* (2nd ed.). Oxford, UK: Blackwell Publishing.

Soane, E., & Chmiel, N. (2005). Are risk preferences consistent? The influence of decision domain and personality. *Personality and Individual Differences*, *38*(8), 1781–1791. doi:10.1016/j.paid.2004.10.005

Solana, E. F. O. (2014). Public private not-for-profit partnerships: Delivering public services to developing countries. *Procedia Engineering*, *78*, 259–264. doi:10.1016/j.proeng.2014.07.065

Soliño, A. S., & Vassallo, J. M. (2009). Using public-private partnerships to expand subways: Madrid-Barajas international airport case study. *Journal of Management Engineering*, *25*(1), 21–28. doi:10.1061/(ASCE)0742-597X(2009)25:1(21)

Tabish, S. Z. S., & Jha, K. N. (2012). Success traits for a construction project. *Journal of Construction Engineering and Management*, *138*(10), 1131–1138. doi:10.1061/(ASCE)CO.1943-7862.0000538

Thamhain, H. (2013). Managing risks in complex projects. *Project Management Journal*, *44*(2), 20–35. doi:10.1002/pmj.21325

Tiwari, R. (2007). The early phases of innovation: Opportunities and challenges in public-private partnership. *Asia Pacific Tech Monitor*, *24*(1), 32–37.

Toor, S., & Ogunlana, S. O. (2010). Beyond the iron triangle: Stakeholder perception of key performance indicators (KPIs) for large-scale public sector development projects. *International Journal of Project Management*, *28*(3), 228–236. doi:10.1016/j.ijproman.2009.05.005

Trafford, S., & Proctor, T. (2006). Successful joint venture partnerships: Public-private partnerships. *International Journal of Public Sector Management*, *19*(2), 117–129. doi:10.1108/09513550610650392

Vlaev, I., Chater, N., & Stewart, N. (2009). Dimensionality of risk perception: Factors affecting consumer understanding and evaluation of financial risk. *Journal of Behavioral Finance*, *10*(3), 158–181. doi:10.1080/15427560903167720

Weeks, R. (2009). *Resiliency management within a globally integrated economic network*. Retrieved from http://actacommercii.co.za/index.php/acta/article/viewFile/92/92

Weeks, R., & Benade, S. (2009). Nurturing a culture of resiliency in the age of fundamental change. *Proceedings of the Portland International Center for Management of Engineering and Technology (PICMET) Conference*, 334–349. doi:10.1109/PICMET.2009.5261860

Weihe, G. (2006). *Public-Private Partnerships: Addressing a nebulous concept*. Working paper No.16. 10th International Symposium on Public Management, Glasgow, UK.

Wibowo, A., & Mohamed, S. (2010). Risk criticality and allocation in privatized water supply projects in Indonesia. *International Journal of Project Management*, *28*(5), 504–513. doi:10.1016/j.ijproman.2009.08.003

Yang, Y., Hou, Y., & Wang, Y. (2013). On the Development of Public Private Partnerships in Transitional Economies; An Explanatory Framework. *The American Society for Public Administration*, *73*(2), 301–310. doi:10.1111/j.1540-6210.2012.02672.x

Yaraghi, N., & Langhe, R. G. (2011). Critical success factors for risk management systems. *Journal of Risk Research*, *14*(5), 551–581. doi:10.1080/13669877.2010.547253

Yu, A. T. W., Shen, Q. P., Kelly, J., & Hunter, K. (2008). Comparative study of the variables in construction project briefing/architectural programming. *Journal of Construction Engineering and Management*, *134*(2), 122–138. doi:10.1061/(ASCE)0733-9364(2008)134:2(122)

Zaharioaie, M. (2012). The utility of using public private partnership for local governments. *Journal of Public Administration, Finance and Law,* 17-24.

Zhang, X. Q. (2005b). Paving the way for public "private partnerships in infrastructure development. *Journal of Construction Engineering and Management, 131*(1), 71–80. doi:10.1061/(ASCE)0733-9364(2005)131:1(71)

Zhong, S., Chew, S. H., Set, E., Zhang, J., Xue, H., Sham, P. C., & Israel, S. et al. (2009). The heritability of attitude toward economic risk. *Twin Research and Human Genetics, 12*(01), 103–107. doi:10.1375/twin.12.1.103 PMID:19210185

Zitron, J. (2006). Public-private partnership projects: Towards a model of contractor bidding decision-making. *Journal of Purchasing and Supply Management, 12*(2), 53–62. doi:10.1016/j.pursup.2006.04.002

Zou, P., Zhang, G., & Wang, J.-Y. (2007). Understanding the key risks in construction projects in China. *International Journal of Project Management, 25*(6), 601–614. doi:10.1016/j.ijproman.2007.03.001

Appendix

List of Abbreviations

AEP……………..Annual Exceedance Probability
ALARP…………As Low As Reasonably Practicable
BBO…………….Buy, Build, Operate
BOO…………….Build, Own, Operate
BOOT…………..Build, Own, Operate, Transfer
BOT…………….Build–Operate–Transfer
BTO…………….Build Transfer Operate
CA……………...Comprehensive Agreement
CDF…………....Cumulative Distribution Function
CIRS……………Critical Incident Reporting System
CREM…………Cost Risk Estimating Management
DBFO…………..Design–Build–Finance– Operate
DA……………...Development Agreement
DDA……………Disposition and Development Agreement
Dr………………Doctor
ELT……………..Executive Leadership Team
EMV…………....Expected Monetary Value
GAAP…………..Generally Accepted Accounting Principle
IRR……………...Internal Rate of Return
IT……………….Information Technology
JVs……………...Joint Ventures
KCI……………..Key Control Indicators
KRI……………..Key Risk Indicators
MDL……………Master Deliverables List
MIGA…………..Multilateral Investment Guarantee Agency
NPM……………New Public Management
NPV…………….Net Present Value
P3..……………… Public Private Partnership
PCM…………….Probability Consequence Matrix
PFI……………...Private Finance Initiative
PMP…………….Project Management Plan

QRA...............Qualitative Risk Analysis
QRA...............Quantitative Risk Analysis
QQIR...............Quantify Qualitative Information on Risks
RAF................Risk Appetite Framework
RAS................Risk Appetite Statements
RBM...............Risk Breakdown Matrix
RBS................Risk Breakdown Structure
RFP.................Request for Proposals
RFQ................Request for Qualifications
RIP.................Rest in Peace
RMP...............Risk Management Plan
SAGB..............Semi-Autonomous Government Bodies
SLAs...............Service Level Agreements
SPV................Special Purpose Vehicle
SR..................Sister
SRM...............Supplier Relationship Management
VFM...............Value for Money
WBS...............Work Breakdown Structure
WPs................Work Packages

Glossary

Acceptable Risk: A risk which everyone impacted is prepared to accept. Action to further reduce such risk is usually not required unless reasonably practicable measures are available at low cost in terms of money, time and effort.

ALARP (As Low as Reasonably Practicable) Principle: That principle which states that risks, lower than the limit of tolerability, are tolerable only if risk reduction is impracticable or if its cost is grossly in disproportion (depending on the level of risk) to the improvement gained.

Annual Exceedance Probability (AEP): The estimated probability that an event of specified magnitude will be exceeded in any year.

Assurance: An evaluated opinion, based on evidence gained from review, on the organization's governance, risk management and internal control framework.

Audit Committee: A Committee appointed to support the Accounting Officer (in NDPBs a Committee of the board to support the Board) in monitoring the corporate governance and control systems in the organization.

Bayes Theorem: A theorem that provides the logical basis for updating a probability on the basis of new information.

Best Value: Means the most overall public benefits as determined through an evaluation of the amount of the concession payment and other appropriate considerations in proposals received from Offerors.

Comprehensive Agreement (CA): Means the Comprehensive Agreement between the private entity and the agency.

Conditional Probability: The probability of an outcome, given the occurrence of some event. For example, given that a flood has reached the crest of an embankment dam, the probability of the dam failing is a conditional probability.

Consequence: In relation to risk analysis, the outcome or result of a hazard being realized.

Contingency Plans: Plans setting out actions that will be undertaken in certain circumstances to limit the impact of risks that materialize or to introduce additional risk capacity.

Countermeasures: All measures taken to counter and reduce a hazard or consequences of a hazard. They most commonly refer to engineering (structural) measures but can also include other non-structural measures and tools designed and employed to avoid or limit the adverse impact of natural hazards and related environmental and technological disasters.

Cumulative Distribution Function (CDF): The integral of the probability density function calculated in the direction of increasing values of the random variable. Thus the probability that the random variable takes on values less than or equal to a particular value can be read from the CDF.

Danger (Threat): The natural phenomenon that could lead to damage, described in terms of its geometry, mechanical and other characteristics. The danger can be an existing one (such as a creeping slope) or a potential one (such as a rock fall). The characterization of a danger or threat does not include any forecasting.

Decision-Maker: The person or organizational unit who decides on a course of action in relation safety.

Deterministic: Describing a process with an outcome that is always the same for a given set of inputs, i.e. the outcome is "determined" by the input. Deterministic contrasts with random, which describes a process with an outcome that can vary even though the inputs are the same. Deterministic analysis contrasts with probabilistic analysis.

Disaster: A serious disruption of the functioning of a community or a society causing widespread human, material, economic or environmental losses which exceed the ability of the affected community or society to cope using its own resources.

Elements at Risk: Population, buildings and engineering works, infrastructure, environmental features and economic activities in the area affected by a hazard.

Emergency Preparedness Plan: Document which contains procedures for dealing with various emergencies which could result from a disaster.

Environmental Risks: Risks to natural ecosystems or to the aesthetics, sustainability or amenity of the natural world.

Event Tree Analysis: Inductive analysis process that utilizes an event tree graphical construct that shows the logical sequence of the occurrence of events in, or states of, a system following an initiating event.

Expected Value: The average or central tendency of a random variable. In risk analysis, the product of the probability of an event and of its consequences, aggregated over all possible values of the variable.

Exposure: The consequences, as a combination of impact and likelihood, which may be experienced by the organization if a specific risk is realized.

Extreme Event: Event, which has a very low annual exceedance probability (AEP). Sometimes defined as an event beyond the credible limit of extrapolation and therefore dependent on the length of record and the quality of the data available.

Factor of Safety: The ratio of system resistance to the peak design loads, often calculated in accordance with established rules.

Failure: The inability of a system, or part thereof, to function as intended. In the context of structural safety (including geotechnical structures), failure is generally confined to issues of structural integrity, and in some contexts to the special case of collapse of the structure or some part of it.

Failure Mechanism: A mechanism describing the physical processes and states that must occur for failure to develop.

Failure Mode: A way that failure can occur, described by the means by which element or component failures must occur to cause loss of the sub-system or system function.

Fault Tree Analysis: A systems engineering method for representing the logical combinations of various system states and possible causes which can contribute to a specified problematic (fault) event (called the top event).

Fragility Curve: Defines the probability of failure as a function of an applied load level; a particular form of the more general system response.

Frequency: A measure of likelihood expressed as the number of occurrences of an event in a given time or in a given number of trials (see also likelihood and probability).

Hazard: Is a dangerous phenomenon, substance, human activity or condition that may cause loss of life, injury or other health impacts, property damage, loss of livelihoods and services, social and economic disruption, or environmental damage.

Horizon Scanning: Systematic activity designed to identify, as early as possible, indicators of changes in risk.

Human Factors: Human factors refer to environmental, organizational and job factors, and human and individual characteristics which influence behavior in a way which can affect safety.

Individual Risk to Life: The increment of risk imposed on a particular individual by the existence of a hazard. This increment of risk is an addition to the background risk to life, which the person would live with on a daily basis if the facility did not exist.

Inherent Risk: Is the risk that exists naturally in any activity and is defined as "the risk existing before the implementation of internal control measures to reduce it" or "all risks that threat the entity/ organization and may be internal or external risks, measurable or immeasurable".

Interim Agreement: Means an agreement, including a memorandum of understanding or binding preliminary agreement, between the private entity and the Responsible Public Entity that provides for the completion of studies and any other activities to advance the development and/or operation of a public private partnership project.

Involuntary Risk: A risk imposed on people by a controlling body and not assumed by free choice of the people at risk.

Joint Probability: The probability that two or more variables will assume certain values simultaneously or within particular time intervals.

Judgment: Contribution to decision-making which depends on a person's experience, technical know-how, and ethical or moral values.

Likelihood: Conditional probability of an outcome given a set of data, assumptions and information. Also used as a qualitative description of probability and frequency.

Limit: In relation to level of risk, that level which, when exceeded, is unacceptable. Higher risks cannot be justified except in extraordinary circumstances (typically where the continuation of the risk has been authorized by government or a regulator in the wider interests of society).

Loss: Any negative consequence, financial or otherwise.

Mitigation: Measures undertaken to limit the adverse impact of, for instance, natural hazards, environmental degradation and technological hazards.

Monte Carlo Simulation: A procedure, which seeks to simulate stochastic processes by random selection of input values to an analysis model in proportion to their joint probability density function.

Natural Hazard: Natural process or phenomenon that may cause loss of life, injury or other health impacts, property damage, loss of livelihoods and services, social and economic disruption, or environmental damage.

Operations and Maintenance (O&M): Means the operational and ongoing maintenance requirements of a facility.

Owner: Legal entity which either holds a government license to operate a facility or retains the legal property title on the facility, and which is responsible for the safety of the facility.

Partners: Are defined as any organizations with which a department works to deliver their objectives, with a formal agreement of roles (contract, funding agreement, Service Level Agreement, etc.). There may often be a long-term relationship.

Partnering: Is more active than traditional 'arms length' contracting, taking more effort, but offering potential benefits including better risk management.

Partnerships: Are defined by the agreements between the partners.

Population at Risk: All those persons who would be directly exposed to the consequences of failure of a structure or facility if they did not evacuate.

Preparedness: Activities and measures taken in advance to ensure effective response to hazards and their consequences.

Prevention: Activities to provide outright avoidance of the hazards and their consequences.

Private Entity: Means any natural person, corporation, general partnership, limited liability company, limited partnership, joint venture, business trust, public benefit corporation, non-profit entity or other business entity.

Probabilistic: A description of procedures, which are based on the application of the laws of probability.

Probability: A measure of the degree of certainty. This measure has a value between zero (impossibility) and 1.0 (certainty). It is an estimate of the likelihood of the magnitude of the uncertain quantity, or the likelihood of the occurrence of the uncertain future event.

Probability Density Function: A function describing the relative likelihood that a random variable will assume a particular value in contrast to taking on other values.

Public-Private Partnership (P3): Means a project or service which is funded and operated through a partnership of government and one or more Private Entities.

Qualitative Risk Analysis: An analysis which uses word form, descriptive or numeric rating scales to describe the magnitude of potential consequences and the likelihood that those consequences will occur.

Quantitative Risk Analysis: An analysis based on numerical values of the probability, vulnerability and consequences, and resulting in a numerical value of the risk.

Random Variable: A quantity, the magnitude of which is not exactly fixed, but rather the quantity may assume any of a number of values described by a probability distribution.

Regulatory Agency (Synonymous with Regulator): Usually a government ministry, department, office, directorate or other unit of government entrusted by law or administrative act with the responsibility for the general supervision of the safe design, construction and operations of structures or facilities, as well as any entity to which all or part of the executive or operational tasks and functions have been delegated by legal power.

Reliability: Likelihood of successful performance of a given project element.

Request for Proposals (RFP): Means the documents constituting the Request for Proposals and identifying the P3 project, the work to be performed and materials to be furnished, in response to which a Proposer may submit a Proposal.

Request for Qualifications (RFQ): Means the documents constituting the Request for Qualifications issued for a P3 project by the agency.

Residual Risk: The exposure arising from a specific risk after action has been taken to manage it and making the assumption that the action is effective.

Retained Risks: Means the Project Risks which are most efficiently managed directly by the Agency and would not be transferred under a P3 project because the Agency has determined that to do so would not provide best value. Examples of Project Risks that are retained or at least shared under almost all P3 projects include the risk of pre-existing hazardous materials, the risk of failure to obtain Right of Way by certain specified dates and the risk of Force Majeure.

Revenue Risk: Means the risks associated with the realization of tolling revenues.

Risk: Uncertainty of outcome, whether positive opportunity or negative threat, of actions and events. It is the combination of likelihood and impact, including perceived importance.

Risk Allocation: Is the assignment of roles and responsibilities for each identified risk.

Risk Analysis: Is a process that is used to understand the nature, sources, and causes of the risks that you have identified and to estimate the level of risk. It is also used to study impacts and consequences and to examine the controls that currently exist.

Risk Appetite: Is the level of exposure that the organization is prepared to accept, namely the risk tolerated by the organization.

Risk Assessment: The process of making a decision recommendation on whether existing risks are tolerable and present risk control measures are adequate, and if not, whether alternative risk control measures are justified or will be implemented.

Risk Attitude: Is organization's approach to assess and eventually pursue, take or refuse risk.

Risk Aversion: Is attitude to turn away from risk.

Risk Aggregation: Is the process to combine individual risks to obtain a more complete understanding of risk.

Risk Avoidance: Means a purposeful decision or strategy to avoid, withdraw from or not to become involved with a risk event or project related activity.

Risk Context: Means the process of establishing the goals, objectives, strategies, scope and parameters of an activity, or part of the organization to which the risk management process is to be applied on a given project. The process should occur at the onset of considering a given project, involve key Stakeholders, and be undertaken with full consideration of the need to balance costs, threats, and opportunities.

Risk-Based Decision Making: Decision making, which has as a main input the results of risk assessment. It involves a balancing of social and other benefits and the residual risks.

Risk Capacity: Is the maximum amount of risk which the organization is technically able to assume before breaching one or more of its capital base, liquidity, and borrowing capacity, reputational and regulatory constraints.

Risk Control: The implementation and enforcement of actions to control risk, and the periodic re-evaluation of the effectiveness of these actions.

Risk Evaluation: The stage at which values and judgment enter the decision process, explicitly or implicitly, by including consideration of the importance of the estimated risks and the associated social, environmental, and economic consequences, in order to identify a range of alternatives for managing the risks.

Risk Identification: Is a process that is used to find, recognize, and describe the risks that could affect the achievement of the project goals and objectives.

Risk Financing: is a form of risk treatments involving contingent arrangements for the provision of funds to meet the financial consequences should they occur.

Risk Management: The systematic application of management policies, procedures and practices to the tasks of identifying, analyzing, assessing, mitigating and monitoring risk.

Risk Management Audit: Is the systematic, independent and documented process for obtaining evidence and evaluating it objectively to determine the extent to which the risk management framework is adequate and effective.

Risk Management Framework: Means the systematic process of deciding how to approach, plan, and execute Risk Management strategies throughout the life of a project. It is intended to minimize or eliminate the consequences of adverse risk events.

Risk Management Plan: Is a detailed plan of action for the management of project risks. The Risk Management Plan is the process to develop and document an organized, comprehensive, and interactive risk management strategy; determine the methods to be used to execute a risk management strategy; and plan for adequate resources.

Risk Management Policy: Overall intentions and direction of an organization related to risk management.

Risk Management Process: Means systematic application of management policies, procedures and practices to the tasks of communicating, consulting, establishing the context, identifying, analyzing, evaluating, treating, monitoring and reviewing risk.

Risk Mitigation: A selective application of appropriate techniques and management principles to reduce either likelihood of an occurrence or its adverse consequences, or both.

Risk Monitoring: Means to supervise and to continually check and critically observe. It means to determine the status and to assess whether or not required or expected performance levels are actually being achieved.

Risk Owner: Is a person or entity that has been given the authority to manage a particular risk and is accountable for doing so.

Risk Profile: Is the description of a set of risks.

Risk Register: Means a detailed table or chart that lists the conceivable quantifiable risks for each project. These risks range from cost overrun and design risks to planning and regulatory risks. Each project risk is described in detail along with the probability of the risk occurring and a range of probable cost and time impacts as a consequence of the risk occurring.

Risk Reporting: Is a form of communication intended to address particular internal or external stakeholders to provide information regarding the current state of risk and its management

Risk Response: Means the process of developing options and actions to enhance opportunities and reduce threats to project objectives. Risk Response documentation should consider possible actions to the identified risk by satisfying the following questions. Can the identified threat be avoided, transferred, mitigated or is it to be accepted? Can the identified opportunity be exploited, shared or enhanced.

Risk Retention: Is the acceptance of the benefit of gain, or burden of loss, from a particular risk.

Risk Sharing (Shared Risk): Means risks that are allocated among two or more parties, where the threat of a loss or the benefit of the gain of a particular risk is proportionally shared as determined by the agreed allocation.

Risk Treatment: Involves selecting and implementing one or more treatment options. There are many treatment options: risk avoidance, risk transfer, risk sharing, and risk acceptance, removing the source of the risk, modifying the consequences, and changing the probabilities. Once a treatment has been implemented, it becomes a control or it modifies existing controls.

Risk Workshop: Is purposefully planned, with a detailed agenda and specific purpose. Workshops may include brainstorming sessions with project team members and extended project team members, such as specialty groups, Stakeholders and regulatory agency representatives is a technique for risk identification. This technique can be scaled for use on the simplest to the most complex projects. This technique can also be tailored to specific areas of interest for the project risk.

Scenario: A unique combination of states. A scenario defines a suite of circumstances of interest in a risk assessment, for example loading scenarios or failure scenarios.

Sensitivity Analysis: An analysis to determine the range over which the result varies, given unit change in one or more input parameters.

Societal Risk: The risk of widespread or large scale detriment from the realization of a defined risk, the implication being that the consequence would be on such a scale as to provoke a socio/political response.

Standards-Based Approach: The traditional approach to engineering, in which risks are controlled by following established rules as to design events and loads, structural capacity, safety coefficients and defensive design measures.

System: Assembly that consists of interacting elements.

Technological Hazard: A hazard originating from technological or industrial conditions, including accidents, dangerous procedures, infrastructure failures or specific human activities, that may cause loss of life, injury, illness or other health impacts, property damage, loss of livelihoods and services, social and economic disruption, or environmental damage.

Temporal Probability: The probability that the element at risk is in the area affected by the danger (threat) at the time of its occurrence.

Tolerable Risk: A risk within a range that society can live with so as to secure certain net benefits. It is a range of risk regarded as non-negligible and needing to be kept under review and reduced further if possible.

Transferable Risks: Mean those risks that are selected to be transferred from the Agency to the private sector delivering the project under a P3 arrangement because to do so would provide value.

Uncertainty: Describes any situation without certainty, whether or not described by a probability distribution. Uncertainty is caused by natural variation and/or incomplete knowledge (lack of understanding or insufficient data).

Unsolicited Proposal: Means a Proposal to develop and/or operate a P3 project submitted by a Private Entity not in response to an RFQ or RFP.

Value-for-Money (VfM): Means the process used to compare the impacts of a P3 project against those for the traditional public delivery alternative. The methodology for carrying out a VfM is discussed in the Value for Money Guidelines.

About the Author

Peter Adoko Obicci, an author, a writer, a management consultant and a philosopher, was born in 1971 in Otaka village, Lamiyo Sub County, Agago district in northern Uganda. He studied philosophy at Bachelor level at Urbaniana Pontificia Universitas-Rome (1995-1998). He has received two Masters degrees from Uganda Management Institute, Kampala-Uganda, in Public Administration and Management (2011) and Public Procurement (2016). He has a Post Graduate Certificate in Research Methods and Writing Skills from Centre of Basic Research (2006). He has two post graduate diplomas in Public Administration and Management from Uganda Management Institute (2009) and Education from Gulu University (2010). He also has two ordinary diplomas in Business Studies from Uganda College of Commerce Pakwach (1995) and Philosophy and Religious studies from Alokolum National Major Seminary (1998). He has certificates in Administrative Law from Law Development Centre (2006), Consultancy from Uganda Management Institute (2009) and SPSS and EpiInfo from Uganda Management Institute (2016). He has worked in a variety of position as lecturer of Office Management, Office Practice and Secretarial Duties at National Teacher's College-Ngetta (2002), teacher at Royal Academy (2002) and a teacher of Business Law at Team Business College-Kisoro and Fort Portal Centers (2003). Outside the classroom, Peter joined the cadre of Ugandan civil service as an Accounts Assistant in Pader District Local Government in 2004. A year later he was elevated to the position of Sub county chief- an administrator and accounting officer in-charge of a Sub County. After the curving of Agago district out of Pader district, he assumed a new title of Assistant Secretary still in charge of the administration of a Sub County in 2010. He lectured political philosophy at Gulu University-Kitgum Campus (2012). He is presently a senior civil servant in the Office of the President- Kampala, Uganda and Executive Director of POA-Kittim Consultants a consultancy firm established in 2014. He has published a book, *Political Decentralization in Uganda: A Case of Agago District* (2014), and more than 15 journal articles in both national and international journals. He is married with five children and lives in Kampala, Uganda.

Index

R

S

T

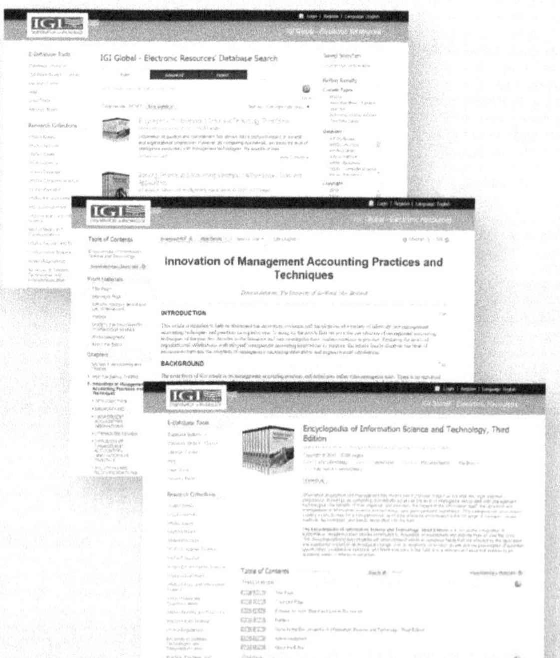
IGI Global - Electronic Resources' Database Search
Innovation of Management Accounting Practices and Techniques
Encyclopedia of Information Science and Technology, Third Edition

www.ingramcontent.com/pod-product-compliance
Lightning Source LLC
LaVergne TN
LVHW062121300926
849161LV00010B/2514